THE
TERRITORIALS
1908–1914

THE TERRITORIALS
1908–1914

A GUIDE FOR MILITARY AND FAMILY HISTORIANS

RAY WESTLAKE

Pen & Sword
MILITARY

First published in Great Britain in 2011 by
Pen & Sword Military
an imprint of
Pen & Sword Books Ltd
47 Church Street
Barnsley
South Yorkshire
S70 2AS

Copyright © Ray Westlake 2011

ISBN 978-1-84884-360-8

Typeset in Ehrhardt by
Mac Style, Beverley, East Yorkshire

Printed and bound in the UK by
CPI

Pen & Sword Books Ltd incorporates the Imprints of Pen & Sword Aviation, Pen &
Sword Maritime, Pen & Sword Military, Wharncliffe Local History, Pen and Sword
Select, Pen and Sword Military Classics, Leo Cooper, Remember When, Seaforth
Publishing and Frontline Publishing.

For a complete list of Pen & Sword titles please contact
PEN & SWORD BOOKS LIMITED
47 Church Street, Barnsley, South Yorkshire, S70 2AS, England
E-mail: enquiries@pen-and-sword.co.uk
Website: www.pen-and-sword.co.uk

Contents

Introduction vi

The Territorial Force 1
Territorial Force Units 8
Territorial Force Gazetteer 65

Further Research 279
Sources of Information and Recommended Further Reading 280
Acknowledgements 281

Introduction

Under the Army Reforms introduced by Secretary of State for War Richard Haldane in 1907, the existing auxiliary forces (the Yeomanry and Volunteer forces) were to be combined (with effect from 1 April 1908) as a new organisation to be known as the Territorial Force. In his Territorial and Reserve Forces Bill, Mr Haldane set up an establishment of fourteen divisions, fourteen mounted brigades, army troops and troops for coastal defence. Organised along similar lines to those of the Regular forces, but for home defence only, the Territorial Force would comprise cavalry (the Yeomanry), artillery, engineers, infantry, supply, transport and medical units. These to be raised and administered locally by a number of Territorial Force Associations. Units were found in the main from existing Yeomanry and Volunteer personnel, the new regiments, battalions, etc. almost, save for a change in name, continuing service as before and bringing with them their history, traditions and battle honours. There would, however, be a number of drastic and unpopular reorganisations which required some infantry to convert to artillery, engineers and other arms of service.

The new conditions of service had to be complied with. A gradual procedure which continued through into the second year of the Territorial Force and, in a number of cases, 1910, before units gained recognition from their Territorial Force Association. As was the case of the Yeomanry and Volunteer forces, the new Territorial Force could not be ordered overseas and was intended for home defence only. Provisions, however, were made in the form of an 'Imperial Service' section which enabled a man, if so volunteered, to proceed overseas if required. There was also a 'Special Service Section' for use in case of national emergency. Essential to the growth of the Yeomanry and Volunteer forces. Likewise, the Territorial Force was the formation by units of a number of affiliated cadet corps made up of boys below military age.

This book is set out in three sections: the first of which, under 'The Territorial Force', offers a brief account of terms and conditions of service, recruiting, general rules, regulations and uniform, together with notes covering the make-up of each arm of service and its permitted establishment. Under 'Territorial Force Units' (the second part) I have set out an order of battle that provides a complete account of all units raised and recognised by the Territorial Force. It is of course, in the space permitted, impossible to provide any form of history for each, however brief, so I have limited information to titles, locations, higher organisation, battle honours (if any) and affiliated cadet units. The final section of the book is titled 'Territorial Force Gazetteer', and this deals with the 3,000 or more locations mentioned in the previous section. In all three cases I have set the entries alphabetically. An obvious approach in the case of the 'Gazetteer', but, it is thought, a more convenient and more easily accessible method in regard of the other two sections.

The Territorial Force

Army Service Corps The Territorial Force element of the Army Service Corps comprised twenty-eight transport and supply columns allotted one each to the fourteen mounted brigades and one each to the fourteen infantry divisions. Mounted brigade transport and supply columns were made up of one company, while those with the divisions comprised four companies – one designated as Divisional Headquarters Company, the others allotted to, and named after, each of the infantry brigades within the division. The peace establishment of a divisional transport and supply column amounted to 512 all ranks, with a lieutenant-colonel in command, while the mounted brigade transport and supply columns had 116 under a captain.

Army Troops Formations attached to, but not required to complete, a division.

Army Veterinary Corps Territorial Force AVC personnel were attached to each of the fourteen TF divisions.

Battle Honours Members of the Yeomanry and former Volunteer Rifle Corps (infantry volunteer battalions) had served on a voluntary basis during the Boer War of 1899–1902, and in recognition of this their regiments or battalions were awarded the battle honour 'South Africa' followed by a date that represented the period spent on active service. Unique within the British Army is the 'Fishguard' battle honour carried by the Pembrokeshire Yeomanry and, among the auxiliary forces, the 'Egypt 1882' which was awarded to the postmen from the old 24th Middlesex Rifle Volunteer Corps that served on that campaign as the Army Post Office Corps. Any battle honours gained prior to 1908 by the Yeomanry or Volunteer Force were carried forward for use by their Territorial successors and are shown in Part Two after the unit title.

Cadets Cadet units were first sanctioned by the government in 1863, and indeed many of the corps mentioned in this record existed prior to the introduction of the Territorial Force in 1908. The reorganisation of that year saw, as far as the cadet forces were concerned, those raised within the several public schools transferred almost immediately to the newly created Officers Training Corps. The OTC was not administered by the county Territorial Force Associations and therefore forms no part of the 'Territorial Force Units' section of this work. It would not be until 1910 that the remaining school and non-school cadet units of the old Volunteer Force were catered for by the formation of a new organisation to be known as the Territorial Cadet Force. Units of the TCF were to be administered by the local Territorial Forces Associations which had been empowered under the *Territorial and Reserve Forces Acts* to establish, or assist, cadet battalions or corps. Regulations required companies to comprise no less than thirty cadets. If membership exceed 100, a second company could be authorised, and in the same way, a third. Four companies were required to form a battalion. When complied with, these regulations, together with others concerning financial details, training facilities, etc, were submitted to the TFAs and, if satisfactory, official recognition would be sanctioned. In the same way, recognition could be withdrawn should strength, etc, fall below requirements. Applications also included details of what, if any, unit of the Territorial Force the cadet corps preferred to be affiliated to. Minimum age requirements varied from unit to unit. However, it was laid down that cadets could not remain with their corps without the express sanction of their county TFA after they had reached the age at which enlistment into the Territorial Force became possible. Also included in the Territorial Cadet Force, and therefore administered by the TFAs, were the several battalions and companies forming the Boys Brigade, Church Lads Brigade and Jewish Lads Brigade. These, however, are not considered to be within the scope of this book.

Cyclist Battalions Raised in 1908 were a total of ten battalions dedicated to a cyclist role: 10th Royal Scots, 6th Norfolk, 7th Devonshire, 5th East Yorkshire, 7th Welsh, 25th London regiments, and four independent battalions designated: Essex and Suffolk, Highland, Kent and Northern. In 1911, however, the Essex and Suffolk was divided to form 6th Suffolk and 8th Essex and in the same year the 9th Hampshire Regiment was raised at Southampton. These were joined in 1914 at St Mary Street, Huntingdon by the Huntingdonshire Cyclist Battalion.

Discipline Officers, NCOs and men were subject to military law when they were being trained or exercised, embodied or called out for actual military service, in the same way as a regular soldier. The standard of discipline required was also on a par, any failures in this direction – disobedience, absent without leave, etc – attracted the same penalties.

Divisions There were fourteen Territorial Force divisions named: East Anglian, Highland, Home Counties, East Lancashire, West Lancashire, 1st London, 2nd London, Lowland, North Midland, South Midland, Northumbrian, West Riding, Welsh and Wessex. Each was made up of three infantry brigades – four battalions in each – and divisional troops supplied by Royal Field Artillery, Royal Garrison Artillery, Royal Engineers, Army Service Corps and Royal Army Medical Corps units of the TF. The naming of these support formations followed that of their division, eg, 1st East Anglian Brigade, RFA; East Anglian RGA, while the infantry brigades were generally named in a way that reflected the regiments from which their component battalions were drawn, eg Argyll and Sutherland Infantry Brigade, Black Watch Infantry Brigade.

Imperial Service Section Although only required to serve as home defence, officers and men of the peacetime Territorial Force could also offer to serve outside of the United Kingdom in time of national emergency. Under the conditions set out for the Imperial Service Section, a Territorial could undertake to serve abroad, but only with his own unit, or part of his own unit. He could not be drafted as an individual to any other regiment or corps, except at his own request. Upon 90% of a unit's strength having volunteered, the words 'Imperial Service' were placed on signboards, in the *Army List* and other official documentation. Members could be identified in uniform by a metal badge. Worn on the right breast, the badge (referred to as a 'broach') comprised a tablet bearing the words 'Imperial Service' surmounted by a crown.

Infantry Territorial Force infantry battalions were included in all English, Scottish and Welsh regiments except for the Royal Fusiliers, King's Royal Rifle Corps and Rifle Brigade. The several Volunteer Corps long associated with these regiments were to continue service in the Territorial Force, however, as battalions of the newly created London Regiment. There were none in the several regiments of Foot Guards or Irish Regiments. Battalions were as a whole numbered on from the Special Reserve (the old Militia) as 4th, 5th etc and varied in number from one to seven in each regiment. There were, however, two battalions that were known by name only: the Brecknockshire Battalion of the South Wales Borderers and the Buckinghamshire Battalion which formed part of the Oxfordshire and Buckinghamshire Light Infantry. In addition, a number of wholly Territorial Force regiments were raised: the Monmouthshire Regiment, which numbered three battalions; the Cambridgeshire, Hertfordshire and Herefordshire Regiments, all three of one battalion each, and, what with its twenty-six battalions would add up to the largest regiment in the British Army, the London Regiment. There was the Inns of Court Officer Training Corps and, dedicated to a cyclist role, the Northern, Highland, Kent and Huntingdonshire Cyclist battalions. Each infantry battalion comprised eight companies (lettered 'A' to 'H') the peace establishment for each numbering 1,009 all ranks under the command of a lieutenant-colonel. Among the other ranks were cooks, pioneers, shoe smiths, armourers, signallers, drivers, medical orderlies and batmen for the officers. Cyclist battalions numbered 523 men.

Infantry Brigades There were forty-five infantry brigades each containing four battalions. Forty-two brigades were allotted, three per division; two served with Coast Defences and one (as Army Troops) was attached to the Welsh Division. Territorial Force Infantry brigades were generally named in a way that reflected the regiments from which they were formed. Alphabetically they were: Argyll and Sutherland, Black Watch, Cheshire, Devon and Cornwall, Durham Light Infantry, East Lancashire, East Midland, Essex, Gloucester and Worcester, Gordon, Hampshire, Highland Light Infantry, Kent, Lancashire Fusiliers, Lincoln and Leicester, Liverpool, 1st London, 2nd London, 3rd London, 4th London, 5th London, 6th London, Lothian, Manchester, Middlesex, Norfolk and Suffolk, North Lancashire, Northumberland, North Wales, Notts and Derby, Scottish Rifle, Seaforth and Cameron, South Lancashire, South Midland, South Scottish, South Wales, South Western, Staffordshire, Surrey, Warwickshire, Welsh Border, 1st West Riding, 2nd West Riding, 3rd West Riding, York and Durham.

Mounted Brigades The fourteen Mounted Brigades each contained: three yeomanry regiments, one battery of Royal Horse Artillery, an ammunition column (supplied by the RHA unit), transport and supply column and a field ambulance. The last three elements were named according to their brigade, eg, Eastern Mounted Brigade Ammunition Column, Eastern Mounted Brigade Transport and Supply Column, Eastern Mounted Brigade Field Ambulance. Created in 1913 were fourteen mounted brigade signal troops. Mounted brigades were named: Eastern, South Eastern, London, Yorkshire, 1st South Western, 2nd South Western, Welsh Border, South Wales, Notts and Derby, North Midland, Highland, Lowland, 1st South Midland and 2nd South Midland.

Officers Applications for appointments to commissions in the lowest officer rank (second lieutenant) of the TF were in the first place to be addressed to the secretaries of Territorial Force Associations. These in turn to be forwarded to the Secretary of State for War. Other applications, those from former Regular or TF officers, went direct to general officers commanding-in-chief who, having satisfied themselves that the applicant's former service had not been terminated due to his character or efficiency, forwarded on in the same way. Candidates for first appointments were to be not under seventeen years of age. Officers were required to retire upon reaching the age of sixty. Two-year extensions were granted, however, but not beyond the age of sixty-five. The use of ranks and the privilege of wearing uniform after retirement was permitted, but only after the completion of fifteen years satisfactory service. Lieutenant-colonel was the highest achievable rank in the TF.

Rates of Pay Paragraph 380 of the *Regulations for the Territorial Force 1908* shows officers' pay which ranges from twenty-one shillings and sixpence per day for a lieutenant-colonel serving with a yeomanry regiment, to the five shilling and three pence of an infantry or ASC second-lieutenant. There would also be allowances for such items as lodgings while at camp and quarters when on instruction courses. Other ranks pay progressed from the one shilling per day of a private, to the four shilling and four pence of a Royal Horse Artillery battery sergeant major. A gratuity of £5 was paid to every officer and man of the TF on joining his unit on embodiment.

Royal Army Medical Corps There were five Territorial Force elements of the RAMC: Mounted Brigade Field Ambulances, which were made up of two sections (designated 'A' and 'B') and allotted one to each of the fourteen mounted brigades; Divisional Field Ambulances, forty-two in number (each had three sections designated 'A', 'B', 'C'), and placed three per division; two Sanitary Companies (named 1st and 2nd London) and twenty-three General Hospitals designated: 1st and 2nd Eastern, 1st to 4th London, 1st to 5th Northern, 1st to 4th Scottish, 1st to 5th Southern, 1st, 2nd, 3rd Western. Formed in 1913 were fourteen Clearing Hospitals (one per division and named accordingly). The peace establishments for the RAMC Territorial Force, as set out in 1908, were for Mounted Brigade Field Ambulances (109 all ranks), Divisional Field Ambulances (195), General

Hospitals (46), Sanitary Company (105). The later were under the command of a major, while the remainder were commanded by lieutenant-colonels.

Royal Engineers – Balloon Company Using a hydrogen-filled balloon attached by a cable to a wagon, only one unit of this type, the London Balloon Company, was raised. Its peace establishment numbering 67 all ranks with a captain in command.

Royal Engineers – Divisional Engineers Allotted to each of the fourteen TF divisions in 1908 were three Royal Engineers companies: two field and one telegraph. Groups was known by the name of their divisions, eg, East Anglian Divisional Royal Engineers; similarly telegraph companies were styled, eg, East Anglian Divisional Telegraph Company. The field companies were numbered within the group, eg, 1st East Anglian Field Company, 2nd East Anglian Field Company. In the Welsh Division, however, the companies were designated Cheshire and Welsh. In 1913 telegraph companies were removed from their divisions and placed in the *Army List* under the heading 'Signal Service'. Each company was now designated as, eg, East Anglian Divisional Signal Company and show as comprising Headquarters and four sections. The 2nd, 3rd and 4th Sections bore the name of the infantry brigade to which it was allotted. Field companies were made up of 216 all ranks under the command of a major, while the telegraph companies had 40 with a captain in command.

Royal Engineers – Electrical Engineers Two units were formed and designated London and Tyne.

Royal Engineers – Fortress Engineers Fortress engineer units were included in Coast Defences and were made up of Works and Electric Lights Companies. The number and type of companies within each formation varied. The several units raised were designated: City of Aberdeen, Cinque Ports, Cornwall, Devonshire, Dorsetshire, City of Dundee, Durham, City of Edinburgh, Essex, Glamorgan, Hampshire, Kent, Lancashire, Northumberland, Renfrewshire, East Riding, North Riding, Sussex and Wiltshire. Peace establishments varied according to local requirements and ranged from 100 to 115 in the case of works companies, and 55 to 136 for electric lights.

Royal Engineers – Railway Battalion Eight company strong, the Cheshire Railway Battalion would be the only unit of this type raised. Peace establishment was 532 all ranks under the command of a lieutenant-colonel.

Royal Engineers – Telegraph/Signal Companies (Army Troops) There were five groups of telegraph companies: London District, Northern Command, Scottish Command, Southern Command and Western Command. Each was made up of one wireless company, one cable company and one airline company, which were designated, eg, London Wireless Telegraph Company. From 1913, 'Signal' was substituted for 'Telegraph' in all instances. Peace establishments were: 70 all ranks under the command of a captain, in the case of a wireless company; the cable companies had 156 men (two of which were shoeing and carriage smiths) with a major in command, and the airline companies, 289 all ranks (one shoeing and carriage smith included), commanded by a major.

Royal Field Artillery Royal Field Artillery brigades were allotted to each of the fourteen Territorial Force divisions. With the exception of the Highland, each included four brigades of which three were field and one a howitzer. The Highland Division had two field and one howitzer, the 4th Highland Brigade being made up of mountain artillery and coming under the Royal Garrison Artillery. Field brigades comprised three batteries each, while howitzer brigades consisted of just two. Batteries were usually designated according to the county in which they were raised. Each brigade had its own ammunition column which was named according to its brigade, eg, 1st East Anglian Ammunition Column. The peace establishment of an RFA brigade totalled 620 all ranks (389 in the case of a howitzer brigade) commanded by a lieutenant-colonel. Trades among the other ranks included a farrier sergeant, shoeing smiths, saddlers and wheelers.

Royal Garrison Artillery – For Defended Ports Units formed by the Territorial Force under the heading Royal Garrison Artillery (for Defended Ports) were located around naval bases and several ports and were required to serve as coastal defences in case of general mobilisation. Each unit varied in size and makeup, some with garrison companies, some with heavy batteries, some with a combination of both. There were seventeen groups in total, all named geographically: Clyde, Cornwall, Devonshire, Dorsetshire, Durham, East Riding, Essex and Suffolk, Forth, Glamorgan, Hampshire, Kent, Lancashire and Cheshire, Orkney, Pembroke, North Scottish, Sussex, Tynemouth. The peace establishment of a heavy battery was 130 all ranks commanded by a major, a farrier sergeant, sadder, wheeler and shoeing smith being among the other ranks. Garrison companies were made up of 80 all ranks under a captain.

Royal Garrison Artillery – Heavy There were fourteen units of the Heavy Section Royal Garrison Artillery, each made up of one heavy battery and an ammunition column. The groups were attached one to each of the TF divisions and were named accordingly. In 1911, however, the East and West Lancashire RGA were grouped together and styled as the Lancashire Brigade containing 1st and 2nd Lancashire Heavy Batteries. Likewise, but in 1912, the two London Batteries (1st and 2nd) were grouped as the London Brigade. There were a number of other heavy batteries, but these were included in the RGA groups 'For Defended Ports'. The peace establishment for a heavy battery and its ammunition column was 214 all ranks under the command of a major. Included among the other ranks was a farrier sergeant, shoeing smiths, saddlers and wheelers.

Royal Garrison Artillery – Mountain Artillery The Territorial Force provided for one mountain artillery unit, the 4th Highland Brigade, which comprised three mountain batteries and an ammunition column. The peace establishment of an RGA mountain brigade and its ammunition column was 804 all ranks commanded by a lieutenant-colonel. Included among the other ranks was a farrier sergeant, shoeing smiths, saddlers and wheelers.

Royal Horse Artillery There were fourteen horse artillery formations, one allotted to each of the fourteen TF Mounted Brigades and made up of one battery and an ammunition column. The later being named according to the mounted brigade in which the group served, eg, Lowland Mounted Brigade Ammunition Column. Twelve of the units came under the Royal Horse Artillery and bore county names – Ayrshire, Berkshire, Essex, Glamorgan, Hampshire, Inverness-shire, Leicestershire, Nottinghamshire, West Riding, Shropshire, Somerset, Warwickshire – and have been recorded as such. The other two, the 1st and 2nd City of London, being found under Honourable Artillery Company. The peace establishment for an RHA battery and ammunition column was 221 all ranks under the command of a major. Trades among the other ranks included a farrier sergeant, shoeing smiths, saddlers and wheelers.

Special Service Section Members of the Territorial Force were invited to enrol into the Special Service Section which enabled the Secretary of State to call out volunteers in the case of a national emergency – even though no order calling out the Territorial Force for actual military service was in force at the time. Service was not to exceed one month; applicants were to undergo special and regular medical examinations and, when called out, were to receive the pay and allowances of their corresponding rank in the regular army. An annual retaining fee of ten shilling was also paid. Members were identified by a special cloth badge worn on the lower left arm made up of the letters 'SSS' within a circle topped by a crown.

Terms of Service The age for enlistment for all sections of the TF was seventeen to thirty-five years. Boys between fourteen and seventeen, however, could be appointed as trumpeters, buglers or bandsmen; but only on approval of their parents or guardians. There were height restrictions which varied according to arm of service (five-foot-three inches the minimum), and the required chest girth, when expanded, began at thirty-two-and-a-half inches. Those not permitted to join the TF included men belonging to either the Regular or Reserve Royal Navy, Special Reserve, the Irish Constabulary or those discharged from any service for misconduct or as being medically unfit for duty. Territorials were exempt (if they so desired) from jury service, from service as peace officer or parish officer, and were not liable as part of a military body to be called out in aid of the Civil Power to preserve peace.

Upon enlistment each soldier, unless excused, was required to attend camp for at least eight days in each year. The number of drills each man had to perform during the course of a Territorial Year varied according to rank, length and arm of service. Forty drills would be about the average, with extra instruction for engineers and medical personnel. Territorials could be called out for service in any part of the United Kingdom, but no part of the TF was to be carried or ordered to go overseas. Term of service was for four years. Re-engagement was possible; this to be within twelve months before the end of the current term of service for a period not exceeding four years. Discharge was possible within the agreed term of service upon the Territorial having given three months notice in writing to his commanding officer and paying an agreed sum to the county association not exceeding £5. A request for discharge was not permitted, however, during a period of embodiment. Normal discharge from the TF was, in the case of sergeants, at the age of fifty years (an extension to fifty-five was possible, but not beyond), and that for other ranks, forty, with extension to forty-five. See also under: 'Officers', 'Imperial Service Section' and 'Special Service Section'.

Territorial Decoration and Territorial Force Efficiency Medal The Territorial Decoration was granted to officers having completed twelve years commissioned service. Previous time in the Yeomanry or Volunteers could be counted. The decoration, which hangs from a green ribbon with yellow stripe down the centre, is an oval silver oak wreath, tied in gold, with, in the centre, the royal cipher surmounted by a crown, both in gold. Recipients were permitted to include the letters 'TD' after their names. Twelve years' service also saw the award to other ranks of the Territorial Force Efficiency Medal; provided they had completed at least twelve trainings. The medal, oval this time and suspended from the same, but slightly narrower ribbon as that for the TD, had the head of the reigning sovereign on the obverse.

Uniform and Badges The only obligatory uniform for officers and men of the Territorial Force was the regulation pattern service dress; authorised patterns of full (or ceremonial) dress were laid down for each unit, but its provision was optional. If and when full dress was to be worn, Territorial Force Regulations clearly set out conditions as to its use. Officers' badges of rank were as those for the Regular Army, the letter 'T', however, being worn on the shoulder cords and straps. In service dress the 'T' was worn below the collar badges.

A distinction of the Volunteer, and subsequently the Territorial, was the rule whereas silver or white metal lace and badges were substituted for any that were gold or gilding metal in the Regular Army. This was never popular and the Territorial, it would seem, was not keen to be seen in the public eye as anything less than a Regular. As this requirement was likely to affect recruiting, the War Office made provisions in TF Regulations for any unit desirous to adopt gold (gilding metal) in lieu of silver (white metal) to seek permission through its County TF Association. Many, but by no means all, units applied, those that did in every case being successful.

The majority of TF infantry full dress uniforms followed the pattern as laid down for its parent regiment. A small number of battalions, however, did have their own distinct style and continued with the greys or rifle-greens they had worn as Volunteers. The Yeomanry retained its full dress, unique to each regiment.

The Yeomanry, independent TF regiments, and a small number of battalions wore their own special badges. Others were permitted the badge of their parent regiment, but with scrolls and tablets bearing battle honours either left blank or inscribed with any distinction that the TF unit possessed

– the South Africa battle honour gained by their Volunteer processors for service in the Boer War usually.

Units were easily identified by means of a metal title placed on each shoulder strap. In the main, shoulder titles were of a three-tier format and comprised at the top, the letter 'T'. Below this appeared arm of service, eg RHA, RFA, RAMC, etc, or in the case of infantry battalions, its number. The lower line would then indicate division, regiment etc. The titles of Yeomanry regiments were made up of the letter 'T', with 'Y' below, then name of regiment, while those of fusilier and light infantry battalions also incorporated either a grenade (fusiliers) or bugle horn (light infantry).

A badge unique to the Volunteer Force, and carried on by the Territorial Force, was the five-pointed star worn on the right forearm by other ranks to indicate that they had been returned as qualified in four successive years. Additional stars were permitted for every further aggregate of four years.

Yeomanry The Yeomanry of 1908–1914 consisted of fifty-seven regiments which were generally part of, or attached to, one or other of the fourteen TF Mounted Brigades. Each regiment was organised on a four squadron basis, the squadrons being lettered 'A' to 'D'. Two regiments, the Lovat's Scouts and Scottish Horse, were double regiments numbered as 1st and 2nd and in each case the squadrons were lettered: 'A' to 'D' (1st Regiment), 'E' to 'H' (2nd Regiment). Yeomanry regiments have been listed under: Ayrshire, Bedfordshire, Berkshire, Buckinghamshire, Cheshire, City of London, County of London (three regiments), Denbighshire, Derbyshire, Dorset, Duke of Lancaster's, Essex, Fife and Forfar, Glamorgan, Gloucestershire, Hampshire, Hertfordshire, King Edward's Horse, Lanarkshire (two regiments), Lancashire, Leicestershire, Lincolnshire, Lothians and Border, Lovat's Scouts (two regiments), Montgomeryshire, Norfolk, North Somerset, Northamptonshire, Northumberland, Nottinghamshire (two regiments), Oxfordshire, Pembrokeshire, Royal 1st Devon, Royal East Kent, Royal North Devon, Royal Wiltshire, Scottish Horse (two regiments), Shropshire, Staffordshire, Suffolk, Surrey, Sussex, Warwickshire, Welsh Horse, West Kent, West Somerset, Westmoreland and Cumberland, Worcestershire, Yorkshire (three regiments). The peace establishment of a yeomanry regiment added up to 468 all ranks commanded by a lieutenant-colonel. Trades among the other ranks include a farrier sergeant, saddlers and shoeing smiths.

Territorial Force Units

Abercarn Territorial Cadet Company Affiliated to 2nd Monmouthshire Regiment. Became part of 1st Cadet Battalion Monmouthshire Regiment in 1912.

Abergavenny Cadet Corps Affiliated to 3rd Monmouthshire Regiment. Became part of 1st Cadet Battalion Monmouthshire Regiment in 1912.

Ackmar School (LCC) Cadet Corps *Headquarters:* The Guildhall, City of London. Formed as two companies of the 2nd (Fulham) Battalion Imperial Cadet Corps which was divided in 1912 to form Ackmar School (LCC) Cadet Corps and New King's School Cadet Corps.

Acton Cadet Company See 10th Middlesex Regiment.

Aldershot Church Cadet Corps See Wessex Divisional Transport and Supply Column.

Allan's School Cadet Unit See 6th Northumberland Fusiliers.

Archbishop Temple's School Cadet Corps Lambeth Road, Lambeth. Recognition was withdrawn under Army Order 49 of 1913.

Ardeer Company See Royal Scots Fusiliers.

Argyll and Sutherland Highlanders Of the regiment's five TF battalions, the 5th was attached to the Black Watch Infantry Brigade, while the remainder made up the Argyll and Sutherland Infantry Brigade of the Highland Division. **5th (Renfrewshire) Battalion:** 'South Africa 1900–02'. *Headquarters:* 34 Union Street, moving to Finnart Street, Greenock in 1911. *Companies:* 'A' to 'D' (Greenock), 'E' (Port Glasgow), 'F', 'G' (Greenock), 'H' (Gourock and Inverkip). **6th (Renfrewshire) Battalion:** 'South Africa 1900–02'. *Headquarters:* 66 High Street, Paisley. *Companies:* 'A', 'B', 'C' (Paisley), 'D' (Renfrew), 'E' (Johnstone), 'F' (Thornliebank), 'G' (Barrhead), 'H' (Pollokshaws). **7th Battalion:** 'South Africa 1900–02'. *Headquarters:* Stirling. *Companies:* 'A' (Stirling, Bannockburn and Bridge of Allan), 'B' (Stenhousemuir and Denny), 'C' (Falkirk and Bonnybridge), 'D' (Lennoxtown and Kilsyth), 'E' (Alloa), 'F' (Alva, Dollar, Tillicoultry and Menstrie), 'G' (Kinross and Kelty), 'H' (Alloa, Sauchie and Clackmannan). **8th (The Argyllshire) Battalion:** 'South Africa 1900–02'. *Headquarters:* Dunoon. *Companies:* 'A' (Inveraray, Lochgoilhead, Auchnagoul, Dalmally, Furnace, Cairndow, Strachur and Kilchrenan), 'B' (Campbeltown), 'C' (Southend, Campbeltown, Glenbarr, Tayinloan, Stewarton and Drumlemble), 'D' (Dunoon and Sandbank), 'E' (Lochgilphead, Kilmartin, Tighnabruaich, Glendaruel, Ardrishaig and Tayvallich), 'F' (Ballachulish, Kinlochleven, Ardgour and Duror), 'G' (Bowmore, Jura, Port Ellen, Bridgend and Ballygrant), 'H' (Easdale, Clachan, Oban, Cullipool, Toberonochy, Benderloch and Ardchattan). *Cadets:* Dunoon Grammar School Cadet Corps. **9th (The Dumbartonshire) Battalion:** 'South Africa 1900–02'. *Headquarters:* Helensburgh, moving to Hartfield, Dumbarton in 1913. *Companies:* 'A' (Helensburgh and Cardross), 'B' (Kirkintilloch, Cumbernauld and Lenzie), 'C' (Dumbarton), 'D' (Milngavie), 'E' (Jamestown and Bonhill), 'F' (Alexandria and Renton), 'G', 'H' (Clydebank).

Argyll and Sutherland Infantry Brigade See Highland Division.

Argyllshire (Mountain) Battery See 4th Highland (Mountain) Brigade RGA.

Arnold House School Cadet Corps See 4th North Lancashire Regiment.

Artists Rifles See 28th London Regiment.

Ashford Grammar School Cadet Corps Ashford, Kent.

Aske's Hatcham School Cadet Corps See 21st London Regiment.

Aylesbury Grammar School Cadet Corps See Buckinghamshire Battalion Oxfordshire and Buckinghamshire Light Infantry.

Ayrshire Batteries See 2nd Lowland Brigade RFA.

Ayrshire Royal Horse Artillery *Headquarters:* Ayr. *Battery* (Ayr). *Ammunition Column* (Ayr). Part of the Lowland Mounted Brigade.

Ayrshire Yeomanry (Earl of Carrick's Own) 'South Africa 1900–02'. *Headquarters:* Ayr. *Squadrons:* 'A' (Ayr), 'B' (Cumnock), 'C' (Kilmarnock), 'D' (Beith). Part of the Lowland Mounted Brigade.

Bablake School (Coventry) Cadet Company See 7th Royal Warwickshire Regiment.

Basingstoke and Eastrop Cadet Corps See 4th Hampshire Regiment.

Battersea Grammar School Cadet Corps St John's Hill, Battersea.

Beccles Cadet Corps See 3rd East Anglian (Howitzer) Brigade RFA.

Bedford Park Cadet Company See 10th Middlesex Regiment.

Bedfordshire Regiment 5th Battalion: 'South Africa 1900–02'. *Headquarters:* Gwyn Street, Bedford. *Companies:* 'A' (Bedford), 'B' and 'C' (Luton), 'D' (Biggleswade, Sandy, Arlesey and St Neots), 'E' (Ampthill and Olney), 'F' (Luton, Dunstable and Leighton Buzzard), 'G' (Fletton and Yaxley), 'H' (Huntingdon, St Ives and Ramsey). Part of the East Midland Infantry Brigade, East Anglian Division. *Cadets:* Dunstable Grammar School Cadet Corps.

Bedfordshire Yeomanry *Headquarters:* St John's Street, moving to Ashburnham Road, Bedford in 1912. *Squadrons:* 'A' (Bedford), 'B' (Biggleswade and Shefford), 'C' (Dunstable, Leighton Buzzard, Woburn and Ampthill), 'D' (Godmanchester, St Neots, Kimbolton, Ramsey, Somersham, Sutton and Chatteris). Attached to Eastern Mounted Brigade.

Berkshire Royal Horse Artillery *Headquarters:* Yeomanry House, Castle Hill, Reading. *Battery* (Reading and Ascot). *Ammunition Column:* (Reading). Part of the 2nd South Midland Mounted Brigade.

Berkshire Yeomanry (Hungerford) 'South Africa 1900–01'. *Headquarters:* Yeomanry House, Castle Hill, Reading. *Squadrons:* 'A' (Windsor, Maidenhead and Wokingham), 'B' (Reading and Wallingford), C' (Newbury, Hungerford and Lambourn), 'D' (Wantage, Abingdon, Faringdon and, from 1913, Didcot). Part of the 2nd South Midland Mounted Brigade.

Birkenhead Cadet Corps, 1st See 4th Cheshire Regiment.

Bishop's Stortford College Cadet Corps See 1st Hertfordshire Regiment.

Black Watch Infantry Brigade *Headquarters:* Perth, 61 George Street, moving to the Bridge Office, then the Soldiers Home. Later to Bell Street, Dundee. *Battalions:* 4th to 7th Black Watch. Part of the Scottish Coast Defences.

Black Watch (Royal Highlanders) The four battalions made up the Black Watch Infantry Brigade which was included in Scottish Coast Defences. An 8th Battalion was planned, but for this see the Highland Cyclist Battalion. **4th (City of Dundee) Battalion:** 'South Africa 1900–02'. *Headquarters:* Dundee. *Companies:* 'A' to 'H' (Dundee). **5th (Angus & Dundee) Battalion:**

'South Africa 1900–02'. *Headquarters:* Arbroath. *Companies:* 'A' (Kirriemuir, Glamis and Newtyle), 'B' (Forfar), 'C' (Montrose and Craigo), 'D' (Brechin and Edzell), 'E' (Arbroath and Friockheim), 'F' (Arbroath, Carnoustie and Monifleth), 'G', 'H' (Dundee). **6th (Perthshire) Battalion:** 'South Africa 1900–02'. *Headquarters:* Tay Street, Perth. *Companies:* 'A', 'B' (Perth), 'C' (Dunblane, Bridge of Allan, Doune and Callander), 'D' (Crieff and Comrie), 'E' (Blairgowrie, Coupar Angus and Alyth), 'F' (Auchterarder, Blackford and Dunning), 'G' (Birnam, Pitlochry, Bankfoot, Ballinluig, Stanley, Luncarty, Strathbraun and Blair Atholl), 'H' (Aberfeldy, Kenmore, Fortingall, Grandtully and Killin). **7th (Fife) Battalion:** 'South Africa 1900–02'. *Headquarters:* St Andrews. *Companies:* 'A' (Dunfermline), 'B' (Lochgelly), 'C' (Kirkcaldy), 'D' (Cowdenbeath), 'E' (Cupar, Newburgh, Auchtermuchty and Abernethy), 'F' (Leven, Colinsburgh and Largoward), 'G' (St Andrews, Guardbridge, Anstruther and Crail), 'H' (Leslie, Markinch and Thornton).

Bolton Artillery See 3rd East Lancashire Brigade RFA.

Border Regiment As Army Troops, the battalions were attached to the East Lancashire Division. **4th (Cumberland and Westmorland) Battalion**: 'South Africa 1900–02'. *Headquarters:* Penrith moving to Kendal in 1909, then Strand Road, Carlisle in 1911. *Companies:* 'A', 'B' (Carlisle), 'C' (Keswick and Brampton), 'D' (Penrith), 'E' (Kirkby Lonsdale, Sedbergh, Endmoor and Milnthorpe, Kirkby Stephen and Appleby), 'F' (Kendal), 'G' (Kendal, Burneside and Staveley), 'H' (Windermere, Ambleside and Elterwater). *Cadets:* Kirkby Lonsdale Cadet Company. **5th (Cumberland) Battalion:** 'South Africa 1901–02'. *Headquarters:* Workington. *Companies:* 'A' (Whitehaven), 'B' and 'C' (Workington), 'D' (Cockermouth), 'E' (Egremont, St Bees and Cleator), 'F' (Wigton), 'G' (Frizington), 'H' (Aspatria, Dearham and Bullgill).

Bradford Postal Telegraph Messengers Cadet Corps See 6th West Yorkshire Regiment.

Brecknockshire Battalion See South Wales Borderers.

Bridgnorth Cadet Corps See 4th King's Shropshire Light Infantry.

Brierley Hill Cadet Corps See 6th South Staffordshire Regiment.

Brighton Brigade Sussex Cadets See 1st Home Counties Brigade RFA.

Brighton Preparatory Schools Cadet Corps See 4th Royal Sussex Regiment.

Broadwater Cadet Corps Broadwater Hall, Broadwater Road, Tooting. Originally called the Broadwater Scouting Corps. Re-designated in 1913.

Broughton Lads' Brigade See 8th Lancashire Fusiliers.

Buckinghamshire Battalion See Oxfordshire and Buckinghamshire Light Infantry.

Buckinghamshire Yeomanry (Royal Bucks Hussars) 'South Africa 1900–01'. *Headquarters:* Buckingham. *Squadrons:* 'A' (Buckingham, Stony Stratford, Bletchley, Newport Pagnell and Akeley), 'B' (Aylesbury, Kimble, Quainton and Wing), 'C' (High Wycombe, Stokenchurch, Taplow and Beaconsfield), 'D' (Chesham, Cholesbury, Chalfont St Peter and Great Missenden). Part of the 2nd South Midland Mounted Brigade.

Buffs (East Kent Regiment) The battalions provided one half of the Kent Infantry Brigade, Home Counties Division. **4th Battalion:** 'South Africa 1900–02'. *Headquarters:* Canterbury. *Companies:* 'A' (Ramsgate, Birchington and Broadstairs), 'B' (Canterbury, Chartham and Ash), 'C' (Canterbury, Littlebourne, Wingham and Nonington), 'D' (Folkestone and Hythe), 'E' (Sittingbourne and Sheerness), 'F' (Herne Bay and Whitstable), 'G' (Margate, St Nicholas at Wade and Westgate-on-Sea), 'H' (Dover). *Cadets:* Chatham House Cadet Corps (Chatham Street,

Ramsgate), Depot Royal Marine Cadets (RM Depot, Deal), Herne Bay College Cadet Corps and New College Herne Bay Cadet Corps. **5th (The Weald of Kent) Battalion:** 'South Africa 1900–02'. *Headquarters:* Ashford. *Companies:* 'A' (Cranbrook and Benenden), 'B' (Hawkhurst and Sandhurst), 'C' (Headcorn, Staplehurst, Marden and Sutton Valence), 'D' (Horsmonden, Goudhurst, Lamberhurst, Brenchley, Yalding and Paddock Wood), 'E' (Ashford, Pluckley, Smarden, Bethersden, Aldington, Boughton Aluph and Ham Street), 'F' (Ashford), 'G' (Tenterden, Lydd, Woodchurch, New Romney, Appledore, Wittersham and Rolvenden), 'H' (Ashford).

Burford Grammar School Cadet Corps See 4th Oxfordshire and Buckinghamshire Light Infantry.

Buteshire (Mountain) Battery See 4th Highland (Mountain) Brigade RGA.

Cadet Battalion of Cornwall, 1st See 4th Duke of Cornwall's Light Infantry.

Cadet Battalion of Hampshire, 1st See 1st Cadet Battalion Hampshire Regiment.

Cadet Norfolk Artillery See 1st East Anglian Brigade RFA.

Cambridgeshire Regiment 1st Battalion: 'South Africa 1900–01'. *Headquarters:* 14 Corn Exchange Street, Cambridge. *Companies:* 'A' (Cambridge, Great Shelford and Burwell), 'B' (Cambridge and Sawston), 'C' (Cambridge and Madingley), 'D' (Cambridge), 'E' (Wisbech), 'F' (Whittlesea, Coates and Thorney), 'G' (March, Chatteris, Benwick and Doddington), 'H' (Ely and Sutton). Part of the East Midland Infantry Brigade, East Anglian Division.

Cameron Highlanders 4th Battalion: 'South Africa 1900–02'. *Headquarters:* Inverness. *Companies:* 'A' (Inverness), 'B' (Nairn, Cawdor, Ardersier, Auldearn, Croy and Petty), 'C' (Inverness and Moy), 'D' (Broadford, Torrin, Elgoll and Raasay), 'E' (Fort William, Corpach, Fort Augustus and Invergarry), 'F' (Kingussie, Dalwhinnie, Newtonmore, Kincraig, Insh, Aviemore and Ardverikie), 'G' (Beauly, Struy, Kiltarlity, Balnain, Inchmore and Drumnadrochit), 'H' (Portree, Glenmore, Bernisdale, Edinbane, Sconser, Tarbert, Kilmuir, Dunvegan and Lochmaddy). Part of the Seaforth and Cameron Infantry Brigade, Highland Division.

Cameronians (Scottish Rifles) The battalions together made up the Scottish Rifle Infantry Brigade, Lowland Division. **5th Battalion:** 'South Africa 1900–02'. *Headquarters:* 261 West Princes Street, Glasgow. *Companies:* 'A' to 'H' (Glasgow). **6th Battalion:** 'South Africa 1900–02'. *Headquarters:* Muir Hall, Hamilton. *Companies:* 'A', 'B' (Hamilton), 'C' (Uddingston), 'D' (Larkhall and Strathaven), 'E' (Bothwell and Palace Colliery), 'F' (Blantyre), 'G', 'H' (Motherwell). **7th Battalion:** 'South Africa 1900–02'. *Headquarters:* Victoria Road, Glasgow. *Companies:* 'A' to 'H' (Glasgow). *Cadets:* Hutcheson's Grammar School Cadet Corps (Crown Street, Glasgow). **8th Battalion:** 'South Africa 1900–02'. *Headquarters:* 149 Cathedral Street, Glasgow. *Companies:* 'A' to 'H' (Glasgow).

Cardiganshire Battery See 2nd Welsh Brigade RFA.

Chatham Cadet Company Royal Marine Light Infantry, 1st See 5th Royal West Kent Regiment.

Chatham House (Ramsgate) Cadet Corps See 4th Buffs (East Kent Regiment).

Chepstow Territorial Cadet Company Affiliated to 1st Monmouthshire Regiment. Became part of 1st Cadet Battalion Monmouthshire Regiment in 1912.

Cheshire Batteries See 3rd Welsh Brigade RFA.

Cheshire Brigade Company See Welsh Divisional Transport and Supply Column.

Cheshire Brigade Royal Field Artillery See 3rd Welsh Brigade RFA.

Cheshire Field Company See Welsh Divisional Engineers.

Cheshire Infantry Brigade See Welsh Division.

Cheshire Railway Battalion *Headquarters:* Wistaston Road, Crewe. Disbanded 1912.

Cheshire Regiment The four battalions together made up the Cheshire Infantry Brigade, Welsh Division. **4th Battalion:** 'South Africa 1901–02'. *Headquarters:* Grange Road, Birkenhead. *Companies:* 'A' to 'D' (Birkenhead), 'E' (Tranmere), 'F', 'G' (Liscard), 'H' (Heswall, Parkgate, West Kirby and Hoylake). *Cadets:* 1st Birkenhead Cadet Corps (St Catherine's Institute, Tranmere), 1st New Brighton Cadet Corps (Mona House), 2nd New Brighton Cadet Corps (65 and 67 Rowson Street), 3rd New Brighton Cadet Corps (Oarside Farm, Mount Pleasant Road), 1st Egremont St John with Columbus Cadet Company (the affiliation was cancelled when the unit became part of the Church Lads Brigade in 1914), Liscard High School Cadet Corps, 1st Oxton Cadet Corps (Birkenhead) and 1st Poulton Cadet Company (St Luke's Parish Hall). **5th (Earl of Chester's) Battalion:** 'South Africa 1900–02'. *Headquarters:* 8 Black Friars, moving to Volunteer Street, Chester in 1912. *Companies:* 'A' (Altrincham and Knutsford), 'B' (Chester and Kelsall), 'C' (Sale and Cheadle), 'D' (Hartford), 'E' (Chester), 'F' (Frodsham and Lymm), 'G' (Runcorn), 'H' (Hartford). **6th Battalion:** 'South Africa 1900–02'. *Headquarters:* The Armoury, Stockport. *Companies:* 'A', 'B' (Stalybridge), 'C' (Hyde), 'D' (Glossop and Hadfield),. 'E' to 'H' (Stockport). **7th Battalion:** *Headquarters:* Congleton, moving to Macclesfield in 1910. *Companies:* 'A' (Congleton), 'B' (Congleton and Bollington), 'C', 'D' (Macclesfield), 'E' (Macclesfield and Winsford), 'F' (Nantwich and Crewe), 'G' (Sandbach, Middlewich and Winsford), 'H' (Wilmslow, Winsford and Middlewich). *Cadets:* Macclesfield Industrial School Cadet Corps and Macclesfield Grammar School Cadet Corps. **1st Territorial Cadet Battalion:** *Headquarters:* 12 St Peter's Square, Stockport. Affiliated to 6th Battalion.

Cheshire Yeomanry (Earl of Chester's) 'South Africa 1900–01'. *Headquarters:* Old Bank Buildings, Chester. *Squadrons:* 'A' (Knutsford, Alderley Edge, Hale and Sale), 'B' (Eaton, Chester, Farndon, Aldford, Pulford, Tattenhall and Kelsall), 'C' (Northwich, Great Budworth, Appleton, Warburton, Nantwich, Winsford, Middlewich, Tarporley and Crewe), 'D' (Macclesfield, Congleton, Stockport and Adlington). Part of the Welsh Border Mounted Brigade.

Christ's College Finchley Cadet Company See 7th Middlesex Regiment.

Church of the Ascension Cadet Corps Victoria Docks See 6th Essex Regiment.

Cinque Ports Cadet Corps, 1st See 5th Royal Sussex Regiment.

Cinque Ports Fortress Engineers *Headquarters:* Castle Street, moving to 16 Bench Street, Dover in 1913. *Electric Lights Company:* No 1 (Dover).

City of Aberdeen Batteries See 1st Highland Brigade RFA.

City of Aberdeen Cadet Battalion *Headquarters:* 31 Adelphi, Aberdeen.

City of Aberdeen Fortress Engineers *Headquarters:* 80 Hardgate, Aberdeen. *Works Company:* No 1 (Aberdeen).

City of Dundee Battery See 2nd Highland Brigade RFA.

City of Dundee Fortress Engineers *Headquarters:* 52 Taylor's Lane, Dundee. *Works Company:* No 1 (Dundee).

City of Edinburgh Batteries See 1st Lowland Brigade RFA.

City of Edinburgh Fortress Engineers *Headquarters:* 46 Albany Street, moving to 28 York Place, Edinburgh in 1911. *Works Company:* No 1 (Edinburgh). *Electric Lights Company:* No 2 (Edinburgh).

City of Glasgow Batteries See 3rd and 4th Lowland Brigades RFA.

City of London Batteries See 1st London Brigade RFA.

City of London Cadet Battalion (Lord Roberts Boys), 1st *Headquarters:* The Guildhall, City of London. Originally called Lord Robert's Boys.

City of London Horse Artillery See Honourable Artillery Company.

City of London Yeomanry (Rough Riders) 'South Africa 1900–02'. *Headquarters:* The Guildhall, moving to 39 Finsbury Square, Finsbury in 1911. *Squadrons:* 'A' to 'D' (Finsbury). Part of the London Mounted Brigade.

Civil Service Cadet Battalion See 2nd (Civil Service) Cadet Battalion London Regiment.

Civil Service Rifles See 15th London Regiment.

Clyde Royal Garrison Artillery *Headquarters:* King William Street, Port Glasgow. *Garrison Companies:* No 1 (Port Glasgow), No 2 (Helensburgh and Dumbarton), No 3 (Dumbarton) and No 4 (Dunoon, Sandbank and Innellan) which was disbanded in 1914.

Colchester Royal Grammar School Cadets See 5th Essex Regiment.

Coldhurst (Oldham) Cadet Corps, 1st See 2nd Cadet Battalion Manchester Regiment.

Collegiate School Cadet Company, Hastings See Home Counties Divisional Engineers and 2nd Home Counties Brigade RFA.

Coopers' Company's School Cadet Corps See 5th London Regiment.

Cornwall Fortress Engineers *Headquarters:* Falmouth. *Electric Lights Company:* No 1 (Falmouth). *Works Companies:* No 2 (Fowey, Lerryn and Lanreath), No 3 (Penryn, Constantine and Ponsanooth).

Cornwall Royal Garrison Artillery (Duke of Cornwall's) *Headquarters:* Falmouth. *Heavy Batteries:* No 1 (Padstow, St Merryn, Charlestown, Bugle and Par), No 2 (Penzance, St Just and St Buryan). *Garrison Companies:* No 3 (Looe), No 4 (Marazion), No 5 (St Ives), No 6 (Falmouth), No 7 (Truro).

County of London Batteries See 2nd to 8th London Brigades RFA.

County of London Yeomanry (Middlesex Hussars), 1st 'South Africa 1900–01'. *Headquarters:* Rutland Yard, Knightsbridge, moving to the Duke of York's Headquarters, King's Road, Chelsea in 1912. *Squadrons:* 'A' to 'D' (as headquarters). Part of the London Mounted Brigade.

County of London Yeomanry (Westminster Dragoons), 2nd 'South Africa 1902'. *Headquarters:* Elverton Street, Westminster. *Squadrons:* 'A' to 'D' (as headquarters). Attached to the London Mounted Brigade.

County of London Yeomanry (Sharpshooter), 3rd 'South Africa 1900–02'. *Headquarters:* 4 Park Village East, Gloucester Gate, Regent's Park, moving to Henry Street, St John's Wood in 1912. *Squadrons:* (as headquarters). Part of the London Mounted Brigade.

Cowes Cadet Company See 8th Hampshire Regiment.

Cowley Cadet Corps See 4th Oxfordshire and Buckinghamshire Light Infantry.

Cranbrook College (Ilford) Cadets See 4th Essex Regiment.

Cumberland Artillery See 4th East Lancashire (Howitzer) Brigade TFA.

Cumberland Howitzer Batteries See 4th East Lancashire (Howitzer) Brigade RFA.

Dartmouth Cadet Company See 7th Devonshire Regiment.

Denbighshire Hussars Yeomanry 'South Africa 1900–01'. *Headquarters:* Denbigh, moving to 1 Erdigg Road, Wrexham in 1911. *Squadrons:* 'A' (Wrexham, Llangollen, Mold and Ruabon), 'B' (Denbigh, Prestatyn, Rhyl and Ruthin), 'C' (Bangor, Carnarvon, Llandudno and Beaumaris), 'D' (Birkenhead). Part of the Welsh Border Mounted Brigade.

Depot Royal Marine Cadet Corps See 4th Buffs (East Kent Regiment).

Derby Post Office Cadet Corps See 5th Sherwood Foresters.

Derbyshire Howitzer Batteries See 4th North Midland (Howitzer) Brigade RFA.

Derbyshire Yeomanry 'South Africa 1900–01'. *Headquarters:* 91 Siddall's Road, Derby. *Squadrons:* 'A' (Chesterfield, Ripley, Belper, Beauchief and Eckington), 'B' (Bakewell, Buxton, Tideswell, Matlock, Youlgreave and Hartington), 'C' (Derby, Osmaston Manor, Duffield and Wirksworth), 'D' (Derby, Ilkeston, Church Gresley and Repton). Part of the Notts & Derby Mounted Brigade.

Devon and Cornwall Brigade Company See Wessex Divisional Transport and Supply Column.

Devon and Cornwall Infantry Brigade See Wessex Division.

Devonshire Batteries See 4th Wessex Brigade RFA.

Devonshire Fortress Engineers *Headquarters:* Mutley Barracks, Plymouth. *Works Companies:* No 1 (Torquay, Newton Abbot and Yealmpton), Nos 2, 3 (Exeter). *Electric Lights Companies:* Nos 4, 5 (Plymouth). *Cadets:* No 1 Cadet Company (Yealmpton), originally called the Yealmpton Cadet Corps and re-designated in 1912; No 2 Cadet Company (Mutley Barracks, Plymouth).

Devonshire Regiment The 4th and 5th Battalions provided one half of the Devon and Cornwall Infantry Brigade, Wessex Division, with the 6th attached The 7th Battalion was attached to Southern Command. **4th Battalion:** 'South Africa 1900–01'. *Headquarters:* Exeter. *Companies:* 'A' (Exeter and Broadclyst). 'B', 'C' (Exeter), 'D' (Exmouth, Budleigh Saltererton and Lympstone), 'E' (Tiverton, Bampton and Dulverton), 'F' (Sidmouth, Ottery St Mary, Newton Poppleford, Honiton and Colyton), 'G' (Cullompton, Whimple, Burlescombe and Uffculme), 'H' (Axminster, Chardstock and Lyme Regis). *Cadets:* Exeter Cathedral School Cadet Company. **5th (Prince of Wales's) Battalion:** 'South Africa 1900–01'. *Headquarters:* Plymouth. *Companies:* 'A' (Plymouth and Tavistock), 'B' (Plymouth), 'C' (Plymouth, Ivybridge and Kingsbridge), 'D' (Devonport), 'E' (Newton Abbot and Chudleigh), 'F' (Teignmouth, Dawlish and Torquay), 'G' (Moreton Hampstead, Bovey Tracey and Chagford), 'H' (Totnes, Ashburton and Buckfastleigh). *Cadets:* Plymouth Lads' Brigade Cadet Corps (79 Embankment Road, Plymouth), Haytor (Newton Abbot) Cadet Corps (Penhurst, Newton Abbot) and Totnes Cadet Company (YMCA, Fore Street, Totnes). **6th Battalion:** 'South Africa 1900–01'. *Headquarters:* Barnstaple. *Companies:* 'A' (Barnstaple and Muddiford), 'B' (Okehampton, Hatherleigh, Bow and Sticklepath), 'C' (Bideford, Appledore, Parkham and Hartland),

'D' (Torrington, St Giles, Holsworthy and Ashwater), 'E' (South Molton, Witheridge, Molland and Chittlehampton), 'F' (Chulmleigh, Winkleigh, King's Nympton, Burrington and Crediton), 'G' (Combe Martin, Berrynarbor, Braunton and Croyde), 'H' (Barnstaple). **7th (Cyclist) Battalion:** *Headquarters:* Exeter. *Companies:* 'A' (Torquay), 'B' (Exeter, Topsham and Woodbury), 'C' (Exeter), 'D' (Cullompton, Bradninch and Silverton), 'E' (Crediton), 'F' (Dartmouth), 'G' (Plymouth), 'H' (Torquay). *Cadets:* Dartmouth Cadet Company (Crothers Hill, Dartmouth).

Devonshire Royal Garrison Artillery *Headquarters:* Devonport, moving to the Artillery Drill Hall, Lambhay Hill, Plymouth in 1912. *Heavy Batteries:* No 1 (Ilfracombe and Lynmouth), No 2 (Devonport, Plympton and Salcombe). *Garrison Companies:* Nos 3, 4 (Devonport), Nos 5, 6 (Plymouth).

Dorsetshire Battery See 3rd Wessex Brigade RFA.

Dorsetshire Fortress Engineers 'Imperial Service'. *Headquarters:* 61 St Thomas Street, Weymouth, moving to Sidney Hall, Weymouth in 1911. *Electric Lights Company:* No 1 (Weymouth and Portland).

Dorsetshire Regiment 4th Battalion: 'South Africa 1900–01'. *Headquarters:* Dorchester. *Companies:* 'A' (Bridport, Beaminster, Chideock and Netherbury), 'B' (Wareham, Corfe Castle, Bere Regis and Wool), 'C' (Dorchester and Broadwey), 'D' (Poole and Parkstone), 'E' (Gillingham and Shaftesbury), 'F' (Wimborne, Witchampton, Broadstone, Horton Heath and Woodlands), 'G' (Sherborne and Milborne Port), 'H' (Blandford, Sturminster Newton and Marnhull). Part of the South Western Infantry Brigade, Wessex Division.

Dorsetshire Royal Garrison Artillery *Headquarters:* Lower St Albans Street, Weymouth. *Garrison Companies:* No 1 (Swanage), No 2 (Poole and Parkstone), No 3 (Portland and Weymouth).

Dorsetshire Yeomanry (Queen's Own) 'South Africa 1900–01'. *Headquarters:* Sherborne. *Squadrons:* 'A' (Dorchester, Bridport, Weymouth, Maiden Newton and Charmouth), 'B' (Sherborne, Yeovil and Pulham), 'C' (Blandford, Wimborne, Wareham and Handley), 'D' (Gillingham, Shaftesbury, Stalbridge and Sturminster Newton). Attached to the 1st South Western Mounted Brigade.

Drax Grammar School Cadet Corps *Headquarters:* Drax, West Riding of Yorkshire.

Duke of Cornwall's Light Infantry The two battalions provided half of the Devon and Cornwall Infantry Brigade, Wessex Division. **4th Battalion:** 'South Africa 1900–01'. *Headquarters:* Truro. *Companies:* 'A' (Penzance), 'B' (Camborne), 'C' (Falmouth), 'D' (Helston), 'E' (Truro), 'F' (Hayle), 'G' (Redruth), 'H' (St Just and Pendeen). *Cadets:* 'A' Company 1st Cadet Battalion of Cornwall (Falmouth). **5th Battalion:** 'South Africa 1900–01'. *Headquarters:* Bodmin. *Companies:* 'A' (Liskeard), 'B' (Saltash and Callington), 'C' (Launceston), 'D' (St Austell and St Stephen), 'E' (Bodmin and Lostwithiel), 'F' (Camelford, Wadebridge and Delabole), 'G' (St Columb and Newquay), 'H' (Bude, Stratton, Kilkhampton and Morwenstow).

Duke of Lancaster's Own Yeomanry 'South Africa 1900–02'. *Headquarters:* Lancaster House, Whalley Road, Whalley Range, Manchester. *Squadrons:* 'A' (Oldham and Rochdale), 'B' (Bolton and Liverpool), 'C' (Whalley Range), 'D' (Preston and Blackpool). Attached to the Welsh Border Mounted Brigade.

Duke of Wellington's (West Riding Regiment) The four battalions together made up the 2nd West Riding Infantry Brigade, West Riding Division. **4th Battalion:** 'South Africa 1900–02'. *Headquarters:* Halifax. *Companies:* 'A', 'B', 'C' (Halifax), 'D' (Brighouse), 'E' (Cleckheaton), 'F' (Halifax), 'G' (Elland), 'H' (Sowerby Bridge). **5th Battalion:** 'South Africa 1900–02'. *Headquarters:*

Huddersfield. *Companies:* 'A' (Huddersfield and Meltham), 'B' to 'E' (Huddersfield), 'F' (Holmfirth), 'G' (Kirkburton), 'H' (Mirfield). **6th Battalion:** 'South Africa 1900–02'. *Headquarters:* Skipton-in-Craven. *Companies:* 'A' (Skipton-in-Craven and Barnoldswick), 'B' (Skipton-in-Craven), 'C' (Guiseley), 'D', 'E' (Keighley), 'F' (Settle and Ingleton), 'G' (Haworth), 'H' (Bingley). *Cadets:* The Settle Cadet Battalion. **7th Battalion:** 'South Africa 1900–02'. *Headquarters:* Milnsbridge. *Companies:* 'A', 'B' (Milnsbridge), 'C' (Slaithwaite), 'D' (Marsden), 'E' (Upper Mill), 'F' (Mossley), 'G' (Lees), 'H' (Mossley).

Dunoon Grammar School Cadet Corps See 8th Argyll and Sutherland Highlanders.

Dunstable Grammar School Cadet Corps See 5th Bedfordshire Regiment.

Durham Batteries See 3rd and 4th Northumbrian (Howitzer) Brigade, RFA.

Durham Fortress Engineers *Headquarters:* Western Road, Jarrow. *Works Companies:* Nos 1, 2 (Jarrow), No 3 (Gateshead).

Durham Light Infantry The 5th Battalion was included in the York and Durham Infantry Brigade, Northumbrian Division, while the 6th to 9th Battalions provided the Durham Light Infantry Brigade, also with the Northumbrian Division. **5th Battalion:** 'South Africa 1900–02'. *Headquarters:* Stockton-on-Tees. *Companies:* 'A', 'B', 'C' (Stockton-on-Tees), 'D', 'E' (Darlington), 'F' (Castle Eden, Coxhoe and Trimdon), 'G' (Castle Eden and West Hartlepool), 'H' (Darlington). **6th Battalion:** 'South Africa 1900–02'. *Headquarters:* Bishop Auckland. *Companies:* 'A' (Bishop Auckland and Coundon), 'B' (Bishop Auckland and West Auckland), 'C' (Spennymoor), 'D' (Crook and Willington), 'E' (Stanhope, St John's Chapel, Rookhope and Wolsingham), 'F' (Barnard Castle, Winston, Staindrop and Gainford), 'G', 'H' (Consett). **7th Battalion:** 'South Africa 1900–02'. *Headquarters:* Livingstone Road, Sunderland. *Companies:* 'A' to 'F' (Sunderland), 'G', 'H' (South Shields). **8th Battalion:** 'South Africa 1900–02'. *Headquarters:* Gilesgate, Durham. *Companies:* 'A' (Gilesgate, Sherburn Hill, Brandon and Sacriston), 'B' (Gilesgate), 'C' (Chester-le-Street), 'D' (Birtley), 'E' (Beamish and Burnhope), 'F' (Stanley), 'G' (Houghton-le-Spring, Pittington and Washington), 'H' (Hamsteels, Langley Park and Sleetburn). **9th Battalion:** 'South Africa 1900–02'. *Headquarters:* Burt Terrace, Gateshead. *Companies:* 'A' to 'D' (Gateshead), 'E' (Felling), 'F' (Chopwell), 'G', 'H' (Blaydon and West Ryton).

Durham Light Infantry Brigade See Northumbrian Division.

Durham Light Infantry Brigade Company See Northumbrian Divisional Transport and Supply Column.

Durham Royal Garrison Artillery *Headquarters:* The Armoury, West Hartlepool. *Heavy Battery:* No 1 (Sunderland). *Garrison Companies:* Nos 2, 3 (Sunderland), Nos 4, 5, 6 (West Hartlepool), No 7 (Hartlepool). In 1913 the two Sunderland companies were disbanded and in consequence Nos 4 to 7 were renumbered as Nos 2 to 5.

Ealing Cadet Company See 8th Middlesex Regiment.

Ealing County School Cadet Company See 8th Middlesex Regiment.

East Anglian Brigades Royal Field Artillery 1st Brigade: *Headquarters:* The Barracks, Surrey Street, Norwich. *Batteries:* 1st Norfolk (Nelson Road, Great Yarmouth), 2nd, 3rd Norfolk (Norwich). *Ammunition Column:* (Great Yarmouth and Norwich). *Cadets:* The Cadet Norfolk Artillery (Surrey Street, Norwich). **2nd Brigade:** *Headquarters:* Artillery House, The Green, Stratford. *Batteries:* 1st Essex (Stratford), 2nd Essex (17 Victoria Road, Romford), 3rd Essex (106 Cromwell Road, Grays moving in 1913 to The Artillery Drill Hall, Grays). *Ammunition Column:*

(Stratford, Romford and Greys). **3rd (Howitzer) Brigade:** *Headquarters:* Beccles, moving in 1913 to Great Gipping Street, Ipswich. *Batteries:* 1st Suffolk (Arnold Road, moving to Beccles Road, Lowestoft in 1911, and Beccles), 2nd Suffolk (Beccles, moving in 1911 to Ipswich). *Ammunition Column:* (Lowestoft and Ipswich). *Cadets:* The Beccles Cadet Corps (Gillingham Rectory, Beccles). Also known as No 1 Cadet Corps Beccles Royal Artillery. **4th Brigade:** *Headquarters:* 28 St Andrew's Street, Hertford. *Batteries:* 1st Hertfordshire (Hertford, moving to the Artillery Buildings, Harpenden Road, St Albans in 1911, Hertford remaining as a drill station), 2nd Hertfordshire (Watford, Berkhamsted and Hemel Hempstead), Northamptonshire (Queen's Road, Peterborough). *Ammunition Column:* (Hertford, St Albans, Watford and Peterborough). *Cadets:* 2nd Hertfordshire (Watford Scouts) Cadet Company (Clarendon Hall, Watford), but transferred to the Hertfordshire Regiment in 1913.

East Anglian Clearing Hospital *Headquarters:* Ipswich.

East Anglian Division *Headquarters:* Claremont House, Warley. *Infantry Brigades:* **Norfolk and Suffolk**, with 4th, 5th Norfolk and 4th, 5th Suffolk Regiments (Brentwood, moving in 1911 to 18a Prince of Wales Road, Norwich); **Essex**, with 4th to 7th Essex Regiment (Epping Place, Epping, moving to Brentwood in 1911) and **East Midland**, with 5th Bedfordshire, 4th Northamptonshire, 1st Cambridgeshire and 1st Hertfordshire Regiments (4 Shaftesbury Avenue, Bedford, moving later to 9 Linden Road, then the Shire Hall).

East Anglian Divisional Royal Engineers *Headquarters:* 13 Hassett Street, moving to Ashburnham Road, Bedford in 1912. *Field Companies:* 1st East Anglian (Bedford), 2nd East Anglian (Bedford and Luton). *Telegraph Company:* (Bedford). In 1913 the Telegraph Company was included in the RE Signal Service, designated as East Anglian Divisional Signal Company and organised as Headquarters and four sections: No 1, No 2 (Norfolk and Suffolk), No 3 (East Midland) and No 4 (Essex).

East Anglian Divisional Telegraph/Signal Company See East Anglian Divisional RE.

East Anglian Divisional Transport and Supply Column *Headquarters:* 182 Kingston Road, moving to 156 High Street, Ilford in 1909. *HQ and Brigade Companies:* HQ (Ilford, Ballingdon and Woolwich), Norfolk and Suffolk Brigade Company (King's Lynn and Downham Market), East Midland Brigade Company (Northampton), Essex Brigade Company (Bay Lodge, The Green, Stratford and Woolwich).

East Anglian Field Ambulances 1st: *Headquarters:* Woodbridge Road, Ipswich. *Sections:* 'A', 'B', 'C' (Ipswich, Woodbridge, Needham Market and Trimley). **2nd:** *Headquarters:* St Giles, Norwich, moving in 1913 to 44 Bethel Street, Norwich. *Sections:* 'A', 'B', 'C' (Norwich, East Dereham and Lowestoft). **3rd:** *Headquarters:* 184 Capworth Street, Leyton, moving by 1909 to 489 Lea Bridge Road, Leyton, then to Walthamstow Lodge, Church Hill, Walthamstow in 1914. *Sections:* 'A', 'B' (Southend-on-Sea), 'C' (Silvertown and Prittlewell).

East Anglian Field Companies See East Anglian Divisional RE.

East Anglian (Heavy) Royal Garrison Artillery (Essex) *Headquarters:* Artillery House, Stratford Green. *Battery:* Stratford Green. *Ammunition Column:* (Stratford Green).

East Ham Secondary School Cadets See 4th Essex Regiment.

East Isle of Wight Cadet Company Affiliated to the 8th Hampshire Regiment when formed and soon absorbed into the 3rd Cadet Battalion Hampshire Regiment.

East Lancashire Brigade Company See East Lancashire Divisional Transport and Supply Column.

East Lancashire Brigades Royal Filed Artillery 1st Brigade: *Headquarters:* 50 King Street, Blackburn. *Batteries:* 4th Lancashire (Blackburn), 5th Lancashire (Church), 6th Lancashire (Burnley). *Ammunition Column:* (Blackburn). **2nd Brigade (The Manchester Artillery):** *Headquarters:* Hyde Road, Manchester. *Batteries:* 15th, 16th, 17th Lancashire (Manchester). *Ammunition Column:* (Manchester). **3rd Brigade (The Bolton Artillery):** *Headquarters:* Bolton. *Batteries:* 18th, 19th, 20th Lancashire (Bolton). *Ammunition Column:* (Bolton). **4th (Howitzer) Brigade (The Cumberland Artillery):** *Headquarters:* Artillery Hall, Albert Hall, Carlisle, moving to Workington in 1909. *Batteries:* 1st Cumberland (Carlisle), 2nd Cumberland (Workington). *Ammunition Column:* (Workington, Maryport and Whitehaven).

East Lancashire Clearing Hospital *Headquarters:* Manchester.

East Lancashire Division *Headquarters:* The Barracks, Preston, moving to Hulme Barracks, Manchester in 1909, then to National Buildings, St Mary's Parsonage, Manchester in 1910. *Infantry Brigades:* **Lancashire Fusiliers**, with 5th to 8th Lancashire Fusiliers (5 Chapel Street, Preston); **East Lancashire**, with 4th, 5th East Lancashire and 9th, 10th Manchester Regiments (Ashton-under-Lyne, then Buxton before moving to 15 Piccadilly, Manchester in 1914) and **Manchester**, with 5th to 8th Manchester Regiment (3 Stretford Road, Manchester).

East Lancashire Divisional Royal Engineers *Headquarters:* 73 Seymour Grove, Old Trafford, Manchester. *Field Companies:* 1st, 2nd East Lancashire (Old Trafford). *Telegraph Company:* (Old Trafford). In 1913 the telegraph company was included in the RE Signal Service, designated as East Lancashire Divisional Signal Company and organised as Headquarters and four sections: No 1, No 2 (Lancashire Fusilier), No 3 (East Lancashire) and No 4 (Manchester).

East Lancashire Divisional Telegraph/Signal Company See East Lancashire Divisional RE.

East Lancashire Divisional Transport and Supply Column *Headquarters:* Hulme Barracks, Manchester. *HQ and Brigade Companies:* HQ, Lancashire Brigade Company and Manchester Brigade Company (Manchester), East Lancashire Brigade Company (Rawtenstall).

East Lancashire Field Ambulances 1st: *Headquarters:* Upper Chorlton Road, Manchester. *Sections:* 'A', 'B' (Manchester), 'C' (Bolton). **2nd:** *Headquarters:* Upper Chorlton Road, Manchester. *Sections:* 'A', 'B' (Manchester), 'C' (Burnley). **3rd:** *Headquarters:* Upper Chorlton Road, Manchester. *Sections:* 'A', 'B' (Manchester), 'C' (Bury).

East Lancashire Field Companies See East Lancashire Divisional RE.

East Lancashire (Heavy) Royal Garrison Artillery See Lancashire Brigade RGA.

East Lancashire Infantry Brigade See East Lancashire Division.

East Lancashire Regiment The two battalions together provided one half of the East Lancashire Infantry Brigade, East Lancashire Division. **4th Battalion:** 'South Africa 1900–02'. *Headquarters:* Blackburn. *Companies:* 'A' to 'E' (Blackburn), 'F', 'G' (Darwen), 'H' (Clitheroe). **5th Battalion:** 'South Africa 1900–02'. *Headquarters:* Burnley. *Companies:* 'A' (Burnley), 'B' (Burnley and Padiham), 'C', 'D' (Burnley), 'E' (Padiham), 'F' (Accrington), 'G' (Haslingden and Ramsbottom), 'H' (Bacup).

East Midland Brigade Company See East Anglian Divisional Transport and Supply Column.

East Midland Infantry Brigade See East Anglian Division.

East Riding Batteries See 2nd Northumbrian Brigade RFA.

East Riding Fortress Engineers *Headquarters:* Colonial Street, Hull. *Works Company:* No 1 (Hull). *Electric Lights Company:* No 2 (Hull).

East Riding of Yorkshire Yeomanry *Headquarters:* Railway Street, Beverley. *Squadrons:* 'A' (Hull), 'B' (Beverley, North Cave, Hornsea and Patrington), 'C' (Fulford and Dunnington), 'D' (Driffield, Hunmanby, Pocklington, Settrington and Bridlington). Part of the Yorkshire Mounted Brigade.

East Riding Royal Garrison Artillery *Headquarters:* Park Street, Hull. *Garrison Companies:* Nos 1, 2, 3, 4 (Hull).

East Surrey Regiment The two battalions together provided one half of the Surrey Infantry Brigade, Home Counties Division. **5th Battalion:** 'South Africa 1900–02'. *Headquarters:* 17 St George's Road, Wimbledon. *Companies:* 'A' (Streatham), 'B' (Leatherhead, Bookham and Walton-on-the-Hill), 'C' (Sutton), 'D' (Mitcham), 'E', 'F', 'G' (Wimbledon), 'H' (Epsom). **6th Battalion:** 'South Africa 1900–02'. 'Imperial Service'. *Headquarters:* Woodville, Surbiton Crescent, Kingston-upon-Thames, moving by 1912 to Orchard Road, Kingston-upon-Thames. *Companies:* 'A' (Esher, Cobham and Hersham), 'B', 'C' (Richmond), 'D', 'E', 'F' (Kingston-upon-Thames), 'G' (Chertsey and Weybridge), 'H' (Egham). *Cadets:* Richmond County School Cadet Corps, Richmond Hill Cadets and Weybridge and District Scout Cadets. Recognition of the latter being withdrawn under Army Order 260 of 1912.

East Yorkshire Regiment 4th Battalion: 'South Africa 1900–01'. *Headquarters:* Londesborough Barracks, Hull. *Companies:* 'A' to 'F' (Hull), 'G', 'H' (East Hull). Part of the York and Durham Infantry Brigade, Northumbrian Division. **5th (Cyclist) Battalion**: *Headquarters:* Park Street, Hull. *Companies:* 'A' to 'D' (Hull), 'E' (Howden, North Cave and Staddlethorpe), 'F' (Beverley, Hessle, Market Weighton and Pocklington), 'G' (Bridlington, Driffield, Hunmanby and Filey), 'H' (Hornsea, Hedon and Withernsea). Attached to Northern Command.

Eastern General Hospitals 1st: *Headquarters:* 1 St Peter's Terrace, later 39 Green Street, Cambridge. **2nd:** *Headquarters:* 117 Gloucester Road, Brighton.

Eastern Mounted Brigade *Headquarters:* The Old School House, Lexden, Colchester moving after 1913 to Belchamp Hall, Sudbury. *Units:* Suffolk, Norfolk, Essex Yeomanries and Essex RHA.

Eastern Mounted Brigade Ammunition Column See Essex RHA.

Eastern Mounted Brigade Field Ambulance *Headquarters:* Durley House, Waldeck Road, until moving in 1909 to Grove Road, Luton. *Sections:* 'A' (Luton and Dunstable), 'B' (Bedford).

Eastern Mounted Brigade Signal Troop *Headquarters:* 8 Head Street, Colchester.

Eastern Mounted Brigade Transport and Supply Column *Headquarters:* Langlands, Railway Street, Chelmsford, moving in 1911 to Market Road, Chelmsford.

Ebbw Vale Territorial Cadet Company Affiliated to 3rd Battalion Monmouthshire. Absorbed into 1st Cadet Battalion Monmouthshire Regiment in 1912.

Egremont (St John with Columbus) Cadet Company, 1st See 4th Cheshire Regiment.

Engineer and Railway Staff Corps *Headquarters:* 15 Dean's Yard, Westminster.

Essex and Suffolk Cyclist Battalion *Headquarters:* Colchester. In 1911 the battalion was divided to form the 6th Suffolk and 8th Essex Regiments. (See under each).

Essex and Suffolk Royal Garrison Artillery *Headquarters:* 6 Church Street, Harwich, moving to Main Road, Dovercourt in 1910. *Garrison Companies:* Nos 1, 2 (Harwich), Nos 3, 4 (Stratford), No 5 (Southend-on-Sea), No 6 (Felixstowe), Nos 7, 8 (Ipswich). In 1913 the establishment of the group was reduced to just four companies and in consequence the resulting composition became:

No 1 (Harwich and Felixstowe), No 2 (Stratford), No 3 (Southend-on-Sea and Leigh-on-Sea), No 4 (Ipswich).

Essex Batteries See 2nd East Anglian Brigade RFA.

Essex Brigade Company See East Anglian Divisional Transport and Supply Column.

Essex Fortress Engineers *Headquarters:* Bank Chamber, New Street, moving to 10 Broomfield Road, then 68 Duke Street and later Market Road, Chelmsford. *Electric Lights Company:* (Chelmsford).

Essex Infantry Brigade See East Anglian Division.

Essex Regiment The 4th to 7th Battalions together made up the Essex Infantry Brigade, East Anglian Division. **4th Battalion:** 'South Africa 1900–02'. *Headquarters:* Brentwood. *Companies:* 'A' (Romford and Harold Wood), 'B' (Manor Park), 'C' (Ilford), 'D' (Barking), 'E' (Loughton, Abridge and Woodford), 'F' (Brentwood, Southminster, Wickford, Billericay, Althorne, Bradwell-on-Sea, Burnham-on-Crouch, Mountnessing and Tillingham), 'G' (Ongar, Epping and Harlow), 'H' (Hornchurch, Dagenham, Rainham and, transferred from 'A' Company in 1913, Harold Wood). *Cadets:* Cranbrook College Cadets (Ilford), Manor Park Cadet Company (63 Carlyce Road, Manor Park), Ongar Grammar School Cadets, Warley Garrison Cadets and East Ham Secondary School Cadets. **5th Battalion:** 'South Africa 1900–02'. *Headquarters:* 35 Salisbury Avenue, Colchester, moving to Association Buildings, Market Road, Chelmsford in 1912. *Companies by 1912:* 'A' (Chelmsford, Broomfield, Writtle and Great Waltham), 'B' (Chelmsford, Boreham, Hatfield and Danbury), 'C' (Colchester), 'D' (Manningtree, Dedham and Bradfield), 'E' (Halstead, Hedingham, Yeldham, Pebmarsh, Earls Colne and Maplestead), 'F' (Braintree, Bocking, Dunmow, Thaxted, Great Bardfield, Felstead and Coggeshall), 'G' (Maldon, Wickham Bishops, Witham, Terling, Tiptree and Tollesbury), 'H' (Clacton-on-Sea, Wivenhoe and Walton-on-the-Naze). *Cadets:* King Edward VI School Cadet Corps (Chelmsford) and Colchester Royal Grammar School Cadets. **6th Battalion:** 'South Africa 1900–02'. *Headquarters:* West Ham. *Companies:* 'A' to 'G' (West Ham), 'H' (Prittlewell and Grays). *Cadets:* Church of the Ascension Cadet Corps (which, according to Army Order 65 of 1911, became 'E' Company of the 1st Cadet Battalion Essex Regiment), Palmer's School Cadet Corps (Grays), Given Wilson Institute Cadets (London Road, Plaistow) and Southend Technical School Cadet Corps (which in 1913 was re-designated as Southend High School). **7th Battalion:** 'South Africa 1900–02'. *Headquarters:* Park Road, Leyton, moving to Walthamstow Lodge, Church Hill, Walthamstow in 1913. *Companies:* 'A', 'B', 'C' (Hackney, moving to Walthamstow in 1913), 'D', 'E' (Leyton, moving to Walthamstow in 1913), 'F' (Silvertown, moving to Walthamstow in 1913), 'G' (Walthamstow), 'H' (Walthamstow and Chingford). *Cadets:* Forest Cadet Corps (Walthamstow), but recognition was withdrawn in 1912, and Walthamstow Cadets (26 Chester Road, Walthamstow). **8th (Cyclist) Battalion:** *Headquarters:* Colchester. *Companies:* 'A' (Leyton), 'B' (West Ham), 'C' (Colchester, Braintree, Dunmow and Maldon), 'D' (Saffron Waldon and Stansted Mountfitchet), 'E' (East Ham), 'F' (Ilford), 'G' (Brentwood), 'H' (Coggeshall). The battalion was originally raised in 1908 as part of the Essex and Suffolk Cyclist Battalion which was divided in 1911. **1st Cadet Battalion:** *Headquarters:* Wellington Street, Canning Town. Formed by the amalgamation of the West Ham, St Gabriel's Canning Town, St Matthew's (Custom House) and Church of the Ascension cadet units.

Essex Royal Horse Artillery *Headquarters:* Chelmsford, Bank Chambers, New Street, moving to 19 Broomfield Road, in 1909, then to 67 Duke Street, later Market Road in 1911. *Battery:* No 1 Section (Colchester), No 2 Section (Chelmsford and Ingatestone). *Ammunition Column:* Eastern Mounted Brigade, 'A' Sub-section (Colchester), 'B' Sub-section (Chelmsford).

Essex Yeomanry *Headquarters:* 17 Sir Isaac's Walk, Colchester. *Squadrons:* 'A' (Colchester, Clacton-on-Sea, Harwich, Walton-on-the-Naze, Great Bentley and Ardleigh), 'B' (Braintree, Halstead, Chelmsford and Tiptree), 'C' (Waltham Abbey, Epping, Loughton, Bishop's Stortford, Newport and Dunmow), 'D' (Southend-on-Sea, Brentwood, Grays, Stratford and Orsett). Part of the Eastern Mounted Brigade.

Exeter Cathedral School Cadet Company See 4th Devonshire Regiment.

Farnham Company West Surrey Cadets See 5th Queen's (Royal West Surrey Regiment).

Fife and Forfar Yeomanry 'South Africa 1900–01'. *Headquarters:* Cupar, moving to Kirkcaldy in 1914. *Squadrons:* 'A' (Cupar, Kirkcaldy, Ladybank and St Andrews), 'B' (Dunfermline, Balfron, Stirling, Kippen, Kelty, Kinross and Alloa), 'C' (Dundee), 'D' (Forfar, Arbroath, Edzell, Montrose and Laurencekirk). Part of the Highland Mounted Brigade.

Fifeshire Battery See 2nd Highland Brigade RFA.

Finsbury Rifles See 11th London Regiment.

First Surrey Rifles See 21st London Regiment.

Flintshire Battery See 3rd Welsh Brigade RFA.

Forest Cadet Corps (Walthamstow) See 7th Essex Regiment.

Forfarshire Battery See 2nd Highland Brigade RFA.

Forth Royal Garrison Artillery *Headquarters:* Edinburgh, 28 York Place moving to Easter Road Barracks in 1911. *Garrison Companies:* Nos 1 to 4 (Edinburgh), No 5 (Kirkcaldy and Kinghorn), No 6 (Burntisland and Inverkeithing).

Friern Barnet School Cadet Company See 7th Middlesex Regiment.

Frimley and Camberley Cadet Corps See 5th Queen's (Royal West Surrey Regiment).

Given Wilson Institute Cadets See 6th Essex Regiment.

Glamorgan Batteries See 1st and 2nd Welsh Brigades RFA.

Glamorgan Fortress Engineers *Headquarters:* Cardiff, 64 Charles Street, Westgate Street, moving later to Park Street. *Works Companies:* No 1 (Cardiff), No 2 (Gladstone Road, Barry and Barry Island). *Electric Lights Companies:* No 3 (Cardiff).

Glamorgan Royal Garrison Artillery *Headquarters:* Cardiff. *Garrison Companies:* Nos 1, 2, 3 (Cardiff), No 4 (Penarth), No 5 (Barry).

Glamorgan Royal Horse Artillery *Headquarters:* Cardiff, moving to Port Talbot in 1909. *Battery:* (Port Talbot). *Ammunition Column:* (Port Talbot). Part of the South Wales Mounted Brigade.

Glamorgan Yeomanry *Headquarters:* Bridgend. *Squadrons:* 'A' (Swansea, Neath, Port Talbot and Reynoldston), 'B' (Bridgend, Maesteg, Cowbridge and Porthcawl), 'C' (Cardiff), 'D' (Pontypridd, Nelson, Llwynypia, Caerphilly, Mountain Ash, Aberdare and Merthyr Tydfil). Part of the South Wales Mounted Brigade.

Glasgow Highlanders See 9th Highland Light Infantry.

Glasgow Postal Telegraph Messengers Cadet Corps See 1st (Glasgow Highland) Cadet Company Highland Light Infantry.

Gloucester and Worcester Brigade Company See South Midland Divisional Transport and Supply Column.

Gloucester and Worcester Infantry Brigade See South Midland Division.

Gloucestershire Batteries See 1st South Midland Brigade RFA.

Gloucestershire Regiment Together, the 4th and 6th Battalions provided half of the Gloucester and Worcester Infantry Brigade, South Midland Division. The 5th Battalion was with the South Midland Infantry Brigade, South Midland Division. **4th (City of Bristol) Battalion:** 'South Africa 1900–02'. *Headquarters:* Queen's Road, Clifton, Bristol. *Companies:* 'A' to 'E' (Clifton), 'F' (Mangotsfield, moving to St George, Bristol in 1913), 'G', 'H' (Bristol). **5th Battalion:** 'South Africa 1900–02'. *Headquarters:* The Barracks, Gloucester. *Companies:* 'A', 'B' (Gloucester), 'C' (Stroud and Cirencester), 'D' (Tewkesbury, Forthampton and Kemerton), 'E', 'F' (Cheltenham), 'G' (Dursley and Wotton-under-Edge), 'H' (Campden, Blockley, Willersey, Shipston-on-Stour, Moreton-in-Marsh, Mickleton and Stow-on-the-Wold). **6th Battalion:** *Headquarters:* St Michael's Hill, Bristol. *Companies:* 'A' to 'H' (Bristol). *Cadets:* 1st and 2nd Cadet Companies (Bristol).

Gloucestershire Yeomanry (Royal Gloucestershire Hussars) 'South Africa 1900–01'. *Headquarters:* The Barracks, Gloucester. *Squadrons:* 'A' (Gloucester, Ledbury, Cheltenham and Winchcombe), 'B' (Stroud, Westonbirt, Yate, Berkeley, Cirencester and Bourton-on-the-Water), 'C' (Newport, Cardiff, Chepstow, Ebbw Vale, Monmouth and Abergavenny), 'D' (Bristol, Broadmead, Tockington and Horfield Barracks). Part of the 1st South Midland Mounted Brigade.

Gordon Boys' Home Cadet Corps West End, Chobham.

Gordon Brigade Company See Highland Divisional Transport and Supply Column.

Gordon Highlanders Together, the four battalions made up the Gordon Infantry Brigade, Highland Division. **4th Battalion:** 'South Africa 1900–02'. *Headquarters:* Aberdeen. *Companies:* 'A' to 'H' (Aberdeen). **5th (Buchan and Formartin) Battalion:** 'South Africa 1900–01'. *Headquarters:* Peterhead. *Companies:* 'A' (Strichen, New Pitsligo, New Aberdour, New Deer and Maud), 'B' (Peterhead, Longside and St Fergus), 'C' (Peterhead, Boddam and Hatton), 'D' (Turriff, Fyvie and Cuminestown), 'E' (Ellon, Auchnagatt, Methlick, Skilmafilly and Newburgh), 'F' (Old Meldrum, Tarves, Newmachar and Pitmedden), 'G' (Fraserburgh and Rosehearty), 'H' (Fraserburgh and Lonmay). **6th (Banff and Donside) Battalion:** 'South Africa 1900–02'. *Headquarters:* Keith. *Companies:* 'A' (Banff, Aberchirder, Cornhill and Portsoy), 'B' (Dufftown, Aberlour, Chapeltown, Glenrinnes and Minmore), 'C' (Keith and Grange), 'D' (Buckie. Findochty and Cullen), 'E' (Inverurie and Pitcaple), 'F' (Alford, Cushnie, Lumsden, Glenbuckat, Strathdon, Corgarff and Towie), 'G' (Bucksburn and Dyce), 'H' (Huntly, Insch and Rhynie). **7th (Deeside Highland) Battalion:** 'South Africa 1900–02'. *Headquarters:* Banchory. *Companies:* 'A' (Banchory, Durris and Torphins), 'B' (Portlethen), 'C' (Stonehaven), 'D' (Laurencekirk, Auchenblae, Bervie, Fettercairn, Fordoun and Marykirk), 'E' (Ballater, Crathie and Braemar), 'F' (Aboyne, Tarland, Finzean and Logie Coldstone), 'G' (Skene, Blackburn, Monymusk and Echt), 'H' (Peterculter and Countesswells). **Shetland Companies:** *Headquarters:* Lerwick. *Companies:* 'A' (Lerwick), 'B' (Lerwick and Scalloway). Attached to Gordon Infantry Brigade.

Gordon Infantry Brigade See Highland Division.

Greenwich Naval Cadet Unit 160 Annandale Road, Greenwich.

Haberdashers (Hampstead) School Cadet Corps Western Road, Cricklewood.

Haddington Cadet Corps See 8th Royal Scots.

Hallamshire Battalion See 4th York and Lancaster Regiment.

Haltwhistle Territorial Cadets See 4th Northumberland Fusiliers.

Hampshire Batteries See 1st, 2nd and 3rd Wessex Brigades RFA.

Hampshire Brigade Company See Wessex Divisional Transport and Supply Column.

Hampshire Fortress Engineers *Headquarters:* Commercial Road, Portsmouth. *Works Companies:* Nos 1, 2, (Hampshire Terrace, Portsmouth), No 3 (Hampshire Terrace, moving to Eastleigh in 1912). *Electric Lights Companies:* Nos 4, 5 (Hampshire Terrace), No 6 (Freshwater, Lymington and East Cowes), No 7 (Gosport). In 1912 one of the Portsmouth electric lights companies was disbanded and subsequently Nos 6 and 7 EL Companies were renumbered as Nos 5 and 6.

Hampshire Infantry Brigade See Wessex Division.

Hampshire Regiment The 4th to 7th Battalions made up the Hampshire Infantry Brigade, Wessex Division. Both the 8th and 9th were unattached in Southern Command. **4th Battalion:** 'South Africa 1900–02'. *Headquarters:* Winchester. *Companies:* 'A', 'B' (Winchester), 'C' (Romsey, Botley, Chandler's Ford, Bishop's Waltham, Hursley, Mottisfont, Twyford, East Tytherley and Newtown), 'D' (Andover, Tidworth, Highclere, Burghclere, Kingsclere, Woodhay, Whitchurch and Cholderton), 'E' (Aldershot, Farnborough, Fleet, Cove and Redfields), 'F' (Yateley, Crowthorne, Blackwater and Eversley), 'G' (Basingstoke, Hartley Wintney, Silchester, Odiham and Strathfieldsaye), 'H' (Alton, Alresford and Selborne). *Cadets:* Peter Symonds School Cadet Corps (Winchester) and the Basingstoke and Eastrop Cadet Company which disappeared from the *Army List* in 1913. **5th Battalion:** 'South Africa 1900–02'. *Headquarters:* Carlton Place, Southampton. *Companies:* 'A' to 'E' (Southampton, Sarisbury, Woolston, Bitterne, Shirley and Westend), 'F' (Eastleigh and Fair Oak), 'G' (Southampton), 'H' (Southampton and Bursledon). **6th (Duke of Connaught's Own) Battalion:** 'South Africa 1900–02'. *Headquarters:* Connaught Hall, Portsmouth. *Companies:* 'A' to 'D' (Portsmouth), 'E' (Gosport and Lee-on-Solent), 'F' (Havant, Waterlooville, South Hayling and Rowlands Castle), 'G' (Petersfield, Greatham, Liphook, Headley and Clanfield), 'H' (Fareham, Titchfield, Swanwick, Wickham and Portchester). **7th Battalion:** 'South Africa 1900–02'. *Headquarters:* 177 Holdenhurst Road, Bournemouth. *Companies:* 'A' (Lymington, East Boldre, Milford-on-Sea, Brockenhurst and South Baddesley), 'B' (Christchurch, Highcliffe and Milton), 'C' (Ringwood, Burley, Fordingbridge and Damerham), 'D' (Totton, Hythe, Fawley and Marchwood), 'E' to 'H' (Bournemouth). *Cadets:* Lymington Cadet Corps. **8th (Isle of Wight Rifles, 'Princess Beatrice's') Battalion:** 'South Africa 1900–01'. *Headquarters:* Newport. *Companies:* 'A' (Ryde, Havenstreet, Binstead and Fishbourne), 'B' (St Helens, Bembridge, Seaview and Brading), 'C' (Newport, Calbourne and Yarmouth), 'D' (Newport, Wootton and Lock's Green), 'E' (Sandown, Shanklin and Newchurch), 'F' (Ventnor and Wroxall), 'G' (Newport, Niton, Whitwell, Godshill, Chillerton and Brighstone), 'H' (Cowes and Northwood). *Cadets:* Ventnor Cadet Company and Cowes Cadet Company. **9th (Cyclist) Battalion:** *Headquarters:* 32 Queen's Terrace, Southampton, moving to Hamilton House, Commercial Road, Southampton in 1914. *Companies:* 'A' (Southampton and Swanwick), 'B' (Bournemouth and Dorchester), 'C' (Romsey), 'D' (Portsmouth), 'E' (Rowland's Castle, Horndean and Petersfield), 'F' (West Meon), 'G' (Basingstoke and Herriard), 'H' (Highclere and Whitchurch). The battalion was formed towards the end of 1911. **1st Cadet Battalion:** *Headquarters:* 41a Union Street, Aldershot. Affiliated to 6th Battalion. Originally called 1st Cadet Battalion of Hampshire (for 'G' and 'H' Companies see Farnham Cadet Corps) and re-designated in 1913. **2nd Cadet Battalion:** *Headquarters:*

Connaught Drill Hall, Portsmouth. Affiliated to 6th Battalion. **3rd (Isle of Wight) Cadet Battalion:** *Headquarters:* Town Hall, Ryde. Affiliated to the 8th Battalion. Formed by the amalgamation in 1915 of the Ventnor, Ryde, Shanklin, East Isle of Wight, Cowes, Sandown and Newport Cadet Companies.

Hampshire Royal Garrison Artillery *Headquarters:* St Mary's Road, Southampton. *Heavy Battery:* No 1 (Southampton and Eastleigh). *Garrison Companies:* No 2 (Southampton), No 3 (Eastleigh and Bishop's Waltham), No 4 (Portsmouth), No 5 (Southampton), No 6 (Woolston and Bitterne), No 7 (Southampton), No 8 (Eastleigh).

Hampshire Royal Horse Artillery *Headquarters:* Southampton. *Battery:* (Southampton). *Ammunition Column:* (Basingstoke). Part of the 1st South Western Mounted Brigade.

Hampshire Yeomanry (Carabiniers) 'South Africa 1900–01'. *Headquarters:* Winchester, 41 Sussex Street, moving to Hyde Close in 1913. *Squadrons:* 'A' (Portsmouth, Freshwater, Newport, Ryde, Petersfield and Titchfield), 'B' (Winchester, Alton, Aldershot, Basingstoke and Bishop's Waltham), 'C' (Southampton, Eastleigh, Andover and Romsey), 'D' (Bournemouth, Stuckton, Highcliffe, Burley and Beaulieu). Part of the 1st South Western Mounted Brigade.

Harringay Cadet Company See 7th Middlesex Regiment.

Harrow Cadet Company See 9th Middlesex Regiment.

Haytor (Newton Abbot) Cadet Corps See 5th Devonshire Regiment.

Herefordshire Regiment 1st Battalion: 'South Africa 1900–02'. *Headquarters:* The Barracks, Hereford. *Companies:* 'A' (Hereford, Peterchurch, Madley, Marden and Burghill), 'B' (Ross-on-Wye and Upton Bishop), 'C' (Ledbury, Colwall, Much Marcle and Bosbury), 'D' (Kington, Presteigne and Eardisley), 'E' (Ruardean and Littledean), 'F' (Leominster and Bromyard), 'G' (Rhayader, Knighton, Chapel Lawn, Newbridge, Bucknell and Llandrindod Wells), 'H' (Hereford). Part of the Welsh Border Infantry Brigade.

Herne Bay College Cadet Corps See 4th Buffs (East Kent Regiment).

Hertfordshire Batteries See 4th East Anglian Brigade RFA.

Hertfordshire Cadets 1st (Chorley Wood) Company, see Hertfordshire Regiment. **2nd (Watford Scouts) Company**, see 4th East Anglian Brigade RFA and 1st Hertfordshire Regiment. **3rd (Stortford School)**, see Hertfordshire Regiment. **4th (St George's School)**, see Hertfordshire Regiment.

Hertfordshire Regiment 1st Battalion: 'South Africa 1900–02'. *Headquarters:* Hertford. *Companies:* 'A' (Hertford, Watton, Hatfield and Berkhamsted), 'B' (St Albans, London Colney and Harpenden), 'C' (Bishop's Stortford, Sawbridgeworth, Braughing, Widford, Ware and Wadesmill), 'D' (Watford and Chorley Wood), 'E' (Royston, Letchworth, Baldock and Ashwell), 'F' (Hemel Hempstead, Great Berkhamsted, Asheridge, Tring and Ivinghoe), 'G' (Hitchin, Welwyn, Stevenage and, from 1913, Whitwell), 'H' (Waltham Cross, Wormley, Cheshunt and Hoddesdon). *Cadets:* 1st (Chorley Wood) Hertfordshire Cadet Company, recognition withdrawn in December 1913, 2nd (Watford Scouts) Hertfordshire Cadet Company (Clarendon Hall, Watford), attached first to 2nd Hertfordshire Battery RFA, transferred in 1913), 3rd (Bishop's Stortford School) Hertfordshire Cadets, 4th Hertfordshire (St George's School) Cadets (Harpenden) and Bishop's Stortford College Cadet Corps. Part of the East Midland Infantry Brigade, East Anglian Division.

Hertfordshire Yeomanry 'South Africa 1900–01'. *Headquarters:* St Albans, moving to Hertford in 1912. *Squadrons:* 'A' (Watford, St John's Wood and Berkhamsted), 'B' (Hertford, Hoddesdon,

Broxbourne, Enfield Lock and Sawbridgeworth), 'C' (St Albans, Harpenden, Hendon, Westminster, Islington, Radlett, Redbourn and Hemel Hempstead), 'D' (High Barnet, Hatfield, Enfield, Finsbury Park, Harringay, Hitchin and Islington). Attached for training to Eastern Mounted Brigade.

Highland Brigades Royal Field Artillery 1st Brigade: *Headquarters:* North Silver Street, Aberdeen. *Batteries:* 1st, 2nd City of Aberdeen (North Silver Street), Banffshire (6 Castle Street, Banff, Macduff, Portsoy and Cullen). *Ammunition Columns:* 1st Highland Brigade (North Silver Street) and Banffshire Small Arm Section (Banff). Disbanded, the Small Arms Section left the brigade in 1910, the Banffshire Battery following in 17 May 1911. The latter being replaced by a new battery designated as 3rd City of Aberdeen. **2nd Brigade:** *Headquarters:* Dudhope Drill Hall, Brown Street, Dundee. *Batteries:* City of Dundee (Brown Street), Forfarshire (Arbroath), Fifeshire (Leven and East Wemyss). *Ammunition Column:* (Aberdeen). **3rd (Howitzer) Brigade:** *Headquarters:* South Street, Greenock. *Batteries:* 1st, 2nd Renfrewshire (South Street). *Ammunition Columns:* 3rd Highland Brigade (Cathcart), Renfrewshire Small Arms Section (Cathcart).

Highland Clearing Hospital Aberdeen.

Highland Cyclist Battalion 'South Africa 1900–02'. *Headquarters:* Birnam, moving in 1912 to Kirkcaldy. *Companies:* 'A' (Kirkcaldy), 'B' (Cowie), 'C' (Tayport), 'D' (Forfar), 'E' (Dunfermline), 'F' (New Scone), 'G' (East Wemyss), 'H' (Bannockburn). Unattached in Scottish Command. It was originally intended in 1908 to call this unit 8th Battalion Black Watch.

Highland Division *Headquarters:* 2 Charlotte Street, Perth. *Infantry Brigades:* **Seaforth and Cameron**, with 4th, 5th, 6th Seaforth Highlands and 4th Cameron Highlanders (Margaret Street, Inverness); **Gordon**, with 4th to 7th Gordon Highlanders (Territorial Barracks, Fonthill, Aberdeen) and **Argyll and Sutherland**, with 6th to 9th Argyll and Sutherland Highlanders (Princess Street, Stirling).

Highland Divisional Royal Engineers *Headquarters:* 80 Hardgate, Aberdeen. *Field Companies:* 1st Highland (21 Jardine Street, Glasgow), 2nd Highland (Aberdeen). *Telegraph Company:* (Aberdeen). In 1913 the Telegraph Company was included in the RE Signal Service, designated as the Highland Divisional Signal Company and organised as Headquarters and four sections: No 1, No 2 (Seaforth and Cameron), No 3 (Gordon) and No 4 (Argyll and Sutherland).

Highland Divisional Telegraph/Signal Company See Highland Divisional RE.

Highland Divisional Transport and Supply Column *Headquarters:* Perth, 16 Victoria Street, moving to 5 Scott Street in 1909. *Companies:* 1st (HQ) (Tay Street, Perth), 2nd (St John Street, Stirling and Grangemouth), 3rd (Gordon Brigade) (Fonthill Road, Aberdeen), 4th (Dundee).

Highland Field Ambulances 1st: *Headquarters:* Fonthill Road, Aberdeen. *Sections:* 'A', 'B', 'C' (Aberdeen). **2nd:** *Headquarters:* Fonthill Road, Aberdeen. *Sections:* 'A', 'B', 'C' (Aberdeen and Inverurie). **3rd:** *Headquarters:* Bell Street, Dundee, moving later to the Dunhope Drill Hall in Brown Street. *Sections:* 'A', 'B', 'C' (Dundee).

Highland Field Companies See Highland Divisional RE.

Highland (Heavy) Royal Garrison Artillery (Fifeshire) *Headquarters:* St Andrew's, moving by 1910 to The Hill, Dunfermline, then, in 1912, to Elgin Street also in Dunfermline. *Battery:* (Dunfermline, Charlestown and Culross). *Ammunition Column:* (Dunfermline).

Highland Light Infantry The 5th, 6th, 7th, 9th Battalions together made up the Highland Light Infantry Brigade, Lowland Division, while the 8th was attached to the Lothian Infantry Brigade, also with the Lowland Division. **5th (City of Glasgow) Battalion:** 'South Africa 1900–02'.

Headquarters: 24 Hill Street, Garnethill, Glasgow. *Companies:* 'A' to 'H' (Garnethill). **6th (City of Glasgow) Battalion:** 'South Africa 1900–02'. *Headquarters:* 172 Yorkhill Street, Glasgow. *Companies:* 'A' to 'H' (Glasgow). **7th (Blythswood) Battalion:** 'South Africa 1900–02'. *Headquarters:* 69 Main Street, Bridgeton, Glasgow. *Companies:* 'A' to 'H' (Bridgeton). **8th (Lanark) Battalion:** 'South Africa 1900–02'. *Headquarters:* Lanark. *Companies:* 'A' (Lesmahagow, Stonehouse, Coalburn and Blackwood), 'B' (Lanark, Biggar, Ponfeigh and Douglas), 'C' (Shotts, Cleland, Salsburgh and Harthill), 'D' (Carluke), 'E' (Forth and Tarbrax), 'F' (Law and Overtown), 'G' (Newmains), 'H' (Wishaw). **9th (Glasgow Highland) Battalion:** 'South Africa 1900–02'. *Headquarters:* 81 Greendyke Street, Glasgow. *Companies:* 'A' to 'H' (Glasgow). **1st (Glasgow Highland) Cadet Company:** *Headquarters:* Head Post Office, Glasgow. Formed as Glasgow Postal Telegraph Messengers Cadet Corps affiliated to 9th Highland Light Infantry and re-designated in 1912.

Highland Light Infantry Brigade See Lowland Division.

Highland Light Infantry Brigade Company See Lowland Divisional Transport and Supply Column.

Highland (Mountain) Brigade Royal Garrison Artillery, 4th *Headquarters:* Tarbert, moving to Russell Street, Rothesay in 1913. *Batteries:* Argyllshire (Campbeltown, Oban and Tobermory), Ross and Cromarty (Lochcarron, Kishorn, Kyle of Lochalsh, Applecross, Plockton, Dornie and Stornoway), Buteshire (Rothesay, Largs and Kilchattan). *Ammunition Column:* Tarbert with 'A' Sub-section (Tarbert), 'B' Sub-section (Millport), 'C' Sub-section, Dingwall.

Highland Mounted Brigade *Headquarters:* Beauly, moving in 1913 to Academy Street, Inverness. *Units:* Fife and Forfar, 1st and 2nd Lovat's Scouts Yeomanries and Inverness-shire RHA.

Highland Mounted Brigade Ammunition Column See Inverness-shire RHA.

Highland Mounted Brigade Field Ambulance *Headquarters:* 15 Douglas Row, Inverness, moving in 1913 to Rose Street, Inverness.

Highland Mounted Brigade Signal Troop *Headquarters:* Academy Street, Inverness.

Highland Mounted Brigade Transport and Supply Column *Headquarters:* Inverness, Margaret Street, moving in 1912 to Academy Street.

Home Counties Brigades Royal Field Artillery 1st Brigade: *Headquarters:* Church Street, Brighton. *Batteries:* 1st, 2nd Sussex (Church Street), 3rd Sussex (Marion Road, Hove and Shoreham). *Ammunition Column:* (Hove, moving to Brighton in 1911, then Worthing in 1913). *Cadets:* Imperial Service Cadet Corps Brighton (35 Temple Street), which was re-designation as 1st Cadet Battalion 1st Home Counties Brigade in 1913; Brighton Brigade Sussex Cadets (Brighton Town Hall) and Steyne School Cadet Corps (Worthing). **2nd Brigade:** *Headquarters:* Hatterly Road, St Leonard's-on-Sea, moving in 1914 to The Goffs, Eastbourne. *Batteries:* 4th Sussex (Eastbourne and Hailsham), 5th Sussex (St Leonards-on-Sea and Hastings), 6th Sussex (The Downs, Bexhill-on-Sea, Pevensey and Ninfield). *Ammunition Column:* (Hailsham). *Cadets:* Imperial Service Cadet Corps (St Cyprian's, Eastbourne), St Leonards Collegiate School Cadet Company (Hastings), first known as the Collegiate School Cadet Company and transferred from the Home Counties Field Company Royal Engineers in 1914 – the unit was re-designated at the same time – and Roborough School Cadet Company (Upper Avenue, Eastbourne). **3rd (Cinque Ports) Brigade:** *Headquarters:* Dover. *Batteries:* 1st Kent (Liverpool Street, Dover), 2nd Kent (Shellon Street, Folkestone), 3rd Kent (Victoria Park, Margate, moving to High Street, Ramsgate in 1911, Margate remained as a drill station). *Ammunition Column:* (Dover, moving to Deal in 1911), with the Gun Section (Deal), Small Arm Section (Sandwich). **4th (Howitzer) Brigade:** *Headquarters:* 'Trevethan', Bexley Road, Erith. *Batteries:* 4th, 5th Kent (Erith). *Ammunition Column:* (Erith).

Home Counties Clearing Hospital *Headquarters:* Surbiton.

Home Counties Division *Headquarters:* Hounslow. *Infantry Brigades:* **Surrey**, with 4th, 5th Queen's and 5th, 6th East Surrey Regiments (Woodhill, Tilford, moving to Shortheath, Farnham, then, in 1912, to Caxton House, Westminster); **Kent**, with 4th, 5th Buffs and 4th, 5th Royal West Kent Regiment (1 Hayes Road, Bromley, moving in 1911 to Tonbridge) and **Middlesex**, with 7th to 10th Middlesex Regiment (22 Holland Street, Kensington, moving to 21 Pelham Place, also in Kensington, and later, 15 Pall Mall East, Westminster).

Home Counties Divisional Royal Engineers *Headquarters:* 40 Junction Road, Eastbourne, moving to Ordnance Yard in 1912. *Field Companies:* 1st Home Counties (Eastbourne and Brighton), 2nd Home Counties (Tower Road West, St Leonards-on-Sea and Bexhill). *Telegraph Company:* (Coombe Road, Brighton). In 1913 the Telegraph Company was included in the RE Signal Service; designated as the Home Counties Divisional Signal Company with headquarters at 23 Gloucester Place, Brighton and organised as Headquarters and four sections: No 1, No 2 (Surrey), No 3 (Kent) and No 4 (Middlesex). Affiliated to the 2nd Field Company were the University School Cadet Company Hastings, and the Collegiate School Cadet Company, also at Hastings. The latter, in 1914, was transferred to the 2nd Home Counties Brigade RFA in 1914.

Home Counties Divisional Telegraph/Signal Company See Home Counties Divisional RE.

Home Counties Divisional Transport and Supply Column *Headquarters:* Hounslow. *HQ and Brigade Companies:* HQ (117 Gloucester Road, Brighton), Surrey Brigade Company (259 Walton Road, Woking), Kent Brigade Company (Church Institute, Union Street, Maidstone) and Middlesex Brigade Company (The Old Court House, Teddington, moving in 1911 to 61 Stanley Road, Teddington, then The Barracks, Barnet in 1912. After the last move, Teddington became a drill station.

Home Counties Field Ambulances 1st: *Headquarters:* The Palace, Maidstone. *Sections:* 'A' (Maidstone), 'B' (Snodland), 'C' (Chatham). **2nd:** *Headquarters:* 3 Adelaide Place, Canterbury, moving to Ashford in 1911. *Sections:* 'A' (Canterbury), 'B' (Ashford and Folkestone), 'C' (Whitstable). **3rd:** *Headquarters:* 24 Claremont Road, Surbiton. *Sections:* 'A', 'B', 'C' (Surbiton).

Home Counties Field Companies See Home Counties Divisional RE.

Home Counties (Heavy) Royal Garrison Artillery (Kent) *Headquarters:* Faversham. *Battery:* (Faversham and Chatham). *Ammunition Column:* (Chatham).

Honourable Artillery Company *Headquarters:* Armoury House, Finsbury. *Artillery:* 'A' Battery (1st City of London Horse Artillery) with London Mounted Brigade Ammunition Column (Finsbury), 'B' Battery (2nd City of London Horse Artillery) with South Eastern Mounted Brigade Ammunition Column (Finsbury). *Infantry:* Four companies (Finsbury). Attached to the 1st London Division.

Hugh Myddelton School Cadet Corps *Headquarters:* The Guildhall, City of London.

Hull Cadet Company St Mark's Church Scouts The vicarage, St Mark's.

Huntingdonshire Cyclist Battalion *Headquarters:* St Mary's Street, Huntingdon. Formed in 1914.

Hutcheson's Grammar School Cadet Corps See 7th Cameronians (Scottish Rifles).

Ilford Church Cadets 193 Mortlake Road, Ilford.

Imperial Cadet Corps See Ackmar School and New King's School Cadet Corps.

Imperial Cadet Yeomanry (City of London) 118–122 Holborn.

Imperial Service Cadet Corps Brighton See 1st Home Counties Brigade RFA.

Imperial Service Cadet Corps Eastbourne See 2nd Home Counties Brigade RFA.

Inns of Court Officers Training Corps 'South Africa 1900–01'. *Headquarters:* 10 Stone Buildings, Lincoln's Inn, Holborn. *Cavalry Squadron:* (Lincoln's Inn). *Infantry:* 'A', 'B', 'C' Companies (Lincoln's Inn).

Inverness-shire Royal Horse Artillery *Headquarters:* Margaret Street, Inverness. *Battery:* (Inverness). *Ammunition Column:* (King Street, Nairn). Part of the Highland Mounted Brigade.

Isle of Wight Rifles See 8th Hampshire Regiment.

Kensington and Hammersmith Navy League Boys' Brigade See 13th London Regiment.

Kensington Cadet Corps See 2nd London Divisional Engineers.

Kent Batteries See 3rd and 4th Home Counties Brigades RFA.

Kent Brigade Company See Home Counties Divisional Transport and Supply Column.

Kent Cyclist Battalion *Headquarters:* Tonbridge. *Companies:* 'A' (Bromley). 'B' (Tonbridge and Pembury), 'C' (Beckenham), 'D' (Maidstone and Chatham), 'E' (Tunbridge Wells), 'F' (Canterbury, Ashford and Whitstable), 'G' (Ramsgate, Margate and Sandwich), 'H' (Sandgate, Hythe, Dover and Folkestone).

Kent Fortress Engineers *Headquarters:* Chatham, moving to the Submarine Mining School at Gillingham in 1911. *Works Companies:* No 1 (Tonbridge and Southborough), No 2 (Ashford), No 3 (Gillingham, moving to Southborough in 1914). *Electric Lights Companies:* No 4 (Gillingham), No 5 (Gillingham and Gravesend), No 6 (Gillingham). *Cadets:* Nos 1 to 4 Cadet Companies. Amalgamation as 1st Cadet Battalion Kent (Fortress) Royal Engineers took place in 1913. Company locations were: Broomhill, Southborough and Tunbridge Wells. 2nd Cadet Battalion (Mathematical School, Rochester). Formed 1914.

Kent Infantry Brigade See Home Counties Division.

Kent Royal Garrison Artillery It was intended, in 1908, to form ten garrison companies under the title of Sussex and Kent RGA and with headquarters at Old Brompton, Chatham. By the beginning of 1910, however, the counties had been separated and were both shown in the *Army List* as independent formations. **Kent RGA:** *Headquarters:* Old Brompton, moving in 1913 to Sheerness. *Companies:* No 1 (Gillingham), No 2 (Gravesend), No 3 (Northfleet), Nos 4, 5 (Sheerness), No 6 (Dover), No 7 (Folkestone). In 1913 the establishment was reduced to three companies: No 1 (Fort Clarence, Rochester and Sheerness), No 2 (Gravesend and Northfleet), No 3 (Dover and Folkestone).

Kilburn Grammar School Cadet Company See 9th Middlesex Regiment.

King Edward VI School Cadet Corps, Chelmsford See 5th Essex Regiment.

King Edward's Grammar School (Aston) Cadet Corps Aston, Birmingham.

King Edward's Horse (The King's Oversea Dominions Regiment) 'Imperial Service'. *Headquarters:* Grove House, Holywood Road, Fulham, moving to the Duke of York's Headquarters,

King's Road, Chelsea in 1911. Made up of Colonial subjects resident in London, the regiment comprised the usual four squadrons and was organised: 'A' (British Asian), 'B' (Canadian), 'C' (Australasian), 'D' (South Africa). There was also a troop in Liverpool and, records Walter Richards in 1910, one contemplated at Manchester and detachments at Oxford and Cambridge. The original title of the regiment was changed from the King's Colonials to the above in 1910. In 1912 (with effect from 21 August) the regiment ceased to be part of the Territorial Force and was transferred to the Special Reserve. Part of the London Mounted Brigade.

King Edward's School (Camp Hill) Cadet Corps Camp Hill, Birmingham.

King Edward's School (Witley) Cadet Corps Witley, Surrey.

King's (Liverpool Regiment) The 5th to 8th Battalions made up the Liverpool Infantry Brigade, West Lancashire Division, while the 9th and 10th provided half of the South Lancashire Infantry Brigade, also with West Lancashire Division. **5th Battalion:** 'South Africa 1900–02'. *Headquarters:* 65 St Anne Street, Liverpool. *Companies:* 'A' to 'H' (Liverpool). **6th (Rifle) Battalion:** 'South Africa 1900–01'. *Headquarters:* Prince's Park Barracks, Upper Warwick Street, Liverpool. *Companies:* 'A' to 'H' (Liverpool). **7th Battalion:** 'South Africa 1900–02'. *Headquarters:* 77 Shaw Street, Liverpool, moving in 1913 to 99 Park Street, Bootle. *Companies:* 'A' to 'D' (Bootle), 'E' (Crosby), 'F' (Bootle), 'G' (Southport), 'H' (Southport and Formby). *Cadets:* Southport Cadet Corps (60 Scarisbrick New Road, Southport). **8th (Irish) Battalion:** 'South Africa 1900–02'. *Headquarters:* Liverpool, 50–52 Everton Brow, moving to 75 Shaw Street in 1912. *Companies:* 'A' to 'H' *(Liverpool)*. **9th Battalion:** 'South Africa 1900–01'. *Headquarters:* 57–61 Everton Road, Liverpool. *Companies:* 'A' to 'E' (Everton Road), 'F' (Ormskirk), 'G' (Everton Road), 'H' (Ormskirk). **10th (Scottish) Battalion:** 'South Africa 1902'. *Headquarters:* 7 Fraser Street, Liverpool. *Companies:* 'A' to 'H' (Liverpool). **1st Territorial Cadet Battalion:** *Headquarters:* 16 South Castle Street, Liverpool. Affiliated to the Liverpool Infantry Brigade. Recognition, however, was withdrawn in 1912. **City of Liverpool Cadet Battalion:** *Headquarters:* Seaton Buildings, 17 Water Street. Affiliated to Liverpool Infantry Brigade.

King's Oversea Dominions Regiment See King Edward's Horse.

King's Own (Royal Lancaster Regiment) The two battalions together provided half of the North Lancashire Infantry Brigade, West Lancashire Division. **4th Battalion:** 'South Africa 1900–02'. *Headquarters:* Ulverston. *Companies:* 'A' (Ulverston and Grange-over-Sands), 'B' (Ulverston, Greenodd, Haverthwaite and Lakeside), 'C' to 'F' (Barrow-in-Furness), 'G' (Dalton-in-Furness and Askam-in-Furness), 'H' (Millom, Broughton-in-Furness, Coniston and Hawkshead). **5th Battalion:** 'South Africa 1900–02'. *Headquarters:* Lancaster. *Companies:* 'A' (Lancaster and Galgate), 'B', 'C', 'D' (Lancaster), 'E' (Morecambe), 'F' (Carnforth, Arnside, Silverdale and Caton), 'G' (Fleetwood, Poulton-le-Fylde, Garstang and Blackpool), 'H' (Fleetwood, Preesall and Thornton).

King's Own Royal Regiment See Norfolk Yeomanry.

King's Own Scottish Borderers The two battalions together provided one half of the South Scottish Infantry Brigade, Lowland Division. **4th (The Border) Battalion:** 'South Africa 1900–02'. *Headquarters:* Melrose, moving to Galashiels in 1910. *Companies:* 'A' (Kelso and Jedburgh), 'B' (Hawick), 'C' (Hawick, Melrose, St Boswells and Newcastleton), 'D' (Duns, Greenlaw, Lauder and Earlston), 'E' (Coldstream, Ayton, Eyemouth, Chirnside, Swinton and Coldingham), 'F', 'G' (Galashiels), 'H' (Selkirk, Melrose and, transferred from 'C' Company in 1914, St Boswells). **5th (Dumfries & Galloway) Battalion:** 'South Africa 1900–02'. *Headquarters:* Dumfries. *Companies:* 'A' (Dumfries and Moniaive), 'B' (Annan, Langholm and Canonbie), 'C' (Lockerbie, Ecclefechan and Moffat), 'D' (Sanquhar, Thornhill and Kirkconnel), 'E' (Maxwelltown), 'F'

(Dalbeattie), 'G' (Castle Douglas, Corsock, Gatehouse and Kirkcudbright), 'H' (Newton Stewart, Wigtown, Creetown, Kirkcowan, Whithorn and Garlieston).

King's Own Yorkshire Light Infantry The battalions together provided one half of the 3rd West Riding Infantry Brigade, West Riding Division. **4th Battalion:** 'South Africa 1900–02'. *Headquarters:* Wakefield. *Companies:* 'A', 'B' (Wakefield), 'C' (Normanton), 'D' (Ossett), 'E', 'F' (Dewsbury), 'G' (Batley), 'H' (Morley). **5th Battalion:** 'South Africa 1900–02'. *Headquarters:* French Gate, Doncaster. *Companies:* 'A' (Pontefract), 'B', 'C' (Doncaster), 'D' (Goole), 'E' (Featherstone), 'F' (Doncaster), 'G' (Conisbrough), 'H' (Castleford).

King's Royal Rifle Corps, 1st Cadet Battalion 'South Africa 1900–02'. *Headquarters:* 42–44 Sun Street, Finsbury, London.

King's School Peterborough Cadet Corps See 4th Northamptonshire Regiment.

King's Shropshire Light Infantry 4th Battalion: 'South Africa 1900–02'. *Headquarters:* Shrewsbury. *Companies:* 'A' (Shrewsbury), 'B' (Whitchurch and Wem), 'C' (Wellington, Market Drayton and Hodnet), 'D' (Ironbridge and Much Wenlock), 'E' (Shifnal, Oakengates and Newport), 'F' (Bridgnorth and Highley), 'G' (Ludlow, Craven Arms, Cleehill and Cleobury Mortimer), 'H' (Oswestry and Ellesmere). Attached to the Welsh Border Infantry Brigade. *Cadets:* Bridgnorth Cadet Company (Eimslea, Bridgnorth).

Kirkby Lonsdale Cadet Company See 4th Battalion Border Regiment.

Kirkcudbrightshire Battery See 2nd Lowland Brigade RFA.

Knutsford (Parish) Cadet Cadets Knutsford, Cheshire.

Lanarkshire Fortress Engineers *Headquarters:* Main Street, Bellshill. *Works Company:* No 1 (Bellshill). Disbanded 1 September 1910.

Lanarkshire Yeomanry 'South Africa 1900–02'. *Headquarters:* Lanark. *Squadrons:* 'A' (Douglas, Auchenheath, Lesmahagow, Douglas Water and Coalburn), 'B' (Lanark, Carluke, Carstairs, Wishaw, Peebles and Biggar), 'C' (Coatbridge and Glasgow), 'D' (Dumfries, Lockerbie, Langholm, Annan, Moffat, Thornhill and Sanquhar). Part of the Lowland Mounted Brigade.

Lanarkshire Yeomanry (Queen's Own Royal Glasgow) 'South Africa 1900–01'. *Headquarters:* Glasgow, 158 Renfrew Street, moving to 26 India Street in 1910, then to Yorkhill Parade, Yorkhill 1912. *Squadrons:* 'A', 'B' (Glasgow), 'C' (Paisley and Greenock), 'D' (Glasgow). Attached to the Lowland Mounted Brigade.

Lancashire and Cheshire Royal Garrison Artillery *Headquarters:* 19 Low Hill, Liverpool. *Garrison Companies:* Nos 1, 2, 3 (Liverpool), No 4 (Liscard), No 5 (New Brighton), Nos 6, 7 (Barrow-in-Furness). In 1909, a new company was raised in Liverpool and designated as No 4 Company. Subsequently Nos 4 to 7 were renumbered as 5 to 8. The two Cheshire companies (now Nos 5 and 6) were later reorganised and relocated at Riverview Road, Seacombe.

Lancashire Batteries See West Lancashire and East Lancashire Brigades RFA.

Lancashire Brigade Royal Garrison Artillery *Headquarters:* Sefton Barracks, Upper Warwick Street, Toxteth Park, Liverpool. *Heavy Batteries:* 1st, 2nd Lancashire (Liverpool). Attached to the East and West Lancashire Divisions respectively.

Lancashire Fortress Engineers *Headquarters:* Liverpool, Dock Board Office, Canning Park, moving to Tramway Road, Aigburth in 1911. *Works Company:* No 1 (Aigburth). *Electric Lights Companies:* Nos 2, 3 (Aigburth).

Lancashire Fusiliers The four battalions together constituted the Lancashire Fusiliers Infantry Brigade, East Lancashire Division. **5th Battalion:** 'South Africa 1900–02'. *Headquarters:* Castle Armoury, Bury. *Companies:* 'A', 'B' (Bury), 'C', 'D' (Heywood), 'E', 'F' (Bury), 'G' (Bury and Radcliffe), 'H' (Bury). **6th Battalion:** 'South Africa 1900–02'. *Headquarters:* Rochdale. *Companies:* 'A' (Middleton), 'B', 'C', 'D' (Rochdale), 'E' (Middleton), 'F' (Rochdale), 'G', 'H' (Todmorden). **7th Battalion:** 'South Africa 1900–02'. *Headquarters:* Cross Lane, Salford. *Companies:* 'A' to 'H' (Salford). **8th Battalion:** 'South Africa 1900–02'. *Headquarters:* Cross Lane, Salford. *Companies:* 'A' to 'H' (Salford). *Cadets:* Broughton Lads' Brigade. Re-designated as 1st Cadet Company 8th Battalion in 1914.

Lancashire Fusiliers Brigade Company See East Lancashire Divisional Transport and Supply Column.

Lancashire Fusiliers Infantry Brigade See East Lancashire Division.

Lancashire Heavy Batteries See Lancashire Brigade RGA.

Lancashire Hussars Yeomanry 'South Africa 1900–02'. *Headquarters:* Prince Alfred Road, Liverpool. *Squadrons:* 'A' (Ashton-in-Makerfield, Wigan and Liverpool), 'B' (St Helens), 'C' (Newton-le-Willows), 'D' (Rainhill). Attached to the Welsh Border Mounted Brigade.

Leeds Postal Telegraph Messengers' Cadet Company See 7th West Yorkshire Regiment and Northern Command Signal Companies.

Leeds Rifles See 7th and 8th West Yorkshire Regiment.

Leicestershire Regiment The two battalions provided half of the Lincoln and Leicester Infantry Brigade, North Midland Division. **4th Battalion:** 'South Africa 1900–02'. *Headquarters:* Oxford Street, Leicester. *Companies:* 'A' (Leicester), 'B' (Leicester and Anstey), 'C' (Leicester and Syston), 'D' to 'G' (Leicester), 'H' (Wigston Magna). **5th Battalion:** 'South Africa 1900–02'. *Headquarters:* Loughborough. 'A' (Ashby-de-la-Zouch and Coalville), 'B' (Oakham, Cottesmore, Whissendine and Uppingham), 'C' (Melton Mowbray, Bottesford, Harby and Wymondham), 'D' (Hinckley), 'E' (Market Harborough, Kibworth and Fleckney), 'F' (Mountsorrel and Woodhouse Eaves), 'G' (Uppingham, Barrowden, Bisbrooke, Shepshed and Ketton), 'H' (Loughborough).

Leicestershire Royal Horse Artillery *Headquarters:* 1 Magazine Square, Leicester. *Battery:* (Leicester). *Ammunition Column:* (Leicester). Part of the North Midland Mounted Brigade.

Leicestershire Yeomanry (Prince Albert's Own) 'South Africa 1900–02'. *Headquarters:* Leicester. *Squadrons:* 'A' (Melton Mowbray, Uppingham, Rearsby, Harby and Oakham), 'B' (Leicester), 'C' (Loughborough, Whitwick, Mountsorrel and Leicester), 'D' (Lutterworth, Market Bosworth, Market Harborough, Wigston Magna, Ibstock and Hinckley). Part of the North Midland Mounted Brigade.

Lewisham Cadet Battalion Hill View, Grove Park, Lewisham.

Lincoln Cadet Battalion, 3rd No 1 Company (Church of England Men's Society), Skegness.

Lincoln and Leicester Infantry Brigade See North Midland Division.

Lincolnshire Batteries See 1st North Midland Brigade RFA.

Lincolnshire Regiment The two battalions made up one half of the Lincoln and Leicester Infantry Brigade, North Midland Division. **4th Battalion:** 'South Africa 1900–02'. *Headquarters:* Lincoln, *Companies:* 'A' (Lincoln), 'B' (Grantham), 'C' (Boston), 'D' (Stamford), 'E' (Lincoln), 'F' (Spalding, Bourne and Sleaford), 'G' (Horncastle and Woodhall Spa), 'H' (Lincoln). **5th Battalion:**

'South Africa 1900–02'. *Headquarters:* Grimsby. *Companies:* 'A', 'B' (Grimsby), 'C' (Spilsby and Skegness), 'D' (Louth and North Thoresby), 'E' (Barton-upon-Humber), 'F' (Alford), 'G' (Frodingham and Brigg), 'H' (Gainsborough).

Lincolnshire Yeomanry *Headquarters:* Old Barracks, Lincoln. *Squadrons:* 'A' (Grantham, Stamford, Bourne and Holbeach), 'B' (Louth, Spilsby, Horncastle, Alford, Skegness and Boston), 'C' (Lincoln, Sleaford, Gainsborough, Market Rasen and Wragby), 'D' (Grimsby, Barton-upon-Humber, Brigg, Scunthorpe and Ulceby). Part of the North Midland Mounted Brigade.

Liscard High School Cadet Corps See 4th Cheshire Regiment.

Liverpool Brigade Company See West Lancashire Divisional Transport and Supply Column.

Liverpool Church Cadet Battalion 22 West Road, Liverpool.

Liverpool Infantry Brigade See West Lancashire Division.

Liverpool Irish See 8th King's (Liverpool Regiment).

Liverpool Scottish See 10th King's (Liverpool Regiment).

London Airline Signal Company See London District Signal Companies.

London Balloon Company Unique within the TF, the London Balloon Company's role was observation and spotting for the artillery. Temporary headquarters were first found in Regency Street, Westminster, but premises in Palmer Street, also in Westminster, were found by the beginning of 1909. The company was disbanded on 31 March 1913.

London Batteries See London Brigades RFA.

London Brigade Companies See London Divisional Transport and Supply Columns.

London Brigades Royal Field Artillery 1st (City of London) Brigade: *Headquarters:* Stains House, Barbican, City of London, moving in 1912 to Handel Street in Bloomsbury. *Batteries:* 1st, 2nd, 3rd City of London (Bloomsbury). *Ammunition Column:* (Bloomsbury). **2nd Brigade:** *Headquarters:* Royal Arsenal, Woolwich. *Batteries:* 4th, 5th County of London (Woolwich), 6th County of London (Woolwich, moving to Eltham in 1914). *Ammunition Column:* (Woolwich and Eltham). *Cadets:* 1st Woolwich Cadet Corps (High Street, Plumstead). **3rd Brigade:** *Headquarters:* Artillery Barracks, Leonard Street, Finsbury. *Batteries:* 7th, 8th, 9th County of London (Finsbury). *Ammunition Column:* (Finsbury). **4th (Howitzer) Brigade:** *Headquarters:* 28 Rhyme Road, Lewisham, moving in 1912 to Ennersdale Road, Lewisham. *Batteries:* 10th, 11th County of London (Lewisham). *Ammunition Column:* (Lewisham). **5th Brigade:** *Headquarters:* 76 Lower Kennington Lane, Lambeth. *Batteries:* 12th, 13th County of London (Lambeth), 14th County of London (Porteous Road, Paddington). *Ammunition Column:* (Lambeth). **6th Brigade:** *Headquarters:* 105 Holland Road, Brixton. *Batteries:* 15th, 16th, 17th County of London (Brixton). *Ammunition Column:* (Brixton). **7th Brigade:** *Headquarters:* Wood Lane, Shepherds Bush, moving in 1911 to High Street, Fulham. *Batteries:* 18th County of London (as headquarters), 19th County of London (Shepherds Bush), 20th County of London (as headquarters). *Ammunition Column:* (as headquarters). **8th (Howitzer) Brigade:** *Headquarters:* Bloomfield Road, Plumstead, moving in 1913 to 'Oaklands', St Margaret's Road, Woolwich. *Batteries:* 21st, 22nd County of London (as headquarters). *Ammunition Column:* (as headquarters).

London Cable Signal Company See London District Signal Companies.

London Clearing Hospitals 1st and 2nd: *Headquarters:* Duke of York's Headquarters, King's Road, Chelsea.

London District Signal Companies *Headquarters:* Regency Street, moving by the beginning of 1909 to Palmer Street, Westminster. *Signal Companies:* London Wireless, Cable and Airline (as headquarters).

London Division, 1st *Headquarters:* Frier's House, New Broad Street, City of London. *Infantry Brigades:* **1st London**, with 1st to 4th London Regiment (34 Walbrook moving to Friar's House, New Broad Street in the City of London by 1909); **2nd London**, with 5th to 8th London Regiment (Buckingham Gate, Westminster) and **3rd London**, with 9th to 12th London Regiment (Buckingham Gate, Westminster).

London Division, 2nd *Headquarters:* Craig's Court House, Charring Cross, Westminster, moving in 1912 to the Duke of York's Headquarters, King's Road, Chelsea. *Infantry Brigades:* **4th London**, with 13th to 16th London Regiment (Buckingham Gate, Westminster); **5th London**, with 17th to 20th London Regiment (Buckingham Gate, Westminster) and **6th London**, with 21st to 24th London Regiment (73 New Street, Lambeth, moving to 14 Cheyne Gardens, Chelsea, then in 1912 to the Duke of York's Headquarters, King's Road, Chelsea).

London Divisional Royal Engineers 1st: *Headquarters:* 10 Victoria Park Square, Bethnal Green. *Field Companies:* 1st, 2nd London (Bethnal Green). *Telegraph Company:* (Bethnal Green). In 1913 the Telegraph Company was included in the RE Signal Service; designated as the 1st London Divisional Signal Company and organised as Headquarters and four sections: No 1, No 2 (1st London), No 3 (2nd London) and No 4 (3rd London). **2nd:** *Headquarters:* 67 College Street, Fulham, moving to the Duke of York's Headquarters, King's Road, Chelsea in 1910. *Field Companies:* 3rd, 4th London (as headquarters). *Telegraph Company:* (as headquarters). *Cadets:* Kensington Cadet Corps which was re-designated as Cadet Company Royal Engineers 2nd London Division (Kensington Cadet Corps) in 1911, then in 1913 to Royal Engineers Cadets (2nd London Division). In 1913 the Telegraph Company was included in the RE Signal Service; designated as the 2nd London Divisional Signal Company and organised as Headquarters and four sections: No 1, No 2 (4th London), No 3 (5th London) and No 4 (6th London).

London Divisional Telegraph/Signal Companies See 1st and 2nd London Divisional RE.

London Divisional Transport and Supply Columns 1st: *Headquarters:* 52 Wellington Street, Woolwich, moving in 1912 to Charles Street, Plumstead. *HQ and Brigade Companies:* HQ, 1st, 2nd and 3rd London Brigade Companies (as headquarters). **2nd:** *Headquarters:* Grove House, Hollywood Road, Fulham, moving in 1912 to the Duke of York's Headquarters. *HQ and Brigade Companies:* HQ, 4th, 5th and 6th Brigade Companies (as headquarters).

London Electrical Engineers *Headquarters:* 46 Regency Street, Westminster. Six companies.

London Field Ambulances 1st (City of London): *Headquarters:* 130 Bunhill Row, moving to the Duke of York's Headquarters, King's Road, Chelsea in 1913. **2nd (City of London):** *Headquarters:* 113 Shaftesbury Street, Shoreditch, moving to the Duke of York's Headquarters, King's Road, Chelsea. **3rd (City of London):** *Headquarters:* 51 Calthorpe Street, Gray's Inn Road, St Pancras, moving in 1913 to the Duke of York's Headquarters, King's Road, Chelsea. **4th:** *Headquarters:* School of Ambulance, Brookhill Road, Woolwich. There were also drill stations at Dartford and Erith. **5th:** 159 Greenwich Road, Greenwich. **6th:** 242 Vauxhall Bridge Road, Westminster, moving to the Duke of York's Headquarters, King's Road, Chelsea in 1913.

London Field Companies See 1st and 2nd London Divisional RE.

London General Hospitals 1st and 2nd: *Headquarters:* 51 Calthorpe Street, St Pancras, moving in 1912 to the Duke of York's Headquarters in King's Road, Chelsea. **3rd:** *Headquarters:*

26 Ivy Lane, City of London, moving to 3 Henry Street, Holborn in 1912. **4th:** *Headquarters:* 148 Harley Street, St Marylebone moving to the Duke of York's Headquarters in 1912.

London Heavy Batteries See London (Heavy) Brigade RGA.

London (Heavy) Brigade Royal Garrison Artillery *Headquarters:* Islington, 2 Barnsbury Park until moving in 1911 to Offord Road. *Heavy Batteries:* 1st, 2nd London which were grouped together under the title London Brigade. The batteries served the 1st and 2nd London Divisions respectively.

London Irish Rifles See 18th London Regiment.

London Mounted Brigade *Headquarters:* Craig's Court House, Charring Cross, Westminster, moving in 1912 to the Duke of York's Headquarters, King's Road, Chelsea. *Units:* City of London, 1st and 3rd County of London Yeomanries, and 'A' Battery Honourable Artillery Company. Prior to its transfer to the Special Reserve in 1912, the King's Colonials formed part of the brigade. It was replaced by 3rd County of London Yeomanry.

London Mounted Brigade Ammunition Column See Honourable Artillery Company.

London Mounted Brigade Field Ambulance *Headquarters:* 242 Vauxhall Bridge Road, Westminster until moving in 1911 to 3 Henry Street, Gray's Inn Road, Holborn.

London Mounted Brigade Signal Troop *Headquarters:* 51 Calthorpe Street, Holborn.

London Mounted Brigade Transport and Supply Column *Headquarters:* 112 Shaftesbury Street, Shoreditch, moving in 1912 to 51 Calthorpe Street, St Pancras.

London Regiment Recruited within the City and Greater (County of) London areas, this solely TF regiment comprised twenty-six battalions – the largest peace-time infantry formation within the British Army. However, each battalion constituted and independent regiment. When the London Regiment was created in 1908, it was intended to include the Honourable Artillery Company and Inns of Court Volunteers as 26th and 27th Battalions respectively. This, however, was not acceptable and these, certainly in the case of the HAC, ancient regiments remained outside (note vacant numbers) of the new formation. The first eight battalions were administered by the City of London TFA, and those from 9th onwards by the County of London TFA. The London Regiment had no direct affiliation to any regular army formation, although all battalions, having prior to 1908 been part of a regimental system, retained strong associations – titles, badges, uniform, traditions etc – with their former parent formation. The battalions were formed from the several Volunteer Battalions, or Volunteer Rifle Corps, attached to the Queen's (Royal West Surrey Regiment), Royal Fusiliers, East Surrey Regiment, Royal West Kent Regiment, King's Royal Rifle Corps and Rifle Brigade. The 1st to 24th Battalions were included in one of other of the two London Divisions: 1st to 4th (1st Brigade, 1st Division), 5th to 8th (2nd Brigade, 1st Division), 9th to 12th (3rd Brigade, 1st Division), 13th to 16th (4th Brigade, 2nd Division), 17th to 20th (5th Brigade, 2nd Division), 21st to 24th (6th Brigade, 2nd Division). **1st (City of London) Battalion (Royal Fusiliers):** 'South Africa 1900–02'. *Headquarters:* 33 Fitzroy Square, St Pancras, moving to Handel Street, St Pancras in 1912. *Companies:* 'A', 'B', 'C' (St Pancras), 'D', 'E' (15 Battersea Square, Battersea), 'F', 'G', 'H' (St Pancras). **2nd (City of London) Battalion (Royal Fusiliers):** 'South Africa 1900–02'. *Headquarters:* 9 Tufton Street, Westminster. *Companies:* 'A' to 'H' (Tufton Street). **3rd (City of London) Battalion (Royal Fusiliers):** 'South Africa 1900–02'. *Headquarters:* 21 Edward Street, St Pancras. *Companies:* 'A' to 'H' (Edward Street), there was also a drill station at 207 Harrow Road, Paddington. *Cadets:* 1st North Paddington Cadets (Pember Hall, Pember Road, Willesden). **4th (City of London) Battalion (Royal Fusiliers):** 'South Africa 1900'.

Headquarters: 112 Shaftesbury Street, Shoreditch. *Companies:* 'A' to 'H' (Shaftesbury Street). **5th (City of London) Battalion (London Rifle Brigade):** 'South Africa 1900–02'. *Headquarters:* 130 Bunhill Row, Finsbury. *Companies:* 'A' to 'H' (Bunhill Row). *Cadets:* Coopers' Company School Cadet Corps (The Guildhall, City of London). **6th (City of London) Battalion (Rifles):** 'South Africa 1900–02'. *Headquarters:* 57a Farringdon Road, Holborn. *Companies:* 'A' to 'H' (Farringdon Road). *Cadets:* 1st Cadet Company (Holborn). **7th (City of London) Battalion:** 'South Africa 1900–02'. *Headquarters:* 24 Sun Street, Shoreditch. *Companies:* 'A', 'B', 'C' (Sun Street), 'D', 'E' (36 Elm Grove, Hammersmith), 'F', 'G', 'H' (Sun Street). **8th (City of London) Battalion (Post Office Rifles):** 'Egypt 1882', 'South Africa 1899–02'. *Headquarters:* 2 Throgmorton Avenue, City of London, moving in 1910 to 130 Bunhill Row, Finsbury. *Companies:* 'A' to 'H' (as headquarters). **9th (County of London) Battalion (Queen Victoria's Rifles):** 'South Africa 1900–02'. *Headquarters:* 56 Davies Street, Westminster. *Companies:* 'A' to 'H' (Davies Street). **10th (County of London) Battalion (Paddington Rifles):** 'South Africa 1900–02'. *Headquarters:* 207 Harrow Road, Paddington. *Companies:* 'A' to 'H' (Harrow Road). Disbanded in 1912. **10th (County of London) Battalion (Hackney):** Formed in 1912. *Headquarters:* 49 The Grove, Hackney. *Companies:* 'A' to 'H' (The Grove). *Cadets:* 10th London Cadet Corps (LCC School in Homerton Row). **11th (County of London) Battalion (Finsbury Rifles):** 'South Africa 1900–02'. *Headquarters:* 17 Penton Street, Finsbury. *Companies:* 'A' to 'H' (Penton Street). **12th (County of London) Battalion (The Rangers):** 'South Africa 1900–02'. *Headquarters:* Chenies Street, Holborn. *Companies:* 'A' to 'H' (Chenies Street). *Cadets:* Polytechnic Schools Cadet Corps (309 Regent Street, Westminster). **13th (County of London) Battalion (Kensington):** 'South Africa 1900–02'. *Headquarters:* Iverna Gardens, Kensington. *Companies:* 'A' to 'H' (Iverna Gardens). *Cadets:* Kensington and Hammersmith Navy League Boys' Brigade (34 Scarsdale Villas, Kensington) and St Peter's Cadet Company (69 Ladbroke Grove, Kensington). **14th (County of London) Battalion (London Scottish):** 'South Africa 1900–02'. *Headquarters:* 59 Buckingham Gate, Westminster. *Companies:* 'A' to 'H' (Buckingham Gate). **15th (County of London) Battalion (Prince of Wales's Own Civil Service Rifles):** 'South Africa 1900–02'. *Headquarters:* Somerset House, Westminster. *Companies:* 'A' to 'H' (Somerset House). *Cadets:* See 2nd Cadet Battalion below. **16th (County of London) Battalion (Queen's Westminster Rifles):** 'South Africa 1900–02'. *Headquarters:* Queen's Hall, 58 Buckingham Gate, Westminster. *Companies:* 'A' to 'H' (Buckingham Gate). *Cadets:* Queen's Westminster Cadet Corps (Westminster City School). **17th (County of London) Battalion (Poplar and Stepney Rifles):** 'South Africa 1900–02'. *Headquarters:* 66 Tredegar Road, Poplar. *Companies:* 'A' to 'H' (Tredegar Road). **18th (County of London) Battalion (London Irish Rifles):** 'South Africa 1900–02'. *Headquarters:* 2 Duke Street, Westminster, moving to the Duke of York's Headquarters, King's Road, Chelsea in 1912. *Companies:* 'A' to 'H' (as headquarters). **19th (County of London) Battalion (St Pancras):** 'South Africa 1900–02'. *Headquarters:* 76 High Street, Camden Town. *Companies:* 'A' to 'H' (76 High Street). **20th (County of London) Battalion (Blackheath and Woolwich):** 'South Africa 1900–02'. *Headquarters:* Holly Hedge House, Blackheath. *Companies:* 'A' to 'H' (Blackheath, there was also a drill station at Woolwich). *Cadets:* St Dunstan's College Cadet Corps (Catford). **21st (County of London) Battalion (First Surrey Rifles):** 'South Africa 1900–02'. *Headquarters:* 4 Flodden Road, Camberwell. *Companies:* 'A' to 'H' (Flodden Road). *Cadets:* St Olave's School Cadet Corps (Tower Bridge, Bermondsey), Aske's Hatcham School Cadet Corps (Pepys Road, New Cross) and South London Cadets (Arch 338, Medlar Street, Camberwell). **22nd (County of London) Battalion (The Queen's):** 'South Africa 1900–02'. *Headquarters:* 2 Jamaica Road, Bermondsey. *Companies:* 'A' to 'H' (Jamaica Road). **23rd (County of London) Battalion:** 'South Africa 1900–02'. *Headquarters:* 27 St John's Hill, Battersea. *Companies:* 'A' to 'H' (St John's Hill). *Cadets:* St Thomas's Cadet Corps (Santos Road, West Hill, Wandsworth).

24th (County of London) Battalion (The Queen's): 'South Africa 1900–02'. *Headquarters:* 71 New Street, Lambeth. *Companies:* 'A' to 'H' (New Street). **25th (County of London) Cyclist Battalion:** *Headquarters:* Fulham House, Putney Bridge, Putney. *Companies:* 'A' to 'H' (Fulham House). Unattached in London District. **28th (County of London) Battalion (Artists Rifles):** 'South Africa 1900–01'. *Headquarters:* Duke's Road, St Pancras. *Companies:* 'A' to 'H' (Duke's Road). Attached to 2nd London Division. **1st (The Queen's) Cadet Battalion:** *Headquarters:* 31 Union Street, Southwark. Formed as 1st Cadet Battalion Queen's (Royal West Surrey Regiment). **2nd (Civil Service) Cadet Battalion:** *Headquarters:* East Wing, Somerset House. Formed as Civil Service Cadet Corps, affiliated to 15th Battalion London Regiment, and re-designated in 1912.

London Rifle Brigade See 5th London Regiment.

London Sanitary Companies 1st (City of London): *Headquarters:* 51 Calthorpe Street, St Pancras, moving in 1912 to the Duke of York's Headquarters, King's Road, Chelsea. **2nd:** *Headquarters:* 33 St John's Road, Putney moving in 1912 to the Duke of York's Headquarters.

London Scottish See 14th London Regiment.

London Wireless Signal Company See London District Signal Companies.

Lord Robert's Boys See 1st City of London Cadet Battalion.

Lothian Infantry Brigade *Headquarters:* 16 George Street, Edinburgh, moving to 28 Rutland Square, Edinburgh in 1914. *Battalions:* 4th, 5th, 8th and 9th Royal Scots. Part of the Scottish Coast Defences.

Lothian Regiment See Royal Scots.

Lothians and Border Horse 'South Africa 1900–01'. *Headquarters:* Edinburgh, 18 Dundonald Street moving to 7 Wemyss Place, in 1914. *Squadrons:* 'A' (Dunbar, Earlston, Greenlaw, North Berwick, Musselburgh, Lauder, Kelso, Berwick-upon-Tweed, Haddington, Tranent, East Linton, Duns and Coldstream), 'B' (Edinburgh, Musselburgh, Dalkeith, Eskbank, Penicuik, Gorebridge, Lasswade and Loanhead), 'C' (Hawick, Galashiels, Jedburgh, Innerleithen, Kelso, Melrose, Newcastleton, Peebles, Selkirk, Stow, Kirk Yetholm and St Boswells), 'D' (Edinburgh, Linlithgow, Bathgate, Broxburn, Hopetoun, Mid Calder, South Queensferry, Ratho and Winchburgh). Part of the Lowland Mounted Brigade.

Lovat's Scouts, 1st 'South Africa 1900–02'. *Headquarters:* Beauly. *Squadrons:* 'A' (Roy Bridge, Fort Augustus, Loch Laggan, Spean Bridge, Glenfinnan, Sheil Bridge and Fort William), 'B' (Lochmaddy, Bayhead, Sollas, Creagorry, Clachan, Torlam and Daliburgh), 'C' (Skeabost, Uig, Portree, Duntulm, Staffin, Glendale, Waternish, Dunvegan and Braes), 'D' (Beauly, Struy, Convinth, Clunes, Beaufort, Dores, Errogie, Whitebridge and Glenurquhart). Part of the Highland Mounted Brigade.

Lovat's Scouts, 2nd 'South Africa 1900–02'. *Headquarters:* Beauly. *Squadrons:* 'E' (Kyle of Lochalsh, Armadale, Aultbea, Glenelg, Strathcarron, Dundonnell, Strathcanaird, Ullapool, Achiltibuie and Achnasheen), 'F' (Dornoch, Brora, Helmsdale, Scourie, Tongue, Melness, Bettyhill, Dunbeath, Latheron and Berriedale), 'G' (Alness, Bonar Bridge, Lairg, Ardgay, Rosehall, Fearn, Edderton, Tain and Contin), 'H' (Inverness, Nairn, Laggan Bridge, Aviemore, Nethy Bridge, Munlochy, Cawdor, Glenferness and Tomatin). Part of the Highland Mounted Brigade.

Lowland Brigades Royal Field Artillery 1st Brigade: *Headquarters:* 30 Grindlay Street, Edinburgh. *Batteries:* 1st, 2nd City of Edinburgh, 1st Midlothian (Grindlay Street). *Ammunition Column:* (Grindlay Street). **2nd Brigade:** *Headquarters:* Kilmarnock, moving to Irvine in 1910.

Batteries: 1st Ayrshire (Irvine), 2nd Ayrshire (Stranraer moving to Kilmarnock in 1909), Kirkcudbrightshire (Kirkcudbright and Gatehouse). *Ammunition Column:* (Kilmarnock, moving to Ardrossan in 1909). **3rd Brigade:** *Headquarters:* 8 Newton Terrace, Charring Cross, Glasgow. *Batteries:* 1st City of Glasgow (Berkeley Street, Charring Cross), 2nd City of Glasgow (Percy Street, Maryhill), 3rd City of Glasgow (Keppochhill in the Springburn area of Glasgow). *Ammunition Column:* (Percy Street). **4th (Howitzer) Brigade:** *Headquarters:* 8 Newton Terrace, Charring Cross, Glasgow. *Batteries:* 4th City of Glasgow (Butterbiggins Road, Govanhill), 5th City of Glasgow (Elder Street, Govan). *Ammunition Column:* (8 Newton Terrace, moving to Butterbiggins Road in 1910).

Lowland Clearing Hospital *Headquarters:* Glasgow.

Lowland Division *Headquarters:* 7 West George Street, Glasgow. *Infantry Brigades:* **South Scottish**, with 4th, 5th Royal Scots Fusiliers, 4th, 5th King's Own Scottish Borderers (Purves, Greenlaw, moving to 7 Wellington Square, Ayr in 1911); **Scottish Rifle**, with 5th to 8th Cameronians (34 Robertson Street, Glasgow) and **Highland Light Infantry**, with 5th, 6th, 7th, 9th Highland Light Infantry (34 Robertson Street, Glasgow).

Lowland Divisional Royal Engineers *Headquarters:* Rutherglen. *Filed Companies:* 1st Lowland 'Imperial Service' (Coatdyke, Coatbridge and Airdrie), 2nd Lowland 'Imperial Service' (Rutherglen, Shettleston and Motherwell). *Telegraph Company:* (192 Main Street, Rutherglen). In 1913 the Telegraph Company was included in the RE Signal Service; designated as the Lowland Divisional Signal Company and organised as Headquarters and four sections: No 1, No 2 (Scottish Rifle), No 3 (Highland Light Infantry), No 4 (South Scottish).

Lowland Divisional Telegraph/Signal Company See Lowland Divisional RE.

Lowland Divisional Transport and Supply Column *Headquarters:* 22 Lochburn Road, Maryhill, Glasgow. *Companies:* 1st (HQ) (Maryhill); 2nd (South Scottish Brigade) (Pitt Street, Edinburgh, moving to Brandon Terrace, Edinburgh in 1912), 3rd (Scottish Rifle Brigade) (Motherwell and Rutherglen) and 4th (Highland Light Infantry Brigade) (22 Lochburn Road, Maryhill, Glasgow, moving in 1914 to Gilbert Street, Yorkhill, Glasgow).

Lowland Field Ambulances 1st, 2nd: *Headquarters:* Glasgow, 21 Gilbert Street, Yorkhill, moving to 17 Royal Terrace West, then Yorkhill Parade, Yorkhill. **3rd:** *Headquarters:* 71 Gilmore Place, Edinburgh, moving in 1909 to Easter Road Barracks, Edinburgh.

Lowland Field Companies See Lowland Divisional RE.

Lowland (Heavy) Royal Garrison Artillery (City of Edinburgh) *Headquarters:* 28 York Place, Edinburgh, moving to McDonald Road, also in Edinburgh, in 1913. *Battery:* (Edinburgh). *Ammunition Column:* (Edinburgh).

Lowland Mounted Brigade *Headquarters:* 28 Rutland Street, Edinburgh, moving in 1911 to 10 Dublin Street, Edinburgh. *Units:* Ayrshire, Lanarkshire, Lothians and Border Horse Yeomanries and Ayrshire RHA.

Lowland Mounted Brigade Ammunition Column See Ayrshire RHA.

Lowland Mounted Brigade Field Ambulance *Headquarters:* 21 Gilbert Street, Yorkhill, Glasgow, moving in 1909 to 17 Royal Terrace West, Glasgow, then to Yorkhill Parade, Yorkhill, Glasgow in 1912.

Lowland Mounted Brigade Signal Troop *Headquarters:* 10 Dublin Street, Edinburgh.

Lowland Mounted Brigade Transport and Supply Column *Headquarters:* 4 Pitt Street, Edinburgh, moving to Brandon Terrace, Edinburgh in 1912.

Lymington Cadet Corps See 7th Hampshire Regiment.

Macclesfield Grammar School Cadet Corps See 7th Cheshire Regiment.

Macclesfield Industrial School Cadet Corps See 7th Cheshire Regiment.

Magdalene Cadet Company Magdalene College, Wyndham Road, Camberwell.

Mall School Cadet Company See 8th Middlesex Regiment.

Manchester Artillery See 2nd East Lancashire Brigade RFA.

Manchester Brigade Company See East Lancashire Divisional Transport and Supply Column.

Manchester Infantry Brigade See East Lancashire Division.

Manchester Regiment The 5th to 8th Battalions together made up the Manchester Infantry Brigade, East Lancashire Division; while the 9th and 10th provided half of the East Lancashire Infantry Brigade, also with East Lancashire Division. **5th Battalion:** 'South Africa 1900–02'. *Headquarters:* Bank Chambers, Wigan. *Companies:* 'A' to 'E' (Wigan), 'F' (Patricroft), 'G' (Leigh), 'H' (Atherton). **6th Battalion:** 'South Africa 1900–02'. *Headquarters:* 3 Stratford Road, Hulme. *Companies:* 'A' to 'H' (Stratford Road). **7th Battalion:** 'South Africa 1900–02'. *Headquarters:* Burlington Street, Manchester. *Companies:* (Burlington Street). **8th (Ardwick) Battalion:** 'South Africa 1900–02'. *Headquarters:* Ardwick. *Companies:* 'A' to 'H' (Ardwick). **9th Battalion:** 'South Africa 1900–02'. *Headquarters:* Ashton-under-Lyne. *Companies:* 'A' to 'H' (Ashton). **10th Battalion:** 'South Africa 1901–02'. *Headquarters:* Oldham. *Companies:* 'A' to 'H' (Oldham). **1st Territorial Cadet Battalion:** *Headquarters:* Poplar Street, Ardwick. Affiliated to the Manchester Infantry Brigade. **2nd Cadet Battalion:** *Headquarters:* Coldhurst, Oldham. Originally called 1st Coldhurst (Oldham) Cadet Corps, re-designated under Army Order 11 of 1912. Affiliated to 10th Manchester Regiment.

Manor Park Cadet Company See 4th Essex Regiment.

Marner School (LCC) Cadet Company *Headquarters:* The Guildhall, City of London.

Middlesex Brigade Company See Home Counties Divisional Transport and Supply Column.

Middlesex Infantry Brigade See Home Counties Division.

Middlesex Regiment The four battalions together made up the Middlesex Infantry Brigade, Home Counties Division. **7th Battalion:** 'South Africa 1900–02'. 'Imperial Service'. *Headquarters:* Priory Road, Hornsey. *Companies:* 'A' (Hampstead), 'B' (Barnet), 'C' (Hornsey), 'D' (Highgate), 'E' (Tottenham), 'F' (Enfield Lock and Enfield Town), 'G' (Tottenham), 'H' (Hornsey). *Cadets:* Christ's College Finchley Cadet Company, Friern Barnet School Cadet Company, Harringay Cadet Company and Tollington School Cadet Company. **8th Battalion:** 'South Africa 1900–02'. 'Imperial Service'. *Headquarters:* Whitton Park, Hounslow, moving in 1911 to 202a Hanworth Road, Hounslow. *Companies:* 'A' (Twickenham), 'B' (Brentford), 'C' (Hounslow), 'D' (Southall), 'E' (Uxbridge), 'F' (Ealing), 'G' (Hampton), 'H' (Stains). *Cadets:* Ealing Cadet Company, Ealing County School Cadet Company and Mall School Cadet Company (185 Hampton Road, Twickenham). **9th Battalion:** 'South Africa 1900–02'. *Headquarters:* Henry Street, St John's Wood, moving in 1911 to Pound Lane, Willesden. *Companies:* 'A', 'B' (Willesden), 'C' (Willesden and Stanmore), 'D', 'E' (Willesden), 'F' (Harrow), 'G' (Wealdstone), 'H' (Hendon). *Cadets:* Harrow Cadet Company, Kilburn Grammar School Cadet Company and Sunbury House School Cadet Company. **10th Battalion:** *Headquarters:*

Stamford Brook Lodge, Ravenscourt Park. *Companies:* 'A' (St John's College, Battersea), 'B' (St Mark's College, Chelsea), 'C' to 'H' (Ravenscourt Park). *Cadets:* Acton Cadet Company and Bedford Park Cadet Company. Recognition of the latter, however, was withdrawn in 1913 (Army Order 187), but then given again in 1914 (Army Order 511).

Middlesex Yeomanry See 1st County of London Yeomanry.

Midlothian Battery See 1st Lowland Brigade RFA.

Monmouth Grammar School Cadet Corps Affiliated to 2nd Monmouthshire Regiment. Became part of the 1st Cadet Battalion Monmouthshire Regiment in 1912.

Monmouthshire Batteries See 4th Welsh Brigade RFA.

Monmouthshire Regiment The three battalions were included in the Welsh Border Infantry Brigade, Welsh Division. **1st Battalion:** 'South Africa 1900–02'. *Headquarters:* Stow Hill, Newport. *Companies:* 'A' (Newport and Caerleon), 'B' (Newport), 'C' (Newport and Rogerstone), 'D' (Newport), 'E' (Chepstow, Sudbrook and Itton Court), 'F' (Aberbargoed), 'G' (Rhymney and New Tredegar), 'H' (Blackwood and Ynysddu). **2nd Battalion:** 'South Africa 1900–02'. *Headquarters:* Osborne Road, Pontypool. *Companies:* 'A' (Pontypool and Goytre), 'B' (Pontypool), 'C' (Pontypool and Garndiffaith), 'D' (Abercarn), 'E' (Blaenavon), 'F' (Llanhilleth), 'G' (Monmouth, Coleford and Usk), 'H' (Crumlin). **3rd Battalion:** 'South Africa 1900–02'. *Headquarters:* Abergavenny. *Companies:* 'A' (Abergavenny), 'B' (Ebbw Vale), 'C' (Cwm), 'D' (Sirhowy), 'E', 'F' (Abertillery), 'G' (Tredegar), 'H' (Blaina). **1st Cadet Battalion:** *Headquarters:* Tal-y-Coed, Formed by the amalgamation of the Usk, Chepstow, Abercarn, Ebbw Vale, Monmouth Grammar School and Abergavenny cadet units. The companies had separate affiliations – 1st Battalion (Chepstow); 2nd Battalion (Abercarn, Monmouth Grammar School, Usk) and 3rd Battalion (Abergavenny, Ebbw Vale).

Montgomeryshire Yeomanry 'South Africa 1901'. *Headquarters:* Welshpool. *Squadrons:* 'A' (Llanfyllin, Meifod, Llanrhaiadr, Llanfihangel, Llangedwyn, Trefonen, Llanfair Caereinion and Llansantffraid), 'B' (Welshpool, Guilsfield, Castle Caereinion, Four Crosses, Chirbury, Berriew, Trewern and Forden), 'C' (Newtown, Church Stoke, Caersws, New Mills, Llanbrynmair, Montgomery, Trefeglwys, Bettws Cedewain, Cemmaes Road, Dolfor and Llangurig), 'D' (Llandrindod Wells, Llanidloes, Builth Wells, Rhayader, Llanbister, Knighton and Hay-on-Wye). Part of the South Wales Mounted Brigade.

Morpeth Grammar School Cadet Company See 7th Northumberland Fusiliers.

New Brighton Cadet Corps See 4th Cheshire Regiment.

New College (Herne Bay) Cadet Corps See 4th Buffs (East Kent Regiment).

New King's School (LCC) Cadet Corps Formed as part of the 2nd (Fulham) Battalion, Imperial Cadet Corps which was divided in 1912 to form Ackmar School (LCC) Cadet Corps and New King's School (LCC) Cadet Corps. Recognition was withdrawn, however, under Army Order 49 of 1913.

Newport Cadet Company Newport, Isle of Wight. Affiliated to the 8th Hampshire Regiment. Absorbed into the 3rd Cadet Battalion Hampshire Regiment.

Newport Market School Cadet Corps 74 Coburg Row, Westminster.

Newport Territorial Cadet Corps See 4th Welsh Brigade RFA.

Norfolk and Suffolk Brigade Company See East Anglian Divisional Transport and Supply Column.

Norfolk and Suffolk Infantry Brigade See East Anglian Division.

Norfolk Batteries See 1st East Anglian Brigade RFA.

Norfolk Regiment The 4th and 5th battalions together provided half of the Norfolk and Suffolk Infantry Brigade, East Anglian Division. The 6th Battalion was attached to Eastern Command. **4th Battalion:** 'South Africa 1900–02'. *Headquarters:* St Giles, Norwich. *Companies:* 'A', 'B' (Norwich), 'C' (Long Stratton, Mulbarton and Saxlingham), 'D' (Diss, Harleston and Tivetshall), 'E' (Attleborough, East Harling, Kenninghall, Banham, Old Buckenham, Hingham and Watton), 'F' (Wymondham, Hethersett, Swardeston, Mulbarton, Colney, Saxlingham and Hingham), 'G' (Brandon, Thetford, Methwold and Feltwell), 'H' (Thorpe St Andrew, Loddon, Blofield, Acle, Burgh St Margaret, Framlingham, Pigot and Coltishall). **5th Battalion:** 'South Africa 1900–02'. *Headquarters:* East Derham. *Companies:* 'A' (King's Lynn), 'B' (Downham Market, Hunstanton, Thornham, Hilgay and Stoke Ferry), 'C' (Fakenham, Wells, Syderstone, Aylsham and Corpusty), 'D' (East Dereham, Castle Acre, Litcham and Swaffham), 'E' (Sandringham, Dersingham, Wolferton, Hillington and West Newton), 'F' (Cromer, Melton Constable, Holt, Sheringham, North Walsham. Westwick, Gunton and Honing), 'G', 'H' (Great Yarmouth). **6th (Cyclist) Battalion:** *Headquarters:* Norwich, York House, Rosary Road moving to Cattle Market Street in 1911. *Companies:* 'A' (Norwich), 'B' (Great Yarmouth), 'C' (King's Lynn and Terrington St Clement), 'D' (Thetford and Attleborough), 'E' (Fakenham, Walsingham, Holkham, Wells and Ryburgh), 'F' (Ditchingham), 'G' (Watton and Swaffham), 'H' (Norwich and Great Yarmouth).

Norfolk Yeomanry (The King's Own Royal Regiment) *Headquarters:* Norwich, 21 Tombland, moving to Cattle Market Hill in 1911. *Squadrons:* 'A' (Norwich, Attleborough, Long Stratton, Loddon, Diss and Harleston), 'B' (North Walsham, Brandiston, Blofield, Coltishall, Cromer, Hanworth, Holt, Marsham, Reepham, Stalham and Great Yarmouth), 'C' (Fakenham, Barwick, Bircham, Brisley, Dersingham, East Dereham, Fransham, Hardingham, Hunstanton, Massingham, Quarles, Summerfield, Swaffham, Watton, Wells, Wymondham and Walsingham), 'D' (King's Lynn, Downham Market, Thetford and Wisbech). Part of the Eastern Mounted Brigade.

North Berwick Cadet Corps See 8th Royal Scots.

North Lancashire Brigade Company See West Lancashire Divisional Transport and Supply Column.

North Lancashire Infantry Brigade See West Lancashire Division.

North Lancashire Regiment The two battalions together provided one half of the North Lancashire Infantry Brigade, West Lancashire Division. **4th Battalion:** 'South Africa 1900–02'. *Headquarters:* St Winifred Street, Preston, moving to 97 Avenham Lane, Preston in 1913. *Companies:* 'A' (Preston), 'B' (Longridge), 'C' (Preston and Bamber Bridge), 'D' (Preston and Leyland), 'E' (Lytham), 'F' (Horwich), 'G', 'H' (Chorley). *Cadets:* Arnold House School Cadet Corps (South Shore, Blackpool). **5th Battalion:** 'South Africa 1900–02'. *Headquarters:* Bolton. *Companies:* 'A', 'B', 'C' (Bolton), 'D' (Farnworth), 'E' (Bolton), 'F' (Astley Bridge), 'G' (Hindley), 'H' (Little Hulton).

North Midland Brigades Royal Field Artillery 1st Brigade: *Headquarters:* Grimsby. *Batteries:* 1st Lincolnshire (Boston), 2nd Lincolnshire (Grimsby), 3rd Lincolnshire (Louth and Grimsby). *Ammunition Column:* (Grimsby, Boston and Louth). **2nd Brigade:** *Headquarters:* Victoria Square, Shelton, Stoke-on-Trent. *Batteries:* 1st, 2nd Staffordshire (Victoria Square), 3rd Staffordshire (Leek). *Ammunition Column:* (Victoria Square and Leek). **3rd Brigade:** *Headquarters:* Wolverhampton, Cleveland Road, moving in 1911 to West Park. *Batteries:* 4th Staffordshire (Wolverhampton). 5th Staffordshire (West Bromwich), 6th Staffordshire (Stafford, Brierley Hill, moving to Bridge Street in 1911, then again to Bailey Street in 1914). *Ammunition Column:* (Wolverhampton, West Bromwich and Stafford). **4th (Howitzer) Brigade:** *Headquarters:* 91 Siddal's Road, Derby. *Batteries:* 1st Derbyshire (Derby and West Hallam), 2nd Derbyshire (Derby). *Ammunition Column:* (Derby).

North Midland Clearing Hospital *Headquarters:* Leicester.

North Midland Division *Headquarters:* Lichfield. *Infantry Brigades:* **Lincoln and Leicester**, with 4th, 5th Lincolnshire, 4th, 5th Leicestershire Regiments (Harrowby House, Grantham, moving to Casthorpe, then Barrowby, then again to Culverthorpe); **Staffordshire**, with 5th, 6th South Staffordshire, 5th, 6th North Staffordshire Regiments (Lichfield, The Friary, moving to White House, then in 1912 to Market Square, Stafford) and **Notts and Derby**, with 5th to 8th Sherwood Foresters (Derby Road, Nottingham).

North Midland Divisional Royal Engineers *Headquarters:* Smethwick, moving in 1912 to Norton Hall, Norton Canes. *Field Companies:* 1st North Midland (Smethwick), 2nd North Midland (Norton Canes). *Telegraph Company:* (Shelton, moving to Victoria Park, Hanley in 1909). In 1913 the Telegraph Company was included in the RE Signal Service; designated as the North Midland Divisional Signal Company and organised as Headquarters and four sections: No 1, No 2 (Staffordshire), No 3 (Notts and Derby), No 4 (Lincoln and Leicester). Moved to Booth Street, Stoke-on-Trent in the following year.

North Midland Divisional Signal Company See North Midland Divisional Engineers.

North Midland Divisional Telegraph/Signal Company See North Midland Divisional RE.

North Midland Divisional Transport and Supply Column *Headquarters:* 15 Belgrave Terrace, Handsworth, moving in 1912 to 7 Magazine Square, Leicester. *HQ and Brigade Companies:* HQ (Handsworth), Lincoln and Leicester Brigade Company (19 Magazine Square, Leicester and Market Harborough), Staffordshire Brigade Company (Handsworth) and Notts and Derby Brigade Company (168 Derby Road, Nottingham, moving in 1909 to Bellevue, Wilford Lane, West Bridgford, then in 1912 to the Drill Hall, Derby Road, Nottingham).

North Midland Field Ambulances 1st: *Headquarters:* 42 Friar Gate, Derby, moving later to 91 Siddals Road, Derby. **2nd:** *Headquarters:* Oxford Street, Leicester. **3rd:** The Deanery, Stafford Street, Wolverhampton. There was also a drill station at Penkridge.

North Midland Field Companies See North Midland Divisional RE.

North Midland (Heavy) Royal Garrison Artillery (Staffordshire) *Headquarters:* Garden Street, Etruria, Stoke-on-Trent, moving in 1910 to 10 Brook Street, then the RGA Drill Hall in Wilfred Place, Hartshill, Stoke-on-Trent in 1911. *Battery:* (Stoke-on-Trent). *Ammunition Column:* (Stoke-on-Trent).

North Midland Mounted Brigade *Headquarters:* Grantham, Bridge House, moving to 163 Dudley Road, then to 7 Magazine Square, Leicester around 1912. *Units:* Leicestershire, Lincolnshire, Staffordshire Yeomanries and Leicestershire RHA.

North Midland Mounted Brigade Ammunition Column See Leicestershire RHA.

North Midland Mounted Brigade Field Ambulance *Headquarters:* Handsworth, 59 Soho Road, moving in 1914 to Nineveh Road. *Sections:* 'A' (Handsworth), 'B' (Swan Village, West Bromwich).

North Midland Mounted Brigade Signal Troop *Headquarters:* 7 Magazine Square, Leicester.

North Midland Mounted Brigade Transport and Supply Column *Headquarters:* 11 The Magazine, Leicester with a drill station at Coalville.

North Paddington Cadets, 1st See 3rd London Regiment.

North Riding Battery See 2nd Northumbrian Brigade RFA.

North Riding Fortress Engineers *Headquarters:* Bright Street, Middlesbrough. *Electric Lights Company:* (Bright Street).

North Scottish Royal Garrison Artillery *Headquarters:* Broughty Ferry. *Garrison Companies:* Nos 1, 2 (North Silver Street, Aberdeen), No 3 (Montrose), No 4 (Broughty Ferry), No 5 (Cromarty, Jemimaville, Newhall and Davidson), No 6 (Stornoway). In 1910, the establishment of the group was reduced when two companies (one at Aberdeen, one at Stornoway) were removed. Subsequently the companies at Montrose and Broughty Ferry were renumbered as 2 and 3 respectively. In 1912 headquarters of No 1 Company were moved from Silver Street to Fonthill Road, Aberdeen.

North Somerset Yeomanry 'South Africa 1900–01'. *Headquarters:* Shepton Mallet, moving to Bath in 1914. *Squadrons:* 'A' (Bath, Bathampton, Farmborough, Frome, Mells and Road), 'B' (Weston-super-Mare, Axbridge, Clevedon, Langford and Nailsea), 'C' (Shepton Mallet, Queen Camel, Ston Easton, Wells, Wincanton and, from 1914, Castle Cary), 'D' (Bristol, Queen Charlton, Barrow Gurney and Keynsham). Part of the 1st South Western Mounted Brigade.

North Staffordshire Regiment The battalions together provided half of the Staffordshire Infantry Brigade, North Midland Division. **5th Battalion:** 'South Africa 1900–02'. *Headquarters:* Hanley. *Companies:* 'A' (Longton), 'B' (Hanley), 'C' (Burslem), 'D' (Tunstall), 'E' (Stoke-on-Trent and Hanley), 'F' (Stone), 'G' (Newcastle-under-Lyme), 'H' (Stoke-on-Trent). **6th Battalion:** 'South Africa 1900–02'. *Headquarters:* Burton-on-Trent. *Companies:* 'A' (Burton-on-Trent), 'B' (Burton-on-Trent and Tutbury), 'C' (Tamworth), 'D' (Rugeley), 'E' (Lichfield), 'F' (Stafford), 'G' (Uttoxeter), 'H' (Burton-on-Trent).

North Wales Brigade Company See Welsh Divisional Transport and Supply Column.

North Wales Infantry Brigade See Welsh Division.

Northampton School Cadet Corps See 4th Northamptonshire Regiment.

Northamptonshire Battery See 4th East Anglian Brigade RFA.

Northamptonshire Regiment 4th Battalion: 'South Africa 1900–02'. *Headquarters:* Northampton, 83 Sheep Street, moving in 1913 to Territorial Headquarters, Clare Street. *Companies:* 'A' (Northampton), 'B' (Northampton, Daventry and Weedon), 'C' (Northampton, Althorp Park, Long Buckby and Harpole), 'D' (Northampton), 'E' (Wellingborough and Finedon), 'F' (Kettering), 'G' (Desborough and Rothwell), 'H' (Higham Ferrers, Rushden and Irthlingborough). Part of the East Midland Infantry Brigade, East Anglian Division. *Cadets:* King's School Peterborough Cadet Corps and Northampton School Cadet Corps (Billing Road).

Northamptonshire Yeomanry *Headquarters:* Northampton, 53 Sheep Street moving to Clare Street in 1911. *Squadrons:* 'A' (Northampton and Cottesbrooke), 'B' (Peterborough, Oundle, Glinton and Thrapston), 'C' (Kettering, Wellingborough, Rushden and Clipston), 'D' (Daventry, Weedon, Blisworth, Blakesley and, from 1913, West Haddon). Part of the Eastern Mounted Brigade.

Northern Airline Signal Company See Northern Command Signal Companies.

Northern Cable Signal Company See Northern Command Signal Companies.

Northern Command Signal Companies *Headquarters:* Leeds. *Companies:* Northern Wireless, Cable and Airline (Leeds). *Cadets:* Leeds Postal Telegraph Messengers Cadet Company. Originally attached to 7th West Yorkshire Regiment, Army Order 86 of 1913 notifying the transfer.

Northern Cyclist Battalion *Headquarters:* Newcastle-upon-Tyne, Cambridge Hall Northumberland Road moving in 1911 to Hutton Terrace, Sandyford Road. *Companies:* 'A', 'B' (Sunderland), 'C' (West Hartlepool), 'D' (Chester-le-Street), 'E' (Newcastle-upon-Tyne), 'F' (Blyth), 'G' (Whitley Bay), 'H' (Newcastle-upon-Tyne).

Northern General Hospitals 1st: *Headquarters:* Hutton Terrace, Newcastle-upon-Tyne. **2nd:** *Headquarters:* Harewood Barracks, Woodhouse Lane, Leeds. **3rd:** *Headquarters:* Sheffield. **4th:** *Headquarters:* 6b Guildhall Street, Lincoln. **5th:** *Headquarters:* Leicester.

Northern Wireless Signal Company See Northern Command Signal Companies.

Northumberland Batteries See 1st Northumbrian Brigade RFA.

Northumberland Brigade Company See Northumbrian Divisional Transport and Supply Column.

Northumberland Fortress Engineers *Headquarters:* Clifford's Fort, North Shields. Originally an electric lights company with the Durham Fortress Engineers, separation came by 1909, but a further reorganisation in 1911 saw the company as part of the Tyne Electrical Engineers.

Northumberland Fusiliers The battalions made up the Northumberland Infantry Brigade, Northumbrian Division. **4th Battalion:** 'South Africa 1900–02'. *Headquarters:* Hexham. *Companies:* 'A' (Hexham and Acomb), 'B' (Bellingham, Plashetts, Otterburn and Wooburn), 'C' (Haydon Bridge, Allendale, Langley and Newbrough), 'D' (Prudhoe and Mickley), 'E' (Corbridge), 'F' (Haltwhistle), 'G' (Newburn and Whorlton), 'H' (Prudhoe). *Cadets:* Haltwhistle Territorial Cadets (Scardeburg, Haltwhistle). **5th Battalion**: 'South Africa 1900–02'. *Headquarters:* Walker, Newcastle-upon-Tyne. *Companies:* 'A', 'B', 'C' (Walker), 'D', 'E', 'F' (Wallsend), 'G' (Gosforth, West Moor and Seaton Burn), 'H' (Gosforth). **6th Battalion:** 'South Africa 1900–02'. *Headquarters:* St George's Drill Hall, Northumberland Road, Newcastle-upon-Tyne). *Companies:* 'A' to 'H' (Northumberland Road). *Cadets:* Allan's School Cadet Unit (Northumberland Road). **7th Battalion:** *Headquarters:* Alnwick. *Companies:* 'A' (Morpeth), 'B' (Ashington), 'C' (Belford, Ford, Wooler and Chatton). 'D' (Alnwick), 'E' (Amble, Broomhill and Warkworth), 'F' (Alnwick and Rothbury), 'G' (Berwick-upon-Tweed), 'H' (Berwick-upon-Tweed and Scremerston). *Cadets:* Morpeth Grammar School Cadet Company.

Northumberland Hussars Yeomanry 'South Africa 1900–02'. *Headquarters:* Northumberland Road, Newcastle-upon-Tyne. *Squadrons:* 'A' (Newcastle-upon-Tyne), 'B' (South Shields, Sunderland, Darlington, Spennymoor and West Hartlepool), 'C' (Morpeth, Alnwick, Ashington, Rothbury, North Shields and Eglingham), 'D' (Hexham, Stanley, Prudhoe, Allendale and Wark-on-Tyne). Part of the Yorkshire Mounted Brigade.

Northumberland Infantry Brigade See Northumbrian Division.

Northumbrian Brigades Royal Field Artillery 1st Brigade: *Headquarters:* Barrack Road, Newcastle-upon-Tyne. *Batteries:* 1st, 2nd, 3rd Northumberland (Barrack Road). *Ammunition Column:* (Barrack Road). **2nd Brigade:** *Headquarters:* Hull. *Batteries:* 1st, 2nd East Riding (Hull), North Riding (Scarborough and Whitby). *Ammunition Column:* (Hull, Scarborough and Whitby). **3rd (County of Durham) Brigade:** *Headquarters:* Seaham Harbour. *Batteries:* 1st Durham (Seaham Harbour), 2nd Durham (Seaham Harbour and Silksworth, after 1913, Durham and Silksworth), 3rd Durham (The Armoury, West Hartlepool). *Ammunition Column:* (Seaham Harbour and Durham). **4th (Howitzer) Brigade (County of Durham):** *Headquarters:* Bolingbroke Street, South Shields. *Batteries:* 4th Durham (Bolingbroke Street), 5th Durham (Hebburn-on-Tyne). *Ammunition Column:* (Bolingbrook Street and Hebburn).

Northumbrian Clearing Hospital *Headquarters:* Newcastle-upon-Tyne.

Northumbrian Division *Headquarters:* The Castle, Richmond. *Infantry Brigades:* **Northumberland**, with 4th to 7th Northumberland Fusiliers (Newcastle-upon-Tyne, 21 Dean Street, moving in 1911 to 6 Elden Square); **York and Durham**, with 4th East Yorkshire, 4th, 5th Yorkshire Regiments and 5th Durham Light Infantry (temporary headquarters were occupied by the brigade in Beverley, and at the 5th Yorkshire Regiment's drill hall in Scarborough until a move was made in 1911 to 12 Castlegate, Malton) and **Durham Light Infantry**, with 6th to 9th Durham Light Infantry (Old Elvet, Durham).

Northumbrian Divisional Royal Engineers *Headquarters:* Barras Bridge, Newcastle-upon-Tyne. *Field Companies:* 1st, 2nd Northumbrian (Barras Bridge). *Telegraph Company:* (Barras Bridge). All three units had in addition the title 'The Newcastle'. In 1913 the Telegraph Company was included in the RE Signal Service, designated as Northumbrian (The Newcastle) Divisional Signal Company and organised as Headquarters and four sections: No 1, No 2 (Northumberland), No 3 (York and Durham) and No 4 (Durham Light Infantry).

Northumbrian Divisional Telegraph/Signal Company (The Newcastle) See Northumbrian Divisional Engineers.

Northumbrian Divisional Transport and Supply Column *Headquarters:* St George's Hall, Newcastle-upon-Tyne. *HQ and Brigade Companies:* HQ (Angus Hall, Gateshead), Northumberland Brigade Company (Newcastle-upon-Tyne), York and Durham Brigade Company (Walton Street, Hull) and Durham Light Infantry Brigade Company (Sunderland).

Northumbrian Field Ambulances 1st: *Headquarters:* 1 Cambridge Hall, Newcastle-upon-Tyne, moving in 1911 to Hutton Terrace, Newcastle-upon-Tyne. **2nd:** *Headquarters:* Larchfield Street, Darlington. *Sections:* 'A', 'B' (Darlington), 'C' (Shildon). **3rd:** *Headquarters:* Eagleton House, Hull, moving in 1910 to Wenlock Barracks, Walton Street, Hull.

Northumbrian Field Companies See Northumbrian Divisional RE.

Northumbrian (Heavy) Royal Garrison Artillery (North Riding) *Headquarters:* Middlesborough. *Battery:* (Middlesbrough and Thornaby). *Ammunition Column:* (Middlesborough).

Nottingham (Church) Cadet Battalion, 1st *Headquarters:* Park Row Chambers, Nottingham. Originally known as 1st Nottingham Cadet Battalion.

Nottinghamshire Royal Horse Artillery *Headquarters:* Nottingham, 116 Raleigh Street moving to Derby Road in 1912. *Battery:* (Nottingham and Wiseton). *Ammunition Column:* (Nottingham). Part of the Notts and Derby Mounted Brigade.

Nottinghamshire Yeomanry (Sherwood Rangers) 'South Africa 1900–02'. *Headquarters:* Retford. *Squadrons:* 'A' (Newark, Sutton-on-Trent and Collingham), 'B' (Mansfield, Chesterfield, Alfreton, Pinxton and Kirkby-in-Ashfield), 'C' (Worksop, Clumber and Normanton), 'D' (Retford, Ranskill, Trent Port, Melton Ross and Misterton). Part of the Notts and Derby Mounted Brigade.

Nottinghamshire Yeomanry (South Notts Hussars) 'South Africa 1900–02'. *Headquarters:* Nottingham, Park Row moving to Derby Road in 1912. *Squadrons:* 'A' (Bingham, Carlton, Plumtree and Southwell), 'B' (Watnall, Arnold and Eastwood), 'C' (Nottingham), 'D' (Wollaton and Long Eaton). Part of the Notts and Derby Mounted Brigade.

Notts and Derby Brigade Company See North Midland Divisional Transport and Supply Column.

Notts and Derby Infantry Brigade See North Midland Division.

Notts and Derby Mounted Brigade *Headquarters:* Derby Road, Nottingham. *Units:* Nottingham (Sherwood Rangers), Nottinghamshire (South Notts Hussars), Derbyshire Yeomanries and Nottinghamshire RHA.

Notts and Derby Mounted Brigade Ammunition Column See Nottinghamshire RHA.

Notts and Derby Mounted Brigade Field Ambulance *Headquarters:* Derby Road, Nottingham. *Sections:* 'A' (Nottingham), 'B' (Grimsby).

Notts and Derby Mounted Brigade Signal Troop *Headquarters:* Derby Road, Nottingham.

Notts and Derby Mounted Brigade Transport and Supply Column *Headquarters:* Chesterfield. There were drill stations at Chatsworth and Bolsover.

Ongar Grammar School Cadets See 4th Essex Regiment.

Oratory Cadet Corps 58 Cromwell Road, Kensington.

Orkney Royal Garrison Artillery *Headquarters:* Kirkwall. *Garrison Companies:* No 1 (Kirkwall), No 2 (Sanday and Stronsay), No 3 (Shapinsay and South Ronaldshay), No 4 (Stromness and Finstown), No 5 (Evie and Birsay), No 6 (Holm, Tankerness and Deerness), No 7 (Kirkwall).

Owen's School (Islington) Cadet Corps Owen Street, Islington.

Oxfordshire and Buckinghamshire Light Infantry The battalions together provided half of the South Midland Infantry Brigade, South Midland Division. The Buckinghamshire Battalion was not numbered. **4th Battalion:** 'South Africa 1900–01'. *Headquarters:* Oxford. *Companies:* 'A' (Oxford), 'B' (Oxford and Thame), 'C' (Banbury and Brackley), 'D' (Henley-on-Thames and Culham), 'E' (Chipping Norton, Kingham, Charlbury, Shipton-under-Wychwood and Stow-on-the-Wold), 'F' (Witney, Woodstock, Burford and Eynsham), 'G' (Banbury and Bicester), 'H' (Oxford and Woodburn). *Cadets:* Burford Grammar School Cadet Corps (14 Holywell Street, Oxford) and Cowley Cadet Corps. **Buckinghamshire Battalion:** 'South Africa 1900–02'. *Headquarters:* Marlow, moving to Aylesbury before the end of 1908. *Companies:* 'A' (Marlow), 'B' (High Wycombe and Winslow), 'C' (Buckingham, Tingewick and Chesham), 'D' (Aylesbury), 'E' (Slough and Datchet), 'F', 'G' (Wolverton), 'H' (High Wycombe). General Swann, in his book, *The Citizen Soldiers of Buckinghamshire,* records how Headquarters in 1908 were moved to Temple Square, Aylesbury, a small shed of corrugated iron being erected in the yard for drill purposes. Most of the battalion stores had to be kept at Wycombe, owing to lack of accommodation. The London & North Western Railway Company continued to find accommodation for the Wolverton Companies ('F' and 'G'), until a new dill hall was opened towards the end of 1914. *Cadets:* Aylesbury Grammar School Cadet Corps.

Oxfordshire Yeomanry (Queen's Own Oxfordshire Hussars) 'South Africa 1900–01'. *Headquarters:* Oxford. *Squadrons:* 'A' (Oxford), 'B' (Woodstock, Witney and Bicester), 'C' (Henley-on-Thames, Watlington, Thame and Goring-on-Thames), 'D' (Banbury, Deddington, Chipping Norton, Shipton-under-Wychwood, Charlbury and Burford). Part of the 2nd South Midland Mounted Brigade.

Oxton (Birkenhead School) Cadet Corps, 1st See 4th Cheshire Regiment.

Paddington Boys' Club and Naval Brigade Guardians' Offices, Harrow Road, Paddington.

Paddington Rifles See 10th London Regiment.

Palmer's School Cadet Corps See 6th Essex Regiment.

Pembroke Royal Garrison Artillery *Headquarters:* Pembroke Dock, moving in 1913 to Milford Haven. *Garrison Companies:* No 1 (Milford Haven), No 2 (Saundersfoot and Tenby), No 3 (Fishguard and Pembroke Dock).

Pembroke Yeomanry (Castlemartin) 'Fishguard', 'South Africa 1900–01'. *Headquarters:* Tenby. *Squadrons:* 'A' (Tenby, Pembroke, St Florence, Manorbier, Kilgetty and Templeton), 'B' (Haverfordwest, Clarbeston Road, Newgale and Fishguard), 'C' (Carmarthen, Whitland, Llanelly, Llandilo, Llangadock, Pantglas and Llandovery), 'D' (Lampeter, Aberystwyth, Tregaron, Llandyssil and Llanybyther). Part of the South Wales Mounted Brigade.

Peter Symonds School Cadet Corps See 4th Hampshire Regiment.

Plymouth Lads' Brigade Cadet Corps See 5th Devonshire Regiment.

Polytechnic Schools Cadet Corps See 12th London Regiment.

Poplar and Stepney Rifles See 17th London Regiment.

Post Office Rifles See 8th London Regiment.

Poulton Cadet Company, 1st See 4th Cheshire Regiment.

Prestonpans Cadet Corps See 8th Royal Scots.

Queen Victoria Rifles See 9th London Regiment.

Queen's Edinburgh Rifles See 4th and 5th Royal Scots.

Queen's (Royal West Surrey Regiment) The battalions together provided half of the Surrey Infantry Brigade, Home Counties Division. **4th Battalion:** 'South Africa 1900–02'. *Headquarters:* Croydon. *Companies:* 'A', 'B' (Croydon), 'C' (Crystal Palace), 'D' (Croydon), 'E' (Caterham and Godstone), 'F' (Croydon), 'G' (Lingfield and Oxted), 'H' (Croydon). *Cadets:* West Croydon Cadets (Drummond Road). **5th Battalion:** 'South Africa 1900–02'. *Headquarters:* Guildford. *Companies:* 'A' (Reigate, Horley and Brockham), 'B' (Camberley, Bagshot and Frimley), 'C' (Guildford and Albury), 'D' (Guildford and Bramley), 'E' (Farnham and Frensham), 'F' (Godalming, Haslemere, Chiddingfold, Witley, Dunsfold, Alfold and Elstead), 'G' (Dorking, Holmwood and Shere), 'H' (Woking, Knap Hill, Byfleet and Send). *Cadets:* Frimley and Camberley Cadet Corps ('Thornhurst', Camberley) and West Surrey Cadets, of which Army Order 233 of 1912 notifies that recognition had been withdrawn for all except the Farnham portion of the unit which was re-designated as the Farnham Company West Surrey Cadets. Yet another change, this time in 1913 (Army Order 273) saw the corps re-designated as 'G' and 'H' (Surrey) Companies of the 1st Cadet Battalion of Hampshire. **1st Cadet Battalion:** *Headquarters:* 31 Union Street, Southwark. Later re-designated as 1st Cadet Battalion London Regiment (The Queen's).

Queen's Westminster Cadet Corps See 16th London Regiment.

Queen's Westminster Rifles See 16th London Regiment.

Rangers See 12th Battalion London Regiment.

Reading Cadet Company See 4th Royal Berkshire Regiment.

Renfrewshire Batteries See 3rd Highland Brigade RFA.

Renfrewshire Fortress Engineers *Headquarters:* Fort Matilda, Greenock. *Works Company:* No 1 (Paisley). *Electric Lights Company:* No 2 (Greenock), which was added in 1911.

Renfrewshire Small Arms Section Ammunition Column See 3rd Highland Brigade RFA.

Richmond County School Cadet Corps See 6th East Surrey Regiment.

Richmond Hill Cadets See 6th East Surrey Regiment.

Roborough School (Eastbourne) Cadet Company See 2nd Home Counties Brigade RFA.

Ross and Cromarty (Mountain) Battery See 4th Highland Brigade RGA.

Rough Riders See City of London Yeomanry.

Royal Berkshire Regiment 4th Battalion: 'South Africa 1900–02'. *Headquarters:* St Mary's Butts, Reading. *Companies:* 'A' (Reading and Englefield), 'B' (Reading), 'C' (Wantage and Wallingford), 'D' (Windsor), 'E' (Newbury, Bucklebury, Aldermaston and Hungerford), 'F' (Abingdon), 'G' (Maidenhead), 'H' (Wokingham). Part of the South Midland Infantry Brigade, South Midland Division. *Cadets:* 1st Cadet Company (Maidenhead County Boys School), Reading Cadet Company (Elm Lodge Avenue) and Windsor Cadet Companies (County Boys' School, Windsor).

Royal 1st Devon Yeomanry 'South Africa 1900–01'. *Headquarters:* 9 Dix's Field in Exeter. *Squadrons:* 'A' (Thorverton, Crediton, Tiverton, Rackenford, Cullompton and Bampton), 'B' (Ottery St Mary, Exmouth, Exeter, Axminster, Sidmouth and Dawlish), 'C' (Totnes, Moreton Hampstead, Bovey Tracey, Newton Abbot, Dartmouth, Kingsbridge and Plymouth), 'D' (Bodmin, Launceston, Camelford, Liskeard, Truro, Helston and Penzance). Part of the 2nd South Western Mounted Brigade.

Royal East Kent Yeomanry 'South Africa 1900–01'. *Headquarters:* Canterbury. *Squadrons:* 'A' (Chatham), 'B' (Faversham, Sheerness, Sittingbourne, Herne Bay and Canterbury), 'C' (Dover, Waldershare, Deal, Margate and Ramsgate), 'D' (Ashford, Folkestone, Tenterden, Bethersden. Headcorn, Wye, New Romney and Westminster). Part of the South Eastern Mounted Brigade.

Royal Engineer Cadets (2nd London Division) *Headquarters:* Duke of York's Headquarters, King's Road, Chelsea. Formed as the Kensington Cadet Corps affiliated to 2nd London Divisional Royal Engineers. Army Order 249 of 1911 notifies re-designation as the Cadet Company Royal Engineers, 2nd London Division (Kensington Cadet Corps) and that numbered 373 of 1913 to Royal Engineer Cadets (2nd London Division).

Royal Fusiliers, 1st Cadet Battalion *Headquarters:* The Harben Armoury, Pond Street, Hampstead.

Royal Highlanders See Black Watch.

Royal North Devon Yeomanry 'South Africa 1900–01'. *Headquarters:* Barnstaple. *Squadrons:* 'A' (Holsworthy, Black Torrington, Hatherleigh, Bratton Clovelly, Tavistock, Woodford Bridge and Bradworthy), 'B' (Barnstaple, Atherington, Bratton Fleming, Blackmore Gate, Fremington, Swimbridge, West Down and Braunton), 'C' (South Molton, West Buckland, Molland, Chittlehampton, Sandyway, Ashreigney and Chulmleigh), 'D' (Torrington, Woolsery, Langtree, Parkham, High Bickington, Bideford and Roborough). Part of the 2nd South Western Mounted Brigade.

Royal Scots (Lothian Regiment) The 4th to 7th Battalions together made up the Lothian Infantry Brigade which had the 8th and 9th attached and formed part of the Scottish Coast Defences.

The 10th Battalion was attached to Scottish Command. **4th and 5th (Queen's Edinburgh Rifles) Battalions:** 'South Africa 1900–02'. *Headquarters:* 28 Forrest Road, Edinburgh, moving to Forrest Hill, Edinburgh in 1910. *Companies:* 'A' to 'H' (Edinburgh). **6th Battalion:** 'South Africa 1901–02'. *Headquarters:* 33 Gilmore Place, Edinburgh. *Companies:* 'A' to 'H' (Edinburgh). **7th Battalion**: 'South Africa 1900–02'. *Headquarters:* Dalmeny Street, Leith. *Companies:* 'A' to 'G' (Leith), 'H' (Musselburgh). **8th Battalion:** 'South Africa 1901'. *Headquarters:* Haddington. *Companies:* 'A' (Haddington, Aberlady, Gifford and Pencaitland), 'B' (Tranent, Ormiston, Elphinstone and Macmerry), 'C' (Prestonpans and Cockenzie), 'D' (North Berwick, East Linton, Dunbar and Gullane), 'E' (Dalkeith, Bonnyrigg, Pathhead and Gorebridge), 'F' (Loanhead and Penicuick), 'G' (Peebles), 'H' (Innerleithen and Walkerburn). *Cadets:* Haddington Cadet Corps (the Knox Institute, Haddington); North Berwick Cadet Corps (High School, North Berwick) and Tranent Industrial School Cadet Corps, Prestonpans Cadet Corps. **9th (Highlanders) Battalion:** 'South Africa 1901–02'. *Headquarters:* 7 Wemyss Road, Edinburgh, moving to 89 East Claremont Street, Edinburgh in 1913. *Companies:* 'A' to 'H' (Edinburgh). **10th (Cyclist) Battalion:** 'South Africa 1901–02'. *Headquarters:* Linlithgow. *Companies:* 'A' (Linlithgow and Phillipstoun), 'B' (Bo'ness and Carriden), 'C' (Armadale, Whitburn, Pumpherston and Blackridge), 'D' (Bathgate), 'E' (Broxburn and Livingstone), 'F' (Fauldhouse and Harthill), 'G' (West Calder and Addiewell), 'H' (Kirkliston, Dalmeny, Winchburgh and Newbridge). **1st (Highland) Cadet Battalion:** *Headquarters:* Forrest Road, Edinburgh.

Royal Scots Fusiliers The two battalions together providing half of the South Scottish Infantry Brigade, Lowland Division. **4th Battalion**: 'South Africa 1900–02'. *Headquarters:* Kilmarnock. *Companies:* 'A' (Kilmarnock), 'B' (Irvine and Kilwinning), 'C' (Stewarton and Kilmaurs), 'D' (Beith, Glengarnock and Lochwinnoch), 'E' (Saltcoats), 'F' (Dalry and Kilbirnie), 'G' (Darvel, Galston and Newmilns), 'H' (Kilmarnock). **5th Battalion:** 'South Africa 1900–01'. *Headquarters:* Ayr. *Companies:* 'A' (Ayr), 'B' (Catrine and Darnconnar), 'C' (Maybole and Girvan), 'D' (Stranraer, Portpatrick and Castle Kennedy), 'E' (Cumnock and New Cumnock), 'F' (Troon), 'G' (Muirkirk and Glenbuck), 'H' (Dalmellington, Waterside and Rankinston). **Ardeer Company:** An independent company attached to 4th Battalion and formed in 1912 from workers employed at Nobel's Explosives Factory in Ardeer. The men came from nearby Kilwinning, Stevenston and Saltcoats. Younger employees provided two companies of 1st Cadet Battalion RSF. **1st Cadet Battalion:** *Headquarters:* The Academy, Ayr. *Companies:* 'A' (Ayr Academy), 'B' (Girvan High School), 'C' (Kilmarnock Academy), 'D' (Royal Academy, Irvine), 'E', 'F' (Nobel's Explosive Works, Ardeer). The companies were affiliated: 'A' and 'D', to 5th Battalion; 'B' and 'C', 4th Battalion; 'E' and 'F', the Ardeer Company.

Royal Sussex Regiment The 4th and 5th Battalions were Army Troops attached to the Home Counties Division, the 6th was unattached in Eastern Command. **4th Battalion:** 'South Africa 1900–02'. *Headquarters:* 34 Tevil's Road, Worthing, moving to Horsham in 1909. *Companies:* 'A' Company (Haywards Heath and Cuckfield), 'B' (Hurstpierpoint, Burgess Hill, Henfield and Steyning), 'C' (East Grinstead, Crawley and Forest Row), 'D' (Petworth, Midhurst, Graffham and North Chapel), 'E' (Horsham and Warnham), 'F' (Arundel, Ashington, Littlehampton and Storrington), 'G' (Chichester, Bognor and Eastergate), 'H' (Worthing). *Cadets:* Brighton Preparatory Schools Cadet Corps and Cottesmore School Cadets. **5th (Cinque Ports) Battalion**: 'South Africa 1900–02'. *Headquarters:* Middle Street, Hastings. *Companies:* 'A' (Hastings, Eastbourne and Hailsham), 'B' (Battle, Dallington, Sedlescombe, Staplecross, Robertsbridge and Bexhill), 'C' (Wadhurst, Burwash, Flimwell, Hurst Green, Ticehurst and Frant), 'D' (Lewes, Glynde and Stanmer), 'E' (Rye, Icklesham, Winchelsea, Peasmarsh and Northiam), 'F' (Uckfield, East Hoathly, Hadlow Down, Nutley, Buxted, Newick and Heathfield), 'G' (Crowborough, Blackham, Hartfield,

Groombridge, Mayfield and Rotherfield), 'H' (Ore and Westfield). *Cadets:* 1st Cinque Ports Cadet Corps (17 Silchester Road, St Leonard's-on-Sea). **6th (Cyclist) Battalion:** Formed in 1912. *Headquarters:* 9 Hampton Place, Brighton, moving to 18 Montpelier Place, Brighton in 1914. *Companies:* 'A', 'B' (Brighton), 'C' (Brighton and Portslade), 'D' (Brighton), 'E' to 'H' (Lewes).

Royal Warwickshire Regiment The battalions together made up the Warwickshire Infantry Brigade, South Midland Division. **5th Battalion:** 'South Africa 1900–02'. *Headquarters:* Thorp Street, Birmingham. *Companies:* 'A' to 'H' (Thorpe Street). **6th Battalions** 'South Africa 1900–02'. *Headquarters:* Thorp Street, Birmingham. *Companies:* 'A' to 'H' (Thorpe Street). **7th Battalion:** 'South Africa 1900–02'. *Headquarters:* Coventry. *Companies:* 'A' to 'D' (Coventry), 'E' (Rugby), 'F' (Leamington), 'G' (Warwick and Kenilworth), 'H' (Nuneaton). *Cadets:* Bablake School Cadet Company (Coventry). **8th Battalion:** *Headquarters:* Aston Manor, Birmingham. *Companies:* 'A' (Aston Manor), 'B' (Saltley), 'C' to 'H' (Aston Manor). **1st Cadet Battalion:** *Headquarters:* The Barracks, Aston Manor, Birmingham. Affiliated to 8th Battalion. **2nd Cadet Battalion:** *Headquarters:* Stevens Memorial Hall, Coventry. Affiliated to 7th Battalion. **3rd Cadet Battalion:** *Headquarters:* The Drill Hall, Thorp Street, Birmingham. Affiliated to 5th Battalion. **4th (Schools) Cadet Battalion:** *Headquarters:* 15–16 Exchange Buildings, Birmingham. Affiliated to 6th Battalion.

Royal Welsh Fusiliers The four battalions together made up the North Wales Infantry Brigade, Welsh Division. **4th (Denbighshire) Battalion:** 'South Africa 1900–02'. *Headquarters:* Wrexham. *Companies:* 'A' (Wrexham), 'B' (Gresford and Wrexham), 'C' (Ruabon), 'D' (Denbigh and Ruthin), 'E' (Coedpoeth), 'F' (Gwersyllt), 'G' (Rhosllanerchrugog), 'H' (Llangollen and Chirk). **5th (Flintshire) Battalion:** 'South Africa 1900–02'. *Headquarters:* Hawarden, moving to Flint in 1911. *Companies:* 'A' (Mold), 'B' (Hawarden and Buckley), 'C' (Rhyl and St Asaph), 'D' (Holywell and Mostyn), 'E' (Flint and Bagillt), 'F' (Caergwle), 'G' (Colwyn Bay and Llanddulas), 'H' (Connah's Quay). **6th (Carnarvonshire & Anglesey) Battalion:** 'South Africa 1900–02'. *Headquarters:* Carnarvon. *Companies:* 'A' (Carnarvon), 'B' (Portmadoc), 'C' (Penygroes and Nantlle), 'D' (Llanberis and Ebenezer), 'E' (Conway and Llandudno), 'F' (Penmaenmawr), 'G' (Pwllheli and Criccieth), 'H' (Holyhead and Menai Bridge). **7th (Merioneth & Montgomery) Battalion:** 'South Africa 1900–01'. *Headquarters:* Newtown. *Companies:* 'A' (Llanidloes, Montgomery, Caersws and Carno), 'B' (Newtown), 'C' (Welshpool, Llanfair Caereinion, Llanfyllin, Llanwddyn, Llansaintffraid and Llanfechain), 'D' (Machynlleth, Llanbrynmair, Cemmaes and Corris), 'E' (Dolgelly, Barmouth and Harlech), 'F' (Towyn, Aberdovey, Abergwynolwyn and Llwyngwril), 'G' (Blaenau Festiniog, Festiniog and Penrhyndeudraeth), 'H' (Bala, Corwen and Glyndyfrdwy).

Royal West Kent Regiment Together the battalions provided one half of the Kent Infantry Brigade, Home Counties Division. **4th Battalion:** 'South Africa 1900–02'. *Headquarters:* Tonbridge. *Companies:* 'A' (Maidstone), 'B' (Maidstone and West Malling), 'C' (Tonbridge and Hadlow), 'D', 'E' (Tunbridge Wells), 'F' (Orpington), 'G' (Sevenoaks), 'H' (Westerham and Edenbridge). *Cadets:* Westerham and Chipstead Cadet Corps. **5th Battalion:** 'South Africa 1900–02'. *Headquarters:* East Street, Bromley. *Companies:* 'A', 'B' (Bromley), 'C' (Dartford), 'D' (Beckenham), 'E' (Sidcup and Dartford), 'F', 'G' (Chatham and Cliffe-at-Hoo), 'H' (Swanley). *Cadets:* 1st Chatham Cadet Company RMLI (RM Barracks, Chatham). **1st Cadet Battalion:** *Headquarters:* 241 Stanstead Road, Forest Hill. Affiliated to 5th Battalion.

Royal Wiltshire Yeomanry 'South Africa 1900–01'. *Headquarters:* Chippenham, Market Yard moving to The Butts, London Road in 1911. *Squadrons:* 'A' (Warminster, Longbridge Deverell, Whiteparish, Salisbury, Amesbury and Trowbridge). 'B' (Chirton, Melksham, Marlborough, Devizes, Lavington, Urchfont and Great Bedwyn), 'C' (Chippenham, Corsham, Wootton Bassett,

Malmesbury, Calne, Purton and Ashton Keynes), 'D' (Swindon). Part of the 1st South Western Mounted Brigade.

Ruthin School Cadet Corps Ruthin, Denbighshire.

Rutland Street (LCC) School Cadet Corps Stepney.

Ryde Cadet Company Affiliated to the 8th Hampshire Regiment. Absorbed into the regiment's 3rd Cadet Battalion.

St Ann's School Cadet Corps 57a Dean Street, Soho, London.

St Christopher's Cadet Corps City of London.

St Dunstan's College Cadet Corps See 20th London Regiment.

St Gabriel's Canning Town Cadet Company Affiliated to 6th Essex Regiment. Became 'C' Company 1st Cadet Battalion Essex Regiment in 1911.

St Leonards Collegiate School Cadet Company See 2nd Home Counties Brigade RFA.

St Mark's (Peckham) Cadet Corps Harders Road, Peckham.

St Matthew's (Custom House) Cadet Corps Re-designated 'D' Company 1st Cadet Battalion Essex Regiment in 1911.

St Olave's School Cadet Corps See 21st London Regiment.

St Peter's Cadet Company See 13th London Regiment.

St Phillip's Arundel Cadet Corps Arundel.

St Thomas's (Wandsworth) Cadet Corps See 23rd London Regiment.

Sandown Cadet Company Affiliated to the 8th Hampshire Regiment. Absorbed into the regiment's 3rd Cadet Battalion.

Sandroyd School Troop of Scouts Cobham.

Scottish Airline Signal Company See Scottish Command Signal Companies.

Scottish Cable Signal Company See Scottish Command Signal Companies.

Scottish Command Signal Companies *Headquarters:* 21 Jardine Street, Glasgow. *Companies:* Scottish Wireless, Cable and Airline Signal (Glasgow).

Scottish General Hospitals 1st: *Headquarters:* Aberdeen. **2nd:** *Headquarters:* 4 Lindsay Place, Edinburgh. **3rd and 4th:** *Headquarters:* 17 Royal Terrace West, Glasgow, moving in 1912 to Yorkhill Parade, Yorkhill, Glasgow.

Scottish Horse, 1st 'South Africa 1900–02'. *Headquarters:* Dunkeld. *Squadrons:* 'A' (Blair Athol, Ballinluig, Pitlochry, Kirkmichael and Kinloch Rannoch), 'B' (Dunkeld, Murthly, Bankfoot, Dupplin, Perth, Clunie and Aberfeldy), 'C' (Couper Angus, Blairgowrie, Alyth and Invergowrie), 'D' (Dunblane, Crieff, Comrie, Lochearnhead, Auchterarder, Muthill, Dunning and Methven). Unattached in Scottish Command.

Scottish Horse, 2nd 'South Africa 1900–02'. *Headquarters:* 142 Great Western Road, Aberdeen. *Squadrons:* 'E' (Elgin, Ballindalloch, Pluscarden, Craigellachie, Cullen, Dallas, Dufftown, Forres, Keith and Archiestown, 'F' (Kintore, Peterhead, Fraserburgh, Ellon, Huntly, Insch, Inverurie, Monymusk, Cluny, Alford, Turriff, Fyvie, Rothienorman, Maud, Mintlaw, Newmachar and

Bucksburn), 'G' (Aberdeen, Torphins, Aboyne, Tarland, Ballater and Braemar), 'H' (Connell, Kilchrenan, Appin, Easdale, Ardrishaig, Taynuilt, Calgary, Tiree, Craignure, Campbeltown, Bunessan, Torloisk, Port Ellen, Port Charlotte, Bowmore and Bridgend). Unattached in Scottish Command.

Scottish Rifle Brigade Company See Lowland Divisional Transport and Supply Column.

Scottish Rifle Infantry Brigade See Lowland Division.

Scottish Rifles See Cameronians.

Scottish Wireless Signal Company See Scottish Command Signal Companies.

Seaford College Cadet Company Seaford.

Seaforth and Cameron Infantry Brigade See Highland Division.

Seaforth Highlanders The battalions, together with the 4th Cameron Highlanders, made up the Seaforth and Cameron Infantry Brigade, Highland Division. **4th (Ross Highland) Battalion:** 'South Africa 1900–02'. *Headquarters:* Dingwall. *Companies:* 'A' (Tain, Nigg, Fearn, Edderton and Portmahomack), 'B' (Dingwall), 'C' (Munlochy, Avoch, Rosemarkie, Culbokie, Muir of Ord and Fortrose), 'D' (Gairloch, Opinan, Poolewe, Kinlochewe and Torridon), 'E' (Ullapool, Coigach and Braemore), 'F' (Invergorden and Kildary), 'G' (Alness and Evanton), 'H' (Maryburgh, Strathpeffer, Garve, Strathconon and Fairburn). **5th (The Sutherland and Caithness Highland) Battalion:** 'South Africa 1900–02'. *Headquarters:* Golspie. *Companies:* 'A' (Golspie, Melvich and Bettyhill), 'B' (Dornoch and Rogart), 'C' (Bonar Bridge, Lairg, Lochinver and Elphine), 'D' (Brora, Helmsdale, Kildonan and Kinbrace), 'E' (Thurso and Reay), 'F' (Wick and Lybster), 'G' (Halkirk, Watten and Westfield), 'H' (Castletown, Dunnet, Mey and Bowermadden). **6th (Morayshire) Battalion:** 'South Africa 1900–02'. *Headquarters:* Elgin. *Companies:* 'A' (Forres and Altyre), 'B' (Elgin, Lossiemouth and Pluscarden), 'C' (Elgin and Lossiemouth), 'D' (Rothes and Archiestown), 'E' (Fochabers and Bogmuir), 'F' (Grantown-on-Spey, Nethy Bridge and Carrbridge), 'G' (Garmouth and Lhanbryde), 'H' (Lossiemouth, Hopeman, Pluscarden and Burghead).

Senior Cadet Battalion, 3rd Included 'A' (Westminster) Company.

Settle Cadet Battalion See 6th Duke of Wellington's Regiment.

Shanklin Cadet Company Affiliated to the 8th Hampshire Regiment. Absorbed into the regiment's 3rd Cadet Battalion.

Sharpshooters See 3rd County of London Yeomanry.

Sherwood Foresters Together the battalions made up the Notts and Derby Infantry Brigade, North Midland Division. **5th Battalion:** 'South Africa 1900–02'. *Headquarters:* Derby. *Companies:* 'A' (Derby), 'B' (Melbourne, moving to Derby c1913), 'C' (Derby), 'D' (Derby, moving to Long Eaton c1913 and, transferred from 'B' Company about the same time, Melbourne), 'E' (Ripley, Codnor Park, Horsley Woodhouse, Kilburn, Alfreton and Butterley), 'F' (Belper, Crich, Horsley and, transferred from 'E' Company c1913, Woodhouse and Kilburn), 'G' (Ilkeston, Long Eaton, Heanor and Langley Mill), 'H' (Swadlincote and Repton). *Cadets:* Derby Post Office Cadet Corps. Recognition, was withdrawn on 6 December 1913. **6th Battalion:** 'South Africa 1900–02'. *Headquarters:* 10 Corporation Street, Chesterfield. *Companies:* 'A' (Chesterfield), 'B' (Chapel-en-le-Frith, Edale, Hathersage, Peak Dale and Chinley), 'C' (Buxton and Ashbourne), 'D' (Bakewell and Stoney Middleton), 'E' (Wirksworth, Cromford and Matlock), 'F' (Staveley, Clowne, Eckington and Brimington), 'G' (Clay Cross, New Tupton and South Wingfield), 'H' (Whaley Bridge, New Mills, Disley and Hayfield). *Cadets:* White Cross Cadet Corps. Recognition withdrawn with effect from 4 September 1911. **7th (Robin Hood) Battalion:** 'South Africa 1900–02'. *Headquarters:* 168 Derby Road, Nottingham. *Companies:* 'A' to 'H' (Nottingham). **8th Battalion:** 'South Africa 1900–02'. *Headquarters:* Newark. *Companies:* 'A' (Retford and Ollerton), 'B' (Newark), 'C' (Sutton-in-Ashfield), 'D' (Mansfield), 'E' (Carlton, Burton Joyce and Bingham), 'F' (Arnold, Basford, Eastwood, Daybrook and Hucknall), 'G' (Worksop and Shireoaks), 'H' (Southwell, Calverton and Farnsfield). *Cadets:* Welbeck Cadet Battalion (Cadet Drill Hall, Mansfield). **1st Cadet Battalion:** *Headquarters:* 48–50 St James's Street, Nottingham. Affiliated to 7th Battalion.

Sherwood Rangers See Nottinghamshire Yeomanry.

Shetland Companies See Gordon Highlanders.

Shropshire Royal Horse Artillery *Headquarters:* Shrewsbury. *Battery:* (Shrewsbury and Wellington). *Ammunition Column:* (Shrewsbury and Church Stretton). Part of the Welsh Border Mounted Brigade.

Shropshire Yeomanry 'South Africa 1900–02'. *Headquarters:* Shrewsbury. *Squadrons:* 'A' (Shrewsbury, Baschurch, Pontesbury, Pulverbach and Wem), 'B' (Oswestry, Whitchurch and Ellesmere), 'C' (Ludlow, Craven Arms, Ross-on-Wye, Hereford, Leominster, Tenbury and Kington), 'D' (Wellington, Much Wenlock, Shifnal, Market Drayton, Newport and Bridgnorth). Part of the Welsh Border Mounted Brigade.

Sir Walter St John's School Cadet Corps High Street, Battersea.

Somerset Light Infantry Together the battalions provided one half of the South Western Infantry Brigade, Wessex Division. **4th Battalion:** 'South Africa 1900–01'. *Headquarters:* Lower Bristol Road, Bath. *Companies:* 'A', 'B' (Bath), 'C' (Keynsham, Brislington, Whitchurch and Bitton), 'D' (Frome, Bruton, Mells and Wanstrow), 'E' (Weston-super-Mare, Winscombe and Cheddar), 'F' (Castle Cary, Shepton Mallet and Evercreech), 'G' (Midsomer Norton, Radstock, Bishop Sutton and Peasedown St John), 'H' (Glastonbury and Wells). **5th Battalion:** 'South Africa 1900–01'. *Headquarters:* Taunton, Old Prison Building, Shuttern moving in 1914 to the County Territorial Hall. *Companies:* 'A' (Taunton), 'B' (Williton, Watchet, Minehead and Washford), 'C' (Bridgwater and North Petherton), D' (Langport, Highbridge and Somerton), 'E' (Yeovil, Martock and Langport), 'F' (Crewkerne and South Petherton), 'G' (Wellington, Milverton and Wiveliscombe), 'H' (Chard and Ilminster).

Somerset Naval Cadet Corps, 1st Location unknown.

Somerset Royal Horse Artillery *Headquarters:* Taunton, Old Prison Buildings, Shuttern, moving to 10 Upper High Street in 1911, the County Territorial Hall 1912. *Battery:* (Taunton and Glastonbury). *Ammunition Column:* (Taunton, Shepton Mallet, Portishead and Wells). Part of the 2nd South Western Mounted Brigade.

South Eastern Mounted Brigade *Headquarters:* 80 Stockwell Road, Lambeth, moving around 1911 to 43 Russell Square, Holborn. *Units:* Royal East Kent, West Kent and Sussex Yeomanries, and 'B' Battery Honourable Artillery Company.

South Eastern Mounted Brigade Ammunition Column See Honourable Artillery Company.

South Eastern Mounted Brigade Field Ambulance *Headquarters:* Victoria Road, Margate. There was a drill station at Ramsgate.

South Eastern Mounted Brigade Signal Troop *Headquarters:* 43 Russell Square, Bloomsbury, London.

South Eastern Mounted Brigade Transport and Supply Column *Headquarters:* Croydon.

South Lancashire Brigade Company See West Lancashire Divisional Transport and Supply Column.

South Lancashire Infantry Brigade See West Lancashire Division.

South Lancashire Regiment Together the battalions provided half of the South Lancashire Infantry Brigade, West Lancashire Division. **4th Battalion:** 'South Africa 1900–02'. *Headquarters:* Warrington. *Companies:* 'A' to 'D' (Warrington), 'E' (Newton-le-Willows), 'F' (Warrington), 'G' (Newton-le-Willows), 'H' (Warrington). **5th Battalion:** 'South Africa 1900–01'. *Headquarters:* St Helens. *Companies:* 'A' (St Helens), 'B' (Prescot), 'C' (St Helens), 'D' (St Helens and Haydock), 'E' (St Helens), 'F' (Prescot), 'G' (St Helens), 'H' (Widness).

South London Cadets See 21st London Regiment.

South Midland Brigade Company See South Midland Divisional Transport and Supply Column.

South Midland Brigades Royal Field Artillery 1st (Gloucestershire) Brigade: *Headquarters:* Bristol. *Batteries:* 1st, 2nd Gloucestershire (Bristol), 3rd Gloucestershire (Gloucester). *Ammunition Column:* (Bristol). **2nd Brigade:** *Headquarters:* 24 Southfield Street, Worcester. *Batteries:* 1st Worcestershire (Worcester), 2nd Worcestershire (George Street, Kidderminster and Great Malvern), 3rd Worcestershire (Easemore Road, Redditch). *Ammunition Column:* (Clarence Road, Great Malvern). **3rd Brigade:** *Headquarters:* Stony Lane, Birmingham. *Batteries:* 1st, 2nd, 3rd Warwickshire (Birmingham). *Ammunition Column:* (Birmingham). **4th (Howitzer) Brigade:** *Headquarters:* Coventry, at the Ordnance Works until 1911, when temporary accommodation was found at the Royal Artillery Barracks, then from 1912, Quinton Road. *Batteries:* 4th Warwickshire (Coventry), 5th Warwickshire (Coventry and Rugby). *Ammunition Column:* (Coventry and Rugby).

South Midland Clearing Hospital *Headquarters:* Birmingham.

South Midland Division *Headquarters:* The Old Barracks, Warwick. *Infantry Brigades:* **Warwickshire**, with 5th to 8th Royal Warwickshire Regiment (Strathfield, Leamington, moving to The Old Barracks, Warwick); **Gloucester and Worcester**, with 4th, 6th Gloucestershire and 7th, 8th Worcestershire Regiment (London, 20a Bute Street, Kensington and 11 Chester Terrace, St Pancras, moving to Sunnyside, Prestbury, Cheltenham in 1910, and Charlecote, Battledown, Cheltenham in 1913) and **South Midland**, with 5th Gloucestershire Regiment, 4th Oxfordshire and Buckinghamshire Light Infantry, Buckinghamshire Battalion and 4th Royal Berkshire Regiment (20 Magdalen Street, Oxford).

South Midland Divisional Royal Engineers *Headquarters:* 32 Park Row, Bristol. *Field Companies:* 1st, 2nd South Midland (Bristol). *Telegraph Company:* (Bristol). In 1913 the Telegraph Company was included in the RE Signal Service, designated as South Midland Divisional Signal Company and organised as Headquarters and four sections: No 1, No 2 (Warwickshire), No 3 (Gloucester and Worcester) and No 4 (South Midland).

South Midland Divisional Telegraph/Signal Company See South Midland Divisional RE.

South Midland Divisional Transport and Supply Column *Headquarters:* Warwick, moving to Aston, Birmingham in 1911. *HQ and Brigade Companies:* HQ (Aston), Warwickshire Brigade Company (Aston, moving in 1911 to Court Oak House, Harborne, Birmingham), Gloucester and Worcester Brigade Company (Wallbridge) and South Midland Brigade Company (Taplow).

South Midland Field Ambulances 1st, 2nd: *Headquarters:* Birmingham, Whitton Road, Aston, moving to Albert Road, also in Aston, and later, the Barracks in Great Brook Street. The 2nd also a drill station at Sutton Coldfield. **3rd:** *Headquarters:* Colston Fort, Montague Place, Kingsdown, Bristol.

South Midland Field Companies See South Midland Divisional RE.

South Midland (Heavy) Royal Garrison Artillery (Warwickshire) *Headquarters:* Metropolitan Works, Saltley, Birmingham. *Battery* (Saltley and Wednesbury). *Ammunition Column:* (Wednesbury).

South Midland Infantry Brigade See South Midland Division.

South Midland Mounted Brigades 1st: *Headquarters:* 12 Northgate Street, Warwick, moving in 1912 to St John's, Warwick. *Units:* Warwickshire, Gloucestershire and Worcestershire Yeomanries, and Warwickshire RHA. **2nd:** *Headquarters:* Reading, moving to The Abbey, Cirencester in 1910, then in 1911 to 12 Lonsdale Road, Oxford. *Units:* Oxfordshire, Buckinghamshire and Berkshire Yeomanries, and Berkshire RHA.

South Midland Mounted Brigade Ammunition Columns See Warwickshire RHA and Berkshire RHA.

South Midland Mounted Brigade Field Ambulances 1st: *Headquarters:* Witton Road, Aston, Birmingham, moving to Albert Road, Aston in 1911, then the Barracks, Great Brook Street, Birmingham in 1912. **2nd:** *Headquarters:* Stony Stratford.

South Midland Mounted Brigade Signal Troops 1st: St John's, Warwick. **2nd:** 12 Lonsdale Road, Oxford.

South Midland Mounted Brigade Transport and Supply Columns 1st: *Headquarters:* Kidderminster, moving in 1909 to 158 Stoney Lane, Birmingham, then in 1912 to Taunton Road, Sparkbrook, Birmingham. **2nd:** *Headquarters:* Yeomanry House, Castle Hill, Reading.

South Nottinghamshire Hussars See Nottinghamshire Yeomanry.

South Scottish Infantry Brigade See Lowland Division.

South Staffordshire Regiment Together the battalions provided one half of the Staffordshire Infantry Brigade, North Midland Division. **5th Battalion:** 'South Africa 1900–02'. *Headquarters:* Walsall. *Companies:* 'A', 'B', 'C' (Walsall), 'D' (Bloxwich), 'E' (Brierley Hill), 'F' (Hednesford), 'G' (Handsworth), 'H' (Wednesbury). **6th Battalion:** 'South Africa 1900–02'. *Headquarters:* Wolverhampton. *Companies:* 'A', 'B' (Wolverhampton), 'C' (Wednesfield), 'D' (Willenhall), 'E' (Tipton), 'F' (Darlaston), 'G' (Bilston), 'H' (Tettenhall). *Cadets:* Brierley Hill Cadet Corps (The Temperance Hall, Brierley Hill).

South Wales Borderers The regiment's only TF battalion was not numbered and included in the South Wales Infantry Brigade, Welsh Division. **Brecknockshire Battalion:** 'South Africa 1900–01'. *Headquarters:* Brecon. *Companies:* 'A' (Brecon), 'B' (Brynmawr), 'C' (Crickhowell), 'D' (Hay-on-Wye), 'E' (Builth Wells and Llanwrtyd Wells), 'F' (Talgarth), 'G' (Cefn-Coed), 'H' (Ystradgynlais, Brynamman and Seven Sisters).

South Wales Brigade Company See Welsh Divisional Transport and Supply Column.

South Wales Infantry Brigade See Welsh Division.

South Wales Mounted Brigade *Headquarters:* Melton Lodge, Whitchurch, Shropshire, moving in 1913 to The Barracks, Carmarthen. *Units:* Pembrokeshire, Montgomeryshire and Glamorgan Yeomanries and Glamorgan RHA.

South Wales Mounted Brigade Ammunition Column See Glamorgan RHA.

South Wales Mounted Brigade Field Ambulance *Headquarters:* The Barracks, Hereford. *Sections:* 'A' (Hereford), 'B' (Hereford and Burghill).

South Wales Mounted Brigade Signal Troop *Headquarters:* Carmarthen.

South Wales Mounted Brigade Transport and Supply Column *Headquarters:* 7 Rutland Street, Swansea.

South Western Brigade Company See Wessex Divisional Transport and Supply Column.

South Western Infantry Brigade See Wessex Division.

South Western Mounted Brigades 1st: *Headquarters:* Petersfield, moving in 1912 to 28a Butcher Row, Salisbury. *Units:* Royal Wiltshire, North Somerset and Hampshire Yeomanries, and Hampshire RHA. **2nd:** *Headquarters:* Lennards Buildings, Goldsmith Street, Exeter. *Units:* 1st Royal Devon, Royal North Devon and West Somerset Yeomanries, and Somerset RHA.

South Western Mounted Brigade Ammunition Columns 1st: See Hampshire RHA. **2nd:** See Somerset RHA.

South Western Mounted Brigade Field Ambulances 1st: *Headquarters:* 40 New Park Street, Devises, moving in 1912 to the drill hall in Church Place, Swindon. By 1912 the sections were located at Swindon, Marlborough, Calne, Pewsey and Devizes. **2nd:** *Headquarters:* Frome. *Sections:* 'A' (Bath), 'B' (Weston-super-Mare).

South Western Mounted Brigade Signal Troops 1st: *Headquarters:* 28a Butcher Row, Salisbury. **2nd**: *Headquarters:* Goldsmith Street, Exeter.

South Western Mounted Brigades Transport and Supply Columns 1st: *Headquarters:* The Armoury, Tisbury with drill stations at Hindon, East Knoyle, Semley, Donhead, Ludwell, Berwick St John, Fovant, Dinton, Salisbury, Longford Park and Amesbury. **2nd:** *Headquarters:* High Street, Weston-super-Mare with a drill station at Wedmore.

Southend High School Cadet Corps See Southend Technical School.

Southend Technical School Cadet Corps See 6th Essex Regiment.

Southern Airline Signal Company See Southern Command Signal Companies.

Southern Cable Signal Company See Southern Command Signal Companies.

Southern Command Signal Companies *Headquarters:* Imperial Buildings, Dale End, Birmingham, moving in 1910 to The Barracks, Great Brook Street. *Companies:* Southern Wireless, Cable and Airline Signal (Birmingham).

Southern General Hospitals 1st: *Headquarters:* Albert Road, Aston, Birmingham, moving in 1912 to Great Brook Street, Birmingham. **2nd:** *Headquarters:* Kingsdown, Colston Fort, Montague Place, Kingsdown, Bristol. **3rd:** *Headquarters:* Oxford. **4th:** *Headquarters:* 11 Athenaeum Chambers, Plymouth, moving in 1912 to the Territorial Barracks, Millbay, Plymouth. **5th:** *Headquarters:* Connaught Drill Hall, Gosport.

Southern Wireless Signal Company See Southern Command Signal Companies.

Southport Cadet Corps See 7th Battalion King's (Liverpool Regiment).

Staffordshire Batteries See 2nd and 3rd North Midland Brigades RFA.

Staffordshire Brigade Company See North Midland Divisional Transport and Supply Column.

Staffordshire Infantry Brigade See North Staffordshire Regiment and formed part of the North Midland Division.

Staffordshire Yeomanry (Queen's Own Royal Regiment) 'South Africa 1900–01'. *Headquarters:* Lichfield, moving to Bailey Street, Stafford in 1914. *Squadrons:* 'A' (Walsall, Birmingham, Tamworth, Lichfield and Sutton Coldfield – the Birmingham drill station was closed down in 1913 and replaced by another at West Bromwich), 'B' (Stoke-on-Trent, Stafford, Leek, Cannock and Newcastle-under-Lyme), 'C' (Burton-on-Trent and Uttoxeter), 'D' (Wolverhampton and Himley). Part of the North Midland Mounted Brigade.

Steyne School Cadet Corps See 1st Home Counties Brigade RFA.

Suffolk Batteries See 3rd East Anglian Brigade RFA.

Suffolk Regiment Together the 4th and 5th Battalions provided half of the Norfolk and Suffolk Infantry Brigade, East Anglian Division. The 6th was unattached in Eastern Command. **4th Battalion:** 'South Africa 1900–02'. *Headquarters:* Portman Road, Ipswich. *Companies:* 'A' to 'D' (Ipswich), 'E' (Lowestoft), 'F' (Halesworth and Saxmundham), 'G' (Framlingham, Woodbridge and Easton), 'H' (Leiston and East Bridge). **5th Battalion:** 'South Africa 1900–02'. *Headquarters:* Bury St Edmunds. *Companies:* 'A' (Stowmarket and Eye), 'B' (Beccles and Bungay), 'C' (Hadleigh and Bildeston), 'D' (Sudbury, Long Melford and Bures), 'E' (Bury St Edmunds and Barrow), 'F' (Bury St Edmunds and Lavenham), 'G' (Haverhill and Clare), 'H' (Newmarket and Mildenhall). **6th (Cyclist) Battalion:** *Headquarters:* Ipswich. *Companies:* 'A', 'B' (Ipswich), 'C' (Ipswich and Brantham), 'D' (Southwold and Aldeburgh), 'E' (Lowestoft), 'F' (Bungay and Beccles), G' (Stowmarket), 'H' (Bury St Edmunds). Originally raised as four companies of the Essex and Suffolk Cyclist Battalion which was divided in 1911 to form 6th Suffolk and 8th Essex Battalions.

Suffolk Yeomanry (Duke of York's Own Loyal Suffolk Hussars) 'South Africa 1900–01'. *Headquarters:* Bury St Edmunds. *Squadrons:* 'A' (Cambridge, Burwell, which was closed in 1913, and Ely), 'B' (Bury St Edmunds, Eye, Thetford, Sudbury and, from 1913, Stowmarket), 'C' (Ipswich, Felixstowe, Framlingham and Woodbridge), 'D' (Beccles, Bungay, Halesworth, Lowestoft and Leiston). Part of the Eastern Mounted Brigade.

Sunbury House School Cadet Company See 9th Middlesex Regiment.

Surrey Brigade Company See Home Counties Divisional Transport and Supply Column.

Surrey Infantry Brigade See Home Counties Division.

Surrey Yeomanry (Queen Mary's Regiment) *Headquarters:* Melbourne House, King's Avenue, Clapham Park, London. *Squadrons:* 'A' (Clapham Park and Aldershot), 'B' (Guildford, Woking and Camberley), 'C' (West Croydon and Clapham), 'D' (Wimbledon and Clapham). *Cadets:* 'E' Cadet Squadron. Part of the South Eastern Mounted Brigade.

Sussex and Kent Royal Garrison Artillery See under each county.

Sussex Batteries See 1st and 2nd Home Counties Brigades RFA.

Sussex Fortress Engineers *Headquarters:* Seaford. *Works Company:* No 1 (Seaford and Newhaven).

Sussex Royal Garrison Artillery The three Sussex garrison companies were, until the beginning of 1910, grouped with the seven from Kent and under the title of Sussex and Kent RGA. Having been made independent, however, headquarters were then placed at 117 Gloucester Road, Brighton and the companies located: Nos 1, 2 (Brighton), No 3 (Lewes). In 1913 one of the Brighton companies was disbanded resulting in Lewes being renumbered as No 2.

Sussex Yeomanry *Headquarters:* Brighton, 9 Hampton Place, moving to Church Street in 1913. *Squadrons:* 'A' (Brighton, Horsham, Worthing, Hayward's Heath and Crawley), 'B' (Lewes, Burgess Hill, Eridge, Brighton, Uckfield, Tunbridge Wells and Groombridge, which was replaced by a drill station at Hayward's Heath in 1913), 'C' (Chichester and Bognor), 'D' (Eastbourne, Battle, which was (replaced by a drill station at St Leonards-on-Sea in 1913, Bexhill and Rye). Part of the South Eastern Mounted Brigade.

Territorial Force Nursing Service Part of Queen Alexandra's Imperial Military Nursing Service. Personnel were attached to each of the Territorial Force General Hospitals.

Tollington School Cadet Company See 7th Middlesex Regiment.

Totnes Cadet Company See 5th Devonshire Regiment.

Tranent Industrial School Cadet Corps See 8th Royal Scots.

Trinity Mission Boys' Club Cadets 285 Albany Road, Camberwell.

Tyne Electrical Engineers *Headquarters:* North Shields. Formed in 1911.

Tynemouth Royal Garrison Artillery *Headquarters:* Military Road, North Shields. *Garrison Companies:* Nos 1 to 4 (North Shields), No 5 (Seaton Delaval), No 6 (Blyth). Two of the North Shields companies were disbanded in 1913 and the Seaton Delaval and Blyth Companies renumbered accordingly.

University School Cadet Company Hastings See Home Counties Divisional Engineers.

Upper Tooting High School Cadet Corps 3 St James Road, Upper Tooting.

Usk Territorial Cadet Corps Affiliated to 2nd Monmouthshire Regiment. Absorbed into 1st Cadet Battalion Monmouthshire Regiment in 1912.

Ventnor Cadet Company Affiliated to the 8th Hampshire Regiment. Absorbed into the regiment's 3rd Cadet Battalion in 1915.

Walthamstow Cadets See 7th Essex Regiment.

Wandsworth Boys' Naval Brigade 37 East Hill, Wandsworth.

Waring Cadet Company 164 Oxford Street, Westminster. Affiliated to the 3rd London Infantry Brigade.

Warley Garrison Cadets See 4th Essex Regiment.

Warminster Cadet Company See 4th Wiltshire Regiment.

Warwickshire Batteries See 3rd and 4th South Midland Brigades RFA.

Warwickshire Brigade Company See South Midland Divisional Transport and Supply Column.

Warwickshire Infantry Brigade See South Midland Division.

Warwickshire Royal Horse Artillery *Headquarters:* Warwick Castle, moving to 9 Clarendon Place, Leamington in 1911. *Battery:* (Leamington and Coventry). *Ammunition Column:* (Leamington and Henley-in-Arden). Part of the 1st South Midland Mounted Brigade.

Warwickshire Yeomanry 'South Africa 1900–01'. *Headquarters:* Warwick, 12 Northgate Street, moving to St John's in 1912. *Squadrons:* 'A' (Birmingham), 'B' (Warwick, Kineton, Wellesbourne, Southam and, from 1913, Brailes), 'C' (Coventry, Rugby and Nuneaton), 'D' (Stratford-upon-Avon, Henley-in-Arden, Salford Priors and Weston-sub-edge). Part of the 1st South Midland Mounted

Brigade. *Cadets:* 1st Cadet Regiment Warwickshire Yeomanry. Recognition withdrawn in December 1913.

Welbeck Cadet Battalion See 8th Sherwood Foresters.

Welsh Border Brigade Company See Welsh Divisional Transport and Supply Column.

Welsh Border Infantry Brigade See Welsh Division.

Welsh Border Mounted Brigade *Headquarters:* Park Street, Denbigh, moving in 1912 to 15 High Street, Shrewsbury. *Units:* Shropshire, Cheshire and Denbighshire Yeomanries, and Shropshire RHA.

Welsh Border Mounted Brigade Ammunition Column See Shropshire RHA.

Welsh Border Mounted Brigade Field Ambulance *Headquarters:* Thomas Street, Chester. There was also a drill station at Ellesmere Port.

Welsh Border Mounted Brigade Signal Troop *Headquarters:* 15 High Street, Shrewsbury.

Welsh Border Mounted Brigade Transport and Supply Column *Headquarters:* 79a Harrowby Road, Birkenhead.

Welsh Brigades Royal Field Artillery 1st (Howitzer) Brigade: *Headquarters:* 42 Castle Street, Swansea. *Batteries:* 1st Glamorgan (Swansea), 2nd Glamorgan (Briton Ferry and Neath). *Ammunition Column:* (Morriston). **2nd Brigade:** *Headquarters:* Cardiff. *Batteries:* 3rd, 4th Glamorgan (Cardiff), Cardiganshire (Aberystwyth). *Ammunition Column:* (Cardiff). **3rd Brigade:** *Headquarters:* Old Prison Yard, Shipgate Street, Chester. *Batteries:* 1st, 2nd Cheshire (Chester), Flintshire (Sandycroft, Chester). *Ammunition Column:* (Chester and Crewe). On 31 October 1912, the Flintshire Battery was disbanded and replaced by a 3rd Cheshire Battery with headquarters at Crewe. Now an all Cheshire formation the 3rd Welsh was subsequently re-designated as the Cheshire Brigade. **4th Brigade:** *Headquarters:* Rodney Parade, Newport, moving to Lime Street in 1913. *Batteries:* 1st Monmouthshire (Newport), 2nd Monmouthshire (Risca), 3rd Monmouthshire (Panteg, moving to Griffithstown in 1913). *Ammunition Column:* (Newport). *Cadets:* Newport Territorial Cadet Corps (Newport Post Office).

Welsh Clearing Hospital *Headquarters:* Cardiff.

Welsh Division *Headquarters:* 11 Granville Street, moving in 1909 to 3 Belmont, Shrewsbury. *Infantry Brigades:* The original three brigades were the Cheshire, North Wales and South Wales. However, in 1910 the Welsh Border Infantry Brigade was formed and subsequently replaced the South Wales which remained attached. **Cheshire Brigade**, with 4th to 7th Cheshire Regiment (Chester, 22 Percy Road, moving to 8 Blackfriars, then the Territorial Drill Hall); **North Wales Brigade**, with 4th to 7th Royal Welsh Fusiliers (The Barracks, Wrexham); **Welsh Border Brigade**, with 1st, 2nd, 3rd Monmouthshire and 1st Herefordshire Regiments (High Street, Shrewsbury) and **South Wales Brigade**, with Brecknockshire Battalion, 4th, 5th, 6th Welsh Regiment (Cardiff, 20 Dumfries Place, moving later to 29 Windsor Place).

Welsh Divisional Royal Engineers *Headquarters:* Old Church Road, Whitchurch, moving in 1910 to 59 Charles Street, Cardiff. *Field Companies:* Cheshire (originally called 1st Welsh Field Company) (79a Harrowby Road, Birkenhead), Welsh (Llanelly, Carmarthen and Garnant). *Telegraph Company:* (Whitchurch, then Cardiff). In 1913 the Telegraph Company was included in the RE Signal Service, designated as Welsh Divisional Signal Company and organised as Headquarters, placed at the Drill Hall, Park Street, Cardiff, and four sections: No 1, No 2 (Cheshire), No 3 (North Wales) and No 4 (Welsh Border).

Welsh Divisional Telegraph/Signal Company See Welsh Divisional Royal Engineers.

Welsh Divisional Telegraph Company See Welsh Divisional Engineers.

Welsh Divisional Transport and Supply Column *Headquarters:* The Barracks, Hereford. *HQ and Brigade Companies:* HQ (Weobley, Kingsland, Hereford and Staunton-on-Wye), Cheshire Brigade Company (79a Harrowby Road, Birkenhead), North Wales Brigade Company (Ruthin, Cerrig-y-Druidion, Caerwys and St Asaph) and South Wales Brigade Company, called Welsh Border from 1911 (Pentre, moving in 1911 to Ystrad).

Welsh Field Ambulances 1st: *Headquarters:* Ebbw Vale. *Sections:* (Ebbw Vale, Newport and Cwm). **2nd:** *Headquarters:* 24 Moira Terrace, Cardiff, moving in 1911 to 15 Newport Road, Cardiff. **3rd:** *Headquarters:* Swansea.

Welsh Field Companies See Welsh Divisional RE.

Welsh (Heavy) Royal Garrison Artillery (Carnarvonshire) *Headquarters:* Bangor. *Battery:* Bangor and Carnarvon). *Ammunition Column:* (Llandudno).

Welsh Horse *Headquarters:* 3–4 Park Place, Cardiff. Formation was well under way by August 1914, the services of the Welsh Horse being accepted by the Glamorgan TFA on the 15th.

Welsh Regiment The 4th, 5th and 6th Battalions were included in the South Wales Infantry Brigade, Welsh Division. **4th Battalion:** 'South Africa 1900–02'. *Headquarters:* Haverfordwest, moving to Llanelly in 1909, then in 1913 to Carmarthen. *Companies:* 'A' (Haverfordwest and Milford Haven), 'B' (Pembroke and Narberth), 'C' (Cardigan), 'D' (Llandilo and Llandovery), 'E' (Carmarthen), 'F' (Llanelly and Tumble), 'G' (Llanelly), 'H' (Ammanford). **5th Battalion:** 'South Africa 1900–02'. *Headquarters:* Pontypridd. *Companies:* 'A', 'B' (Pontypridd), 'C', 'D' (Mountain Ash), 'E' (Aberdare), 'F' (Treharris), 'G' (Merthyr Tydfil and Dowlais), 'H' (Merthyr Tydfil). **6th (Glamorgan) Battalion:** 'South Africa 1900–02'. *Headquarters:* Swansea. *Companies:* 'A' (Maesteg), 'B', 'C', 'D' (Swansea), 'E' (Hafod and Morriston), 'F' (Neath), 'G' (Gorseinon and Clydach), 'H' (Gorseinon). **7th (Cyclist) Battalion:** *Headquarters:* 28 Park Road, Cardiff, moving to 11 Newport Road, Cardiff in 1911. *Companies:* 'A', 'B' (Cardiff), 'C' (Barry), 'D' (Bridgend), 'E', 'F' (Swansea), 'G' (Neath), 'H' (Aberavon).

Wessex Brigades Royal Field Artillery 1st Brigade: *Headquarters:* St Paul's Road, Portsmouth. *Batteries:* 1st, 2nd Hampshire (Portsmouth). 3rd Hampshire (Walpole Road, Gosport). *Ammunition Column:* (Portsmouth) **2nd (Howitzer) Brigade:** *Headquarters:* Ryde. *Batteries:* 4th Hampshire (Ventnor and Ryde), 5th Hampshire (Freshwater and Newport). *Ammunition Column:* (Ryde, Binstead and Ventnor). **3rd Brigade:** *Headquarters:* The Armoury, Prospect Place, Swindon. *Batteries:* 6th Hampshire (Victoria Drill Hall, Bournemouth), Dorsetshire (Bridport, Uploders and Dorchester), Wiltshire (Swindon). *Ammunition Column:* (Malmesbury, Swindon and Tetbury). **4th Brigade:** *Headquarters:* Exeter. *Batteries:* 1st Devonshire (Exeter and Exmouth), 2nd Devonshire (Paignton, Torre and Dartmouth), 3rd Devonshire (Tavistock, Lydford and Milton Abbot). *Ammunition Column:* (Exeter, Crediton and Teignmouth).

Wessex Clearing Hospital *Headquarters:* Exeter.

Wessex Division *Headquarters:* 19 Cathedral Close, Exeter. *Infantry Brigades:* **Devon and Cornwall**, with 4th, 5th Devonshire Regiment and 4th, 5th Duke of Cornwall's Light Infantry (Exeter, 57 High Street, moving to Lennards Buildings in Goldsmith Street); **South Western**, with 4th, 5th Somerset Light Infantry, 4th Dorsetshire and 4th Wiltshire Regiments (18 Manor Road, Yeovil, moving to 14 Gay Street, Bath, then Silvermead, 1 Fons George Road, 4 Park Street and the County Territorial Hall, all of which are in Taunton) and **Hampshire**, with 4th to 7th Hampshire Regiment (Southampton, Netley Castle, moving to 32 Queen's Terrace in 1911, then 30 Carlton Place 1913).

Wessex Divisional Royal Engineers *Headquarters:* Upper Bristol Road, Bath. *Field Companies:* 1st Wessex (Bath and Long Ashton), 2nd Wessex (Churchill Road, Weston-super-Mare and Clevedon). *Telegraph Company:* (The Priory, Colleton Crescent, Exeter). In 1913 the Telegraph Company was included in the RE Signal Service, designated as Wessex Divisional Signal Company and organised as Headquarters and four sections: No 1, No 2 (Devon and Cornwall), No 3 (South Western) and No 4 (Hampshire).

Wessex Divisional Telegraph/Signal Company See Wessex Divisional Royal Engineers.

Wessex Divisional Transport and Supply Column *Headquarters:* ASC Office, Higher Barracks, Exeter, moving in 1911 to 14 Oxford Road, Exeter. *HQ and Brigade Companies:* HQ (Andover, Barton Stacey, St Mary Bourne and Winchester), Devon and Cornwall Brigade Company (Mutley Barracks, Plymouth), South Western Brigade Company (Bridgwater) and Hampshire Brigade Company (Aldershot, Church Crookham and Farnborough). *Cadets:* Aldershot Church Cadet Corps. Affiliated to the Hampshire Brigade Company.

Wessex Field Ambulances 1st: *Headquarters:* 4 Priory Road, Heavitree, Exeter, moving in 1914 to 71 Holloway Street, Exeter. *Sections:* 'A', 'B' (Exeter), 'C' (Teignmouth). **2nd:** *Headquarters:* 3 Sussex Terrace, Plymouth, moving in 1911 to Millbay, Plymouth. **3rd:** *Headquarters:* Portsmouth. *Sections:* 'A' (Portsmouth), 'B' (Whitchurch, Overton, Andover, Sutton Scotney, Basingstoke and Winchester), 'C' (Southampton).

Wessex Field Companies See Wessex Divisional RE.

Wessex (Heavy) Royal Garrison Artillery (Hampshire) *Headquarters:* Cosham. *Battery:* Cosham and Fareham. *Ammunition Column:* Cosham.

West Croydon Cadets See 4th Queen's (Royal West Surrey Regiment).

West Ham Cadets Affiliated to 6th Essex Regiment. Absorbed as 'A' Company 1st Cadet Battalion Essex Regiment.

West Kent Yeomanry (Queen's Own) 'South Africa 1900–01'. *Headquarters:* Union Street, Maidstone. *Squadrons:* 'A' (Bromley, Catford and Woolwich), 'B' (Dartford, Rochester, Gravesend, Sevenoaks and Woolwich), 'C' (Tunbridge Wells, Tonbridge and Hawkhurst), 'D' (Maidstone, West Malling, Westminster and Woolwich). Part of the South Eastern Mounted Brigade.

West Lancashire Brigades Royal Field Artillery 1st Brigade: *Headquarters:* Windsor Barracks, Spekeland Street, Liverpool. *Batteries:* 1st, 2nd, 3rd Lancashire (Liverpool). *Ammunition Column:* (Liverpool). **2nd Brigade:** *Headquarters:* 46 Miller Arcade, Lancaster Road, Preston, moving to Stanley Street, Preston in 1911. *Batteries:* 9th Lancashire (26 Fishergate, Preston, moving to Stanley Street, Preston in 1911), 10th Lancashire (Dallas Road, Lancaster), 11th Lancashire (Yorkshire Street, Blackpool and Bamber Bridge). *Ammunition Column:* (Dallas Road, Lancaster, moving to Stanley Street, Preston in 1911). **3rd Brigade:** *Headquarters:* 65 Admiral Street, Liverpool. *Batteries:* 12th Lancashire (65 Admiral Street, Liverpool), 13th Lancashire (65 Admiral Street, Liverpool, moving to 1 Earp Street, Garston in 1912), 14th Lancashire (65 Admiral Street, Liverpool, moving to 1 Earp Street in 1909, then Widnes in 1913). *Ammunition Column:* (Liverpool, Garston and Widnes). **4th (Howitzer) Brigade:** *Headquarters:* Edge Lane, Liverpool. *Batteries:* 7th, 8th Lancashire (Edge Lane). *Ammunition Column:* (Edge Lane).

West Lancashire Clearing Hospital *Headquarters:* Kendal.

West Lancashire Division *Headquarters:* 21 Islington, Liverpool. *Infantry Brigades:* **North Lancashire**, with 4th, 5th King's Own Royal Lancaster and 4th, 5th North Lancashire Regiments

(16 Castle Park, Lancaster); **Liverpool**, with 5th to 8th King's Liverpool Regiment (Shaw Street, Liverpool) and **South Lancashire**, with 9th, 10th King's Liverpool, 4th, 5th South Lancashire Regiments, (11 Eshe Road, Blundellsands, moving to 21 Victoria Street, Liverpool in 1911).

West Lancashire Divisional Royal Engineers *Headquarters:* Engineer Hall, Croppers Hill, St Helens. *Field Companies:* 1st West Lancashire (St Helen's), 2nd West Lancashire (St Helens and Widnes). *Telegraph Company:* (St Helen's). All three units carried the additional title 'St Helens'. In 1913 the Telegraph Company was included in the RE Signal Service; designated as the West Lancashire Divisional Signal Company and organised as Headquarters and four sections: No 1, No 2 (South Lancashire), No 3 (Liverpool), No 4 (North Lancashire).

West Lancashire Divisional Telegraph/Signal Company See West Lancashire Divisional RE.

West Lancashire Divisional Transport and Supply Column *Headquarters:* Liverpool, then to Derby Road, Southport by 1909. *HQ and Brigade Companies:* HQ (Southport), North Lancashire Brigade Company (Tramway Road, Aigburth), Liverpool Brigade Company (Tramway Road, Aigburth) and South Lancashire Brigade Company (Bath Street, moving in 1909 to 46 Legh Street, Warrington).

West Lancashire Field Ambulances 1st: *Headquarters:* 73 Shaw Street, Liverpool, moving in 1910 to Tramway Road, Liverpool. **2nd:** *Headquarters:* 19 Low Hill, Liverpool, moving in 1910 to 14 Harper Street, Liverpool. **3rd:** *Headquarters:* St Helens. *Sections:* 'A' (St Helen's), 'B' (Kendal), 'C' (Blackpool). In 1911, the Blackpool Section was disbanded and the unit was reorganised: 'A' and 'C' Sections (Croppers Hill, St Helens), 'B' Section (Kendal and Barrow-in-Furness).

West Lancashire Field Companies See West Lancashire Divisional RE.

West Lancashire (Heavy) Royal Garrison Artillery See Lancashire Brigade RGA.

West Riding Batteries See 1st to 4th West Riding Brigades RFA.

West Riding Brigade Companies See West Riding Divisional Transport and Supply Column.

West Riding Brigades Royal Field Artillery 1st Brigade: *Headquarters:* Fenton Street, Leeds. *Batteries:* 1st West Riding (Leeds), 2nd West Riding (Leeds, Bramley from 1910), 3rd West Riding Battery (Leeds). *Ammunition Column:* (Leeds). **2nd Brigade:** *Headquarters:* Valley Parade, Bradford. *Batteries:* 4th West Riding (Bradford), 5th West Riding (Halifax), 6th West Riding (Heckmondwike). *Ammunition Column:* (Bradford and Halifax). **3rd Brigade:** *Headquarters:* Edmund Road, Sheffield, moving in 1911 to Norfolk Barracks, Sheffield. *Batteries:* 7th, 8th, 9th West Riding (Sheffield). *Ammunition Column:* (Sheffield). **4th (Howitzer) Brigade:** *Headquarters:* Otley. *Batteries:* 10th West Riding (Otley), 11th West Riding (Burley and Ilkley). *Ammunition Column:* (Burley and Ilkley).

West Riding Clearing Hospital *Headquarters:* Leeds.

West Riding Division *Headquarters:* 9 St Leonards, York. *Infantry Brigades:* **1st West Riding**, with 5th to 8th West Yorkshire Regiment (9 St Leonard's Crescent, York, moving to 3 Tower Street, York in 1912); **2nd West Riding**, with 4th to 7th Duke of Wellington's Regiment (Skipton-in-Craven) and **3rd West Riding**, with 4th, 5th King's Own Yorkshire Light Infantry, 4th and 5th York and Lancaster Regiment (12 East Parade, Sheffield, moving to 7 Bank Court Chambers, Sheffield in 1912).

West Riding Divisional Royal Engineers *Headquarters:* Glossop Road, Sheffield. *Field Companies:* 1st, 2nd West Riding (Sheffield). *Telegraph Company:* (Sheffield) In 1913 the Telegraph Company was included in the RE Signal Service, designated as West Riding Divisional Signal Company and organised as Headquarters and four sections: No 1, No 2 (1st West Riding), No 3 (2nd West Riding) and No 4 (3rd West Riding).

West Riding Divisional Telegraph/Signal Company See West Riding Divisional RE.

West Riding Divisional Transport and Supply Column *Headquarters:* 6 Tower Street, York, moving in 1912 to Harewood Barracks, Woodhouse Lane, Leeds. *HQ and Brigade Companies:* HQ (6 Tower Street, York, moving in 1911 to Lumley Barracks, Burton Stone Lane, York), 1st West Riding Brigade Company (Leeds), 2nd West Riding Brigade Company (Shipley, moving to Leeds in 1911) and 3rd West Riding Brigade (Leeds).

West Riding Field Ambulances 1st: *Headquarters:* Harewood Barracks, Woodhouse Lane, Leeds. **2nd:** *Headquarters:* Harewood Barracks, Woodhouse Lane, Leeds. There was also a drill station at Shipley. **3rd:** *Headquarters:* Brook House, 2 Gell Street, Sheffield.

West Riding Field Companies See West Riding Divisional RE.

West Riding (Heavy) Royal Garrison Artillery *Headquarters:* York.

West Riding Infantry Brigades See West Riding Division.

West Riding Royal Horse Artillery *Headquarters:* Wentworth Woodhouse, Rotherham. *Battery:* (Rotherham). *Ammunition Column:* (Rotherham). Part of the Yorkshire Mounted Brigade.

West Somerset Yeomanry 'South Africa 1900–01'. *Headquarters:* Taunton. *Squadrons:* 'A' (Wellington, Minehead, Wiveliscombe, Washford, Dulverton and Williton), 'B' (Taunton, Churchingford, Buckland St Mary, Bishop's Lydeard, Churchstanton and Hatch Beauchamp), 'C' (Bridgwater, Highbridge, Glastonbury, Langport, Nether Stowey and North Petherton), 'D' (Yeovil, Crewkerne, Chard, Ilminster, South Peterton and Martock). Part of the 2nd South Western Mounted Brigade.

West Surrey Cadets See 5th Queen's (Royal West Surrey Regiment).

West Yorkshire Regiment Together the battalions made up the 1st West Riding Infantry Brigade, West Riding Division. **5th Battalion:** 'South Africa 1900–02'. *Headquarters:* York. *Companies:* 'A' (York and Tadcaster), 'B', 'C' (York), 'D' (Selby), 'E' (Harrogate), 'F' (Harrogate and Wetherby), 'G' (Knaresborough, Boroughbridge and Starbeck), 'H' (Ripon and Pateley Bridge). **6th Battalion:** 'South Africa 1900–02'. *Headquarters:* Belle View Barracks, Bradford. *Companies:* 'A' to 'H' (Bradford). *Cadets:* Bradford Postal Telegraph Messengers' Cadet Corps. **7th and 8th Battalions (Leeds Rifles):** 'South Africa 1900–02'. *Headquarters:* Carlton Barracks, Leeds. *Companies:* (Leeds, there was also a drill station attached to the 8th Battalion at Pudsey). *Cadets:* Leeds Postal Telegraph Messengers Cadet Company. Affiliated to 7th Battalion, Army Order 86 of 1913, however, notified transfer of affiliated to Northern Command Signal Companies.

Westerham and Chipstead Cadet Corps See 4th Royal West Kent Regiment.

Western Airline Signal Company See Western Command Signal Companies.

Western Cable Signal Company See Western Command Signal Companies.

Western Command Signal Companies *Headquarters:* 38 Mason Street, Edge Hill, Liverpool. *Companies:* Western Wireless, Cable and Airline (Edge Hill).

Western General Hospitals 1st: *Headquarters:* 73 Shaw Street, Liverpool. **2nd**: *Headquarters:* Manchester. **3rd: 1** *Headquarters:* 5 Newport Road, Cardiff.

Western Wireless Signal Company See Western Command Signal Companies.

Westminster Cadet Company *Headquarters:* The Guildhall, London.

Westminster Dragoons See 2nd County of London Yeomanry.

Westminster Rifles See 16th London Regiment.

Westmorland and Cumberland Yeomanry 'South Africa 1900–01'. *Headquarters:* Penrith. *Squadrons:* 'A' (Kendal, Carnforth, Kirkby Lonsdale, Ulverston and Windermere), 'B' (Penrith, Keswick, Temple Sowerby and Cockermouth), 'C' (Whitehaven, Workington, Maryport and Barrow-in-Furness), 'D' (Carlisle, Wigton and Alston). Attached to the Welsh Border Mounted Brigade.

Weybridge and District Scout Cadets See 6th East Surrey Regiment.

Weymouth Secondary School Cadets Weymouth.

White Cross Cadet Corps See 6th Sherwood Foresters.

Wiltshire Battery See 3rd Wessex Brigade RFA.

Wiltshire Fortress Engineers *Headquarters:* Church Road, Swindon. *Works Company:* No 1 (Swindon).

Wiltshire Regiment 4th Battalion: 'South Africa 1900–02'. *Headquarters:* Warminster, moving to Fore Street, Trowbridge in 1909. *Companies:* 'A' (Salisbury and Farley), 'B' (Wilton, Wishford and Barford St Martin), 'C' (Trowbridge and Steeple Ashton), 'D' (Chippenham and Calne), 'E' (Devizes, Lavington and Bromham), 'F' (Warminster, Westbury, Chitterne, Horningsham, Dilton March and Heytesbury), 'G' (Bradford-on-Avon, Melksham and Holt), 'H' (Swindon and Marlborough. Part of the South Western Infantry Brigade, Wessex Division. *Cadets:* Warminster Cadet Company.

Wimbledon Boys Naval Brigade The Institute, Bridges Road, South Wimbledon.

Windsor Cadet Companies See 4th Royal Berkshire Regiment.

Woolwich Cadet Corps, 1st See 2nd London Brigade RFA.

Woolwich Scout Cadet Company, 2nd 'Oakleigh', Hill Street, Woolwich.

Worcestershire Batteries See 2nd South Midland Brigade RFA.

Worcestershire Regiment Together the battalions provided one half of the Gloucestershire and Worcestershire Infantry Brigade, South Midland Division. **7th Battalion:** 'South Africa 1900–01'. *Headquarters:* Kidderminster. *Companies:* 'A' (Kidderminster), 'B' (Tenbury, Kidderminster and Bockleton), 'C' (Stourport and Bewdley), 'D' (Stourport and Kinver), 'E' (Oldbury), 'F' (Halesowen), 'G', 'H' (Dudley). **8th Battalion:** 'South Africa 1900–02'. *Headquarters:* Silver Street, Worcester. *Companies:* 'A', 'B' (Worcester), 'C' (Pershore, Great Malvern, Upton-upon-Severn, Elmley Castle and Fladbury), 'D' (Evesham and Badsey), 'E' (Droitwich and Stoke Works), 'F' (King's Norton and Rubery), 'G' (Bromsgrove), 'H' (Redditch). **2nd (Dudley Grammar School) Cadet Battalion:** Affiliated to 7th Battalion. **3rd (Kidderminster Grammar School) Cadet Battalion:** Affiliated to 7th Battalion.

Worcestershire Yeomanry (Queen's Own) 'South Africa 1900–02'. *Headquarters:* Worcester. *Squadrons:* 'A' (Kidderminster, Bewdley, Dudley and Witley), 'B' (Camp Hill, Birmingham, Bromsgrove, Redditch and King's Heath), 'C' (Great Malvern, Upton-upon-Severn, Leigh Sinton and Ledbury), 'D' (Worcester, Droitwich and Pershore). Part of the 1st South Midland Mounted Brigade.

Yealmpton Cadet Corps See Devon Fortress Engineers.

York and Durham Brigade Company See Northumbrian Divisional Transport and Supply Column.

York and Durham Infantry Brigade See Northumbrian Division.

York and Lancaster Regiment Together the battalions provided half of the 3rd West Riding Infantry Brigade, West Riding Division. **4th (Hallamshire) Battalion:** 'South Africa 1900–02'. *Headquarters:* Sheffield. *Companies:* 'A' to 'H' (Sheffield). **5th Battalion:** 'South Africa 1900–02'. *Headquarters:* Rotherham. *Companies:* 'A', 'B' (Rotherham), 'C' (Barnsley), 'D' (Wath-upon-Dearne, Wombwell and Mexborough), 'E' (Barnsley), 'F' (Rotherham), 'G' (Treeton), 'H' (Birdwell).

Yorkshire Dragoons (Queen's Own) 'South Africa 1900–02'. *Headquarters:* Doncaster. *Squadrons:* 'A' (Sheffield and Rotherham), 'B' (Wakefield, Dewsbury and Pontefract), 'C' (Doncaster, Barnsley, Snaith, and Goole), 'D' (Bradford, Huddersfield and Halifax). Part of the Yorkshire Mounted Brigade.

Yorkshire Hussars (Alexandra, Princess of Wales's Own) 'South Africa 1900–02'. *Headquarters:* 30 New Walk Terrace, York. *Squadrons:* 'A' (Leeds and Ilkley), 'B' (York, Bedale, Thirsk, Helmsley and Malton), 'C' (Knaresborough, Harrogate, Bradford, Easingwold and Ripon), 'D' (Middlesbrough and Scarborough). Part of the Yorkshire Mounted Brigade. *Cadets:* Yorkshire Squadron Imperial Cadet Yeomanry (103 North Street, Leeds).

Yorkshire Mounted Brigade *Headquarters:* 9 St Leonard's, York. *Units:* Yorkshire Hussars, Yorkshire Dragoons and East Riding of Yorkshire Yeomanries, and West Riding RHA.

Yorkshire Mounted Brigade Ammunition Column See West Riding RHA.

Yorkshire Mounted Brigade Field Ambulance *Headquarters:* Grove House, Wakefield, moving in 1912 to the drill hall in Vicarage Street, Wakefield. *Sections:* 'A' (Wakefield), 'B' (Halifax).

Yorkshire Mounted Brigade Signal Troop *Headquarters:* 9 St Leonard's, York.

Yorkshire Mounted Brigade Transport and Supply Column *Headquarters:* 6 Tower Street, York, moving in 1910 to 29 St Saviourgate, York, Lumley Barracks, York in 1912. There were also drill stations at Malton and Scarborough.

Yorkshire Regiment Together the battalions provided one half of the York and Durham Infantry Brigade, Northumbrian Division. **4th Battalion:** 'South Africa 1900–02'. *Headquarters:* Northallerton. *Companies:* 'A', 'B' (Middlesbrough), 'C' (Yarm-on-Tees, Great Ayton, Stokesley and Hutton Rudby), 'D' (Guisborough, Eston, South Bank and Grangetown), 'E' (Richmond, Catterick, Eppleby and Reeth), 'F' (Redcar and Marske-by-the-Sea), 'G' (Skelton, Carlin How, Lingdale and Loftus), 'H' (Northallerton, Bedale, Thirsk, Easingwold, Brompton and Helperby). **5th Battalion:** 'South Africa 1900–02'. *Headquarters:* Scarborough. *Companies:* 'A' (Market Weighton, Pocklington, Newbald and Stamford Bridge), 'B' (Bridlington, Filey, Hunmanby and Flamborough), 'C' (Beverley and Cottingham), 'D' (Driffield and Sledmere), 'E', 'F' (Scarborough), 'G' (Pickering, Helmsley, Kirby Moorside, Grosmont, Ebberston and Thornton Dale), 'H' (Malton, Sand Hutton, Sheriff Hutton and Hovingham).

Yorkshire Squadron Imperial Cadet Yeomanry See Yorkshire Hussars Yeomanry.

Territorial Force Gazetteer

Listed in this section are all locations (cities, towns. villages, hamlets) known to have been associated with the Territorial Force – divisional, regimental, brigade, battalion, battery, company headquarters; outlying drill stations and recognised cadet corps. Geographical details have been given, as well as brief notes on local trade, employment, railways – all important aspects of a Territorial's daily civilian life. Also noted are important events – the opening or restoration of a new church, public building, unveiling of a notable statue – which fall within the memory of these that served in the TF between 1908–1914. A certain amount of personal knowledge has been used, but in the main my main source of information has been gleaned from guides published as near to the period 1908–1914 as possible. Certainly no earlier than 1890, and not later than 1930. Each place name ends with a listing of units local to it.

Aberavon District of Port Talbot in Glamorgan on the right bank of the River Afan near its mouth on Swansea Bay. The area thrived from its dock trade, coal mines, copper works, rolling mills, tinplate manufacture and railway development. The Aberavon Harbour Company began in 1834 and sixty years later commenced expansion as the Port Talbot Railway and Docks Company. Here is St Mary's Church. *Territorials:* 7th Welsh Regiment.

Aberbargoed Monmouthshire coal mining village in the Rhymney Valley, twenty miles from Newport and with a station on the Brecon & Merthyr Railway. The colliery owned by the Powell Duffryn Company was, by 1910, employing some 1,943 miners and as such was one of the largest in South Wales. One guidebook published about the same time noted that Aberbargoed was 'still in the process of making'. *Territorials:* 1st Monmouthshire Regiment.

Abercarn Town in Monmouthshire with station on the Great Western Railway ten miles from Newport. Many were employed in collieries, iron and tinplate works – Abercarn's most important colliery, the Prince of Wales, was sunk in 1862. The town's St Luke's Church was built in 1853 at the expense of Sir Benjamin Hall of Llanover for the purpose of carrying on services in Welsh. In London, 'Big Ben' was named after him. *Territorials:* 2nd Monmouthshire Regiment and Abercarn Territorial Cadet Company.

Aberchirder A planned Banffshire village in the valley of the Burn of Auchintoul, nine miles from Banff, founded in 1764 by Alexander Gordon of Auchintoul. Close by is Kinnairdy Castle. *Territorials:* 6th Gordon Highlanders.

Aberdare Industrial and market town in Glamorgan on the Great Western Railway, four miles from Merthyr Tydfil at the head of the Cynon Valley. Prosperity came with the iron and coal industries. The Gadlys Ironworks opened in 1827, steam-coal production ten years after that. Major employers in the area were David Davis & Sons, the Nixon Navigation Company and Powell Duffryn. Council-ran trams came to Aberdare in October 1913. Laid out in 1860, Aberdare Park was the venue in the following year for the very first National Eisteddfod. *Territorials:* Glamorgan Yeomanry and 5th Welsh Regiment.

Aberdeen Maritime and university city situated between the mouths of the Dee and Don and made up of two towns: Old and New Aberdeen. Fishing provided much employment, as did the Rubislaw Quarry to the west of the city which gave the granite that led to Aberdeen being called the 'Granit City'. But the railway, in its posters, referred to Aberdeen as the 'Silver City by the Sea'. In one we see a clean, tidy beech with fields beyond. Through the fields come a steady stream of buses bringing passengers to the sea. The city itself, indeed, looks silver in the picture. Cleary distinguishable on the skyline is Marischal College, St Machar's Cathedral and His Majesty's Theatre. The production of paper in Aberdeen began in 1694. In 1897, while visiting Aberdeen, Minnie Palmer became Britain's first women driver. The city was served by the Caledonian Railway. In the Senior Division of the OTC, Aberdeen University maintained one field ambulance section. *Territorials:* Gordon Infantry Brigade, 2nd Scottish Horse, 1st Highland Brigade RFA, North Scottish RGA, Highland Divisional Engineers, City of Aberdeen Fortress Engineers, 4th Gordon Highlanders, Highland Divisional Transport and Supply Column, 1st and 2nd Highland Field Ambulances, Highland Clearing Hospital, 1st Scottish General Hospital and City of Aberdeen Cadet Battalion.

Aberdovey Seaport and holiday resort on the Dyfi estuary in Merionethshire, the area around the town being known for its several large slate quarries and numerous lead and copper mines. Aberdovey, however, grew up around the shipbuilding industry and was served by the branch of the Cambrian Railway that ran from Dovey Junction along the coast to Pwllheli. *Territorials:* 7th Royal Welsh Fusiliers.

Aberfeldy Village on the Tay in Perthshire, with station on the Highland Railway, said to have been the place where the 42nd Regiment (1st Black Watch) was first embodied. A monument erected in 1887 on one side of General Wade's bridge of 1733 tells the story. On the western outskirts of Aberfeldy is a gorge made famous in a Robert Burns poem, 'The Birks of Aberfeldy'. *Territorials:* 1st Scottish Horse and 6th Black Watch.

Abergavenny Market town at the confluence of the Gavenny and Usk rivers in Monmouthshire, just over seventeen miles from Newport and served by both the Western and London & North Western railway companies. Overlooked by the Sugarloaf Mountain, the area in and around Abergavenny gave employment in agriculture, a number of breweries, iron foundries and an engine works. The poet Samuel Taylor Coleridge once stayed the night at Abergavenny and complained of vile food and accommodation. Born in Abergavenny was Thomas Monaghan who won the Victoria Cross during the Indian Mutiny, and John Williams (born Fielding), another VC, this time from the 1879 Rorke's Drift action in Zululand. At St Mary's Church lie the Herberts, Sir William Herbert thought to be the most powerful man in Wales in his day. *Territorials:* Gloucestershire Yeomanry, 3rd Monmouthshire Regiment and Abergavenny Cadet Corps.

Abergwynolwyn Merionethshire village in the Dysynni valley, seven miles from Towyn and chiefly inhabited by workers in the slate quarries at Bryn Eglwys. It was for the transportation of the slate to the coast at Towyn that the Talyllyn Railway opened from Abergwynolwyn in October 1866. *Territorials:* 7th Royal Welsh Fusiliers.

Aberlady Coastal village in Haddingtonshire, on the Firth of Forth sixteen miles from Edinburgh, its station being opened by the Aberlady, Gullane & North British Railway Company in April 1898. Aberlady parish church was built in 1887. *Territorials:* 8th Royal Scots.

Aberlour Banffshire village seventeen miles from Keith on the Great North of Scotland Railway. Here, Joseph Walker of Walkers Shortbread Ltd opened his bakery in 1898. The parish is separated from Elginshire by the River Spey, the village (its proper name, Charlestown of Aberlour) being founded in 1812 by Charles Grant. Here is St Margaret's Episcopal Church. *Territorials:* 6th Gordon Highlanders.

Abernethy Perthshire town on the River Nethy and North British Railway, just under nine miles from Perth. Abernethy station was opened in 1848 by the Edinburgh & Northern Railway Company. Here is the parish church of St Bridget and, looking like a factory chimney, Abernethy's round tower. One of only two in Scotland. *Territorials:* 7th Black Watch.

Abertillery Monmouthshire town on the Great Western Railway, fifteen miles from Newport. Development came with the opening of a tinplate works in 1846; collieries and ironworks also employed many throughout the area. Here, in Church Street, is the parish church of St Michael. *Territorials:* 3rd Monmouthshire Regiment.

Aberystwyth Cardiganshire coastal town, at the mouth of the rivers Ystwyth and Rheidol, where both the Great Western and Cambrian Railway Companies once brought holiday makers to the long Marine Terrace and students to the nearby University of Wales. The National Library of Wales, designed by Sidney Greenslade, was opened in 1911. Employment for many was in the area's several iron foundries and from a busy timber trade. Opened in 1896 was the Aberystwyth Cliff Railway. Here is the parish church of St Michael, completed in 1890 and the third to be built and, finished about the same time in Stanley Street, Holy Trinity. Aberystwyth University College maintained an OTC contingent. *Territorials:* Pembrokeshire Yeomanry and 2nd Welsh Brigade RFA.

Abingdon Berkshire market town on the Great Western Railway where the Thames flows under the seven arches of Burford Bridge and the tall spire of St Helen's Church at the south end of East Street is reflected in the river. Buried there is Thomas Trapham, a military surgeon in Cromwell's time and the sewer back on of Charles I's head after execution. The Wilts & Berks Canal once linked Abingdon with Semington and the Kennet & Avon. At Abingdon are Radley College and Roysse's School, both of which maintained OTC infantry contingents. Abingdon is six miles from Oxford. *Territorials:* Berkshire Yeomanry and 4th Royal Berkshire Regiment.

Aboyne Village at the foot of the Grampians in Aberdeenshire, where the River Dee is crossed by a suspension bridge and the North of Scotland Railway called on its way from Ballater to Aberdeen. *Territorials:* 2nd Scottish Horse and 7th Gordon Highlanders.

Abridge Essex village on the River Roding, just to the south of Epping, the Great Eastern Railway one mile to the north at Theydon Bois. Here is Holy Trinity Church which was built in 1833 without a churchyard. *Territorials:* 4th Essex Regiment.

Accrington Lancashire industrial and cotton town on the River Hinburn and served by the Lancashire and Yorkshire Railway. The Accrington Corporation Steam Tramways opened in April 1886. Once famous, the Accrington Stanley Football Club took its name from its origins in the town's Stanley Street. *Territorials:* 5th East Lancashire Regiment.

Achiltibuie Ross and Cromarty hamlet on the Coigach Coast of north-west Scotland, ten miles from Ullapool and overlooking Loch Broom and the Summer Isles. *Territorials:* 2nd Lovat's Scouts.

Achnasheen Ross and Cromarty village at the north-eastern tip of the Ledgowan Forest, served by the Highland Railway as it journeyed from Kyle of Lochalsh to Dingwall. The railway, originally the Dingwall & Skye, had reached the village in 1870. *Territorials:* 2nd Lovat's Scouts.

Acle Small Norfolk town on the River Bure and Norfolk Broads, served by the Great Eastern Railway on its way to and from Great Yarmouth. Acle station was opened in March 1883. Here, with its round tower, is St Edmund's Church. *Territorials:* 4th Norfolk Regiment.

Acomb Just one mile from Hadrian's Wall, Acomb in Northumberland lies close to Hexham and, according to one source, was 'a chaotic mixture of a mining settlement with prosperous lead and coal mines...an agricultural village with pens and stockyards spilling out on to the main street.' Here, on a hillside, is the church of St John Lee. *Territorials:* 4th Northumberland Fusiliers.

Acton West London district where railway stations once numbered five and many were employed by the Great Western Railway at its massive Old Oak Common engine sheds. A clean place; with its

180 laundries at the turn of the twentieth century, Acton was known locally as 'Soapsuds Island'. Here, at the corner of Horn Lane and close to Acton Central station, is St Mary's Church where registers date from 1538. *Territorials:* 10th Middlesex Regiment and Acton Cadet Company.

Addiewell Served by both the Caledonian and North British Railway companies, the Midlothian town of Addiewell, just under two miles from West Calder, sprang up from the chemical works – ammonia, paraffin and candles were made – established in the area in 1866. *Territorials:* 10th Royal Scots.

Adlington Small Cheshire town on the River Bollin, five miles from Macclesfield, served by the London & North Western Railway. Nearby Adlington Hall was under siege by Cromwell's forces for two weeks during the Civil War. *Territorials:* Cheshire Yeomanry.

Aigburth Suburb of Liverpool where, according to one guide, its houses were occupied mainly by wealthy merchants – four of them being responsible in 1836–37 for the building of St Anne's Church in Aigburth Road. The railway station, called Mersey Road and Aigburth, was maintained by the Cheshire Line Committee. *Territorials:* Lancashire Fortress Engineers and West Lancashire Divisional Transport and Supply Column.

Airdrie Lanarkshire market town, eleven miles from Glasgow and served by both the North British and Caledonian railways, once important in the iron and coal industries. Territorials would no doubt remember the 1911 opening of the Pavilion Music Hall in Graham Street and, in the year after that, the new Sir John Wilson Town Hall. The Airdrie & Coatbridge Tramways Company, with their maroon and cream trams, began service in February 1904. *Territorials:* Lowland Divisional Engineers.

Akeley Buckinghamshire village three miles from Buckingham. Here St James's Church dates from 1154, but was rebuilt by John Tarring in 1854. *Territorials:* Buckinghamshire Battalion.

Albury Surrey village in the Tillingbourne Valley, four miles from Guildford and just over one mile from the railway at Chilworth station. It seems that Mr Henry Drummond bought the original village of Albury in 1819, but his desire for privacy at his Albury Park seat caused him to move the inhabitants to what was then a small hamlet called Weston Street. There existed in the old village St Peter and St Paul's Church, but this became disused when a replacement was built at Weston Street in 1842. *Territorials:* 5th Queen's Royal West Surrey Regiment.

Aldeburgh Suffolk seaport served by the Great Eastern Railway, six miles from Saxmundham, where many were employed in fishing and boatbuilding. Drake's *Golden Hind* and *Pelican* were built at Aldeburgh, most of their crews being local seamen. In 1899 seven Aldeburgh men put to sea in a lifeboat, and seven men did not return. They are remembered by a fine memorial in the churchyard of St Peter and St Paul's which overlooks the sea. Inside the church is a memorial to one of its rectors: George Crabbe, who gave us the poem 'The Borough' from which Aldeburgh resident, the composer Benjamin Britten, took Peter Grimes for his opera. *Territorials:* 6th Suffolk Regiment.

Alderley Edge Cheshire village, three miles from Macclesfield, with station on the London & North Western Railway opened by the former Manchester & Birmingham Railway Company in 1842. Several references note how it was the railway that brought about the name of the village. The Manchester & Birmingham, in order to draw in business, had offered Manchester businessmen free twenty-year season tickets if they built houses in the Chorley area within one mile of the then Alderley station. A name change to Alderley and Chorley followed in 1853, but this was not liked by the railway so yet another change came in 1876, this time to Alderley Edge. Here, built in 1853, is St Philip's Church. *Territorials:* Cheshire Yeomanry.

Aldermaston Berkshire village, just over eight miles from Reading, served by the Great Western Railway. Running through, close by Aldermaston Court, is the Kennet and Avon Canal. In St Mary's Church is the fine alabaster tomb of Sir George Foster, who died in 1526, and his wife whose robe is being tugged by a small dog. Around the tomb are the figures of twelve sons and eight daughters. *Territorials:* 4th Royal Berkshire Regiment.

Aldershot The military came to Aldershot in 1854 and soon after that this quiet Hampshire village became the important garrison town often now referred to as 'The Home of the British Army'. The railway came, churches and other public building sprang up, the Post Office in Station Road opened in 1902, the building in Grosvenor Road of the Town Hall took place in 1904, St Augustine's Church in North Lane came in 1907 and the town's Roman Catholic St Josephs in 1913. The Aldershot & Farnborough Tramway, with its red and white trams, opened c1882, but was closed down in 1906. *Territorials:* Surrey Yeomanry, Hampshire Yeomanry, 4th Hampshire Regiment, Wessex Divisional Transport and Supply Column, 1st Cadet Battalion Hampshire Regiment and Aldershot Church Cadet Company.

Aldford Cheshire village on the east bank of the Dee, six miles to the south of Chester. Here, St John's was built on the sight of an earlier church in 1866, from which came a memorial to Lieutenant Job Watson who was killed in 1812 at the battle of Badajoz. *Territorials:* Cheshire Yeomanry.

Aldington Seen far out to sea, and used as a landmark for ships, is the tower of Aldington's St Martin's Church. To the west of Hythe, this Kent village lies on high ground and looks across to Romsey Marsh. *Territorials:* 5th Buffs East Kent Regiment.

Alexandria Situated on the River Leven to the north of Dumbarton, the inhabitants of Alexandria were mostly employed in the area's bleaching, printing and dyeing works and, opened in 1906, the Argyll Motor Company. The town is linked to neighbouring Bonhill by an iron suspension bridge, its railway, that ran by the Dumbarton & Balloch Joint. *Territorials:* 9th Argyll and Sutherland Highlanders.

Alfold Surrey village, on the border with Sussex and nine miles from Godalming, where a paved way leads past the village stocks to the white walls of St Nicholas's Church. The railway did not reach Alfold, its nearest station being four miles to the west at Baynard. *Territorials:* 5th Queen's Royal West Surrey Regiment.

Alford (Aberdeenshire) The railway, in the form of the Vale of Alford line, came to this quiet Aberdeenshire village in 1859 just as the predecessor of the Territorial Force, the old Volunteer Force, was springing to life in the county. Skirting the village, which gives its name to a Civil War battle of 1645, is the River Don; while looking down on the area are the hills of Bennachie and Coreen. *Territorials:* 2nd Scottish Horse and 6th Gordon Highlanders.

Alford (Lincolnshire) The chief trades of this market town are noted as: iron founding, brewing, tanning, rope and brick making. Bow-windowed shops, Georgian houses, thatched cottages and a thatched inn line the long main street. Alford was served by the East Lincolnshire Railway as it came to, and from, Louth in the north-west. A tramway, linking Alford to the seaside resort of Sutton (seven miles off), was opened in April 1884, but had closed by December 1889. Here at the fourteenth-century St Wilfrid's Church, there are memorials to the Christopher family. *Territorials:* Lincolnshire Yeomanry and 5th Lincolnshire Regiment.

Alfreton Derbyshire market town, ten miles from Chesterfield with station on the Midland Railway. At Alfreton, many were employed in local potteries, collieries, stone quarries and ironworks. Here is St Martin's Church which has memorials to the Morewood family. *Territorials:* Nottinghamshire Yeomanry (Sherwood Rangers) and 5th Sherwood Foresters.

Allendale South Northumberland town situated at the termination of the North Eastern Railway out of Newcastle-upon-Tyne. Catton Road Station (renamed Allendale in May 1898) being opened on 1 March 1869. Allendale, ten miles south-west of Hexham, was lit by electricity in 1889, and was once active in the production of lead. *Territorials:* Northumberland Yeomanry and 4th Northumberland Fusiliers.

Alloa This Clackmannanshire seaport, market and industrial town, lies on the north bank of the Forth and gave employment to many in its production of wool, glass and iron. Also in the area were breweries (George Younger the first here in 1764, the Thistle Brewery building still dominates the town), distilleries, saw mills and a large engineering works. The Town Hall was opened in 1887. Alloa was served by both the North British and Caledonian Railway companies. *Territorials:* Fife and Forfar Yeomanry and 7th Argyll and Sutherland Highlanders.

Alness This Ross-shire village, with its numerous distilleries, lies by the River Alness as it makes its way down to the Cromarty Firth. Alness station on the Highland Railway was the last stop before the line reached Invergordon Harbour having come from Inverness. *Territorials:* 2nd Lovat's Scouts and 4th Seaforth Highlanders.

Alnwick Small Northumberland market town on the River Aln, with station on the North Eastern Railway. Here battles against the Scots were fought – there are several memorials commemorating – Alnwick Castle on the right bank of the river playing an important part. Here, on the wall of the Falconer's Tower, a cross remembers the Hon Henry Hugh Manvers Percy who won the Victoria Cross at the Crimea in 1854. The town was once noted for its production of tobacco and snuff. Situated at the top of a hillside is St Michael and All Angels Church. *Territorials:* Northumberland Yeomanry and 7th Northumberland Fusiliers.

Alresford There is Old Alresford and New Alresford, the two being joined by a dam built across the River Alre by Bishop of Winchester, Godfrey de Lucy. Once an important Hampshire wool town, Alresford, on the London & South Western Railway, went on to make a name in watercress. Here, in Old Alresford, is St Mary's Church. *Territorials:* 4th Hampshire Regiment.

Alston Cumberland market town and lead-mining centre on the South Tyne to the south-west of Hexham. Here the North Eastern Railway terminated after its thirteen-mile journey down from Haltwhistle, and the tall spire of St Augustine's Church still looks down to the river. *Territorials:* Westmorland and Cumberland Yeomanry.

Althorne Essex village on the northern bank of the River Crouch, with station on the Great Eastern Railway's branch that opened from Woodham Ferrers to Southminster in 1889. Here is the chiefly sixteenth-century St Andrew's Church where the registers date from 1734. *Territorials:* 4th Essex Regiment.

Althorp Park Northamptonshire hamlet and seat of the Spencer family since the early sixteenth century with its own railway station opened by the London & North Western in 1881. *Territorials:* 4th Northamptonshire Regiment.

Alton Hampshire market town where for some time the inhabitants were chiefly employed in the brewery trade, and at a large paper mill. Alton saw two fights during the Civil War; one of which saw fierce fighting at St Laurence's Church during the night of 12–13 December 1643. The dead were buried in a pit just outside and a plaque inside tells how the Royalist commander on the day was overcome as he stood in the pulpit. The London & South Western Railway Company served Alton and, opened in 1901, the Basingstoke & Alton. *Territorials:* Hampshire Yeomanry and 4th Hampshire Regiment.

Altrincham Cheshire market town south of the River Mersey and to the south-west of Manchester where many were employed in local iron foundries, saw mills and, after the Bridgewater Canal reached Altrincham in 1765, market gardening. The railway came in 1849, the original station being closed and replaced in 1881. Here is St Margaret's Church, its vicar from 1908 to 1924, Hewlett Johnson (1874–1966) who later, as Dean of Canterbury, acquired the nickname 'the Red Dean' due to his political views. *Territorials:* 5th Cheshire Regiment.

Altyre Locality forming part of Rafford in Elginshire and situated two miles to the south-east of Forres. *Territorials:* 6th Seaforth Highlanders.

Alva In Clackmannanshire, and situated at the southern foot of the Ochil Hills, Alva employed many from the area in its manufacture of blankets, serges, tartans and tweeds. The North British Railway Company served the town via the short branch line that came up from Alloa, just across the River Devon to the South. *Territorials:* 7th Argyll and Sutherland Highlanders.

Alyth Through this Perthshire town runs the Alyth Burn which is crossed by a seventeenth-century packhorse bridge. Situated at the foot of Alyth Hill, Alyth had a railway station on the Caledonian Railway branch line that terminated at the town and employed a number in its linen and woollen mills. *Territorials:* 1st Scottish Horse and 6th Black Watch.

Amble Northumberland coastal town, to the south-east of Alnwick, situated at the mouth of the River Coquet and looking across to Coquet Island. Here, many were employed in fishing and shipbuilding, but Amble's prosperity came from coal. A branch of the North Eastern Railway brought the line up from Amble Junction. *Territorials:* 7th Northumberland Fusiliers.

Ambleside On the main road through the Lake District, Westmorland's Ambleside lies at the foot of Wansfell Pike close to the head of Lake Windermere. Thread, spinning, and other bobbins were manufactured here. Associated with Ambleside are William Wordsworth who, as Distributor of Stamps for Westmorland, had an office there, and the Arnold family – Dr Thomas Arnold of Rugby School, his son, the poet Matthew Arnold. *Territorials:* 4th Border Regiment.

Amesbury Wiltshire market town on Salisbury Plain seven miles north of Salisbury on the River Avon. Amesbury was not reached by the railway until the London & South Western branched out to Bulford in 1901. Here is the church of St Mary and St Melor. *Territorials:* Wiltshire Yeomanry and 1st South Western Mounted Brigade Transport and Supply Column.

Ammanford Carmarthenshire market town with collieries, tinplate, paint and oil works served by the Great Western Railway. There survives still, the large stone building once used by the Aberlash Tinplate Works (built 1888) and, at the bottom of Quay Street and completed in 1909, the premises of the Ammanford Electric Supply Company. There are many churches in the town, but St Michael's in Wind Street and All Saints, Brynmawr Avenue are recent – work beginning on the latter in 1911. *Territorials:* 4th Welsh Regiment.

Ampthill Market town seven miles south of Bedford and reached by the Midland Railway main line out of St Pancras. Thatched cottages built for workers on Lord Ossory's estate at Ampthill Park line Woburn Street. The area employed many in its extensive ironworks and a large brewery. At St Andrew's Church is a fine monument to Colonel Richard Nicolls who, having captured New Amsterdam, thought it better named New York. The cannonball at the base of the memorial is thought to be that responsible for the colonel's death at Sole Bay in 1672. *Territorials:* Bedfordshire Yeomanry and 5th Bedfordshire Regiment.

Andover Both the London & South Western and Midland & South Western railway companies served this Hampshire market town situated on the River Anton to the north-east of Salisbury. An important place in the medieval wool trade. Placed on a hill above the town sits the knapped flint and stone St Mary's Church that was built for Andover by a former headmaster at Winchester College. *Territorials:* Hampshire Yeomanry, 4th Hampshire Regiment, Wessex Divisional Transport and Supply Column. and 3rd Wessex Field Ambulance.

Annan Dumfriesshire seaport and market town at the mouth of the River Annan, off the Solway Firth, served by both the Caledonian and Glasgow & South Western railway companies. Trains coming and going over a viaduct that crosses the river. One guide notes the town's principal industries as cotton, a distillery, tannery, sawmills, shipbuilding, fishing and a bacon curing establishment. *Territorials:* Lanarkshire Yeomanry and 5th King's Own Scottish Borderers.

Anstey Large Leicestershire village, four miles north-west of Leicester, its main industry being the manufacture of boots and shoes. Here on Bradgate Road is the parish church of St Mary. *Territorials*: 4th Leicestershire Regiment.

Anstruther Fifeshire seaport and market town situated at the entrance of the Firth of Forth and served by the North British Railway as it passed along the coast to Leven. Once an important fishing port, many though were employed in shipbuilding and tanning. *Territorials:* 7th Black Watch.

Appin Argyllshire village and port on Appin Bay to the north–north-east of Oban and served by the Callander & Oban Railway branch that opened between Connel Ferry and Ballachulish in 1903. At Edinburgh Castle are the Colours of the Appin Regiment which fought at Culloden – these the only Jacobite example to survive the battle. *Territorials:* 2nd Scottish Horse.

Appleby Westmorland's Appleby is situated on the River Eden, its wide main street having Appleby Castle at the south end and Sir Robert Smirk's Cloisters at the north. Both the Stockton & Darlington and Midland railways served the town. Here is St Lawrence's Church. *Territorials:* 4th Border Regiment.

Applecross Ross-shire fishing village on Applecross Bay, west coast of Scotland, of which one guide published in the 1890s noted that 'the Gaelic-speaking population are chiefly engaged in salmon and herring fishing. *Territorials:* 4th Highland Brigade RGA.

Appledore (Devonshire) Fishing, ship and boatbuilding are the main industries of this Devonshire seaport and market town situated on the western bank of the River Torridge where it meets the Taw. On the quay, and dating from 1838, is St Mary's Church, the tower, however, not being added until 1909. The railway, in the form of the Bideford, Westward Ho! & Appledore line, reached the town in 1908. *Territorials:* 6th Devonshire Regiment.

Appledore (Kent) Village on the old Royal Military Canal where a boy who fought at Waterloo lies buried in St Peter and St Paul's churchyard. Served by the South Eastern & Chatham Railway, Appledore station is situated just before the line once branched off towards Dungeness. *Territorials:* 5th Buffs East Kent Regiment.

Appleton Cheshire village close to the Bridgwater Canal and three miles south-east of Warrington, its station being opened by the St Helens & Runcorn Gap Railway Company in 1833. Here is the red sandstone St Cross Church which was built and paid for by Rowland Egerton-Warburton of Arley Hall in 1886. *Territorials:* Cheshire Yeomanry.

Arbroath Forfarshire market town and seaport at the mouth of the River Brothock and served by the North British and Caledonian railways. Fisheries were important to Arbroath, but many were also employed in the production of chemicals, tar and asphalt. One guide notes twenty-two churches in the town. Born here was the inventor of the adhesive postage stamp, James Chalmers (1782–1853), and, the American car manufacturer, David Dunbar Buick (1854–1929). *Territorials:* Fife and Forfar Yeomanry, 2nd Highland Brigade RFA and 5th Black Watch.

Archiestown Elginshire village in the south-east of the county situated below the Elchies Forest on the Moor of Ballintomb. Named after its founder, Sir Archibald Grant, Archiestown and the surrounding area is best known for its distilleries. *Territorials:* 2nd Scottish Horse and 6th Seaforth Highlanders.

Ardchattan Argyllshire parish in the mountainous north of the county and situated on Loch Etive seven miles from Oban. Here, founded as a Valliscaulian Priory around 1230, is Ardchattan Priory. *Territorials:* 8th Argyll and Sutherland Highlanders.

Ardeer Area in Ayrshire, one mile south of Stevenston, occupied by Nobel's Explosives Factory. Alfred Nobel (1833–96), inventor of Dynamite and instigator of the Nobel Peace Prize. *Territorials:* Ardeer Company and 1st Cadet Battalion Royal Scots Fusiliers.

Ardersier Small, former fishing village, on the Moray Firth, Inverness-shire close to Fort George and reached via General Wade's Military Road. *Territorials:* 4th Cameron Highlanders.

Ardgay Small Ross-shire village on the north-west shore of the Dornoch Firth, its station (called Bonnar Bridge) opened by the Inverness & Aberdeen Junction Railway Company in October 1864. *Territorials:* 2nd Lovat's Scouts.

Ardgour Argyllshire village on the western shore of Loch Linhhe, ten miles south-west of Fort William. *Territorials:* 8th Argyll and Sutherland Highlanders.

Ardleigh Essex village, four miles from Colchester, its station being opened by the Eastern Union Railway Company (became the Great Eastern in 1862) in June 1846. Here, in the centre of the village by the crossroads, is St Mary's Church where the registers date from 1555. *Territorials:* Essex Yeomanry.

Ardrishaig Argyllshire seaport on the west side of Loch Fyne and at the termination of the Crinan Canal. Fishing gave employed to many from the area, one guide also noting brisk steamer traffic and a vast shipping trade in cattle and sheep. *Territorials:* 2nd Scottish Horse and 8th Argyll and Sutherland Highlanders.

Ardrossan Ayrshire seaport and holiday resort, six miles from Irvine, where fishing and boatbuilding provided employment. The Caledonian and Glasgow & South Western Railway companies served Ardrossan, both also providing ferry services to the Isle of Arran, Isle of Man and Belfast. *Territorials:* 2nd Lowland Brigade RFA.

Ardverikie Seat on the south shore of Loch Laggan, Inverness-shire, occupied by Sir John William Ramsden, Bart (Hon Colonel, 1st West Riding Brigade RFA, TF) who in 1907 installed electricity on the estate. *Territorials:* 4th Cameron Highlanders.

Ardwick Industrial district of Manchester with station opened by the Sheffield, Ashton-under-Lyme & Manchester Railway Company in November 1842. Once important here was the Birch family, one of them, Samuel Birch building St Thomas's Church in 1741. *Territorials:* 8th Manchester Regiment and 1st Territorial Cadet Battalion Manchester Regiment.

Arlesey Bedfordshire village on the border with Hertfordshire, four miles south of Biggleswade and served by the Great Northern Railway. A Brickworks, where 'Arlesey White Bricks' were produced, and the Portland Cement Works provided employment for the area. Here is St Peter's Church. *Territorials:* 5th Bedfordshire Regiment.

Armadale (Linlithgowshire) Served by the North British Railway, Armadale lies close to Bathgate and for some time gave its inhabitants employment in the production of bricks, chemicals and paraffin. *Territorials:* 10th Royal Scots.

Armadale (Sutherlandshire) Fishing village on the Sleat Peninsular, Isle of Skye. *Territorials:* 2nd Lovat's Scouts.

Arnold Nottinghamshire lace-making town, four miles north-east of Nottingham and served by the Great Northern Railway's Daybrook station. Arnold was a centre for framework knitting and the scene in 1811 of Luddite riots. One major employer was the Home Brewery which opened in 1875. Here is St Mary's Church. *Territorials:* Nottinghamshire Yeomanry (South Notts) and 8th Sherwood Foresters.

Arnside Westmorland costal village and seaside resort looking across Morecambe Bay which was reached by the Furness Railway over a viaduct across the River Kent. Built by Miles Thompson in 1866, Arnside's St James's Church was enlarged in 1905, and again in 1914. *Territorials:* 5th King's Royal Lancaster Regiment.

Arundel West Sussex market town on the River Arun to the east of Chichester, where the castle and the flint and Pulborough sandstone St Nicholas's parish church overlooks ancient streets and buildings. In 1880, after a lawsuit, it was decided that the chancel at St Nicholas's was the private property of the Duke of Norfolk who, as a Roman Catholic, had a wall built separating it from the rest of the church. Arundel was served by the London, Brighton & South Coast Railway. *Territorials:* 4th Royal Sussex Regiment and St Phillip's Arundel Cadet Corps.

Ascot Berkshire town to the south-west of Windsor where the London & South Western Railway Company's Ascot station (called 'Ascot and Sunninghill' until 1921) brought many to the races. The 'Royal Ascot' horseracing event introduced by Queen Anne in 1711. Here, the red-brick All Saints Church dates from 1864 and All Souls, at the south end of the town and also red-brick, 1896–97. *Territorials:* Berkshire RHA.

Ash Town in Kent, on the road between Canterbury and Sandwich, not reached by the railway until the South Eastern & Chatham Company extended their line up from Eastry in 1912. Ash Town station opening in 1916. Here is St Nicholas's Church. *Territorials:* 4th Buffs East Kent Regiment.

Ashbourne Derbyshire market town on the River Dove and southern edge of the Peak District where mother of the Salvation Army, Catherine Booth, was born. Here for centuries, the locals have taken part in the annual Royal Shrovetide two-day football match which has the town as a pitch and the goals three miles apart. At the west end of town, the central tower and spire of St Oswald's is referred to as the 'Pride of the Peak'. Novelist George Elliot thought it the finest parish church in England. Both the London & North Western and North Staffordshire railway companies served the town – Ashbourne station being closed in August 1899 and a new one opened just to the north-east of the original. At Compton, a suburb of the town, there was a large stay factory. *Territorials:* 6th Sherwood Foresters.

Ashburton Just through the richly-worked iron gates of Ashburton's St Andrew's Church, lies a young French officer – a POW of the Napoleonic wars – and close by him, Miriam Adams, the town's postwoman for forty-four years. A Devonshire market town on the River Yeo to the south-west of Newton Abbot, Ashburton's station was situated at the end of the Great Western branch line that ran up from Totnes. *Territorials:* 5th Devonshire Regiment.

Ashby-de-la-Zouch To the town, and its Ivanhoe Baths, came invalids and sufferers from rheumatism to 'take the waters' that came up from the three-mile-distant Moira Springs. Local inhabitants worked at the Moira Colliery, a number of them also finding employment on the Ashby-de-la-Zouch Canal. Situated on the River Mease to the north-west of Leicester, the town was served by the Midland Railway. Here, on the north side of the town's ruined castle, is St Helen's Church. *Territorials:* 5th Leicestershire Regiment.

Asheridge Small Buckinghamshire hamlet in the Chiltern Hills, two miles north-west of Chesham. *Territorials:* Hertfordshire Regiment.

Ashford Market town in Kent where a factory making agricultural implements provided many with jobs and the South Eastern Railway Company's locomotive and carriage works employed more than a thousand. Ashford is located fourteen miles south-west of Canterbury on the River Great Stour. Here, with its central tower, is St Mary's Church. *Territorials:* Royal East Kent Yeomanry, Kent Fortress Engineers, 5th Buffs East Kent Regiment, Kent Cyclist Battalion, 2nd Home Counties Field Ambulance and Ashford Grammar School Cadet Corps.

Ashington (Northumberland) Mining town in the north of the county served by the North Eastern Railway. Ashington is bounded on the south side by the River Wansbeck, its Church of the Holy Sepulchre dating from 1888. *Territorials*: Northumberland Yeomanry and 7th Northumberland Fusiliers.

Ashington (Sussex) West Sussex village on the London-Worthing road just to the north of the Downs and about five miles north-west of Steyning. Here is St Peter and St Paul's Church. *Territorials:* 4th Royal Sussex Regiment.

Ashreigney Devonshire village in the north of the county four miles from Chulmleigh. Here is St James's Church, which was restored in 1889 and, built by the Bible Christians in 1906, the Zion Methodist Chapel which replaced an older building. *Territorials:* Royal North Devon Yeomanry.

Ashton-in-Makerfield Lancashire township to the north-west of Warrington, well known for its production of locks, bolts, hinges and screws. There were also numerous collieries in the area – William Keneally, who won the Victoria Cross at Gallipoli in 1915, working in one of them. Holy Trinity Church in Rectory Road dates from 1838, the red sandstone St Thomas's being completed in 1893. Ashton-in-Makerfield station was not opened until 1900, the town library six years later in 1906. *Territorials:* Lancashire Hussars.

Ashton Keynes North Wiltshire village on the River Thames close to the border with Gloucestershire and four miles west of Cricklade. The village was served by the Midland & South Western Junction Railway at two stations: Cerney and Ashton Keynes to the north, and Minety and Ashton Keynes to the south. Both some two miles distant. Here is the church of the Holy Cross. *Territorials:* Wiltshire Yeomanry.

Ashton-under-Lyne Market and industrial town on the River Tame to the east of Manchester where many were employed in cotton mills, collieries and engineering works – Ashton Colliery once the deepest in the world. Near the town is Dukinfield Junction where three canals meet: the Ashton, Peak Forest and Huddersfield Narrow. The town's corporation tramway was opened in August 1902. *Territorials:* East Lancashire Infantry Brigade and 9th Manchester Regiment.

Ashwater Devonshire village on the River Carey with station opened by the North Cornwall Railway Company in July 1886. Here is St Peter ad Vinchla (St Peter in Chains), which dates from 1250. *Territorials:* 6th Devonshire Regiment.

Ashwell Hertfordshire village served by the Great Northern Railway in which springs contribute to the source of the River Cam and the four-stage tower of St Mary's Church rises to 176 ft. Always an attraction is the church's 600-year-old graffiti. One item shows the original St Paul's Cathedral, before its spire fell down in 1561, another takes the form of a master mason's harsh comment (in Latin) of some poor workmanship. *Territorials:* Hertfordshire Regiment.

Askam-in-Furness Lancashire coastal village, six miles from Barrow-in-Furness, where its street names reflect the area's connection with the steel industry: Steel Street and Sharp and Crossley streets which were named after early investors in the business – Joseph Sharpe and William Crossley. Called the 'Iron Church' (it was built partly from the proceeds of iron) St Peter's Church is situated high above the village. *Territorials:* 4th King's Royal Lancaster Regiment.

Aspatria Cumberland town bounded on the south by the River Ellen, with a view across the Solway Firth towards Scotland. Aspatria station was opened in 1841 by the old Maryport & Carlisle Railway Company, the town's church being dedicated, unusually, to St Kentigern. *Territorials:* 5th Border Regiment.

Astley Bridge Many from this Bolton suburb were employed in cotton spinning or at a large local bleach works. All Souls Church in Astley Street dates from 1881 and, in Blackburn Road, the Congregational Church from 1895. The town library was built in 1912. *Territorials:* 5th North Lancashire Regiment.

Aston Large suburb of Birmingham of which one visitor remarked, 'after the mean streets of the city', we were delighted at the sight of the Jacobean turrets and chimneys of Aston Hall and the spire of the church as it rose up from its sixteenth-century tower.' Founded at the Villa Cross Wesleyan Chapel in 1874 was the Aston Villa Football Club. *Territorials:* South Midland Divisional Transport and Supply Column, 1st South Midland Mounted Brigade Field Ambulance and King Edward's Grammar School (Aston) Cadet Corps.

Atherington Devonshire village to the south-east of Barnstaple. Here is St Mary's Church which is noted for its 400-year-old carved screen and gallery. *Territorials:* Royal North Devon Yeomanry.

Atherton Lancashire town where the inhabitants were chiefly employed in the cotton trade, collieries and ironworks. Atherton station was served by the London & North Western Railway, while Atherton Central belonged to the Lancashire & Yorkshire. The Council Officers were opened in 1900, St Anne's Church in Tyldesley Road completed in 1901 and the Library in York Street finished 1905. *Territorials:* 5th Manchester Regiment.

Attleborough Norfolk market town sixteen miles south-west of Norwich, its station opened by the Norfolk Railway (Great Eastern from 1862) in July 1854. A major employer at Attleborough was Gaymer's Cider which set up a plant by the railway in 1896. Here is St Mary's Church. *Territorials:* Norfolk Yeomanry, 4th and 6th Norfolk Regiment.

Auchenblae Readers of the Lewis Grassic Gibbon (1901–35) novel *Sunset Song* will be familiar with Auchenblae. Close to Bervie Water, this Kincardineshire village lies to the south-west of Stonehaven. *Territorials:* 7th Gordon Highlanders.

Auchenheath Coal produced by this south Lanarkshire village was supplied to Glasgow for the manufacture of gas. Auchenheath lies on the River Nethan to the west of Lanark and had a station on the Caledonian Railway. *Territorials:* Lanarkshire Yeomanry.

Auchnagatt Aberdeenshire village on the Ebrie Burn between Ellon and New Deer, its station opened by the Formartine & Buchan Railway Company (later Great North of Scotland) in July 1861. *Territorials:* 5th Gordon Highlanders.

Auchnagoul Argyllshire hamlet just over two miles south-west of Inveraray. *Territorials:* 8th Argyll and Sutherland Highlanders.

Auchterarder Small Perthshire market town, fourteen miles south-west of Perth, with station on the Caledonian Railway. In view of its long main street, the town became known locally as 'Lang Toon'. The parish church dates from 1784. *Territorials:* 1st Scottish Horse and 6th Black Watch.

Auchtermuchty Fifeshire market town, served by the North British Railway to the north-east of Kinross, familiar, perhaps, to viewers of the TV series *Doctor Finlay's Casebook* as 'Tannochbrae'. The town is divided by Loverspool, which flows through it, and is noted as giving employment in its bleach fields, distillery and linen mill. *Territorials:* 7th Black Watch.

Auldearn Site of the battle in May 1645, Auldearn village in Nairnshire looks across the Moray Firth. Auldearn station, to the north, was located on the Highland Railway between Nairn and Brodie. *Territorials:* 4th Cameron Highlanders.

Aultbea Fishing village on the east side of Loch Ewe, Ross and Cromarty, its communication with Glasgow and the Clyde being by steamboat. *Territorials:* 2nd Lovat's Scouts.

Aviemore Inverness-shire village in the north-east of the county and within the Cairngorms National Park, said to have expanded in the 1890s when the Highland Railway opened its line up from Aviemore towards Inverness. *Territorials:* 2nd Lovat's Scouts and 4th Cameron Highlanders.

Avoch Coastal village on the Black Isle, Ross and Cromarty, which maintained a fishing fleet, produced wool and operated several grain mills. Avoch station was the last on the line before the Highland Railway terminated at Fortrose. *Territorials:* 4th Seaforth Highlanders.

Axbridge Small Somerset market town on the River Axe where the Bristol and Exeter Railway (later the Great Western) had called since 1869. Once a wool town specialising in hosiery. Here is St John's Church. *Territorials:* North Somerset Yeomanry.

Axminster Devonshire market town on the River Axe, twenty-five miles north-east of Exeter, where the internationally know carpets that bear the town's name were first made in Silver Street. The railway reached Axminster in 1860, the London & South Western opening a branch line down to Lyme Regis from the town in 1903. Here is St Mary's Church and, in Lyme Street, the Roman Catholic church is also called St Mary's. *Territorials:* Royal 1st Devon Yeomanry and 4th Devonshire Regiment.

Aylesbury Buckinghamshire market town, to the south-east of Buckingham, once a Parliament-arian stronghold during the Civil War and where local hero of that period, John Hampden, is remembered by a statue in Market Square. He is in good company with Prime Minister Disraeli who stands close by. A large printing works once employed many from the town, which was well served by the railway: the London & North Western, Great Western & Great Central Joint and Metropolitan & Great Central Joint all maintaining services. Here, in the centre of town, is the thirteenth-century St Mary's and, in Cambridge Street, the red brick St John's which was began in 1881. *Territorials:* Buckinghamshire Yeomanry, Buckinghamshire Battalion and Aylesbury Grammar School Cadet Corps.

Aylsham With its two railway stations: one to the north of the town ran by the Midland & Great Northern Joint Company, the other in the south by the Great Eastern, Norfolk's Aylsham employed many in its grain and timber trades. The town lies on the River Bure, twelve miles from Norwich, the tower of its St Michael and All Angels Church dominating the market place. *Territorials:* 5th Norfolk Regiment.

Ayr William Wallace is remembered in this county and market town by a tall tower, as too is Robert Burns who was born just three miles away at Alloway. His statue stands in a square and is now in good company with the war memorial. A busy seaport where much shipbuilding took place, Ayr was served by the Glasgow & South Western Railway. The trains entering the town across a substantial viaduct. Territorials will remember the extensive repairs carried out to the ancient Auld Bridge in 1911 and the opening of the Pavilion the following year. Born at Ayr in 1756 was John McAdam who we must now thank for our smooth roads. *Territorials:* South Scottish Infantry Brigade, Ayrshire Yeomanry, Ayrshire RHA, 5th Royal Scots Fusiliers and 1st Cadet Battalion Royal Scots Fusiliers.

Ayton Berwickshire village served by the North British Railway just before it reached Burnmouth and travelled down the east coast towards Berwick-upon-Tweed. Ayton station was opened in June 1846, the parish church twenty years after that. *Territorials:* 4th King's Own Scottish Borderers.

Bacup Lancashire market, industrial and cotton town, twenty miles north of Manchester, high in the south Pennines and within the Forest of Rossendale. Yorkshire Street its main thoroughfare, Bacup is situated at the end of the line began by the old East Lancashire Railway (later Lancashire & Yorkshire) in 1846. Here, St John's Church dates from 1788, Christ Church, 1854 and St Saviour's, 1865. The Roman Catholic St Mary's opening in 1857. *Territorials:* 5th East Lancashire Regiment.

Badsey Worcestershire village in the Vale of Evesham and close to the River Avon. Badsey was served by the Great Western's Littleton & Badsey station, its St James's Church being restored in 1885. In the church there is a monument to Richard Hoby (died 1617) and his wife Margaret. Below the two figures are their children who, because they were from Margaret's first marriage, are facing west, not east as is usual. *Territorials:* 8th Worcestershire Regiment.

Bagillt Flintshire village with collieries and lead-smelting works on the Dee estuary, its station being opened by the Chester & Holyhead Railway Company in 1849. Here is St Mary's Church. *Territorials:* 5th Royal Welsh Fusiliers.

Bagshot Surrey town three miles south of Ascot and close to the border with Berkshire. Here, in red brick, is St Anne's Church where a window remembers Sir Howard Elphinstone who won the Victoria Cross during the Crimean War. The London & South Western Railway reached Bagshot in 1878. *Territorials:* 5th Queen's Royal West Surrey Regiment.

Bakewell Derbyshire market town on the Wye, twenty-five miles north-west of Derby, where many were employed in the turning and polishing of the marble quarried in the neighbourhood. Here, with its octagonal tower and monuments to the Vernon family, is All Saints Church. Bakewell station, on the Midland Railway, lies just to the south of Haddon Tunnel. *Territorials:* Derbyshire Yeomanry and 6th Sherwood Foresters.

Bala Merionethshire market town at the north end of Bala Lake, eleven miles south-west of Corwen, where Christ Church dates from 1857. The Bala & Festiniog Railway opened in 1882, the line taken over by the Great Western in 1910. Bala was once famous for its knitwear. *Territorials:* 7th Royal Welsh Fusiliers.

Baldock Hertfordshire market town to the north-east of Hitchin where the principle industries are noted as malting and brewing – Simpson's Georgian premises are in the High Street. To the north of the town, Baldock station was on the Great Northern Railway. Here is St Mary's Church. *Territorials:* Hertfordshire Regiment.

Balfron Stirlingshire village on the Endrick, just over twenty-four miles north-west of Glasgow, where a number were employed in the cotton industry. The town was served by the old Forth & Clyde Junction Railway. *Territorials:* Fife and Forfar Yeomanry.

Ballachulish Argyllshire village on Loch Leven, sixteen miles south of Fort William, where the parish church was enlarged in 1880. Slate quarries were established in the area in 1760, and in 1893 some 600 men out of a total population of 1,045 are recorded as being employed in them. Ballachulish was at the end of the line opened in 1903 by the Callander & Oban Railway. *Territorials:* 8th Argyll and Sutherland Highlanders.

Ballater Aberdeenshire village on the River Dee, to the south-west of Aberdeen, reached by the Aboyne & Braemar Railway Company in 1866. A popular line with the royal family, Ballater being the closest station to Balmoral Castle. *Territorials:* 2nd Scottish Horse and 7th Gordon Highlanders.

Ballindalloch Banffshire hamlet, twelve miles north-east of Grantown, best known for its whiskey distilleries and castle. Ballindalloch station was opened by the Strathspey Railway Company in July 1863. *Territorials:* 2nd Scottish Horse.

Ballingdon Suffolk village on the edge of Sudbury and border with Essex. Ballingdon lies on the River Stour, the bridge here being the only crossing for several miles in either direction. *Territorials:* East Anglian Divisional Transport and Supply Column.

Ballinluig Perthshire village on the River Tummel, four miles south-east of Pitlochry, its station being opened by the Inverness & Perth Junction Railway Company in June 1863. *Territorials:* 1st Scottish Horse and 6th Black Watch.

Ballygrant Hamlet on the Isle of Islay, Inner Hebrides. *Territorials:* 8th Argyll and Sutherland Highlanders.

Balnain Inverness-shire hamlet in Glen Urquhart to the west of Loch Ness. *Territorials:* 4th Cameron Highlanders.

Bamber Bridge Lancashire cotton village, three miles south-east of Preston, served by the Lancashire & Yorkshire Railway. Set up here in 1764 was Lancashire's first calico printing works. Another employer was the Withy Trees Mill. Owned by Eccles & Co, their premises were burnt down with the loss of 250 jobs in October 1859. Here are two parish churches: St Saviour's on Church Road, and in Station Road, St Aidan's. *Territorials:* 2nd West Lancashire Brigade RFA and 4th North Lancashire Regiment.

Bampton Devonshire market town, seven miles north of Tiverton on the River Batherm close to the Somerset border, reached by the Tiverton & North Devon Railway in 1884. Here is St Michael's Church. *Territorials:* 1st Royal Devon Yeomanry and 4th Devonshire Regiment.

Banbury Oxfordshire municipal borough and market town to the north of Oxford on the River Cherwell and Oxford and Birmingham Canal. Guides note the town's principal industries as being the manufacture of agricultural implements, tent, rope, brick and tile making. The town was served by both the Great Western and London & North Western railways. Here is St Mary's Church where reindeer, a walrus, polar bears, Arctic foxes, Eskimos and an ice-bound ship feature in a window dedicated to the memory of early Arctic explorer, Admiral Sir George Back, RN. *Territorials:* Oxfordshire Yeomanry and 4th Oxfordshire and Buckinghamshire Light Infantry.

Banchory Kincardineshire village on the River Dee, seventeen miles south-west of Aberdeen, served by the Great North of Scotland line that ran from Aberdeen to Ballater. *Territorials:* 7th Gordon Highlanders.

Banff Banffshire seaport and market town on the Moray Firth at the mouth of the Deveron and served by the Great North of Scotland Railway. Connected to Macduff by a bridge of seven arches, Banff became a popular holiday resort. Its main industries being fishing and the production of woollens, leather, rope and bricks. There was also breweries and distilleries. *Territorials:* 1st Highland Brigade RFA and 6th Gordon Highlanders.

Bangor Carnarvonshire town close to the Menai Strait and just over eight miles north-east of Caernarfon and served by the London & North Western Railway. In July 1907 the foundation stone of the University College of North Wales was laid by King Edward VII, the building formally opened by George V four years later. The area around Bangor contained numerous slate quarries. Here is the medieval Bangor Cathedral, and Bangor University College which maintained an OTC contingent. *Territorials:* Denbighshire Yeomanry and Welsh RGA.

Banham Norfolk village in the south of the county, seven miles from Diss, noted for its production of cider, bricks, tiles and chimney pots. Here is St Mary's Church. *Territorials:* 4th Norfolk Regiment.

Bankfoot Perthshire village on the Corral Burn to the north of Perth. *Territorials:* 1st Scottish Horse and 6th Black Watch.

Bannockburn Stirlingshire town to the south-east of Stirling on the Caledonian Railway, noted as a busy manufacturing centre turning out large quantities of woollens, tweeds, tartans, carpets and leather. Here was fought the great battle of 24 June 1314. *Territorials:* 7th Argyll and Sutherland Highlanders and Highland Cyclist Battalion.

Barford St Martin Wiltshire village on the River Nadder, just over five miles from Salisbury. Although the London & South Western line ran within yards of the church, villagers had to journey the two miles to Wilton for the train. At St Martin's Church there is a monument to Alice Walker and here eleven children. *Territorials:* 4th Wiltshire Regiment.

Barking Essex market town, seven miles east of London, with a powder magazine and chemical manure works – the North London Main Drainage Works being on the west side of Barking Creek. Barking station was opened by the London, Tilbury & Southend Railway in 1854. Here is St Margaret's Church where the registers date from 1558 and Captain James Cook married Elizabeth Batts in 1762. *Territorials:* 4th Essex Regiment.

Barmouth Merionethshire seaport and market town at the mouth of the River Mawddach, ten miles west of Dolgelly and reached by the longest railway viaduct (Cambrian Railway) in Wales. Barmouth grew up around the shipbuilding industry, much was also made from the gold ('Welsh Gold') taken from the hills above. With their dark red and white trams, the Barmouth Junction & Arthog Tramways Company began operations in August 1899. *Territorials:* 7th Royal Welsh Fusiliers.

Barnard Castle Durham market town on the River Tees to the west of Darlington and served by the North Eastern Railway. Here, notes one late Victorian guide, 'carpets were once made, but the town is now chiefly employed in the manufacture of flax thread'. The Bows Museum opened at Bernard Castle in June 1892. In Dickens's *Nicholas Nickleby*, Newman Nobbs recommends the King's Head ('where there is good ale') at Barnard Castle. Here is St Mary's Church, and the North Eastern County School which maintained two OTC infantry companies. *Territorials:* 6th Durham Light Infantry.

Barnet Hertfordshire market town eleven miles north of central London – the battle fought nearby (Wars of the Roses), and a horse fair is held on the common. An important coaching stage on the Great North Road, Dickens's Oliver Twist met the Artful Dodger at Barnet while passing through. Barnet station, on the Great Northern Railway, was renamed New Barnet in 1884. Here, in the Market Place, is St John's Church and, on St Alban's Road, Christ Church. *Territorials:* 7th Middlesex Regiment and Home Counties Divisional Transport and Supply Column.

Barnoldswick West Yorkshire township on the Leeds and Liverpool Canal to the south-west of Skipton, where numerous mills produced cotton – Bancroft Mill being one of them. Barnoldswick station was opened in 1871 when the Midland Railway extended their line from Barnoldswick Junction. Here is the church of St Mary-le-Gill. *Territorials:* 6th Duke of Wellington's Regiment.

Barnsley West Yorkshire borough and market town best known for its coal production, but once an important centre for glass making. The town was well served by the Great Central, Midland, London & North Western, Great Northern and North Eastern railways. The green and white trams of the Barnsley & District Electric Tramway carried their first passengers from its depot off Upper Sheffield Street in October 1902. Here, among the town's several churches, is St Mary's which replaced an older building in 1821. *Territorials:* Yorkshire Dragoons and 5th York and Lancaster Regiment.

Barnstaple Situated on the River Taw, Barnstable in Devon made lace, gloves and had several tanneries, flour mills and potteries. Local inhabitants would have seen first-hand Gilbert Scott's restoration at St Peter and St Paul's church, between High Street and Bouthport Street, which began in 1866 and went on right into the 1880s. It was to Barnstaple that Captain Jorgan went to see his lawyer in Dickens's *A Message from the Sea*. The Great Western and London & South Western railways served the town. *Territorials:* Royal North Devon Yeomanry and 6th Devonshire Regiment.

Barrhead Renfrewshire town on the River Leven and Glasgow & South Western Railway, seven miles south-west of Glasgow, where the chief industries were shawl and calico printing, dying, cotton-spinning, bleaching and brass founding. *Territorials:* 6th Argyll and Sutherland Highlanders.

Barrow Suffolk village six miles west of Bury St Edmunds. Ignored by the railway, villagers had to make the two-mile journey to Higham and the Great Eastern. Barrow's All Saints Church, where there are memorials to the Heigham family, is about half that distance from the village. *Territorials:* 5th Suffolk Regiment.

Barrow Gurney Somerset hamlet, five miles south-west of Bristol, where a number were employed by the Bristol Waterworks. Here is Barrow Court, and attached to the house, St Mary and St Edward's Church. *Territorials:* North Somerset Yeomanry.

Barrow-in-Furness Lancashire seaport, manufacturing and shipbuilding town, at the extremity of the Furness Peninsular across from the Isle of Walney, where the Naval Construction and Armament Company employed many. There was also the Bessemer steel works, the Tubular Frame Wagon Company, the Paper Pulp Manufacturing Company and the Yarlside Mining Company. To house their employees in 1898, Vickers, who owned Barrow Docks, began construction of Vickerstown. The Barrow Corporation Tramway opened in July 1885. Here, among the town's numerous churches, are St George's and St James's. *Territorials:* Westmorland and Cumberland Yeomanry, Lancashire and Cheshire RGA, 4th King's Own Royal Lancaster Regiment and 3rd West Lancashire Field Ambulance.

Barrowby Lincolnshire village two miles west of Grantham. Here at All Saints Church, its vicars settled in: Jonathan Kendal staying forty-seven years, until 1849, his replacement, George Earle Welby, putting in fifty-one years. *Territorials:* Lincoln and Leicester Infantry Brigade.

Barrowden Rutlandshire village on the River Welland to the east of Uppingham served by Wakerley & Barrowden station (London & North Western Railway) just to the south east. Here is St Peter's Church. *Territorials:* 5th Leicestershire Regiment.

Barry Glamorganshire coastal town seven miles south-west of Cardiff and served by the Barry Railway which opened in 1889. This same year saw the building of the town's docks which became important in the export of coal. A small iron church was completed in 1890 for the use of Norwegian and German seaman. Here too was the British Seaman's Institute. *Territorials:* Glamorgan RGA, Glamorgan Fortress Engineers and 7th Welsh Regiment.

Barry Island Separated from Barry by a narrow channel passable at low water. Here, the docks employed many, the railway reaching the island when the Barry line was extended in 1896. *Territorials:* Glamorgan Fortress Engineers.

Barton Stacey Hampshire village on the road between Winchester and Marlborough, five miles south-east of Andover. Barton Stacey was ignored by the railway, but there was a choice: two miles to the south-east at Sutton Scotney was the Didcot, Newbury & Southampton Railway; while the same distance to the north-west brought villagers to Longparish station and the London & South Western. Here is All Saints Church. *Territorials:* Wessex Divisional Transport and Supply Column.

Barton-upon-Humber Lincolnshire market town on the Great Central Railway, six miles south-west of Hull, where a windmill looks down on the market place. Tanning was an important trade in the town; rope, bricks and tiles were also made. Born here in 1911 was founder of the Samaritans, Chad Varah. Here is St Mary's Church. *Territorials:* Lincolnshire Yeomanry and 5th Lincolnshire Regiment.

Barwick Norfolk village nine miles north-west of Fakenham. Ignored by the railway, Barwick's nearest station was at Stanhoe on the Great Eastern. The church, All Saints, was also at Stanhoe. *Territorials:* Norfolk Yeomanry.

Baschurch Shropshire village, to the north-west of Shrewsbury, its station opened by the Shrewsbury & Chester (Great Western from 1854) in October 1848. A report of 1790 noted that the church at Baschurch (All Saints) was 'so ruinous that the parishioners cannot assemble therein without danger of their lives …' All Saints was rebuilt that year, and again in 1894. *Territorials:* Shropshire Yeomanry.

Basford North-western suburb of Nottingham served by both the Midland and Great Northern railways. Here the Norman church is dedicated, unusually, to St Leodegarius. *Territorials:* 8th Sherwood Foresters.

Basingstoke Hampshire market town where the Great Western Railway terminated and passengers were connected to the London & South Western. Basingstoke's churches include St Michael and All Angels, St Mary's in Eastrop Lane and the Roman Catholic Church of the Holy Ghost which opened at Chapel Hill in 1902. Here begins the Basingstoke Canal. Just over fourteen miles south-west of Reading, Basingstoke was the centre of an agricultural district. Breweries, foundries and several large clothing factories also gave employment – one in New Street, then later, London Street, being the premises where a local draper, Thomas Burberry, first made garments from a waterproofed material which he called 'Gabardine'. *Territorials:* Hampshire Yeomanry, Hampshire RHA, 4th, 9th Hampshire Regiment, 3rd Wessex Field Ambulance and Basingstoke and Eastrop Cadet Corps.

Bath Somerset's Bath lies on the River Avon and Kennet and Avon Canal to the south-east of Bristol. Always and important tourist attraction – Bath Abbey, the Pump Room, Wood's Georgian architecture – Bath was served by the Great Western, Midland and Somerset & Dorset railway companies. The Bath Tramway Company began operations from their London Road depot in December 1880. At the King Edward's School in Bath there was one OTC infantry company. *Territorials:* South Western Infantry Brigade, North Somerset Yeomanry, Wessex Divisional Engineers, 4th Somerset Light Infantry and 2nd South Western Mounted Brigade Field Ambulance.

Bathampton Somerset village and suburb of Bath on the River Avon and Kennet & Avon Canal, served by the Great Western Railway. William Harbutt invented plasticine in 1897 and employed many at his Bathampton factory. Here, by the side of the canal, is St Nicholas's which has an Australian chapel. Arthur Philip (1738–1814), the first Governor of New South Wales, is buried there. *Territorials:* North Somerset Yeomanry.

Bathgate Linlithgowshire market town to the south-west of Edinburgh and once busy in the production of large quantities of lime, iron and paraffin – James Young opened his first commercial paraffin refinery at Bathgate in 1851. Much of Bathgate's prosperity was due to the coming of the railway – the Edinburgh & Glasgow in 1849. *Territorials:* Lothians and Border Horse and 10th Royal Scots..

Batley West Yorkshire township, just to the north of Dewsbury, served by both the Great Northern and London & North Western railways. In the town were iron foundries; stone being quarried from the surrounding area. Batley was also the centre for the 'Shoddy' trade – a process where old woollen garments and rag was recycled into blankets, carpets and clothing. By the middle of the nineteenth century there were some thirty mills in existence. Batley Corporation Tramways, with its green and cream trams, opened in October 1903. Here is All Saints Church. *Territorials:* 4th King's Own Yorkshire Light Infantry.

Battersea London borough on the south bank of the Thames. Among the many establishments employing large numbers were: the Morgan Crucible Company and, on York Road, Price's Candle Works from where many enrolled as Territorials. Battersea Park, opened in 1853, was an attraction for Victorian cyclists. *Territorials:* 10th Middlesex Regiment, 1st, 23rd London Regiment, Sir Walter St John's School Cadet Corps and Battersea Grammar School Cadet Corps.

Battle East Sussex market town six miles north-west of Hastings and served by the South Eastern & Chatham Railway. Battle Abbey was built on the site of, and shortly after, the Battle of Hastings in 1066 (it took place at Battle, not Hastings), work on St Mary's, just to the north, beginning a little later in 1107. The town lays claim to having established the first gunpowder factory in Britain – John Hammond's works employing many at Powdermill Lane. *Territorials:* Sussex Yeomanry and 5th Sussex Regiment.

Bayhead Village on North Uist, Outer Hebrides, Inverness-shire, twelve miles west of Lochmaddy. *Territorials:* 1st Lovat's Scouts.

Beaconsfield Buckinghamshire market town, to the south of Amersham which was reached by the Great Western & Great Central Joint Railway in March 1906. Benjamin Disraeli (later Earl Beaconsfield) was member of parliament here. Here is St Mary and All Saints Church, St Michael's, in the New Town area, being built in 1914. *Territorials:* Buckinghamshire Yeomanry.

Beaminster Dorsetshire market town, six miles north of Bridport, where the tower of St Mary's Church is said to be one of the most spectacular in the county. Here are memorials to the Strode and Oglander families. Also in the town is Holy Trinity and, in East Street, a Congregational Church. The River Brit runs close to the main street. Readers of Thomas Hardy's *Tess of the D'Urbervilles* will be familiar with Beaminster which he called 'Emminster'. *Territorials:* 4th Dorsetshire Regiment.

Beamish Durham village, six miles south-west of Gateshead and reached by the North Eastern Railway in 1894. Here is St Andrew's Church which dates from 1876. *Territorials:* 8th Durham Light Infantry.

Beauchief Derbyshire village, just to the south-west of Sheffield, situated on a hill overlooking the River Sheaf and where the Midland Railway arrived in 1870. Here is Beamish Abbey which was founded in 1183. *Territorials:* Derbyshire Yeomanry.

Beaufort Inverness-shire seat of Lord Lovat, four miles to the south-west of Beauly. *Territorials:* 1st Lovat's Scouts.

Beaulieu Hampshire village on the Beaulieu River six miles from Lymington. Here, with its wagon-shaped plaster roof, is the church of The Blessed Virgin and Holy Child. In the churchyard a tombstone remembers the master carpenter of HMS *Agamemnon*, Michael Silver (1732–78). *Territorials:* Hampshire Yeomanry.

Beauly Inverness-shire town on the River Beauly, ten miles west of Inverness, its principal trade being in coal, lime, timber, grain and fish. Here the Highland Railway crossed the river via a viaduct, an old stone bridge being destroyed in a flood in 1891. *Territorials*: Highland Mounted Brigade, 1st and 2nd Lovat's Scouts and 4th Cameron Highlanders.

Beaumaris Seaport and market town on the Menai Strait, Isle of Anglesy, producing slate and a rock which, ground down, was worked into china. Built at Beaumaris in 1829 was its Goal, the architect being the inventor of the Hansom Cab, Joseph Hansom. Here is St Mary's Church. *Territorials:* Denbighshire Yeomanry.

Beccles Suffolk market town on the River Waveney, to the west of Lowestoft, where the manufacture of agricultural implements, pottery, bricks, tiles and tobacco pipes gave employment to many from the area. There was also a large coach building works. Beccles was served by the Great Eastern Railway. Much of the town was destroyed by fire in the sixteenth and seventeenth centuries. Here is St Michael's Church, said to be unique is the four staircases (one in each corner) of its 92 ft detached bell-tower. *Territorials:* Suffolk Yeomanry, 3rd East Anglian Brigade RFA, 5th, 6th Suffolk Regiment and Beccles Cadet Corps.

Beckenham Town, two miles west of Bromley in Kent, with three stations served by the South Eastern & Chatham Railway. Once a village, Beckenham grew rapidly after the railway came; the Park Langley district of the town being built around 1908, then Elmers End in 1911. In the centre of town is Beckenham's main church, St George's, which replaced an earlier building in 1886. *Territorials:* 5th Royal West Kent Regiment and Kent Cyclist Battalion.

Bedale North Yorkshire market town on the west bank of Bedale Beck to the south-west of Northallerton, its station being opened by the York, Newcastle & Berwick Railway Company (later North Eastern) in February 1855. Here is St Gregory's Church. *Territorials:* Yorkshire Hussars and 4th Yorkshire Regiment.

Bedford County town on the River Ouse served by both the London & North Western and Midland railways. Noted as a major employer is the Britannia Iron Works, the production of agricultural implements and portable railways also being important to the town. John Bunyan did much of his writing in Bedford and now looks out from St Peter's Green. Not far from Bunyan's statue, and outside the Swan Hotel, a bronze soldier remembers those from the town that lost their lives in South Africa during the Boer War. St Mary's Church has a fourteenth-century central tower, St Paul's, though, is the largest church in Bedford. Both Bedford Grammar School and Bedford Modern School maintained contingents in the OTC. *Territorials:* East Midland Infantry Brigade, Bedfordshire Yeomanry, East Anglian Divisional Engineers, 5th Bedfordshire Regiment and Eastern Mounted Brigade Field Ambulance.

Bedford Park West London garden suburb close to Turnham Green station built between 1875–81, firstly by E W Godwin, then Norman Shaw. Noted as a 'middle-class commuting village' – it was said to contain many 'arty' types – Bedford Park saw St Michael's Church added in 1880. In G K Chesterton's *The Man Who Was Thursday*, Bedford Park becomes Saffron Park. *Territorials:* Bedford Park Cadet Company.

Beith Ayrshire market town in the north of the county to the south-west of Glasgow, where the production of coal, leather goods, furniture, cheese, silk dying and printing gave employment. The town was served by two railway companies: the Glasgow and South Western, which arrived in 1840, and the Glasgow, Barrhead & Kilmarnock Joint which terminated at Beith having opened in 1873. *Territorials:* Ayrshire Yeomanry and 4th Royal Scots Fusiliers.

Belford In the north of Northumberland, Belford's railway station lies to the east of the township on the North Eastern line just as it begins its journey inland from the North Sea. It was opened by the Newcastle & Berwick Railway Company in March 1847. Here is St Mary's Church. *Territorials:* 7th Northumberland Fusiliers.

Bellingham Small Northumberland market town on the North Tyne and served by the North British Railway. Erected in 1903 was J Milburn's memorial to those local members of the Yeomanry and Volunteers that fought in South Africa during the Boer War of 1899–1902. Close to the river is St Cuthbert's Church, its stone roof over the nave said to be unique in its construction. *Territorials:* 4th Northumberland Fusiliers.

Bellshill North Lanarkshire town to the east of Glasgow and served by both the Caledonian and North British railways. Extensive coal and iron mines in the neighbourhood employed many. Lithuanian prisoners from the Crimean War settled permanently in Bellshill. *Territorials:* Lanarkshire Fortress Engineers.

Belper Derbyshire market town on the Derwent, to the north of Derby, served by the North Midland Railway. The old trade of nail making is said to have been declining in Belper by 1908; but all around, coal, limestone, iron and lead were mined. It was, however, the cotton and textile mills that employed most – Arkwright's and Strutt's being just two of the many in the town. Here is St Peter's Church of 1824. *Territorials:* Derbyshire Yeomanry and 5th Sherwood Foresters.

Bembridge Village on the Isle of Wight to the north-east of Brading, its dark blue and red-brick station being opened in 1882 when the Isle of Wight Railway started its branch line up from Brading. Here is the church of Holy Cross which was built 1845–46. *Territorials:* 8th Hampshire Regiment.

Benderloch District on the peninsular between Loch Etive and Loch Creran, West Argyllshire and to the north-east of Oban. A popular resort, Benderloch station was opened by the Callander & Oban Railway in 1903. *Territorials:* 8th Argyll and Sutherland Highlanders.

Benenden Village, three miles south-east of Cranbrook, where the green is said to be one of the biggest in Kent. Opened in 1907 by a group of trade unions, was the Benenden Chest Hospital. Here is St George's Church where the monuments include a brass to Admiral Sir John Norris, and others to the Hodges family. *Territorials:* 5th Buffs East Kent Regiment.

Benwick Cambridgeshire village on the Isle of Ely, six miles south-west of March, where the Great Eastern Railway's goods line that ran down from Three Horse Shoes Junction terminated. Here is St Mary's Church. *Territorials:* Cambridgeshire Regiment.

Bere Regis Dorsetshire township, ten miles from Dorchester, called by Thomas Hardy, 'Kingsbere'. The Turberville Chapel at St John the Baptist's Church remembers the family from which he based his *Tess* novel. *Territorials:* 4th Dorsetshire Regiment.

Berkeley Gloucestershire market town on the River Severn, twenty-four miles north of Bristol, where there was trade in coal, timber, malt and cheese. The town lies close to the Gloucester and Sharpness Canal. Near to Berkley Castle is the church of St Mary the Virgin with its detached bell-tower. The north door of the church still shows shot and axe marks sustained during the Roundhead assault of 1645 – they latter set up a battery in the churchyard from which they bombarded the castle. Inside there are memorials to the Jenner family, one of them, Dr Edward Jenner (1749–1823), an early pioneer of a vaccination against smallpox. Here too is what is thought to have been the last court jester in England. Dicky Pearce falling from the minstrel gallery at Berkeley Castle in 1728. The Midland Railway's Berkley station was opened in 1876. *Territorials:* Gloucestershire Yeomanry.

Berkhamsted Hertfordshire market town, to the north-west of Watford, through which runs the Grand Junction Canal and London & North Western Railway. Cassell's notes that in the 1890s there was a brisk trade in coals, malt, timber and brushes. There were also manufactures of straw plait and articles of carved and turned wood. Born here were the poet William Cowper (1731–1800), his father a local rector and, in 1904, the writer Graham Green whose father was headmaster at Berkhamsted Collegiate School. Here is St Peter's Church. Berkhamsted School maintain a contingent of the OTC. *Territorials:* Hertfordshire Yeomanry, 4th East Anglian Brigade RFA and Hertfordshire Regiment.

Bermondsey London borough, south of the Thames, where many were employed in the docks and warehouses – Chamberlain's, Hay's, Butler's, St Saviour's among the many. There was the Leather Market in Weston Street and next door the Leather, Hide and Wool Exchange. Sarson's Malt Vinegar Company employed a good number in its Tanner Street works. Here is St Olave's Church. *Territorials:* 22nd London Regiment and St Olave's School Cadet Corps.

Bernisdale Hamlet near the head of Loch Snizort Beag, Isle of Skye. *Territorials:* 4th Cameron Highlanders.

Berriedale Coastal parish and hamlet at the mouth of the rivers Berriedale and Langwell, Caithness-shire. *Territorials:* 2nd Lovat's Scouts.

Berriew Montgomeryshire village, to the north-west of Montgomery, where an aqueduct carries the Montgomeryshire Canal across the River Rhiw. Here the church is dedicated to St Beuno. *Territorials:* Montgomeryshire Yeomanry.

Berrynarbor Devonshire coastal village, three miles to the east of Ilfracombe, with steep streets and, in its St Peter's Church, the squire's pew complete with fireplace, fire-tongs and a mantelpiece. In the churchyard lies Captain Roger Turpie who served on ships belonging to the London Missionary Society. *Territorials:* 6th Devonshire Regiment.

Bervie Seaport and market town at the mouth of the River Bervie in Kincardineshire, thirteen miles north-east of Montrose. The main trade at Bervie was in cattle and corn – flax woollens, sacking and chemicals being manufactured in the surrounding area. Bervie station was at the termination of the North British Railway up from Aberdeen. *Territorials:* 7th Gordon Highlanders.

Berwick St John South Wiltshire village, to the south-east of Shaftesbury, its nearest station being just over six miles to the north on the London & South Western line at Tisbury. At St John's Church there are memorials to the Grove family. *Territorials:* 1st South Western Mounted Brigade Transport and Supply Column.

Berwick-upon-Tweed Northumberland seaport and market town where the railway crosses the river via Robert Stevenson's bridge of twenty-eight arches and many were employed in the shipping trade. Here at Berwick's station, the North Eastern Railway terminated and the North British began. Without a tower, without a steeple, is Holy Trinity Church. *Territorials:* 7th Northumberland Fusiliers and Lothians and Border Horse.

Bethersden Small village in Kent, on the road from Ashford to Tenterden, well known for quarries producing paludina (or freshwater marble) and the manufacture of bell ropes. Ignored by the railway, the nearest station to Bethersden was three miles to the north on the South Eastern & Chatham line at Pluckley. Here is St Margaret's Church. *Territorials:* Royal East Kent Yeomanry and 5th Buffs East Kent Regiment.

Bethnal Green East London borough once well known for its silk weaving and production of furniture and ceremonial clothing. Among the churches here are: St Matthew's, built 1746, and St John's which dates from 1828. *Territorials:* 1st London Divisional Engineers and 1st London Divisional Signal Company.

Bettws Cedewain Montgomeryshire village on the River Bechan north of Newtown. Ignored by the railway, the nearest service to the village was two miles away at the Caledonian Railway's Abermule station. Here is St Beuno's Church. *Territorials:* Montgomeryshire Yeomanry.

Bettyhill Sutherlandshire fishing hamlet near the mouth of the River Naver, west of Thurso on Scotland's north coast. *Territorials:* 2nd Lovat's Scouts and 5th Seaforth Highlanders.

Beverley East Yorkshire market town, to the north-west of Hull, noted for its tanning industry. There were also foundries, breweries and a chemical works in the area. The Hull & Selby (later North Eastern) Railway came in 1846. In a painting by transport artist Malcolm Root, we see a bus from the 1950s making its way through the narrow Gothic arch of Beverly Bar. There is just inches to spare, even with the specially-shaped bus roof. Here, with its twin towers and collection of carved medieval musical instruments, is the Minster Church of St John the Evangelist, and at St Mary's there are some 600 roof bosses. *Territorials:* York and Durham Infantry Brigade, East Riding Yeomanry, 5th East Yorkshire Regiment and 5th Yorkshire Regiment.

Bewdley Georgian market town on the River Severn in Worcestershire, to the south-west of Kidderminster, noted for its working of horn – combs, powder flasks among the many items made. Here, one of Telford's bridges crosses the river, and St Anne's Church looks along the wide Load Street. The Seven Valley Railway reached the town in 1862. Bewdley was the birthplace in 1867 of Stanley Baldwin. *Territorials:* Worcestershire Yeomanry and 7th Worcestershire Regiment.

Bexhill-on-Sea Sussex coastal resort, five miles south-west of Hastings, served by the London, Brighton & South Coast Railway. A second station was opened by the Crowhurst, Sidley & Bexhill Railway in 1902, this becoming the South Eastern & Chatham in 1907. The Parade at Bexhill stretches for two miles with views over Pevensey Bay. Here is St Peter's Church. *Territorials:* Sussex Yeomanry, 2nd Home Counties Brigade RFA, Home Counties Divisional Engineers and 5th Royal Sussex Regiment.

Bicester Oxfordshire market town, twelve miles north-east of Oxford, where much employment came from a brewery and tannery. But the principal trade was in cattle fairs. There were two stations: the London & North Western, and, opened in 1910, the Great Western. In Bicester's St Eadburg's Church, there is a memorial window to General Gordon. *Territorials:* Oxfordshire Yeomanry and 4th Oxfordshire and Buckinghamshire Light Infantry.

Bideford Here at Bideford in North Devonshire, the River Torridge is crossed by a bridge of twenty-four arches. From the town's small port ran frequent ferry services; trade in the area including the manufacture of cuffs and collars. There were also tanneries and potteries. The London & South Western Railway served the town, a new line being opened by the Bideford, Westward Ho! & Appledore Company in 1901. Here, in Church Walk, is St Mary's Church. *Territorials:* Royal North Devon Yeomanry and 6th Devonshire Regiment.

Biggar Lanarkshire town, on the eastern border of the county, served by the Caledonian Railway – Biggar station being opened by the Symington, Biggar & Broughton Company in November 1860. Albion Motors, at one time the biggest manufacture of commercial vehicles, began at Biggar. *Territorials:* Lanarkshire Yeomanry and 8th Highland Light Infantry.

Biggleswade Bedfordshire market town on the River Ivel, ten miles from Bedford, served by the Great Northern Railway which carried locally grown vegetables to the London market. Another main employer was the Ivel Cycle Works. Those that attended St Andrew's Church in Biggleswade would have seen the installation of its Venetian mosaic reredos in 1877. *Territorials:* Bedfordshire Yeomanry and 5th Bedfordshire Regiment.

Bildeston Small Suffolk town, six miles north-west of Hadleigh, once well known for its production of cloth and blankets. Here is St Mary's Church where lies buried Captain Edward Rotherham who commanded the *Royal Sovereign* at Trafalgar. *Territorials:* 5th Suffolk Regiment.

Billericay Essex market town, east of Brentwood, reached by the Great Eastern Railway in 1888. Here is the church of St Mary Magdalen and, in Chapel Street, a chapel founded in 1672. Across the road from the chapel is Mayflower Hall where a plaque remembers several from Billericay that sailed in the *Mayflower* to America. *Territorials:* 4th Essex Regiment.

Bilston Staffordshire market town, to the south-east of Wolverhampton, served by the Great Western Railway. Bilston's chief employment was in the production of boilers, buckets, chains, fireproof safes and wood screws – Bilston Steelworks was to the west of the town. Iron, coal and stone were also mined locally. Here is St Leonard's Church. *Territorials:* 6th South Staffordshire Regiment.

Bingham Nottinghamshire market town, to the east of Nottingham, served by the old Nottingham & Grantham Railway and Canal Company. A new station called Bingham Road, just to the south-west of the town, was opened by the Great Northern & London & North Western in 1879. Here is St Mary's Church. *Territorials:* Nottinghamshire Yeomanry (South Notts) and 8th Sherwood Foresters.

Bingley West Yorkshire market, woollen and textile town, to the north-west of Bradford, situated on the River Aire and Leeds and Liverpool Canal. Bingley station, on the Midland Railway between Shipley and Keighley, was opened by the Leeds & Bradford Company in March 1847. Here is All Saints Church, which underwent restoration in 1871, and Holy Trinity, built 1866. *Territorials:* 6th Duke of Wellington's Regiment.

Binstead Isle of Wight coastal village west of Ryde, where many were employed in a quarries and brickworks. At Holy Cross Church there is a scene carved on a gravestone that shows a smuggler's attempt to outsail the law. He lost, and was shot on board his own ship. *Territorials:* 2nd Wessex Brigade RFA and 8th Hampshire Regiment.

Bircham Norfolk parish, twelve miles north-east of King's Lynn, made up of three villages: Great Bircham (St Mary's Church), Bircham Newton (St Mary's) and Bircham Tofts (St Andrew's). *Territorials:* Norfolk Yeomanry.

Birchington Coastal village in Kent, two miles south-west of Margate, served by the South Eastern & Chatham Railway. Opened in 1896 by Major P H G Powell-Cotton in Quex Park, was a museum exhibiting artefacts acquired by him during his African and Asian travels. Here, at All Saints Church, Dante Gabriel Rossetti lies buried in the churchyard. *Territorials:* 4th Buffs East Kent Regiment.

Birdwell West Yorkshire hamlet, south of Barnsley, its station (Birdwell and Hoyland Common) opened by the South Yorkshire Railway & River Dun Navigation Company in 1855. Dun is an old spelling of Don, and the station for a short time was called Hangman's Stone. The Wharncliffe Silkstone Colliery was nearby. *Territorials:* 5th York and Lancaster Regiment.

Birkenhead Cheshire seaport on the left bank of the River Mersey looking across to Liverpool, where many were employed in the docks (Mersey Docks & Harbour Board) and Cammell Laird's shipbuilding yards. Moving to Birkenhead from Shrewsbury in 1900, his father (Tom) had been appointed as stationmaster at the town's Woodside station, was the seven-year-old, and future war poet,

Wilfred Owen. The Mersey Railway Tunnel was opened in 1886. Here is St Mary's Church. *Territorials:* Denbighshire Yeomanry, Welsh Divisional Engineers, 4th Cheshire Regiment, Welsh Border Mounted Brigade Transport, Welsh Divisional Transport and Supply Column and Supply Column.

Birmingham City and busy junction involving several railway companies. Commercially, notes one reference, Birmingham may be described as the birthplace of the brass trade, and the centre of almost every important branch of metal work except cutlery. Here originated the manufacture of badges and buttons (Gaunt's supplied the British Army with all aspects of insignia), steel pens, bicycles, gas-fittings, metal bedsteads, and the process of electro-plating. There were also extensive glass and steam engine works. Guns have been made and tested at the Birmingham Gun Barrel Proof House on the Fazeley Canal since 1813. Unveiled in 1905 at Cannon Hill Park – the parade attended by local Yeomanry and Volunteers – was Albert Toft's South African War Memorial. Birmingham University was represented in the OTC, as were King Edward's School and the Oratory School at Edgbaston. *Territorials:* Staffordshire Yeomanry, Warwickshire Yeomanry, Worcestershire Yeomanry, 3rd South Midland Brigade RFA, South Midland RGA, Southern Command Telegraph/Signal Companies 5th, 6th and 8th Royal Warwickshire Regiment, 1st South Midland Mounted Brigade Transport and Supply Column, South Midland Divisional Transport and Supply Column, 1st South Midland Mounted Brigade Field Ambulance, 1st and 2nd South Midland Field Ambulances, South Midland Clearing Hospital, South Midland General Hospital, 1st, 3rd and 4th Cadet Battalions Royal Warwickshire Regiment.

Birnam Perthshire village on the River Tay, to the south-east of Dunkeld, served by the Highland Railway's Dunkeld and Birnam station. The railway had reached Birnam in 1856. *Territorials:* 6th Black Watch and Highland Cyclist Battalion.

Birsay Coastal village, twenty miles to the north-west of Kirkwall, in the north-west corner of mainland Orkney. Here are the ruins of Earl's Palace, built by Robert Stewart, the 1st Earl of Orkney who died in 1593. *Territorials:* Orkney RGA.

Birtley Durham town, to the south-east of Gateshead, reached by the North Eastern Railway in 1868. Major employers were the Birtley Ironworks, a colliery, and close to the station, the Birtley Brick Works. Here is St John's Church. *Territorials:* 8th Durham Light Infantry.

Bisbrooke Rutlandshire village, just to the east of Uppingham, where the houses stood among orchards and gardens. In his book *Bisbrooke: Into the Next Millennium*, Tony Cutting recalls the importance of the village in the production of strawberries and other soft fruit. He also notes how Bisbrooke had no railway station, but unperturbed, locals were able to leave the train (Seaton to Uppingham line) as it slowed down at a steep embankment called 'Spion Kop' (after the Boer War battle), just to the south. *Territorials:* 5th Leicestershire Regiment.

Bishop Auckland South Durham market town and busy industrial area at the confluence of the Wear and Gaunless rivers to the south-west of Durham. The North Eastern Railway served the town, its station being built at the south end of Newgate Street. Employment for the vast majority of the population was in local coal mines or ironworks. Here is the chiefly thirteenth-century St Andrew's church, and the small medieval St Helen's. *Territorials:* 6th Durham Light Infantry.

Bishop Sutton Somerset village, nine miles south of Bristol, where Jesse Lovell & Sons employed many in their coal pit. Here is Holy Trinity Church which was built in 1848. *Territorials:* 4th Somerset Light Infantry.

Bishop's Lydeard Somerset village, on the West Somerset Railway to the north-west of Taunton, where the houses and St Mary's Church are built from local red sandstone. Bishop's Lydeard station was opened in March 1862. *Territorials:* West Somerset Yeomanry.

Bishop's Stortford Hertfordshire market town on the River Stort and Great Eastern Railway to the north-east of Hertford, its chief industries being noted as malting, brewing, brick and sack making. There was also a coachworks and foundry. Here is St Michael's Church, Cecil Rhodes being born at the vicarage in 1853. *Territorials:* Essex Yeomanry, Hertfordshire Regiment, Bishop's Stortford College Cadet Corps and 3rd (Bishop's Stortford School) Hertfordshire Cadets.

Bishop's Waltham Hampshire market town at the head of the River Humble, to the south-east of Winchester, served by the London & South Western Railway. A large brickworks gave employment to many in the area. During the Napoleonic wars a large number of French prisoners were kept at Bishop's Waltham. Here is St Peter's Church. *Territorials:* Hampshire Yeomanry, Hampshire RGA and 4th Hampshire Regiment.

Bitterne Hampshire village on the London & South Western Railway close to the eastern side of Southampton. Here, in Bursledon Road, is the church of the Holy Saviour. Bitterne station was opened in March 1866. *Territorials:* Hampshire RGA and 5th Hampshire Regiment.

Bitton Gloucestershire township on the River Boyd, six miles south-east of Bristol, served by the Midland Railway which arrived in August 1869. Here is St Mary's Church. *Territorials:* 4th Somerset Light Infantry.

Black Torrington Devonshire village on the River Torridge, to the north-west of Hatherleigh, well known for its glove making. Here is St Mary's Church. *Territorials:* Royal North Devon Yeomanry.

Blackburn (Aberdeenshire) Village nine miles north-west of Aberdeen. *Territorials:* 7th Gordon Highlanders.

Blackburn (Lancashire) Cotton town in which some 140 mills were noted – Duke Street, Fountains, Malvern, Pioneer and the Bannister Eccles in Jubilee Street among them. Numerous engineering firms also gave employment – Rowland Baguley & Company in Addison Street making shuttles and other machinery for the textile trade. Running through the town is the Leeds & Liverpool Canal, on the edge of which is the Daisyfield Mill with its tall, twin, red-brick towers. Railway services were provided by the Lancashire & Yorkshire, trams by the Blackburn & Over Daren Tramway Company from their depot in Lorne Street. Blackburn's Stonyhurst College maintained an OTC contingent of three infantry companies. *Territorials:* 1st East Lancashire Brigade RFA, 4th East Lancashire Regiment and Arnold House School Cadet Corps.

Blackford Perthshire village on the River Danny, ten miles from Dunblane, served by the Caledonian Railway's line between Perth and Stirling. There were breweries here – one of them being Sharpe's Brewery – as well as wool and flax businesses. *Territorials:* 6th Black Watch.

Blackham Sussex hamlet to the west of Tunbridge Wells, its All Saints Church being built close to the railway in 1902. Nearest station, Ashurst on the London, Brighton & South Coast Railway. *Territorials:* 5th Royal Sussex Regiment.

Blackheath Part of the South East London borough of Lewisham. Here, in 1870, a roller-skating rink was opened which also had seating for concerts; but the performances were said to have been spoilt by the noise of the nearby railway. The Conservatoire of Music was founded at Blackheath in 1881, and an art school about the same time. *Territorials:* 20th London Regiment.

Blackmore Gate In Devonshire, to the north-east of Barnstaple, and the western gateway to the Exmore National Park. Here was Blackmore station which was opened by the Lynton & Barnstaple Railway Company in May 1898. *Territorials:* Royal North Devon Yeomanry.

Blackpool North Lancashire coastal resort served by the former London & North Western Railway. Street lighting came to Blackpool in 1879 and with that, the 'Illuminations'. Further attractions for visitors were the electric tramway which, beginning in 1885, first ran from Cocker Street to Dean Street, and the opening to the public of the Blackpool Tower in May 1894. *Territorials:* Duke of Lancaster's Yeomanry, 2nd West Lancashire Brigade RFA, 5th King's Own Royal Lancaster Regiment and 3rd West Lancashire Field Ambulance.

Blackridge Linlithgowshire village, just over five miles west of Bathgate, served by the North British Railway's station at Westcraigs. Blackridge Church was opened in the Main Street in 1901. *Territorials:* 10th Royal Scots.

Blackwater Hampshire village to the west of Camberley, its station opened by the Reading, Guildford & Reigate Railway Company in July 1849. Here is Holy Trinity Church which was built in 1837. *Territorials:* 4th Hampshire Regiment.

Blackwood (Lanarkshire) Village just to the south of Stonehouse and served by the Caledonian Railway which arrived in December 1866. A new station replaced the original in 1905. *Territorials:* 8th Highland Light Infantry.

Blackwood (Monmouthshire) Town to the south-west of Pontypool, on the London & South Western Railway, with collieries and an iron foundry. Here in Blackwood, St Margaret's Church was completed in 1876, other churches opening: Mount Pleasant Baptists, Cefn Road, in 1891; the Central Methodists, also in Cefn Road, 1898, and, in Highland Terrace in 1904, the Primitive Methodist. *Territorials:* 1st Monmouthshire Regiment.

Blaenau Festiniog Merionethshire village situated among the mountains of Snowdonia, noted as one of the great slate-quarrying centres of Wales. Here ran the London & North Western Railway, the old Bala & Fesiniog coming within the Great Western in 1910. *Territorials:* 7th Royal Welsh Fusiliers.

Blaenavon Monmouthshire town to the north-west of Pontypool, where the production of iron, steel, coal and brick making gave employment to most. Blaenavon was served by both the Great Western and London & North Western railways. Here is St Peter's Church. *Territorials:* 2nd Monmouthshire Regiment.

Blaina Monmouthshire town with tinplate works and several collieries, two miles from Brynmawr. One guide noted in 1909 that 'modern Blaina...is a mere jumble of minors' cottages, collieries, and ironworks.' Blaina station was opened by the Great Western Railway in December 1850, the town's Institute and Library in 1892. *Territorials:* 3rd Monmouthshire Regiment.

Blair Atholl Perthshire village at the confluence of the Tilt and Garry, to the north-west of Perth, served by the Highland Railway. Blair Atholl station opened in September 1863. Here is Blair Castle, the home of the Dukes of Athol, the only private individuals in the British Isles allowed to maintain a private army – the Athol Highlanders. *Territorials:* 1st Scottish Horse and 6th Black Watch.

Blairgowrie Perthshire market town on the River Ericht situated at the termination of the Caledonian Railway's branch line that up from Couper Angus and was opened in August 1855. Here were jute mills and others producing linen and flax. *Territorials:* 1st Scottish Horse and 6th Black Watch.

Blakesley South Northamptonshire township, five miles to the west of Towcester, served by the Stratford-upon-Avon & Midland Junction Railway which opened its station in July 1873. Here is St Mary's Church. *Territorials:* Northamptonshire Yeomanry.

Blandford Dorsetshire market town on the River Stour, sixteen miles north-east of Dorchester, served by the Somerset & Dorset Railway. There has been a military camp and training ground in the area since the eighteenth century. An important employer in the town was Hall & Woodhouse's Badger Brewery. Fire destroyed the town and the church in 1731. A local family of builders (the Bastards) undertook the rebuilding work, the new St Peter and St Paul's being completed in 1739. Connected to Blandford by a bridge over the Stour is Blandford St Mary. Here the Pitt family resided at Down House and are buried at the church. *Territorials:* Dorsetshire Yeomanry and 4th Dorsetshire Regiment.

Blantyre South Lanarkshire town on the Clyde, three miles north-west of Hamilton, served by the Caledonian Railway. Born here in 1813 was the explorer David Livingstone who for a time worked in one of Blantyre's cotton mills. Coal was mined in the area – William Dixon's pit being the scene of Scotland's worst mine disaster when in October 1877 more than 200 men and boys lost their lives. There was also an extensive dye works in the town. *Territorials:* 6th Cameronians.

Blaydon Durham town on the Tyne, five miles west of Gateshead, served by the North Eastern Railway. An important industrial area, Blaydon produced coal, chemicals, bottles, sanitary pipes, iron and bricks – here since 1730 was Joseph Cowen's Upper and Lower Brickworks. *Territorials:* 9th Durham Light Infantry.

Bletchley Buckinghamshire town and important junction of the London & North Western Railway to the south-east of Milton Keynes. Bletchley station was opened by the London & Birmingham Company in June 1839. Here is the mainly fifteenth-century St Mary's Church. *Territorials:* Buckinghamshire Yeomanry.

Blisworth Northamptonshire village on the London & North Western Railway, five miles south-west of Northampton, and the location of the Grand Union Canal's, almost two-mile- long, Blisworth Tunnel. Stone quarries and the production of iron ore gave employment. *Territorials:* Northamptonshire Yeomanry.

Blockley Although a Worcestershire village, Blockley, served by the Great Western Railway, lay detached to the east in the north Cotswolds area of Gloucester (the parish transferred to Gloucestershire in 1931). Blockley station was opened by the Oxford, Worcester & Wolverhampton Railway Company in June 1853. Here is St Peter and St Paul's Church. *Territorials:* 5th Gloucestershire Regiment.

Blofield Norfolk village, five miles to the east of Norwich, served by the Great Eastern's Brundal station just to the south of the village. Here is St Andrew and St Peter's Church, which has memorials to the Paston family. *Territorials:* Norfolk Yeomanry and 4th Norfolk Regiment.

Bloomsbury Central London district and fashionable area in the Borough of Holborn, associated with the arts, education, publishing, museums and medicine. The British Museum began there in 1755, the 'Bloomsbury Group' of writers and artists existing in the early part of the twentieth century. Here is the parish church of St George's and, in Woburn Square, Christ Church. *Territorials:* 1st London Brigade, RFA, South Eastern Mounted Brigade Signal Troop and 1st London Regiment.

Bloxwich Staffordshire village on the London & North Western Railway close to Walsall. Bloxwich grew up around coal and iron, the area also active in the manufacture of horse furniture, keys, locks and chains. Here in High Street is All Saints Church. *Territorials:* 5th South Staffordshire Regiment.

Blyth Northumberland seaport and market town, nine miles south-east of Morpeth, served by the former North Eastern Railway. Much trade was handled by the town's three docks (coal from the surrounding area going abroad), ships were built and almost everything to do with them manufactured

– ropes, masts, chain cables, anchors, sails. *Territorials:* Tynemouth RGA and Northern Cyclist Battalion.

Bocking Essex village on the River Blackwater close to Braintree, served by the Great Eastern Railway. Braintree station was renamed Braintree and Bocking in 1910. Here, adjoining Bocking Hall, is St Mary's Church. *Territorials:* 5th Essex Regiment.

Bockleton Worcestershire village on the Herefordshire border to the east of Leominster. Here is St Michael's Church which has a memorial to local a squire, William Prescott, who died from infection caught while attending to his sick gamekeeper. *Territorials:* 7th Worcestershire Regiment.

Boddam Aberdeenshire coastal village, to the south of Peterhead, where many were employed in the fishing industry. It was not until 1897, when the Great North of Scotland Company opened its branch from Ellon, that the railway reached Boddam. *Territorials:* 5th Gordon Highlanders.

Bodmin Cornwall market town on the Great Western Railway. Here is the mainly medieval St Petrock's, the largest parish church in Cornwall. During the Civil War, Bodmin changed hands a number of times and was, in May 1643, the scene of bitter fighting in its streets. *Territorials:* Royal 1st Devon Yeomanry and 5th Duke of Cornwall's Light Infantry.

Bogmuir Banffshire hamlet three miles north of Fochabers. *Territorials:* 6th Seaforth Highlanders.

Bognor Sussex seaside resort to the south-east of Chichester, about half-way between Selsey Bill and the mouth of the River Arun, served by the London, Brighton & South Coast Railway. The line being brought down from Barnham Junction in 1864. Here in London Road is the church of St John the Baptist. *Territorials:* Sussex Yeomanry and 4th Royal Sussex Regiment.

Bollington Cheshire town on the River Dean and Macclesfield Canal to the north of Macclesfield, its station opened by the Macclesfield, Bollington & Marple Railway in August 1869. Bollington was a cotton town: the Adelphi, Clarence, the Antrobus family's Lowerhouse and on Queen Street, the Bollington, being a few of the many mills that gave employment in the town. Here is St John's Church. *Territorials:* 7th Cheshire Regiment.

Bolsover Derbyshire town, east of Chesterfield, served by both the Midland and Great Central railways. There was a colliery locally, but Bolsover was once well known for its production of buckles and spurs. Here is St Mary's Church which has monuments to the Cavendish family. *Territorials:* Notts and Derby Mounted Brigade Transport and Supply Column.

Bolton Lancashire cotton and industrial town where one source in 1898 noted some 140 factories employing 28,000 hands; a characteristic of the place being its 'forest of chimneys'. Dobson and Barlow in Kay Street are mentioned as a major employer, the Bolton Iron and Steel Company, Atlas Forge and numerous collieries being others. The same reference records how the Colours of the old Bolton Volunteers of 1794–1802 hang in St Peter's Church. Painful in the memories of Bolton's Territorials would have been the Hulton Colliery Company's Pretoria pit disaster of 21 December 1910, in which some 344 lost their lives. Bolton Corporation Tramways opened in September 1880. *Territorials:* Duke of Lancaster's Own Yeomanry, 3rd East Lancashire Brigade RFA, 5th North Lancashire Regiment and 1st East Lancashire Field Ambulance.

Bonar Bridge Sutherlandshire village on the north bank of the Kyle of Sutherland and served by the former Highland Railway. Here in January 1892, the bridge was swept away in a flood (it was replaced in the following year) and in May 1900, a hoard of bronze-age jewellery and other artefacts (the 'Migdale Hoard') was discovered. *Territorials:* 2nd Lovat's Scouts and 5th Seaforth Highlanders.

Bo'ness Linlithgowshire seaport and industrial town on the Firth of Forth served by the North British Railway. Borrowstounness, to give the place its full name, numbered among its industries: shipbuilding, fisheries, the production of coal, iron, salt, soap and bricks. There was also distilleries, potteries and sandstone quarries. *Territorials:* 10th Royal Scots.

Bonhill Dumbartonshire town to the north of Dumbarton, where an iron suspension bridge takes you across the River Leven to the larger Alexandria and the railway. Of Bonhill, one Edwardian guide notes that some 4,000 in the town were employed at the 'Turkey red dye, calico printing and bleaching works'. *Territorials:* 9th Argyll and Sutherland Highlanders.

Bonnybridge Stirlingshire town to the west of Falkirk, served by both the Caledonian and North British railway companies. In the area were peppermills, chemical works, a sawmill and several ironworks – the Smith and Wellstold Foundry was well known. Goods produced by the town were transported via the railway, or the nearby Forth & Clyde Canal. Bonny Water flows through the place. *Territorials:* 7th Argyll and Sutherland Highlanders.

Bonnyrigg Midlothian town, just under ten miles from Edinburgh, served by the North British Railway which arrived in 1855. *Territorials:* 8th Royal Scots.

Bookham The Surrey villages of Great Bookham and Little Bookham lie between Leatherhead and Guildford, just over four miles north-west of Dorking. Serving both, and arriving in 1885, was the London & South Western Railway. At Little Bookham, notes one Edwardian guide, there was an establishment 'preparing pupils for army examinations.' At Great Bookham is St Nicholas's, the dedication of the church at Little Bookham, however, is unknown. *Territorials:* 5th East Surrey Regiment.

Bootle Lancashire industrial town at the mouth of the River Mersey adjoining Liverpool which, according to one guide, included some 370 acres of the Liverpool Docks and the loading berths of the American liners. Industrially, Bootle maintained timber yards, Jute factories, foundries and corn mills. The London & South Western Railway also employed a number. *Territorials:* 7th King's Liverpool Regiment.

Boreham Essex village on the River Chelmer three miles to the north-east of Chelmsford. Here, in the centre of the village and next to the Queen's Head Inn, is St Andrew's Church where there are memorials to the Radcliffe family, and registers dating from 1559. *Territorials:* 5th Essex Regiment.

Boroughbridge West Yorkshire market town on the Rive Ure to the north-east of Harrogate, served by the North Eastern Railway. Edward II defeated the Earls of Lancaster and Hereford at Boroughbridge in March 1322. Here is St James's Church. *Territorials:* 5th West Yorkshire Regiment.

Bosbury Herefordshire village on the River Leadon four miles from Ledbury. Here the red sandstone Holy Trinity Church has a detached tower and in its churchyard, the Victorian novelist Edna Lyall. *Territorials:* Herefordshire Regiment.

Boston Lincolnshire town on the River Witham, thirty miles from Lincoln and served by the Great Northern Railway. At Boston there is a small port; agricultural implements and rope were made; there was brewing, tanning, brickfields and a deep-sea fishing company. But it was wool that built the town. Boston's St Botolph's Church is thought to be one of the largest parish churches in England, its 272 ft lantern tower seen as far away as Lincoln. *Territorials:* Lincolnshire Yeomanry, 1st North Midland Brigade RFA and 4th Lincolnshire Regiment.

Bothwell Lanarkshire industrial town on the River Clyde, to the south-east of Glasgow and served by both the Caledonian and North British railways. Fought here, in June 1679, was the Battle of Bothwell Brig. *Territorials:* 6th Cameronians.

Botley Hampshire market town on the River Hamble, to the south-west of Bishop's Waltham, served by the London & South Western Railway. Trade was carried on in flour and timber – Botley Mill at the bottom of High Street. Here is All Saints Church. *Territorials:* 4th Hampshire Regiment.

Bottesford Leicestershire village on the River Devon and Nottingham and Grantham Canal, situated to the north-west of Grantham and served by the Great Northern Railway. Here, at the medieval St Mary's Church, the highest spire in the county (210 ft) towers above the tombs and memorials of the Dukes of Rutland. *Territorials:* 5th Leicestershire Regiment.

Boughton Aluph Village in Kent, four miles from Ashford, the nearest railway station being two miles to the south-east on the South-Eastern & Chatham Railway at Wye. Here is the mainly thirteenth-century All Saints Church. *Territorials:* 5th Buffs East Kent Regiment.

Bourne Lincolnshire market town to the west of Spalding and served by the Midland and Great Northern Joint Railway. When the railway reached Bourne in 1859, the Great Northern Company set up its station in an Elizabethan building (The Old Red House) once owned by the Digby family and said to be where the Gunpowder Plot was hatched. Here is St Peter and St Paul's Church. *Territorials:* Lincolnshire Yeomanry and 4th Lincolnshire Regiment.

Bournemouth Hampshire resort reached by the Ringwood, Christchurch & Bournemouth Railway in 1870. The Town Hall in St Stephen's Road was opened ten years after that. Here, in the churchyard of St Peter's, lies the wife of the poet Shelly. In addition to St Peter's, Nicholas Pevsner and David Lloyd ('Buildings of England Series') list some thirty churches and nonconformist chapels in the town: St Ambrose in West Cliff Road (1898–1900), St Albans, Charminster Road (1907–09) and St Andrews in Florence Road (1907–08) being three of the more recent. Charles Rolls, of Ross-Royce car fame, was killed in what was to be the first aero fatality at Bournemouth's Hengistbury Aerodrome on 12 July 1910. Bournemouth School maintained a contingent of the OTC. *Territorials:* Hampshire Yeomanry, 3rd Wessex Brigade RFA, 7th and 9th Hampshire Regiment.

Bourton-on-the-Water Gloucestershire Cotswolds village on the River Windrush, to the east of Cheltenham, served by the Great Western Railway. At Bourton, picturesque low bridges cross the river as it flows down the main street, the one leading to Victoria Street being a 1911 addition. Here is St Lawrence's Church which dates from 1794. *Territorials:* Gloucestershire Yeomanry.

Bovey Tracey Devonshire village south-west of Exeter on the Great Western Railway, where there were lignite works and yards making bricks and drainpipes. There was also a type of pottery named 'Chudleigh ware' associated with the village – the Bovey and Candy's Potteries are mentioned in local directories. There were micaceous haematite mines too, Pevsner noting several to the north of Bovey near Hawkmoor Hospital that were worked from 1890 to around 1911 – Plumley, Shaptor, and Hawkmoor. Hawkmoor Hospital for chest complaints was opened in 1913. At Bovey, in 1646, the English Civil War battle of Bovey Heath was fought, the event reflected, perhaps, in the naming of the local inn, 'The Cromwell Arms'. Uphill to the east of the town is the church of St Peter, St Paul and St Thomas of Canterbury. *Territorials:* Royal 1st Devon Yeomanry and 5th Devonshire Regiment.

Bow Devonshire village on the River Yeo, to the north-east of Exeter, served by the London & South Western Railway – the two-story station of Dartmoor granite dating from around 1865. William Carter Pedler's Congregational Church was opened in 1898. *Territorials:* 6th Devonshire Regiment.

Bowermadden Caithness-shire locality south-east of Thurso, the nearest railway station being on the Highland Railway at Bower. *Territorials:* 5th Seaforth Highlanders.

Bowmore Argyllshire seaport on Loch Indal, Islay Island, noted around 1900 as a 'fairly prosperous place with a distillery and a considerable shipping trade.' *Territorials:* 2nd Scottish Horse and 8th Argyll and Sutherland Highlanders.

Brackley Northamptonshire market town on the River Ouse, seven miles from Buckingham, served by the London & North Western Railway – the Great Central arriving in 1899. Lace making was Brackley's principal industry, but several breweries also gave employment. *Territorials:* 4th Oxfordshire and Buckinghamshire Light Infantry.

Bradfield Essex village on high ground overlooking the River Stour, three miles to the east of Manningtree, served by the Great Eastern Railway. Here, opposite the Strangers Home public house, is St Lawrence's Church, its registers dating from 1695. *Territorials:* 5th Essex Regiment.

Bradford West Yorkshire municipal borough, market town and, from 1887, a city well served by several railway companies and stations. One late Victorian guide notes Bradford, with its 300 mills, as being the centre of the worsted yarn spinning and weaving industry – Lister's and Salt's being the grandest perhaps. Both men have statues in the city. The Bradford Canal reached the city centre having travelled through ten locks from the Leeds & Liverpool. Here is the parish church of St Peter's. *Territorials:* Yorkshire Dragoons, Yorkshire Hussars, 2nd West Riding Brigade RFA, 6th West Yorkshire Regiment and Bradford Postal Telegraph Messengers Cadet Corps.

Bradford-on-Avon Wiltshire market town in the west of the county, nine miles south-east of Bath, served by the Great Western Railway. For many years important in the woollen textile industry, but the last of thirty mills in and around the town closed in 1905. The five-story Abbey Mill on the river bank of the river was built in 1875. The Kennet & Avon Canal runs through Bradford, its parish church, Holy Trinity, being old, but the Saxon St Laurence's across the road is even older. There is a memorial at Holy Trinity to Henry Shrapnel (1761–1842) who invented the shell that ejected deadly fragments as it exploded. *Territorials:* 4th Wiltshire Regiment.

Brading Town on the Isle of Wight, to the south of Ryde, reached by the railway in 1864. Important Roman remains were found at Brading in 1880 and James Newman's New Town Hall was opened in 1903. Here, standing at one end of the town, is the church of St Mary the Virgin which has memorials to the Oglander family. *Territorials:* 8th Hampshire Regiment.

Bradninch Devonshire village, to the north-east of Exeter, served by the Great Weston's Hele and Bradninch station. After the demise of the cloth trade in Bradninch, the Hele Paper Mill on the River Culm got underway in 1762. Here is St Disen's Church. *Territorials:* 7th Devonshire Regiment.

Bradwell-on-Sea Essex village on the River Blackwater, the nearest railway station being fifteen miles away at Maldon. At Bradwell, some trade was carried on in corn and coals. Here is the ancient church of St Peter-on-the-Wall. Built in 654 from the stones of an old Roman fort, there was a period when the church was used by smugglers and as a barn by a local farmer. *Territorials:* 4th Essex Regiment.

Bradworthy Devonshire village on the River Waldon, the nearest railway station being seven miles away at Holsworthy. Here is St John's Church where, in the churchyard, there is a inscription telling how one John Cann died in the village aged 101 having fought through all the battles of the Peninsular War and, after that, Waterloo. *Territorials:* Royal North Devon Yeomanry.

Braemar Aberdeenshire village, its closest railway station being eighteen miles to the north-east at Ballater, where since 1832 the Braemar Royal Highland Society have held games. The Duke of Fife donating grounds for the event in 1906. Braemar is officially on record as the coldest place in Britain. One winter here, Robert Louis Stevenson began his *Treasure Island* classic. *Territorials:* 2nd Scottish Horse and 7th Gordon Highlanders.

Braemore Ross and Cromarty seat and deer forest, twelve miles south-east of Ullapool. *Territorials:* 4th Seaforth Highlanders.

Braes Village on the Isle of Skye where the inhabitants were almost all engaged in crofting and fishing. Here, in 1882, took place the 'Battle of the Braes'. Threatened with eviction, a protest by several of the crofters resulted in fifty Glasgow policemen being brought in to keep the peace. *Territorials:* 1st Lovat's Scouts.

Brailes South Warwickshire village, its closest railway station being just over five miles off at the Great Western's Hook Norton station. Here is St George's Church. *Territorials:* Warwickshire Yeomanry.

Braintree Essex market town on the River Blackwater to the north-east of Chelmsford. An important agricultural and textile centre – George Coutald started a silk factory here – Braintree was served by the Great Eastern Railway. Braintree station being renamed Braintree and Bocking in 1910. Here is St Michael's Church which dates from the beginning of the thirteenth century. *Territorials:* Essex Yeomanry, 5th and 8th Essex Regiment.

Bramley (Surrey) Village to the south-east of Guildford served by the London, Brighton & South Coast Railway – Bramley station being renamed Bramley and Wonersh in 1888. Here is Holy Trinity Church. *Territorials:* 5th Queen's Royal West Surrey Regiment.

Bramley (Yorkshire) Town in the West Riding, just over two miles west of Leeds, served by the Great Northern Railway. Chief industries are noted as being the manufacture of woollen cloths, tanning, currying, iron founding and shoemaking. There were also several quarries in the area. *Territorials:* 1st West Riding Brigade RFA.

Brampton Cumberland market town, nine miles from Carlisle, served by the North Eastern Railway. Tweeds and cotton were manufactured at Brampton and ale was brewed. Brampton's St Martin's Church, with its William Morris stained-glass, was built by public subscription in 1878. *Territorials:* 4th Border Regiment.

Brandiston Norfolk village, to the north-west of Norwich, its closest railway station being three miles to the north-west at Reepham. St Nicholas's Church at Brandiston has a round tower. *Territorials:* Norfolk Yeomanry.

Brandon (County Durham) Durham mining village three miles south-west of Durham – the Bell Brothers Browney Colliery and Straker and Love's Brandon Colliery, employing large numbers from the area. On the North Eastern Railway, Brandon station was renamed Brandon Colliery in 1896. *Territorials:* 8th Durham Light Infantry.

Brandon (Suffolk) Market town on the River Ouse and border with Norfolk, served by the Great Eastern Railway. Barges, notes one guide, go between King's Lynn and Brandon carrying corn and coal, and there was a good trade in malt and timber. *Territorials:* 4th Norfolk Regiment.

Brantham Suffolk village on the River Stour to the south-west of Ipswich, its closest railway station being on the Great Eastern just to the north-east at Bentley. The village was almost entirely agricultural until 1887 and the building then by the British Xylonite Company of a factory nearby. Houses for its workforce were also built. *Territorials:* 6th Suffolk Regiment.

Bratton Clovelly Devonshire village to the south-west of Oakhampton, its nearest station being on the London & South Western Railway at Ashbury. Here is St Mary's Church. *Territorials:* Royal North Devon Yeomanry.

Bratton Fleming Devonshire village, to the north-east of Barnstaple, served by the Lynton & Barnstaple Railway whose eight-arched Chelfham Viaduct spans the valley of the River Yeo close by. Here is St Peter's Church. *Territorials:* Royal North Devon Yeomanry.

Braughing Hertfordshire village on the River Quin, to the west of Bishop's Stortford, served by the Great Eastern Railway. Here, schoolchildren still sweep the leaves from Fleece Lane every 2 October on 'Old Man's Day'. *Territorials:* Hertfordshire Regiment.

Braunton Devon village six miles from Barnstaple at the mouth of the River Taw, served by the London & South Western Railway. Here, high up in the roof of St Brannock's Church, there is a carving of a sow with a litter of pigs and, in a side chapel, newlyweds sign the register on a sixteenth-century Portuguese chest. *Territorials:* Royal North Devon Yeomanry and 6th Devonshire Regiment.

Brechin At Brechin, businesses made paper, flax, linen and sailcloth. Several breweries and distilleries also provided employment. In Forfarshire, Brechin lies on the River Esk five miles west of Montrose, and was served by the Caledonian Railway. Here, with its 106 ft round tower, is Brechin Cathedral. *Territorials:* 5th Black Watch.

Brecon The Duke of Wellington stands in the square outside St Mary's Church in this county town situated at the confluence of the Usk and Honddu rivers. At the Church of St John the Baptist (Brecon Cathedral) a fine east window remembers those of the 24th Regiment (later South Wales Borderers) that perished at Isandlhwana and Rorke's Drift during the Zulu War of 1879 – their depot in the town. Brecon was served by the Great Western Railway. Here too is the termination of the Monmouthshire & Brecon Canal. *Territorials:* Brecknockshire Battalion.

Brenchley Village in south-west Kent, six miles north-east of Tunbridge Wells, its closest railway station being just to the north at Paddock Wood. Here is the sixteenth-century All Saints Church. *Territorials:* 5th Buffs East Kent Regiment.

Brentford West London area on the River Brent which connects the Grand Junction Canal to the Thames. At Brentford there were distilleries, breweries, timber yards, a soap works and pottery. Brentford was served by the Great Western Railway. *Territorials:* 8th Middlesex Regiment.

Brentwood Brentwood's church of St Thomas the Martyr was opened in 1883. Brewing and brick making were the chief industries of the town, and there was also a large factory making agricultural tools owned by William Burges and Sir K G Key. Both men were keen supporters of the Volunteers, and later, Territorials. An Essex market town to the south-west of Chelmsford, Brentwood was served by the Great Eastern Railway. *Territorials:* Norfolk and Suffolk Infantry Brigade, Essex Infantry Brigade, Essex Yeomanry, 4th and 8th Essex Regiment.

Bridge of Allan Stirlingshire town on Allan Water, to the north of Stirling, served by the Caledonian Railway. Seen on stations around 1910, was a poster showing the town and offering it as 'An all the year round health and holiday resort.' The mineral wells at Bridge of Allan brought Victorian development which saw the building of grand houses and hotels for visitors. But here too were manufacturers of paper and an industry in dyeing and bleaching. *Territorials:* 6th Black Watch and 7th Argyll and Sutherland Highlanders.

Bridgend (Argyllshire) Village on Islay Island at the head of Loch Andail. *Territorials:* 2nd Scottish Horse and 8th Argyll and Sutherland Highlanders.

Bridgend (Glamorgan) Market town served by the Great Western Railway to the west of Cardiff, where many were employed in a steam joinery works, brewery, an agricultural implement factory, tannery, iron and brass foundries. Here, in the Newcastle district of Bridgend, is the medieval

St Illtyd's Church and, on Merthyr Mawr Road, St Marys which was opened in 1887. *Territorials:* Glamorganshire Yeomanry and 7th Welsh Regiment.

Bridgnorth Shropshire market town on the Severn, to the south-west of Wolverhampton, served by the Great Western Railway. The town's main source of employment was the manufacture of carpets and brewing. Here is the church of St Mary Magdalen where a French general captured during the Napoleonic Wars lies buried in the churchyard and, at the other end of town, St Leonard's where there are memorials to the Bellett family – one of them a commander in the Royal Navy, anther a local rector. At Bridgnorth there is 'Old Town' and 'New Town', the two divided by a red sandstone cliff. *Territorials:* Shropshire Yeomanry, 4th King's Shropshire Light Infantry and Bridgnorth Cadet Corps.

Bridgwater Somerset market town and seaport on the River Parrett to the south-west of Bristol, where the chief industries are noted as: brewing, malting, foundry work and the manufacture of oil cake. Bridgwater was served by the Great Western Railway – a line ran by the Bridgewater Railway Company reaching the town in 1890. Here is St Mary's Church. *Territorials:* West Somerset Yeomanry, 5th Somerset Light Infantry and Wessex Divisional Transport and Supply Column.

Bridlington East Yorkshire seaport, market town and holiday resort to the north-east of Driffield, served by the North Eastern Railway. Here, with its sixteen carvings of mice by Robert Thompson, is the Priory Church of St Mary the Virgin. The American privateer John Paul Jones did not like Bridlington so, in 1779, he bombarded it. A later visitor, in the form of Charlotte Brontë, was so taken back with the place that she cried. Bridlington Grammar School maintained a contingent of the OTC. *Territorials:* East Riding Yeomanry, 5th East Yorkshire Regiment and 5th Yorkshire Regiment.

Bridport Dorsetshire seaport and market town, west of Dorchester, where the manufacture of beer, rope, fishing nets, sailcloth and twines provided much employment. Bridport station on the Great Western Railway was opened in November 1857. Here is St Mary's Church where there is a brass to a member of the Coker family killed during the Monmouth rebellion in 1685. *Territorials:* Dorsetshire Yeomanry, 3rd Wessex Brigade RFA and 4th Dorset Regiment.

Brierley Hill Staffordshire market town on the River Stour, to the north-east of Stourbridge, served by the Great Western Railway. At Brierley Hill there were factories making anchor chains, nails and bottles – the Round Oak Steelworks employing many. In the town, E W Pugin's St Mary's Church was opened in 1873; St Michael's, earlier in 1765. *Territorials:* 3rd North Midland Brigade RFA, 5th South Staffordshire Regiment and Brierley Hill Cadet Corps.

Brigg North Lincolnshire market town on the River Ancholme south-east of Scunthorpe, served by the Great Central Railway. Brigg station was opened in November 1848 by the Manchester, Sheffield & Lincolnshire Company. Here is St John's Church. *Territorials:* Lincolnshire Yeomanry and 5th Lincolnshire Regiment.

Brighouse West Yorkshire town, just over five miles north of Huddersfield on the Lancashire & Yorkshire Railway, where woollen, worsted, silk and cotton goods were manufactured. There were also flourmills and factories producing wire, carpets and soap. Here is St Martin's Church. *Territorials:* 4th Duke of Wellington's Regiment.

Brighstone Village on the south-west coast of the Isle of Wight six miles from Newport. Here is St Mary's Church. *Territorials:* 8th Hampshire Regiment.

Brighton South coast of Sussex resort and market town on the London, Brighton & South Coast Railway. At the Metropole Hotel in 1896 was the finish of the first ever London to Brighton car run;

the destruction in a storm of the old Chain Pier occurring about the same time. In St Nicholas's Church, about 200 yards west of Queen Street, is a memorial to the Duke of Wellington. George IV liked the place and made it popular. Doctor Johnson, however, did not and referred to it as 'the World's End'. At Brighton College there was a contingent of the OTC. *Territorials:* Sussex Yeomanry, 1st Home Counties Brigade RFA, Sussex RGA, Home Counties Divisional Engineers, 6th Royal Sussex Regiment, Home Counties Divisional Transport and Supply Column, 2nd Eastern General Hospital, Brighton Brigade Sussex Cadets, Imperial Service Cadet Corps (later called 1st Cadet Battalion 1st Home Counties Brigade RFA) and Brighton Preparatory Schools Cadet Corps.

Brimington Derbyshire village two miles to the north-east of Chesterfield. Here is a chapel dedicated to St Michael. *Territorials:* 6th Sherwood Foresters.

Brisley Norfolk village to the north-west of East Dereham. Here is St Bartholomew's Church. *Territorials:* Norfolk Yeomanry.

Brislington Somerset village, two miles from Bristol, served by the Great Western Railway. Brislington station was opened by the Bristol & North Somerset Railway Company in September 1873. Here is St Luke's Church. *Territorials:* 4th Somerset Light Infantry.

Bristol City, seaport and market town on the River Avon, and a busy junction for the Great Western and Midland railways. Chief industries noted around the turn of the twentieth century were: import and export, shipbuilding and sugar refining. There were also tanneries, chemical works, glass and soap manufacturers. Here among the many churches is St Mary Redcliffe which, like much of Bristol, was built from the generosity of wealthy merchants. In the churchyard is a memorial to the church cat. At Bristol University and Bristol Grammar School there were contingents of the OTC. In his painting, *St Augustine's Parade, Bristol*, transport artist Eric Bottomley depicts a scene that would be familiar to the Territorial of 1908–14. Here we see the blue-and-white livery of Bristol's trams and buses. Turning right at Husbands the opticians is a steam-powered vehicle belonging to a local firm of hauliers, Davey & Co; while emerging out of the same street comes, horse-drawn this time, a cart from one of Bristol's leading employers, cigarette manufacturer, W D & H O Wills. Next to Husbands in St Augustine's Parade, pianos could be purchased from W Brunt & Sons; played to perfection, no doubt, at the Hippodrome which opened in 1912. Its roof-top globe just visible. *Territorials:* Gloucestershire Yeomanry, North Somerset Yeomanry, 1st South Western Brigade RFA, South Midland Divisional Engineers, 4th, 6th Gloucestershire Regiment, 3rd South Midland Field Ambulance and 2nd Southern General Hospital.

Briton Ferry Glamorgan town, at the mouth of the River Neath, served by the Great Western Railway. Employing many were such concerns as the Albion Steel Works, Briton Ferry Ironworks, Crown Smelter Works, Baglan Bay Tinplate Works and Gwalia Tinplate Works. Here, in Church Street is At Mary's and, on Neath Road, St Clements. *Territorials:* 1st Welsh Brigade RFA.

Brixton Part of the South London borough of Lambeth reached by the London, Chatham & Dover Railway in 1862. Resident in the area around the turn of the twentieth century were music hall artist Dan Leno and the film producer Fred Karno. In Coldharbour Lane the Ritzy was opened as the 'Electric Pavilion' in 1910 – one of the first purpose-built cinemas in the country. Here is St Matthew's Church, built in 1823 to celebrate victory at Waterloo. *Territorials:* 6th London Brigade RFA.

Broadclyst Devonshire village, to the north-east of Exeter, served by the London & South Western Railway which opened its station in July 1860. Here is the church of St John the Baptist. *Territorials:* 4th Devonshire Regiment.

Broadford Inverness-shire fishing village and the second largest community on the Isle of Skye. *Territorials:* 4th Cameron Highlanders.

Broadmead Locality in Bristol. *Territorials:* Gloucestershire Yeomanry.

Broadstairs Coastal town and holiday resort in Kent, to the north-east of Ramsgate on the Isle of Thanet, served by the South Eastern & Chatham Railway. Broadstairs has a number of literary connections: Charles Dickens wrote *David Copperfield* there in 1849–50, it gets a mention in the Grossmith's *The Diary of A Nobody*, and John Buchan began his *Thirty-Nine Steps* while staying in the town. Here is Holy Trinity Church. *Territorials:* 4th Buffs East Kent Regiment.

Broadstone Dorsetshire village and junction of the London & South Western and Somerset & Dorset railways just to the north of Poole. Guides around 1900 note the production of lavender oil in the area. Here is the church of St John the Baptist, which was built in 1888. *Territorials:* 4th Dorsetshire Regiment.

Broadwey Dorsetshire village on the River Wey, three miles from Weymouth, served by the Great Western Railway at its Upwey Junction station. Here is St Nicholas's Church. *Territorials:* 4th Dorsetshire Regiment.

Brockenhurst Hampshire village in the New Forest, between Lyndhurst and Lymington, served by the London & South Western Railway. Set on a wooded knoll is the Norman St Peter's Church where a yew in the churchyard is thought to be the oldest tree in the New Forest. *Territorials:* 7th Hampshire Regiment.

Brockham Surrey village on the River Mole, just to the east of Dorking, where until its closure in 1910, the Brockham Brick Company employed many. Here is Christ Church. *Territorials:* 5th Queen's Royal West Surrey Regiment.

Bromham Wiltshire village, four miles to the north-west of Devises, where the Irish poet and close friend of Byron, Thomas Moore, is buried at St Nicholas's Church. Ignored by the railway, Bromham's nearest station was three miles to the north-east at Seend. *Territorials:* 4th Wiltshire Regiment.

Bromley Market town in Kent, on the River Ravensbourne to the north-east of Croydon, with station on the South Eastern & Chatham Railway. Borne there in 1866 was the writer H G Wells. Here is St John's Church which was built in 1880. *Territorials:* Kent Infantry Brigade, West Kent Yeomanry, 5th Royal West Kent Regiment and Kent Cyclist Battalion.

Brompton North Yorkshire village, two miles north of Northallerton, served by the North Eastern Railway which opened its station in June 1852. Once an important centre for the manufacture of linen, there were eight mills in the village at one time. Here is St Thomas's Church. *Territorials:* 4th Yorkshire Regiment.

Bromsgrove Worcestershire market town north-east of Worcester. Many from Bromsgrove were employed at the Midland Railway's carriage works, but Cassell's for 1893 notes that the chief industry was the making of nails. Here, in red sandstone and reached by a long flight of steps, is the church of St John the Baptist. In the churchyard are the graves of what appear to be two footplate men ('Engineers'), killed when the boiler of their Birmingham & Gloucester Railway locomotive blew up in 1840. At Bromsgrove School there was a contingent of the OTC. *Territorials:* Worcestershire Yeomanry and 8th Worcestershire Regiment.

Bromyard Herefordshire market town on the River Frome seventeen miles west of Worcester. The area all around Bromyard was mainly agricultural. There was, however, a firm in the 1890s making spade and shovel handles. The railway, in the form of the Worcester, Bromyard & Leominster line, reached the town in October 1877. Here is the Norman church of St Peter. *Territorials:* Herefordshire Regiment.

Broomfield Essex village on the River Chelmer two miles north of Chelmsford. Here, next to the King's Arms, is St Mary's Church which has registers dating from 1546. *Territorials:* 5th Essex Regiment.

Broomhill (Kent) Parish both in Kent and Sussex. One late Victorian guide notes that 'the church has been swallowed up by the sea.' *Territorials:* 1st Cadet Battalion Kent Fortress Engineers.

Broomhill (Northumberland) Colliery village, just inland from the sea to the north-east of Morpeth, served by the North Eastern Railway. Broomhill station was opened by the York, Newcastle & Berwick Railway Company in September 1849. *Territorials:* 7th Northumberland Fusiliers.

Brora Sutherlandshire fishing village, just under five miles to the north-east of Golspie, served by the Highland Railway. Here at Brora there were collieries, brickworks and a long established distillery. *Territorials:* 2nd Lovat's Scouts and 5th Seaforth Highlanders.

Broughton Part of the borough of Salford in Lancashire. Here is the church of St John the Evangelist. *Territorials:* Broughton Lads' Brigade.

Broughton-in-Furness Lancashire market town, close to the River Dudden to the north-west of Ulverston, served by the Furness Railway. Many at Broughton were employed in the production of hoops and brush stocks. Here is the church of St Mary Magdalene. *Territorials:* 4th King's Own Royal Lancaster Regiment.

Broughty Ferry Forfarshire seaport and fishing town, on the Firth of Tay to the east of Dundee, served by the North British and Caledonian railways. In the nineteenth century, many of Dundee's rich merchants and industrialist built houses at Broughty Ferry. *Territorials:* North Scottish RGA.

Broxbourne Hertfordshire village, to the south-east of Hertford, where St Augustine's Church sits close to the bank of the River Lea and a name was made in the manufacture of terracotta decorative items. Broxbourne was served by the North Eastern Railway. *Territorials:* Hertfordshire Yeomanry.

Broxburn Linlithgowshire town, twelve miles west of Edinburgh, served by the North British Railway. Situated on the Broxburn and Union Canal, Broxburn had collieries and produced oil-shale and bricks. *Territorials:* Lothians and Border Horse and 10th Royal Scots.

Bruton Somersetshire market town on the River Brue, two miles east of Bridgewater, served by the Great Western Railway. The town prospered from textile manufacture, workers in the trade being housed in narrow alleyways called Bartons. Here, on the edge of the town and with two towers, is St Mary's Church. King's School in Bruton had a contingent in the OTC. *Territorials:* 4th Somerset Light Infantry.

Brynamman Carmarthenshire village on the edge of the Black Mountains, its station opened by the Swansea Vale Railway in March 1868. Henllys Vale Colliery was a major employer in the area. Here, built 1880–01, is St Catherine's Church. *Territorials:* Brecknockshire Battalion.

Brynmawr Brecknockshire town to the south-west of Abergavenny with extensive collieries and ironworks. Brynmawr station was opened by the Merthyr, Tredegar & Abergavenny Railway in October 1862. Here is St Mary's Church. *Territorials:* Brecknockshire Battalion.

Buckfastleigh Small Devonshire market town on the River Dart, north-west of Totnes, served by the Great Western Railway. Here is Buckfastleigh Abbey, taken over by French Benedictine monks in 1906. *Territorials:* 5th Devonshire Regiment.

Buckie Banffshire fishing town, to the north of Keith, served by the Great North of Scotland Railway. Buckie had manufacturers of sails, ropes and gas, its railway station being opened in May 1886. *Territorials:* 6th Gordon Highlanders.

Buckingham Buckinghamshire market town on the Great Ouse and Grand Junction Canal served by the London & North Western Railway. Seventeen miles from Aylesbury, Buckingham is noted as an agricultural centre with several maltings, a brewery, artificial manure factory and manufacturer of pillow lace. Here is St Peter and St Paul's Church. *Territorials:* Buckinghamshire Yeomanry and Buckinghamshire Battalion.

Buckland St Mary Somerset village five miles to the north-west of Chard. St Mary's Church, a replacement for a former building, was completed in 1863. Remembered here is the story of a man who was crushed to death by his wagon which was carrying stone to build the church. *Territorials:* West Somerset Yeomanry.

Bucklebury Berkshire village in the upper valley of the Pang to the north-east of Newbury. Here in St Mary's Church are monuments to the Stephens, Stone and Winchcombe families, old high box pews and a three-decker pulpit. *Territorials:* 4th Royal Berkshire Regiment.

Buckley Flintshire town to the east of Mold noted for its manufacture of course earthenware, firebricks and tiles. Buckley station was opened by the Wrexham, Mold & Connahs Quay Railway in May 1866. Here is St Matthew's Church. *Territorials:* 5th Royal Welsh Fusiliers.

Bucknell Village, part in Shropshire, part in Herefordshire, on the River Redlake and London & North Western Railway. Bucknell station was opened by the Knighton Railway in October 1860. Here is St Mary's Church. *Territorials:* Herefordshire Regiment.

Bucksburn Village on the north-western edge of Aberdeen served by the Great North of Scotland Railway which opened its station in January 1897. *Territorials:* 2nd Scottish Horse and 6th Gordon Highlanders.

Bude Small Cornwall seaside resort at the mouth of the River Neet, served by the London & South Western Railway which reached the town in 1898. The Bude Canal began here and ran to Launceston. Here is St Michael and All Angels Church which was built in 1835. *Territorials:* 5th Duke of Cornwall's Light Infantry.

Budleigh Salterton Village at the mouth of the River Otter, on the south coast of Devon fifteen miles south of Exeter, and the scene of Sir John Everett Millais's 1871 painting *The Boyhood of Raleigh*. Sir Walter born just to the north of Budleigh in 1552. The railway, in the form of the London & South Western, did not reach the village until 1897. *Territorials:* 4th Devonshire Regiment.

Bugle Cornwall village, about four miles inland from St Austell, served by the Great Western Railway and once a centre for the production of china-clay. The railway had come to Bugle via the Treffry Tramway in 1842. *Territorials:* Cornwall RGA.

Builth Wells The railway reached Builth in September 1864, which no doubt brought more visitors to 'take the waters.' The town sits on the River Wye, fourteen miles north of Brecon, its ancient bridge of six arches taking you across to Radnorshire. Here is St Mary's Church. *Territorials:* Montgomeryshire Yeomanry and Brecknockshire Battalion.

Bullgill Cumberland locality, four miles to the north-east of Maryport, served by the Maryport & Carlisle Railway which opened its station in July 1840. *Territorials:* 5th Border Regiment.

Bunessan Crofters and fishing village on Ross of Mull, Mull Island in Argyllshire. *Territorials:* 2nd Scottish Horse.

Bungay Suffolk market town, to the west of Beccles, served by the Great Eastern Railway. Bungay lies on the River Waveney, on which much trade was done from local flourmills. There was in the town, a large print works and iron foundry. Here, with its circular tower, is Holly Trinity Church. *Territorials:* Suffolk Yeomanry and 5th Suffolk Regiment.

Bures Small town on the Great Eastern Railway, with the River Stour here forming the border between Essex and Suffolk. Part in each, Bures at one time was represented by two county councils, and two members of parliament. Here is St Mary's Church. *Territorials:* 5th Suffolk Regiment.

Burford Oxfordshire market town on the River Windrush to the north-west of Oxford. To the east of High Street, and almost on the banks of the river, is the church of St John the Baptist where lie buried many of the wealthy wool merchants that once lived in the town. Here, in May 1649 and around the Crown in Sheep Street, a mutiny by Cromwell's troops was quelled and some 350 rebellious troops were imprisoned in the church overnight. Next morning the ringleaders – Thompson, Perkins and Church – were shot in the churchyard. By-passed by the railway, Burford's nearest station was five miles to the north at Shipton. *Territorials:* Oxfordshire Yeomanry, 4th Oxfordshire and Buckinghamshire Light Infantry and Burford Grammar School Cadet Corps.

Burgess Hill Sussex town, eighteen miles north of Brighton, on the main line served by the London, Brighton & South Coast Railway. The population here grew rapidly along with the development of several brick and tile manufacturers: in Station Road were Messrs Meeds & Son, William Norman's brickyard could be found to the east of London Road, and close to this another owned by Mr Gravett. Here, opened in 1863, is St John's Church which has memorials to the Cruden family. *Territorials:* Sussex Yeomanry and 4th Royal Sussex Regiment.

Burgh St Margaret Norfolk village (sometimes called Fleggburgh) seven miles from Great Yarmouth. St Margaret's Church has a fine Norman doorway and was restored in 1876. *Territorials:* 4th Norfolk Regiment.

Burghclere Hampshire village, to the south of Newbury, reached by the Didcot, Newbury & Southampton Railway in 1885. Here is All Saints Church. *Territorials:* 4th Hampshire Regiment.

Burghead Elginshire town and seaport where the production of agricultural chemicals, boatbuilding and fishing are noted as the chief industries. The Highland Railway served the town. *Territorials:* 6th Seaforth Highlanders.

Burghill Herefordshire village three miles north-west of Hereford. Here is St Mary's Church. *Territorials:* Herefordshire Regiment and South Wales Mounted Brigade Field Ambulance.

Burlescombe Devonshire village bordering on Somerset to the south-west of Wellington, served by the Great Western Railway. In the neighbourhood were limekilns and quarries. Here is St Mary's Church. *Territorials:* 4th Devonshire Regiment.

Burley (Hampshire) New Forrest village, to the west of Brockenhurst, where forest ponies can be seen roaming the streets. Here is the church of St John the Baptist and, at Burley Lodge, twelve oak trees known locally as the Twelve Apostles. *Territorials:* Hampshire Yeomanry and 7th Hampshire Regiment.

Burley (Yorkshire) West Riding village, to the north-west of Leeds, where carpets and woollen goods were manufactured – the Victorian mill owners building for their workers a hall, library and reading room. Burley was served by the Midland and North Eastern railways. *Territorials:* 4th West Riding Brigade RFA.

Burneside Westmorland village on the River Kent, to the north of Kendal, served by the London & North Western Railway. The station was opened in April 1847 by the Kendal & Windermere

Railway Company. Many in Burneside were employed at James Cropper's paper mill which opened in 1845. Here is St Oswald's Church. *Territorials:* 4th Border Regiment.

Burnham Somerset town and seaside resort on the Bristol Channel, served by the Somerset & Dorset Railway which arrived in May 1858. Here is St Andrew's Church. *Territorials:* 5th Somerset Light Infantry.

Burnham-on-Crouch Essex town to the south-east of Maldon, its chief industry noted as the cultivation of oysters. Herring fishing also employed a number, while on the Crouch there were several boat and shipbuilding yards. The town was served by the Great Eastern Railway. Here, on the edge of town, is St Mary's Church, its registers dating from 1559. *Territorials:* 4th Essex Regiment.

Burnhope Durham village just to the south-east of Stanhope. *Territorials:* 8th Durham Light Infantry.

Burnley Lancashire industrial town on the River Calder and Leeds and Liverpool Canal, served by the London & North Western Railway. Burnley was a cotton town, but there was also much employment in its foundries, machine works, quarries and collieries. *Territorials:* 1st East Lancashire Brigade RFA, 5th East Lancashire Regiment and 2nd East Lancashire Field Ambulance.

Burntisland Fifeshire town and seaport on the Firth of Forth and North British Railway, where many were employed in the production of whiskey, shipbuilding, coal and iron mining. The docks at Burntisland were important to the Fifeshire coalfields centered around Cowdenbeath and Lochgelly. *Territorials:* Forth RGA.

Burrington Devon village to the south-east of Barnstaple. Here is Holy Trinity Church. *Territorials:* 6th Devonshire Regiment.

Bursledon South Hampshire village on the River Humble to the south-east of Southampton, served by the London & South Western Railway. Once a thriving dockyard building ships for the Royal Navy, this trade had disappeared by 1870 and the production of arable agriculture became the main source of income to the area. Opening at Bursledon in 1897 was the Bursledon Brickworks. *Territorials:* 5th Hampshire Regiment.

Burslem Staffordshire pottery town served by the North Staffordshire Railway. At James Macintyre & Co, William Moorcroft was employed who later, in 1912, branched out on his own with a factory at Sandbach Road. Burgess & Leigh took over the Middleport Pottery adjoining the Trent & Mersey Canal in 1899. Born in the town, Josiah Wedgwood's statue is in Queen Street. Here, at Cross Hill, is St John's Church. *Territorials:* 5th North Staffordshire Regiment.

Burton Joyce South Nottinghamshire village on the River Trent, to the north-east of Nottingham, served by the Midland Railway which arrived in August 1846. Here is St Helen's Church. *Territorials:* 8th Sherwood Foresters.

Burton-on-Trent Staffordshire town where railway lines leading to the breweries that employed more than 7,000 people crossed the streets in all directions. Always strong supporters of the Volunteer and Territorial Forces, a glance at an *Army List* will show names from old brewing families: Tenant, Bass, Worthington and Ind. 'Say, for what were hop-yards meant,/Or why was Burton built on Trent?' (from *A Shropshire Lad* by A E Housman). Here too were copper works, cement mills, and the Marmite Food Company which started in Burton in 1902 but moved to London in 1907. Burton Corporation began its overhead electric tram service in August 1903. Here is St Modwen's Church. *Territorials:* Staffordshire Yeomanry and 6th North Staffordshire Regiment.

Burwash Sussex village situated on high ground between the rivers Rother and its affluent the Dudwell and once an important centre of the iron industry. Burwash was the home of Rudyard Kipling from 1902 until his death in 1936. Here, in 1906–07, he wrote *Puck of Pook's Hill* which is based around the area and a hill visible from his home called 'Bateman's'. Here is St Bartholomew's Church. *Territorials:* 5th Royal Sussex Regiment.

Burwell Cambridgeshire village on the Burwell Lode, four miles from Newmarket, where many were employed in Colchester and Ball's Patent Manure Works and a number by Prentice Brothers who built barges. Here is St Mary's Church which sits next to a windmill. *Territorials:* Suffolk Yeomanry and Cambridgeshire Regiment.

Bury Lancashire industrial town on the River Irwell and Bury and Bolton Canal, served by the London & North Eastern Railway. Cotton mills employed many, but other local industries included: bleaching and dying, boiler making, coal mining and stone quarrying. At Bury Grammar School there was a contingent of the OTC. Unveiled in the Market Place on 18 March 1905 was George Frampton's memorial to those Lancashire Fusiliers from the town (Regulars, Militia and Volunteers) that lost their lives in South Africa during the Boer War of 1899–1902. Here is St George's Church. *Territorials:* 5th Lancashire Fusiliers and 3rd East Lancashire Field Ambulance.

Bury St Edmunds Suffolk market town on the River Lark served by the Great Eastern Railway, its chief industry noted as being the manufacture of agricultural implements. Also in Bury since 1799 is the Green King Westgate Brewery. In the town was the Depot of the 12th (later Suffolk) Regiment. Here is the Cathedral Church of St James and, built 1424–33, St Mary's. King Edward's Grammar School in Bury St Edmunds maintained one OTC infantry company. *Territorials:* Suffolk Yeomanry, 5th and 6th Suffolk Regiment.

Butterley At Butterley, which is ten miles south-east of Derby, there were numerous coal mines, blast furnaces, foundries and a boiler works. Cannon and shot were produced for the Woolwich Arsenal. The Midland Railway's Butterley station was opened on 1 May 1875. *Territorials:* 5th Sherwood Foresters.

Buxted Sussex village, close to Uckfield, served by the London, Brighton & South Coast Railway and once important in the iron industry – the first cannon in East Sussex was cast here in 1543. Here is St Margaret's Church. *Territorials:* 5th Royal Sussex Regiment.

Buxton Derbyshire market and spa town on the River Wye, east of Macclesfield, served by the London & North Western and Midland railways. The Town Hall and Library were built 1888–89, and Frank Matcham's Opera House in 1903. Here is the church of St John the Baptist which was opened in 1811. *Territorials:* East Lancashire Infantry Brigade, Derbyshire Yeomanry and 6th Sherwood Foresters.

Byfleet Surrey village on the River Wey, to the north-east of Guildford, served by the London & South Western Railway. G T Tarrant arrived in Byfleet in 1895 and soon rose to become its largest employer with his stonemason yard, joinery, wrought iron and leaded lights workshops. Here is St Mary's Church. *Territorials:* 5th Queen's Royal West Surrey Regiment.

Caergwle Flintshire town once important for its manufacture of spades and shovels. Caergwle Station, which opened in 1866 as part of the Wrexham, Mold & Connah's Quay Railway, was renamed Hope Village in January 1899. *Territorials:* 5th Royal Welsh Fusiliers.

Caerleon Monmouthshire town on the north bank of the River Usk close to Newport and with a station on the Great Western Railway. For 300 years, the headquarters of the 2nd Roman Legion, its barracks and amphitheatre still to be seen. Here is St Cadoc's Church. *Territorials:* 1st Monmouthshire Regiment.

Caerphilly Glamorganshire market town, to the north of Cardiff, with station on the Great Western Railway which opened in March 1858. Chief industries: collieries and a large ironworks. Here is St Martin's Church which was built 1877–79. *Territorials:* Glamorgan Yeomanry.

Caersws Montgomeryshire village on the River Severn, four miles to the west of Newtown, served by the Cambrian and Van railways. Here is St Mary's Church. *Territorials:* Montgomeryshire Yeomanry and 7th Royal Welsh Fusiliers.

Caerwys Flintshire market town, six miles from St Asaph, with station opened by the Mold & Denbigh Junction Railway in September 1869. Here is St Michael's Church. *Territorials:* 7th Royal Welsh Fusiliers and Welsh Divisional Transport and Supply Column.

Cairndow Argyllshire coastal hamlet on Loch Fyne. *Territorials:* 8th Argyll and Sutherland Highlanders.

Calbourne Isle of Wight village with station on the Isle of Wight Central Railway which opened in July 1889. Here is All Saints Church. *Territorials:* 8th Hampshire Regiment.

Calgary Village on Mull Island, Argyllshire. *Territorials:* 2nd Scottish Horse.

Callander Perthshire market town on the River Teith. At the foot of the Trossachs, and the scene of Scott's *Lady of the Lake*, Callander is sixteen miles north-west of Stirling; Its station, Callander Dreadnought, being opened by the Callander & Oban Railway Company in June 1870. *Territorials:* 6th Black Watch.

Callington Cornwall market town, nine miles from Liskeard, with station on the London & South Western Railway. Once a prosperous town with mines and a woollen trade – the tall chimney of Kit Hill mine is there still. Here is St Mary's Church. *Territorials:* 5th Duke of Cornwall's Light Infantry.

Calne Wiltshire market town, six miles from Chippenham, with station on the Great Western Railway. Flour, flax and paper mills gave employment, but Calne's chief industry was in bacon curing – Harris's Bacon Factory was founded in 1770. Here is St Mary's Church. A lithograph exists which shows Calne High Street c1840. Here on one side of the road are the Lansdowne Arms and King's Arms, in-between the two, the old Town Hall which was demolished in 1883. Three shops are clearly identified: Mead the saddler, Sutton the chemist and Baily's printing office. *Territorials:* Wiltshire Yeomanry, 4th Wiltshire Regiment and 1st South Western Mounted Brigade Field Ambulance.

Calverton Nottinghamshire village on the River Doverbeck, seven miles from Nottingham, where Inventor of the stocking frame, William Lee, was once curate at St Wilfrid's Church. *Territorials:* 8th Sherwood Foresters.

Camberley West Surrey town with station on the London & South Western Railway. Close by is the Royal Military College, later to be called Royal Military Academy, Sandhurst. Camberley was once called Cambridge Town in honour of the Duke of Cambridge, but this confused the Post Office, so it was changed in 1877. *Territorials:* Surrey Yeomanry, 5th Queen's Royal West Surrey Regiment and Frimley and Camberley Cadet Corps.

Camberwell South London borough. Dan Leno's Oriental Palace of Varieties was opened on Denmark Hill in 1896, the Camberwell School of Arts and Crafts in Peckham Road, the same year. Here is Wilson's School, which maintained an OTC contingent of one infantry company, and St Giles's Church which replace a former building burnt down in 1841. *Territorials:* 21st London Regiment, Magdalene Cadet Company, South London Cadet, and Trinity Mission Boys' Club Cadets.

Camborne Cornwall market town, three miles from Redruth, with station on the Great Western Railway. Here were tin and copper mines – the Dolcoath Mine, for many years one of the deepest in the world, and South Crofty which went on until 1998. The large manufacturer of industrial equipment, Holman Brothers, also employed many. The Camborne & Redruth Tramway, with its dark green and cream trams, began operating between the two towns in November 1902. Camborne's church, St Martin and St Meriadocus, stands at the end of the town. *Territorials:* 4th Duke of Cornwall's Light Infantry.

Cambridge 'For Cambridge people rarely smile,/Being urban, squat, and packed with Guile;' (from 'The Old Vicarage, Grantchester' by Rupert Brooke, 1912). One major employer, as well as the university, was H J Gray and Sons, makers of sports equipment since 1855. Cambridge was served by the Great Eastern Railway, the red and cream vehicles of the Cambridge Street Tramways Company operating from the station as far as the Post Office opposite Christ's College from October 1880. Of the many churches in Cambridge, All Saints in Jesus Lane and Great St Andrew's, with its monument to Captain Cook, are of note. OTC contingents in Cambridge were to be found at the University, and at the Cambridge County, Leys and Perse schools. *Territorials:* Suffolk Yeomanry, Cambridgeshire Regiment and 1st Eastern General Hospital.

Camden Town North London district in the Borough of St Pancras where much local trade and employment revolved around the Regent's Canal. *Territorials:* 19th London Regiment.

Camelford Cornwall market town on the River Camel, twelve miles to the north of Bodmin and reached by the old North Cornwall Railway in August 1893. *Territorials:* Royal 1st Devon Yeomanry and 5th Duke of Cornwall's Light Infantry.

Camp Hill Area in south-east Birmingham with station on the Midland Railway which opened in December 1840. *Territorials:* Worcestershire Yeomanry and King Edward's School (Camp Hill) Cadet Corps.

Campbeltown From Campbeltown, on the coast of Kintyre in Argyllshire, distilleries exported whisky all around the world. Coal and iron were produced, ships were built, and a number were involved in the fishing industry. The Campbeltown & Machrihanish Light Railway opened to passengers in 1906 (it had previously been owned by the Argyll Coal & Canal Company). *Territorials:* 2nd Scottish Horse, 4th Highland Brigade RGA and 8th Argyll and Sutherland Highlanders.

Canning Town Part of the Borough of West Ham in Essex with station on the Great Eastern Railway. Employment was in the Victoria and Albert Docks – the area all around built to house the Dockers – and at works producing chemicals and creosote. Here are Holy Trinity, St Luke's and St Gabriel's churches. *Territorials:* St Gabriel's Cadet Corps and 1st Cadet Battalion Essex Regiment.

Cannock Staffordshire town with station on the London & North Western Railway, where the mining of coal and the manufacture of bricks, titles and paving material employed many. Here is St Luke's Church. *Territorials:* Staffordshire Yeomanry and North Midland Divisional Engineers.

Canonbie Dumfrieshire village on the River Esk, two miles north of Scotland's border with England, with station on the North British Railway that opened in May 1862. *Territorials:* 5th King's Own Scottish Borderers.

Canterbury Cathedral city in east Kent served by the South Eastern & Chatham Railway, its chief industries noted as brewing, malting, tanning, brick making, linen weaving and rope making. Magnificent is the cathedral, but so too is St Mary's Church; parts of which date from AD560. King's School and St Edmund's School in Canterbury both maintained OTC infantry companies. *Territorials:* Royal East Kent Yeomanry, 4th Buffs East Kent Regiment, Kent Cyclist Battalion and 2nd Home Counties Field Ambulance.

Cardiff Seaport, the Bute Docks employing many, and county market town on the River Taff in Glamorgan. As the coal trade increased, so did the railways: the Taff Vale arriving in 1841, South Wales and Great Western in 1850, the Rhymney in 1858. Here is St John's Church and, in Charles Street dating from 1887, the Roman Catholic St David's. *Territorials:* South Wales Infantry Brigade, Gloucestershire Yeomanry, Glamorgan Yeomanry, Welsh Horse, Glamorgan RHA, 2nd Welsh Brigade RFA, Glamorgan RGA, Welsh Divisional Engineers, Glamorgan Fortress Engineers, 7th Welsh Regiment, 2nd Welsh Field Ambulance and 3rd Western General Hospital.

Cardigan County and market town situated on the River Teifi and served by the Great Western Railway. Many from the town were employed in the manufacture of tiles, bricks, agricultural implements and woollen garments. Then part of the Whitland & Cardigan Railway Company, Cardigan's station was opened on 1 September 1886. *Territorials:* 4th Welsh Regiment.

Cardross Dumbartonshire village on the Firth of Clyde, four miles north-west of Dumbarton, served by the North British Railway. Born here in 1896 was the novelist A J Cronin. *Territorials:* 9th Argyll and Sutherland Highlanders.

Carlin How North Yorkshire village four miles south-east of Saltburn-on-Sea. Ironstone was extensively worked in the area. *Territorials:* 4th Yorkshire Regiment.

Carlisle Cumberland county and market town. In 1880, Carlisle's Her Majesty's Theatre became the first in England to be lit by electricity. Chief sources of employment were cotton goods, print and dye works, iron foundries and tanneries. The City of Carlisle Electric Tramways opened in June 1900. Here is the Cathedral Church of the Holy and Undivided Trinity. *Territorials:* Westmorland and Cumberland Yeomanry, 4th East Lancashire Brigade RFA and 4th Border Regiment.

Carlton Nottingham suburb served by the Great Northern Railway where, noted the guides, many of the inhabitants were employed in the manufacture of hosiery and lace. Here is St Paul's Church. *Territorials:* Nottinghamshire Yeomanry (South Notts) and 8th Sherwood Foresters.

Carluke South Lanarkshire town with station on the Caledonian Railway opened in March 1860. *Territorials:* Lanarkshire Yeomanry and 8th Highland Light Infantry.

Carmarthen General Picton, who fell at Waterloo, was a native of Carmarthen and a monument to his memory now looks down on the town from a hill. Another hero, this time General Nott of Ghuznee, stands in Nott Square. Carmarthen lies on the Towy, about twenty-eight miles from Swansea, its main industry being the export of timber, slates, marble, lead and tin-plate. Salmon fishing was also important to the town. The Carmarthen and Cardigan Railway Company began on 1 March 1860, the original station closing in 1902 and replaced just to the south by the Great Western on 1 July. *Territorials:* South Wales Mounted Brigade, Pembrokeshire Yeomanry, Welsh Divisional Engineers South Wales Mounted Brigade Signal Troop and 4th Welsh Regiment.

Carnarvon Seaport and market town on the Menai Strait served by the London & North Western and North Wales Narrow Gauge railways. Victorian guides note the parish church as being 'modern' and the existence in the town of the North Wales Training College for Schoolmasters. *Territorials:* Denbighshire Yeomanry, Welsh RGA and 6th Royal Welsh Fusiliers.

Carnforth North Lancashire town on Morecambe Bay with extensive ironworks. Carnforth was a major railway junction where three railway companies met: the London & North Western, Furness and Midland. Familiar to many will be the station, much featured in the 1945 film *Brief Encounter*. Here is Christ Church. *Territorials:* Westmorland and Cumberland Yeomanry and 5th King's Own Royal Lancaster Regiment.

Carno Montgomeryshire village, north-west of Newtown, served by the Cambrian Railway. Situated at the foot of the Clorin hillside lies the church of St John the Baptist which was completed in 1863. *Territorials:* 7th Royal Welsh Fusiliers.

Carnoustie Coastal town in Fifeshire, ten miles from Dundee, served jointly by the North British and Caledonian Railways. Golf, as now, brought much business to the town; a good number were also employed in the production of linens at the Penmure Works, and shoes in John Winter's factory. *Territorials:* 5th Black Watch.

Carrbridge Inverness-shire village on the Dulnan Water, to the north of Aviemore, reached by the Highland Railway in 1892. *Territorials:* 6th Seaforth Highlanders.

Carriden Locality on the eastern side of Bo'ness in Linlithgowshire. *Territorials:* 10th Royal Scots.

Carstairs Lanarkshire village on the River Clyde with station on the Caledonian Railway which opened in February 1848. *Territorials:* Lanarkshire Yeomanry.

Casthorpe Hamlet two miles west of Grantham in Lincolnshire. *Territorials:* Lincoln and Leicester Infantry Brigade.

Castle Acre Norfolk village on the River Nar four miles north of Swaffham. Here is St James's Church. *Territorials:* 5th Norfolk Regiment.

Castle Caereinion Montgomeryshire village to the south-west of Welshpool, with station on the Cambrian Railway opened in April 1903. Here is St Garmon's Church. *Territorials:* Montgomeryshire Yeomanry.

Castle Cary Somerset market town on the River Cary, to the north-west of Wincanton, served by the Great Western Railway. Here among the town's several industries were brick and tile works, a twine factory, and manufacturers of horsehair seating. Here is All Saints Church. *Territorials:* North Somerset Yeomanry and 4th Somerset Light Infantry.

Castle Douglas Cassel's in the 1890s noted that Castle Douglas in Kircudbrightshire was the chief business centre in the whole of the Galloway area. There were manufactures of iron, leather, farm implements and mineral water. The town was served by two railway stations: Castle Douglas, opened by the old Castle Douglas & Dumfries Railway in November 1859, and the Kirkcudbright Company's Castle Douglas St Andrew Street in March 1864. *Territorials:* 5th King's Own Scottish Borderers.

Castle Eden Just under ten miles from Durham on the North Eastern Railway, the village of Castle Eden mined coal, made bricks, tiles, ropes, and brewed beer. Here is St James's Church. *Territorials:* 5th Durham Light Infantry.

Castle Kennedy Wigtownshire village to the south-east of Stranraer, close to White Loch and Black Loch, served by the Glasgow & South Western and Portpatrick & Wigtownshire Joint railways. *Territorials:* 5th Royal Scots Fusiliers.

Castleford West Yorkshire town close to Pontefract, served by the Great Northern, North Eastern and London & North Western railways. Glass and earthenware production was important to the town. Here is All Saints Church. *Territorials:* 5th King's Own Yorkshire Light Infantry.

Castletown Caithness-shire village on Dunnet Bay, five miles to the south-east of Thurso, where the flagstone quarries owned by the Traill family provided much employment. *Territorials:* 5th Seaforth Highlanders.

Caterham Surrey town, to the south of Croydon, served by the South Eastern & Chatham Railway. On a hill overlooking the town from 1877 was a barracks used for training recruits to the several regiments of foot guards. Here is St Lawrence's Church. *Territorials:* 4th Queen's Royal West Surrey Regiment.

Catford Locality in the London Borough of Lewisham served by the South Eastern & Chatham Railway. Here is St Lawrence's Church, and St Dunstan's College which maintained two OTC infantry companies. *Territorials:* West Kent Yeomanry and St Dunstan's College Cadet Corps.

Cathcart Renfrewshire town on the White Cart Water, three miles south of Glasgow, served by the Caledonian Railway. The parish church dates from 1831. *Territorials:* 3rd Highland Brigade RFA.

Caton Lancashire village on the River Lune, to the east of Lancaster, served by the Midland Railway. Caton station was opened in November 1849. Here is St Paul's Church. *Territorials:* 5th King's Own Royal Lancaster Regiment.

Catrine East Ayrshire village on the River Sorn, reached by the Glasgow & South Western Railway in 1903, where there were manufacturers of cotton and a brewery. *Territorials:* 5th Royal Scots Fusiliers.

Catterick North Yorkshire town on the River Swale, just over four miles south-east of Richmond, served by the North Eastern Railway. Catterick Bridge station was opened in September 1846. Here is St Ann's Church. *Territorials:* 4th Yorkshire Regiment.

Cawdor Nairnshire village five miles from Nairn. *Territorials:* 2nd Lovat's Scouts and 4th Cameron Highlanders.

Cefn Coed A tall, fifteen-arched railway viaduct of 1865–1866 towers above the houses of this small Brecknockshire town which was served by the Brecon & Merthyr London & North Western Joint Railway. Here, dating from 1888, is St Tudor's Church. *Territorials:* Brecknockshire Battalion.

Cemmaes Montgomeryshire village served by the Cambrian Railway. Here is St Tydecho's Church. *Territorials:* 7th Royal Welsh Fusiliers.

Cemmaes Road Montgomery village served by the Cambrian Railway. *Territorials:* Montgomeryshire Yeomanry.

Cerrig-y-Druidion Denbighshire village to the south-west of Denbigh. Here is St Mary Magdalene's Church. *Territorials:* Welsh Divisional Transport and Supply Column.

Chagford Devonshire market town on the edge of Dartmoor near the River Teign, four miles from Moreton Hampstead and the railway. During a Civil War engagement at Chagford in February 1643, the Royalist poet Sidney Godolphin was shot in the leg and subsequently bled to death at the Three Crowns inn. Here is the fifteenth-century, granite-built St Michael's Church. *Territorials:* 5th Devonshire Regiment.

Chalfont St Peter Buckinghamshire village to the south-east of Amersham. Here, St Peter's Church dates from 1726, the much younger All Saints not being built until 1912. *Territorials:* Buckinghamshire Yeomanry.

Chandler's Ford Hampshire village on the Winchester to Southampton road served by the London & South Western Railway. Here many were employed in an extensive brickworks. *Territorials:* 4th Hampshire Regiment.

Chapel-en-le-Frith Small Derbyshire market town, to the north of Buxton, served by the Midland and London & North Western railways. The chief industries of the town were paper and wadding making, and there was also a brewery. Here is St Thomas's Church which was founded in 1225 by the foresters and keepers of the nearby old Forest of the Peak – frith meaning forest. During September 1648, some 1,500 prisoners of the Scots army (just defeated at Preston) were imprisoned in the church. More than fifty of their number appear in the church records as having died in captivity and subsequently buried in the churchyard. *Territorials:* 6th Sherwood Foresters.

Chapel Lawn South-west Shropshire village to the north-east of Knighton. Here is St Mary's, an Edward Haycock church of 1844. *Territorials:* 1st Herefordshire Regiment.

Chapeltown Banffshire village eighteen miles south-west of Dufftown. Close by is the Braes of Glenlivet distillery. *Territorials:* 6th Gordon Highlanders.

Chard Somerset market town, close to the border with Devonshire to the south-west of Yeovil, served by the Great Western and London & South Western railways. Chief industries: lace, linen and collar manufacture. Here is St Mary's Church. *Territorials:* West Somerset Yeomanry and 5th Somerset Light Infantry.

Chardstock East Devonshire village on the River Kitbridge four miles from Axminster. Chardstock parish was part of Dorset until 1896. Here is St Andrew's Church. *Territorials:* 4th Devonshire Regiment.

Charlbury Oxfordshire market town on the River Evenlode, to the south-east of Chipping Norton, served by the Great Western Railway. Here is St Mary's Church. *Territorials:* Oxfordshire Yeomanry and 4th Oxfordshire and Buckinghamshire Light Infantry.

Charlestown (Cornwall) Village and port, just under two miles from St Austell, well known for its production of china clay. Here is St Paul's Church which opened in 1849. *Territorials:* Cornwall RGA.

Charlestown (Fifeshire) Village and seaport on the Firth of Forth, just under four miles south-west of Dunfermline, where the chief industries were in coal and limestone. *Territorials:* Highland RGA.

Charmouth Dorsetshire village on the River Char six miles south-east of Axminster. Here is St Andrew's Church of 1836–38 which has memorials to the Breton family. *Territorials:* Dorsetshire Yeomanry.

Chartham East Kent village on the River Stour to the south-west of Canterbury, served by the South Eastern & Chatham Railway. From the river, power has been taken for the Chartham Paper Mill since the late eighteen century. Here is St Mary's Church. *Territorials:* 4th Buffs East Kent Regiment.

Chatham Kent town and seaport where several thousand were employed at the docks. Here, St John's Church dates from 1821, St Mary's being mostly rebuilt in 1896–98 and 1908. *Territorials:* Royal East Kent Yeomanry, Home Counties RGA, Kent Fortress Engineers, 5th Royal West Kent Regiment, Kent Cyclist Battalion, 1st Home Counties Field Ambulance and 1st Chatham Cadet Company RMLI.

Chatsworth Derbyshire parish on the River Derwent. Chatsworth House, the seat of the Cavendishes, Dukes of Devonshire. *Territorials:* Notts and Derby Mounted Brigade Transport and Supply Column.

Chatteris Market town in the Fenland district of Cambridgeshire, seven miles south of March, served by the Great Eastern Railway. Beer was brewed at Chatteris, matting and ropes were made. Here is St Peter's Church. *Territorials:* Bedfordshire Yeomanry and Cambridgeshire Regiment.

Chatton North Northumberland village on the River Till, three miles to the east of Wooler, where many were employed in the quarrying of limestone. Here is the church of Holy Cross. *Territorials:* 7th Northumberland Fusiliers.

Cheadle Cheshire town near the River Mersey, three miles south-west of Stockport, served by the Cheshire Lines and North Staffordshire railways. There were printing and bleaching works in the town. Here is St Mary's Church. *Territorials:* 5th Cheshire Regiment.

Cheddar Somerset village on the southern edge of the Mendip Hills, to the south-east of Axbridge, served by the Great Western Railway. Buried in the churchyard at St Andrew's Church in Cheddar is the hymn writer William Chatterton Dix (1837–98). *Territorials:* 4th Somerset Light Infantry.

Chelmsford *Cassell's Gazetteer* for 1895 noted that Chelmsford's corn market was the most extensive in the country. Other chief industries were: electrical engineering, agricultural implement making, iron founding, tanning and brewing. Marconi opened the world's first radio factory in Hall Street Chelmsford in 1899. Chelmsford in Essex was served by the Great Eastern Railway. Here is St Mary's Church, elevated to the status of a cathedral in 1913 (its registers dating from 1558) and Dean Close School which had an OTC contingent. *Territorials:* Essex Yeomanry, Essex RHA, Essex Fortress Engineers, 5th Essex Regiment, Eastern Mounted Brigade Transport and Supply Column and Chelmsford King Edward VI School Cadet Corps.

Chelsea London borough on the left bank of the Thames and the home of the Royal Hospital for army veterans. Here too is Chelsea Barracks, and at St Luke's Church in Sydney Street, the registers date from 1559. Some of the more recent entries include the marriages of both Charles Dickens and, author of *Three Men in a Boat*, Jerome K Jerome. *Territorials:* 2nd London Division, London Mounted Brigade, 6th London Infantry Brigade, 1st County of London Yeomanry, King Edward's Horse, 2nd London Divisional Engineers, 10th Middlesex Regiment, 18th London Regiment, 2nd London Divisional Transport and Supply Column, 1st, 2nd, 3rd, 6th London Divisional Filed Ambulances, 1st, 2nd London Clearing Hospitals, 1st, 2nd London General Hospitals, 1st, 2nd London Sanitary Companies, Royal Engineers Cadets (2nd London Division).

Cheltenham Gloucestershire market town where the Public Library was opened in Clarence Street in 1887, an art gallery in 1899, and museum in 1907. Served by the Great Western and Midland railways, Cheltenham owed its prosperity to its mineral springs. All around the walls at Christ Church there are memorials to soldiers of the British and Indian armies. Many of them from the Gaitskill family. There are sailors too. One of them being Captain John McNeill Boyd who perished at Kingstown in Ireland while trying to save others in a storm. In the centre of town there is St Mary's Church, where a young corporal in the Volunteers is remembered having died while serving in South Africa 1901. At Cheltenham College there was a contingent of the OTC. *Territorials:* Gloucester and Worcester Infantry Brigade, Gloucestershire Yeomanry and 5th Gloucestershire Regiment.

Chepstow Monmouthshire river port and market town served by the Great Western Railway, where two bridges across the Wye take you from Wales and into England. Here at St Mary's Church there are memorials to the Kirby family. *Territorials:* Gloucestershire Yeomanry, 1st Monmouthshire Regiment and Chepstow Territorial Cadet Company.

Chertsey Surrey market town on the Thames, to the south-west of London, served by the London & South Western Railway. Here is St Peter's Church where Blanch Heriot delayed the execution of her lover by hanging onto the clapper of the bell. Her action allowing sufficient time for his pardon to come from the king. In fiction, Chertsey was the scene of the attempted burglary by Bill Sikes and Toby Crackit in *Oliver Twist* by Charles Dickens. *Territorials:* 6th East Surrey Regiment.

Chesham Buckinghamshire market town on the River Chess, five miles south-west of Berkhamstead, served by the Metropolitan & Great Central Joint Railway which arrived in July 1889. Thanks to the abundance of beech trees, much employment was enjoyed from the making of wooden ware such as hoops, bowls, brushes and small dairy utensils – the Chiltern Toy Works opened in Bellingdon Road in 1908. Here is the medieval St Mary's Church. *Territorials:* Buckinghamshire Yeomanry and Buckinghamshire Battalion.

Cheshunt Hertfordshire village on the River Lea served by the Great Eastern Railway, Cheshunt station being opened by the Northern & Eastern Railway Company in May 1846. At Cheshunt there were large nurseries, market gardens and brickfields. Here is St Mary's Church. *Territorials:* Hertfordshire Regiment.

Chester The railway was a major employer in Chester; the London & North Western, Great Western, Great Central, North Staffordshire and Cheshire Lines companies all providing services. On the right bank of the River Dee, Chester businesses were involved in the manufacture of boots, shoes, paint and furniture. Here is Chester Cathedral and the Norman St John's Church. *Territorials:* Cheshire Infantry Brigade, Cheshire Yeomanry, 3rd Welsh Brigade RFA, 5th Cheshire Regiment and Welsh Border Mounted Brigade Field Ambulance.

Chester-le-Street Five miles north of Durham, the area employed many in its numerous collieries and ironworks. Here the church is dedicated to St Mary and St Cuthbert. *Territorials:* 8th Durham Light Infantry and Northern Cyclist Battalion.

Chesterfield Derbyshire market town, at the junction of the Rivers Hipper and Rother and on the Trent Canal, served by the Midland and Great Central railways. The chief industries of the town included tanning, iron and brass founding and the manufacture of engines and agricultural implements. Chesterfield stands in the centre of a large colliery area. Here, with its twisted spire and memorials to the Foljambe family, is St Mary and All Saints Church and at Holy Trinity, the remains of 'Father of the Railways', George Stephenson. *Territorials:* Derbyshire Yeomanry, Nottinghamshire Yeomanry (Sherwood Rangers), 6th Sherwood Foresters and Notts and Derby Mounted Brigade Transport and Supply Column.

Chichester Sussex cathedral city on a branch of the Arundel and Portsmouth Canal and served by the London, Brighton & South Coast Railway. In addition to the cathedral, in Chichester there were ten parish churches. *Territorials:* Sussex Yeomanry and 4th Royal Sussex Regiment.

Chiddingfold West Surrey village on the border with Sussex, four miles north-east of Haslemere. Here is St Mary's Church. *Territorials:* 5th Queen's Royal West Surrey Regiment.

Chideock South-west Dorsetshire coastal village just under three miles west of Bridport. Here is St Giles's Church. *Territorials:* 4th Dorsetshire Regiment.

Chillerton Village on the Isle of Wight to the south-west of Newport. Good news in 1907 when residents were granted free water. Victorian and Edwardian Guides note Chillerton as consisting of scattered farms and cottages. *Territorials:* 8th Hampshire Regiment.

Chingford West Essex village between the River Lea and Epping Forest served by the Great Eastern Railway. Here, at Chingford Green, is All Saints Church which replaced an earlier building abandoned in 1844. *Territorials:* 7th Essex Regiment.

Chinley Derbyshire village two miles north of Chapel-en-le-Frith on the western edge of the Peak District National Park. Served by the Midland Railway, Chinley's main sources of employment lay in paper, cotton wool, coal and grit stone. *Territorials:* 6th Sherwood Foresters.

Chippenham A thirsty Volunteer in 1879 may well have been the first to take refreshment from the town fountain opened that year and which, some forty-two years later, was used to show the names of those that did not return from the Great War. In the town, much was sent out, and brought in, via the great Wilts and Berks Canal wharf that once stood in Timber Street where the bus station is now situated. Chippenham brewed beer, made cheese, farm machinery, a firm called Hathaway made churns there, and another by the name of Rowland Brotherhood produced railway wagons. Nestlé made condensed milk and the Westinghouse Brake and Signal Co Ltd made all things for the railway. Hunts of Chippenham made the 30-million bricks used to line the interior of Box Tunnel (1836–41). Here is St Andrew's Church. *Territorials:* Wiltshire Yeomanry and 4th Wiltshire Regiment.

Chipping Campden Gloucestershire village, south-east of Evesham, served by the Great Western Railway. Here is St James's Church which was built from the profits made by William Grevel of Chipping Campden, once one of the richest wool merchants in England. *Territorials:* 5th Gloucestershire Regiment.

Chipping Norton Oxfordshire market town, south-west of Banbury, situated on a branch line ran by the Oxford, Worcester & Wolverhampton, later, Great Western Railway. Gloves were made here, beer was brewed at Hitchman's in Albion Street, and woollens made at Bliss Mill on the western side of the town. In the winter of 1913–14, the workers at Bliss Mill struck for eight weeks. Here is St Mary's Church, which dates from the thirteenth century. *Territorials:* Oxfordshire Yeomanry and 4th Oxfordshire and Buckinghamshire Light Infantry.

Chirbury Shropshire village on the border with Montgomeryshire three miles north-east of Montgomery. Here is St Michael's Church. *Territorials:* Montgomeryshire Yeomanry.

Chirk Denbighshire market town nine from Wrexham. The Llangollen Canal crosses the Ceiriog here via an aqueduct, the railway over a viaduct by its side. Chirk station, on the Great Western and Glynn Valley Tramroad, was opened on 15 March 1891. Employment was in coal, lime and the manufacture of paper. Here is St Mary's Church. *Territorials:* 4th Royal Welsh Fusiliers.

Chirnside Small Berwickshire village, about five miles from Duns, served by the North British Railway. Here, paper was made at Cousin's Chirnside Bridge Paper Mill. *Territorials:* 4th King's Own Scottish Borderers.

Chirton Wiltshire village, its rail connection being just to the north at the Great Western Railway's Patney and Chirton station which opened in 1900. Here is the church of St John the Baptist. *Territorials:* Wiltshire Yeomanry.

Chitterne Wiltshire village on Salisbury Plain four miles from Heytesbury. Here is All Saints Church of 1863. *Territorials:* 4th Wiltshire Regiment.

Chittlehampton Devonshire village on the River Taw seven miles from Barnstaple. Here the church (St Hieritha, or Urith) is dedicated to a local saint murdered by the villagers c700. *Territorials:* Royal North Devon Yeomanry and 6th Devonshire Regiment.

Chobham Surrey village on the River Bourne four miles north-west of Woking. Here is St Laurence's Church. *Territorials:* Gordon Boys Home Cadet Corps.

Cholderton Wiltshire village in the Bourne Valley four miles from Amesbury. Here is St Nicholas's Church which was completed in 1850. *Territorials:* 4th Hampshire Regiment.

Cholesbury Buckinghamshire village in the Chiltern Hills on the border with Hertfordshire. Here is St Laurence's Church. *Territorials:* Buckinghamshire Yeomanry.

Chopwell Durham mining community, a major employer being the Consett Iron Company. *Territorials:* 9th Durham Light Infantry.

Chorley Lancashire market town served by the London & North Western Railway. On the Leeds and Liverpool Canal, Chorley gave employment to many in its cotton mills, iron foundries, railway wagon works and breweries. Here is St Lawrence's Church; St George's, built in 1825; St Peter's, dating from 1850, and St James's which opened in 1878. *Territorials:* 4th North Lancashire Regiment.

Chorley Wood Hertfordshire village, three miles from Rickmansworth, reached by the extension of the Metropolitan Railway out of London in 1889. Here, built 1869–70, is Christ Church. *Territorials:* Hertfordshire Regiment and 1st (Chorley Wood) Hertfordshire Cadet Company.

Christchurch Hampshire town and seaport situated at the head of the estuary formed by the Rivers Avon and Stour, its chief industry being the manufacture of watch and clock fuse chains. Many of the inhabitants, though, were employed in salmon fishing and the hosiery trade. The Ringwood, Christchurch & Bournemouth Railway opened Christchurch Station in November 1862. Here, looking across the harbour, is the Priory Church of The Holy Trinity, its porch the largest of any parish church in Great Britain. *Territorials:* 7th Hampshire Regiment.

Chudleigh Devonshire market town on the River Teign, to the south-west of Exeter, served by the Great Western Railway which arrived in 1874. Here is St Mary and St Martin's Church. *Territorials:* 5th Devonshire Regiment.

Chulmleigh Devonshire market town on the River Taw to the south of South Molton. Here is the mainly fifteenth-century church of St Mary Magdalene. *Territorials:* Royal North Devon Yeomanry and 6th Devonshire Regiment.

Church Lancashire town on the Leeds and Liverpool Canal, one mile west of Accrington and served by the London & North Western Railway, where a large print and dye works employed many. Chemicals and iron implements were manufactured and coal was extensively mined. It was here that Windham Sadler, an early balloonist, fell to his death in 1823 close to St James's Church. *Territorials:* 1st East Lancashire Brigade RFA.

Church Crookham Hampshire village on the Basingstoke Canal close to Fleet. Here is Christ Church, built in 1841. *Territorials:* Wessex Divisional Transport and Supply Column.

Church Gresley Derbyshire village close to Swadlincote and served by the Midland Railway. Coal mining and the manufacture of fire-bricks, encaustic tiles, and pottery are noted as its chief industries. The Gresley family, from nearby Drakelowe, are remembered in St George's Church which was founded in the reign of Henry I. *Territorials:* Derbyshire Yeomanry.

Church Stoke Montgomeryshire village on the River Camlad close to the English/Welsh border. Here is St Nicholas's Church. *Territorials:* Montgomeryshire Yeomanry.

Church Stretton Shropshire market town, to the south-west of Shrewsbury, its first station being opened by the Shrewsbury & Hereford Joint Railway in April 1852. Here is St Lawrence's Church. *Territorials:* Shropshire RHA.

Churchingford Somersetshire hamlet close to the River Bolham, just over seven miles from Taunton. *Territorials:* West Somerset Yeomanry.

Churchstanton Somersetshire village on the River Otter five miles south of Taunton. Here, almost a mile from the village, is St Peter and St Paul's Church. *Territorials:* West Somerset Yeomanry.

Cirencester Gloucestershire market town on the River Churn and Thames and Severn Canal, served by the Great Western and Midland & South Western railways. In the market place is the church of St John the Baptist, its three-story south porch once used as a Town Hall. During a Civil War action fought at Cirencester on 2 February 1643, Royalist forces took 1,000 Parliamentarian prisoners which were then held captive in the church. In the Trinity Chapel, on the north side of the church, those that brought prosperity to the town with the wool trade are remembered. Here is the Royal Agricultural College which maintained an OTC contingent. *Territorials:* 2nd South Midland Mounted Brigade, Gloucestershire Yeomanry and 5th Gloucestershire Regiment.

Clachan (Argyllshire) Hamlet on the Clachan Sound, Seil Island, Firth of Lorne. *Territorials:* 8th Argyll and Sutherland Highlanders.

Clachan (North Uist) Village ten miles from Lochmaddy. *Territorials:* 1st Lovat's Scouts.

Clackmannan County town on the River Black Devon, two miles from Alloa and served by the North British Railway. Clackmannan station was opened by the Stirling & Dunfermline Railway Company in August 1850. Coal and the quarrying of sandstone provided employment. *Territorials:* 7th Argyll and Sutherland Highlanders.

Clacton-on-Sea Essex coastal town and seaside resort, to the south-east of Colchester, served by the Great Eastern Railway. Here is St James's Church and, opened in 1875, St Paul's. *Territorials:* Essex Yeomanry and 5th Essex Regiment.

Clanfield Hampshire village to the south-west of Petersfield. Here is St James's Church which was built in 1875. *Territorials:* 6th Hampshire Regiment.

Clapham Area in the London borough of Wandsworth. The railway arrived in 1839 and later, with some 2,500 trains passing each day, Clapham Junction became the busiest in the world. Here, with its domed tower, is Holy Trinity dating from 1776, and, opened in 1864, St Saviour's. *Territorials:* Surrey Yeomanry.

Clapham Park Locality in the London borough of Wandsworth. *Territorials:* Surrey Yeomanry.

Clarbeston Road Pembrokeshire village, to the north-east of Haverfordwest, served by the Great Western Railway. Clarbeston station was opened by the South Wales Railway in January 1854. Here is St Martin's Church. *Territorials:* Pembrokeshire Yeomanry.

Clare Suffolk market town on the north bank of the River Stour, west of Long Melford, served by the Great Eastern Railway which arrived in 1865. Here is St Peter and St Paul's Church. *Territorials:* 5th Suffolk Regiment.

Clay Cross Derbyshire town, south of Chesterfield and served by the Midland Railway, where many were employed in several coal pits and ironworks. Both coal and iron were discovered by George Stephenson while constructing the railway. Clay Cross station was opened in April 1841. Here is St Bartholomew's Church. *Territorials:* 6th Sherwood Foresters.

Cleator Cumberland village on the River Ehen, four miles from Whitehaven and served by the London & North Western and Furness Joint Railway, where the chief industries are noted as: linen thread, flax, iron and coal. Here is St Leonard's Church. *Territorials:* 5th Border Regiment.

Cleckheaton West Yorkshire town, five miles from Bradford, served by the London & North Western Railway. Woollens, flannels, chemicals and wire cord were manufactured, noted the guides of c1900, and there were many coalmines. Cleckheaton Town Hall was opened in 1892. Here are St John's and St Luke's churches. *Territorials:* 4th Duke of Wellington's Regiment.

Cleehill Small village within the Clee Hills range near Ludlow in Shropshire. *Territorials:* 4th King's Shropshire Light Infantry.

Cleland Lanarkshire village on South Calder Water, to the north-east of Motherwell, served by the Caledonian Railway. The neighbouring coal and iron mines gave employment to most of the inhabitants. *Territorials:* 8th Highland Light Infantry.

Cleobury Mortimer Shropshire market town on the Rive Rea to the north-east of Tenbury, its station being opened by the Cleobury Mortimer & Ditton Priors Railway Company in November 1908. Here is St Mary's Church. *Territorials:* 4th King's Shropshire Light Infantry.

Clevedon Somerset coastal town, sixteen miles from Bristol, and the terminus of the Great Western Railway's Yatton to Clevedon branch opened in July 1847. The town was also served by the Weston, Clevedon & Portishead Light Railway. Here is St Andrew's Church. *Territorials:* North Somerset Yeomanry and Wessex Divisional Engineers.

Cliffe-at-Hoo North Kent village, six miles from Gravesend, served by the South Eastern & Chatham Railway. The Francis & Co (later the Portland) Cement Works and the Alpha Cement Works opened in 1910, and explosives were made at Curtis & Harvey's. Here is St Helen's Church. *Territorials:* 5th Royal West Kent Regiment.

Clifton Bristol suburb overlooking the Avon and served by the Great Western Railway. Here, over the Avon Gorge, is Isambard Kingdom Brunel's Clifton Suspension Bridge which opened in 1864. Clifton College maintain a contingent in the OTC. Here is St Andrew's Church. *Territorials:* 1st South Midland Brigade RFA and 4th Gloucestershire Regiment.

Clipston Northamptonshire village, four miles from Market Harborough, served by the London & North Western Railway which arrived in 1859. The station, Clipston and Oxenden, was two miles from the village on the Market Harborough to Northampton branch line. Here is All Saints Church. *Territorials:* Northamptonshire Yeomanry.

Clitheroe Lancashire market town on the River Ribble, ten miles from Blackburn, served by the London & North Western Railway. At Clitheroe there were cotton and paper mills, a print works, foundries, breweries and a company producing cement. *Territorials:* 4th East Lancashire Regiment.

Clowne East Derbyshire locality to the south-west of Worksop, served by the Great Central and Midland railways, where the Southgate Colliery provided employed for most. Here is the church of St John the Baptist. *Territorials:* 6th Sherwood Foresters.

Clumber Seat of the Duke of Newcastle near Worksop Nottinghamshire. Here is St Mary's Church. *Territorials:* Nottinghamshire Yeomanry (Sherwood Rangers).

Clunes Inverness-shire village on Beauly Firth, to the west of Inverness, served by the Highland Railway. *Territorials:* 1st Lovat's Scouts.

Clunie Perthshire village on the western shore of Loch of Clunie to the south-west of Blairgowrie. *Territorials:* 1st Scottish Horse.

Cluny Aberdeenshire village nine miles from Kintore. *Territorials:* 2nd Scottish Horse.

Clydach Glamorgan village to the north of Swansea served by the Midland Railway. In 1902 Ludwig Mond's Clydach Nickel Refinery opened and by 1910 employed almost half of the village's population. Here is St John's Church. *Territorials:* 6th Welsh Regiment.

Clydebank Just under six miles from Glasgow, most of the population of Clydebank were employed in shipyards. John Brown & Co came to Clydebank in 1899, the company launching the Cunard liner

Lusitania in 1906. Clydebank was served by both the Caledonian and North British Railways. Here is St James's Church. *Territorials:* 9th Argyll and Sutherland Highlanders.

Coalburn Lanarkshire mining village, three miles from Lesmahagow, served by the Caledonian Railway. *Territorials:* Lanarkshire Yeomanry and 8th Highland Light Infantry.

Coalville Leicestershire village, five miles south-east of Ashby-de-la-Zouch, served by the London & North Western Railway. The area maintained several large collieries. Employment was also provided in the production of iron objects, railway wagons, bricks, tiles and silk. Here is Christ Church. *Territorials:* 5th Leicestershire Regiment and North Midland Mounted Brigade Transport and Supply Column.

Coatbridge Cassel's notes that Coatbridge, on the Monkland Canal and Caledonian and North British railways just under ten miles east of Glasgow, was in the 1890s the principle seat of the iron trade in Scotland. Railway wagons and boilers were manufactured. *Territorials:* Lanarkshire Yeomanry and Lowland Divisional Engineers.

Coatdyke North Lanarkshire village, one mile south-west of Airdrie, its station in Quarry Street being served by the North British Railway. *Territorials:* Lowland Divisional Engineers.

Coates Cambridgeshire village three miles from Whittlesey. Here is Holy Trinity Church. *Territorials:* Cambridgeshire Regiment.

Cobham Surrey town on the River Mole, west of Epsom, served by the London & South Western Railway. Here, with its Norman west tower, is St Andrew's Church. *Territorials:* 6th East Surrey Regiment and Sandroyd School Troop of Scouts.

Cockenzie Haddingtonshire fishing village on the Firth of Forth one mile from Prestonpans. Much trade was carried on from Port Seton, and coal and salt were produced in the area. *Territorials:* 8th Royal Scots.

Cockermouth West Cumberland market town at the confluence of the Derwent and Cocker, served by the London & North Western and Furness Railways. In the town were woollen factories and tanneries. Here is All Saints Church where a window remembers William Wordsworth. *Territorials:* Westmorland and Cumberland Yeomanry and 5th Border Regiment.

Codnor Park East Derbyshire locality on the Erewash and Cromford Canal to the east of Ripley. Here most of the population helped produced coal, steel and iron; the area served by the Midland and Great Northern Railways. *Territorials:* 5th Sherwood Foresters.

Coedpoeth Denbighshire village west of Wrexham served by the Great Western Railway which arrived in 1897. Main industries here were in lead, lime, coal and steel: the Minera lead mines, Minera limeworks, Brymbo steel mill, Vron colliery and John Wilkinson's Brenham ironworks employing many. *Territorials:* 4th Royal Welsh Fusiliers.

Coggeshall Essex market town on the River Blackwater, to the east of Braintree, where the economy centred around the woollen industry. Here, next to the Woolpack Inn, is the church of St Peter-ad-Vincula, which was built by the town's prosperous wool merchants around 1400–25. *Territorials:* 5th and 8th Essex Regiment.

Coigach Ross and Cromarty coastal hamlet to the north-west of Ullapool. *Territorials:* 4th Seaforth Highlanders.

Colchester Essex market town on the south bank of the River Colne. The town's oyster fishery gave employment, as did firms manufacturing boots, shoes and clothing – see inside St Peter's

Church on North Hill for memorials to the many wealthy cloth merchants that once lived in the town. The church was damaged, along with more than 1,000 other buildings in Colchester, during an earthquake which took place on 22 April 1884. Colchester was served by the Great Eastern Railway and, opened in 1904 was the Colchester Corporation Tramway which operated from its depot in Magdalen Street. There is a painting by transport artist Malcolm Root which shows Tram No 10 ascending Lexden Hill. The several advertisements on the front of the vehicle including one for Graves ('For Furs and Umbrellas') whose premises were opposite the Town Hall. *Territorials:* Eastern Mounted Brigade, Essex Yeomanry, Essex RHA, Eastern Mounted Brigade Signal Troop, 5th, 8th Essex Regiment, Essex and Suffolk Cyclist Battalion and Colchester Royal Grammar School Cadets.

Coldhurst Suburb of Manchester. Here is Holy Trinity Church which dates from 1848. *Territorials:* 1st Coldhurst (Oldham) Cadet Corps (later called 2nd Cadet Battalion Manchester Regiment).

Coldingham Berwickshire coastal village three miles north of Eyemouth. Here is the priory dedicated to St Cuthbert, St Mary and St Ebba. *Territorials:* 4th King's Own Scottish Borderers.

Coldstream Town in Berwickshire where in 1650, General Monk raised the regiment that would later be known as Coldstream Guards. On the Tweed, to the north-east of Kelso, Coldstream was served by the North Eastern Railway. Here the parish church dates from 1795. *Territorials:* Lothians and Border Horse and 4th King's Own Scottish Borderers.

Coleford Gloucestershire market town in the midst of the mining district of the Forest of Dean to the south-east of Monmouth. The Severn & Wye, Great Western and Midland railways served the town. Here is St John's Church. *Territorials:* 2nd Monmouthshire Regiment.

Colinsburgh East Fifeshire market village named after Colin, 3rd Earl of Balcarras. *Territorials:* 7th Black Watch.

Collingham Nottinghamshire village on the River Trent, six miles from Newark, served by the Midland Railway which arrived in August 1846. Here is All Saints Church. *Territorials:* Nottinghamshire Yeomanry (Sherwood Rangers).

Colney Norfolk village on the River Yare three miles west of Norwich. Here is St Andrew's Church. *Territorials:* 4th Norfolk Regiment.

Coltishall Norfolk village on the River Bure, eight miles to the north-east of Norwich, served by the Great Eastern Railway. Coltishall station was opened by the East Norfolk Railway in July 1879. Here is the church of St John the Baptist. *Territorials:* Norfolk Yeomanry and 4th Norfolk Regiment.

Colwall Herefordshire village on the border with Worcestershire, to the north-east of Ledbury, served by the Great Western Railway which arrived in September 1861. Here is the church of St James the Great. *Territorials:* Herefordshire Regiment.

Colwyn Bay Denbighshire town and seaside resort served by the London & North Western Railway, the station being opened by the Chester & Holyhead Company in October 1849. Colwyn Bay was host to the 1910 National Eisteddfod. Here, in Abergele Road, is St Paul's Church which replaced an earlier building destroyed by fire in 1886. *Territorials:* 5th Royal Welsh Fusiliers.

Colyton Devonshire market town on the River Coly, five miles from Axminster, served by the London & South Western Railway. Trade in the town was mostly agricultural. Paper was made there, and a tannery still exists. Here is St Andrew's Church. *Territorials:* 4th Devonshire Regiment.

Combe Martin North Devon coastal village five miles east of Ilfracombe. Close by is the Knap Down Mine which was worked until 1875. Here is St Peter's Church. *Territorials:* 6th Devonshire Regiment.

Comrie Perthshire market town on the River Earn served by the Caledonian Railway. Cassell's notes of Comrie, just over six miles west of Crieff, that the place was subject to frequent earthquakes and severe shocks. *Territorials:* 1st Scottish Horse and 6th Black Watch.

Congleton Congleton in Cheshire is situated in the valley of the Dane and gave employment to many in what was described as its main industry, 'fustian cutting'. Fustian a kind of thick hard-wearing twilled cloth. There were also extensive collieries and stone quarries in the area. The town was served by the North Staffordshire Railway. Here, with its galleries on three sides and box-pews, is St Peter's Church of 1742. *Territorials:* Cheshire Yeomanry and 7th Cheshire Regiment.

Conisbrough West Yorkshire village on the River Don, five miles south-west of Doncaster, served by the Midland and Great Central railways. Local employment was in the production of hooks, sickles, scythes, bottles, pipes, bricks and tiles. Here is St Peter's Church. *Territorials:* 5th King's Own Yorkshire Light Infantry.

Coniston North Lancashire village, on the west side of Coniston Water, served by the Furness Railway which opened its first station in June 1859. Copper mines have been worked on and off since the reign of Elizabeth I. Here is St Andrew's Church where lies buried John Ruskin. *Territorials:* 4th King's Own Royal Lancaster Regiment.

Connah's Quay Flintshire coastal village, on the estuary of the River Dee, served by the London & North Western Railway which arrived in 1870. Here is St Mark's Church, built 1836–35, and St David's which opened in 1914. *Territorials:* 5th Royal Welsh Fusiliers.

Connell Argyllshire village at the mouth of Loch Etive, six miles to the north-east of Oban, served by the Caledonian Railway – Connell Ferry station opened by the Callander & Oban Railway Company in 1880, North Connell in 1904. *Territorials:* 2nd Scottish Horse.

Consett Durham town on the River Derwent served by the North Eastern Railway, where the Consett Ironworks employed more than 6,000 people. The same company also owned collieries in the area. Here is Christ Church. *Territorials:* 6th Durham Light Infantry.

Constantine Cornwall village on the River Helford to the south-west of Falmouth, where oyster fishing and the quarrying of granite gave employment to many. Here is St Constantine's Church. *Territorials:* Cornwall Fortress Engineers.

Contin East Ross and Cromarty village to the south-west of Dingwall. *Territorials:* 2nd Lovat's Scouts.

Convinth Inverness-shire locality to the south-west of Beauly. *Territorials:* 1st Lovat's Scouts.

Conway Caernarvonshire market town and seaport on the left bank of the Conwy, served by the London & North Western Railway. Here is St Mary's Church where a grave in the churchyard is thought to have inspired Wordsworth's poem 'We are Seven'. *Territorials:* 6th Royal Welsh Fusiliers.

Corbridge South Northumberland town on the north bank of the Tyne to the east of Hexham, served by the North Eastern Railway. Here is St Andrew's Church. *Territorials:* 4th Northumberland Fusiliers.

Corfe Castle Small Dorsetshire town on the Isle of Purbeck and the London & South Western Railway's branch from Wareham to Swanage. The area produced marble, and large quantities of potters' clay. Here is the church of St Edward the Martyr. *Territorials:* 4th Dorsetshire Regiment.

Corgarff West Aberdeenshire hamlet on the River Don just over seven miles west of Strathdon. *Territorials:* 6th Gordon Highlanders.

Cornhill Banffshire village, its station situated just before the Great North of Scotland line branched off to Banff Harbour. *Territorials:* 6th Gordon Highlanders.

Corpach Inverness-shire village on Loch Eil and Telford's Caledonian Canal, three miles from Fort William. Corpach was served by the North British Railway which arrived in 1901. *Territorials:* 4th Cameron Highlanders.

Corpusty North Norfolk village on the River Bure, sixteen miles from Norwich, served by the Midland & Great Northern Joint Railway. Here is St Peter's Church. *Territorials:* 5th Norfolk Regiment.

Corris Merionethshire village, to the south-west of Dolgelly, served by the narrow gauge Corris Railway which opened in August 1879. Here, many were employed in local slate quarries and iron mines. Here is Holy Trinity Church. *Territorials:* 7th Royal Welsh Fusiliers.

Corsham Wiltshire town, four miles south-west of Chippenham on the Great Western Railway, where many were employed in the underground quarrying of Bath stone. Here is St Bartholomew's Church. *Territorials:* Wiltshire Yeomanry.

Corsock Kirkcudbrightshire village on Urr Water eight miles to the north of Castle Douglas. *Territorials:* 5th King's Own Scottish Borderers.

Corwen Merionethshire market town at the foot of the Berwyn Mountains. Twelve miles to the north-east of Bala and situated on the River Dee, Corwen was served by both the Great Western and London & North Western railways. Here is St Julien's Church. *Territorials:* 7th Royal Welsh Fusiliers.

Cosham Hampshire village, four miles to the north of Portsmouth, served by the London & South Western Railway which arrived in 1848. *Territorials:* Wessex RGA.

Cottesbrooke Northamptonshire village two miles to the north-west of Northampton. All Saints Church is set in the centre of the village in a little wooded hollow. Here, the Langham family are remembered in wood, stone and glass – they even have their own pew: two storeys and with built-in fireplace. *Territorials:* Northamptonshire Yeomanry.

Cottesmore North Rutland village four miles to the north-east of Oakham. Here is St Nicholas's Church. *Territorials:* 5th Leicestershire Regiment.

Cottingham East Yorkshire village, four miles to the north-west of Hull, served by the North Eastern Railway. Cottingham station was opened by the York & North Midland Railway Company in October 1846 which encouraged many wealthy Hull merchants to set up home in the area. Here is St Mary's Church. *Territorials:* 5th Yorkshire Regiment.

Coundon South Durham mining village, two miles to the east of Bishop Auckland, served by the North Eastern Railway which arrived in 1885. Here is St James's Church. *Territorials:* 6th Durham Light Infantry.

Countesswells Estate in east Aberdeenshire to the west of Aberdeen. *Territorials:* 7th Gordon Highlanders.

Coupar Angus Perthshire market town near the River Isla, to the south of Blairgowrie, served by the Caledonian Railway. Chief industries: corn and the manufacture of course linens and leather. *Territorials:* 1st Scottish Horse and 6th Black Watch.

Cove Hampshire village one mile west of Farnborough. Here, in St John's Road, is the church of St John the Baptist which was built in 1844. *Territorials:* 4th Hampshire Regiment.

Coventry Many from Coventry were employed in the manufacture of bicycles – the Coventry Machinists Company producing the first English-made machine in 1870. The city was also well known for its art metal works, one of which was the Albert Memorial in London. Coventry was served by the London & North Western and Midland railways. Victorian and Edwardian guides note three ancient churches in Coventry: St Michael's, Holy Trinity and St John's. *Territorials:* Warwickshire Yeomanry, Warwickshire RHA, 4th South Midland Brigade RFA, 7th Royal Warwickshire Regiment, 2nd Cadet Battalion Royal Warwickshire Regiment and Bablake School Cadet Company.

Cowbridge South Glamorgan market town, to the south-west of Cardiff, served by the Taff Vale Railway which opened its first station in September 1865. *Territorials:* Glamorganshire Yeomanry.

Cowdenbeath Fifeshire coal mining town, east of Dunfermline, served by the North British Railway. The Fife Coal Company was a major employer. In the town was the Fife Mining School, and opened in Victoria Street in October 1910 was the offices of the Miners Association. The first mine rescue station started at Stenhouse Street in the following November. *Territorials:* 7th Black Watch.

Cowes Seaport on the north coast of the Isle of Wight, served by the Isle of Wight Central Railway, where many were employed in shipping and shipbuilding. Here, in West Cowes next to Northwood House, is St Mary's Church and, built in 1909 in Newport Road, St Faith's. *Territorials:* 8th Hampshire Regiment and Cowes Cadet Company.

Cowie Kincardineshire fishing village just to the north of Stonehaven. *Territorials:* Highland Cyclist Battalion.

Cowley Oxfordshire town, just over two miles to the south-east of Oxford, where William Morris began his car production in 1912 at the premises previously occupied by the Oxford Military College. The Great Western Railway called at Littlemore, some distance from the town, but in 1908 the closer Garsington Bridge Halt station was opened. Here is St James's Church. *Territorials:* Cowley Cadet Corps.

Coxhoe Mining village, five miles from Durham, served by the North Eastern Railway – Coxhoe Bridge station half-mile to the north. The surrounding collieries employed most, but there were also limekilns and manufacturers of brown pottery. East of the village is Coxhoe Hall, the birthplace in 1806 of Elizabeth Barrett Moulton Barrett, the future wife of the poet Robert Browning. Here is St Mary's Church. *Territorials:* 5th Durham Light Infantry.

Craigellachie West Banffshire village on the River Spey, thirteen miles south-east of Elgin, served by the Great North of Scotland Railway which crosses the river via Telford's iron bridge. There are whiskey distilleries in the area. *Territorials:* 2nd Scottish Horse.

Craignure Argyllshire village and ferry port at the head of Loch Don, Mull Island. *Territorials:* 2nd Scottish Horse.

Craigo Forfarshire village on the River North Esk, five miles to the north-west of Montrose, served by the Caledonian Railway. Craigo station was opened by the Aberdeen Railway Company in November 1849. *Territorials:* 5th Black Watch.

Crail East Fifeshire town and seaport at the mouth of the Firth of Forth, ten miles to the south-east of St Andrews, served by the North British Railway. Crab and lobster fishing was important to the town. *Territorials:* 7th Black Watch.

Cranbrook On the River Crane in mid-Kent, Cranbrook lies six miles south of Staplehurst. The Cranbrook & Paddock Wood Railway opened its station there in September 1893. Here is

St Dunstan's Church and Cranbrook School which maintained an OTC contingent. *Territorials:* 5th Buffs East Kent Regiment.

Crathie Aberdeenshire village on the River Dee, to the west of Ballater, where many were employed by the close by Balmoral estate. Here are monuments to Prince Albert and John Brown. The latter, servant to Queen Victoria, is buried in the village church. The Royal Lochnagar Distillery was also near Crathie. *Territorials:* 7th Gordon Highlanders.

Craven Arms South Shropshire market town, seven miles from Church Stretton, served by the London & North Western and Great Western Joint Railway. Once a small village shown on the maps as 'Newton', the town grew with the arrival of the railways – Shrewsbury & Hereford in 1852, Knighton in 1860 – and took its name from the Craven Arms inn located at the junction of the A49 and B4368 roads. *Territorials:* Shropshire Yeomanry and 4th King's Shropshire Light Infantry.

Crawley Sussex village on the main road from London to Brighton, to the north-east of Horsham and two mile south of the Surrey border. The London, Brighton & South Coast Railway called at Crawley station which was opened in 1848. Here is the church of St John the Baptist. *Territorials:* Sussex Yeomanry and 4th Royal Sussex Regiment.

Creagorry Village on South Uist, Outer Hebrides. *Territorials:* 1st Lovat's Scouts.

Crediton Devonshire market town, to the north-west of Exeter, served by the London & South Western Railway. Agriculture and the manufacture of boots, shoes, tinplate ware and confectionary were important to the town. Born here was General Sir Redvers Buller (1839–1908) who won the Victoria Cross during the Zulu War of 1879. He is buried in the churchyard of Crediton's Holy Cross Church. *Territorials:* Royal 1st Devon Yeomanry, 4th Wessex Brigade RFA, 6th and 7th Devonshire Regiment.

Creetown Seaport on Wigtown Bay at the mouth of the River Cree, Kirkcudbrightshire. Served by the Portpatrick & Wigtownshire Joint Railway, many from Creetown were employed in local quarries. *Territorials:* 5th King's Own Scottish Borderers.

Crewe Important to the town, since it came in 1843, was the London & North Western Railway with its locomotive and carriage works. Some 7,000 were employed, according to one source in the 1890s. Cassell's noted about the same time that Crewe 'consists almost entirely of the artisans and officials in the company's service.' Christ Church was built by the railway in 1845, St Paul's, in 1869. St Barnabas's, 1885 and the Roman Catholic St Mary's five years after that. *Territorials:* Cheshire Yeomanry, 3rd Welsh Brigade RFA, Cheshire Railway Battalion and 7th Cheshire Regiment.

Crewkerne South Somerset market town on the River Parret to the south-west of Yeovil. Served by the London & South Western Railway, Crewkerne residents were chiefly employed in the manufacture of webbing, horsehair seating and sails for the Royal Navy. Here is St Bartholomew's Church. *Territorials:* West Somerset Yeomanry and 5th Somerset Light Infantry.

Criccieth Carnarvonshire town on Cardigan Bay, to the south-west of Tremadoc, served by the Cambrian Railway. Criccieth station was opened by the Aberystwyth & Welsh Coast Railway in September 1867. Prime Minister David Lloyd George grew up in nearby Llanystumdwy and prior to the First World War practiced as a solicitor in Criccieth. Here is St Catherine's Church. *Territorials:* 6th Royal Welsh Fusiliers.

Crich Derbyshire mining village, on the Cromford Canal to the north of Belper, where the quarrying of limestone employed many. Here is St Mary's Church. *Territorials:* 5th Sherwood Foresters.

Crickhowell Brecknockshire town situated about fourteen miles to the south-east of Brecon in the valley of the Usk. The area is mostly agricultural. Here is St Edmund's Church. *Territorials:* Brecknockshire Battalion.

Cricklewood North London district where many were employed by the Midland Railway in its locomotive works, the Phoenix Telephone Company, and aircraft manufacturer, Handley Page. *Territorials:* Haberdashers (Hampstead) School Cadet Corps.

Crieff Perthshire town on the River Earn, eighteen miles west of Perth, served by the Caledonian Railway. In one of the Caledonian Railway's posters issued in 1910, the artist provides a view of Crieff as seen from the 'new' eighteen-hole golf course. Here is Morrison's Academy which maintained one OTC infantry company. *Territorials:* 1st Scottish Horse and 6th Black Watch.

Cromarty Fishing town on the southern shore of Cromarty Firth, just under twenty miles from Inverness. *Territorials:* North Scottish RGA.

Cromer Norfolk coastal town, to the north of Norwich, served by the Great Eastern and Midland & Great Northern Joint railways. Cromer employed a number in its fishing industry, but tourism has been the main source of income to the town since Victorian times and the coming of the railway. Here is St Peter and St Paul's Church. *Territorials:* Norfolk Yeomanry and 5th Norfolk Regiment.

Cromford Derbyshire market town on the Cromford Canal, served by the Midland Railway where, with help from the River Derwent, the first cotton mill was opened by Sir Richard Arkwright in 1771. John Smedley's clothing factory also employing many from the town. The Arkwright family are remembered in St Mary's Church, founded by Sir Richard in 1792. *Territorials:* 6th Sherwood Foresters.

Crook Durham mining village six miles from Bishop Auckland. Crook's first station was opened by the Bishop Auckland & Weardale Railway Company in November 1843. Here is St Catherine's Church. *Territorials:* 6th Durham Light Infantry.

Crosby Lancashire town, at the mouth of the River Mersey to the north-west of Liverpool, its station opened by the Liverpool, Crosby & Southport Railway Company in July 1848. Both in Liverpool Road, St Luke's Church was built 1853–54, the Roman Catholic St Peter and St Paul's, 1892–94. *Territorials:* 7th King's Liverpool Regiment.

Crowborough Sussex town, seven miles to the south-west of Tunbridge Wells, served by the London, Brighton & South Coast Railway. Those leaving the station ('Crowborough and Jarvis Brook') facing a weary climb of almost two miles to the town centre and All Saints Church of 1744. *Territorials:* 5th Royal Sussex Regiment.

Crowthorne Berkshire village to the south-east of Wokingham. The Roman Road called Duke's Drive took villagers to the nearest railway station which was one mile off at Wellington College. Here is St John's Church, red-brick and built in 1873, and the Broadmoor Asylum. *Territorials:* 4th Hampshire Regiment.

Croy Hamlet in both Inverness-shire and Nairnshire, ten miles to the north-east of Inverness. *Territorials:* 4th Cameron Highlanders.

Croyde North Devon coastal village to the north-west of Barnstable. Built in 1874 was St Mary's Church. *Territorials:* 6th Devonshire Regiment.

Croydon Surrey market town on the River Wandle, ten miles south of London, served by the London, Brighton & South Coast and South Eastern & Chatham railways. The Croydon Tramways Company began operations from its Thornton Heath Pond depot in October 1879. Noted among the town's main industries were breweries, shoe factories, a cloth factory and bell foundry. Here, and almost destroyed by fire in 1867, is St John's Church (the guides note some eleven other churches in the town) and Whitgift Grammar School which maintained an OTC contingent of two infantry companies. *Territorials:* 4th Queen's Royal West Surrey Regiment and South Eastern Mounted Brigade Transport and Supply Column.

Crumlin Monmouthshire town five miles to the south-west of Pontypool in the Ebbw Valley. Towering more than 200 ft above Crumlin was the steel viaduct built for the Taff Vale extension of the Newport, Abergavenny & Herefordshire Railway. Here too was the terminus of the Crumlin Arm of the Monmouthshire Canal. Coal was important to Crumlin, the Navigation Colliery beginning in 1907. *Territorials:* 2nd Monmouthshire Regiment.

Crystal Palace Area in Sydenham, Kent seven miles south of London Bridge. The cast-iron and glass Crystal Palace was erected in London's Hyde Park in 1851 to house the Great Exhibition. The building was then moved to Sydenham Hill in 1854 and with it came the London, Brighton & South Coast Railway. *Territorials:* 4th Queen's Royal West Surrey Regiment.

Cuckfield Sussex market town, two miles to the west of Hayward's Heath, on the Southern Forest Ridge. Here at Cuckfield Park, one of an avenue of limes leading up to the house is said to shed a bough whenever any member of the family (the Bowyers and later the Sergisons) was about to die. Here is Holy Trinity Church where there are memorials to the Neville family. *Territorials:* 4th Royal Sussex Regiment.

Culbokie East Ross and Cromarty village on the Cromarty Firth to the north-east of Conon Bridge. *Territorials:* 4th Seaforth Highlanders.

Culham South Oxfordshire village, situated on a bend of the Thames to the south-east of Abingdon, served by the Great Western Railway. Here is St Paul's Church, Victorian save for its tower which underwent restoration in 1710. *Territorials:* 4th Oxfordshire and Buckinghamshire Light Infantry.

Cullen Banffshire coastal and fishing town on Cullen Bay and served by the Great North of Scotland Railway which arrived in 1886. *Territorials:* 2nd Scottish Horse, 1st Highland Brigade RFA and 6th Gordon Highlanders.

Cullipool Village on Luing Island, West Argyllshire, twelve miles south-west of Oban. *Territorials:* 8th Argyll and Sutherland Highlanders.

Cullompton Devonshire market town on the River Culm, twelve miles from Exeter, its station being opened by the Bristol & Exeter Railway in June 1841. Several paper and flour mills gave employment. A landmark in the area is the 100 ft sandstone tower of St Andrew's Church. One who made much from the wool trade here was John Lane, his 1526 aisle on the south side of the church having angel corbels holding the tools of his trade. *Territorials:* Royal 1st Devon Yeomanry, 4th and 7th Devonshire Regiment.

Culross Fifeshire seaport on the Firth of Forth. *Territorials:* Highland RGA

Culverthorpe Lincolnshire hamlet near Sleaford. *Territorials:* Lincoln and Leicester Infantry Brigade.

Cumbernauld Village on the Forth and Clyde Canal, to the north-east of Glasgow, served by the Caledonian Railway which arrived in 1848. Employment was mostly in the production of coal, limestone and iron. *Territorials:* 9th Argyll and Sutherland Highlanders.

Cuminestown Aberdeenshire village six miles to the east of Turriff. *Territorials:* 5th Gordon Highlanders.

Cumnock Ayrshire market town, seventeen miles to the east of Ayr, served by the Glasgow & South Western Railway which arrived in 1872. Employment was in coal and iron. *Territorials:* Ayrshire Yeomanry and 5th Royal Scots Fusiliers.

Cupar Fifeshire market town on the River Eden, to the west of St Andrews, served by the North British Railway which arrived in 1847. Cupar provided employment in brewing and the manufacture of linen, flax, leather and cloth. Part of the St Andrews University Press was located in the town. *Territorials:* Fife and Forfar Yeomanry and 7th Black Watch.

Cushnie Locality in Aberdeenshire to the south-west of Alford. *Territorials:* 6th Gordon Highlanders.

Cwm Monmouthshire town, three miles from Ebbw Vale, served by the Great Western Railway. Local collieries gave employment to most in the area. Here is St Paul's Church. *Territorials:* 3rd Monmouthshire Regiment and 1st Welsh Field Ambulance.

Dagenham Essex town, five miles to the east of Barking, served by the London, Tilbury & Southend Railway which opened its station in May 1885. The station at the busy Dagenham Docks was opened in July 1908. Here is St Peter and St Paul's Church. *Territorials:* 4th Essex Regiment.

Dalbeattie South Kirkcudbrightshire town, five miles to the east of Castle Douglas, served by the Glasgow & South Western Railway. Several large granite quarries employed many from the area. *Territorials:* 5th King's Own Scottish Borderers.

Daliburgh Village three miles inland on South Uist, Inverness-shire. *Territorials:* 1st Lovat's Scouts.

Dalkeith Just under seven miles from Edinburgh, Dalkeith employed many in the production of iron, brushes and carpets. The town was served by the North British Railway. *Territorials:* Lothians and Border Horse and 8th Royal Scots.

Dallas Elginshire village on the River Lossie, to the south-east of Forres, with extensive grouse moors. *Territorials:* 2nd Scottish Horse.

Dallington Sussex village, six miles to the north-west of Battle and just over five miles from the railway at Heathfield. Dallington sits high on a hill, the (rare in Sussex) short reassessed stone spire of St Giles's Church having a view of the sea. *Territorials:* 5th Royal Sussex Regiment.

Dalmally Argyllshire village on the River Orchy close to the north-east head of Loch Awe and to the east of Oban. Dalmally was served by the Caledonian Railway. *Territorials:* 8th Argyll and Sutherland Highlanders.

Dalmellington Ayrshire village, to the south-east of Ayr and served by the Glasgow & South Western Railway, where most were employed in local collieries and ironworks. *Territorials:* 5th Royal Scots Fusiliers.

Dalmeny Linlithgowshire village on the Firth of Forth to the north-west of Edinburgh. Residents of Dalmeny would have seen, or even worked on, the construction of the Forth Bridge. The North British Railway had arrived in 1866, the service being transferred to the Forth Bridge Company upon the opening of the bridge in 1890. *Territorials:* 10th Royal Scots.

Dalry On the River Garnock, Dalry lies just under eighteen miles north-north-west of Ayr and was served by the Glasgow & South Western Railway. The manufacture of woollens and worsteds are noted as being the town's main industries. *Territorials:* 4th Royal Scots Fusiliers.

Dalton-in-Furness Lancashire market town served by the Furness Railway, where iron, malting and brewing were the main sources of employment. Dalton station was opened in August 1846. Here is St Mary's Church. *Territorials:* 4th King's Own Royal Lancaster Regiment.

Dalwhinnie Inverness-shire village, one mile from the north-east head of Loch Ericht, served by the Highland Railway. Dalwhinnie station was opened by the Inverness & Perth Junction Railway in September 1863. *Territorials:* 4th Cameron Highlanders.

Damerham Hampshire village close to the border with Wiltshire and Dorsetshire and four miles from Cranborne. Here is St George's Church. *Territorials:* 7th Hampshire Regiment.

Danbury Essex village four miles to the south-east of Chelmsford. Here is the church of St John the Baptist which stands on the site of a Danish camp and has registers dating from 1673. *Territorials:* 5th Essex Regiment.

Darlaston Staffordshire town on the Bentley Canal (part of the Birmingham Navigation Canal) where the principal items of manufacture were bolts, nuts, screws, gunlocks, railway ironworks, bridges and girders. Close to Wednesbury, Darlaston was situated within the South Staffordshire Coalfields and was served by the London & North Western Railway. Here is St Lawrence's Church. *Territorials:* 6th South Staffordshire Regiment.

Darlington The North Eastern Railway was Darlington's major employer – locomotives being made in the town from the very beginning of railway history. Planned here, and brought to fulfilment, was Edward Pearse and George Stephenson's Stockton and Darlington Railway which opened for public traffic in 1825. Unveiled in the grounds of St Cuthbert's Church on 5 August 1905 was the Leeds Slate and Granite Company's memorial to those from Darlington that had volunteered for service in South Africa 1899–1902. St Cuthbert's Church stands on the west bank of the River Skerne. *Territorials:* Northumberland Yeomanry, 5th Durham Light Infantry and 2nd Northumbrian Field Ambulance.

Darnconnar Ayrshire mining village just over two miles from Auchinleck. *Territorials:* 5th Royal Scots Fusiliers.

Dartford Market town on the River Darent in Kent, seventeen miles from London and served by the South Eastern & Chatham Railway. The chief industries of Dartford were the manufacture of steam engines – Richard Trevethick the engineer is buried at Holy Trinity Church in the centre of town – and the making of gunpowder. The first English paper mill was established at Dartford. Here, on the marches between Dartford and the Thames estuary, were the Long Reach, Orchard and Joyce Green isolation hospitals. Dartford Grammar School had an OTC contingent. *Territorials:* West Kent Yeomanry, 5th Royal West Kent Regiment and 4th London Field Ambulance.

Dartmouth Devonshire seaport and market town served by the Great Western Railway. Here is the Royal Naval Cadet Training College and St Saviour's Church where tragedies at sea, and those that were involved, are remembered among its memorials. Founded by Edward I in 1286, the church is close enough to the harbour for ships to tie-up to the churchyard wall. Here too is the church of St Petrox, used during the Civil War as a magazine and store by the Royalists. *Territorials:* Royal 1st Devon Yeomanry, 4th Wessex Brigade RFA, 7th Devonshire Regiment and Dartmouth Cadet Company.

Darvel Ayrshire town, nine miles east of Kilmarnock on the River Irvine, where the Glasgow and South Western Railway arrived in June 1896. The manufacture of muslins, lace and carpets are noted as the main sources of employment. *Territorials:* 4th Royal Scots Fusiliers.

Darwen Lancashire town, two miles from Blackburn, served by the London & North Western Railway. Darwen's chief industries are noted as stone quarrying, cotton spinning and the manufacture of artificial manure. Here, on a hillside above the station, is St James's Church. *Territorials:* 4th East Lancashire Regiment.

Datchet Buckinghamshire village on the River Thames, two miles from Windsor, served by the London & South Western Railway which arrived in 1849. Here is St Mary's Church. *Territorials:* Buckinghamshire Battalion.

Daventry The town, twelve miles north-west of Northampton, gave employment to many in its several shoe and boot factories. Daventry Station, on the old London & North Western Railway, was opened in March 1888. There are nice Georgian streets here and, built by a Warwick designer, Holy Cross Church. *Territorials:* Northamptonshire Yeomanry and 4th Northamptonshire Regiment.

Davidston Inverness-shire locality just over three miles from Cromarty. *Territorials:* North Scottish RGA.

Dawlish Devon seaside town served by the Great Western Railway, three miles north-east of Teignmouth. Dawlish station was opened by the South Devon Railway in May 1846. Here, at the bottom of Barton Road, is St Gregory's Church. *Territorials:* Royal 1st Devon Yeomanry and 5th Devonshire Regiment.

Daybrook Nottinghamshire village, three miles from Nottingham, served by the Great Northern Railway which arrived in 1876. Here is St Paul's Church. *Territorials:* 8th Sherwood Foresters.

Deal Seaport and fishing town in Kent with a station on the South Eastern & Chatham Railway between Dover and Ramsgate. There is a memorial to Nelson at St George's Church, and here too in the town is the medieval St Leonard's. *Territorials:* Royal East Kent Yeomanry, 3rd Home Counties Brigade RFA and Depot Royal Marine Cadet Corps.

Dearham Cumberland village served by the Maryport & Carlisle Railway, five miles to the north-west of Cockermouth. The area had extensive coal mines, brick and title works. The church here is undedicated. *Territorials:* 5th Border Regiment.

Deddington Oxfordshire market town on the River Cherwell and close to the Oxford Canal, sixteen miles north of Oxford. Deddington's nearest station was two miles to the east at Aynho, its church dedicated to St Peter and St Paul. *Territorials:* Oxfordshire Yeomanry.

Dedham Essex village on the River Stour, just over three miles to the north-west of Manningtree, once an important centre for the woollen trade. Often painted by Constable, St Mary's Church by the Sun Inn has a font cover made of timber from HMS *Royal George* which sank in 1782 with the loss of 800 lives. The church registers date from 1560. *Territorials:* 5th Essex Regiment.

Deerness Locality on mainland Orkney Islands nine miles to the south-east of Kirkwall. *Territorials:* Orkney RGA.

Delabole Cornwall village on the London & South Western Railway, two miles from Camelford, where slate quarries provided employment for many. Here is St John's Church, built c1800. *Territorials:* 5th Duke of Cornwall's Light Infantry.

Denbigh County and market town on the London & North Western Railway where many were employed in the manufacture of boots and shoes. There were also quarries for slate and lime. Of churches, one late Victorian guide notes the ancient parish church of S Marcellus as being in ruins; St Hilary's, an old garrison chapel attended by men only, and St Mary's which opened in 1874. *Territorials:* Welsh Border Mounted Brigade, Denbighshire Yeomanry and 4th Royal Welsh Fusiliers.

Denny Served by the Caledonian Railway, Denny is on the River Carron to the south of Stirling, its collieries, ironworks, paper mills and chemical works once employing many from the town. The railway arrived in Denny in 1858. *Territorials:* 7th Argyll and Sutherland Highlanders.

Derby County and market town on the River Derwent, its main industries being silk mills, pottery, and the workshops and locomotive works of the Midland Railway which employed more than 10,000. Here are All Saints; St Alkmund, which dates from 1846; St Andrew's, 1866, and St Luke's, which was finished in 1871. Derby School had an OTC contingent. *Territorials:* Derbyshire Yeomanry, 4th North Midland Brigade RFA, 5th Sherwood Foresters, 1st North Midland Field Ambulance, North Midland Division School of Instruction and Derby Post Office Cadet Corps.

Dersingham Norfolk village, to the north-east of King's Lynn, served by the Great Eastern Railway. Dersingham station was opened by the Lynn & Hunstanton Railway in October 1862. Here is St Nicholas's Church. *Territorials:* Norfolk Yeomanry and 5th Norfolk Regiment.

Desborough Northamptonshire town, five miles south-east of Market Harborough overlooking the upper part of the Isle Valley, served by the Midland Railway which arrived in 1857. Local trade was in the manufacture of boots and shoes. Here is St Giles's Church. *Territorials:* 4th Northamptonshire Regiment.

Devises North Wiltshire market town on the Kennet and Avon Canal and served by the Great Western Railway. At Devises, agricultural steam engines were manufactured, the corn market there being well known all over the West of England. The Wadworth Brewery of 1885 can still be seen in Market Place. In *Crime Statistics of Fisherton Goal*, there is an account of the trail and subsequent execution at Devises in 1849 of Rebecca Smith. A mass murderer who killed seven of here young children by smearing poison on her nipples. Here are the medieval churches of St John's and St Mary's, both extensively damaged during the Civil War – one side striping the lead from the roofs to make bullets, the other bombarding the buildings with cannonballs. St Peter's, in Bath Road, was completed in 1867. *Territorials:* Wiltshire Yeomanry, 4th Wiltshire Regiment and 1st South Western Mounted Brigade Field Ambulance.

Devonport Two miles from Plymouth, Devonport is the home of the Royal Dockyard which gives employment to many from the town. Devonport was served by both the Great Western and London & South Western railways. *Territorials:* Devonshire RGA and 5th Devonshire Regiment.

Dewsbury West Yorkshire market town on the River Calder, to the south of Leeds, served by both the Great Northern and London & North Western railways. The Woollen industry was important to Dewsbury, blankets, carpets, rugs, jerseys and serges being its speciality. On the hillside to the west of the town lies the seventy-acre Crow Nest Park, opened in 1892 and the site after 1918 of the war memorial. Here is All Saints Church. *Territorials:* Yorkshire Dragoons and 4th King's Own Yorkshire Light Infantry.

Didcot Berkshire town on the Great Western Railway, to the south of Abingdon, liked, and disliked, by visitors – the old 'villagey' Didcot, with its All Saints Church, is preferred to the 'uninteresting' St Peter's Church (finished in 1898) and houses south of the railway's 'grimy' station at 'New Town', notes one. *Territorials:* Berkshire Yeomanry.

Dilton March Wiltshire village two miles from Westbury. Here is Holy Trinity Church. *Territorials:* 4th Wiltshire Regiment.

Dingwall Ross and Cromarty market town and Highland Railway junction on the Cromarty Firth to the north-west of Inverness. Dingwall station was opened by the Inverness & Ross-shire Railway in June 1862. *Territorials:* 4th Highland Brigade RGA and 4th Seaforth Highlanders.

Dinton South Wiltshire village on the River Nadder, eight miles from Salisbury, served by the London & South Western Railway. Dinton station was opened by the Salisbury & Yeovil Railway in May 1859. Here is St Mary's Church. *Territorials:* 1st South Western Mounted Brigade Transport and Supply Column.

Disley Cheshire village, served by the London & North Western Railway, to the south of Stockport and close to the border with Derbyshire. The Peak Forest Canal passes along the edge of the village. Here is St Mary's Church. *Territorials:* 6th Sherwood Foresters.

Diss South Norfolk market town on the River Waveney, just under twenty miles south-west of Norwich and served by the Great Eastern Railway. At Diss, noted the guides, there was a brewery and a factory making matting. Here is St Mary's Church. *Territorials:* Norfolk Yeomanry and 4th Norfolk Regiment.

Ditchingham South Norfolk village on the River Waveney to the north of Bungay and served by the Great Eastern Railway which arrived in 1863. Here is St Mary's Church. *Territorials:* 6th Norfolk Regiment.

Doddington North Cambridgeshire village four miles south of March. Here is St Mary's Church which has memorials to the Peyton, Richards and Harding families. *Territorials:* Cambridgeshire Regiment.

Dolfor Montgomeryshire village two miles south-west of Newtown. Here is St Paul's Church. *Territorials:* Montgomeryshire Yeomanry.

Dolgelly Merionethshire market town, on the north side of the Calder Idris at the confluence of the Rivers Aran and Wnion, served by the Cambrian Railway. Dolgelly, noted the guides, was long famed for its manufacture of course woollens, especially the kind called 'Welsh webs'. Here is St Mary's Church. *Territorials:* 7th Royal Welsh Fusiliers.

Dollar Clackmannanshire village at the foot of the Ochil Hills on the River Devon, six miles to the north-east of Alloa, served by the North British Railway. Dollar station was opened by the Devon Valley Railway Company in May 1869. Here is the Dollar Institution, which had an OTC contingent. *Territorials:* 7th Argyll and Sutherland Highlanders.

Doncaster West Yorkshire market town and important railway junction on the River Don. The Great Northern Railway Company, a major employer, had extensive carriage and locomotive works in the town. Doncaster Corporation Tramways, with their maroon and cream trams, opened for business in June 1902. The old parish church of St George was completely destroyed by fire in 1853, but replaced in the following year. *Territorials:* Yorkshire Dragoons and 5th King's Own Yorkshire Light Infantry.

Donhead There is Donhead St Andrew and Donhead St Mary, both Wiltshire villages on the River Nadder and within four miles of Salisbury. *Territorials:* 1st South Western Mounted Brigade Transport and Supply Column.

Dorchester County and market town served by both the Great Western and London & South Western railways. The Eldridge Pope Brewery in Weymouth Avenue, which dates from 1880, gave employment to many from the town. Here in the centre of town is St Peter's Church. Dorchester Grammar School had an OTC contingent, the barracks in Bridport Road being built 1876–77. *Territorials:* Dorsetshire Yeomanry, 3rd Wessex Brigade RFA, 9th Hampshire Regiment and 4th Dorsetshire Regiment.

Dores Village on east side of Loch Ness seven miles to the south-west of Inverness. *Territorials:* 1st Lovat's Scouts.

Dorking Surrey market town, to the east of Guildford, served by both the London, Brighton & South Coast and South Eastern & Chatham railways. Here is St Martin's Church. *Territorials:* 5th Queen's Royal West Surrey Regiment.

Dornie Fishing village at the mouth of Loch Long, Ross and Cromarty, seven miles to the south of Strome Ferry. *Territorials:* 4th Highland Brigade RGA.

Dornoch Seaport and county town of Sutherlandshire on the Dornoch Firth fourteen miles to the east of Bonar Bridge. The town's church has long been the burial place of the Sutherland family. *Territorials:* 2nd Lovat's Scouts and 5th Seaforth Highlanders.

Douglas South Lanarkshire village on Douglas Water, just under eleven miles south-west of Lanark, served by the Caledonian Railway which arrived in 1864. The Kirk of St Bride, founded in the twelfth century, for many years the burial place of the Douglas family. *Territorials:* Lanarkshire Yeomanry and 8th Highland Light Infantry.

Douglas Water Small Lanarkshire mining village, five miles from Douglas, built early in the twentieth century close to the railway by the Coltness Iron Company. The Caledonian Railway reached the small village of Ponfeigh in 1864, historical references giving Ponfeigh and Douglas Water as one in the same. *Territorials:* Lanarkshire Yeomanry.

Doune South Perthshire village on the River Teith served by the Caledonian Railway. Pride of place among the possessions of pistol and sporran collectors would be items made at Doune. Doune, its castle being mentioned in Scott's *Waverley* and more recently the location of *Monty Python and the Holy Grail*, is to the north-west of Stirling. *Territorials:* 6th Black Watch.

Dover Kent seaport and market town served by the South Eastern & Chatham Railway. Opened in September 1897, with its green and ivory vehicles, was the Dover Corporation Tramways. At Dover the Town Hall was opened in 1883 and the new Promenade Pier on Whitson Monday ten years after that. This was also the year when the Volunteers were among those that provided the guard of honour on the occasion of the Prince of Wales laying the foundation stone of the new Commercial Harbour. Here is St Mary's Church, which adjoins an ancient Roman lighthouse, and Dover College which maintained an OTC contingent. *Territorials:* Royal East Kent Yeomanry, 3rd Home Counties Brigade RFA, Kent RGA, Cinque Ports Fortress Engineers, 4th Buffs East Kent Regiment and Kent Cyclist Battalion.

Dovercourt East Essex town at the mouth of the River Stour, just to the south of Harwich, served by the Great Eastern Railway. Some 300 British and German troops returning from the ill-fated Walcheren campaign of 1809–10 suffering from fever, were buried at Dovercourt's All Saints Church. A lichgate was dedicated to their memory in September 1899. *Territorials:* Essex and Suffolk RGA.

Dowlais Close to Merthyr Tydfil in Glamorgan, the Dowlais Iron Company is said to have employed close to 10,000 in its production of iron, tin bars, rails and other articles of steel. Here, on Union Street and dating from 1827, is St John's Church. *Territorials:* 5th Welsh Regiment.

Downham Market West Norfolk market town on the River Ouse, eleven miles south of King's Lynn, served by the Great Eastern Railway. Here is St Edmund's Church. *Territorials:* Norfolk Yeomanry, 5th Norfolk Regiment and East Anglian Divisional Transport and Supply Column.

Drax West Yorkshire village on the River Ouse served by the Hull & Barnsley Railway which arrived in 1885. Here is St Peter and St Paul's Church. *Territorials:* Drax Grammar School Cadet Company.

Driffield East Yorkshire market town, twenty miles from Hull, served by the North Eastern Railway. Artificial manures and linseed cakes, notes the guides, were manufactured at Driffield on a large scale. Here is All Saints Church. *Territorials:* East Riding Yeomanry, 5th East Yorkshire Regiment and 5th Yorkshire Regiment.

Droitwich Worcestershire market town on the River Salwarpe, seven miles from Worcester, served by the Great Western Railway. Popular in the town for centuries were the salt springs. The old brine baths just to the north of Queen Street, and John Corbett's St Andrew's Brine Baths in Victoria Street easing the aches and pains, no doubt, of many. Here is St Andrew's Church; St Peter's, with its memorials to the Nash family, and on Ombersley Street, St Nicholas's. *Territorials:* Worcestershire Yeomanry and 8th Worcestershire Regiment.

Drumlemble Argyllshire mining community, four miles west of Campbeltown, served by the Campbeltown & Machrihanish Light Railway which began operating in 1906. *Territorials:* 8th Argyll and Sutherland Highlanders.

Drumnadrochit Inverness-shire village on the Caledonian Canal fourteen miles to the south-west of Inverness. *Territorials:* 4th Cameron Highlanders.

Dudley Worcestershire market town on the Dudley Canal, to the north-west of Birmingham, served by the Great Western and London & North Western railways. There were numerous collieries and ironworks in the Dudley area. Chains, nails and bicycles were among the many products linked with the town. A soldier, his bayonet fixed, defends a wounded bugler at his feet on Dudley's South African War memorial which was unveiled in September 1904. Here is the parish church of St Thomas. *Territorials:* Worcestershire Yeomanry, 7th Worcestershire Regiment and 2nd Cadet Battalion Worcestershire Regiment.

Duffield Derbyshire market town on the River Derwent, four miles from Derby, served by the Midland Railway. Here is St Alkmund's Church where there is a monument to Anthony Bradshaw (1600), his two wives and twenty children. *Territorials:* Derbyshire Yeomanry.

Dufftown Banffshire village served by the Great North of Scotland Railway and founded in 1817 by James Duff, 4th Earl of Fife. Here the chief industry was whisky – Glenfiddich Distillery, owned by the Grant family, opened in 1887. *Territorials:* 2nd Scottish Horse and 6th Gordon Highlanders.

Dulverton West Somerset market town on the River Barle, to the west of Taunton, served by the Great Western Railway. Here is All Saints Church. *Territorials:* West Somerset Yeomanry and 4th Devonshire Regiment.

Dumbarton County town and seaport on the Clyde and Leven, sixteen miles north-west of Glasgow, served by the North British and Caledonian Railways. Dumbarton was one of the chief shipbuilding centres – William Denny and Brothers, who built the *Cutty Sark*, probably the most famous yard. *Territorials:* Clyde RGA and 9th Argyll and Sutherland Highlanders.

Dumfries County and market town on the River Nith, served by the Glasgow & South Western and Caledonian railways. Tweeds, hosiery, clogs, baskets, iron implements, leather and carriages were all manufactured in the area. *Territorials:* Lanarkshire Yeomanry and 5th King's Own Scottish Borderers.

Dunbar Haddingtonshire seaport and market town to the east of Edinburgh, served by the North British Railway, where fishing, boatbuilding and the production of whiskey, malt, ropes and agricultural implements employed many. *Territorials:* Lothians and Border Horse and 8th Royal Scots.

Dunbeath Caithness-shire fishing village on the River Dunbeath twenty miles to the south-west of Wick. *Territorials:* 2nd Lovat's Scouts.

Dunblane South Perthshire market town on Allan Water five miles north of Stirling. Served by the Caledonian and North British railways, Dunblane's woollen mills provided employment for many. *Territorials:* 1st Scottish Horse and 6th Black Watch.

Dundee As a thriving seaport, the City of Dundee employed many in its dockyards and numerous industries – flax, carpets, sails, rope and, of course, marmalade, were all made locally. The newspaper publishers D C Thomson, who would later give us the *Dandy* and *Beano*, began in Dundee in 1905. Winston Churchill was member of parliament for Dundee 1908–22. There were a number of railway companies serving Dundee, the North British coming in from the south via the Tay Bridge. *Territorials:* Black Watch Infantry Brigade, Fife and Forfar Yeomanry, 2nd Highland Brigade RFA, City of Dundee Fortress Engineers, 4th, 5th Black Watch, Highland Divisional Transport and Supply Column and 3rd Highland Field Ambulance.

Dundonnell Ross and Cromarty village on the south side of Loch Broom to the south of Ullapool. *Territorials:* 2nd Lovat's Scouts.

Dunfermline Fifeshire town on the North British Railway, sixteen miles north-west of Edinburgh. The manufacture of table linen, brass utensils, machinery, soap, terracotta articles and rope were among the Dunfermline's main sources of employment. There were also bleach works, corn mills and breweries in the area. The bright green and cream trams of the Dunfermline & District Tramways Company were first seen on the streets in November 1909. Born here was Andrew Carnegie who, having emigrated to America and made his fortune, afterwards did much to benefit Dunfermline. Dunfermline Abbey, the last resting place of several King's and Queen's of Scotland, was began around 800 AD. *Territorials:* Fife and Forfar Yeomanry, Highland RGA, 7th Black Watch and Highland Cyclist Battalion.

Dunkeld Perthshire market town where the choir of the old cathedral is used as the parish church and has a memorial to those of the Black Watch that lost their lives in the Crimea and Indian Mutiny. The Highland Railway served the town, which is connected to Birnam across the River Tay by a Telford bridge of 1809. Here is Dunkeld Cathedral, fortunately a survivor from the Jacobite burning of the town. *Territorials:* 1st Scottish Horse.

Dunmow Essex market town (called Great Dunmow) on the River Chelmer to the north-west of Chelmsford and served by the Great Eastern Railway. Here is St Mary's Church. *Territorials:* Essex Yeomanry, 5th and 8th Essex Regiment.

Dunnet North Caithness-shire coastal village on Pentland Firth nine miles to the north-east of Thurso. Dunnet Head is the most northerly point on the Scottish mainland. *Territorials:* 5th Seaforth Highlanders.

Dunning Perthshire village ten miles south-west of Perth served by the Caledonian Railway. Dunning station was opened by the Scottish Central Railway Company in May 1848. *Territorials:* 1st Scottish Horse and 6th Black Watch.

Dunnington East Yorkshire village, four miles east of York, served by the Derwent Valley Light Railway which was opened in 1913. Dunnington was well known for its manufacture of farm implements. Here is St Nicholas's Church. *Territorials:* East Riding Yeomanry.

Dunoon Argyllshire town on the west shore of the Firth of Clyde twenty-seven miles from Glasgow. The guides note that Dunoon was a popular residence for a number of Glasgow merchants. The railways came nowhere near the town. Access by road was difficult, so visitors to Dunoon usually came by sea. *Territorials:* Clyde RGA, 8th Argyll and Sutherland Highlanders and Dunoon Grammar School Cadet Corps.

Duns Berwickshire market town, to the west of Berwick-upon-Tweed, served by the North British Railway which arrived in 1849. *Territorials:* Lothians and Border Horse and 4th King's Own Scottish Borderers.

Dunsfold Surrey village to the south-east of Godalming where, notes the guides, bricks and titles were made. Here, just on a half-mile from the village, is the church of St Mary and All Saints, the most beautiful, according to William Morris, 'country church in all England.' *Territorials:* 5th Queen's Royal West Surrey Regiment.

Dunstable Bedfordshire market town, five miles east of Luton, served by the Great Northern and London & North Western railways. Dunstable's large printing works employed a good number from the town, which also made straw hats. St Peter's Church has a Norman nave of 1150 and in June 1644 was subject to a raid by Royalists who disrupted the service and took pot-shots at the minister. They missed him, but not so lucky was the landlord of the Red Lion in the High Street who was killed. *Territorials:* Bedfordshire Yeomanry, 5th Bedfordshire Regiment, Eastern Mounted Brigade Field Ambulance and Dunstable Grammar School Cadet Corps.

Duntulm Hamlet on Loch Scour, Isle of Skye, Inverness-shire. *Territorials:* 1st Lovat's Scouts.

Dunvegan Coastal village on the Isle of Skye, Inverness-shire. *Territorials:* 1st Lovat's Scouts and 4th Cameron Highlanders.

Dupplin Locality, and site of the 1332 battle, just over five miles from Perth. *Territorials:* 1st Scottish Horse.

Durham Cathedral and university city served by the North Eastern Railway. The Durham coalfields were noted as the most important in England, the area also providing employment in shipbuilding, ironworks and the production of carpet, chemicals, glass, earthenware and paper. *Territorials:* Durham Light Infantry Brigade, 3rd Northumbrian Brigade RFA and 8th Durham Light Infantry.

Duror Argyllshire village, five miles south-west of Ballachulish, served by the Caledonian Railway. Duror station was opened by the Calendar & Oban Railway Company in August 1903. *Territorials:* 8th Argyll and Sutherland Highlanders.

Durris North Kincardineshire village on the River Dee to the south-west of Aberdeen. *Territorials:* 7th Gordon Highlanders.

Dursley Gloucestershire market town on the River Cam, fifteen miles to the south-west of Gloucester, served by the Midland Railway. At Dursley, there were rope works, breweries and a tannery. Here is the church of St James, much altered and restored in 1867. *Territorials:* 5th Gloucestershire Regiment.

Dyce Aberdeenshire village on the River Don, six miles to the north-west of Aberdeen, served by the Great North of Scotland Railway which arrived in 1854. Many here were involved in the quarrying of granite. *Territorials:* 6th Gordon Highlanders.

Ealing West London suburb, its first station being opened by the Great Western Railway in December 1838. Just north of South Ealing station is St Mary's Church where the registers date back to 1582. *Territorials:* 8th Middlesex Regiment, Ealing County School Cadet Company and Ealing Cadet Company.

Eardisley Herefordshire village, fourteen miles north-west of Hereford, served by the Great Western and Hereford, Hay & Brecon railways. Here is the church of St Mary Magdalene. *Territorials:* Herefordshire Regiment.

Earls Colne Essex village, three miles south-east of Halstead, served by the Colne Valley & Halstead Railway. A silk-winding factory was opened in 1883, the large Hunt engineering works also employing a good number. Here is St Andrew's Church which has a memorial to Richard Harlakenden and his four wives. The registers date from 1559. *Territorials:* 5th Essex Regiment.

Earlston Berwickshire market town on Leader Water, ten miles south-west of Greenlaw, served by the North British Railway. Earlston station was opened by the Berwickshire Railway Company in November 1863. *Territorials:* Lothians and Border Horse and 4th King's Own Scottish Borderers.

Easdale West Argyllshire village, partly on Easdale and Seil Islands. *Territorials:* 2nd Scottish Horse and 8th Argyll and Sutherland Highlanders.

Easingwold North Yorkshire market town, ten miles to the south-east of Thirst, reached by the Easingwold Railway in July 1891. Here is the church of St John the Baptist and All Saints. *Territorials:* Yorkshire Hussars and 4th Yorkshire Regiment.

East Boldre South Hampshire village in the New Forest to the north-east of Lymington. One reference notes of East Boldre that most were employed on the nearby Beaulieu estate. Here is St Paul's Church which was built in 1839. *Territorials:* 7th Hampshire Regiment.

East Bridge Suffolk hamlet just over four miles north-east of Saxmundham. Here is the Ells Foot Inn, once a favourite of local smugglers, which dates from 1533. *Territorials:* 4th Suffolk Regiment.

East Cowes The Rive Medina divides the town of Cowes on the north coast of the Isle of Wight, its station being opened by the Cowes & Newport Railway Company in June 1862. Here is St James's, a John Nash church of 1831–33. *Territorials:* Hampshire Fortress Engineers.

East Dereham At East Dereham, sixteen miles north-west of Norwich, there were iron foundries, breweries, a factory making shoes, and a coachworks. Here at St Nicholas's Church we see two towers, one added because the original was thought not to be strong enough to hold the bells. The addition also came in useful to hold French prisoners from the Napoleonic wars. One of them, not too happy about the situation, was shot while trying to escape and now lies buried in the churchyard. *Territorials:* Norfolk Yeomanry, 5th Norfolk Regiment and 2nd East Anglian Field Ambulance.

East Grinstead Sussex market town, fourteen miles north-east of Horsham, served by the London, Brighton & South Coast Railway. Here, noted the guides, there was breweries, and works producing bricks and titles. The town sits high on a hill with fine views to the south of Forest Ridge. St Swithun's Church in the High Street dates from 1789, but St Mary's in Windmill Street is a little younger having been completed in 1912. *Territorials:* 4th Royal Sussex Regiment.

East Ham East London district just over six miles from Fenchurch Street on the Midland Railway. The chocolate and cream trams of the East Ham Corporation Tramway first ran in June 1901. Here, close to the docks, is the church of St Mary Magdalene. *Territorials:* 8th Essex Regiment and East Ham Secondary Schools Cadets.

East Harling Norfolk market town, eight miles north-east of Thetford, served by the Great Eastern Railway at its Harling Road station about one mile to the north-west. Here is St Peter and St Paul's Church. *Territorials:* 4th Norfolk Regiment.

East Hoathly East Sussex village just over four miles south-east of Uckfield. Here the church displays the arms of the Pelhams (Lord Chichester's family), and E T Kemp, killed in the Indian Mutiny, has a shako and sabre monument. *Territorials:* 5th Royal Sussex Regiment.

East Hull TF Returns show this location as being three miles by road from central Hull. *Territorials:* 4th East Yorkshire Regiment.

East Knoyle Wiltshire village five miles from Shaftesbury. Born here in 1632 was Sir Christopher Wren, his father being rector of East Knoyle and St Mary's Church. *Territorials:* 1st South Western Mounted Brigade Transport and Supply Column.

East Linton Haddingtonshire village, five miles east of Haddington, served by the North British Railway which arrived in December 1864. *Territorials:* Lothians and Border Horse and 8th Royal Scots.

East Tytherley Hampshire village six miles south-west of Stockbridge. Here is St Peter's Church. *Territorials:* 4th Hampshire Regiment.

East Wemyss Fifeshire village on the Firth of Forth, five miles north-east of Kirkcaldy, served by the North British Railway at its Wemyss Castle station which was opened by the Wemyss & Buckhaven Railway Company in August 1881. *Territorials:* 2nd Highland Brigade RFA and Highland Cyclist Battalion.

Eastbourne Coastal town which grew in a short space of time to be the third largest in Sussex and one of the most popular seaside resorts in the south of England. The advance no doubt helped by the coming of the London, Brighton & South Coast Railway in 1849. Here, in Church Street, stands the ancient and quite large St Mary's; some of the more recent church additions to Eastbourne being: All Saints in Carlisle Road (1878–80); in Susan's Road, All Souls (1882); the Roman Catholic Our Lady of Ransom (1901–02) by F A Walter in Grange Road, and St Michael's in Willington Road which was finished in 1911. Eastbourne College maintained an OTC contingent. *Territorials:* Sussex Yeomanry, 2nd Home Counties Brigade RFA, Home Counties Divisional Engineers, Cinque Ports Fortress Engineers, 5th Royal Sussex Regiment, Roborough School Cadet Company and Imperial Service Cadet Corps.

Eastergate West Sussex village five miles to the east of Chichester and a mile from the railway at Barnham Junction. Here, the heavily restored St George's Church is described as small and plain, but the chancel is Saxon and part of the south wall shows Roman brick. *Territorials:* 4th Royal Sussex Regiment.

Eastleigh South Hampshire town to the south-east of Southampton served by the London & South Western Railway. The railway employed many from the town after the L&SW transferred its wagon works from London's Nine Elms in 1891, followed by the same company's locomotive works in 1909. Here is the Church of the Resurrection, a railwaymen's' church built in 1868, and in Derby Road, All Saints which was opened in 1910. *Territorials:* Hampshire Yeomanry, Hampshire RGA, Hampshire Fortress Engineers and 5th Hampshire Regiment.

Easton Suffolk village on the River Deben three miles south of Framlingham. Here is All Saints Church which has memorials to the Wingfield family. *Territorials:* 4th Suffolk Regiment.

Eastrop North Hampshire village on the Basingstoke Canal forming an eastern suburb of Basingstoke. Here is St Mary's Church. *Territorials:* Basingstoke and Eastrop Cadet Corps.

Eastwood Nottinghamshire town on the Erewash Canal, nine miles from Nottingham, where most were employed in local collieries. There was also rope and brick making. Eastwood station was opened by the Manchester & Leeds Railway Company in January 1841. Born here in 1885 was the writer D H Lawrence. Here is St Mary's Church. *Territorials:* Nottinghamshire Yeomanry (South Notts) and 8th Sherwood Foresters.

Eaton Cheshire village on the Rive Dane, close to the Macclesfield Canal, where the manufacture of lace provided much employment. Here is Christ Church. *Territorials:* Cheshire Yeomanry.

Ebberston North Yorkshire village close to the River Derwent, fourteen miles from Scarborough, served by the North Eastern Railway. Here is St Mary's Church. *Territorials:* 5th Yorkshire Regiment.

Ebbw Vale Monmouthshire town, two miles from Tredegar, served by the Great Western and London & Great Western railways. Here, most of the population were employed in local collieries, iron and steel works. High up on Briery Hill and overlooking the town is Christ Church, built by the Ebbw Vale Ironworks Company 1860–61. *Territorials:* Gloucestershire Yeomanry, 3rd Monmouthshire Regiment, 1st Welsh Field Ambulance and Ebbw Vale Territorial Cadet Company.

Ebenezer Carnarvonshire village four miles north-east of Carnarvon. *Territorials:* 6th Royal Welsh Fusiliers.

Ecclefechan Dumfrieshire village six miles by rail from Lockerby on the Caledonian Railway. Born here, and buried in the parish church, was the author Thomas Carlyle (1795–1881). *Territorials:* 5th King's Own Scottish Borderers.

Echt Aberdeenshire village in the south-east of the county, twelve miles west of Aberdeen. Echt church was built in 1804. *Territorials:* 7th Gordon Highlanders.

Eckington Derbyshire town to the south-east of Sheffield served by the Midland and Great Central Railways. On the River Rother, the town was known for its manufacture of sickles and scythes. There were also collieries in the area. Here, with its thirteenth-century tower, is St Peter and St Paul's Church. *Territorials:* Derbyshire Yeomanry and 6th Sherwood Foresters.

Edale North Derbyshire village on the River Edale nineteen miles by rail from Sheffield on the Midland Railway. Here is Holy Trinity Church which dates from around 1886. *Territorials:* 6th Sherwood Foresters.

Edderton Ross and Cromarty village on the south shore of Dornoch Firth, just over five miles by rail on the Highland Railway from Tain. *Territorials:* 2nd Lovat's Scouts and 4th Seaforth Highlanders.

Edenbridge Kent market town on the River Eden, five miles south of Westerham, served by the South Eastern & Chatham and London, Brighton & South Coast railways. Here is St Peter and St Paul's Church. *Territorials:* 4th Royal West Kent Regiment.

Edinbane Hamlet at the head of Loch Greshinish, Isle of Skye. *Territorials:* 4th Cameron Highlanders.

Edinburgh The capital of Scotland, Edinburgh lies on the south side of the Firth of Forth. In one of Francis Frith's photos of the city taken in 1897 we see Grassmarket, the scene of the Porteous Riots in 1736 and where many were once executed. We see Dodd's Beehive Hotel, which stands next-door to the possibly more downmarket Black Bull Lodgings for Travellers and Working Men. The eye then moves above the rooftops to a Victorian block of flats, lines of washing all along the balconies, and then to Edinburgh Castle itself. Opened in Edinburgh in October 1902 was the 300-roomed hotel built by the North British Railway Company. The OTC was well represented in Edinburgh: the Royal (Dick) Veterinary College, Edinburgh University, George Herlot's School, George Watson's Boys' College, the Edinburgh Academy, Merchiston Castle School and Fettes College all maintained contingents. *Territorials:* Lowland Mounted Brigade, Lothian Infantry Brigade, Lothians and Border Horse, 1st Lowland Brigade RFA, Lowland RGA, Forth RGA, Lowland Mounted Brigade Signal Troop, City of Edinburgh Fortress Engineers, 4th, 5th, 6th, 9th Royal Scots, Lowland Mounted Brigade Transport and Supply Column, Lowland Divisional Transport and Supply Column, 3rd Lowland Field Ambulance, 2nd Scottish General Hospital, 2nd Scottish General Hospital and 1st (Highland) Cadet Battalion 10th Royal Scots.

Edzell Forfarshire village on the North Esk, six miles to the north of Brechin, served by the Caledonian Railway. Edzell station was opened by the Brechin & Edzell Railway Company in June 1896. *Territorials:* Fife and Forfar Yeomanry and 5th Black Watch.

Egham West Surrey town just to the west of Stains, from which it is separated by the Thames, served by the London & South Western Railway. Opened here by Queen Victoria in 1886 was the Royal Holloway College. Here is the church of St John the Baptist. *Territorials:* 6th East Surrey Regiment.

Eglingham North Northumberland village between the rivers Alne and Breamish six miles to the north-east of Alnwick. Eglingham's church is dedicated to St Maurice. *Territorials:* Northumberland Yeomanry.

Egremont (Cheshire) Town and steamboat station on the River Mersey looking across to Liverpool. Egremont was served by the Wirral Railway's Seacombe and Egremont station. Here is St John's Church. *Territorials:* 1st New Brighton Cadet Company and 1st Egremont Cadet Company.

Egremont (Cumberland) Market town on the River Ehen five miles to the south-east of Whitehaven, its station being opened by the Whitehaven, Cleator & Egremont Railway Company in July 1857. Iron ore and limestone were quarried in the area. Here is St Mary's Church. *Territorials:* 5th Border Regiment.

Elgin County and market town, Elgin lies on the banks of the River Lossie served by the Highland and Great North of Scotland railways. Sandstone was quarried and well known throughout the world was Elgin's production of woollens, tweeds, plaiding and leather. *Territorials:* 2nd Scottish Horse and 6th Seaforth Highlanders.

Elgoll West Inverness-shire hamlet of the Isle of Skye to the north-west of Broadford. *Territorials:* 4th Cameron Highlanders.

Elland West Yorkshire town on the River Calder, four miles from Halifax, served by the London & North Western Railway. The area here was well known for its production of flagstones and fire clay goods. Here is All Saints Church. *Territorials:* 4th Duke of Wellington's Regiment.

Ellesmere Shropshire market town and important agricultural centre served by the Cambrian Railway, which ran down from Whitchurch, and the Wrexham & Ellesmere which reached the town in 1895. Here also is the Ellesmere Canal, St Mary's Church and Ellesmere College which was built 1879–83 and maintained an OTC contingent. *Territorials:* Shropshire Yeomanry and 4th King's Shropshire Light Infantry.

Ellesmere Port Cheshire town seven miles from Chester at the junction of the Ellesmere Canal with the Manchester Ship Canal. With large docks and warehouses, the town was served by the Great Western and London & North Western Joint Railway. Here is Christ Church. *Territorials:* Welsh Border Mounted Brigade Field Ambulance.

Ellon East Aberdeenshire village on the River Ythan, to the south-west of Peterhead, served by the Great North of Scotland Railway. Ellon station was opened by the Formartine & Buchan Railway Company in July 1861. *Territorials:* 2nd Scottish Horse and 5th Gordon Highlanders.

Elmley Castle Worcestershire village to the south-west of Evesham. Here in the church of St Mary the Virgin are memorials to the Savage family. *Territorials:* 8th Worcestershire Regiment.

Elphine Sutherlandshire hamlet twenty-three miles to the south-east of Lochinver. *Territorials:* 5th Seaforth Highlanders.

Elphinstone Haddingtonshire mining village two miles to the south-west of Tranent. *Territorials:* 8th Royal Scots.

Elstead West Surrey village on the River Wey, five miles west of Godalming, served by the London & South Western Railway. Elstead station was opened by the Petersfield Railway company in September 1864. Here is St James's Church. *Territorials:* 5th Queen's Royal West Surrey Regiment.

Elterwater Westmorland village, four miles from Ambleside, where many were once employed in the production of gunpowder. There were also slate quarries. *Territorials:* 4th Border Regiment.

Eltham South-east London suburb between Blackheath and Sidcup in Kent about ten miles from Charring Cross on the South Eastern & Chatham Railway. Here is the medieval church of St John the Baptist. *Territorials:* 2nd London Brigade RFA.

Ely Dominated by it great octagon-towered cathedral, Cambridgeshire's Ely stands on almost the highest part of the Fenland, bounded to the south by the River Ouse. Ely was served by the Great Eastern Railway. *Territorials:* Suffolk Yeomanry and Cambridgeshire Regiment.

Endmoor Westmorland village three miles to the north-east of Milnthorpe. *Territorials:* 4th Border Regiment.

Enfield Middlesex market town on the New River, eleven miles north of London, served by the Great Northern (a new station was opened in 1910) and the Great Eastern railways. Here, in 1908, the Royal Small Arms Factory was producing more than 1,800 rifles each day. The medieval St Andrew's Church is on the market place, its registers dating from 1550. *Territorials:* Hertfordshire Yeomanry and 7th Middlesex Regiment.

Englefield Berkshire village six miles from Reading and just over one mile from Theale station. Here in St Mark's Church former lords of the manor are remembered: the Benyons, and before them, the Englefields. *Territorials:* 4th Royal Berkshire Regiment.

Epping Essex market town sixteen miles by rail from Liverpool Street, London. Here, alongside the High Street, is the church of St John the Baptist which dates from 1832. *Territorials:* Essex Infantry Brigade, Essex Yeomanry and 4th Essex Regiment.

Eppleby North Yorkshire village nine miles north of Richmond. *Territorials:* 4th Yorkshire Regiment.

Epsom Surrey market town at the foot of Banstead Downs, fourteen miles from London, served by the London & South Western and London, Brighton & South Coast railways. St Martin's Church is in Church Street, Christ Church, on Epsom Common. Here too is Epsom College which had two companies of infantry with the OTC. *Territorials:* 5th East Surrey Regiment.

Eridge East Sussex village, four miles south-west of Tunbridge Wells, served by the London, Brighton & South Coast Railway. Eridge station was opened by the Brighton, Uckfield & Tunbridge Wells Railway in August 1868. Here is Holy Trinity Church which was built in 1852–56. *Territorials:* Sussex Yeomanry.

Erith West Kent town on the south bank of the Thames fourteen miles by rail from London's Charing Cross on the South Eastern & Chatham Railway. Station built in 1849. A tram service was opened by the Erith Urban District Council Tramways, with its apple-green and primrose vehicles, in August 1905. Here, the Maxim Nordenfelt gun factory employed many, as well as large engineering, gunpowder, oil and glue manufacturing works. Here is St John's Church and, on Victoria Road, Christ Church which was opened in 1874. *Territorials:* 4th Home Counties Brigade RFA and 4th London Field Ambulance.

Errogie Inverness-shire hamlet just over two miles from Inverfarigaig. *Territorials:* 1st Lovat's Scouts.

Esher North Surrey village fourteen miles by rail from London's Waterloo on the London & South Western Railway. Here, just behind the Bear Hotel, is St George's Church. *Territorials:* 6th East Surrey Regiment.

Eskbank Village eight miles by rail from Edinburgh on the North British Railway. *Territorials:* Lothians and Border Horse.

Eston North Yorkshire village near the River Tees four miles by rail from Middlesbrough on the North Eastern Railway. Well known, note the guides, was the Easton ironstone quarries. Here were large blast furnaces, iron foundries and iron and steel works, the largest of their kind in the world. Here, built in 1884, is Christ Church. *Territorials:* 4th Yorkshire Regiment.

Evanton Ross and Cromarty village on the Cromarty Firth seven miles to the north-east of Dingwell. *Territorials:* 4th Seaforth Highlanders.

Evercreech Somerset village three miles by rail from Shepton Mallet on the Somerset & Dorset Railway. Here is St Peter's Church. *Territorials:* 4th Somerset Light Infantry.

Eversley Hampshire village to the north-east of Basingstoke. Territorials would no doubt have remembered the author Charles Kinsley who was rector at St Mary's, Eversley until his death in January 1875. He lies buried with his wife Fanny by the door. *Territorials:* 4th Hampshire Regiment.

Evesham Worcestershire market town on the River Avon, to the south-east of Worcester, served by the Great Western and Midland Railways. Market gardens extend for many miles over the district. Here since 714 is Evesham Abbey, and within its precinct two churches: All Saints and St Lawrence. *Territorials:* 8th Worcestershire Regiment.

Evie Locality just to the north of Finstown, Orkney. *Territorials:* Orkney RGA.

Exeter Devonshire county town served by the Great Western and London & South Western railways, where the cathedral towers throw down shadows onto busy streets. Macaulay called it the 'Metropolis of the West', and the Volunteer ancestors of the Territorials are remembered at Northernhay Gardens. Here, in 1887, a great fire destroyed the theatre with the loss of come 200 lives. Beatrix Potter (1866–1943) came to Exeter in 1892 with her parents who were booked to stay at the Peple's Hotel in High Street. But the family were not impressed, so moved on to the Royal Clarence in Cathedral Place. Opened in April 1882, the Exeter Tramway Company operated from its depot in New North Street. Exeter School had a company of infantry in the OTC. *Territorials:* Wessex Division, 2nd South Western Mounted Brigade, Devon and Cornwall Infantry Brigade, Royal 1st Devon Yeomanry, 4th Wessex Brigade RFA, Devonshire Fortress Engineers, Wessex Divisional Telegraph/Signal Company, 2nd South Western Mounted Brigade Signal Troop, 4th and 7th Battalions Devonshire Regiment, Wessex Divisional Transport and Supply Column, 1st Wessex Field Ambulance, Wessex Clearing Hospital and Exeter Cathedral School Cadet Company.

Exmouth East Devon seaport and holiday resort on the east side of the River Ex, ten miles to the south-east of Exeter, served by the London & South Western Railway. Here, in Rolle Road, is Holy Trinity Church and, on Exeter Road, All Saints which dates from 1887. *Territorials:* Royal 1st Devon Yeomanry, 4th Wessex Brigade RFA and 4th Devonshire Regiment.

Eye Suffolk market town twenty miles north of Ipswich served by the Great Eastern Railway. At Eye, breweries and a small iron foundry gave employment. Here is St Peter and St Paul's Church. *Territorials:* Suffolk Yeomanry and 5th Suffolk Regiment.

Eyemouth Berwickshire fishing town, eight miles from Berwick-upon-Tweed, served by the North British Railway which arrived in 1891. *Territorials:* 4th King's Own Scottish Borderers.

Eynsham Oxfordshire village on the River Thames, seven miles by rail from Oxford, where the guides note streets of grey stone cottages radiating from the Market Square. Here the church is dedicated to St Leonard. Eynsham station was opened by the Witney Railway in November 1861. *Territorials:* 4th Oxfordshire and Buckinghamshire Light Infantry.

Fair Oak South Hampshire village three miles from Eastleigh. Here is St Thomas's Church which was built in 1863. *Territorials:* 5th Hampshire Regiment.

Fairburn Estate and county seat on the Orrin, Ross and Cromarty. *Territorials:* 4th Seaforth Highlanders.

Fakenham North Norfolk market town on the River Wensum served by the Great Eastern and Midland & Great Northern Joint railways. Here is St Peter and St Paul's Church. *Territorials:* Norfolk Yeomanry, 5th and 6th Norfolk Regiment.

Falkirk Stirlingshire market town twenty-two miles from Glasgow served by the North British and Caledonian Railways. The town, note the guides, stands amidst ironworks and collieries – Here was the Grahamston Iron Company and, opened in 1759, the Carron Ironworks. Made here were guns for Nelson's navy, and artillery for Wellingtons army. Henry Shrapnel (1761–1842) developed his artillery shell at Falkirk. Opened in October 1905 was the Falkirk & District Tramway Company. *Territorials:* 7th Argyll and Sutherland Highlanders.

Falmouth Cornwall market town and once busy seaport on the south Cornwall coast eleven miles south of Truro. Beatrix Potter (1866–1943) once noted on a visit that the town was very cosmopolitan (British and foreign seamen were loitering about) with very narrow and steep streets full of all things nautical – a notice in a barber's shop window 'was in five languages'. Falmouth was served by the Great Western Railway. All around are remembered the Killigrews. Sir Peter paid for much of the King Charles the Martyr Church (1662–64). All Saints of 1887–90 is in Killigrew Street, the Roman Catholic St Mary's in Killigrew Road since 1869. *Territorials:* Cornwall RGA, Cornwall Fortress Engineers, 4th Duke of Cornwall's Light Infantry and 'A' Company 1st Cadet Battalion of Cornwall.

Fareham Hampshire market town and seaport, nine miles to the north-west of Portsmouth and served by the London & South Western Railway, where a brickworks produced bricks known as 'Fareham Reds'. Here is St Peter and St Paul's Church. *Territorials:* Wessex RGA and 6th Hampshire Regiment.

Faringdon Berkshire market town on the Great Western Railway's Uffington to Farringdon branch line that opened in June 1864. Nine miles from Wantage, Faringdon lies on the slope of a hill overlooking the Thames Valley, the town's trade being noted as bacon, corn, cattle and sheep. Here were two important families: Unton, who lived at Wadley House, and Pye who occupied Farringdon House just to the north of All Saints Church where there are monuments to both. One of the Pye family (Henry James) was appointed poet laureate in 1790, his uncle, Admiral Sir Thomas Pye was called 'Nosey' and believed every women he met fell in love with him. *Territorials:* Berkshire Yeomanry.

Farley South Wiltshire hamlet, six miles to the east of Salisbury, where founder of the Chelsea Hospital, Sir Stephen Fox, was born. Here, All Saints Church built by Sir Stephen was completed in 1690. *Territorials:* 4th Wiltshire Regiment.

Farmborough Somerset village six miles to the south-west of Bath on the road to Wells. Here is All Saints Church. *Territorials:* North Somerset Yeomanry.

Farnborough Hampshire village on the Surrey border close to Aldershot's North Camp and served by the London & South Western and South Eastern & Chatham railways. The Aldershot & Farnborough Tramway, with its red and white trams, opened c1882, but was closed down in 1906. Here is St Peter's Church. *Territorials:* 4th Hampshire Regiment and Wessex Divisional Transport and Supply Column.

Farndon Cheshire village on the River Dee eight miles to the south of Chester. Close by, on the road to Chester, stands a stone obelisk in memory of Major Roger Barnston who fought in the Crimea and died in 1857, and his brother Major William Barnston who lived until 1872. There was a Civil War battle fought here which is remembered at St Chad's Church by a window showing in great detail Royalist soldiers of Colonel Sir Francis Gamul's Regiment, their weapons, armour and equipment. *Territorials:* Cheshire Yeomanry.

Farnham West Surrey market town on the River Wey, three miles from Aldershot, served by the London & South Western Railway. Born at Farnham in 1740 was Augustus Toplady, author of 'Rock of Ages', and William Cobbett who toured Britain and wrote down what he saw in *Rural Rides on Horseback* (1821–26). Here is St Andrew's Church and, on East Street, St James's. *Territorials:* Surrey Infantry Brigade, 5th Queen's Royal West Surrey Regiment, and West Surrey Cadets (later 'G' and 'H' Companies 1st Cadet Battalion of Hampshire.

Farnsfield Nottinghamshire village eight miles by rail on the Midland Railway from Mansfield. Farnsfield station was opened in March 1871. Here is St Michael's Church, which was rebuilt 1859–60 after a fire. *Territorials:* 8th Sherwood Foresters.

Farnworth Lancashire town, three miles by rail from Bolton on the London & North Western Railway, which gave employment in its paper mills, iron foundries, cotton mills, collieries and brick works. Farnworth Council opened a tram service in January 1902. St James's Church in St James's Street was built 1862–65, and the Roman Catholic St Gregory's opened on Preston Street in 1875. *Territorials:* 5th North Lancashire Regiment.

Fauldhouse Linlithgowshire town twenty-four miles by rail from Glasgow on the Caledonian Railway. The guides note of Fauldhouse that its existence was dependant on the coal, ironstone and paraffin industries. *Territorials:* 10th Royal Scots.

Faversham Kent market town and river port nine miles by rail on the South Eastern & Chatham Railway from Canterbury. Here is the church of Our Lady of Charity. *Territorials:* Royal East Kent Yeomanry and Home Counties RGA.

Fawley Hampshire village on the west side of Southampton Water just over five miles from Southampton. Here is All Saints Church. *Territorials:* 7th Hampshire Regiment.

Fearn Ross and Cromarty village four miles by rail from Tain on the Highland Railway. *Territorials:* 2nd Lovat's Scouts and 4th Seaforth Highlanders.

Featherstone West Yorkshire village two miles by rail from Pontefract on the London & North Western Railway. Here, note the guides, the inhabitants were principally occupied in the neighbouring collieries, and in the great coal strike of 1893 demonstrators were fired upon by soldiers. Two were killed and several wounded. Here is All Saints Church. *Territorials:* 5th King's Own Yorkshire Light Infantry.

Felixstowe Suffolk coastal town, twelve miles from Ipswich, served by the Great Eastern Railway which arrived in 1877. Here is the church of St Peter and St Paul. *Territorials:* Suffolk Yeomanry and Essex and Suffolk RGA.

Felling Durham village, and the first station out of Gateshead on the North Eastern Railway's line to Sunderland. Employment at Felling was in the production of paper and, from a colliery close to the station, coal. Here, an explosion in May 1812 took seventy-one lives. Christ Church was built in 1866. *Territorials:* 9th Durham Light Infantry.

Felstead West Essex village eleven miles by rail from Bishop's Stortford on the Great Eastern Railway. Here is Holy Cross Church which has memorials to the Rich family. Richard, Lord Rich founded Felstead public school in 1564 which had two infantry companies in the OTC. *Territorials:* 5th Essex Regiment.

Feltwell Norfolk village six miles to the north-west of Brandon. Here are the churches of St Mary and St Nicholas. *Territorials:* 4th Norfolk Regiment.

Festiniog Merionethshire town served by the Great Western Railway where many were employed in local slate quarries. Here is St Michael's Church which was built in 1845. *Territorials:* 7th Royal Welsh Fusiliers.

Fettercairn Kincardineshire village just over four miles to the north–west of Laurencekirk. A number from the village were employed in its distillery. *Territorials:* 7th Gordon Highlanders.

Filey East Yorkshire fishing and market town, eight miles from Scarborough, served by the North Eastern Railway. At Filey, the fishermen went to sea and their wives stayed home and made them 'Guernseys' to keep them warm. Thick knitted jerseys (sometimes called Ganseys), the initials of the wearer formed part of the pattern which varied from family to family. Men lost at sea, and latter washed ashore, have often been identified only by their Guernsey. *Territorials:* 5th East Yorkshire Regiment and 5th Yorkshire Regiment.

Finchley North London suburb on the Great Northern line out of King's Cross. In Hendon Lane, close to Finchley Central station, is the old parish church of St Mary where the registers date from 1558. *Territorials:* Christ's College Finchley Cadet Company.

Findochty Banffshire fishing village, just over three miles north-east of Buckie, served by the Great North of Scotland Railway which arrived in 1886. *Territorials:* 6th Gordon Highlanders.

Finedon Northamptonshire village overlooking the Isle Valley, three miles from Wellingborough, served by the Midland Railway which arrived in 1857. Here is St Mary's Church. *Territorials:* 4th Northamptonshire Regiment.

Finsbury London borough to the north and north-west of the City. Whitbread's brewery in Chiswell Street was a major employer. *Territorials:* City of London Yeomanry, Honourable Artillery Company, 3rd London Brigade RFA, 5th, 8th, 11th London Regiment, 1st London Field Ambulance and 1st Cadet Battalion King's Royal Rifle Corps.

Finsbury Park North London area, to the north of Highbury, served by the Great Northern and Metropolitan Railways. Here are St John and St Thomas's churches. *Territorials:* Hertfordshire Yeomanry.

Finstown Coastal village and seaport at the mouth of the Bay of Firth, Orkney, six miles from Kirkwall. Here, many were employed in local flagstone quarries. *Territorials:* Orkney RGA.

Finzean Aberdeenshire seat six miles south-east of Aboyne. *Territorials:* 7th Gordon Highlanders.

Fishbourne Hamlet on the north coast of the Isle of Wight situated at the mouth of the River Wootton just over two miles west of Ryde. *Territorials:* 8th Hampshire Regiment.

Fishguard North Pembrokeshire seaport and market town at the mouth of the Gwaen fourteen miles north of Haverfordwest. Served by the Great Western Railway, Fishguard's main employment was in agriculture, fishing and from local slate quarries. Here is St Mary's Church which was built in 1857. *Territorials:* Pembrokeshire Yeomanry and Pembroke RGA.

Fladbury Worcestershire village on the River Avon, three miles north-west of Evesham, served by the Great Western Railway. Fladbury station was opened by the Oxford, Worcester & Wolverhampton Railway in May 1852. Here is the church of St John the Baptist. *Territorials:* 8th Worcestershire Regiment.

Flamborough Large fishing village, four miles from Bridlington in East Yorkshire, served by the North Eastern Railway. Here is St Oswald's Church. *Territorials:* 5th Yorkshire Regiment.

Fleckney South Leicestershire village seven miles north-west of Market Harborough, its principal industry being noted as framework knitting and the production of bricks. Here is St Nicholas's Church. *Territorials:* 5th Leicestershire Regiment.

Fleet Hampshire village three miles by rail from Farnborough on the London & South Western Railway. All Saints in Church Road dates from 1862. *Territorials:* 4th Hampshire Regiment.

Fleetwood North Lancashire seaport on the mouth of the River Wyre overlooking Morecambe Bay, served by the London & North Western Railway. Here, many were employed in deep sea fishing. At Rossall School in Fleetwood there was a contingent of the OTC. Here is St Peter's Church which was built in 1841. *Territorials:* 5th King's Own Royal Lancaster Regiment.

Fletton Huntingdonshire village just to the south of Peterborough. Here is St Margaret's Church. *Territorials:* 5th Bedfordshire Regiment.

Flimwell East Sussex village just over two miles from Ticehurst close to the border with Kent. Here is St Augustine's Church. *Territorials:* 5th Royal Sussex Regiment.

Flint County and market town, on the south-west bank of the estuary of the Dee, served by the London & North Western Railway. The manufacture of chemical products was important to the town, employment was also available at the area's several copper works, paper mills and brick making establishments. Here is St Mary's Church, built 1848, St David's, 1872, and St Thomas's, which opened in 1874. *Territorials:* 5th Royal Welsh Fusiliers.

Fochabers Elginshire town and tourist centre, on the mouth of the River Spey, served by the Highland Railway. In the town was George Baxter's grocery shop, his son later to make his name from his 'Royal Game' and other soups. *Territorials:* 6th Seaforth Highlanders.

Folkestone Kent seaport and market town five miles from Dover on the South Eastern & Chatham Railway. Here is St Saviour's Church. *Territorials:* Royal East Kent Yeomanry, 3rd Home Counties Brigade RFA, Kent RGA, 4th Buffs East Kent Regiment, Kent Cyclist Battalion and 2nd Home Counties Field Ambulance.

Ford North Northumberland village on the River Till six miles to the north-west of Wooler. Here is St Michael's Church. *Territorials:* 7th Northumberland Fusiliers.

Forden Montgomeryshire village on the River Severn, four miles north of Montgomery, served by the Great Western Railway. Here is St Michael's Church. *Territorials:* Montgomeryshire Yeomanry.

Fordingbridge Hampshire town on the River Avon, close to the borders with Wiltshire and Dorset, fourteen miles by rail from Salisbury on the London & South Western Railway. Here is St Mary's Church. *Territorials:* 7th Hampshire Regiment.

Fordoun Kincardineshire hamlet three miles by rail from Laurencekirk on the Caledonian Railway. *Territorials:* 7th Gordon Highlanders.

Forest Hill London suburb, part of Lewisham, just over five miles by rail from London Bridge on the London, Brighton and South Coast Railway. St Dunstan's College at Catford Bridge was opened in 1888. Here is Christ Church and St Paul's churches. *Territorials:* 1st Cadet Battalion Royal West Kent Regiment.

Forest Row Sussex village near the Ashdown Forest, three miles from East Grinstead, served by the London, Brighton & South Coast Railway. Here is Holy Trinity Church. *Territorials:* 4th Royal Sussex Regiment.

Forfar County and market town to the north-east of Dundee served by the Caledonian Railway. The manufacture of course linen gave employment, as well as several bleach fields and iron works. *Territorials:* Fife and Forfar Yeomanry, 5th Black Watch and Highland Cyclist Battalion.

Formby Lancashire coastal town, seven miles from Stockport, served by the London & South Western Railway. Close to the sea is St Peter's Church of 1736. *Territorials:* 7th King's Liverpool Regiment.

Forres Elginshire market town on the River Findhorn, twelve miles from Elgin, served by the Highland Railway. Woollens, boots, shoes, carriages and chemicals were made in the area. *Territorials:* 2nd Scottish Horse and 6th Seaforth Highlanders.

Fort Augustus Inverness-shire village on the Caledonian Canal and North British Railway at the head of Loch Ness. *Territorials:* 1st Lovat's Scouts and 4th Cameron Highlanders.

Fort Matilda Situated on the River Clyde in Renfrewshire, one mile north-east of Gourock, and served by the Caledonian Railway. *Territorials:* Renfrewshire Fortress Engineers.

Fort William Small Inverness-shire town at the foot of Ben Nevis on the Caledonian Canal and east side of Loch Linnhe. Fort William itself was dismantled and sold by the Government in 1860, the site passing into the hands of the West Highland Railway, which employed many from the town, in 1892. Two distilleries are noted as important employers, the Nevis and Ben Nevis producing a then famous whisky called 'Long John'. *Territorials:* 1st Lovat's Scouts and 4th Cameron Highlanders.

Forth Lanarkshire mining village one mile from Wilsontown. *Territorials:* 8th Highland Light Infantry.

Forthampton Gloucestershire village, three miles from Tewkesbury, bounded on the east by the River Severn and on three other sides by Worcestershire. Here is St Mary's Church, much admired for it pyrographic picture on the south wall. *Territorials:* 5th Gloucestershire Regiment.

Fortingall Perthshire village on the River Lyon, nine miles to the south-west of Aberfeldy. *Territorials:* 6th Black Watch.

Fortrose Ross and Cromarty town on the Moray Firth just over ten miles from Inverness. Fortrose lies at the termination of the Black Isle branch of the Highland Railway which came up from Muir of Ord in 1894. *Territorials:* 4th Seaforth Highlanders.

Four Crosses Village on the Carnarvonshire/Montgomeryshire border three miles to the north-east of Pwllheli. *Territorials:* Montgomeryshire Yeomanry.

Fovant South Wiltshire village on the River Avon seven miles from Wilton. Here is St George's Church. *Territorials:* 1st South Western Mounted Brigade Transport and Supply Column.

Fowey Small Cornwall fishing town near the mouth of the River Fowey, twenty-one miles from Plymouth, served by the Great Western Railway. What remained of the Parliamentary Army under the Earl of Essex surrender at Fowey on 2 September 1644. Here is St Nicholas's Church. *Territorials:* Cornwall Fortress Engineers.

Framingham Pigot Norfolk village four miles to the south-east of Norwich. Here is St Andrew's Church. *Territorials:* 4th Norfolk Regiment.

Framlingham East Suffolk market town to the west of Saxmundham, served by the Great Eastern Railway. Here at St Michael's Church the Howards are remembered; one of them saved from losing his head by a few hours, another not so lucky. On his tomb, a coronet lies by his side to remind us. Framlingham College maintained one OTC infantry company. *Territorials:* Suffolk Yeomanry and 4th Suffolk Regiment.

Fransham Norfolk village, divided as Great Fransham and Little Fransham, six miles to the west of East Dereham and served by the Great Eastern Railway. Here at Great Fransham is All Saints Church, and at Little Fransham, St Mary's. *Territorials:* Norfolk Yeomanry.

Frant East Sussex village two miles south of Tunbridge Wells and 600 ft above sea level. Most of the houses are set around a large green and the old archery butts. A short street leads from the green to St Alban's Church which was completed in 1822. The South Eastern & Chatham Railway's Frant station was opened in September 1851. *Territorials:* 5th Royal Sussex Regiment.

Fraserburgh Aberdeenshire seaport on the Great North of Scotland Railway. *Cassell's Gazetteer* for 1895 noted that 'The Wine Tower' on a crag overlooking the sea, has a cave under it which 'now serves as a Volunteer armoury and store'. Fraserburgh is at the north-eastern tip of the county where the Moray Firth meets the North Sea. *Territorials:* 2nd Scottish Horse and 5th Gordon Highlanders.

Fremington North Devon village and small port on the Taw Estuary, three miles from Barnstaple, served by the London & South Western Railway. Fremington station was opened by the Bideford Extension Railway in November 1855. Here is St Paul's Church. *Territorials:* Royal North Devon Yeomanry.

Frensham West Surrey village on the River Wey four miles to the south of Farnham. Here is St Mary's Church. *Territorials:* 5th Queen's Royal West Surrey Regiment.

Freshwater Coastal town at the western extremity of the Isle of Wight where the Freshwater, Yarmouth & Newport Railway began in 1889. Alfred Lord Tennyson moved to Farringford House, Freshwater shortly after he was made Poet Laureate in 1850 and resided there until his death in 1892. Here is All Saints Church and, built by Isaac Jones on Freshwater Bay in 1908, the low thatched St Agnes's. *Territorials:* Hampshire Yeomanry, 2nd Wessex Brigade RFA and Hampshire Fortress Engineers.

Friern Barnet North Middlesex locality served by the Great Northern Railway. Here, on Friern Barnet Lane, is the church of St James the Great which has registers dating from 1674. *Territorials:* Friern Barnet School Cadet Company.

Frimley West Surrey village on the River Blackwater, just over seven miles from Farnham, served by the London & South Western Railway. Here is St Peter's Church. *Territorials:* 5th Queen's Royal West Surrey Regiment.

Friockheim Forfarshire village on the Lunan served by the Caledonian Railway. At Friockheim, just under seven miles from Arbroath, there were bleach fields and several manufacturers of textile materials. *Territorials:* 5th Black Watch.

Frizington West Cumberland village, three miles from Whitehaven, served by the London & North Western and Furness Joint Railway and where many were employed in coal and iron mines. Here is St Paul's Church which was built 1867–68. *Territorials:* 5th Border Regiment.

Frodingham Lincolnshire village, nine miles from Brigg, served by the Great Central Railway and where, note the guides, there were numerous smelting works employing great numbers. Here is St Lawrence's Church. *Territorials:* 5th Lincolnshire Regiment.

Frodsham Cheshire town served by the London & North Western and Great Western Joint Railway. Frodsham is on the road from Warrington to Chester and lies close to the Rivers Mersey and Weaver. Here is St Laurence's Church. *Territorials:* 5th Cheshire Regiment.

Frome East Somerset market town on the River Frome just over twenty-four miles by rail from Bristol on the Great Western Railway. At Frome the leading industry was once the manufacture of fancy cloth. There were also art-metal works, a large printing establishment, iron foundries and breweries. On a hillside is St John's Church in which there is a memorial to local clothier, Richard Antrum. *Territorials:* North Somerset Yeomanry, 4th Somerset Light Infantry and 2nd South Western Mounted Brigade Field Ambulance.

Fulford Village on the southern edge of York, the River Ouse and in sight of the eleventh-century Battle of Fulford. There has been a barracks here since 1795. Here is St Oswald's Church. *Territorials:* East Riding Yeomanry.

Fulham South-west London borough between Putney and Chelsea, served by the London & North Western Railway. Here is All Saints Church, and Fulham Palace, once the home of the Bishops of London. *Territorials:* King Edward's Horse, 7th London Brigade RFA and 2nd London Divisional Transport and Supply Column.

Furnace Argyllshire village on Loch Fyne, eight miles to the south-west of Inveraray, where many were employed in local granite quarries. *Territorials:* 8th Argyll and Sutherland Highlanders.

Fyvie Aberdeenshire parish on the River Ythan seven miles from Turriff served by the Great North of Scotland Railway. Fyvie station was opened by the Banff, Macduff and Turriff Junction Railway Company in September 1857. *Territorials:* 2nd Scottish Horse and 5th Gordon Highlanders.

Gainford Durham village on the North Eastern Railway eight miles west of Darlington where St Mary's church lies close enough to the River Tees that its sound can be heard from within the building. *Territorials:* 6th Durham Light Infantry.

Gainsborough Lincolnshire market town and river port on the east bank of the River Trent, Gainsborough lies fifteen miles north-west of Lincoln. Served by the Great Central and Great Northern & Great Eastern Joint railways, Gainsborough's principal industries are noted as malting and the manufacture of linseed cake and oil. Here is All Saints Church. *Territorials:* Lincolnshire Yeomanry and 5th Lincolnshire Regiment.

Gairloch West Ross and Cromarty village with steamboat pier at the head of Gair Loch. *Territorials:* 4th Seaforth Highlanders.

Galashiels Selkirkshire town served by the North British Railway on both sides of the Gala extending to within a short distance of its confluence with the Tweed. Twenty-two woollen factories were noted in the area around 1890. There was also a yard where skins were tanned and dressed, said to be the largest in Scotland. *Territorials:* Lothians and Border Horse and 4th King's Own Scottish Borderers.

Galgate North Lancashire village on the Lancaster Canal, four miles to the south of Lancaster, served by the London & North Western Railway. Galgate station was opened by the Lancaster & Preston Junction Railway in June 1840. The area around the village is well known for its production of rhubarb. *Territorials:* 5th King's Own Royal Lancaster Regiment.

Galston Ayrshire town on the River Irvine, five miles east of Kilmarnock, served by the Caledonian Railway. Coal was the main source of employment. *Territorials:* 4th Royal Scots Fusiliers.

Garlieston Small Wigtownshire seaport to the south of Whithorn. *Territorials:* 5th King's Own Scottish Borderers.

Garmouth Elginshire village and seaport served by the Caledonian Railway which arrived in 1884. Garmouth is on the west bank of the River Spey to the north of Fochabers. *Territorials:* 6th Seaforth Highlanders.

Garnant Glamorgan mining village served by the Great Western Railway, ten miles from Neath. *Territorials:* Welsh Divisional Engineers.

Garndiffaith Monmouthshire village to the north of Pontypool where most were employed in the production of coal and iron. *Territorials:* 2nd Monmouthshire Regiment.

Garstang North Lancashire market town on River Wyre to the south of Lancaster, served by the Knott End Railway. Here is St Thomas's Church. *Territorials:* 5th King's Own Royal Lancaster Regiment.

Garston South-west Lancashire seaport on the River Mersey, five miles from Liverpool, served by the London & North Western Railway. Garston's inhabitants were mostly employed in the docks. Here is St Michael's Church. *Territorials:* 3rd West Lancashire Brigade RFA.

Garve Hamlet at the mouth of Strath Garve, Ross and Cromarty, twelve miles by rail from Dingwall on the Highland Railway. *Territorials:* 4th Seaforth Highlanders.

Gatehouse Small river port and town on the River Fleet, Kirkcudbrightshire, served by the Portpatrick & Wigtownshire Railway. Many were once employed here in the town's several cotton mills. *Territorials:* 2nd Lowland Brigade RFA and 5th King's Own Scottish Borderers.

Gateshead *Cassell's Gazetteer* for 1896 notes that the principal locomotive works of the North Eastern Railway Company were located at Gateshead. Employment was also given at the town's shipbuilding yards, and several iron works producing anchors and chain cables. Here, outside Low Fell Post Office in Durham Road, stands a memorial to a sergeant and four troopers, all members of the Imperial Yeomanry, who fell during the South African War 1899–1902. St Edmund's and St Mary's churches are in the town. *Territorials:* Durham Fortress Engineers, 9th Durham Light Infantry and Northumbrian Divisional Transport and Supply Column.

Gifford Haddingtonshire village on Gifford Water twenty-one miles by rail from Edinburgh on the North British Railway. *Territorials:* 8th Royal Scots.

Gillingham (Dorset) Market town on the Stour where it joins the Lidden, served by the London & South Western Railway. At Gillingham, bricks, tiles, rope and twine were made and beer brewed at Wyke Brewery, still to be seen just a mile west of the town. Here is St Mary's Church. *Territorials:* Dorsetshire Yeomanry and 4th Dorsetshire Regiment.

Gillingham (Kent) Town on the south bank of the River Medway adjoining Chatham, served by the South Eastern & Chatham Railway. Here is St Mary's Church. *Territorials:* Kent RGA and Kent Fortress Engineers.

Girvan Ayrshire seaport twenty-two miles from Aye by rail on the Glasgow & South Western Railway. Fishing was the main industry of Girvan which looks across the Firth of Clyde to tall Ailsa Craig from where locals brought back granite to turn into curling stones. *Territorials:* 5th Royal Scots Fusiliers and 1st Cadet Battalion Royal Scots Fusiliers.

Glamis Forfarshire village on Glamis Burn, eleven miles north of Dundee on the Caledonian Railway. *Territorials:* 5th Black Watch.

Glasgow From the very beginning of the Volunteer Movement in 1859, Glasgow residents were involved in part-time soldiering; managers and clerks from the banks, shopkeepers, men from the legal profession, the shipping lines and the great shipyards, all joined. And the railways too. Here were the North British, Glasgow & South Western, London & North Western and Caledonian. Unveiled at Kelvingrove Park on 28 September 1906 was William Birnie Rhind's memorial to those of the Highland Light Infantry that fell in the South African war of 1889–1902. Glasgow was well represented in the OTC: the University, Glasgow Academy, Glasgow High School, Kelvinside Academy and Hillhead High School, all maintaining contingents. *Territorials:* Lowland Division, Scottish Rifle Infantry Brigade, Highland Light Infantry Brigade, Lanarkshire Yeomanry, Lanarkshire (Royal Glasgow) Yeomanry, 3rd, 4th Lowland Brigades RFA, Highland Divisional Engineers, Scottish Command Signal Companies, 5th, 7th, 8th Cameronians, 5th, 6th, 7th, 9th Highland Light Infantry, Lowland Divisional Transport and Supply Column, Lowland Mounted Brigade Field Ambulance, 1st, 2nd Lowland Field Ambulances, 3rd, 4th Scottish General Hospitals, Lowland Clearing Hospital, Highland Division School of Instruction, Glasgow Postal Telegraph Messengers Cadet Corps (later called 1st Cadet Company Highland Light Infantry), and Hutcheson's Grammar School Cadet Corps.

Glastonbury Mid Somerset market town on the River Brue six miles by rail from Wells on the Somerset & Dorset Railway. Here, noted the guides, the town's principal industries were the manufacture of sheepskin rugs, gloves and other leather goods. At the top of Glastonbury Tor is St Michael's Tower, said to be one of the entrances to the underworld. Here is Glastonbury Abbey. *Territorials:* West Somerset Yeomanry, Somerset RHA and 4th Somerset Light Infantry.

Glenbarr South Argyllshire hamlet on Barr Water, west coast of Kintyre, six miles to the south of Tayinloan. *Territorials:* 8th Argyll and Sutherland Highlanders.

Glenbuck Ayrshire village just over three miles to the north-east of Muirkirk, served by the Caledonian Railway. In 1802, two large reservoirs were made to supply water to the Catrine Cotton mills where many from Glenbuck worked. Extensive lime works and collieries also provided employment. *Territorials:* 5th Royal Scots Fusiliers.

Glenbuckat Village on the west Aberdeenshire border sixteen miles from Alford. *Territorials:* 6th Gordon Highlanders.

Glendale Seat on the Isle of Skye, Inverness-shire, eight miles north-west of Dunvegan. *Territorials:* 1st Lovat's Scouts.

Glendaruel Argyllshire hamlet north of the head of Loch Riddon. *Territorials:* 8th Argyll and Sutherland Highlanders.

Glenelg West Inverness-shire village on Sound of Sleat, ten miles to the south of Strome Ferry. *Territorials:* 2nd Lovat's Scouts.

Glenferness Seat of the Earl of Leven on the Findhorn, Nairnshire. *Territorials:* 2nd Lovat's Scouts.

Glenfinnan South-west Inverness-shire hamlet on Loch Shiel, eighteen miles by rail from Fort William on the North British Railway. *Territorials:* 1st Lovat's Scouts.

Glengarnock Ayrshire village on Kilbirnie Loch, to the north-east of Dalry, served by the Caledonian and Glasgow & South Western railways. Here, extensive iron and steel works provided employment. *Territorials:* 4th Royal Scots Fusiliers.

Glenmore Hamlet of the Isle of Skye, west Inverness-shire, five miles from Portree. *Territorials:* 4th Cameron Highlanders.

Glenrinnes Banffshire locality five miles from Dufftown. *Territorials:* 6th Gordon Highlanders.

Glenurquhart Inverness-shire locality seven miles to the west of Drumnadrochit. *Territorials:* 1st Lovat's Scouts.

Glinton Northamptonshire village three miles to the south-east of Market Deeping. Ignored by the railway, the nearest station was one mile away at Peakirk. Here is St Benedict's Church. *Territorials:* Northamptonshire Yeomanry.

Glossop Derbyshire market and manufacturing town, ten miles from Stockport, served by the Great Central Railway. The Library and Public Hall at Glossop in Derbyshire date from 1887; Woods Hospital in Howard Park, from the same year. Cotton was produced in Glossop, there was also paper mills and a calico printing works in the area. Opened in August 1903, the Glossop Tramways service was mainly used by the town's textile workers; the long, winding route deliberately planned so as to take in as many mills as possible. Here is All Saints Church. *Territorials:* 6th Cheshire Regiment.

Gloucester Cathedral city, county and market town on the River Severn, 114 miles by rail on the Great Western Railway's main line from London. The Gloucester Tramway Company began operating in January 1879. Railway locomotives, carriages and wagons were made in Gloucester. *Territorials:* Gloucestershire Yeomanry, 1st South Midland Brigade RFA and 5th Gloucestershire Regiment.

Glynde Sussex village, three miles south-east of Lewis, served by the London, Brighton & South Coast Railway which arrived in 1846. Here is St Mary's Church which was built 1763–65. *Territorials:* 5th Royal Sussex Regiment.

Glyndyfrdwy Village on the River Dee and north-east border of Merionethshire, three miles east of Corwen, served by the Great Western Railway. Glyndyfrdwy station was opened by the Llangollen & Corwen Railway in May 1865. Here is St Thomas's Church. *Territorials:* 7th Royal Welsh Fusiliers.

Godalming West Surrey market town on the Rive Wye just over thirty-four miles on the London & South Western main line from London. Godalming gave employment in the production of timber, paper, leather goods, gloves and hosiery. Here is St Peter and St Paul's Church, and Charterhouse School which had an OTC contingent. *Territorials:* 5th Queen's Royal West Surrey Regiment.

Godmanchester Huntingdonshire market town on the River Ouse, just under a mile from Huntingdon, served by the Great Eastern Railway. Here is St Mary's Church. *Territorials:* Bedfordshire Yeomanry.

Godshill Village on the River Medina, five miles north-west of Ventnor, Isle of Wight. Godshill was reached by the Newport, Godshill & St Lawrence Railway in 1897 which was absorbed into the Isle of Wight Central in 1913. The walk up the hill to All Saints Church is between thatched cottages. *Territorials:* 8th Hampshire Regiment.

Godstone Surrey village on the main Eastbourne road twenty-eight miles by rail from London's Charing Cross on the South Eastern & Chatham Railway. Here is St Nicholas's Church. *Territorials:* 4th Queen's Royal West Surrey Regiment.

Golspie Sutherlandshire fishing village on the Moray Firth seventeen miles from Helmsdale on the Highland Railway. *Territorials:* 5th Seaforth Highlanders.

Goole West Yorkshire market town, twenty-three miles from Hull, served by the North Eastern and Lancashire & Yorkshire Railways. Goole stands where the Don meets the Ouse, an iron bridge built in 1890 crossing the former river. There are docks from where the Aire and Calder Navigation Company operated. The smart brick and terracotta bank of Messrs Beckett and Co was opened in 1892, in the upper portion of which were to be found the offices of many leading shipping companies. It would be the canal company that, in part, was responsible for the building at Goole of the church of St John the Evangelist in 1844. The Market Hall was destroyed by fire in 1891. *Territorials:* Yorkshire Dragoons and 5th King's Own Yorkshire Light Infantry.

Gorebridge Midlothian village on Gore Water twelve miles by rail from Edinburgh on the North British Railway. *Territorials:* Lothians and Border Horse and 8th Royal Scots.

Goring-on-Thames Village on the south Oxfordshire border nine miles by rail from Reading on the Great Western Railway main line. Here is the church of St Thomas of Canterbury which dates from the early part of the twelfth century. Much younger is the Roman Catholic, Our Lady and St John, which was opened in Ferry Lane in 1893. *Territorials:* Oxfordshire Yeomanry.

Gorseinon Glamorganshire hamlet eight miles by rail from Swansea on the London & North Western Railway. Here is St Catherine's Church which was built 1911–13. *Territorials:* 6th Welsh Regiment.

Gosforth South Northumberland village, just over two miles by rail north of Newcastle-upon-Tyne on the Great Eastern Railway, and the residences of many Newcastle merchants. Here is All Saints Church which was built in 1887. *Territorials:* 5th Northumberland Fusiliers.

Gosport Hampshire seaport, naval base and market town four miles by rail from Fareham on the London & South Western Railway. The Barracks at Gosport were completed in 1859, a Soldiers' Home in 1884 and the Thorngate Memorial Hall, built in memory of local merchant William Thorngate, opened in 1885. 'Seamen's' biscuits were made in the town for the Royal Navy. In July 1882 the emerald-green and cream vehicles of the Gosport Street Tramways Company were seen for the first time. Here at Holy Trinity Church is an organ used by Handel. *Territorials:* 1st Wessex Brigade RFA, Hampshire Fortress Engineers, 6th Hampshire Regiment and 5th Southern General Hospital.

Goudhurst Small town in Kent four miles by rail from Cranbrook. Opened in 1892, Goudhurst (first called Hope Mill) Station on the Cranbrook & Paddock Wood line served both Goudhurst and Lamberhurst. Rife in the town was smuggling. Centered around the Eagle Inn, the smugglers were linked to St Mary's Church by an underground passage. In the churchyard in 1747, the authorities did battle with a gang which resulted in three of the smugglers being killed. *Territorials:* 5th Buffs East Kent Regiment.

Gourock Renfrewshire coastal town on the south shore of the Firth of Clyde two miles below Greenock. The town was reached by the Caledonian Railway's service from Glasgow in June 1889. Here in Royal Street is Gourock and Ashton Parish Church. *Territorials:* 5th Argyll and Sutherland Highlanders.

Govan Glasgow suburb on the south side of the Clyde and seat of an immense shipbuilding and engineering industry. *Territorials:* 4th Lowland Brigade RFA.

Goytre Monmouthshire village on the River Usk and Brecon and Abergavenny Canal, four miles to the north-east of Pontypool. Here is St Peter's Church. *Territorials:* 2nd Monmouthshire Regiment.

Graffham West Sussex village four miles to the south-east of Midhurst and a little over two miles from the railway at Selham. Here St Giles's Church was practically rebuilt by G E Street, 1874–87. *Territorials:* 4th Royal Sussex Regiment.

Grandtully Perthshire locality just over four miles by rail from Aberfeldy on the Highland Railway. *Territorials:* 6th Black Watch.

Grange Banffshire locality, four miles to the east of Keith, served by the Great North of Scotland Railway. *Territorials:* 6th Gordon Highlanders.

Grange-over-Sands North Lancashire seaside resort on the estuary of the River Kent and Morecambe Bay. Just over nine miles from Ulverston, the town was served by the Furness Railway which arrived in 1857. Here is St Paul's Church. *Territorials:* 4th King's Own Royal Lancaster Regiment.

Grangemouth East Stirlingshire seaport town on the Firth of Forth and entrance to the Forth and Clyde Canal, three miles north-east of Falkirk by rail on the North British Railway. With the opening of the canal in 1790, much employment came to the town in the form of import and export, ship and boat building. There was also the Carron Ironworks. *Territorials:* Highland Divisional Transport and Supply Column.

Grangetown North Yorkshire village four miles from Middlesbrough by rail on the North Eastern Railway. Here, notes the guides, the inhabitants were chiefly employed in iron and steel production. An important employer being Bolckow and Vaughan. Here is St Matthew's Church. *Territorials:* 4th Yorkshire Regiment.

Grantham Lincolnshire market town on the main Great Northern line from King's Cross, twenty-five miles from Lincoln. There were paper mills in the town, tanneries and a business manufacturing carriages. One visitor passing through by train noticed the 282 ft crocketed spire of St Wulfram's Church, 'but the town', he commented, 'is mostly notable for the gigantic ironworks of Messrs, Richard Hornsby & Sons.' King's School, at 54 High Street, maintained one OTC infantry company. *Territorials:* North Midland Mounted Brigade, Lincoln and Leicester Infantry Brigade, Lincolnshire Yeomanry and 4th Lincolnshire Regiment.

Grantown-on-Spey Elginshire market town served by the Great North of Scotland Railway. Queen Victoria and Prince Albert wrote of the 'excellent golf course' at Grantown and no doubt enjoyed the whiskey that was distilled there. Two stations served the area. Both opened in 1863, one to the west of the town was opened by the Inverness & Perth Junction line, the other, across the Spey to the east, by the Strathspey Railway. *Territorials:* 6th Seaforth Highlanders.

Gravesend North-west Kent market town and river port on the south bank of the Thames to the east of Dartford. Served by the South Eastern & Chatham Railway, Gravesend employed many in its fishing industry, boats were also built, and soap and bricks made. Vessels passing up the river take on pilots and customs officials at Gravesend. Here are St George's, and St James's churches. *Territorials:* West Kent Yeomanry, Kent RGA and Kent Fortress Engineers.

Grays Essex town on the north bank of the Thames to the south-east of London. Bricks and cement were made at Grays, many of its inhabitants no doubt making the just over one mile by rail journey to work at the Tilbury Docks. The town was served by the London, Tilbury & Southend Railway which became the Midland in 1912. The training ships *Exmouth* and *Shaftesbury* were here. Another training ship, the *Goliath*, was burnt at Grays in 1875 with the loss of a schoolmaster and nineteen boys. There is a monument to their memory at St Peter and St Paul's Church at the bottom of High Street, close to the railway. *Territorials:* Essex Yeomanry, 2nd East Anglian Brigade RFA, 6th Essex Regiment and Palmer's School Cadet Corps.

Great Ayton North Yorkshire village just over eight miles by rail on the North Eastern Railway from Middlesborough. Here are the churches of All Saints and, not built until 1876, Christ Church. *Territorials:* 4th Yorkshire Regiment.

Great Bardfield North-west Essex village on the River Blackwater six miles to the north-east of Dunmow. Here is St Mary's Church. *Territorials:* 5th Essex Regiment.

Great Bedwyn Wiltshire village close to the Kennet and Avon Canal, five miles south-west by rail from Hungerford on the Great Western Railway. Here is St Mary's Church. *Territorials:* Wiltshire Yeomanry.

Great Bentley North-east Essex village served by the Great Eastern Railway eight miles to the south-east of Colchester. Here is St Mary's Church, its registers dating from 1558. *Territorials:* Essex Yeomanry.

Great Budworth Cheshire village two miles to the north of Northwich. Here, perched on a hill, is the church of St Mary and All Saints. *Territorials:* Cheshire Yeomanry.

Great Malvern Worcestershire town served by the Great Western and Midland railways, just over seven miles to the south-west of Worcester. Mineral water is produced in the area around Malvern, and just outside the town since 1909, the hand-built Morgan sports car. Here in the centre of town is the Priory Church of St Mary and St Michael where a window on the north aisle depicts Queen Victoria at here Jubilee calibration. Shown among the guests is Kaiser Wilhelm II of Germany, thought to be the only representation of him in a British church. At Malvern College there were three OTC infantry companies. *Territorials:* Worcestershire Yeomanry, 2nd South Midland Brigade RFA and 8th Worcestershire Regiment.

Great Maplestead Essex village three miles from Halsted. Here is St Giles's Church, its registers dating from 1678. *Territorials:* 5th Essex Regiment.

Great Missenden Buckinghamshire village four miles from Chesham and twenty-nine from London, Baker Street on the Metropolitan & Great Central Railway. Here is St Peter and St Paul's Church. *Territorials:* Buckinghamshire Yeomanry.

Great Shelford Cambridgeshire village on the River Cam, four miles from Cambridge and just over fifty-two from Liverpool Street on the Great Eastern Railway. Here is St Mary's Church which has an altar dedicated to a soldier killed on the Indian Frontier. *Territorials:* Cambridgeshire Regiment.

Great Waltham Essex village on the River Chelmer five miles from Chelmsford. Here is the church of St Mary and St Lawrence which has pews dating from c1420. *Territorials:* 5th Essex Regiment.

Great Yarmouth The most easterly town on the Norfolk coast, Great Yarmouth gave employment to many in its fishing and shipbuilding industries. The Great Eastern Railway would have brought you the 122 miles from London's Liverpool Street Station. The town's first tram service (Yarmouth & Gorleston Tramways) was opened in March 1875. Here is St George's Church of 1714. *Territorials:* Norfolk Yeomanry, 1st East Anglian Brigade RFA, 5th and 6th Norfolk Regiment.

Greatham Hampshire village five miles from Petersfield. Here is the church of St John the Baptist which was built in 1875. *Territorials:* 6th Hampshire Regiment.

East Riding of Yorkshire Yeomanry. The regimental badge of a fox in full cry can be seen in the caps of this group at camp. The badge reflecting the regiment's 1903 origins from within the fox-hunting landowners and farmers of the county. The motto of the regiment, 'Forrard', also has hunting connections and comes from the term 'Hark Forrard'. The lancer-style tunics are maroon with light-blue fronts, collars and cuffs.

Gordon Highlanders. The three-tiered shoulder title and two efficiency stars on the lower right arm identify this sergeant as a member of the Territorial Force. The Royal Tiger collar badges placing his regiment as the Gordon Highlanders. Another badge of the regiment is a stag's head with the motto 'Bydand' (watchful, according to one translation; stand fast, another), unseen in the glengarry cap on this occasion, but clearly visible as a sporran decoration. On his scarlet doublet, proudly displayed, is a medal awarded for service in South Africa during the war of 1899–1902.

Unit and Headquarters.	Company.	Distribution of Serjt.-Instructors. Acting Serjt.-Major.	Others.	Company Head-Quarters.	Miles from Head-Quarters of Unit. By road.	By rail.	Outlying Drill Stations.	Miles from Head-Quarters of Company. By road.	By rail.	Remarks.
7th Bn. Gordon Highlanders— *Banchory*	A	1	..	Banchory	..	..	Durris ..	6½	3 (a)	(a) And 3¼ by road
							Torphins	7	7	
	B	..	1	Portlethen	16	26		..	..	
	C	..	1	Stonehaven	18	34		..	..	
	D	..	1	Laurencekirk	48	48	Auchenblae	6	..	
							Bervie ..	9	20	
							Fettercairn	5	..	
							Fordoun	4	3½ (b)	(b) And 1 by road.
							Marykirk	4	4	
	E	..	1	Ballater	26½	26½	Crathie..	8	..	
							Braemar	17	..	
	F	..	1	Aboyne	15	15½	Tarland	6	..	
							Finzean	8	..	
							Logie Coldstone	5	..	
	G	..	1	Kemnay	9	35	Skene ..	7½	..	
							Blackburn	5	..	
							Monymusk	3½	3	
							Echt ..	10	..	
	H	..	1	Peterculter	12	12	Countesswells ..	5	..	
Shetland Companies Gordon Highlanders—*Lerwick*	A	..	1	Lerwick	..	..		..	..	
	B	..	..	Lerwick	..	..	Scalloway	6½	..	
4th Bn. Cameron Highlanders—*Inverness*	A	1	..	Inverness	..	..		..	..	
	B	..	1	Nairn ..	15¾	15½	Cawdor	6	..	
							Ardersier	7	7	
							Auldearn	3	2½	
							Croy ..	8	..	
							Petty ..	10	..	
	C	..	..	Inverness	..	..	Moy ..	12	15	
	D	..	1	Broadford	85 (c)	..	Torrin ..	6	..	(c) 85 by road and steamer.
							Elgol ..	15	..	
							Raasay ..	..	12 (d)	(d) 12 by steamer.
	E	..	1	Fort William ..	66 (e)	60	Corpach ..	5	4	(e) 60 by steamer.
							Fort Augustus..	32	30	
							Invergarry	23	24 (f)	(f) 23 by steamer.
	F	..	1	Kingussie	44	47	Newtonmore	3	3	
							Kincraig, or Inch	8	6	
							Aviemore	12	12	
							Ardverikie (Loch Laggan)	21	..	
	G	..	1	Beauly ..	12	10	Struy ..	11	..	
							Kiltarlity	5	..	
							Balnain	20	31 (g)	(g) By road, rail and steamer.
							Inchmore	6	..	
							Drumnadrochit	14	25 (g)	
	H	..	1	Portree..	110 (h)	..	Glenmore	6	..	(h) 110 by road and steamer
							Bernisdale	8	..	
							Edinbane	14	..	
							Sconser	12	..	
							Tarbert (Harris)	..	51 (i)	(i) By steamer
							Kilmuir	20	..	

4/7/13

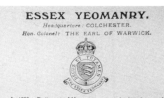

Essex Yeomanry. Published after 1914, this postcard provides much information regarding the regiment's history. Both full dress (dark blue with scarlet facings and helmet plume) and khaki service dress are shown.

Essex Royal Horse Artillery at Lydd artillery range in Kent.

Devonshire Royal Garrison Artillery manoeuvring a 4.7 inch gun.

4th London Brigade Royal
Field Artillery, drivers and
trumpeters at camp in Kent,
1910. Note the leather and
steel leg-protectors worn on
the right legs of the drivers.

Royal Field Artillery Territorials
detraining at Okehampton, 1911.
Note the use of hired civilian
transport.

Royal Garrison Artillery (Territorial Force). A 1910
colour plate by R Caton Woodville taken from *His
Majesty's Territorial Army* by Walter Richards. One of
the heavy, fix-position, guns of the RGA is seen in the
background.

Telegraph Company, 2nd London Divisional Engineers.

Highland Divisional Engineers, Piper.

Cheshire Railway Battalion. A 1910 colour plate by R Caton Woodville taken from *His Majesty's Territorial Army* by Walter Richards. As railway work goes on in the background, the central figure poses in full dress uniform of the Royal Engineers: scarlet jacket, blue collar, cuffs and trousers. The white metal locomotive collar badges, however, were unique to the battalion.

Cheshire Field Company, Welsh Divisional Engineers. On the left is Sergeant-Major Jackson, a long-serving member of both the Volunteers and Territorials (note his collection of efficiency stars).

London Balloon Company at summer camp, Farnborough, 1909. (Courtesy Peter Wright)

4th Battalion Queen's (Royal West Surrey Regiment) leaving Croydon for its war station shortly after mobilisation in August 1914.

5th Battalion Buffs (East Kent Regiment). Father and son perhaps? The gentleman seated wears the crossed axes of a Pioneer. Jackets are scarlet, the collars and cuffs being buff (the title of the regiment comes from this).

Cover from the first issue (1909) of *The Territorial Year Book*.

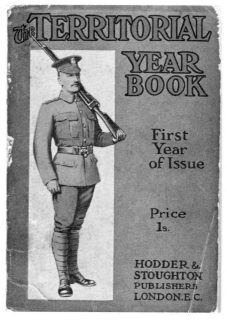

Davies Street, Berkeley Square, headquarters of the 9th (County of London) Battalion London Regiment (Queen Victoria's Rifles). Built at a cost of £16,000, the building was opened on 6 December 1890.

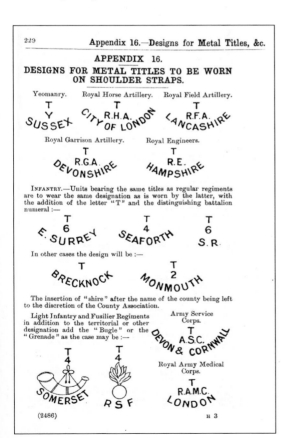

Designs for metal shoulder titles as directed by *Regulations for the Territorial Force, 1908.*

5th Battalion Royal Welsh Fusiliers. In this study from John Player & Sons cigarette card series *Uniforms of the Territorial Army* we see a Pioneer of the battalion with Rhuddlan Castle in the background.

Sample entries from the *Army List*. Here, in this edition for February 1912, three battalions of the London Regiment are featured, each listed along with its battle honour, headquarters address, names, ranks and commission dates of officers and uniform detail.

London Small Arms Company advertisement published in 1909.

10th London Regiment (Paddington Rifles) headquarters, 207–209 Harrow Road. The property was acquired by the old 18th Middlesex Rifle Volunteer Corps in 1895.

Above: 10th London Regiment (Paddington Rifles) at Longmore camp, August 1910.

Right: 28th London Regiment (Artists Rifles), Abergavenny camp, 1913.

Brecknockshire Battalion South Wales Borderers, Mhow, India, sometime in 1915. Many in the photograph are original members of the battalion. One of the first TF units to move overseas in the Great War, the Brecknocks had left Southampton on 29 October 1914, arrived Bombay on 3 December, where they transhipped for Aden, then returned to India August 1915.

22nd London Regiment (The Queen's). In this photograph taken in 1909, the drums still bear the pre-1908 designation '3rd Volunteer Battalion Queen's (Royal West Surrey Regiment)'.

8th Cameronians (Scottish Rifles), Machine Gun Section, December 1914. The battalion would leave for Gallipoli in the following May.

Corporal John Herbert Spencer, 'H' Company 1st Battalion Monmouthshire Regiment. From Cwmgelli close to Blackwood, John Spencer is seen here in this photograph taken on 21 September 1914, less than five months before he sailed with his battalion for France, less than a year before he met his death at Belgium's Hill 60.

Cornwall Fortress Engineers. The Lerryn detachment of No 2 Works Company are seen here having returned from the memorial service held at Fowey for King Edward VII in 1910.

1st Cadet Battalion Cheshire Regiment. With headquarters in St Peter's Square, Stockport, the battalion wore the designation 1/C/Cheshire on the shoulder straps.

2nd London Regiment (Royal Fusiliers) at their Tufton Street, Westminster, headquarters shortly after receiving the battalion's first set of Colours in 1909.

Drummer Robert Harper of the 6th Gloucestershire Regiment. The scarlet jacket here displays the additional lace, shoulder cords and wings of a drummer. On the right breast can be seen an Imperial Service badge, and on the lower left arm two awards for good shooting: Best shot in the band (top), best shot, junior ranks, in the battalion (bottom).

1st Cadet Battalion Royal Fusiliers at its Pond Street, Hampstead headquarters.

5th Argyll and Sutherland Highlanders shortly after having received its first set of Colours in 1909. Note the sporrans with their badger heads.

ritorial Force Nursing Service. Grey capes are
here with scarlet edging, the letter 'T' being
ed at each point, and white aprons hide grey
sses. On the capes, and suspended from a red
on with a central white stripe, are badges
ring the intertwined cipher of Queen
xandra. The nurse on the right is a Sister, this
g indicated by the two rings (scarlet again)
nd the lower sleeves.

(Cyclist) Battalion London Regiment. The battalion's vehicle, clearly
ked and laden with cycles and stretchers, is seen here returning from
ual camp in 1913.

8th (Irish) Battalion King's (Liverpool Regiment). Black metal shoulder title.

Important to the Territorial Force were the railways that provided the means of transporting the troops, together with their horses, guns and equipment, to and from camps. Here a regular soldier of the Army Service Corps (far left) looks on, his vehicle bearing chalk marks showing its allocation to the 4th and 5th York and Lancaster Regiment, as the Territorials transfer stores from a railway wagon.

4th King's Own Scottish Borderers. The piper wears Buccleugh tartan.

13th London Regiment. The battalion lines the road during a royal visit to South London in 1911.

5th Gloucestershire Regiment. Note how the rifles are secured to the cycles.

Notts and Derby Mounted Brigade Transport and Supply Column. Brass shoulder title.

Southern Command Airline Signal Company. Having left their headquarters at Great Brook Street in Birmingham, the men are photographed here with their equipment at annual camp. Carried on the wagons behind them is the wire, and the necessary equipment (ladders being essential) to position it high up in trees.

Attestation document of Harry Allen of the 6th Battalion North Staffordshire Regiment. A typical example which, in this case, reveals Harry's address, occupation, name of employer, his former service as a Volunteer, and the fact that he was prepared to continue with the Territorial Force for another four years. (Courtesy The National Archives).

Base drummer, 2nd Home Counties Field Ambulance.

1908 recruiting poster issued by the County of London Territorial Force. (Courtesy Mike and Linda Jackson).

A lifetime of service before and through two world wars as seen in the medals of Company Sergeant Major J J Scrivener of the 10th Middlesex Regiment. Left to right: British War Medal and Territorial Force War Medal for the Great War, Territorial Force Efficiency Medal and bar, and Special Constabulary Long Service Medal. (Courtesy Mike and Linda Jackson).

7th Middlesex Regiment, Drums and Fifes at Falmer Camp near Brighton 1912. As an 'Imperial Service' battalion (90% or more having volunteered to serve outside of the United Kingdom if required), perhaps not surprisingly at least twelve men are seen here wearing Imperial Service badges (see insert) on their right breast.

Greenlaw About seven miles south-west of Duns in Berwickshire, Greenlaw lies on the River Blackadder and produced woollens and agricultural implements. The town was served by the North British Railway. *Territorials:* South Scottish Infantry Brigade, Lothians and Border Horse and 4th King's Own Scottish Borderers.

Greenock On the south bank of the Clyde, Greenock's chief industries were shipbuilding, marine and general engineering. In the 1890s, notes Cassel's, there were about a dozen large sugar refineries giving employment to several thousand. Both the Caledonian and Glasgow & South Western railways had stations in the town. But one visitor arriving in Greenock by train was not impressed. He preferred Helensburgh across the Firth of Clyde to 'grimy Greenock', a 'crow facing a swan.' *Territorials:* Lanarkshire Yeomanry (Royal Glasgow), 3rd Highland Brigade RFA, Renfrewshire Fortress Engineers and 5th Argyll and Sutherland Highlanders.

Greenodd North Lancashire village on the estuary of the Lune just over three miles by rail from Ulverston on the Furness Railway. *Territorials:* 4th King's Own Royal Lancaster Regiment.

Greenwich London borough on the south bank of the Thames just over five miles by rail from Charring Cross on the South Eastern & Chatham Railway. At Greenwich, the home of the Royal Naval College and Royal Observatory, the Metropolitan Gas Company had extensive works. Other employers made chemicals and soap. Here is St Alfege's Church. *Territorials:* 5th London Field Ambulance and Greenwich Naval Cadet Unit.

Gresford East Denbighshire village three miles north-east of Wrexham by rail on the Great Western Railway. Coal mines and brickworks gave employment. Here is All Saints Church. *Territorials:* 4th Royal Welsh Fusiliers.

Griffithstown Monmouthshire town on the Monmouthshire and Brecon Canal, two miles to the south of Pontypool, where many were employed in the engine sheds of the Great Western Railway. Here, on the corner of Sunnybank Road and Kemys Street, is St Hilda's Church. *Territorials:* 4th Welsh Brigade RFA.

Grimsby Important Lincolnshire fishing port on the right bank of the River Humber, served by the Great Central Railway. Here, many were employed in the docks – the Union, Alexander and Royal – and the fisheries which around 1900 was noted as having some 900 vassals at sea. Here is St James's Church, and Grimsby Municipal College which maintained an infantry company in the OTC. *Territorials:* Lincolnshire Yeomanry, 1st North Midland Brigade RFA, 5th Lincolnshire Regiment and Notts and Derby Mounted Brigade Field Ambulance.

Groombridge Sussex village on the London, Brighton & South Coast Railway just over three miles from Tunbridge Wells. Here is St Thomas's Church. *Territorials:* Sussex Yeomanry and 5th Royal Sussex Regiment.

Grosmont North Yorkshire village on the River Esk, six miles to the south-west of Whitby, served by the North Eastern Railway. One guide written in 1904 noted that 'the hideous blast furnaces have disappeared, and the slag heaps are now slowly disappearing...' Close to the station, a brickworks employed many. Here is St Matthew's Church. *Territorials:* 5th Yorkshire Regiment.

Guardbridge Fifeshire village to the north-west of St Andrew's where a six-arched bridge built in 1420 spans the River Eden. Guardbridge station was on the North British Railway and opened in July 1852. *Territorials:* 7th Black Watch.

Guildford Surrey market town on the River Wey served by the London & South Western, London, Brighton & South Coast and South Easter & Chatham railways. A major Victorian employer at Guildford was the Friary Brewery, its red-brick tower of the 1860s still to be seen in Commercial

Road. Here on Stag Hill is Guildford Cathedral and, on High Street, Holy Trinity Church. Guildford's Royal Grammar School of King Edward VI maintained one OTC infantry company. *Territorials:* Surrey Yeomanry and 5th Queen's Royal West Surrey Regiment.

Guilsfield Montgomeryshire village three miles from Welshpool bounded to the east by the River Severn. Here is the church of St Aelhaiarn. *Territorials:* Montgomeryshire Yeomanry.

Guisborough North Yorkshire market town, ten miles by rail from Middlesborough, on the North Eastern Railway. *Cassell's Gazetteer* for the 1890s notes that the area was rich in ironstone, most of the inhabitants being employed in that industry. An engagement was fought here in January 1643 during the Civil War. Here is St Nicholas's Church. *Territorials:* 4th Yorkshire Regiment.

Guiseley West Yorkshire village two miles to the south of Otley by rail on the North Eastern Railway. Standing on high ground between the Aire and the Wharfe, Guiseley's mills gave employment to many from the area. Here is St Oswald's Church. *Territorials:* 6th Duke of Wellington's Regiment.

Gullane Haddingtonshire village on Gullane Bay four miles to the south-west of North Berwick. The railway did not reach Gullane until the North British extended its line up from Aberlady Junction in 1898. *Territorials:* 8th Royal Scots.

Gunton North Norfolk village five miles by rail from Cromer on the Great Eastern Railway. Here is St Andrew's Church which was built by Robert Adam in 1769. *Territorials:* 5th Norfolk Regiment.

Gwersyllt Denbighshire village three miles to the north-west of Wrexham where much of the population was employed in local ironworks and coal mines. The railway came to the town in 1886, the Wrexham, Mold & Connahs Quay line opening Gwersyllt Station on 1 May of that year. Here is Holy Trinity Church. *Territorials:* 4th Royal Welsh Fusiliers.

Hackney North-east London borough on the west side of the River Lea served by the London & North Western Railway. Only the tower of the old Gothic church of St Augustine remains, the rest being demolished in 1798 to make way for a new church, St John's, which was opened in 1794. *Territorials:* 7th Essex Regiment and 10th London Regiment.

Haddington County and market town on the River Tyne, just over seventeen miles to the east of Edinburgh, where several small businesses provided employment in the manufacture of woollen goods, agricultural implements and sacking. Haddington station was at the termination of a North British Railway's branch that opened in 1846. Here is St Martin's, the longest parish church in Scotland. *Territorials:* Lothians and Border Horse, 8th Royal Scots and Haddington Cadet Corps.

Hadfield Derbyshire cotton village on the border with Cheshire, about a mile by rail to the north-west of Glossop on the Great Central Railway. Major employers here were once the Sidebottoms, they went out of business in 1896; Bridge Mill, which was destroyed by fire in 1899; Waterside Mill, and Station Mill, built by the Platt brothers in 1834. Here is St Andrew's Church, its font sent by a former parishioner all the way from New Zealand. *Territorials:* 6th Cheshire Regiment.

Hadleigh Suffolk market town on the River Bret, ten miles from Ipswich where cocoanut matting was manufactured. Here is St Mary's Church, Hadleigh station being at the terminus of the Great Eastern Railway's branch from Bentley. *Territorials:* 5th Suffolk Regiment.

Hadlow West Kent village four miles from the railway at Tonbridge. Here is St Mary's Church, the guides noting brick making and brewing as Hadlow's main industries. *Territorials:* 4th Royal West Kent Regiment.

Hadlow Down East Sussex village three miles from the railway at Buxted. Here is St Mark's Church. *Territorials:* 5th Royal Sussex Regiment.

Hafod District on the River Tawe to the north of Swansea, where many were employed in the Hafod Copperworks, opened by J H Vivian in 1810, and William Foster & Co's Hafod Morfa Copperworks. Here, on Odo Street and built 1878–80, is St John's Church. *Territorials:* 6th Welsh Regiment.

Hailsham East Sussex market town served by the London, Brighton & South Coast Railway. One early twentieth-century guide notes Hailsham as a prosperous little town, with a rope manufactory and a large cattle market. Here, in 1870, a south isle was added to St Mary's Church. *Territorials:* 2nd Home Counties Brigade RFA and 5th Royal Sussex Regiment.

Hale Cheshire village, six miles from Knutsford, served by the Cheshire Lines Committee Railway. The station was opened in May 1862 and called Bowden Peel Causeway until 1899 when it was shown in railway timetables as Peel Causeway. The change to Hale station came in 1902. *Territorials:* Cheshire Yeomanry.

Halesowen North Worcestershire market town on the River Stour seven miles to the south-west of Birmingham. Halesowen station was opened in March 1878 and during the period 1908–14 was served by the Midland & Great Western Joint Railway. Manufactured in the town were gun barrels, anchors, metal tools, perambulators and horn buttons. Here is the church of St John the Baptist. *Territorials:* 7th Worcestershire Regiment.

Halesworth East Suffolk market town on the River Blyth ten miles to the south-east of Bungay. The Great Eastern Railway served the town, a new line ran by the Southwold Railway and branching south-east to Southwold opening up in September 1879. In the town were carriage works, malthouses and breweries; a large trade was also carried on in cotton. Here is St Mary's Church. *Territorials:* Suffolk Yeomanry and 4th Suffolk Regiment.

Halifax West Yorkshire market, cotton and industrial town situated in the valley of the Hebble about two miles from where it meets the Calder. A busy railway junction, the town's trade lay in cotton, chemicals, machinery of all kinds and the clothing industry. The Akroyd Museum and Art Gallery at Harley Hill was opened in 1886 in the former seat of Edward Akroyd, an early member of the Volunteer Force. To the east of the town is the church of St John the Baptist which underwent restoration in 1878. *Territorials:* Yorkshire Dragoons, 2nd West Riding Brigade RFA, 4th Duke of Wellington's Regiment and Yorkshire Mounted Brigade Field Ambulance.

Halkirk Caithness-shire village on the River Thurso, ten miles from Thurso town, served by the Highland Railway. Here, flagstones were quarried. *Territorials:* 5th Seaforth Highlanders.

Halstead Essex market town on the River Colne thirteen miles from Colchester. Halstead was served by the Colne Valley and Halstead Railway which opened in April 1860. Here, at the end of High Street, is St Andrew's Church; mainly fourteenth century with memorials to the Bourchier family. Its registers date from 1564. Employment for many in the town was in large silk and crape mills. There is a painting by transport artist Malcolm Root which shows Halstead around 1930, but the scene would have been little different twenty years before. Here, as the road bends round into the High Street, we see Simmons Brothers the draper and milliner; across the road J H Joyce the family butcher and, perhaps on its way to or from its Tidings Hill depot, a delivery van belonging to local brewer, G E Cook & Sons. *Territorials:* Essex Yeomanry and 5th Essex Regiment.

Haltwhistle Northumberland market town on the north bank on the Tyne, to the west of Hexham, served by the North Eastern Railway. Many from the town were employed in local collieries and brickworks. Here is the church of the Holy Cross which was restored around 1870. *Territorials:* 4th Northumberland Fusiliers and Haltwhistle Territorial Cadets.

Ham Street East Kent village, its railway station ('Ham Street and Oriestone') being on the South Eastern & Chatham Railway which ran south from Ashford. *Territorials:* 5th Buffs East Kent Regiment.

Hamilton Lanarkshire mining and market town at the confluence of the rivers Avon and Tyne. A busy junction of the Caledonian Railway, Hamilton lies ten miles south-east of Glasgow. *Territorials:* 6th Cameronians.

Hammersmith West London borough on the Thames which is crossed by a suspension bridge built by Sir Joseph Bazalgette 1883–87. The railway reached Hammersmith in 1858, the London Electric station being opened in December 1906. Here, on Glenthorne Road and built 1857–59. is the church of St John the Evangelist, and in Paddenswick Road, Holy Innocents which opened in 1887. *Territorials:* 7th London Regiment.

Hampstead North-west London suburb well known for its artists, musicians and literary residents. The railway reached Hampstead in 1851, but in 1907 came the Charring Cross, Euston & Hampstead line which became the London Electric in 1910. University College School at Frognal maintained three OTC infantry companies. Here is the old parish church of St John's. *Territorials:* 7th Middlesex Regiment, 1st Cadet Battalion Royal Fusiliers.

Hampton Middlesex village on the north bank of the Thames served by the London & South Western Railway. Here were the pumping rooms and filtering beds of the Grand Junction, West Middlesex, Southwark and Vauxhall Water Companies. A little to the south-east, and with its own stations, is Hampton Court Palace. In white brick is St Mary's Church, its registers dating from 1555. *Territorials:* 8th Middlesex Regiment.

Hamsteels Durham locality two miles from the railway at Lanchester. Here is the small stone church of St John the Baptist. *Territorials:* 8th Durham Light Infantry.

Handley Dorsetshire village (sometimes called 'Sixpenny Handley') on the Wiltshire border five miles north-west of Cranborne. A fire in 1892 almost destroyed the village. Here is St Mary's Church, the nearest railway station being eight miles to the south at Verwood. *Territorials:* Dorsetshire Yeomanry.

Handsworth South Staffordshire residential district to the north-west of Birmingham. On a hill looking down on the town, St Mary's Church was restored and partly rebuilt in 1877. The offices of the Local Board were opened in Soho Street in 1879 and the London & North Western Railway's station (Handsworth Wood) in April 1889 – the Great Western had reached the town in 1854. Here is Handsworth Grammar School which maintained an infantry company in the OTC. *Territorials:* 5th South Staffordshire Regiment, North Midland Divisional Transport and Supply Column and North Midland Mounted Brigade Field Ambulance.

Hanley North Staffordshire market and potteries town just two miles up the line (North Staffordshire Railway) from Stoke. Here in Town Road is St John's Church and, in Leek Road All Saints. *Territorials:* North Midland Divisional Engineers and 5th North Staffordshire Regiment.

Hanworth Norfolk village just over two miles from the railway to the east at Gunton. Here is St Bartholomew's Church. *Territorials:* Norfolk Yeomanry.

Harborne Suburb of Birmingham served by the London & North Western Railway where the chief industries are noted as market gardening, brick making and the manufacture of wrenches, hammers and spectacle. Here is St Peter's Church. *Territorials:* South Midland Divisional Transport and Supply Column.

Harby Leicestershire village on the Grantham and Nottingham Canal nine miles to the north of Melton Mowbray. The station at Harby ('Harby and Strathern') was on the Great Northern & London & North Western Joint Railway. Here is St Mary's Church. *Territorials:* Leicestershire Yeomanry and 5th Leicestershire Regiment.

Hardingham Norfolk village two stations from Wymondham on the Great Eastern Railway. Here is St George's Church where there is a memorial to Captain William Foster of the 11th Hussars, who died in 1911 and was one of the Light Brigade at Balaclava. *Territorials:* Norfolk Yeomanry.

Harlech Merionethshire coastal town overlooking Tremadoc Bay ten miles up from Barmouth on the Cambrian Railway. Most of the male population at Harlech were employed in the neighbouring quarries at Blaenau Ffestiniog. Here, in the centre of the town, is St Tanwg's Church. *Territorials:* 7th Royal Welsh Fusiliers.

Harleston South Norfolk market town ten miles to the north-east of Diss on the Great Eastern Railway. Here is the church of St John the Baptist. *Territorials:* Norfolk Yeomanry and 4th Norfolk Regiment.

Harlow West Essex market town on the Great Eastern Railway, just over twenty-three miles from London's Liverpool Street station, where the chief industries are noted as engineering, dry glazing and brewing. Here are the churches of St Mary the Virgin, St John the Baptist and, in Potter Street, St Mary Magdalen. *Territorials:* 4th Essex Regiment.

Harold Wood Essex hamlet three miles from Romford and fifteen from London's Liverpool Street on the Great Eastern Railway. *Territorials:* 4th Essex Regiment.

Harpenden Hertfordshire village five miles to the south-east of Luton served by the Midland and Great Northern railways. Here is St Nicholas's Church. *Territorials:* Hertfordshire Yeomanry, Hertfordshire Regiment and 4th Hertfordshire (St George's School) Cadets.

Harpole Northamptonshire village four miles from the nearest railway at Northampton. Here is All Saints Church. *Territorials:* 4th Northamptonshire Regiment.

Harringay Area in north London served by the Great Northern and Midland railways. Here, on the corner of Wightman Road and Burgoyne Road, is St Paul's Church where the registers go back to 1884. *Territorials:* Hertfordshire Yeomanry and Harringay Cadet Company.

Harrogate West Yorkshire market town on the North Eastern Railway, much advertised in their posters as 'Britain's Health Resort' and 'The British Spa'. Harrogate's Royal Baths in Crescent Road opened in 1897. Here is Christ Church, St Mary's and, opened in 1876, St Peter's Church. A statue to Queen Victoria was unveiled in Station Square in 1887. *Territorials:* Yorkshire Hussars and 5th West Yorkshire Regiment.

Harrow Middlesex town to the north-west of London served by the Metropolitan and Great Central Railways. Here, lying on John Peachey's tomb in St Mary's churchyard, Byron wrote a number of his earlier poems. He was a pupil at Harrow School at the time. The school, a strong supporter of the Volunteer Movement since 1859, after 1908 maintained three infantry companies in the OTC. *Territorials:* 9th Middlesex Regiment and Harrow Cadet Company.

Hartfield East Sussex village on the upper course of the Medway, a little north of Ashdown Forest. At St Mary's Church there is a lych gate with a timber-built cottage attached, which has the date

1520. Hartfield was served by the London, Brighton & South Coast Railway. *Territorials:* 5th Royal Sussex Regiment.

Hartford Cheshire village on the River Weaver, to the south-west of Northwich, served by the London & North Western and Cheshire Lines Railways. Here is St John's Church. *Territorials:* 5th Cheshire Regiment.

Harthill Lanarkshire mining village on the River Almond two miles from the railway at Westcraigs. *Territorials:* 10th Royal Scots and 8th Highland Light Infantry.

Hartington Small Derbyshire market town on the Staffordshire border just over nine miles south-west of Bakewell. On the London and North Western Railway, Hartington Station was placed over a mile to the east and opened on 4 August 1899. Here, on high ground to the north of the town, is St Giles's Church. *Territorials:* Derbyshire Yeomanry.

Hartland Devonshire village on the south side of Barnstaple Bay where the nearest railway stations was thirteen miles to the east at Barnstaple. The tall tower of Hartland's St Nectan's looks out to the Atlantic. *Territorials:* 6th Devonshire Regiment.

Hartlepool Durham seaport and market town served by the North Eastern Railway, where many were employed in local collieries, in the docks (which exported much of the coal), in shipbuilding yards, engine and boiler works. In the summer of 1644 at Hartlepool, the Royalist surrendered to the Scottish army. Here is Holy Trinity Church, St Andrew's, which was opened in 1886 and, at the east end of the town near the sea and docks, St Hilda's. *Territorials:* Durham RGA.

Hartley Wintney Hampshire village nine miles from Basingstoke. The closest railway station was at Winchfield (London & South Western), a mile to the south. Here is the church of St John Evangelist which was completed in 1870. *Territorials:* 4th Hampshire Regiment.

Hartshill Northern district of Stoke-on-Trent, North Staffordshire. Here is Holy Trinity Church. *Territorials:* North Midland RGA.

Harwich Essex seaport and market town on the south side of the River Stour where it meets the Orwell. The Great Eastern Railway served the town, its inhabitant largely employed in the fishing industry, docks and shipbuilding. Here, close to the waterfront and next-door to the Three Cups Inn, is St Nicholas's Church where can be seen a memorial to an officer and a number of soldiers that died from fever contracted while serving in the Walcheren expedition of 1809–10. Here too are remembered the Cox family – the well-known army agents. The church registers date from 1539. *Territorials:* Essex Yeomanry and Essex and Suffolk RGA.

Haslemere South-west Surrey village close to the borders with Hampshire and Sussex and on the London & South Western main line from Waterloo. Here is St Bartholomew's Church, and the Tudor-style Aldworth House were Poet Laureate Lord Tennyson died in 1892. *Territorials:* 5th Queen's Royal West Surrey Regiment.

Haslingden East Lancashire market town just under twenty miles from Manchester on the London & North Western Railway. Cotton mills were the main employer, there were also collieries, iron works and quarries in the area. Here are St James's, St Stephen's and, finished in 1886, St John's churches. *Territorials:* 5th East Lancashire Regiment.

Hastings A popular East Sussex seaside resort then, as it is now, Victorian Hastings saw the restoration of All Saints Church in 1871 and St Clement's, where a cannonball fired into the town by a French ship in 1720 could be seen in the wall of the tower, in 1875. A Russian gun taken at Sebastopol was exhibited on the seafront which, as Hastings meets St Leonards, extends for almost three miles. Charles Lamb thought the town 'detestable', but Byron, when he came in 1814, enjoyed the place. Hastings was served by the London, Brighton & South Coast and the South Eastern & Chatham railways. The Hastings & District Electric Tramways Company, with its maroon and cream vehicles, began operating in July 1905. *Territorials:* 2nd Home Counties Brigade RFA, 5th Royal Sussex Regiment, University School Cadet Company and Collegiate School Cadet Company.

Hatch Beauchamp Somerset village to the south-east of Taunton served by the Great Western Railway. Here is St John's Church. *Territorials:* West Somerset Yeomanry.

Hatfield Small Hertfordshire town (sometimes called 'Bishop's Hatfield') five miles from St Albans on the main Great Northern line from London's King's Cross. Here the church is dedicated to St Etheldreda. *Territorials:* 5th Essex Regiment, Hertfordshire Yeomanry and Hertfordshire Regiment.

Hatherleigh North Devon market town on Lew Stream near its junction with the Torridge, eight miles from the railway at Okehampton station. Here is the church of St John the Baptist, and close by at Hatherleigh Moor, a monument in memory of Crimean War hero, and resident of the parish, Lieutenant Colonel Morris, CB. *Territorials:* Royal North Devon Yeomanry and 6th Devonshire Regiment.

Hathersage Derbyshire village on the River Derwent where many were employed in the production of needles, pins and hooks. Hathersage station on the Midland Railway, just over eleven miles from Sheffield, was opened in 1894. Here is St Michael's Church where two tall stones mark the spot where Robin Hood's companion Little John is believed to have been buried. Remembered here too are members of the Eyre family, among them Robert and Joan with their fourteen children. *Territorials:* 6th Sherwood Foresters.

Hatton Aberdeenshire village just over ten miles from Peterhead on the Great North of Scotland branch from Ellon to Boddam which opened in 1897. *Territorials:* 5th Gordon Highlanders.

Havant Hampshire market town on Langston Harbour served by the London, Brighton & South Coast and London & South Western railways. Parchment was made at Havant. Here is St Faith's Church. *Territorials:* 6th Hampshire Regiment.

Havenstreet Small hamlet on the Isle of Wight, three miles south-west of Ryde, reached by the railway (Isle of Wight Central) in 1875. Here is St Peter's Church. *Territorials:* 8th Hampshire Regiment.

Haverfordwest Market town, river port and county town of Pembrokeshire situated on the Western Cleddau and served by the Great Western Railway, Employment was mainly agricultural, the area also having a paper mill and brewery. Here are St Martin's, St Mary's and St Thomas's churches. *Territorials:* Pembrokeshire Yeomanry and 4th Welsh Regiment.

Haverhill Suffolk market town to the south of Newmarket with two stations, one served by the Great Eastern Railway, the other, a small branch ran by the Colne Valley & Halstead Company. The town had a large factory employing some 3,000 in the manufacture of clothing and mats; there were also firms producing silk, boots, shoes and bricks. Here is St Mary's Church. *Territorials:* 5th Suffolk Regiment.

Haverthwaite North Lancashire village on the River Levan two stations from Ulverston on the Furness Railway. Here, overlooking the river, is St Anne's Church, and in the neighbourhood a factory producing gunpowder that employed a good number. *Territorials:* 4th King's Own Royal Lancaster Regiment.

Hawarden Flintshire market town close to the River Dee, six miles from Chester on the Great Central Railway. A fountain was erected at the village cross in 1889 to commemorate the Golden

Wedding of several times Prime Minister W E Gladstone and his wife (heiress to Hawarden Castle Catherine Glynn) who were married at Hawarden. Their son was a former Volunteer officer. The church here is dedicated to St Deiniol. *Territorials:* 5th Royal Welsh Fusiliers.

Hawick Roxburghshire market town on the North British Railway forty-five miles from Carlisle. Employment in the area was provided by numerous clothing manufactures, saw mills and quarries. Here is St Mary's Church, restored after a fire in 1880, and St John's which was built in the same year. Ten years later, the old Wilton Lodge Estate was formed into a public park. *Territorials:* Lothians and Border Horse and 4th King's Own Scottish Borderers.

Hawkhurst Kent village where Babies' Castle, one of Doctor Barnardo's institutions, was opened in 1886. The railway came in September 1893, but the old Cranbrook & Paddock Wood branch station, however, was sited some two miles north of the village. Here, since the reign of Edward III, is St Lawrence's Church; All Saints a little younger having been completed in 1861. *Territorials:* West Kent Yeomanry and 5th Buffs East Kent Regiment.

Hawkshead Small north Lancashire town five miles from Ambleside and four from the railway at Coniston. On high ground, St Michael's Church has fine views towards Grasmere, the town well known to William Wordsworth and his brother who were educated here. *Territorials:* 4th King's Own Royal Lancaster Regiment.

Haworth West Yorkshire village situated on the slope of a steep hill. At the top is St Michael and All Angels Church where there is a memorial tablet to the Brontë family who came to Haworth in 1820. All around there were mills much written about, of course, by the sisters. Haworth was served by the Midland Railway. *Territorials:* 6th Duke of Wellington's Regiment.

Hay-on-Wye Brecknockshire market town seven miles from Brecon and just across the river from Radnorshire on the Neath & Brecon Railway. Here is St Mary's Church and, close by, the Black Mountains. *Territorials:* Montgomeryshire Yeomanry and Brecknockshire Battalion.

Haydock South-west Lancashire village on the Great Central Railway, three miles from St Helen's, from where many were employed in local collieries. Here since 1866, and enlarged in 1891, is St James's Church. *Territorials:* 5th South Lancashire Regiment.

Haydon Bridge South Northumberland village on the South Tyne, served by the North Eastern Railway, seven miles west of Hexham. Here since 1797 is St Cuthbert's Church. *Territorials:* 4th Northumberland Fusiliers.

Hayfield North Derbyshire village, on the Great Central Railway just over eighteen miles from Manchester, where many were employed in a local calico printing works and paper making factory. Here is St Matthew's Church where John Wesley preached in 1755. *Territorials:* 6th Sherwood Foresters.

Hayle Hayle was a busy seaport four miles from St Ives in Cornwall on the Great Western Railway and well known for its manufacture of mining machinery. Some of the largest ever pumping machines were made there. The work of the same architect that built Holy Trinity in Sloan Street, London (J D Sedding), St Elwyn's Church at Hayle was completed in 1888. *Territorials:* Cornwall RGA and 4th Duke of Cornwall's Light Infantry.

Haywards Heath East Sussex town on the main line (London, Brighton & South Coast) from London, Victoria to Brighton. The railway had arrived in 1841 and soon after it, as the town grew, St Wilfrid's Church. Here is Ardingly College which maintained a contingent of the OTC. *Territorials:* Sussex Yeomanry and 4th Royal Sussex Regiment.

Headcorn Kent village on the River Beult, nine miles south-east of Maidstone, to which both the South Eastern & Chatham and Kent & East Sussex railways brought Londoners for the hop picking. Here too, bricks and tiles were made. Headcorn's church is dedicated to St Peter and St Paul. *Territorials:* Royal East Kent Yeomanry and 5th Buffs East Kent Regiment.

Headley East Hampshire village three miles to the east of Bordon and the nearest railway station. Headley is situated in the Woolmer Forest, its church being dedicated to All Saints. *Territorials:* 6th Hampshire Regiment.

Heanor Derbyshire town, served by both the Great Northern and Midland railways, just over five miles from Belper. Here were ironworks, collieries, and a large factory manufacturing hosiery. Born at Heanor in January 1890 was William Gregg who would receive the Victoria Cross, Distinguished Conduct and Military medals during the First World War. Heanor's church is dedicated to St Lawrence. *Territorials:* 5th Sherwood Foresters.

Heathfield Sussex village on the line opened by the London, Brighton & South Coast Railway in 1880. Heathfield Park was the home of General Eliot (later Lord Heathfield) the defender of Gibraltar 1779–82. He is buried in a vault at nearby All Saints Church. *Territorials:* 5th Royal Sussex Regiment.

Hebburn-on-Tyne North Durham manufacturing town on the south bank of the river just over five miles on the North Eastern Railway from Newcastle. Employment in Hebburn, which was divided into three parishes: St Cuthbert's, St John's and St Oswald's, was cantered around a large colliery, shipbuilding, engineering and the production of cement and lead. *Territorials:* 4th Northumbrian Brigade RFA.

Heckmondwike West Yorkshire market town on the London & North Easter Railway two miles to the north-west of Dewsbury. The production of blankets and carpets are noted as the town's chief industries, but many were also employed in collieries, chemical, iron and engineering works. Here, since 1831, is St James's Church; the Roman Catholic St Patricks opening forty years after that. *Territorials:* 2nd West Riding Brigade RFA.

Hedingham Essex villages – Castle Hedingham to the north, Sible Hedingham in the south – on the River Colne served by the Colne Valley & Halstead Railway. Here at Castle Hedingham is St Nicholas's Church, and at Sible, that dedicated to St Peter. *Territorials:* 5th Essex Regiment.

Hednesford Staffordshire town on the Cannock Chase and London & North Western Railway with numerous collieries, brick and tile works. Here on Church Hill is St Peter's Church. *Territorials:* 5th South Staffordshire Regiment.

Hedon East Yorkshire town just over eight miles east of Hull on the North Eastern Railway, where many were employed in the production of tiles and bricks. Hedon consists of one main street, in the centre of which stands St Augustine's Church. *Territorials:* 5th East Yorkshire Regiment.

Helensburgh Dumbartonshire town on the north shore of the Firth of Clyde forming the terminus of the Glasgow & Helensburgh branch of the North British Railway, and the eastern terminus of the West Highland Railway which came in from Fort William in 1894. 'The Brighton of Glasgow', was one reference to Helensburgh, 'the favourite resting place of the busy city man...' Born at Helensburgh in 1888 was John Logie Baird, the pioneer of television. *Territorials:* Clyde RGA and 9th Argyll and Sutherland Highlanders.

Helmsdale Sutherlandshire fishing village on the mouth of the Helmsdale served by the Highland Railway. *Territorials:* 2nd Lovat's Scouts and 5th Seaforth Highlanders.

Helmsley North Riding of Yorkshire market town on the River Rye just under thirty-two miles from York on the North Eastern Railway. Here is the Norman All Saints Church and, founded in 1132, Rievaulx Abbey. *Territorials:* Yorkshire Hussars and 5th Yorkshire Regiment.

Helperby North Riding of Yorkshire village on the River Swale, three miles north-east of Boroughbridge, served by the North Eastern Railway just to the north at Brafferton. The area was well known for its barley and had busy breweries and malthouses. Here were Wesleyan and Primitive Methodist chapels. *Territorials:* 4th Yorkshire Regiment.

Helston Cornwall town, three miles from the sea on the River Cober, the Gwinear Road to Helston Railway having been opened by the Great Western on 9 May 1887. Inhabitants wishing to travel to The Lizard from 17 August 1903 would have done so via the first ever railway-operated bus service. Here is St Michael's Church which dates from 1763 – an earlier building having been destroyed by lightening – and a grammar school at which Derwent Coleridge, the poet's son, was once headmaster. *Territorials:* Royal 1st Devon Yeomanry and 4th Duke of Cornwall's Light Infantry.

Hemel Hempstead Hertfordshire market town on the River Gade, and close to the Grand Junction Canal, three miles by rail from Harpenden on the Midland Railway. At Hemel Hempstead there were large paper mills, iron foundries and breweries. Here is the twelfth-century St Mary's Church. *Territorials:* Hertfordshire Yeomanry, 4th East Anglian Brigade RFA and Hertfordshire Regiment.

Hendon North-west London suburb in Middlesex and on the border with Hertfordshire, its station being on the Midland Railway between Cricklewood and Mill Hill. Here is St Mary's Church which dates from the seventeenth century. *Territorials:* Hertfordshire Yeomanry and 9th Middlesex Regiment.

Henfield West Sussex village above the River Adur and north of the Downs, where, notes one guide, most of the vegetables for the Brighton market were grown. Henfield was served by the London, Brighton & South Coast Railway just over fourteen miles from Brighton, its church being dedicated to St Peter. *Territorials:* 4th Royal Sussex Regiment.

Henley-in-Arden Small Warwickshire town just over eight miles by rail from Stratford-upon-Avon on the Great Western Railway. Here is the church of St John the Baptist. *Territorials:* Warwickshire Yeomanry and Warwickshire RHA.

Henley-on-Thames Oxfordshire town just over twenty-three miles from Oxford on the Great Western Railway. *Cassell's* notes that malting, brewing and a large trade in corn, flour and timber gave employment to the area. Here, in flint and stone, is St Mary's Church, Holy Trinity and, opened in Reading Road in 1907, the United Reform Church by Hampden W Pratt. *Territorials:* Oxfordshire Yeomanry and 4th Oxfordshire and Buckinghamshire Light Infantry.

Hereford County and market town served by the Great Western and London & North Western railways. Dominating the town is Hereford Cathedral, close by is All Saints, which underwent restoration in 1892, and the Norman St Peter's which had work done seven years before that. St Paul's, in Church Road, was opened in 1865, St James's in Green Street, 1869, Holy Trinity, 1883. Hereford in 1908–14, as now, was strongly associated with the making of cider, Bulmers a major employer. Hereford Cathedral School maintained one company of infantry in the OTC. *Territorials:* Shropshire Yeomanry, Herefordshire Regiment, Welsh Divisional Transport and Supply Column and South Wales Mounted Brigade Field Ambulance.

Herne Bay Seaside resort of the Kent north coast, just to the west of Margate, served by the South Eastern & Chatham Railway. Here is Christ Church. *Territorials:* Royal East Kent Yeomanry, 4th

Buffs East Kent Regiment, Herne Bay College Cadet Corps and New College (Herne Bay) Cadet Corps.

Herriard Hampshire village five miles south-east of Basingstoke. The railway did not reach Herriard until the opening by the London & South Western of their branch between Alton and Basingstoke in 1901. Here is St Mary's Church. *Territorials:* 9th Hampshire Regiment.

Hersham North Surrey village on the River Mole, close to Walton-on-Thames, served by the London & South Western Railway's Walton and Hersham station. Here is St Peter's Church. *Territorials:* 6th East Surrey Regiment.

Hertford County and market town on the River Lea just over twenty-four miles by rail from London on the Great Eastern Railway. Here there were iron foundries, breweries, malthouses, brickfields and limekilns. The town for a long time, well known for its paper making – John Tate establishing the first paper mill in Britain at Sele Mill in 1494. All Saints and St Andrews are parishes. Hertford Grammar School maintained one infantry company in the OTC. *Territorials:* Hertfordshire Yeomanry, 4th East Anglian Brigade RFA and Hertfordshire Regiment.

Hessle East Riding of Yorkshire town on the River Humber, just over four miles from Hull and served by the North Eastern Railway, where many were employed in shipyards and the quarrying of chalk. All Saints Church lies just off the town square, the Town Hall at the top of South Lane being opened in 1897. *Territorials:* 5th East Yorkshire Regiment.

Heswall West Cheshire town on the River Dee and the London & North Western and Great Western Joint Railway between Neston and West Kirby. Here is St Peter's Church. *Territorials:* 4th Cheshire Regiment.

Hethersett Norfolk village just over six miles by rail on the Great Eastern Railway from Norwich. Here the church is dedicated to St Remigius. *Territorials:* 4th Norfolk Regiment.

Hexham Northumberland market town on the south bank of the Tyne and North Eastern Railway to the west of Newcastle, once known for its manufacture of gloves, saddles and other leather items. Here, at Beaumont Street in March 1904, was unveiled a memorial to Colonel G E Benson who had been killed at the Battle of Brankenlaaghe 30 October 1901. Dominating the town and is narrow, irregular streets, is Hexham Abbey Church of St Andrew which lies at the west end of the market place. *Territorials:* Northumberland Yeomanry and 4th Northumberland Fusiliers.

Heytesbury Wiltshire village on the River Wiley and Great Western Railway four miles to the south-east of Warminster and close to Salisbury Plain. Here is the church of St Peter and St Paul. *Territorials:* 4th Wiltshire Regiment.

Heywood South-east Lancashire town on the River Roch, three miles from Bury on the London & North Western Railway. Sir Robert Peel brought cotton mills to the town, other chief industries being the production of railway plant, boilers, iron and brass founding. Here are St Luke's and St James's churches. *Territorials:* 5th Lancashire Fusiliers.

High Barnet South Hertfordshire town (sometimes called 'Chipping Barnet') on the Great North Road between London and St Albans and served by the Great Northern Railway out of King's Cross. Here is the church of St John the Baptist and, in St Albans Road, Christ Church. *Territorials:* Hertfordshire Yeomanry.

High Bickington Devonshire village on the River Taw, just over seven miles east of Torrington and two from the railway at the London & South Western Railways Portsmouth Arms station. Here the twelfth-century St Mary's Church sits on a hill top. *Territorials:* Royal North Devon Yeomanry.

High Wycombe Buckinghamshire market town, on the River Wye, just over twenty-six miles by rail from London, Paddington on the Great Western Railway, where the making of chairs was once an important industry. There exists a photograph dated May 1901 which shows members of the Buckinghamshire Yeomanry marching from the station upon their return from South Africa. The Buckinghamshire Battalion line the route. Here is All Saints Church of 1273, and the Royal Grammar School which maintained one OTC infantry company. *Territorials:* Buckinghamshire Yeomanry and Buckinghamshire Battalion.

Higham Ferrers Northamptonshire town on the south side of the Nene Valley important in the manufacture of boots and shoes. There were two railway stations: one served by the Midland, the other, on the London & North Western line. Here is St Mary's Church. *Territorials:* 4th Northamptonshire Regiment.

Highbridge Small Somerset town on the River Brue, six miles from Bridgewater, served by the Great Western and Somerset & Dorset railways. Many from Highbridge were employed in a locomotive works, and in the production of bricks and tiles. Here, with its lofty spire and red and black tile roof, is St John's Church. *Territorials:* West Somerset Yeomanry and 5th Somerset Light Infantry.

Highclere North Hampshire village to the south of Newbury on the Western Railway's Didcot, Newbury & Southampton branch that opened in 1885. Here is St Michael and All Angels Church which dates from 1870. *Territorials:* 4th and 9th Hampshire Regiment.

Highcliffe South Hampshire seaside resort three miles from the railway at Christchurch. Here is St Mark's Church of 1843. *Territorials:* Hampshire Yeomanry and 7th Hampshire Regiment.

Highgate North London suburb served by the Great Northern and London Electric railways. Born at Highgate in 1904 was poet laureate Sir John Betjeman who attended Highgate Junior School where T S Elliot was one of the teachers. Here are St Michael's, St Anne's, All Saints and St Augustine's churches. Highgate School maintained one infantry company in the OTC. *Territorials:* 7th Middlesex Regiment.

Highley South Shropshire village on the River Severn and Great Western Railway, seven miles from Bridgnorth, where a colliery employed many. Here is St Mary's Church which underwent restoration in 1880. *Territorials:* 4th King's Shropshire Light Infantry.

Hilgay West Norfolk village on the left bank of the River Wissey and Great Eastern Railway, four miles from Downham. Here is All Saints Church. *Territorials:* 5th Norfolk Regiment.

Hillington Norfolk village just over ten miles by rail on the Midland & Great Northern Joint Railway. Here is St Mary's Church. *Territorials:* 5th Norfolk Regiment.

Himley Staffordshire village four miles to the west of Dudley and three from the railway at Brierley Hill. Here is St Michael's Church. *Territorials:* Staffordshire Yeomanry.

Hinckley Leicestershire market town, twelve miles to the south-west of Leicester, served by the Midland and London & North Western railways. Inhabitants may have been employed in the production of Hinckley's famous course cotton stockings, or perhaps in one or other of the many boot and shoe factories in and around the area. Here are St Mary's and Holy Trinity churches, the Ashby-de-la-Zouch Canal about a mile to the south-west. *Territorials:* Leicestershire Yeomanry and 5th Leicestershire Regiment.

Hindley Lancashire town, just over two miles from Wigan on the London & North Western Railway, where many were employed in its coal mines, iron works and cotton mills. Here are All Saints and St Peter's churches. *Territorials:* 5th North Lancashire Regiment.

Hindon Wiltshire village four miles from the railway at the London & North Weston's station at Tisbury. Here is the church of St John the Baptist. *Territorials:* 1st South Western Mounted Brigade Transport and Supply Column.

Hingham Norfolk village six miles west of Wymondham and two from the railway at Hardingham station. Here is St Andrew's Church which dates from 1316. *Territorials:* 4th Norfolk Regiment.

Hitchin Hertfordshire town thirty-two miles by rail on the Great Northern Railway from London's King's Cross. The town was also served by the Midland's line that came down from Bedford. Here, in the centre of the town, is St Mary's Church where iron railings once stood to keep out the bodysnatchers. They did not return after going to help with the Second World War; but neither did the bodysnatchers. *Territorials:* Hertfordshire Yeomanry and Hertfordshire Regiment.

Hoddesdon Small Hertfordshire town situated on a slope west of the Rive Lea, seventeen miles by rail on the Great Eastern Railway from London's King's Cross. Hoddesdon was well known to Izaak Walton who fished the nearby Lea. Here is St Catherine's Church. *Territorials:* Hertfordshire Yeomanry and Hertfordshire Regiment.

Hodnet Shropshire village close to the River Tern and served by the Great Western Railway five miles south-west of Market Drayton. Here, on high ground to the north-west of the village, is St Luke's Church. *Territorials:* 4th King's Shropshire Light Infantry.

Holbeach South Lincolnshire market town seven miles by rail from Spalding on the Midland & Great Northern Joint Railway. Here, with its 180 ft spire, is All Saints Church. *Territorials:* Lincolnshire Yeomanry.

Holborn London borough, business and law centre – here are the Inns of Court, Lincoln's and Gray's Inns – where a church is dedicated to St Etheldreda. *Territorials:* South Eastern Mounted Brigade, London Mounted Brigade Signal Troops, 6th, 12th London Regiment, Inns of Court OTC, London Mounted Brigade Field Ambulance, 3rd London General Hospital and Imperial Cadet Yeomanry.

Holkham North Norfolk village served by the Great Eastern Railway two miles west of Wells-on-Sea. Here, the church is dedicated to St Withberga. *Territorials:* 6th Norfolk Regiment.

Holm Fishing village on Holme Sound, Orkney some twenty-five miles from the railway at Thurso. *Territorials:* Orkney RGA.

Holmfirth West Riding of Yorkshire town just over six miles by rail from Huddersfield on the London & North Western Railway. Holmfirth, the scene of the TV series *Last of the Summer Wine*, stands in the valley where the Holme and Ribble meet and was once important in the cloth industry. Barmforth & Co produced their saucy seaside postcards at their printing works in Station Road, the company, and the town, also well known for its contribution to the early film industry. Here is Holy Trinity Church of 1777, and the Gothic-style St John's which was completed in 1847. *Territorials:* 5th Duke of Wellington's Regiment.

Holmwood South Surrey village served by the London, Brighton & South Coast Railway two miles south of Dorking. Here, on the highest part of Holmwood Common, stands St Mary Magdalene's Church of 1838, and to the north of the village, St John's. *Territorials:* 5th Queen's Royal West Surrey Regiment.

Holsworthy West Devon village served by the London & South Western Railway, fourteen miles west of Hatherleigh. Here, greatly restored and enlarged in 1884, is St Peter's and St Paul's Church. *Territorials:* Royal North Devon Yeomanry and 6th Devonshire Regiment.

Holt (Norfolk) Market town in the north of the county of which one guide describes as a 'cheerful little town and well paved'. Holt lies on the branch line began by the Eastern & Midlands Railway in 1884 which ran between Melton Constable and Cromer. Here is St Andrew's Church, and Gresham's School which maintained an OTC contingent. *Territorials:* Norfolk Yeomanry and 5th Norfolk Regiment.

Holt (Wiltshire) Village just over two miles from Bradford-on-Avon served by the Great Western Railway. Here, with its saddle-back roof, is St Katherine's Church. *Territorials:* 4th Wiltshire Regiment.

Holyhead Market town and busy seaport on the north side of Holyhead Island, Anglesey where, note the guides, the inhabitants are mostly involved with the railway and steamer services (London & North Midland). Here is St Cybi's Church, and the Gothic-style St Seiriol's. *Territorials:* 6th Royal Welsh Fusiliers.

Holywell Flintshire market town, fifteen miles north-west of Chester, where the several industries noted include: lead mining, copper and iron production. There were also paper mills, cement works, collieries and lime quarries. Holywell station was served by the London & North Western Railway and was re-named Holywell Junction when the line was extended closer to the town (the new station called 'Holywell Town') in 1912. Here is St James's Church and the Roman Catholic, St Winefride's. *Territorials:* 5th Royal Welsh Fusiliers.

Honing North Norfolk village, four miles south-east of North Walsham, served by the Midland & Great Northern Joint Railway. Here is St Peter and St Paul's Church. *Territorials:* 5th Norfolk Regiment.

Honiton East Devon market town, seventeen miles from Exeter, served by the London & South Western Railway and well known for its production of lace and butter. Bricks, tiles and brown pottery were also made. Here are St Paul's and St Michael's churches, and All Hallows School which maintained a contingent of the OTC. *Territorials:* 4th Devonshire Regiment.

Hopeman Fishing village on the Moray Firth in Elginshire reached by the Highland Railway when its line extended east from Burghead in 1892. *Territorials:* 6th Seaforth Highlanders.

Hopetoun Estate and seat of the Earl of Hopetoun on the Firth of Forth, in Linlithgowshire, three miles from South Queensferry. *Territorials:* Lothians and Border Horse.

Horfield South Gloucestershire village and suburb of Bristol. Born here in 1904 was the Hollywood film actor Cary Grant (real name Archibald Leach). Here is Holy Trinity and St Edmund's churches. *Territorials:* Gloucestershire Yeomanry.

Horley Surrey village on the River Mole five miles south of Reigate on the London, Brighton & South Coast Railway. Here is St Bartholomew's Church. *Territorials:* 5th Queen's Royal West Surrey Regiment.

Horncastle Lincolnshire market town on the Rive Bain, twenty-one miles from Lincoln, reached by the Great Northern Railway when it opened its branch from Kirkstead to Horncastle in 1855. Here is Holy Trinity and St Mary's churches. *Territorials:* Lincolnshire Yeomanry and 4th Lincolnshire Regiment.

Hornchurch Essex village, two miles from Romford, reached by the London, Tilbury & Southend Railway in 1885. The main offices of the South Essex Waterworks were to be found at Hornchurch, as well as a factories making bicycles and agricultural implements. Here is St Andrew's Church. *Territorials:* 4th Essex Regiment.

Horndean South Hampshire village on the road from Petersfield to Portsmouth, four miles to the north-west of Havant. Established at Horndean in 1850, and the town's largest employer, was Gale's Brewery. *Territorials:* 9th Hampshire Regiment.

Horningsham South Wiltshire village, four miles south-west of Warminster. Here is St John's Church. *Territorials:* 4th Wiltshire Regiment.

Hornsea East Riding of Yorkshire coastal town on the North Sea, sixteen miles by rail from York on the North Eastern Railway. A popular seaside resort, Hornsea was always advertised as 'Lakeland by the Sea', due to the 467-acre lake 'Hornsea Mere' which was just inland from the coast. Here is St Nicholas's Church. *Territorials:* East Riding Yeomanry and 5th East Yorkshire Regiment.

Hornsey North London, Middlesex, suburb, which sprang up after the coming of the Great Northern Railway in 1850 – one Edwardian developer offering homes for London's 'clerks and skilled workers'. Here is St Mary's Church which was built in 1888. Hornsey station lies just over four miles out of King's Cross. *Territorials:* 7th Middlesex Regiment.

Horsham West Sussex market town and important junction on the London, Brighton & South Coast Railway, where the four main streets meet at the Carfax. St Mary's at the south end of the Causeway, St Mark's in North Street. At West Horsham, Christ's Hospital School had an OTC contingent. *Territorials:* Sussex Yeomanry and 4th Royal Sussex Regiment.

Horsley Woodhouse Derbyshire village to the south-west of Heanor and a mile from the nearest railway station at Kilburn. Here the church is dedicated to St Susanna. *Territorials:* 5th Sherwood Foresters.

Horsmonden Kent village on the Paddock Wood to Hawkhurst branch of the South Eastern & Chatham Railway opened in 1892. Here, some distance from the village, is the church of St Margaret of Antioch. Remembered in the south aisle is the rector's gardener is John Reid who died in 1847 having invented the stomach pump in 1823. *Territorials:* 5th Buffs East Kent Regiment.

Horton Heath South Hampshire village five miles to the north-east of Southampton. *Territorials:* 4th Dorsetshire Regiment.

Horwich Lancashire town just over seven miles by rail from Bolton. The railway arrived in 1868 and established soon was the locomotive works of the Lancashire and Yorkshire Railway which went on to employ some 3,500 staff. There were also cotton mills, collieries, bleaching works and manufacturers of bricks and titles. Here are Holy Trinity and St Catherine's churches. *Territorials:* 4th North Lancashire Regiment.

Houghton-le-Spring North Durham market and mining town six miles north-east of Durham, the nearest railway being two miles to the west at Fencehouses station. Here is St Michael's Church. *Territorials:* 8th Durham Light Infantry.

Hounslow Middlesex town, three miles from Brentford, served by the Metropolitan & District Railway. To the south-west, a gunpowder works called Hounslow Mills employed many from the area. Here are Holy Trinity, St Paul's and St Stephen's churches. *Territorials:* Home Counties Division, 8th Middlesex Regiment and Home Counties Divisional Transport and Supply Column.

Hove Western suburb of Brighton, Sussex served by the London, Brighton & South Coast Railway. Here at St Andrew's Church, a memorial remembers a man who fell to his death from the western tower of Ely Cathedral in 1845, and another, Admiral George Augustus Westphal who was with Nelson on the *Victory* at Trafalgar. All Saints replaced St Andrew's as the parish church in 1892. *Territorials:* 1st Home Counties Brigade RFA.

Hovingham North Riding of Yorkshire village served by the North Eastern Railway eight miles from Malton. Here is All Saints Church. *Territorials:* 5th Yorkshire Regiment.

Howden East Riding of Yorkshire market town twenty-one miles by rail from Hull on the North Eastern Railway. Here, dominating the area with its 135 ft tower, is St Peter and St Paul's Church. The town is twenty-five miles west of Hull. *Territorials:* 5th East Yorkshire Regiment.

Hoylake West Cheshire fishing town and seaside resort just over seven miles by rail from Birkenhead on the Wirral Railway. Here is Holy Trinity Church. *Territorials:* 4th Cheshire Regiment.

Hucknall Nottinghamshire town ten miles by rail from Nottingham on the Great Northern Railway, where a large colliery employed many. Cigars and Stockings were also made. Here, in the centre of town, is the church of St Mary Magdalene and St John the Evangelist, where Lord Byron is buried along with twenty-seven members of his family. *Territorials:* 8th Sherwood Foresters.

Huddersfield West Riding of Yorkshire town and busy railway junction of the Midland and London & North Western railways. The woollen trade employed many in Huddersfield, the machinery for the mills, as well as locomotive boilers, was made in the town's several foundries. Silk spinning also went on. Three firms: Leonard & Sons, Day & Sons, E T Monk & Co, were all supporters of the Volunteer and Territorial forces. Trams began to run in Huddersfield in January 1883. *Territorials:* Yorkshire Dragoons and 5th Duke of Wellington's Regiment.

Hull East Riding of Yorkshire town on the north bank of the Humber and either side of the River Hull – Kingston-upon-Hull its proper name. The building of ships, many for the Royal Navy, and fishing were the main industries in Hull. Here is the spacious Holy Trinity and Holy Apostles Church, and Hymers College which maintained one infantry company in the OTC. *Territorials:* East Riding Yeomanry, 2nd Northumbrian Brigade RFA, East Riding RGA, East Riding Fortress Engineers, 4th, 5th East Yorkshire Regiment, Northumbrian Divisional Transport and Supply Column, 3rd Northumbrian Field Ambulance and Hull Cadet Company St Mark's Church Scouts.

Hulme Manchester suburb where many were employed in cotton mills. Here is St George's Church, built by Francis Goodwin 1826–27; in Chichester Road and by J S Crowther (1856–58), St Mary's, and in Birchvale Close, Pugin's Roman Catholic St Wilfrid's. *Territorials:* 6th Manchester Regiment.

Hungerford Berkshire market town on the Kennet & Avon Canal and Great Western Railway close to the border with Wiltshire. Here, St Lawrence's Church of 1814–16 stands close to the canal. *Territorials:* Berkshire Yeomanry and 4th Royal Berkshire Regiment.

Hunmanby East Riding of Yorkshire village served by the North Eastern Railway twelve miles by rail form Scarborough. The guides note the area as mostly agricultural, but bricks and rope was made in the village. Here is All Saints Church. *Territorials:* East Riding Yeomanry, 5th East Yorkshire Regiment and 5th Yorkshire Regiment.

Hunstanton Norfolk town and seaside resort on the Great Eastern Railway fifteen miles from King's Lynn. Here we have New Hunstanton, with its St Edmund's Church and, just on a mile away, Old Hunstanton where in the churchyard of St Mary's can be seen the graves of William Webb, a soldier of the 15th Dragoons, and Customs Officer William Green. Both killed during an encounter with local smugglers in 1784. *Territorials:* Norfolk Yeomanry and 5th Norfolk Regiment.

Huntingdon County and market town on the north bank of the River Ouse, served by the Great Northern and Great Eastern railways, where breweries and a large carriage works employed many. Here is St John's, whose register records the baptism there in 1599 of Oliver Cromwell, and St Benedict's and St Mary's churches. *Territorials:* 5th Bedfordshire Regiment and Huntingdonshire Cyclist Battalion.

Huntley Aberdeenshire market town just over forty miles by rail from Aberdeen on the Great North of Scotland Railway. In the north-west of the county, Huntly gave employment in the manufacture of agricultural machinery, bricks and titles. There were two woollen mills and a stocking factory. Gordon School, founded in 1840, is close to Huntly Lodge and was enlarged in 1888. *Territorials:* 2nd Scottish Horse and 6th Gordon Highlanders.

Hursley Hampshire village four miles from Winchester and three from the nearest railway at Chandlers Ford station. Here is All Saints Church in which lies the body of hymn writer and local vicar, John Keble. Remembered at All Saints are the Cromwell family, descendants of Oliver Cromwell. *Territorials:* 4th Hampshire Regiment.

Hurst Green East Sussex hamlet just to the north-west of Etchingham. Here is L W Ridge's red-brick Holy Trinity Church of 1884. *Territorials:* 5th Royal Sussex Regiment.

Hurstpierpoint East Sussex village just under two miles from the railway at Hassocks. Within Sir Charles Barry's Holy Trinity Church, which was completed in 1845, there is a memorial to Bishop Hannington who was murdered in October 1885 by natives when leading an expedition in Africa. Here, in Hurstpierpoint, lived Percy Bysshe Shelly's friend, Elizabeth Hitcher. Hurstpierpoint College maintained one infantry company in the OTC. *Territorials:* 4th Royal Sussex Regiment.

Hutton Rudby Large village in the North Riding of Yorkshire on the River Leven four miles from Stokesley. Here is All Saints Church. *Territorials:* 4th Yorkshire Regiment.

Hyde Cheshire market town on the River Tame and Peak Forest Canal, just over seven miles by rail from Manchester on the Great Central Railway. The main source of employment in the town was from cotton, the Sidebotham, Hibbert, Horsfield and Ashton family-owned mills being the major employers. There were also several iron foundries and engineering works. Here is St George's Church, which was built in 1822. *Territorials:* 6th Cheshire Regiment.

Hythe (Hampshire) Large village on the west side of Southampton Water and just over two miles from the railway at Southampton in the south of the county. Here is the red-brick St John's Church. *Territorials:* 7th Hampshire Regiment.

Hythe (Kent) Hythe is five miles west of Folkestone and was served by the South Eastern & Chatham Railway's branch that came down from Sandling Junction in 1874. There was a tram service ran by the Folkestone, Hythe & Sandgate Tramway Company which opened in May 1891 and had a deport in Red Lion Square. Here, set on a hill and looking down on the town, is St Leonard's Church where Lionel Lukin, the inventor of the life boat, is buried in the churchyard. The Royal Military Canal begins just east of Hythe. *Territorials:* 4th Buffs East Kent Regiment and Kent Cyclist Battalion.

Ibstock Leicestershire village just over thirteen miles by rail from Loughborough on the London & North Western and Midland Joint Railway. Coal and the production of bricks, tiles and sanitary earthenware was Ibstock's main industries. Here is St Deny's Church. *Territorials:* Leicestershire Yeomanry.

Icklesham East Sussex village just under two miles to the west of Winchelsea. Here is All Saints Church which has a Norman north tower. *Territorials:* 5th Royal Sussex Regiment.

Ilford Almost London, Ilford in Essex lies on the Roding just over seven miles by rail from Liverpool Street Station. The Ilford Urban District Council Tramways service began operating in March 1903. Here is St Mary's Church, built in 1830, and St Clement's which dates from 1896. *Territorials:* 8th Essex Regiment, East Anglian Divisional Transport and Supply Column, Ilford Church Cadets and Cranbrook College Cadets.

Ilfracombe North Devon seaport, market town and seaside resort reached by the railway when the London & South Western came up from Barnstaple in 1874. Here, in the west of the town, is Holy Trinity Church; in St James's Place by the harbour, St Philip and St James and, in Highfield Road and opened in 1903, St Peter's. Beatrix Potter (1866–1943) on a visit to Illfracombe was not too impressed. She thought it may have been its many Welsh visitors that upset the place. *Territorials:* Devonshire RGA.

Ilkeston Derbyshire market town served by the Great Northern Railway, eight miles from Derby, where the Maxwell family's business made soap flakes, soda crystals and other cleaning products. Hosiery, lace and needles were made in the town, but the main source of employment was in local collieries. The town lies close to the Erewash Canal where there were iron works and brickfields. From their deport in Park Road, the maroon and cream trams of the Corporation Tramways began service in May 1903. Here are the churches of St Mary; Holy Trinity, which opened in 1890, and St John's which was completed four years after that. *Territorials:* Derbyshire Yeomanry and 5th Sherwood Foresters.

Ilkley West Riding of Yorkshire town on the south bank of the River Wharfe, twelve miles from Bradford, served by the Midland and North Eastern Railways – the 'Gateway to the Yorkshire Dales', as advertised on railway posters. Here is All Saints and St Margaret's churches. *Territorials:* Yorkshire Hussars and 4th West Riding Brigade RFA.

Ilminster South Somerset market town on the River Isle, five miles from Chard, served by the Great Western Railway. Here, collars and cuffs, flax, rope and bricks were made; and at St Mary's Church the Wadham family – one of them founded Wadham College, Oxford – are remembered. *Territorials:* West Somerset Yeomanry and 5th Somerset Light Infantry.

Inchmore Inverness-shire locality to the west of Inverness. *Territorials:* 4th Cameron Highlanders.

Ingatestone Essex village on the Great Eastern Railway to the south-west of Chelmsford. A million bricks, it is said, went to build the tower at St Mary and St Edmund's Church. The Petre family lie, and are remembered all around the church – Sir William Petre being Henry VIII's Secretary of State. Registers date from 1558. *Territorials:* Essex RHA.

Ingleton West Riding of Yorkshire village where the Midland and Lancaster & Carlisle railways met. Railway posters refer to Ingleton as the 'Land of Waterfalls'. Arthur Mee wrote of the village that it was the gateway to some of the finest scenery in the north of England. High up, about ten miles from Settle, the village looks down on the River Greta which is spanned by a seven-arched railway viaduct. Here is the church of St Mary the Virgin. *Territorials:* 6th Duke of Wellington's Regiment.

Innellan Argyllshire village on the Firth of Clyde four miles from Dunoon. *Territorials:* Clyde RGA.

Innerleithen Peebleshire town on the Leithen Water, close to where it meets the Tweed, served by the North British Railway. Innerleithen prospered, it is said, from its mineral spa and woollen mills. The spring is supposed to be the 'St Ronan's Well' of Scott's novel. Here are the ruins of Horsbrugh Castle. *Territorials:* Lothians and Border Horse and 8th Royal Scots.

Insch Aberdeenshire village just over twenty-seven miles by rail on the Great North of Scotland Railway from Aberdeen. There were slate quarries in the area. *Territorials:* 2nd Scottish Horse and 6th Gordon Highlanders.

Insh Inverness-shire village eight miles from Kingussie close to the River Spey and Loch Insh. *Territorials:* 4th Cameron Highlanders.

Inveraray County town of Argyllshire, fifteen miles from Dalmally. Inveraray is situated at the lower end of a small bay where the River Aray enters Loch Fyne and was well known for its herring fishery – there were also granite quarries in the area. Here is Inveraray Castle, the seat of the Dukes of Argyll. *Territorials:* 8th Argyll and Sutherland Highlanders.

Invergarry Inverness-shire village on Loch Oich at the mouth of the River Garry, seven miles from Fort Augustus. The Invergarry & Fort Augustus Railway arrived in 1903 (renamed North British in 1914) and the Caledonian Canal is close by. *Territorials:* 4th Cameron Highlanders.

Invergordon Ross and Cromarty town and port, thirteen miles north-east of Dingwall on the north shore of the Cromarty Firth, served by the Highland Railway. *Territorials:* 4th Seaforth Highlanders.

Invergowrie Perthshire village on the north bank of the Firth of Tay, three miles west of Dundee, served by the Caledonian Railway. Here is All Souls Episcopal Church, paper being made in the village at the Bullionfield Mill. *Territorials:* 1st Scottish Horse.

Inverkeithing Fifeshire seaport on the Firth of Forth, just east of the Forth Bridge and thirteen miles by rail from Edinburgh on the North British Railway. The town had a busy harbour, and also produced leather goods, rope and paper. Here, in July 1651, was the Battle of Inverkeithing. The parish church of St Peter stands on the east side of Church Street. *Territorials:* Forth RGA.

Inverkip Renfrewshire coastal village just under twenty-nine miles by rail from Glasgow on the Caledonian Railway. Here lies buried Dr James Young, the chemist who did much towards the production of paraffin. *Territorials:* Argyll and Sutherland Highlanders.

Inverness County town on the River Ness where it enters the Moray Firth. The headquarters of the Highland Railway were at Inverness, the town also forming the eastern terminus of the Caledonian Canal. St Andrew's Cathedral was consecrated in 1869, the Town Hall built in 1882, and certainly the Volunteers would have taken part in the unveiling ceremony ten years later of the white stone monument to those officers and men of the Cameron Highlanders who fell in the Egyptian campaign. There was shipbuilding at Inverness, also brewing and distilling. One guide notes that the shopkeeping business of the town was extensive. *Territorials:* Highland Mounted Brigade, Seaforth and Cameron Infantry Brigade, 2nd Lovat's Scouts, Inverness-shire RHA, Highland Mounted Brigade Signal Troop, 4th Cameron Highlanders, Highland Mounted Brigade Transport and Supply Column and Highland Mounted Brigade Field Ambulance.

Inverurie Aberdeenshire market town situated at the confluence of the rivers Don and Urie, served by the Great North of Scotland Railway who opened a locomotive works in the town in 1905. A large paper mill also gave much employment. Here, in 1307, was the Battle of Inverurie. The parish church of St Andrew lies close to the River Don. *Territorials:* 2nd Scottish Horse, 6th Gordon Highlanders and 2nd Highland Field Ambulance.

Ipswich Suffolk seaport, county and market town situated on the left bank of the River Gipping as it meets the Orwell, served by the Great Eastern Railway. Here, Ransome's employed many in their production of agricultural tools; their lawn mowers still produced today. Thomas Wolsey (1475–1530) was the son of an Ipswich butcher, and in 1837, Mr Pickwick (in *Pickwick Papers*) encountered Miss Witherfield in her bedroom at the town's Great White Horse Hotel. Ipswich School maintained one infantry company in the OTC. *Territorials:* Suffolk Yeomanry, 3rd East Anglian Brigade RFA, Essex and Suffolk RGA, 4th and 6th Suffolk Regiment, 1st East Anglian Field Ambulance and East Anglian Clearing Hospital.

Ironbridge Shropshire town on the River Severn served by the Great Western Railway. Up a steep slope from the river comes the town, its brick-built St Luke's Church of 1836 almost at the top. In

1778, at his Coalbrookdale foundry, Abraham Darby cast the world's first cold-cast iron bridge. *Territorials:* 4th King's Shropshire Light Infantry.

Irthlingborough Northamptonshire town on the north side of the River Nene, three miles from Wellingborough, served by the London & North Western Railway. Important to Irthlingborough was the manufacture of boots and shoes, and the quarrying of ironstone. Here, with its semi-detached bell tower and octagonal lantern looking like a lighthouse, is St Peter's Church. *Territorials:* 4th Northamptonshire Regiment.

Irvine Seaport and market town on the north bank of the River of the same name, Irvine lies eleven miles north of Ayr. Served by both the Caledonian and Glasgow & South Western railways, the town's principle sources of employment were in chemicals, shipbuilding, engineering, coal and iron. *Territorials:* 2nd Lowland Brigade RFA, 1st Cadet Battalion and 4th Royal Scots Fusiliers.

Islington North London borough just over three miles by rail from Broad Street station. Here since the middle of the seventeenth century is the famous 'Angel Hotel', and the birthplace of cartoonist and illustrator William Heath Robinson (1872–1944). Islington's parish church is St Mary's, St Peter's being built in 1835. *Territorials:* Hertfordshire Yeomanry, London Brigade RGA and Owen's School Cadet Corps.

Itton Court Seat of the Curre family. Itton village lies three miles from Chepstow in Monmouthshire on the Great Western Railway, its church being dedicated to St Deiniol. *Territorials:* 1st Monmouthshire Regiment.

Ivinghoe East Buckinghamshire market town, close to the Hertfordshire border and the Grand Junction Canal, situated nine miles from Aylesbury and two from the railway at Cheddington. Here is St Mary's Church which dates from 1220. *Territorials:* Hertfordshire Regiment.

Ivybridge Small Devon town on the River Erme and southern edge of Dartmoor, just over ten miles by rail from Plymouth of the Great Western Railway. Come the railway in 1848, come the Stowford paper mill which still employs many from the town. The ivy-covered bridge, from which the town takes its name, was painted by Turner in 1813. Here is St John's Church and the birthplace of Surgeon Major Edmund Barron Hartley (1847–1919) who won the Victoria Cross during the Basuto War of 1879. *Territorials:* 5th Devonshire Regiment.

Jamestown Small Dumbartonshire town on the River Leven, just south of Loch Lomond, between Balloch and Bonhill and served by the old Forth & Clyde Junction Railway. Jamestown employed many in its large print works. *Territorials:* 9th Argyll and Sutherland Highlanders.

Jarrow-on-Tyne Here, on the south bank of the Tyne, Charles Palmer's shipbuilding yard employed some eighty-percent of the town's workforce. Others made a living from local collieries, marine engineering and chemical works. Jarrow was served by the North Eastern Railway, a statue erected in 1903 by shipyard workers in memory of Charles's Palmer is situated close to the station. An inscription at St Paul's Church gives a dedication date of AD685. This was the Venerable Bede's church, his chair still there. *Territorials:* Durham Fortress Engineers.

Jedburgh Jedburgh Abbey looks down on the town which played an important part in Scotland's woollen industries. The county town of Roxburghshire, Jedburgh is situated on Jed Water and opened its station when the Jedburgh Railway (later North British) brought a line down from Roxburgh in 1856. *Territorials:* Lothians and Border Horse and 4th King's Own Scottish Borderers.

Jemimaville Village on South side of Cromarty Firth, Ross and Cromarty. *Territorials:* North Scottish RGA.

Johnstone Cotton and engineering town on the south bank of Black Cart Water in Renfrewshire, three miles west of Paisley on the Glasgow & South Western Railway. *Territorials:* 6th Argyll and Sutherland Highlanders.

Jura Island among the Inner Hebrides, Argyllshire, almost divided in two by Loch Tarbert. With just two principle towns: Craighouse, where there is a distillery, in the south, and Ardlussa in the north, one reference notes that on Jura, deer outnumber people by twenty-five-to-one. *Territorials:* 8th Argyll and Sutherland Highlanders.

Keighley West Riding of Yorkshire market town just over thirteen miles by rail from Bradford on the Great Northern Railway. Keighley, which is situated at the confluence of the Aire and Worth rivers, prospered in the textile industry and became well known for its manufacture of a worsted material called 'Bradford Stuffs'. The machines much needed by the mills to make the cloth were made here, as well as sewing machines to work the finished article. Close by is the Leeds and Liverpool Canal. In North Street a cinema has the date '1913' above its door, making it one of the oldest in the country. From its depot in South Street, the Keighley Tramways Company began service in May 1889. Here are St Andrew's and St Peter's churches. *Territorials:* 6th Duke of Wellington's Regiment.

Keith Banffshire town on the River Isla, ten miles from Huntly, where the Great North of Scotland Railway up from Aberdeen terminated and the Highland Railway took over to take travellers on to Inverness. Blankets, tweeds, boots, shoes and agricultural implements were manufactured in the area. There were also flour mills, a lime works and distilleries – the town's Strathisla distillery being the oldest (legal anyway) in the Highlands. *Territorials:* 2nd Scottish Horse and 6th Gordon Highlanders.

Kelsall Cheshire agricultural village on the edge of the Delamere Forest eight miles from Chester. Here, at St Peter's Church, one visitor remarked that much of the rough stonework suggested that the sculptor had possibly forgotten to finish his work. *Territorials:* Cheshire Yeomanry and 5th Cheshire Regiment.

Kelso Roxburghshire market town, twelve miles east of Melrose at the confluence of the rivers Teviot and Tweed. In *A Tour Through the Whole Island of Great Britain* (1724–26), Daniel Defoe remarked of the dangers of the Tweed, '... it is not very strange to them at Kelso, to hear of frequent disaster, in the passage, to men and cattle.' On the North British Railway, the town's main industries were: coach building, agricultural machinery, cabinet and upholstery works. *Territorials:* Lothians and Border Horse and 4th King's Own Scottish Borderers.

Kelty Fifeshire mining town twenty-four miles by rail from Edinburgh on the North British Railway. *Territorials:* Fife and Forfar Yeomanry and 7th Argyll and Sutherland Highlanders.

Kemerton North Gloucestershire village on the border with Worcestershire five miles from Tewksbury. Here is St Nicholas's Church, built, except for the tower, in 1847. *Territorials:* 5th Gloucestershire Regiment.

Kemnay Aberdeenshire village on the River Don just over thirteen miles by rail from Aberdeen on the Great North of Scotland Railway. Kemnay enjoyed much prosperity from the quarrying of granite. *Territorials:* 7th Gordon Highlanders.

Kendal Westmorland town on the River Kent, to the south-east of Lake Windermere, served by the London & North Western Railway. Wool was Kendal's main industry, a cloth called 'Kendal Green' being a speciality of the town whose motto roughly translates as 'Wool is my Bread'. There were also iron foundries and businesses producing snuff, tobacco, paper, boots and shoes. At Holy

Trinity Church, high up on the north wall, is a helmet thought to have belonged to Royalist Sir Robert Phillipson, known to some as 'Robin the Devil'. *Territorials:* Westmorland and Cumberland Yeomanry, 4th Border Regiment, West Lancashire Clearing Hospital and 3rd West Lancashire Field Ambulance.

Kenilworth Warwickshire market town, five miles from Coventry, served by the London & North Western Railway where, noted the guides, most of the inhabitants were employed in tanning. Here is St Nicholas's and St John's churches, and the twelfth-century Kenilworth Castle which Elizabeth I gave to Lord Dudley in 1563. Read all about it in *Kenilworth* by Sir Walter Scott. *Territorials:* 7th Royal Warwickshire Regiment.

Kenmore Perthshire village situated where the River Tay meets Loch Tay, six miles from Aberfeldy. *Territorials:* 6th Black Watch.

Kenninghall Norfolk village six miles from Diss. Here is St Mary's Church. *Territorials:* 4th Norfolk Regiment.

Kensington West London borough and birthplace (at Kensington Place) of Queen Victoria. Here, in Victoria Road, is Christ Church, on the north side of Kensington High Street, St Mary Abbot's, and St Paul's School, which maintained two OTC infantry companies. *Territorials:* Gloucester and Worcester Infantry Brigade, Middlesex Infantry Brigade, 13th London Regiment, Kensington and Hammersmith Navy League Boys' Brigade, St Peter's Cadet Company, Oratory Cadet Corps and Kensington Cadet Corps (later called Royal Engineers Cadet Company 2nd London Division.

Keswick Cumberland market town, fifteen miles from Penrith on the Cockermouth, Keswick & Penrith Railway, famous for its production of lead pencils. Keswick is near the confluence of the Gretna and Derwent and just a half-mile from the north end of Wordsworth's Derwentwater. Here is St John's Church. *Territorials:* Westmorland and Cumberland Yeomanry and 4th Border Regiment.

Kettering Northamptonshire market town on high ground overlooking the Isle Valley, important in the manufacture of boots and shoes. Also providing much employment were works producing agricultural implements, clothing and brushes. Kettering was served by the Midland main line out of London's St Pancras. Here is St Peter and St Paul's Church. *Territorials:* Northamptonshire Yeomanry and 4th Northamptonshire Regiment.

Ketton Rutlandshire village, three miles from Stamford, served by the London & North Western Railway. Here is St Mary's Church. *Territorials:* 5th Leicestershire Regiment.

Keynsham Somerset market town on the River Chew near its confluence with the Avon, just under five miles from Bristol. Its station served by the Great Western main line. Here is St John's Church. *Territorials:* North Somerset Yeomanry and 4th Somerset Light Infantry.

Kibworth Leicestershire town, five miles from Market Harborough, served by the Midland main line out of London's St Pancras. Here is St Wilfrid's Church. *Territorials:* 5th Leicestershire Regiment.

Kidderminster Worcestershire market town, fifteen miles from Wolverhampton, on the River Stour and Staffordshire and Worcestershire Canal and Great Western Railway. Born in the town was Sir Rowland Hill (1795–1879) who gave us the Penny Postage system. Here many were employed in the production of carpets, for which the town became famous. The local newspaper is called the *Kidderminster Shuttle,* which celebrates the connection. Her is St Mary's Church which sits within stone throwing distance of the canal. *Territorials:* Worcestershire Yeomanry, 2nd South Midland Brigade RFA, 7th Worcestershire Regiment, 1st South Midland Mounted Brigade Transport and Supply Column and 3rd Cadet Battalion Worcestershire Regiment.

Kilbirnie North Ayrshire town on the River Garnock, just over eleven miles from Paisley, served by the Glasgow & South Western and Caledonian railways. Here, many were employed in the production of flannel goods, rope, engineering, iron and steel. *Territorials:* 4th Royal Scots Fusiliers.

Kilburn (Derbyshire) Mining village just over seven miles by rail from Derby on the Midland Railway which arrived in 1856. *Territorials:* 5th Sherwood Foresters.

Kilburn (London) District of north-west London in the borough of Willesden. Holy Trinity in Brondesbury Road was built in 1867, and who in Kilburn did not do their shopping at B B Evans's department store in the High Street. Opened in 1897, burnt down January 1910. *Territorials:* Kilburn Grammar School Cadet Company.

Kilchattan Village on Bute Island, south of Rothesay. *Territorials:* 4th Highland Brigade RGA.

Kilchrenan Argyllshire village on west side of Loch Awe, seven miles from Taynuilt. *Territorials:* 2nd Scottish Horse and 8th Argyll and Sutherland Highlanders.

Kildary Ross and Cromarty hamlet on the River Balnagown, just over five miles from Inverness. Kildary was served by the Highland Railway, its viaducts panning the river. *Territorials:* 4th Seaforth Highlanders.

Kildonan Sutherlandshire village on the River Helmsdale just over twenty miles by rail from Brora on the Highland Railway. Here, by the river, is St Donan's Church. *Territorials:* 5th Seaforth Highlanders.

Kilgetty Pembrokeshire village five miles from Tenby by rail on the Great Western Railway. Kilgetty and Begelly station was opened by the Pembroke & Tenby Railway in September 1866. *Territorials:* Pembrokeshire Yeomanry.

Kilkhampton Cornwall village six miles from Bude. Here, at St James's Church in the centre of the village, are memorials to the Grenville family, including one to Civil War Royalist Commander Sir Bevil Grenville. *Territorials:* 5th Duke of Cornwall's Light Infantry.

Killin Perthshire village situated on the River Lochay where it meets the Dochart, close to the western extremity of Loch Tay. Well known for its manufacture of tweeds, Killin was served by the Caledonian Railway. *Territorials:* 6th Black Watch.

Kilmarnock Ayrshire market town situated on Kilmarnock Water where it meets the Irvine, just over twenty-four miles by rail from Glasgow on the Glasgow & South Western Railway. A 'manufacturing' town, note the guides. Walker's 'Kilmarnock' Whiskey was already well known, but when Johnnie's son, Alexander, took over in 1859, the business grew to become the largest whisky firm in the world. Robert Burns is associated with the town, his book, *Poems Chiefly in the Scottish Dialect*, published there by John Wilson and called 'The Kilmarnock Edition'. *Territorials:* Ayrshire Yeomanry, 2nd Lowland Brigade RFA, 4th Royal Scots Fusiliers and 1st Cadet Battalion Royal Scots Fusiliers.

Kilmartin Argyllshire village on Loch Craignish, seven miles from Balloch. *Territorials:* 8th Argyll and Sutherland Highlanders.

Kilmaurs Small Ayrshire town on Carmel Water, two miles from Kilmarnock, served by the Glasgow & South Western Railway. At Kilmaurs, which was once famous for its production of cutlery and swords, the parish church is dedicated to St Maurs. *Territorials:* 4th Royal Scots Fusiliers.

Kilmuir Hamlet on the Isle of Skye, Inverness-shire, twelve miles north of Portree. Here, in the churchyard, is buried the Jacobite heroin, Flora MacDonald (1722–90). *Territorials:* 4th Cameron Highlanders.

Kilsyth Kilsyth is to the north-east of Kirkintilloch and has to the north, the River Carron, to the south, the Kelvin, and just beyond that, the Forth and Clyde Canal. There were collieries and ironstone quarries in the area. The sport of curling began here and, note the guides, the first potatoes in Scotland were grown near Kilsyth. The North British Railway brought the trains up from Glasgow, the Caledonian taking them on to Bonnybridge. *Territorials:* 7th Argyll and Sutherland Highlanders.

Kiltarlity Small Inverness-shire village twelve miles to the west of Inverness. *Territorials:* 4th Cameron Highlanders.

Kilwinning North Ayrshire town on the River Garnock just over twenty-six miles by rail from Glasgow on the Glasgow & South Western Railway. Here were extensive engineering works, coal mining and textile production. Well known for its archery since possibly 1483, there still exists the Ancient Society of Kilwinning Archers which has regular competitions in the grounds of Kilwinning Abbey. The Masonic Lodge in Kilwinning is thought to be the oldest in the world, its roll number being '0'. *Territorials:* 4th Royal Scots Fusiliers.

Kimble In Buckinghamshire there is Little Kimble, with its All Saints Church and railway station on the Great Western & Great Central Joint Railway just over four miles from Aylesbury, and, just to the south-east, Great Kimble where can be found St Nicholas's Church. *Territorials:* Buckinghamshire Yeomanry.

Kimbolton Huntingdonshire market town on the River Kym and Bedfordshire border, eight miles from St Neots. Here at St Andrew's Church are monuments to the earls and dukes of Manchester, the Midland Railway's Kimbolton station being just over two miles from the town. *Territorials:* Bedfordshire Yeomanry.

Kinbrace Small Sutherlandshire village, fourteen miles from Helmsdale, served by the Highland Railway. *Territorials:* 5th Seaforth Highlanders.

Kincraig Village on the River Spey, Inverness-shire, just under six miles from Kingussie on the Highland Railway's main line from Perth to Inverness. *Territorials:* 4th Cameron Highlanders.

Kineton Warwickshire market town, nine miles from Stratford-upon-Avon, served by the Stratford-upon-Avon & Midland Junction Railway. Here is St Peter's Church. *Territorials:* Warwickshire Yeomanry.

Kingham Oxfordshire village, just over four miles from Chipping Norton, where a long street leads from the green to St Andrew's Church and its unusual stone bench ends. Kingham station, on the Great Western Railway, was called Chipping Norton Junction until 1909. *Territorials:* 4th Oxfordshire and Buckinghamshire Light Infantry.

Kinghorn South Fifeshire town on the north shore of the Firth of Forth, just over twenty-two miles from Edinburgh by rail on the North British Railway. When Daniel Defoe visited Kinghorn in the 1720s, he noted men shooting porpoises, the fat from which was then boiled into oil. *Territorials:* Forth RGA.

King's Heath Worcestershire village, three miles from Birmingham, served by the Midland Railway. Here is All Saints Church. *Territorials:* Worcestershire Yeomanry.

King's Lynn Norfolk market town and port on the Wash and Great Ouse served by the Great Eastern and Midland & Great Northern Joint railways. Standing in the marketplace in the town centre is St Margaret's Church with its twin towers. *Territorials:* Norfolk Yeomanry, 5th, 6th Norfolk Regiment and East Anglian Divisional Transport and Supply Column.

King's Norton Southern suburb of Birmingham on the Midland Railway and Birmingham and Worcester Canal. Here, with its crocketed spire, is St Nicholas's Church. *Territorials:* 8th Worcestershire Regiment.

King's Nympton Devonshire village on the Rive Mole, about four miles from Chulmleigh on the southern edge of Exmoor. Here is St James's Church, the London & South Western Railway's station being called South Molton Road. *Territorials:* 6th Devonshire Regiment.

Kingsbridge Devonshire seaport and market town, three miles north of Salcombe, served by Kingsbridge & Salcombe Railway (later Great Western) which arrived in December 1893. Here is St Edmund's Church and the birthplace in 1705 of William Cookworthy who found china clay and from it made the first porcelain in England. *Territorials:* 1st Devon Yeomanry and 5th Devonshire Regiment.

Kingsclere Hampshire village seven miles from Newbury and well known for its training stables. While staying at Kingsclere, King John shared a room with a bed-bug which did not please him. To show his disgust of the place he ordered that a model of the insect be displayed on the tower of St Mary's Church as a warning to travellers to keep away. But the bed-bug weathervane had the opposite effect. *Territorials:* 4th Hampshire Regiment.

Kingsland Herefordshire village on the River Lug, just over three miles from Leominster, served by the Great Western Railway. Here is St Michael and All Angels Church and, just to the north-west of the village at Kingsland Field in 1461, the sight of the Battle of Mortimer's Cross. *Territorials:* Welsh Divisional Transport and Supply Column.

Kingston-upon-Thames Surrey market town, and south-west London suburb, where Thomas Sopwith set up the Sopwith Aviation Company in June 1912. Kingston is just over twelve miles by rail from Waterloo on the London & South Western Railway. Here is All Saints Church. *Territorials:* 6th East Surrey Regiment.

Kington Herefordshire market town on the River Arrow and Great Western Railway just before it terminated at New Radnor. Here, St Mary's Church sits on a hill overlooking the town which employed a number in agriculture and the production of Nails. *Territorials:* Shropshire Yeomanry and Herefordshire Regiment.

Kingussie Inverness-shire village on the River Spey just over forty-six miles by rail from Inverness. Kingussie prospered as a summer resort after the coming of the Highland Railway in 1863. *Territorials:* 4th Cameron Highlanders.

Kinloch Rannoch Perthshire village at the east end of Loch Rannoch, thirteen miles from Struan. *Territorials:* 1st Scottish Horse.

Kinlochewe Hamlet near the head of Loch Maree, Ross and Cromarty. *Territorials:* 4th Seaforth Highlanders.

Kinlochleven Argyllshire village at the eastern end of Loch Leven, seven miles from Ballachulish. Here, in 1907, the construction of a hydroelectric dam created the Blackwater Reservoir in connection with the British Aluminium Company which employed some 700 persons. *Territorials:* 8th Argyll and Sutherland Highlanders.

Kinross County and market town on the west side of Loch Leven and bust junction of the North British Railway. Here linen was produced, and there were several woollen mills. *Territorials:* Fife and Forfar Yeomanry and 7th Argyll and Sutherland Highlanders.

Kintore Small Aberdeenshire town on the River Don, just over thirteen miles by rail from Aberdeen on the Great North of Scotland Railway. *Territorials:* 2nd Scottish Horse.

Kinver Small Staffordshire town on the River Stour and Stafford Canal four miles from Stourbridge. A overhead electric tram service called the Kinver Light Railway was opened in April 1901. Here is St Peter's Church. *Territorials:* 7th Worcestershire Regiment.

Kippen Stirlingshire village on the River Forth, nine miles from Stirling, on the North British Railway. *Territorials:* Fife and Forfar Yeomanry.

Kirby Moorside North Riding of Yorkshire market town on the River Dove, seven miles by rail from Pickering on the North Eastern Railway. Here is All Saints Church. *Territorials:* 5th Yorkshire Regiment.

Kirk Yetholm Roxburghshire village on Bowmont Water, eight miles from Kelso in the Scottish Border country, once the headquarters of Romani gipsies in Scotland – their last king being crowned there in 1898. The church here dates from the thirteenth century. *Territorials:* Lothians and Border Horse.

Kirkburton West Riding of Yorkshire market town just over six miles by rail from Huddersfield on the London & North Western Railway. Here, many were employed in collieries, woollen mills, and a company called Carter that made edge tools and shovels. In George Street, with its Elizabethan and Jacobean pews, is All Hallows Church. *Territorials:* 5th Duke of Wellington's Regiment.

Kirkby-in-Ashfield Nottinghamshire market town, just over thirteen miles by rail from Nottingham on the Midland Railway, where many were employed in local collieries. Here are St Wilfrid's and St John's churches. *Territorials:* Nottinghamshire Yeomanry (Sherwood Rangers).

Kirkby Lonsdale Westmorland market town on the River Lune, eleven miles from Kendal, serve by the London & North Western Railway. An ancient stone bridge of three arches ('Devil's Bridge') crosses the river just below the town. Here is St Mary's Church, the view from its churchyard being noted by art critic and writer on architecture, John Ruskin (1819–1900), as the finest in England. *Territorials:* Westmorland and Cumberland Yeomanry, 4th Border Regiment and Kirkby Lonsdale Cadet Company.

Kirkby Stephen Westmorland market town on the River Eden, nine miles from Appleby, served by both the North Eastern and Midland Railways. Here is St Stephen's Church, and in Kirkby Stephen Cemetery a memorial to the fourteen killed in a railway accident that took place close by in 1913. *Territorials:* 4th Border Regiment.

Kirkcaldy Fifeshire seaport and market town, on the Firth of Forth twenty-six miles from Edinburgh by rail on the North British Railway. Linoleum was manufactured at Kirkcaldy, the docks giving employment to many in shipbuilding and other jobs connected with sea trade. Born at Kirkcaldy was the architect Robert Adam (1728–92), and at Kirkcaldy High School there was one OTC infantry company. *Territorials:* Fife and Forfar Yeomanry, Forth RGA, 7th Black Watch and Highland Cyclist Battalion.

Kirkconnel Dumfrieshire mining village on the River Nith, just over three miles by rail from Sanquhar on the Glasgow & South Western Railway. *Territorials:* 5th King's Own Scottish Borderers.

Kirkcowan Wigtownshire village with railway station (Portpatrick & Wigtownshire Joint Committee) on Tarf Water, just over seven miles from Wigtown. *Territorials:* 5th King's Own Scottish Borderers.

Kirkcudbright County and market town on the east side of the River Dee, thirty miles by rail from Dumfries on the Glasgow & South Western Railway. Active in the area, c1880–1910, was the 'Glasgow Boys' and Scottish Colourists' art movements, and in the churchyard is a memorial to a man believed to have been 120 years old when he died. *Territorials:* 2nd Lowland Brigade RFA and 5th King's Own Scottish Borderers..

Kirkintilloch Dumbartonshire town on the River Luggie where it meets the Kelvin, and Forth of Clyde Canal. Situated eight miles by rail from Glasgow on the North British Railway, Kirkintilloch employed many in its chemical works and iron foundries – the Lion and Star foundries being probably the largest. Here, the parish church of St Mary's dominates the town, its opening in 1914 being captured on newsreel film. Alcohol was forbidden in the town until the 1970s. *Territorials:* 9th Argyll and Sutherland Highlanders.

Kirkliston Linlithgowshire village on the River Almond, just under ten miles by rail from Edinburgh on the North British Railway which crosses the river by means of a viaduct of thirty-six arches. A whiskey distillery was set up in the village in 1795, a speciality being the production of Drambuie. *Territorials:* 10th Royal Scots.

Kirkmichael Perthshire village on the River Ardle, thirteen miles from Blairgowrie. *Territorials:* 1st Scottish Horse.

Kirkwall Seaport and county town of Orkney where, notes one guide, the inhabitants were mostly of the professional, shopkeeping, fishing and labouring classes. Here is St Magnus's Cathedral which dates from 1137. *Territorials:* Orkney RGA.

Kirriemuir Forfarshire market town on the Gairie Burn where creator of Peter Pan, J M Barrie, was born at 9 Brechin Road in 1860. Here too, just one year after the Territorials were formed, is the birthplace of film actor David Niven. The town was once an important weaving centre, and at Marywell Works there was an extensive jute mill. Kirriemuir station lay at the terminus of the Caledonian branch that ran from Forfar via Kirriemuir Junction. *Territorials:* 5th Black Watch.

Kishorn Hamlet on Loch Kishorn, Ross and Cromarty, five miles from Lochcarron. *Territorials:* 4th Highland Brigade RGA.

Knap Hill Surrey village just over two miles from Woking. Here are army barracks, and Brookwood Mental Hospital. *Territorials:* 5th Queen's Royal West Surrey Regiment.

Knaresborough West Riding of Yorkshire market town, four miles by rail from Harrogate on the North Eastern Railway, the trains coming and going via a tall three-arched railway viaduct crossing the River Nidd. Here, in St John's Church, the Slingsby family are remembered; one of them, the Royalist Sir Henry, being executed in 1658, another to be drowned in 1869. *Territorials:* Yorkshire Hussars and 5th West Yorkshire Regiment.

Knighton Radnorshire market town on the south bank of the River Teme looking across to Shropshire, served by the London & North Western Railway. Here is St Edward's Church. *Territorials:* Montgomeryshire Yeomanry and Herefordshire Regiment.

Knightsbridge West London district, it Underground station being opened in 1906. Here is Knightsbridge Barracks, home of the Horse Guards for many years, and some of London's prestige stores: Harvey Nichols, since 1813, and Harrods where a number of employees joined the Territorials. *Territorials:* 1st County of London Yeomanry.

Knutsford Cheshire market town twenty-four miles by rail from Chester on the Cheshire Lines Committee Railway. Knutsford and its inhabitants feature widely in Elizabeth Cleghorn Gaskell's *Cranford* and other novels. She was buried in the churchyard of the town's Unitarian Chapel in 1865. Here too is the church of St John the Baptist. *Territorials:* Cheshire Yeomanry, 5th Cheshire Regiment and Knutsford (Parish) Cadet Company.

Kyle of Lochalsh Small town across from Skye, Inverness-shire and the terminus of the Highland Railway which arrived in 1897. *Territorials:* 2nd Lovat's Scouts and 4th Highland Brigade RGA.

Ladybank Small Fifeshire town and important railway junction (North British) with lines radiating to Edinburgh, Dundee, Perth and Stirling. Just under six miles from Cupar, the town's most important industries were in linen weaving, coal and malting. *Territorials:* Fife and Forfar Yeomanry.

Laggan Bridge Inverness-shire locality on the River Spey, ten miles from Kingussie. *Territorials:* 2nd Lovat's Scouts.

Lairg Sutherlandshire village on Loch Shin, seventeen miles from Dornoch, served by the Highland Railway's line from Inverness to Wick. *Territorials:* 2nd Lovat's Scouts and 5th Seaforth Highlanders.

Lakeside Locality at the southern end of Lake Windermere reached by the Furness Railway's branch that ran up from Leven Junction and was opened in 1869. Station called Windermere Lakeside. *Territorials:* 4th King's Own Royal Lancaster Regiment.

Lamberhurst Small town on the River Teise in Kent where brewing is noted as an important industry. Here is St Mary's Church. *Territorials:* 5th Buffs East Kent Regiment.

Lambeth London borough on the south bank of the Thames and at one time, one of the poorest areas of the capital. Royal Doulton ceramics began in Lambeth in 1815 and the government centre, County Hall, was built in 1912. Here too is Lambeth Palace, the London residence of the archbishops of Canterbury; the Oval Cricket Ground, opened in 1846; the 'Lambeth Walk', St Mary's parish church and Bedlam Hospital which became the Imperial War Museum. Born in the area in 1889 was Charlie Chaplin. *Territorials:* South Eastern Mounted Brigade, 6th London Infantry Brigade, 5th London Brigade RFA, 24th London Regiment and Archbishop Temple's School Cadet Corps.

Lambourn Small Berkshire town on the River Lambourn in the heart of the Chalk Downs twelve miles from Newbury, well known for its association with racehorse training stables. Close by is Lambourn Down and the Gallops. The railway came in the form of the Lambourn Valley line, which came up from Newbury in 1898. Here is St Michael and All Angels Church where remembered are three important Lambourn families: Eastbury, Garrard and Essex. In the churchyard lies buried John Carter who was executed in 1833 for setting fire to two places in Lambourn. *Territorials:* Berkshire Yeomanry.

Lampeter Cardiganshire market town close to the banks of the River Teifi and just over thirteen miles by rail from Aberayron. The line was opened by the Manchester & Milford Railway and became the Great Western in 1911. Here is St Peter's Church and St David's University College. *Territorials:* Pembrokeshire Yeomanry.

Lanark County town of Lanarkshire close to the Rive Clyde and just over thirty-two miles by rail from Glasgow on the Caledonian Railway. Here is St Leonard's Church and the Roman Catholic, St Mary's. *Territorials:* Lanarkshire Yeomanry and 8th Highland Light Infantry.

Lancaster Seaport, county and market town situated on the slope of a hill rising from the south bank of the River Lune, served by both the London & North Western and Midland railways. Many in Lancaster were employed in the manufacture of furniture, linoleum and railway plant. Here is St Mary's Church, the Roman Catholic St Peter's, and Lancaster Castle which now serves as the county goal. Lancaster's Royal Grammar School maintained one OTC infantry company. *Territorials:* North Lancashire Infantry Brigade, 2nd West Lancashire Brigade RFA and 5th King's Own Royal Lancaster Regiment.

Langford Somerset village six miles from Axbridge. *Territorials:* North Somerset Yeomanry.

Langholm Dumfrieshire market town on the River Esk, fifteen miles from Annan, served by the North British Railway. Many here were employed in the production of tweeds. There were also distilleries. *Territorials:* Lanarkshire Yeomanry and 5th King's Own Scottish Borderers.

Langley Northumberland village on the North Eastern Railway branch began in 1867 between Hexham and Allendale. *Territorials:* 4th Northumberland Fusiliers.

Langley Mill Nottinghamshire village on the River Erewash, just under seventeen miles by rail from Nottingham on the Midland Railway. Here, a number were employed in the manufacture of railway wagons. *Territorials:* 5th Sherwood Foresters.

Langley Park Durham colliery village six miles from Durham. *Territorials:* 8th Durham Light Infantry.

Langport Somerset market town on the River Parret served by the Great Western Railway. A new station named Langport East was opened in October 1906 which required the old Bristol & Exeter Railway's 'Langport' to be renamed as Langport West. Here is All Saints Church. *Territorials:* West Somerset Yeomanry and 5th Somerset Light Infantry.

Langtree Devonshire village just over three miles from Torrington. Here is All Saints Church. *Territorials:* Royal North Devon Yeomanry.

Lanreath Cornwall village, five miles from Looe, where the church is dedicated to St Marnarck and St Dunstan. Here are monuments to the Grylls family. *Territorials:* Cornwall Fortress Engineers.

Largoward Fifeshire village three miles from Colinsburgh. *Territorials:* 7th Black Watch.

Largs Ayrshire resort town on the Firth of Clyde, twelve miles from Greenock, at the termination of the Glasgow & South Western Railway's line that came up from Glasgow in 1885. Here is the birthplace of Sir Thomas Brisbane (1773–1860), who gave his name to the Australian city, and a fine view across the water to Great Cumbrae Island. There exists a railway poster showing the seafront at Largs in which can be seen a church spire close enough to the water's edge to be troubled by the sound of waves. *Territorials:* 4th Highland Brigade RGA.

Larkhall Lanarkshire town near the right bank of the River Avon, just under three miles by rail from Hamilton on the Caledonian Railway. Many in Larkhall were employed in local collieries and bleach works. *Territorials:* 6th Cameronians.

Lasswade Small Midlothian town on the north bank of the River Esk, just under ten miles by rail from Edinburgh on the North British Railway. Here were paper mills and a factory making carpets. *Territorials:* Lothians and Border Horse.

Latheron Caithness-shire fishing village at the mouth of Latheronwheel Burn, eighteen miles from Wick. *Territorials:* 2nd Lovat's Scouts.

Lauder Berwickshire town on Leader Water which brought many to the area for trout fishing – no doubt by the Lauder Light Railway which opened Lauder station on 2 July 1901. Lauder is twenty-two miles from Edinburgh. *Territorials:* Lothians and Border Horse and 4th King's Own Scottish Borderers.

Launceston A Cornwall town, eleven miles from Tavistock, Launceston looks down from the side of a steep hill to the River Tamar. David St John Thomas, in his book *The Country Railway*, tells how those present at the opening ceremony of the Launceston & South Devon Railway in July 1865 were soaked to the skin by torrential rain. After that, a rainy day in Launceston was referred to by the locals as 'railway weather'. A better day, perhaps, when the North Cornwall came to the town in 1886. Here is St Mary Magdalene's Church. *Territorials:* Royal 1st Devon Yeomanry and 5th Duke of Cornwall's Light Infantry.

Laurencekirk Small Kincardineshire town ten miles by rail from Montrose. Both the North British and Caledonian railways served Laurencekirk which was famous for making snuffboxes. *Territorials:* Fife and Forfar Yeomanry and 7th Gordon Highlanders.

Lavenham Suffolk village, just over eleven miles by rail from Bury St Edmunds on the Great Eastern Railway, once an important centre of the wool trade; a blue broadcloth being a speciality. Here, a cathedral in miniature some say, is St Peter and St Paul's Church with its memorials to the de Veres and Spryngs. Two wealthy wool merchants who built much of the church. *Territorials:* 5th Suffolk Regiment.

Law Lanarkshire village which sprang up around 1877 and was chiefly inhabited by colliers and persons engaged in neighbouring quarries and brickworks. Served by the Caledonian Railway, Law is just over two miles from Wishaw. *Territorials:* 8th Highland Light Infantry.

Leamington A Warwickshire town, Leamington (or Royal Leamington Spa) lies on the River Leam, Grand Union Canal and Great Western and London & North Western railways. One guide notes that Leamington's production of cooking ranges had brought 'celebrity' to the place. Here is All Saints Church. *Territorials:* Warwickshire RHA and 7th Royal Warwickshire Regiment.

Leatherhead Surrey town on the River Mole, five miles from Dorking, served by both the London & South Western and London, Brighton & South Western railways. Here is St Mary and St Nicholas's Church, and St John's School, which maintained one OTC infantry company. *Territorials:* 5th East Surrey Regiment.

Ledbury Herefordshire market town, to the west of the Malvern Hills and fifteen miles from Hereford, served by the Great Western Railway. Here a narrow street of half-timbered houses leads to St Michael and All Angels Church with its detached tower and spire and memorial to Mr and Mrs Edward Moulton Barrett, the parents of the poet Elizabeth Barrett Browning. Well represented too, in stone, glass and metal, is the Biddulph family. The quarrying of limestone and production of cider was important to the area. The poet John Masefield (1878–1967) was born in Ledbury. *Territorials:* Gloucestershire Yeomanry, Worcestershire Yeomanry and Herefordshire Regiment.

Lee-on-Solent Hampshire seaside resort on Southampton Water which became popular with the coming of the London & South Western Railway in 1894. *Territorials:* 6th Hampshire Regiment.

Leeds Situated on the River Aire and Leeds and Liverpool Canal, Leeds grew from the wool trade – a golden fleece is featured in the city's coat of arms. But much more went on in Leeds. Coal and iron were important. There was the Leeds pottery, and Thomas Chippendale's furniture-making business. Here too was a market stall ran by Michael Marks, which grew somewhat after he teamed up with Mr Spencer. The Yorkshire Penny Bank opened in Leeds in 1894, and what is thought to be some of the first moving pictures were shot in Leeds by film pioneer Loius Alme Augustin le Prince. Leeds University and the Leeds Grammar School both maintained contingents in the OTC. At St Peter's Church there is a memorial to those from Leeds that were killed in the Crimean War. *Territorials:* Yorkshire Hussars, 1st West Riding Brigade RFA, Northern Command Telegraph Companies, Northern Command Signal Companies, 7th, 8th West Yorkshire Regiment, West Riding Divisional Transport and Supply Column, 1st, 2nd West Riding Field Ambulances, 2nd Northern General Hospital, West Riding Clearing Hospital, Yorkshire Squadron Imperial Cadet Yeomanry and Leeds Postal Telegraph Messengers Cadet Company.

Leek Staffordshire market town on the River Churnet, ten miles from Stoke-on-Trent, served by the North Staffordshire Railway. Many in the town were employed in the manufacture of silk and in the clothing trade. Bringing visitors to the town around the time of the summer solstice, is the curious phenomenon that appears at a hill on the west side of Leek which gives the impression that the sun has set twice on the same day. The so called 'Double Sunset' is a feature of the town's coat of arms. Here is the church of St Edward the Confessor. *Territorials:* Staffordshire Yeomanry and 2nd North Midland Brigade RFA.

Lees Lancashire town, just to the east of Oldham and close to the border with the West Riding of Yorkshire, served by the London & North Western Railway. One source describes the place as a 'factory town', another mentions some eleven cotton mills. *Territorials:* 7th Duke of Wellington's Regiment.

Leicester County and market town on the River Sour and Grand Union Canal. Leicester's main industries were the manufacture of boots, shoes, elastic webbing, hats and cigars. An early public parade attended by the Leicester Territorials would have been the unveiling by Field Marshal Lord Grenfell on 1 July 1909 of the South Africa war memorial at the corner of Every Street and Horsefair Street. Here, with masonry and tiles recycled from a Roman building, is St Nicholas's Church. *Territorials:* North Midland Mounted Brigade, Leicestershire Yeomanry, Leicestershire RHA, North Midland Mounted Brigade Signal Troop, 4th Leicestershire Regiment, North Midland Mounted Brigade Transport and Supply Column, North Midland Divisional Transport and Supply Column, 2nd North Midland Field Ambulance, North Midland Clearing Hospital and 5th Northern General Hospital.

Leigh Lancashire market town, eight miles from Wigan, on the Bridgewater Canal and London & North Western Railway. Leigh's principle industries were coal mining, cotton mills, brewing and the manufacture of agricultural implements. James Hilton, the author of *Goodbye Mr* Chips, was born in Leigh and would have been just eight years old when the local Territorials held their first parade. Here is St Mary's Church. *Territorials:* 5th Manchester Regiment.

Leigh-on-Sea Essex fishing town and seaside resort on the Thames estuary, three miles from Southend, served by the Midland Railway. Many London businessmen had homes here, and seafaring men too. Here, in the churchyard of St Clement's Church, lie Admiral Sir Richard Haddock (1629–1715) and his son, Admiral Nicholas Haddock (1686–1746). Registers date from 1684. *Territorials*: Essex and Suffolk RGA.

Leigh Sinton Worcestershire hamlet in the Malvern Hills three miles from Great Malvern. *Territorials:* Worcestershire Yeomanry.

Leighton Buzzard Bedfordshire market town on the River Ouzel and Grand Junction Canal, seven miles by rail from Dunstable on the London & North Western Railway. Here is All Saints Church which was began in the thirteenth century. *Territorials:* Bedfordshire Yeomanry and 5th Bedfordshire Regiment.

Leiston Suffolk village, four miles by rail from Saxmundham on the Great Eastern Railway. Agricultural machinery and implements, and steam boilers were made at Leiston, Garrett's 'Long Shop', thought to be the first purpose-built assembly line in the world. Here is St Margaret's Church. *Territorials:* Suffolk Yeomanry and 4th Suffolk Regiment.

Leith Busy seaport close to Edinburgh on the Firth of Forth, Leith provided employment in shipbuilding, brewing, distilling, engineering and at a large chemical works. The Leith Corporation Tramway service opened in October 1904. *Territorials:* 7th Royal Scots.

Lennoxtown Stirlingshire town just over eleven miles by rail from Glasgow on the North British Railway. An industrial town with printing and chemical works, some coal mining and limestone quarrying. *Territorials:* 7th Argyll and Sutherland Highlanders.

Lenzie Dumbartonshire village close to Kirkintilloch and just over six miles by rail from Glasgow on the North British Railway. *Territorials:* 9th Argyll and Sutherland Highlanders.

Leominster Herefordshire market town at the confluence of the rivers Pringle and Lugg, just over thirteen miles by rail from Hereford on the Great Western Railway. Here is St Peter and St Paul's Church, half-timbered buildings and the beginning of the Leominster Canal. Cider is produced, and there were brickfields. *Territorials:* Shropshire Yeomanry and Herefordshire Regiment.

Lerryn Village on the River Lerryn, Cornwall, four miles from Fowey. Two bridges cross the river here, both sixteenth century. *Territorials:* Cornwall Fortress Engineers.

Lerwick Fishing town and busy ferry port situated on Bressay Sound, Shetland Islands. First developed by the Dutch for their fishing fleet, Lerwick is the most northerly town in the British Isles. *Territorials:* Shetland Companies.

Leslie Fifeshire market town on the River Leven, seven miles from Kirkcaldy, served by the North British Railway. Here, many were employed in flax spinning, bleaching and the manufacture of paper. *Territorials:* 7th Black Watch.

Lesmahagow Lanarkshire village (also called Abbey Green) on the River Nethan, six miles from Lanark, served by the Caledonian Railway. Coal is noted as the principal industry, but there were also large weaving and hosiery factories. *Territorials:* Lanarkshire Yeomanry and 8th Highland Light Infantry.

Letchworth Hertfordshire village close to the border with Bedfordshire that in 1903 was developed into the world's first 'garden city'. The idea of town planner Ebenezer Howard, Letchworth Garden City offered wide, clean streets, open spaces and no overcrowding. The Great Northern Railway arrived in 1903, a new station replacing the original ten years after that. Opened in 1912, and providing much employment, was the Spirella corset factory. Here is St Mary's Church. *Territorials:* Hertfordshire Regiment.

Leven Fifeshire town on the River Leven, nine miles along the coast from Kirkcaldy, served by the North British Railway. Many here were employed in local collieries, the town a popular seaside resort after the coming of the railway in 1854. *Territorials:* 2nd Highland Brigade RFA and 7th Black Watch.

Lewes The county town of Sussex and busy junction on the London, Brighton & South Coast Railway, Lewes is placed on the right bank of the Ouse. Here, from the station and up steep St Mary's Street, is the castle, and in High Street, St Michael's Church which underwent much restoration in 1885, as did St Anne's, a little further up the road in 1889. *Territorials:* Sussex Yeomanry, Sussex RGA and 5th and 6th Royal Sussex Regiment.

Lewisham South-east London borough on the River Ravensbourne noted as a 'solid, middle-class suburb' soon after the coming of the railway in 1849. Here is the ancient church of St Mary, the Roman Catholic St Saviour and St John opening in 1909. *Territorials:* 4th London Brigade RFA and Lewisham Cadet Battalion.

Leyland Lancashire town, five miles from Preston, served by the London & North Western Railway. Here were cotton mills, a factory producing rubber and, started in 1896, the Lancashire Steam Motor Company which became Leyland Motors in 1907. Much remembered in the town, and at St Andrew's Church, is the Farlington family. *Territorials:* 4th North Lancashire Regiment.

Leyton Essex town and north-east London suburb on the River Lea where may were employed by the railway; the Great Eastern opening a wagon works at Temple Mills in 1897. Opened in June 1905 was the Leyton Urban District Council Tramway service. Here is All Saints Church, and St Mary's, where there are monuments to the Hickes family. *Territorials:* 7th, 8th Essex Regiment and 3rd East Anglian Field Ambulance.

Lhanbryde Elginshire village, just under four miles from Elgin, served by the Highland Railway. *Territorials:* 6th Seaforth Highlanders.

Lichfield Staffordshire cathedral city just over sixteen miles by rail from Birmingham on the London & North Western Railway. Commander Edward John Smith, Captain of the *Titanic* is remembered in Kathleen Scott's memorial unveiled in Beacon Park, Lichfield on 29 July 1914. Doctor Samuel Johnson (1709–84) has a statue outside his birthplace and father's bookshop on the corner of Market Place. The actor David Garrick (1717–79) born here too. Lichfield Cathedral has three spires, all three badly damaged during the Civil War. *Territorials:* North Midland Division, Staffordshire Infantry Brigade, Staffordshire Yeomanry and 6th North Staffordshire Regiment.

Lincoln Cathedral city and busy railway junction on the River Witham. Here in the High Street is St Benedict's Church, and the earliest church in the city, St Mary's. *Territorials:* Lincolnshire Yeomanry, 4th Lincolnshire Regiment and 4th Northern General Hospital.

Lingdale North Riding of Yorkshire mining village, just over four miles from Guisborough, which developed for the pit workers in the 1870s. *Territorials:* 4th Yorkshire Regiment.

Lingfield Surrey village just over twenty-six miles by rail from London Victoria on the London, Brighton & South Coast Railway. Here is St Peter and St Paul's Church in which all around are memorials and tombs to the Cobhams. One has the first Lord Cobham (c1295–1361) with his head resting of a Saracen's head, his feet on another. Opened in 1890 was the Lingfield Park racecourse. *Territorials:* 4th Queen's Royal West Surrey Regiment.

Linlithgow County and market town on the Avon, just over seventeen miles by rail from Edinburgh on the North British Railway. At St Michael's Church, where James IV had a vision warning him against his journey to England, and Mary Queen of Scots was baptised, restoration went on in 1894–1895. Here in 1819, the Linlithgow Mortsafe Society was formed which rented out cages that could be placed over graves to defeat the bodysnatchers. *Territorials:* Lothians and Border Horse and 10th Royal Scots.

Liphook Hampshire village, eight miles from Petersfield on the London & South Western Railway, and well known coaching halt on the old London-Portsmouth road with several inns. Samuel Pepys stayed at one of them in 1668 and noted 'good honest people'. *Territorials:* 6th Hampshire Regiment.

Liscard Cheshire town, two miles from Birkenhead, reached by the Wirral Railway in 1895. Here is St Mary's Church. *Territorials:* Lancashire and Cheshire RGA, 4th Cheshire Regiment, 3rd New Brighton Cadet Corps and Liscard High School Cadet Corps.

Liskeard Cornwall market town served by the Great Western Railway and one of the county's several 'Stannary' towns – that is one that had special powers to set up courts to try those working in tin mines for most cases except murder, assault and disputes over land. At Liskeard, just under twelve miles from Bodmin, the restoration of St Martin's Church, the second largest in Cornwall, went on over the period 1879–1903. *Territorials:* Royal 1st Devon Yeomanry and 5th Duke of Cornwall's Light Infantry.

Litcham Norfolk village seven miles from Swaffham. Here is All Saints Church. *Territorials:* 5th Norfolk Regiment.

Little Berkhamstead Hertfordshire village five miles from Hertford. Here is St Andrew's Church. *Territorials:* Hertfordshire Regiment.

Little Hulton South Lancashire mining town close to Salford with many collieries, including Madam's Wood, Ashton's Field and Peel House. The London & North Western Railway came in 1879. Here is St Paul's Church. *Territorials:* 5th North Lancashire Regiment.

Littlebourne Kent village four miles from Canterbury where the church is dedicated to St Vincent of Saragossa. *Territorials:* 4th Buffs East Kent Regiment.

Littledean Gloucestershire village on the edge of the Forest of Dean once important in the production of coal and iron. Here is St Ethelbert's Church, Roman roads and a Roman camp. *Territorials:* Herefordshire Regiment.

Littlehampton West Sussex seaside resort at the mouth of the River Arun over which a swing bridge was built in 1909 connecting the town with Bognor and Chichester. The church of St Mary the Virgin by G Draper dates from 1826, the Brighton & Chichester Railway (latter London, Brighton & South Coast) arriving in 1863. *Territorials:* 4th Royal Sussex Regiment.

Liverpool Shortly after the opening to the public of St John's Gardens in June 1904, a fine monument to those of the King's Liverpool Regiment that had lost their lives in campaigns, 1878 through to the South African War of 1899–1902, was erected by the city. Also remembered, this time on the corner of Princes Road and Upper Parliament Street, is Florence Nightingale; Charles John Allen's bas-relief sculpture being unveiled on 2 October 1913. Here, in 1904, work began on the Anglican Liverpool Cathedral, Noel Chavasse, the son of its bishop, later going on as a Territorial to twice win the Victoria Cross in the Great War. The OTC was well represented in Liverpool with contingents at Liverpool College and Liverpool Institute. *Territorials:* West Lancashire Division, Liverpool Infantry Brigade, South Lancashire Infantry Brigade, Duke of Lancaster's Own Yeomanry, Lancashire Hussars, 1st, 3rd, 4th West Lancashire Brigade RFA, Lancashire RGA, Lancashire and Cheshire RGA, Lancashire Fortress Engineers, Western Command Signal Companies, 5th, 6th, 7th, 8th, 9th, 10th King's Liverpool Regiment, West Lancashire Divisional Transport and Supply Column, 1st, 2nd West Lancashire Field Ambulance, 1st Western General Hospital, West Lancashire School of Instruction, 1st Territorial Cadet Battalion King's Liverpool Regiment, Liverpool Church Cadet Battalion and City of Liverpool Cadet Battalion.

Livingstone Linlithgowshire village on the River Almond just under sixteen miles by rail from Edinburgh on the North British Railway. Here were paper mills and shale was produced. *Territorials:* 10th Royal Scots.

Llanberis Carnarvonshire village where many were employed in slate queries. The church of St Padarn was built in 1886, the much older St Peris's, with its fifteenth-century timber roof, being restored in 1893. Llanberis, where those wishing to get to the top of Mount Snowdon came, was reached by the London & North Western Railway, the Snowdon Mountain Tramway taking you on to almost the summit. *Territorials:* 6th Royal Welsh Fusiliers.

Llanbister Radnorshire village, ten miles from Rhayader, served by the London & North Western Railway. Here, on the bank of the River Ithon, is St Cynllo's Church. *Territorials:* Montgomeryshire Yeomanry.

Llanbrynmair Montgomeryshire village, nine miles from Machynlleth, served by the Cambrian Railway. There were lead mines in the area, and flannel was produced. Here is St Mary's Church. *Territorials:* Montgomeryshire Yeomanry and 7th Royal Welsh Fusiliers.

Llanddulas Denbighshire coastal village on the Irish Sea, five miles from Colwyn Bay, served by the London & North Western Railway. Here the church is dedicated to St Cyndryd, many from the village being employed in local limestone quarries. *Territorials:* 5th Royal Welsh Fusiliers.

Llandilo Carmarthenshire market town on the River Towy, just over eleven miles by rail from Llandovery on the London & North Western Railway. Here there was a large trade in corn and flour. There was also brewing, tanning, saw and woollen mills. The church is dedicated to St Teilo. *Territorials:* Pembrokeshire Yeomanry and 4th Welsh Regiment.

Llandovery Carmarthenshire market town on the River Towy where it meets the Brân, eighteen miles from Brecon, served by the London & North Western Railway. The ancient church of St Mary is a little to the north of the town. *Territorials:* Pembrokeshire Yeomanry and 4th Welsh Regiment.

Llandrindod Wells Radnorshire spa town on the River Ithon six miles from Builth Wells. The London & North Western Railway brought the visitors to the town, its waters recommended by the Victorian guidebooks as being beneficial to those suffering from lung complaints. The old Llandrindod parish church of Holy Trinity, just to the south-east of the town, was rebuilt in 1894 and greatly extended in 1911. But in the town, in 1871, came another, also called Holy Trinity. There is a Roman fort in the area where much excavation was undertaken in 1913. *Territorials:* Montgomeryshire Yeomanry and Herefordshire Regiment.

Llandudno Just over three miles from Conway, the London & North Western Railway brought the visitors to this Carnarvonshire seaside town – the most popular in North Wales, according to the guide books. The Grand Hotel sits handy for the pier, the Great Ormes Tramway opening in July 1902. Here is St George's Church and, perched high up on the cliffs, St Tudno's. *Territorials:* Denbighshire Yeomanry, Welsh RGA and 6th Royal Welsh Fusiliers.

Llandyssil Cardiganshire village on the River Teifi, fourteen miles from Lampeter and served by the Great Western Railway, where many were employed in a number of small woollen producing factories. Here is St Tyssil's Church. *Territorials:* Pembrokeshire Yeomanry.

Llanelly Carmarthenshire market town and busy seaport, eleven miles from Swansea, served by the Great Western Railway. Many from the town were employed in the tinplate works (the largest in the world at one time), docks, collieries, copper, iron or lead mines. There are a number of churches in the town, one being dedicated to St Elli, mostly of 1904–06 construction, and another, All Saints in Goring Road, which dates from 1874. *Territorials:* Pembrokeshire Yeomanry, Welsh Divisional Engineers and 4th Welsh Regiment.

Llanfair Caereinion Montgomeryshire market town at the terminus of the light railway opened by the Cambrian from Welshpool in 1903. Here is St Mary's Church. *Territorials:* Montgomeryshire Yeomanry and 7th Royal Welsh Fusiliers.

Llanfechain Montgomeryshire village on the Llanfyllin branch of the Cambrian Railway. Here is St Garmon's Church. *Territorials:* 7th Royal Welsh Fusiliers.

Llanfihangel Montgomeryshire village six miles from Llanfyllin. Here is St Michael's Church. *Territorials:* Montgomeryshire Yeomanry.

Llanfyllin Montgomeryshire market town, nine miles from Welshpool, at the terminus of a Cambrian Railway branch that opened in 1863. Brewing, malting and tanneries were the chief industries, the church here being dedicated to St Myllin. *Territorials:* Montgomeryshire Yeomanry and 7th Royal Welsh Fusiliers.

Llangadock Carmarthenshire market town, six miles from Llandovery on the London & North Western Railway. Here is St Cadog's Church. *Territorials:* Pembrokeshire Yeomanry.

Llangedwyn Denbighshire village on the River Tanat, four miles from Llanfyllin, served by the Cambrian Railway. Here the church is dedicated to St Cedwyn *Territorials:* Montgomeryshire Yeomanry.

Llangollen Denbighshire market town on the River Dee, nine miles from Wrexham, served by the Great Western Railway. Many were employed here by local flannel and slate manufacturers. The Llangollen Canal makes its way to join the Shropshire Union and in doing so crosses nearby Thomas Telford's aqueduct – the longest in Britain. Llangollen was the home of Lady Eleanor Butler (1739–1829) and the Hon Sarah Ponsonby (1755–1832) – the 'Ladies of Llangollen'. An unusual relationship for the time, but one that attracted many visitors to their home: Wordsworth, Shelly, Byron, Scott, among the many writers; Josiah Wedgwood and the Duke of Wellington. See a memorial to the 'Ladies' in the churchyard at St Collen's, Llangollen. *Territorials:* Denbighshire Yeomanry and 4th Royal Welsh Fusiliers.

Llangurig Montgomeryshire village where many were employed in the production of flannel. Here, in the early part of the twentieth century, 'white witches' made a good living charging local farmers a fee to protect their property and animals from the more feared black variety. Llangurig means Church of St Curig. *Territorials:* Montgomeryshire Yeomanry.

Llanhilleth Monmouthshire village on the River Ebbw, four miles from Pontypool, served by the Great Western Railway. Most at Llanhilleth, where the church is dedicated to St Ithel, were employed in local collieries. *Territorials:* 2nd Monmouthshire Regiment.

Llanidloes Montgomeryshire market town on the River Severn, eleven miles from Newtown, served by the Cambrian Railway. Many were employed in the town's flannel factory, or local lead mines. Llanidloes means Church of St Idloes. *Territorials:* Montgomeryshire Yeomanry and 7th Royal Welsh Fusiliers.

Llanrhaiadr Montgomeryshire village on the River Rhaiadr and Tanat Valley Light Railway which opened in 1904. Here is St Dogvan's Church. *Territorials:* Montgomeryshire Yeomanry.

Llansaintffraid Montgomeryshire village on the River Vyrnwy, five miles from Llanfyllin, served by the Cambrian Railway. Here is St Bride's Church. *Territorials:* Montgomeryshire Yeomanry and 7th Royal Welsh Fusiliers.

Llanwddyn Montgomeryshire village in the Vyrnwy Valley, ten miles from Llanfyllin, built to replace an earlier settlement evacuated when the river was dammed so as to create a water supply for Liverpool. Work on the dam began in 1881 and was completed in 1888. Old engravings show a quiet village, the post office, Cross Guns Inn and parish church of St Wddyn. All this levelled, the dam completed and the area flooded, the villagers were then relocated lower down the valley at the new Llanwddyn. *Territorials:* 7th Royal Welsh Fusiliers.

Llanwrtyd Wells Small Brecknockshire spar town, ten miles from Builth Wells, served by the London & North Western Railway. Once simply Llanwrtyd, but the name extended to include Wells after the discovery by the town's vicar that a well was producing water with healing properties. Local people called the well 'Ffynnon Ddrewllydd', the 'Stinking Well'. Came the visitors, came the Belle Vue Hotel in 1843, came the railway with more visitors in 1867. Here is St David's Church. *Territorials:* Brecknockshire Battalion.

Llanybyther Carmarthenshire village on the River Teifi, five miles by rail from Lampeter on the Great Western Railway. The rail service was originally ran by the Manchester & Milford Company, but the Great Western took over in 1911. Here is St Peter's Church. *Territorials:* Pembrokeshire Yeomanry.

Llwyngwril Merionethshire coastal village, just over five miles from Towyn on the Cambrian Railway. *Territorials:* 7th Royal Welsh Fusiliers.

Llwynypia Glamorgan mining village, five miles from Pontypridd, served by the Taff Vale Railway. Here is St Andrew's Church. *Territorials:* Glamorgan Yeomanry.

Loanhead Midlothian town, close to the North Esk, on the North British Railway just over ten miles from Edinburgh. Here, the Polton paper mill employed many, shale was produced until 1909, the Burdiehouse Limeworks ceased production two years after that, and coal was mined. *Territorials:* Lothians and Border Horse and 8th Royal Scots.

Loch Laggan Inverness-shire, sixteen miles from Kingussie. *Territorials:* 1st Lovat's Scouts.

Lochcarron Fishing village on Loch Carron, Ross and Cromarty, twenty-seven miles from Fort Augustus. *Territorials:* 4th Highland Brigade RGA.

Lochearnhead Perthshire village at the foot of Glen Ogle close to Loch Earn, served by the Caledonian Railway. *Territorials:* 1st Scottish Horse.

Lochgelly Fifeshire mining town close to Loch Gelly six miles from Kirkcaldy, served by the North British Railway. Lochgelly is noted as once being famous for its gypsy population, and for the production of the 'loanhead', a leather strap with thongs used in Scottish schools to administer punishment. *Territorials:* 7th Black Watch.

Lochgilphead Argyllshire town at the head of Loch Gilp, two miles from Ardrishaig. Once a village, Lochgilphead prospered at the coming of the Crinan Canal in 1801. Here too was the Argyll and Bute Lunatic Asylum. *Territorials:* 8th Argyll and Sutherland Highlanders.

Lochgoilhead Argyllshire village at the head of Loch Goil just over eleven miles from Inveraray. *Territorials:* 8th Argyll and Sutherland Highlanders.

Lochinver Sutherlandshire village on Loch Inver popular for its fishing, many anglers no doubt arriving via the many steamers that called in regularly from Glasgow. *Territorials:* 5th Seaforth Highlanders.

Lochmaddy Village on Loch Maddy, North Uist, Inverness-shire which takes its name from the dog-shaped rock at the loch entrance called the 'Maddies'. With its regular steamer connection to Skye and the mainland, Lochmaddy became an important trade centre for a large part of the Outer Hebrides. *Territorials:* 1st Lovat's Scouts and 4th Cameron Highlander.

Lochwinnoch Small Renfrewshire town on the River Calder at the west end of Castle Semper Loch. Lochwinnoch, which could be reach by the Glasgow & South Western Railway, manufactured chairs, carried on silk weaving and printing, and had a large steam laundry. *Territorials:* 4th Royal Scots Fusiliers.

Lockerbie Dumfrieshire market town, twelve miles from Dumfries, served by the Caledonian Railway. *Territorials:* Lanarkshire Yeomanry and 5th King's Own Scottish Borderers.

Lock's Green Village on the Isle of Wight, five miles from Newport. *Territorials:* 8th Hampshire Regiment.

Loddon Norfolk market town seven miles from Beccles. Here is Holy Trinity Church. *Territorials:* Norfolk Yeomanry and 4th Norfolk Regiment.

Loftus Small town in the North Riding of Yorkshire, nine miles from Guisborough and served by the North Eastern Railway, where bricks and tiles were produced. Here is St Leonard's Church. *Territorials:* 4th Yorkshire Regiment.

Logie Coldstone Aberdeenshire village just over four miles from Dinnet. *Territorials:* 7th Gordon Highlanders.

London, City of Small area of just over one square mile and major world business and financial centre. At the Guildhall on 17 January 1908, F W Pomeroy's memorial to those of the Royal Fusiliers that had lost their lives in South Africa 1899–1902 was unveiled. Merchant Taylors' School, at Charterhouse Square, maintained two OTC infantry companies. *Territorials:* 1st London Division, 1st London Infantry Brigade, City of London Yeomanry, 1st London Brigade RFA, 8th London Regiment, 3rd London General Hospital, Ackmar School Cadet Corps, Hugh Myddelton School Cadet Corps, Coopers' Company School Cadet Corps, Marner School (LCC) Cadet Company and 1st City of London Cadet Battalion.

London Colney Hertfordshire village on the River Colne, six miles from Barnet. Here is St Peter's Church. *Territorials:* Hertfordshire Regiment.

Long Ashton Somerset village, three miles from Bristol, where many were employed in local stone quarries, coal and iron mines. Here is All Saints Church. *Territorials:* Wessex Divisional Engineers.

Long Buckby Northamptonshire village, five miles from Daventry, served by the London & North Western Railway. Here is St Lawrence's Church, the village once employing many in the manufacture of boots and shoes. *Territorials:* 4th Northamptonshire Regiment.

Long Eaton Derbyshire town on the Nottinghamshire border, just over seven miles by rail from Nottingham on the Midland Railway. A large railway carriage works employed many from Long Eaton, which also made its contribution to the famous Nottingham Lace industry. Here is St Lawrence's Church and Trent College which had an OTC contingent of one infantry company. *Territorials:* Nottinghamshire Yeomanry (South Notts) and 5th Sherwood Foresters.

Long Melford Suffolk village close to the border with Essex, three miles from Sudbury and served by the Great Eastern Railway. Local wool merchants brought wealth to the area and left a good number of fine houses. Here, in the churchyard of the cathedral-like Holy Trinity Church, is the grave of First World War poet and author, Edmund Blunden. *Territorials:* 5th Suffolk Regiment.

Long Stratton Norfolk village, just over ten miles from Norwich. Here is St Mary's Church, the village sometimes referred to as Stratton St Mary. *Territorials:* Norfolk Yeomanry and 4th Norfolk Regiment.

Longbridge Deverell Wiltshire village three miles from Warminster. Here is the church of St Peter and St Paul. *Territorials:* Wiltshire Yeomanry.

Longford Park Wiltshire Locality seventeen miles from Tisbury. *Territorials:* 1st South Western Mounted Brigade Transport and Supply Column.

Longridge Lancashire town, six miles from Preston, served by the London & north Western Railway. Stone was quarried here, and after the railway came in 1840, cotton mills brought even more prosperity. Here is St Lawrence's Church. *Territorials:* 4th North Lancashire Regiment.

Longside Aberdeenshire village on the River Ugie, six miles from Peterhead, served by the Great North of Scotland Railway. Here is St John's Church, many at Longside being employed in local granite quarries. *Territorials:* 5th Gordon Highlanders.

Longton Staffordshire market town, three miles from Stoke-on-Trent, served by the North Staffordshire Railway. A major producer of pottery, with Star's Paragon and the Roslyn Gladstone works among the largest employers. Still seen in the town are the Phoenix Works; in Caroline Street, the Caroline Pottery, and the Salisbury China Company in Chadwick Street. Arnold Bennett wrote about the town, but in his book *Five Towns*, called it 'Longshaw'. Here in King Street is St John's Church. *Territorials:* 5th North Staffordshire Regiment.

Lonmay Small Aberdeenshire village, four miles from Fraserburgh, served by the Great North of Scotland Railway. *Territorials:* 5th Gordon Highlanders.

Looe Town in Cornwall, where the river divides the place into two (East and West Looe), and of which the novelist Wilkie Collins once referred to as 'one of the prettiest and most primitive places in England' where there was 'no such thing as a straight street in the place'. Here in East Looe is St Ann's Church, and in West Looe, St Nicholas's. Looe was served by the Great Western Railway. *Territorials:* Cornwall RGA.

Lossiemouth Elginshire seaport and fishing town, five miles from Elgin and situated where the River Lossie joins the Moray Firth. Lossiemouth, served by the Great North of Scotland Railway, was the birth place of the former Labour prime minister, Ramsay Macdonald (1866–1937). *Territorials:* 6th Seaforth Highlanders.

Lostwithiel Market town on the River Fowey once the capital of Cornwall and leading centre of the tin trade. The Great Western Railway called at Lostwithiel, the company having workshops in the town. Dating from the twelfth century is St Bartholomew's Church where a horse was once christened in the font. He was named 'Charles'. *Territorials:* 5th Duke of Cornwall's Light Infantry.

Loughborough Leicestershire market town on the River Soar and Loughborough Canal, ten miles from Leicester. Loughborough made locomotives for the railway and bells for the church. 'Great Paul', now in St Paul's Cathedral and the largest bell in Britain, was cast at Taylor's, Loughborough in 1881. An important railway town, the old Charnwood Forest line terminated at Loughborough's Derby Road Station (it later became the London & North Western) and the Great Central and Midland both passed through. Here is All Saints Church and, founded in 1909, Loughborough College. *Territorials:* Leicestershire Yeomanry and 5th Leicestershire Regiment.

Loughton Small Essex town on the River Roding and eastern edge of Epping Forest. Loughton was reached by the Great Eastern Railway, just over eleven miles from London's Fenchurch Street. Here are three churches: St John's, brick-built in 1746; St Nicholas (1877), and St Mary's of 1871. *Territorials:* Essex Yeomanry and 4th Essex Regiment.

Louth Lincolnshire market town on the River Lud, twenty-six miles from Lincoln, served by the Great Northern Railway. St James's Church, with its 295 ft spire, dominates the town. Employment was in iron foundries, breweries and rope making. Alfred Lord Tennyson attended Louth Grammar School which, from 1908, maintained one OTC infantry company. *Territorials:* Lincolnshire Yeomanry, 1st North Midland Brigade RFA and 5th Lincolnshire Regiment.

Lowestoft Suffolk seaport and market town with a large fishing industry, ship and boat building yards and a coachworks. A soft-past porcelain ('Lowestoft') was made here, and composer Benjamin Britten was born in the town in 1913. A popular seaside resort, the town is situated at the most easterly point in Britain and was served by the Great Eastern and other railways. A splendid sight must have been the Tuscan-red, chocolate, primrose and cream trams ran by the Lowestoft Corporation from July 1903 until May 1931. Here is St Margaret's Church. *Territorials:* Suffolk Yeomanry, 3rd East Anglian Brigade RFA, 4th and 6th Suffolk Regiment and 2nd East Anglian Field Ambulance.

Ludlow Shropshire market town close to the border with Herefordshire and the point where the Corve river meets the Teme. Here is St Laurence's Church with its rare hexagonal porch and Commandments window. Panels show all ten of them being broken. The railway service at Ludlow was provided by the Great Western and London & North Western Joint. 'Or come you home of Monday/When Ludlow market hums ...' (from 'The Recruit' and *A Shropshire Lad* by A E Housman). *Territorials:* Shropshire Yeomanry and 4th King's Shropshire Light Infantry.

Ludwell Wiltshire hamlet three miles from Shaftesbury. *Territorials:* 1st South Western Mounted Brigade Transport and Supply Column.

Lumsden Aberdeenshire village twelve miles from Huntly. *Territorials:* 6th Gordon Highlanders.

Luncarty Perthshire village, four miles from Perth, served by the Caledonian Railway. *Territorials:* 6th Black Watch.

Luton Bedfordshire town on the River Lea, nineteen miles from Bedford, served by both the Midland and Great Northern railways. In the north transept of St Mary's Church, among some fifteenth and sixteenth-century brasses, Captain Crawley's (an old Volunteer) family arms appear on a stone shield. Well known for its manufacture of straw hats and bonnets, when the town's football team got started in 1885 it soon acquired the nickname 'the Hatters'. Here too was the Vauxhall motor works which began production in 1905. Bedfordshire's only tramway system was operated by Luton Corporation, the trams running on overhead electric wires from their deport in Bailey Street. *Territorials:* East Anglian Divisional Engineers, 5th Bedfordshire Regiment and Eastern Mounted Brigade Field Ambulance.

Lutterworth Leicestershire market town on the River Swift, eight miles from Rugby, reached by the Great Central Railway in March 1899. Canon John Wycliffe (1329–84) of Lutterworth's St Mary's Church produced what is believed to be the first translation of the Bible from Latin into English. His efforts, it would seem, were not appreciated, and thirty years after his death his body was dug up and thrown into the Swift. Here too was the Religious Tract Society, later to develop into the Lutterworth Press of whom we must thank for the *Boy's Own Paper* and other learned publications. *Territorials:* Leicestershire Yeomanry.

Lybster Caithness-shire fishing village, thirteen miles from Wick, at the termination of the Wick & Lybster Light Railway which opened in 1903. *Territorials:* 5th Seaforth Highlanders.

Lydd Market town on the Romney Marsh in Kent, three miles from New Romney and served by the South Eastern & Chatham Railway. An important military training area for artillery from the late 1880s. Explosives were tested here and 'Lyddite' invented. Here is All Saints Church, the 'Cathedral of Romney March'. *Territorials:* 5th Buffs East Kent Regiment.

Lydford Devonshire village on the Rive Lyd and western edge of Dartmoor, just over seven miles from Tavistock, served by both the Great Western and London & South Western railways. Lydford was once important in the production of tin and conditions in its castle so bad that, those awaiting trial there often died before they appeared in court. This 'jeddart' form of justice, whereas a person is hanged first and tried afterwards, led to an alternative expression 'Lydford law'. Here is St Petrock's Church. *Territorials:* 4th Wessex Brigade RFA.

Lyme Regis Dorset market town and seaside resort, nine miles from Bridport, reached by the railway in August 1903 when the London & South Western ran a branch off its main line down from Axminster. Here, perched on the edge of a cliff, is St Michael and All Angels Church in which part of the north aisle pavement bears the name of nineteen-year-old William Hewling – one of Judge Jefferies victims. *Territorials:* 4th Devonshire Regiment.

Lymington Hampshire seaport and market town on the River Lymington, just under twelve miles from Southampton, served by the London & South Western Railway. An important yachting centre, here at the top of High Street is St Thomas's Church. *Territorials:* Hampshire Fortress Engineers, 7th Hampshire Regiment and Lymington Cadet Corps.

Lymm Cheshire town on the Bridgewater Canal, five miles from Warrington, served by the London & North Western Railway. Here is St Mary's Church. *Territorials:* 5th Cheshire Regiment.

Lympstone Devonshire fishing village on the east bank of the Exe estuary, seven miles from Exeter, served by the London & South Western Railway. Oysters were once a speciality, and Honiton lace was produced. Here is St Mary's Church. *Territorials:* 4th Devonshire Regiment.

Lynmouth Village and seaside resort on the north Devon coast at the point where the East and West Lyn rivers meet. Nineteen miles from Illfracombe, Lynmouth was served by the Lynton & Barnstaple Railway which arrived in 1898. The poet Shelly spent his honeymoon here in 1812 and when teacher and lecturer Walter Raleigh (1861–1922) came in 1889 he found the Lyndale Hotel not to his liking so moved on to the more humble Rising Sun. Opened in April 1890 was the Lynton & Lynmouth Cliff Railway which linked the two places via a 300-yard double track up the cliff. Here is the Church of St John the Baptist. *Territorials:* Devonshire RGA.

Lytham Lancashire town on the north shore of the Ribble estuary, seven miles from Blackpool, served by the London & North Western Railway. Here are St Cuthbert's and St John's churches. Lytham was merged with St Ann's in 1922 to become Lytham St Anne's. *Territorials:* 4th North Lancashire Regiment.

Macclesfield Cheshire market town on the River Bollin, fifteen miles from Manchester, where much of the town's prosperity once came from the silk and cotton trade. There were also coal, slate mines and stone quarries in the area. The London & North Western, North Staffordshire and Great Central railways served the town. Here is St Michael's Church and, with its box-pews, Christ Church. *Territorials:* Cheshire Yeomanry, 7th Cheshire Regiment, Macclesfield Industrial School Cadet Corps and Macclesfield Grammar School Cadet Corps.

Macduff Banffshire seaport and fishing town on the Moray Firth, eleven miles from Banff, served by the Great North of Scotland Railway. *Territorials:* 1st Highland Brigade RFA.

Machynlleth Montgomeryshire market town on the River Dovey, seventeen miles from Dolgelly, served by the Cambrian and Corris railways. Flannel was manufactured, slate was quarried and lead mined. Here are Christ Church and St Peter's churches. *Territorials:* 7th Royal Welsh Fusiliers.

Macmerry Haddingtonshire village just over fourteen miles by rail from Edinburgh on the North British Railway. *Territorials:* 8th Royal Scots.

Madingley 'And things are done you'd not believe/At Madingley on Christmas Eve.' (from 'The Old Vicarage, Grantchester' by Rupert Brooke, 1912). Cambridgeshire village four miles from Cambridge. Here is the church of St Mary Magdalene. *Territorials:* Cambridgeshire Regiment.

Madley Herefordshire village just over five miles from Herford. Here is the church of the Nativity of St Mary the Virgin where once the vicar and the squire were involved in a lawsuit over the altar. *Territorials:* Herefordshire Regiment.

Maesteg Glamorgan town on the River Llynvi, eight miles from Neath on the Great Western and Port Talbot Railway and Docks railways, where the inhabitants were mostly employed in collieries and ironworks. Here, in Castle Street, is St David's Church; St Michael and All Angels is in Church Place. The Roman Catholic St Michael and St Patrick's being built in Monica Street 1906–7. *Territorials:* Glamorgan Yeomanry and 6th Welsh Regiment.

Maiden Newton Dorset village on the River Frome, eight miles from Dorchester, and the junction for the Great Western Railway branch line to Bridport. Here is the twelfth-century St Mary's Church. *Territorials:* Dorsetshire Yeomanry.

Maidenhead Berkshire market town on the right bank of the Thames six miles to the north-west of Windsor, Maidenhead is connected with Taplow and Buckinghamshire on the opposite bank by a seven-arched stone bridge and a viaduct built by Brunel for the Great Western Railway (see Turner's painting *Rain, Steam and Speed*). Maidenhead was thought to be 'too snobby in Jerome K Jerome's *Three Men in a Boat*. Here is the church of St Andrew and St Mary Magdalene (1822–25), and on Boyne Hill, All Saints of 1854–57. *Territorials:* Berkshire Yeomanry, 4th Royal Berkshire Regiment and 1st Cadet Company 4th Royal Berkshire Regiment.

Maidstone Market town on the Medway in Kent, twenty-four miles from Canterbury, served by the South Eastern & Chatham Railway. Many in Maidstone were employed in the production of paper – leading mill owners, John Hollingworth and R J Balston were members of the old 1st Kent Rifle Volunteer Corps. A tram service began operating in the town in July 1904, one of its routes terminating at the Tovil paper mill. Here, overlooking the river and built in 1395, is the parish church of All Saints where the Ashley family are remembered; as too is Lieutenant-Colonel William Havelock who was killed in India in 1848. At Maidstone Grammar School there was a one OTC infantry company. *Territorials:* West Kent Yeomanry, 4th Royal West Kent Regiment, Kent Cyclist Battalion, Home Counties Divisional Transport and Supply Column and 1st Home Counties Field Ambulance.

Maldon Essex river port and market town at the confluence of the Chelmer and Blackwater, ten miles from Chelmsford and served by the Great Eastern Railway. Here there was a busy shipping trade, oyster fisheries and a salt production plant. The Maldon Crystal Salt Company was founded in 1882. At the top of High Street, next to the Blue Boar inn, stands All Saints Church with its triangular tower – the only one in England. The registers date from 1536, and there is a memorial window in the church to a relative of American president George Washington. Here too in Maldon is St Peter's and, known as the 'Seaman's Church', St Mary's which has registers from 1558. *Territorials:* 5th and 8th Essex Regiment.

Malmesbury Wiltshire market town on the River Avon, nine miles from Chippenham, served by the Great Western Railway. Here in Malmesbury Abbey, a window tells how Elmer the monk thought he could fly. With paper wings attached to his arms, from one of the towers he jumped; only to crash to the ground breaking both his legs in the process and no doubt looking a bit silly. In the burial ground a headstone tells how in 1703 Hannah Twynnoy, a maid at the White Lion Inn, was killed by a tiger. *Territorials:* Wiltshire Yeomanry and 3rd Wessex Brigade RFA.

Malton North Riding of Yorkshire market town on the River Derwent, twenty-one miles by rail from York on the North Eastern Railway. Here is the chiefly Norman St Leonard's Church. *Territorials:* York and Durham Infantry Brigade, York and Lancaster Infantry Brigade, Yorkshire Hussars, 5th Yorkshire Regiment and Yorkshire Mounted Brigade Transport and Supply Column.

Manchester Where the damp and soft water was good for cotton and the locals called the place 'Cottonopalis'. The Manchester Territorials were formed in time to attend the unveiling in St Ann's Square on 26 October 1908 of William Hamo Thornycroft's memorial to those of the Manchester Regiment that lost their lives in South Africa 1899–1902. Manchester University and the Manchester Grammar School both maintained contingents in the OTC. *Territorials:* East Lancashire Division, East Lancashire Infantry Brigade, Manchester Infantry Brigade, Duke of Lancaster's Own Yeomanry, 2nd East Lancashire Brigade RFA, East Lancashire Divisional Engineers, 6th, 7th Manchester

Regiment, East Lancashire Divisional Transport and Supply Column, 1st, 2nd, 3rd East Lancashire Field Ambulances, 2nd Western General Hospital, East Lancashire Clearing Hospital and East Lancashire School of Instruction.

Mangotsfield Gloucestershire village five miles from Bristol. Here is St James's Church, almost entirely rebuilt in 1850. *Territorials:* 4th Gloucestershire Regiment.

Manningtree Small Essex market town on the River Stour, eight miles from Colchester, served by the Great Eastern Railway. Here is St Michael's Church and the headquarters of Matthew Hopkins – the 'witch-hunter'. *Territorials:* 5th Essex Regiment.

Manor Park London district described as Victorian terraces between Forest Gate and Ilford. Born there in 1890 was the actor Stanley Holloway. *Territorials:* 4th Essex Regiment and Manor Park Cadet Company.

Manorbier Pembrokeshire coastal village, four miles from Tenby, served by the Great Western Railway. Here is St James's Church. *Territorials:* Pembrokeshire Yeomanry.

Mansfield Nottinghamshire market town on the River Maun, thirteen miles from Nottingham, served by the Great Central and Midland railways. Employment in and around the town was mostly from the manufacture of boots and shoes. There were also large iron foundries and engine works. Operating in the town from July 1905 until October 1932, were the red and cream (later light green and cream) tramcars of the Mansfield and District Light Railway company. Here is St Mark's Church of 1897. *Territorials:* Nottinghamshire Yeomanry (Sherwood Rangers), 8th Sherwood Forester and Welbeck Cadet Battalion.

Marazion Small town and port on Mounts Bay, Cornwall, three miles from Penzance. Market gardening is noted as the chief industry at Marazion which was once called Market Jew. Here is All Saints Church which dates from 1861. *Territorials:* Cornwall RGA.

March Cambridgeshire market town on the River Nene, fourteen miles from Peterborough. Much trade in coal, timber and corn was carried out on the river. In the town there was an extensive engineering works and a factory producing agricultural implements. An important railway junction, trains entered and left March belonging to the Eastern Counties, Great Eastern and Great Northern railways. Here is St Wendreda's Church, its high spire visible for miles across the Fenlands. *Territorials:* Cambridgeshire Regiment.

Marchwood Hampshire village on Southampton Water, two miles from Southampton. Here is the church of St John the Apostle, a Royal Naval ordnance dept and barracks. *Territorials:* 7th Hampshire Regiment.

Marden (Hereford) Village on the River Lugg, four miles from Hereford. Here is St Mary's Church. *Territorials:* Herefordshire Regiment.

Marden (Kent) Village nine miles from Tunbridge served by the South Eastern & Chatham Railway. Here is St Michael's Church. *Territorials:* 5th Buffs East Kent Regiment.

Margate Kent seaside resort, fifteen miles from Canterbury, served by the South Eastern & Chatham Railway. Here, in 1753, local glove maker and Quaker Benjamin Beale, invented the bathing machine. Here is the parish church of St John the Baptist. *Territorials:* Royal East Kent Yeomanry, 3rd Home Counties Brigade RFA, 4th Buffs East Kent Regiment, Kent Cyclist Battalion and South Eastern Mounted Brigade Field Ambulance.

Market Bosworth Leicestershire market town, eight miles from Nuneaton, served by the London & North Western and Midland railways. Close by is the Ashby-de-la-Zouch Canal. Here is St Peter's

Church and at the grammar school, Doctor Samuel Johnson was one on the staff. *Territorials:* Leicestershire Yeomanry.

Market Drayton Shropshire market town on the River Tern and Shropshire Union Canal, nine miles from Whitchurch and served by the North Staffordshire Railway. An important agricultural centre with ironworks and factories producing tools to work the land. Here is St Mary's Church and the birthplace of Robert Clive (Clive of India) in 1725. *Territorials:* Shropshire Yeomanry and 4th King's Shropshire Light Infantry.

Market Harborough Leicestershire market town on the River Welland and Union Canal, fourteen miles from Leicester, served by the Midland and London & North Western railways. There were brickfields, boot and shoe factories and a plant manufacturing rubber goods. The liberty bodice for ladies, produced by R & W H Symington, began at Market Drayton in around 1910. Here is St Dionysius's church. *Territorials:* Leicestershire Yeomanry, 5th Leicestershire Regiment and North Midland Divisional Transport and Supply Column.

Market Lavington Wiltshire village (sometimes called East Lavington), five miles from Devises. Here is St Mary's Church. *Territorials:* Wiltshire Yeomanry and 4th Wiltshire Regiment.

Market Rasen Lincolnshire market town on the River Rase, thirteen miles from Lincoln, served by the Great Central Railway. Here is St Thomas's Church and a well known racecourse. *Territorials:* Lincolnshire Yeomanry.

Market Weighton East Riding of Yorkshire market town, ten miles from Beverly, served by the North Eastern Railway. The Market Rasen Canal begins here and runs down to the Humber. Here, at All Saints Church, the 'Yorkshire Giant' is remembered. William Bradley: seven feet, nine inches tall, and twenty-seven stone in weight, he died in 1820 when just twenty. *Territorials:* 5th East Yorkshire Regiment and 5th Yorkshire Regiment.

Markinch Small Fifeshire town, eight miles from Kirkcaldy, served by the North British Railway. Here were collieries, bleach fields, paper mills and distilleries. *Territorials:* 7th Black Watch.

Marlborough Wiltshire market town on the River Kennet, ten miles from Swindon, served by the Great Western and Midland & South Western Junction railways. Rope and sacking were made, and there was brewing, malting and tanning. Here are St Mary's and St Peter and St Paul's churches, and Marlborough College which was founded in 1843 and from 1908 maintained an OTC contingent. *Territorials:* Wiltshire Yeomanry, 4th Wiltshire Regiment and 1st South Western Mounted Brigade Field Ambulance.

Marlow Buckinghamshire market town on the River Thames, four miles from Maidenhead, served by the Great Western Railway. Principal sources of employment at Marlow were: paper mills, a brewery, the manufacture of chairs and lace making. Here is All Saints Church. *Territorials:* Buckinghamshire Battalion.

Marnhull Dorset village on the River Stour, three miles from Sturminster Newton. Brewing, malting and quarrying were local industries. Marnhull is Thomas Hardy's 'Marlott' in *Tess of the D'Urbervilles*. Here is St Gregory's Church. *Territorials:* 4th Dorsetshire Regiment.

Marsden West Riding of Yorkshire town on the River Colne, seven miles from Huddersfield, served by the London & North Western Railway. There were woollen mills here, Luddite trouble occurring in 1812 which saw the fatal shooting of a Marsden mill owner. Here is St Bartholomew's Church and a canal tunnel more than three miles in length. *Territorials:* 7th Duke of Wellington's Regiment.

Marsham Norfolk village, ten miles from Norwich. Here is All Saints Church. *Territorials:* Norfolk Yeomanry.

Marske-by-the-Sea North Riding of Yorkshire village on the North Sea, two miles from Redcar, served by the North Eastern Railway. Here is St Mark's Church of 1867 and, on the Cliff edge, the more ancient St Germain's. *Territorials:* 4th Yorkshire Regiment.

Martock Somerset village on the River Parret, seven miles from Yeovil, served by the Great Western Railway. Martock was well known for its manufacture of gloves. Here is All Saints Church, built with stone from the nearby Ham Hill quarries. *Territorials:* West Somerset Yeomanry and 5th Somerset Light Infantry.

Maryburgh Ross and Cromarty village on the River Conon just above where it enters Cromarty Firth. Here, noted the guides, the population consisted chiefly of artisans and crofters. *Territorials:* 4th Seaforth Highlanders.

Maryhill North-west Glasgow locality. Here is Maryhill Barracks. *Territorials:* Lowland Divisional Transport and Supply Column.

Marykirk Kincardineshire village on the North Esk river, four miles from Laurencekirk, served by the Caledonian Railway. *Territorials:* 7th Gordon Highlanders.

Maryport Cumberland seaport and market town at the mouth of the River Ellen, five miles from Workington, served by the Maryport & Carlisle Railway. Once a small fishing village called Ellenfoot, it prospered when Humphrey Senhouse built a dock for the export of his coal and renamed the place after his wife. Thomas Ismay, born in the town in 1836, also made some money when he began his White Star shipping line. Here is Christ Church and St Mary's Church. *Territorials:* Westmorland and Cumberland Yeomanry and 4th East Lancashire Brigade RFA.

Massingham Great Massingham and Little Massingham; both in Norfolk within twelve miles of King's Lynn and sharing the same railway station – Massingham, on the Midland and Great Northern Joint. Here in Great Massingham is St Mary's Church, and in Little Massingham, St Andrew's. *Territorials:* Norfolk Yeomanry.

Matlock Derbyshire market and spa town on the River Derwent, nine mile from Chesterfield, served by the Midland Railway. Paper, cotton and corn mills, a bleach works and stone quarries provided employment. Opened in March 1893, with its royal blue and white vehicles, was the Matlock Cable Tramway. Here is the parish church of St Giles. *Territorials:* Derbyshire Yeomanry and 6th Sherwood Foresters.

Maud Aberdeenshire village, twelve miles from Peterhead, served by the Great North of Scotland Railway. *Territorials:* 2nd Scottish Horse and 5th Gordon Highlanders.

Maxwelltown Kirkcudbrightshire town on the right bank of the River Nith, served by the Glasgow & South Western Railway, once called Bridgend. The town is connected to Dumfries by bridges across the river and in 1810 one Marmaduke Maxwell was important enough to have the name changed. Here were tweed mills, a dye works and a factory making hosiery. *Territorials:* 5th King's Own Scottish Borderers.

Maybole Ayrshire market town, eight miles from Ayr, served by the Glasgow & South Western Railway. Here boots, shoes and agricultural implements were made. *Territorials:* 5th Royal Scots Fusiliers.

Mayfield Sussex town, eight miles from Tunbridge Wells, served by the London, Brighton & South Coast Railway. Here is St Dunstan's Church. *Territorials:* 5th Royal Sussex Regiment.

Meifod Montgomeryshire village on the River Vyrnwy six miles from Welshpool. Here is St Tysilio's Church. *Territorials:* Montgomeryshire Yeomanry.

Melbourne Small Derbyshire town, seven miles from Derby, served by the Midland Railway. Boots, shoes and silk were made in the area. Here is the church of St Michael and St Mary, and in 1808, the birthplace of travel agent Thomas Cook. *Territorials:* 5th Sherwood Foresters.

Melksham Wiltshire market town on the River Avon, five miles from Trowbridge, served by the Great Western Railway. Rope and sacking were produced. Here is St Michael's Church and, running to the east of the town is the Wilts & Berks Canal. *Territorials:* Wiltshire Yeomanry and 4th Wiltshire Regiment.

Mells Somerset village, three miles from Frome and served by the Great Western Railway. Mells was noted for its production of good quality scythes and other edge tools. Here is St Andrew's Church and the seat of the Horner family who made much from local mineral workings. *Territorials:* North Somerset Yeomanry and 4th Somerset Light Infantry.

Melness Sutherlandshire village on the west side of Kyle of Tongue, thirty-five miles from Lairg. *Territorials:* 2nd Lovat's Scouts.

Melrose Roxburghshire town on the River Tweed, four miles from Galashiels, served by the North British Railway. Opened in 1872, the Waverley Hydropathic Establishment stands on Skirmish Hill, the site of a Border fight in 1526. Popular here is rugby, the seven-a-side version ('Sevens') having originated at Melrose in 1883. *Territorials:* Lothians and Border Horse and 4th King's Own Scottish Borderers.

Meltham West Riding of Yorkshire village, five miles from Huddersfield, served by the London & North Western Railway. There was woollen and cotton mills. Here is St Bartholomew's Church. *Territorials:* 5th Duke of Wellington's Regiment.

Melton Constable Norfolk village, five miles from Holt, served by the Midland and Great Northern Joint Railway which had large locomotive and carriage repair shops in the area. Here is St Peter's Church. *Territorials:* 5th Norfolk Regiment.

Melton Mowbray Leicestershire market town, thirteen miles from Leicester, situated at the junction of the Wreak and Eye and served by both the Midland and Great Northern railways. Famous is the town for its pork pies and Stilton cheese. Here is St Mary's Church. *Territorials:* Leicestershire Yeomanry and 5th Leicestershire Regiment.

Melton Ross Lincolnshire village five miles from Brigg. Here is the church of the Holy Ascension. *Territorials:* Nottinghamshire Yeomanry (Sherwood Rangers).

Melvich Sutherlandshire village at the mouth of the River Halladale. *Territorials:* 5th Seaforth Highlanders.

Menai Bridge Village at the north end of the Menai Suspension Bridge on Anglesey, four miles from Beaumaris, served by the London & North Western Railway. Here is St Tysilio's Church, the village being well known once for its manufacture of tombstones and writing slates. *Territorials:* 6th Royal Welsh Fusiliers.

Menstrie Clackmannanshire village at the foot of the Ochil Hills, three miles from Alloa where blankets and other woollen articles were made. *Territorials:* 7th Argyll and Sutherland Highlanders.

Merthyr Tydfil Glamorgan industrial town at the head of the Taff Valley and served by both the Great Western and London & North Western railways. Cassell's *Gazetteer* for 1895 notes that nearly all the inhabitants of Merthyr Tydfil were employed in coal mining and the manufacture of iron and steel. Indeed, by the middle of the nineteenth century, the Dowlais Ironworks was employing some 10,000 from the area. In 1804 the world's first steam railway began here and ran from Merthyr to

Abercynon. Of the town's many churches, we find both St David's and St Tydfil's in the High Street, and in Aberdare Road, Christ Church which was opened in 1857. *Territorials:* Glamorgan Yeomanry and 5th Welsh Regiment.

Methlick Aberdeenshire village on the River Ythan seventeen miles from Peterhead. *Territorials:* 5th Gordon Highlanders.

Methven Perthshire village, six miles from Perth and served by the Caledonian Railway. *Territorials:* 1st Scottish Horse.

Methwold Norfolk village three miles from Stoke Ferry. Here is St George's Church. *Territorials:* 4th Norfolk Regiment.

Mexborough West Riding of Yorkshire town on the River Don, five miles from Rotherham, served by the Great Central Railway. Wheels for the railway, bottles and grindstones were made at Mexborough. The Mexborough & Swinton Tramways Company, with its bright red and cream trams, opened in February 1907. Here is the church of St John the Baptist. *Territorials:* 5th York and Lancaster Regiment.

Mey Caithness village six miles from John O' Groats. *Territorials:* 5th Seaforth Highlanders.

Mickleton Gloucestershire village three miles from Chipping Campden. Here is St Lawrence's Church. *Territorials:* 5th Gloucestershire Regiment.

Mickley Northumberland mining village nine miles from Hexham. Here is St George's Church. *Territorials:* 4th Northumberland Fusiliers.

Mid Calder Midlothian village on the River Almond, eleven miles from Edinburgh, served by the Caledonian Railway. Here were large manufacturers of mineral oil, chemicals and paper. *Territorials:* Lothians and Border Horse.

Middlesbrough North Riding of Yorkshire port and industrial town on the south bank of the Tees. Once a small village, the coming of the railway in 1830 saw rapid growth and the establishment of the steel industry. Among the several companies giving employment, the Vaughan and Bolckon steel works was reckoned to be the most extensive in the world. The town has several Gothic style churches. Churchlike, with their towers, are the Ironmasters' and General Exchange (1866–68) and Town Hall (1889) buildings. *Territorials:* Yorkshire Hussars, Northumbrian RGA, North Riding Fortress Engineers and 4th Yorkshire Regiment.

Middleton Lancashire market town, three miles from Oldham, served by the London & North Western Railway. Coal production was important to Middleton, there was also silk weaving, cotton spinning, calico printing and a chemical works. The crimson and primrose trams of the Middleston Electric Tramway began work in the town in March 1902. Here is St Leonard's Church. *Territorials:* 6th Lancashire Fusiliers.

Middlewich Cheshire town, four miles from Sandbach, served by the London & North Western Railway. The Trent and Mersey and Shropshire Union canals meet here, their presence being important to the town's salt industry. The suffix 'wich' means saltworks, 'middle distinguishing the place from the area's other salt producing towns: Nantwich and Northwich. Chemicals were also made, and condensed milk. Here is St Michael and All Angels Church where, under siege during the Civil War, a Royalist party led by Colonel Ellis were forced to surrender. There are marks from Parliamentary cannon-fire on the tower still. *Territorials:* Cheshire Yeomanry and 7th Cheshire Regiment.

Midhurst Sussex market town on the River Rother, ten miles from Chichester, served by both the London & South Western and London, Brighton & South Coast railways. Author, H G Wells

(1866–1946) had strong connections with Midhurst. Went to school there, later taught there, and featured the town, under the name Wimblehurst, in his novel *Tono-Bungay* (1909). Here the much restored in 1882 church is dedicated to St Mary Magdalene and St Denys. *Territorials:* 4th Royal Sussex Regiment.

Midsomer Norton Somerset village, eight miles from Bath, served by both the Great Western and Somerset & Dorset railways. Here the church is dedicated to St John the Baptist. *Territorials:* 4th Somerset Light Infantry.

Milborne Port Somerset town, three miles from Sherborne, served by the London & South Western Railway. Gloves and other leather goods were made at Milborne Port, and here is the church of St John the Evangelist. *Territorials:* 4th Dorsetshire Regiment.

Mildenhall Suffolk village on the River Lark, eleven miles from Thetford, served by the Great Eastern Railway which arrived in 1885. Here is the church of St Mary and St Andrew. *Territorials:* 5th Suffolk Regiment.

Milford Haven Pembrokeshire town on the estuary of the East and West Cleddau rivers, served by the Great Western Railway. A large seaport – the 'finest in Christendom' according to Lord Nelson. Founded in 1793 by Quakers from the USA as a whaling centre, the town had numerous shipyards giving employment, and a large fishing industry. Here is St Catherine's Church. *Territorials:* Pembrokeshire RGA and 4th Welsh Regiment.

Milford-on-Sea Hampshire village three miles from Lymington. Here is All Saints Church which has a memorial to Admiral Sir William Cornwallis who lived at the nearby Newlands estate. *Territorials:* 7th Hampshire Regiment.

Millom Cumberland town on the Duddon estuary, seven miles from Barrow-in-Furness, served by the Furness Railway. An important centre in the iron and smelting industry – the Hodbarrow Steelworks employing many. Here is Holy Trinity Church. *Territorials:* 4th King's Own Royal Lancaster Regiment.

Millport Seaside resort on the south coast of Great Cumbrae Island, Firth of Clyde, Buteshire. Here is William Butterfield's small Cathedral of the Isles with its forty-ft by twenty-ft nave and seats for just 100 people. *Territorials:* 4th Highland Brigade RGA.

Milngavie Dumbartonshire town, five miles from Glasgow, served by the North British Railway. There were bleaching and dying businesses, a print works and large paper mill. *Territorials:* 9th Argyll and Sutherland Highlanders.

Milnsbridge West Riding of Yorkshire village, two miles from Huddersfield, served by the London & North Western Railway. Woollen mills and stone quarries gave employment. Here is St Luke's Church. *Territorials:* 7th Duke of Wellington's Regiment.

Milnthorpe Westmorland market town on the mouth of the River Kent, seven miles from Carnforth, served by the London & North Western Railway. A busy river port, the town's main industries are noted as the making of combs, and the malting of barley. Here is St Thomas's Church. *Territorials:* 4th Border Regiment.

Milton Hampshire village seven miles from Lymington. Here the church is dedicated to St Mary Magdalene. *Territorials:* 7th Hampshire Regiment.

Milton Abbot Devonshire village six miles from Tavistock. Here remembered at St Constantine's Church are members of the Doidge family who resided in Milton Abbot for centuries. *Territorials:* 4th Wessex Brigade RFA.

Milverton Somerset town, seven miles from Taunton, served by the Great Western Railway. Here is St Michael's Church. *Territorials:* 5th Somerset Light Infantry.

Minehead Somerset seaside resort and market town on the south shore of the Bristol Channel and served by the Great Western Railway. Here, high up on North Hill, is St Michael's Church where the Quirck family have memorials, and in Wellington Square, St Andrew's. *Territorials:* West Somerset Yeomanry and 5th Somerset Light Infantry.

Minmore Locality in Glenlivet area, close to the distillery, Banffshire. *Territorials:* 6th Gordon Highlanders.

Mintlaw Aberdeenshire village, eight miles from Peterhead, served by the Great North of Scotland Railway. *Territorials:* 2nd Scottish Horse.

Mirfield West Riding of Yorkshire town on the River Calder, five miles from Huddersfield, served by the London & North Western Railway. The collieries and the production of woollen cloths, cottons, carpets and blankets gave employment to the area. Here the Brontë sisters attended school, Charlotte returning in 1835 as a teacher while Anne was employed as a governess at nearby Blake Hall. Here is St Mary's Church. *Territorials:* 5th Duke of Wellington's Regiment.

Misterton Nottinghamshire village on the Chesterfield Canal, five miles from Gainsborough, served by the Great Northern & Great Eastern Joint Railway. Bricks, chemicals and copper were produced. Here is All Saints Church. *Territorials:* Nottinghamshire Yeomanry (Sherwood Rangers).

Mitcham District to the south-west of London in Surrey, on the River Wandle, where the chief industries are noted as being the production of cordials, perfumes and medicinal herbs. Here, at Cricket Green, is St Peter and St Paul's Church. *Territorials:* 5th East Surrey Regiment.

Moffat Dumfries-shire market town on the River Annan, twenty miles from Dumfries, served by the Caledonian Railway. The discovery in the seventeenth century of springs containing iron salts brought many visitors to Moffat. John Loudon McAdam, who we must thank for our smooth 'tarmacadam' roads, was born here in 1756 and, in 1882, the head of Fighter Command in the Second World War, Lord Hugh Downing. *Territorials:* Lanarkshire Yeomanry and 5th King's Own Scottish Borderers.

Mold Flintshire market town on the River Alyn, eleven miles from Chester, served by the London & North Western Railway. In the area were collieries, lead mines, tin-plate works, a nail factory and a company making fire bricks. Hear is St Mary's Church where, just by the north door, lies the body of landscape painter Richard Wilson who died in 1782. *Territorials:* Denbighshire Yeomanry and 5th Royal Welsh Fusiliers.

Molland Devonshire village on the River Yeo, seven miles from South Moulton, served by the Great Western Railway. Here is St Mary's Church. *Territorials:* Royal North Devon Yeomanry and 6th Devonshire Regiment.

Moniaive Dumfrieshire village at the junction of Dalwhat and Craigdarroch waters, seven miles from Thornhill. *Territorials:* 5th King's Own Scottish Borderers.

Monifieth Forfarshire town on the north shore of the Firth of Tay, six miles from Dundee, served by the North British and Caledonian Joint Railway. *Territorials:* 5th Black Watch.

Monmouth Monmouthshire county and market town situated at the confluence of the Wye, Monnow and Trothy rivers, nineteen miles from Hereford and served by the Great Western Railway. Born here at the castle was Henry V – there is an Agincourt Square in the town – and in 1877, Charles Rolls who, with his friend Mr Royce, gave some of us our cars. Here is St Mary's Church. *Territorials:*

Gloucestershire Yeomanry, 2nd Monmouthshire Regiment and Monmouth Grammar School Cadet Corps.

Montgomery Montgomeryshire county and market town, seven miles from Welshpool, served by the Cambrian Railway. Here is St Nicholas's Church. *Territorials:* Montgomeryshire Yeomanry and 7th Royal Welsh Fusiliers.

Montrose Forfarshire seaport and market town at the mouth of the South Esk River, eleven miles from Arbroath, served by the North British and Caledonian railways. Canvas, rope, machinery and chemicals were made here. The town is on record as having the widest High Street in Scotland and being the location of Britain's first operational military airfield which was opened by the Royal Flying Corps in 1912. *Territorials:* Fife and Forfar Yeomanry, North Scottish RGA and 5th Black Watch.

Monymusk Aberdeenshire village on the River Don, seven miles from Inverurie, served by the Great North of Scotland Railway. *Territorials:* 2nd Scottish Horse and 7th Gordon Highlanders.

Morecambe Lancashire seaside resort on Morecambe Bay four miles from Lancaster. So dangerous are part of the sands that since the fourteenth century a guide ('The Queen's Guide to the Sands') has been appointed to escort visitors. Among the town's several churches is Holy Trinity which dates from 1745. *Territorials:* 5th King's Own Royal Lancaster Regiment.

Moreton Hampstead Devon market town twelve miles from Exeter on the eastern edge of Dartmoor and at the terminus of the Moretonhampstead & South Devon Railway (later Great Western) branch that opened from Newton Abbot in 1866. Here is St Andrew's Church. *Territorials:* Royal 1st Devon Yeomanry and 5th Devonshire Regiment.

Moreton-in-Marsh Gloucestershire market town, seven miles from Chipping Norton, served by the Great Western Railway. Here is the thirteenth-century St David's Church. *Territorials:* 5th Gloucestershire Regiment.

Morley West Riding of Yorkshire town, five miles from Leeds, served by the Great Northern and London & North Western railways. There were collieries, but the wool trade was most important. Here in 1803 was born one of the leaders in that business, Titus Salt. H H Asquith, who served as prime minister 1908–16, also came from Morley. *Territorials:* 4th King's Own Yorkshire Light Infantry.

Morpeth Northumberland town on the Wansbeck, fifteen miles from Newcastle, served by the North Eastern and North British railways. Breweries, brick and tile manufacturers gave employment to the area. Here at St Mary's Church on Kirk Hill is the grave of Emily Davidson, the suffragette who was killed having thrown herself under the feet of the king's horse during the 1913 Derby. *Territorials:* Northumberland Yeomanry, 7th Northumberland Fusiliers and Morpeth Grammar School Cadet Company.

Morriston Glamorgan village, three miles from Swansea, served by the Great Western Railway. The place takes its name from Sir John Morris who built Morriston to house the workers on his estate. Here were collieries and tin-plate works. *Territorials:* 1st Welsh Brigade RFA and 6th Welsh Regiment.

Morwenstow Village on the north coast of Cornwall six miles from Bude. A short walk inland is the remote church of St John the Baptist where for forty years (1834–74) the poet Robert Stephen Hawker was the vicar. He introduced the idea for the harvest festival, and buried shipwrecked seamen washed up on the shores of the parish in his churchyard. *Territorials:* 5th Duke of Cornwall's Light Infantry.

Mossley Lancashire manufacturing town on the River Tame and Huddersfield Canal, ten miles from Manchester and served by the London & North Western Railway. Here is St George's Church, and from 1863, the world's first fish and chip shop. *Territorials:* 7th Duke of Wellington's Regiment.

Mostyn Flintshire village and port on the estuary of the River Dee, four miles from Holywell, served by the London & North Western Railway. There were collieries and ironworks that gave employment. Here is Christ Church and the birthplace in 1905 of actor and playwright Emlyn Williams. *Territorials:* 5th Royal Welsh Fusiliers.

Motherwell Lanarkshire industrial town on South Calder Water, two miles from Hamilton, served by the Caledonian Railway. Prior to 1914 the largest steel works in Britain was here, but the guides note that most were employed in coalmines. *Territorials:* Lowland Divisional Engineers, 6th Cameronians and Lowland Divisional Transport and Supply Column.

Mottisfont Hampshire village on the River Test, twelve miles from Southampton, served by the London & South Western Railway. Here is St Andrew's Church. *Territorials:* 4th Hampshire Regiment.

Mountain Ash Glamorgan mining and industrial town, four miles from Aberdare, served by the Great Western Railway. Here is St Margaret's Church. *Territorials:* Glamorgan Yeomanry and 5th Welsh Regiment.

Mountnessing Essex village four miles from Brentwood. Here is St Giles's Church. *Territorials:* 4th Essex Regiment.

Mountsorrel Leicestershire market town on the River Soar seven miles from Leicester. The Mountsorrel Granit Company employed many, its pinkish-brown granite much used in road making. Here at the north end of town is St Peter's Church and, at the south end, Christ Church. *Territorials:* Leicestershire Yeomanry and 5th Leicestershire Regiment.

Moy Inverness-shire village on Loch Moy twelve miles from Inverness. *Territorials:* 4th Cameron Highlanders.

Much Marcle Herefordshire village four miles from Ledbury. Employing many since 1878 is the cider producer Weston's. Here is St Bartholomew's Church. *Territorials:* Herefordshire Regiment.

Much Wenlock Shropshire market town, twelve miles from Shrewsbury, served by the Great Western Railway. Once there was considerable trade in coal and iron, but much wealth in the area came from its limestone. Here is Holy Trinity Church. *Territorials:* Shropshire Yeomanry and 4th King's Shropshire Light Infantry.

Muddiford Devonshire village three miles from Barnstaple. *Territorials:* 6th Devonshire Regiment.

Muir of Ord Ross and Cromarty village, three miles from Beauly, served by the Highland Railway. *Territorials:* 4th Seaforth Highlanders.

Muirkirk Ayrshire town, eight miles from Cumnock, served by the Caledonian and Glasgow & South Western railways. Here many were employed in coal mining, lime-burning, chemical and iron production. The inventor of the road surface, John Loudon McAdam (1756–1836) had tar-pits near Muirkirk and constructed Furness Road there, one of the first to use the new material. Here too was the Muirkirk Coke and Gaslight Company which placed the town in the record books as being the first in Britain to be lit by gas. *Territorials:* 5th Royal Scots Fusiliers.

Mulbarton Norfolk village two miles from Norwich. Here is the church of St Mary Magdalen. *Territorials:* 4th Norfolk Regiment.

Munlochy Fishing village on the Black Isle, Ross and Cromarty, five miles from Fortrose. The railway arrived in 1894 when the Highland line branched across from Muir of Ord. *Territorials:* 2nd Lovat's Scouts and 4th Seaforth Highlanders.

Murthly Perthshire village, four miles from Dunkeld, served by the Highland Railway. Here was the Perthshire Lunatic Asylum. *Territorials:* 1st Scottish Horse.

Musselburgh Midlothian town at the mouth of the River Esk and Firth of Forth, five miles from Edinburgh, served by the North British Railway. Here golf is played and horses raced, the place so well known for its mussels that it put them in its coat of arms. The making of nets, twine and paper also went on. Here is Loretto School, which maintained two OTC infantry companies. *Territorials:* Lothians and Border Horse and 7th Royal Scots.

Muthill Perthshire village on the River Earn, nineteen miles from Stirling, served by the Caledonian Railway. *Territorials:* 1st Scottish Horse.

Nailsea Somerset village, nine miles from Bristol, served by the Great Western Railway. Here is Holy Trinity Church. *Territorials:* North Somerset Yeomanry.

Nairn Seaside resort, market and county town of Nairnshire on the River Nairn and Moray Firth served by the Highland Railway. *Territorials:* 2nd Lovat's Scouts, Inverness-shire RHA and 4th Cameron Highlanders.

Nantlle Carnarvonshire village, eight miles from Carnarvon on the lake of the same name, served by the London & North Western Railway. Here many were employed in slate quarries. *Territorials:* 6th Battalion Royal Welsh Fusiliers.

Nantwich Cheshire market town on the River Weaver, four miles from Crewe, served by the Great Western and London & North Western railways. Thomas Telford's aqueduct takes the Shropshire Union Canal through the town, which made its name in the production of salt. Boots, shoes and clothing were also manufactured. Here is the red sandstone St Mary's Church, which managed to escape the great Nantwich fire of 1583. In the Civil War, St Mary's saw much action; a force of Royalists making a stand there in January 1644 before being forced to surrender. *Territorials:* Cheshire Yeomanry and 7th Battalion Cheshire Regiment.

Narberth Pembrokeshire market town, ten miles from Haverfordwest, served by the Great Western Railway. Samuel Taylor Coleridge visited Narberth in 1802 and remembers his stay at the White Hart Inn where a large dog entered via a closed window and landed on the poet. Here is St Andrew's Church. *Territorials:* 4th Welsh Regiment.

Neath Glamorgan industrial and market town on the River Neath, seven miles from Swansea, served by the Great Western Railway. The town employed many at its tinplate works, collieries, iron and brass foundries. Neath Corporation Tramways opened in 1875. Here is St Thomas's Church. *Territorials:* Glamorgan Yeomanry, 1st Welsh Brigade RFA, 6th and 7th Welsh Regiment.

Needham Market Suffolk market town on the River Gipping, three miles from Stowmarket, served by the Great Eastern Railway. Here is the church of St John the Baptist. *Territorials:* 1st East Anglian Field Ambulance.

Nelson Glamorgan village two miles from Hengoed. *Territorials:* Glamorgan Yeomanry.

Nether Stowey Somerset village in the Quantock Hills, nine miles from Bridgewater. Here were the 'Broom Squires', a nickname given to the inhabitants who made birch-brooms. Samuel Taylor Coleridge lived at Nether Stowey from 1796 to 1798 and wrote probably his most famous poem,

'The Rime of the Ancient Mariner', there in 1798. Mentioned is the village church of St Mary's. *Territorials:* West Somerset Yeomanry.

Netherbury Dorset village on the River Brit just over a mile from Beaminster. Here is St Mary's Church which has a memorial to Admiral Sir Samuel Hood and his two brothers who were born in the parish. *Territorials:* 4th Dorsetshire Regiment.

Nethy Bridge Inverness-shire village, five miles from Grantown on the edge of the Abernethy Forest, reached by the Strathspey Railway (absorbed by the Great North of Scotland in 1866) in 1863. *Territorials:* 2nd Lovat's Scouts and 6th Seaforth Highlanders.

New Aberdour Aberdeenshire village on the Moray Firth coast, eight miles from Fraserburgh, where St Drostan's Church was founded in 580 AD. *Territorials:* 5th Gordon Highlanders.

New Brighton Cheshire holiday resort on the Irish Sea, five miles from Birkenhead, served by the Wirral Railway which arrived in 1888. Here, notes one guide, 'beautiful residences and marine villas were occupied by Liverpool men of business'. Here is St James's Church. *Territorials:* Lancashire and Cheshire RGA, 1st, 2nd New Brighton Cadet Corps.

New Cross District of south-east London reached by the South Eastern Railway in 1876. The poet Robert Browning lived in New Cross during the 1840s. *Territorials:* Aske's Hatcham School Cadet Corps.

New Cumnock Ayrshire mining town at the confluence of the rivers Afton and Nith, twenty-one miles from Kilmarnock, which was reached by the Glasgow, Paisley, Kilmarnock & Ayr Railway in 1850. *Territorials:* 5th Royal Scots Fusiliers.

New Deer Aberdeenshire village thirteen miles from Peterhead. *Territorials:* 5th Gordon Highlanders.

New Mills (Derbyshire) Town on the border with Cheshire at the confluence of the rivers Goyt and Sett, eight miles from Stockport and reached by the Stockport, Disley & Whaley Bridge Railway in 1857. Collieries, cotton spinning, bleaching and calico printing have provided employment. Here is St George's Church, built in 1831, and St James's, which opened in 1880. *Territorials:* 6th Sherwood Foresters.

New Mills (Montgomery) Montgomeryshire hamlet four miles from Llanfair. *Territorials:* Montgomeryshire Yeomanry.

New Pitsligo Aberdeenshire town four miles from Strichen. Close by there were several granite quarries. *Territorials:* 5th Gordon Highlanders.

New Romney Town, fourteen miles from Ashford in Kent, served by the South Eastern & Chatham Railway. Here is St Nicholas's Church. *Territorials:* Royal East Kent Yeomanry and 5th Buffs East Kent Regiment.

New Scone Perthshire village on the River Tay two miles from Perth. *Territorials:* Highland Cyclist Battalion.

New Tredegar Monmouthshire mining village on the River Rhymney, four miles from Tredegar, served by the Great Western Railway. Here the church is dedicated to St Dingat. *Territorials:* 1st Monmouthshire Regiment.

New Tupton Derbyshire village just over one mile from Claycross. *Territorials:* 6th Sherwood Foresters.

Newark Nottinghamshire port and market town on the River Trent, seventeen miles from Nottingham, served by the Great Northern and Midland railways. There were numerous iron and brass foundries in the area, the manufacture of plaster also being important to the town. Here the 252 ft spire of St Mary's Church towers over the town from the top of Kirkgate. *Territorials:* Nottinghamshire Yeomanry (Sherwood Rangers) and 8th Sherwood Foresters.

Newbald Two villages, North and South, in the East Riding of Yorkshire four miles south-east of Market Weighton. *Territorials:* 5th Yorkshire Regiment.

Newbridge (Midlothian) Hamlet on the River Almond eight miles from Edinburgh. *Territorials:* 10th Royal Scots.

Newbridge (Radnorshire) Village on the River Wye, five miles from Builth Wells, its station (Newbridge-on-Wye) being opened by the Mid Wales Railway in September 1864. The bridge connecting the village with Breconshire was re-built in ferro-concrete in 1910. Here is All Saints Church. *Territorials:* Herefordshire Regiment.

Newbrough Northumberland village on the River Tyne six miles from Hexham. There were lead mines in the area. Here is St Peter's Church. *Territorials:* 4th Northumberland Fusiliers.

Newburgh (Aberdeenshire) Port and village on the River Ythan thirteen miles from Aberdeen. *Territorials:* 5th Gordon Highlanders.

Newburgh (Fifeshire) Port and market town on the Firth of Tay, eight miles from Perth, served by the North British Railway. Salmon fisheries were important. *Territorials:* 7th Black Watch.

Newburn Northumberland village on the northern bank of the Tyne, five miles from Newcastle, served by the North Eastern Railway. Here were collieries, a large works produced steel castings, and salmon fisheries. At St Michael's Church in 1802, George Stephenson was married. *Territorials:* 4th Northumberland Fusiliers.

Newbury Berkshire market town on the River Kennet and Kennet and Avon Canal, seventeen miles by rail from Reading on the Great Western Railway. There was fighting here during the Wars of the Roses, and again (twice) during the Civil War. Once one of the three most important cloth towns in Berkshire, important to the trade was Thomas Dolman But it is John Smallwood, alias Wynchcombe, alias 'Jack of Newbury' who is best known and probably made the most money. Some of what he made went to build the town's St Nicholas's Church c1500–32. *Territorials:* Berkshire Yeomanry and 4th Royal Berkshire Regiment.

Newcastle-under-Lyme Staffordshire market town, sixteen miles from Stafford, served by the North Staffordshire Railway. Bricks and tiles were made here, and clothing for the army at the Enderley Mills. Here is St Giles's Church, which dates from 1876, and Newcastle-under-Lyme High School which maintained one OTC infantry company. *Territorials:* Staffordshire Yeomanry and 5th North Staffordshire Regiment.

Newcastle-upon-Tyne County town of Northumberland, busy seaport and railway junction. Important here was the coal and shipbuilding trades. Stephenson's ironworks also employed many in its production of locomotives and other heavy machinery. Probably the first public parade of the Newcastle Territorials was the unveiling next to Haymarket Metro station on 22 June 1908 of the memorial to those of all Northumberland regiments that lost their lives in South Africa 1899–1902. Here is the cathedral church of St Nicholas, and the Royal Grammar School which maintained one OTC infantry company. Durham University's OTC contingent was found at Armstrong College in Newcastle. *Territorials:* Northumberland Infantry Brigade, Northumberland Yeomanry, 1st Northumbrian Brigade RFA, Northumbrian Divisional Engineers, 6th Northumberland Fusiliers,

Northern Cyclist Battalion, Northumbrian Divisional Transport and Supply Column, 1st Northumbrian Field Ambulance, 1st Northern General Hospital, Northumbrian Clearing Hospital, Northumbrian School of Instruction and Allan's School Cadet Corps.

Newcastleton Roxburghshire village on Liddel Water, seven miles from Langholm, served by the North British Railway. *Territorials:* Lothians and Border Horse and 4th King's Own Scottish Borderers.

Newchurch Village on the Isle of Wight, three miles from Sandown, served by the Isle of Wight Central Railway. Here is All Saints Church which has memorials to the Dillington and Bissett families. *Territorials:* 8th Hampshire Regiment.

Newgale Location on St Bride's Bay, Pembrokeshire, seven miles from St David's. *Territorials:* Pembrokeshire Yeomanry.

Newhall Seat on the Cromarty Firth. Ross and Cromarty, looking across to Invergordon. *Territorials:* North Scottish RGA.

Newhaven Sussex port at the mouth of the Ouse, the town itself being just under a mile inland, nine miles from Brighton and served by the London, Brighton & South Coast Railway. The port here once provided the main ferry service to the Continent. On a hill is St Michael's Church. In its churchyard a monument to an old sea captain who was wrecked with his crew in 1800, and a gravestone inscribed in verse with the story of local brewer Thomas Tipper. *Territorials:* Sussex Fortress Engineers.

Newick Sussex village on the River Ouse, eight miles from Lewis, served by the London, Brighton & South Coast Railway. The station ('Newick and Chailey'), which was opened in 1882, lies a mile to the east of the village. Here, in 1886–87, the nave of St Mary's Church was lengthened and the chancel rebuilt. *Territorials:* 5th Royal Sussex Regiment.

Newmachar Aberdeenshire hamlet, seven miles from Aberdeen, served by the Great North of Scotland Railway. *Territorials:* 2nd Scottish Horse and 5th Gordon Highlanders.

Newmains Lanarkshire town, two miles from Wishaw, served by the Caledonian Railway. Here, many were employed by the Coltness Iron Company. *Territorials:* 8th Highland Light Infantry.

Newmarket Suffolk town on the Cambridgeshire border served by the Great Eastern Railway. Well known for its racecourse and training centre, Newmarket was where Stubbs came to paint the finest horses in the country. All Saints Church sits at the Cambridge end of the High Street. *Territorials:* 5th Suffolk Regiment.

Newmilns Ayrshire town on the River Irvine, twenty-four miles from Glasgow, served by the Glasgow & South Western Railway. Here, many were employed in the production of muslins and lace. *Territorials:* 4th Royal Scots Fusiliers.

Newport (Essex) Village on the River Cam, three miles from Saffron Walden, served by the Great Eastern Railway. Standing on high ground in the centre of the village is the church of St Mary the Virgin. *Territorials:* Essex Yeomanry.

Newport (Isle of Wight) Market town and holiday resort, five miles from Cowes, served by the Isle of Wight Central Railway. Here the church is dedicated to St Thomas the Apostle. *Territorials:* Hampshire Yeomanry, 2nd Wessex Brigade RFA, 8th Hampshire Regiment and Newport Cadet Company.

Newport (Monmouthshire) Busy port, county and market town at the mouth of the River Usk and served by the Great Western Railway. The Volunteers were present at the opening in 1906 of

Newport's Transporter Bridge. Crossing the Usk, and high enough to allow high-masted ships through, it is one of only two such bridges in the country and was built so as Mr J Lysaght's workers could get quicker to their jobs at his steel works on the east side of the river. In 1839 a Chartist march reached the Westgate Hotel where it met the police and a detachment of the 45th Regiment. The town mayor was wounded, some twenty of the marchers being shot dead. St Woolos Church, at the top of Stow Hill, is partly Norman. *Territorials:* Gloucestershire Yeomanry, 4th Welsh Brigade RFA, 1st Monmouthshire Regiment, 1st Welsh Field Ambulance and Newport Territorial Cadet Corps.

Newport (Shropshire) Served by the London & North Western Railway, with the Shropshire Union Canal running to the north, Newport employed a number in the manufacture of agricultural implements and machinery. But fish once brought income to the town. Its coat of arms feature three fishes and, in the centre of Newport, the church is named after St Nicholas, the patron saint of fishermen. *Territorials:* Shropshire Yeomanry and 4th King's Shropshire Light Infantry.

Newport Pagnell Buckinghamshire market town situated at the confluence of the rivers Ouse and Lovat, four miles from Olney and served by the London & North Western Railway. Here the church is dedicated to St Peter and St Paul. *Territorials:* Buckinghamshire Yeomanry.

Newquay Cornwall port and holiday resort, eleven miles from Truro, served by the Great Western Railway. Here is St Michael's Church. *Territorials:* 5th Duke of Cornwall's Light Infantry.

Newton Abbot Devon market town on the Teign estuary six miles from Torquay. An important railway junction, the Great Western had carriage-building workshops at Newton Abbot. Consecrated in 1428 was All Saints Church, located in the Highweek area of Newton Abbot, while, St Leonard's, dating from 1835, is to be found in Wolborough Street. *Territorials:* Royal 1st Devon Yeomanry, Devonshire Fortress Engineers, 5th Devonshire Regiment and Haytor (Newton Abbot) Cadet Corps.

Newton-le-Willows Lancashire industrial town, five miles from St Helens, served by the London & North Western Railway. A large foundry employed some 750 and a print works more than 500. There were also paper mills, glass works and collieries. Here is St Peter's and the Emmanuel churches. *Territorials:* Lancashire Hussars and 4th South Lancashire Regiment.

Newton Poppleford Devon village on the River Otter, four miles from Sidmouth, reached by the Budleigh Salterton Railway (absorbed into the London & South Western in 1911) in 1899. Here is St Luke's Church. *Territorials:* 4th Devonshire Regiment.

Newton Stewart Wigtownshire market town on the River Cree, eight miles from Wigtown, the Portpatrick Railway Company reaching Newton Stewart in 1861. *Territorials:* 5th King's Own Scottish Borderers.

Newtonmore Inverness-shire village on the Rive Spey, three miles from Kingussie, served by the Highland Railway. *Territorials:* 4th Cameron Highlanders.

Newtown (Hampshire) Village on the edge of Southampton. Here is St Luke's Church. *Territorials:* 4th Hampshire Regiment.

Newtown (Montgomeryshire) Montgomeryshire market town on the River Severn, eight miles from Montgomery, served by the Cambrian Railway. Much of Newtown's prosperity came from the manufacture of flannel. One to prosper in this was Pryce Pryce-Jones who would extend his business to mail order. As one of the first to do so, he would no doubt have employed many from Newtown to look after the 100,000 customers that he had acquired by 1900. Also beginning here (in 1792) was newsagent W H Smith. *Territorials:* Montgomeryshire Yeomanry and 7th Royal Welsh Fusiliers.

Newtyle Forfarshire village, five miles from Couper Angus, served by the Caledonian Railway. *Territorials:* 5th Black Watch.

Nigg On the Cromarty Firth, Ross and Cromarty, the Highland Railway's Nigg station being some four miles from the village. *Territorials:* 4th Seaforth Highlanders.

Ninfield Sussex village nine miles from Hastings. Here is St Mary's Church where cast iron stocks can be seen on the main road just to the north. *Territorials:* 2nd Home Counties Brigade RFA.

Niton Village on the Isle of Wight, five miles from Ventnor, where at Knowles Farm there is a stone telling how Marconi established a wireless experimental station there in 1900. Here the church is dedicated to St John the Baptist. *Territorials:* 8th Hampshire Regiment.

Nonington Village in Kent, seven miles from Sandwich, where there is an oak tree said to be (with a girth of thirty-six ft) the largest in England. Here is St Mary's Church. *Territorials:* 4th Buffs East Kent Regiment.

Normanton (Nottinghamshire) Locality six miles to the south-east of Worksop. *Territorials:* Nottinghamshire Yeomanry (Sherwood Rangers).

Normanton (West Riding of Yorkshire) Mining town on the River Calder, five miles from Wakefield, served by the Midland and North Eastern railways. Here is All Saints Church. *Territorials:* 4th King's Own Yorkshire Light Infantry.

North Berwick Haddingtonshire town and port at the entrance to the Firth of Forth, twenty-three miles from Edinburgh, served by the North British Railway. *Territorials:* Lothians and Border Horse, 8th Royal Scots and North Berwick Cadet Corps.

North Cave East Riding of Yorkshire village, seven miles from Market Weighton, served by the Hull & Barnsley Railway. Here in All Saints Church are memorials to the Metham family. *Territorials:* East Riding Yeomanry and 5th East Yorkshire Regiment.

North Chapel Sussex village five miles from Petworth near the Surrey border. Brick making was important to the village, a brickworks being established at Colhook Common in 1779. Here the church is dedicated to St John the Baptist. *Territorials:* 4th Royal Sussex Regiment.

North Petherton Somerset village three miles from Bridgewater and close to the edge of Sedgemoor. Here is St Mary's Church. *Territorials:* West Somerset Yeomanry and 5th Somerset Light Infantry.

North Shields Busy seaport and industrial town on the mouth of the River Tyne, eight miles from Newcastle, served by the North Eastern Railway. Here is Christ Church. *Territorials:* Northumberland Yeomanry, Tynemouth RGA, Durham Fortress Engineers, Northumberland Fortress Engineers and Tyne Electrical Engineers.

North Thoresby Lincolnshire village, seven miles from Grimsby, served by the East Lincolnshire Railway. Here is St Helen's Church. *Territorials:* 5th Lincolnshire Regiment.

North Walsham Norfolk market town, fourteen miles from Norwich, served by the Great Eastern and Midland & Great Northern Joint railways. Many were employed in a factory manufacturing agricultural implements. Here is St Nicholas's Church, and Horatio Nelson went to school in North Walsham 1768–71. *Territorials:* Norfolk Yeomanry and 5th Norfolk Regiment.

Northallerton North Riding of Yorkshire market town, seventeen miles from Ripon, served by the North Eastern Railway. Here is All Saints Church. Close by Northallerton, on Cowton Moor in 1138, was fought the battle of The Standard. *Territorials:* 4th Yorkshire Regiment.

Northampton County and market town of Northamptonshire, twenty-one miles from Bedford, served by the London & North Western and Midland railways. An important town in the manufacture of boots and shoes supplying the army since Cromwell's time – the Ocean Works a main employer – Northampton lies on the north bank of the River Nene. Also here was one of the oldest firms of bookbinders in Britain, large leather and tanning factories, foundries and paper mills. The Northampton Street Tramways Company began its services in June 1881. Inside one of the town's four parish churches, Holy Sepulchre in Sheep Street, there can still be seen bullet marks left from fighting during the Civil War. *Territorials:* Northamptonshire Yeomanry, 4th Northamptonshire Regiment, East Anglian Divisional Transport and Supply Column and Northampton School Cadet Corps.

Northfleet Kent village on the Thames, two miles from Gravesend, served by the South Eastern & Chatham Railway. Here many were employed in paper mills and a large cement works. Here is St Botolph's Church and, in Perry Street, All Saints of 1870. *Territorials:* Kent RGA.

Northiam Sussex village, eight miles from Rye, reached by the Rother Valley Light Railway in 1900 – the station situated a mile to the north-east. Here at St Mary's Church are memorials to the Frewen family. *Territorials:* 5th Royal Sussex Regiment.

Northwich Cheshire market town situated at the confluence of the rivers Weaver and Dane and served by the London & North Western and Cheshire Lines railways. Important to Northwich was its salt and rock salt mines, the finished product being carried to the Trent and Mersey Canal via the Anderson Boat Lift which was constructed in 1865 to connect the canal to the river some fifty feet below. Major work had to be carried out in 1892 when part of the High Street was raised six feet due to it having sunk below the level of the River Weaver. *Territorials:* Cheshire Yeomanry.

Northwood Village on the Isle of Wight two miles from Newport. Here is the church of St John the Baptist. Close by is Parkhurst Prison. *Territorials:* 8th Hampshire Regiment.

Norton Canes Staffordshire village six miles from Walsall. Here is St James's Church. *Territorials:* North Midland Divisional Engineers.

Norwich Norfolk city served by the Great Eastern and Midland & Great Northern Joint railways. Here there were more medieval churches than anywhere else in Europe – one for every Sunday of the year it was said. Among the products manufactured in the city were clothing, wire netting, iron fencing and gates. Colman's English Mustard was made there since the early nineteenth century. The maroon and ivory trams of the Norwich Electric Tramways Company operated in the town from July 1900 until December 1935. *Territorials:* Norfolk and Suffolk Infantry Brigade, Norfolk Yeomanry, 1st East Anglian Brigade RFA, 4th, 6th Norfolk Regiment, 2nd East Anglian Field Ambulance and Cadet Norfolk Artillery.

Nottingham Jesse Boot opened his first chemist shop ('Boots') in Nottingham in 1877 and the cyclists of the town would all have known of the premises in Raleigh Street that began to make 'Raleigh' bicycles towards the end of the 1890s. Nottingham, of course, would be best known for its production of lace. Nottingham University College and the Nottingham High School both maintained contingents in the OTC. Of Nottingham's many churches, St Peter's near the Market Place is the oldest. *Territorials:* Notts and Derby Mounted Brigade, Notts and Derby Infantry Brigade, Nottinghamshire Yeomanry (South Notts), Nottinghamshire RHA, Notts and Derby Mounted Brigade Signal Troop, 7th Sherwood Foresters, North Midland Divisional Transport and Supply Column, Notts and Derby Mounted Brigade Field Ambulance, 1st Cadet Battalion Sherwood Foresters and 1st Nottingham (Church) Cadet Battalion.

Nuneaton Warwickshire market town on the River Anker and Coventry Canal, nine miles from Coventry, served by the London & North Western and Midland railways. Many were employed in the manufacture of bricks, tiles and drain-pipes. Unveiled at Coton Road by General Sir Redvers

Buller VC on 28 January 1905 was Adolphus Rost's memorial to those from the area that had volunteered for service in the Boer War 1889–1902. Here in the town is St Nicholas's Church where among the memorials are several to the Stratford and Truman families. *Territorials:* Warwickshire Yeomanry and 7th Royal Warwickshire Regiment.

Nutley Sussex village three miles from Maresfield. Here is St James's Church. *Territorials:* 5th Royal Sussex Regiment.

Oakengates Coal and ironstone were mined at Oakengates in Shropshire, the town being served by both the Great Western and London and North Western Railway companies. Here is Holy Trinity Church, built 1855. *Territorials:* 4th King's Shropshire Light Infantry.

Oakham Here, on the walls of the great hall (all that is left of Oakham Castle) are displayed horseshoes paid as a toll over centuries by visiting royalty and peers of the realm. Close by, All Saints Church has a memorial to Lieutenant John Bullivant who served with Sir John Moore at Corunna. The county town of Rutland, Oakham was served by the former Midland Railway and, according to one source, once carried on an extensive trade in coal, corn, malt and 'the knitting of fancy hosiery'. At Oakham School there was a contingent of the OTC. *Territorials:* Leicestershire Yeomanry and 5th Leicestershire Regiment.

Oban This Argyllshire town on the Firth of Lorne, grew up around its distillery; the whiskey, along with locally produced wool and slate, being exported from its port. At the terminus of the Callander & Oban Railway, Oban was also the centre of much steamer and tourist traffic. There is an Edwardian poster issued by the railway in which we see the town within a sheltered bay, the steamers coming and going, and the Awe Hotel where the majority of visitors were guests. *Territorials:* 4th Highland Brigade RGA and 8th Argyll and Sutherland Highlanders.

Odiham Just outside this Hampshire market town, along the road to Winchfield, is Frenchman's Oak, so called because it marked the permitted limit to which Napoleonic prisoners could walk. Overlooking the town is All Saints Church. *Territorials:* 4th Hampshire Regiment.

Okehampton At the end of an avenue of elms, the churchyard of All Saints has tombstones engraved in French which mark the last resting places of prisoners from the Napoleonic Wars. A Devonshire market town, Oakhampton lies on the north border of Dartmoor and at the confluence of the East and West Okement rivers. Built on the wool trade, the town was served by the London & South Western Railway, its Territorials perhaps remembering the opening of Lloyds Bank in 1908 and, in the year before that, Simmons Park. The older Okehampton Park was taken over for military use in Victorian times. *Territorials:* 6th Devonshire Regiment.

Old Brompton Locality close to Chatham and Gillingham in Kent. *Territorials:* Kent RGA.

Old Buckenham South Norfolk village to the south-east of Attleborough where its church, All Saints, has a thatched roof. *Territorials:* 4th Norfolk Regiment.

Old Meldrum Small Aberdeenshire market town in the north-eastern part of the county where many were employed in the distilling and brewing trades. *Territorials:* 5th Gordon Highlanders.

Oldbury Village in south-east Shropshire just over twelve miles from Kidderminster. *Territorials:* 7th Worcestershire Regiment.

Oldham Well served by the railways, Oldham's 250 cotton mills at the beginning of the twentieth century were employing more than 35,000. Other inhabitants mined the coal that provided the power to run the looms, some helped in the manufacture of gas meters and hats. On the south side of the town, the Oldham Canal was opened and ran south-west to where it joined the Rochdale Canal.

Among Oldham's several churches, St Paul's near the centre of the town is the oldest. *Territorials:* Duke of Lancaster's Own Yeomanry and 10th Manchester Regiment.

Ollerton Small Nottinghamshire town on the River Maun, nine miles from Mansfield and served by the Lancashire, Derbyshire & East Coast Railway Company which, in 1907, became the Great Central. Here is St Giles's Church. *Territorials:* 8th Sherwood Foresters.

Olney Buckinghamshire market town in the valley of the Ouse and five miles north of Newport Pagnell. Principally one long high street with many Georgian houses, Olney thrived on agriculture, had a large brewery and made boots and shoes. The railway reached the town in 1872 when the line from Bedford (later Midland Railway) branched off at Oakley Junction and made for Northampton. Here in the town lived the poet William Cowper, his house on the south side of Market Square being opened up as a museum in 1900. At St Peter and St Paul's Church are the graves of John and Mary Newton who were first buried in 1807 and 1790 respectively at St Mary, Woolnoth Church in London. The remains were reburied at Olney in January 1893. *Territorials:* 5th Bedfordshire Regiment.

Ongar Small Essex market town on the River Roding eleven miles south-west of Chelmsford, the railway arriving there when the Great Eastern extended its line from Loughton in 1865. At St Martin's church in 1637 was buried Jane, the daughter of Oliver Cromwell. *Territorials:* 4th Essex Regiment and Ongar Grammar School Cadets.

Opinan Ross and Cromarty fishing village on the west coast of Scotland. *Territorials:* 4th Seaforth Highlanders.

Ore Part of the district of Hastings, Ore station was opened by the old South Eastern and Chatham Railway in 1888. Here is medieval St Helen's Church. *Territorials:* 5th Royal Sussex Regiment.

Ormiston Haddingtonshire mining village (the Ormiston Coal company) on the north bank of the River Tyne. *Territorials:* 8th Royal Scots.

Ormskirk West Lancashire market town just over twelve miles from Liverpool, where many were employed in the manufacture of rope and twine. Here, and almost unique (there are just two other examples in England), is the side-by-side tower and spire of the Church of St Peter and St Paul. Both the Lancashire & Yorkshire, and London & North Western railways called at Ormskirk Station on the east side of the town. *Territorials:* 9th King's Liverpool Regiment.

Orpington Kent village to the south-west of Dartford where hops were grown and much fruit was sent to the London markets. Served by the South Eastern & Chatham Railway, perhaps Orpington is best known for the breed of chicken that originated there in 1886. Here is All Saints Church. *Territorials:* 4th Royal West Kent Regiment.

Orsett Essex village four miles from Grays station. Here is St Giles and All Saints Church. *Territorials:* Essex Yeomanry.

Osmaston Manor The seat of Sir Peter Carlaw Walker, Bart (officer commanding Derbyshire Yeomanry), Osmaston Manor in Derbyshire dates from 1849, Osmaston village itself, with its thatched cottages built to house estate workers, being just over two miles from Ashbourne station. *Territorials:* Derbyshire Yeomanry.

Ossett Municipal borough on the River Calder in West Yorkshire, situated between Dewsbury and Wakefield. Important in the manufacture of woollen garments – much was produced for both the Navy and Army – the town was served by the Great Northern Railway. Here is Holy Trinity Church and Christ Church, which dates from 1851. *Territorials:* 4th King's Own Yorkshire Light Infantry.

Oswestry Here, in this Shropshire market town, many were employed by the Cambrian Railway in its engine and carriage works. The Shrewsbury & Chester Railway Company also maintained a station. Oswestry lies close to the border with Wales some eighteen miles north-west of Shrewsbury. The Montgomery Canal is close by. Born here in 1893 was the poet Wilfred Owen. Badly damaged in the Civil War, St Oswald's Church lies facing High Street. *Territorials:* Shropshire Yeomanry and 4th King's Shropshire Light Infantry.

Otley The Eastern Railway came to Otley in 1865, but sixteen years before that some forty railwaymen were laid to rest in the town's All Saints Church after an accident that occurred during the cutting of Bramhope Tunnel (Leeds & Thirsk Railway) just to the south east. In West Yorkshire, Otley is situated on the River Wharfe ten miles north of Bradford, its principal employment being in worsted spinning and printing. *Territorials:* 4th West Riding Brigade RFA.

Otterburn Located on the bank of the River Rede, and within the Cheviot Hills, the Northumberland village of Otterburn was the scene of a battle between the English and Scottish armies in 1388. A small woollen factory and a colliery gave employment. Here is St John's Church, built in 1857. *Territorials:* 4th Northumberland Fusiliers.

Ottery St Mary Devonshire market town on the River Otter, the elder relatives of the Territorials there no doubt being witness to the disastrous fire of 1866 in which some 111 houses were destroyed resulting in over 500 persons being made homeless. The railway reached the town when the Sidmouth Railway Company opened its line in 1874. St Mary's Church dates from 1342. *Territorials:* Royal 1st Devon Yeomanry and 4th Devonshire Regiment.

Oundle Northamptonshire market town, overlooking the Nene Valley, thirteen miles south-west of Northampton, served by the London & North Western Railway. Seen for miles around is the spire of St Peter's Church. At Oundle School there was a contingent of the OTC. *Territorials:* Northamptonshire Yeomanry.

Overton Hampshire village on the River Test, eight miles west of Basingstoke, served by the London & South Western Railway. Here is St Mary's Church. *Territorials:* 3rd Wessex Field Ambulance.

Overtown Lanarkshire village on the Caledonian Railway, the inhabitants chiefly employed in the neighbouring ironworks. *Territorials:* 8th Highland Light Infantry.

Oxford University city lying between the Cherwell and Thames (called Isis here) served by both the Great Western and London & North Western railway companies. Her too is the Oxford Canal and, opening up premises to make bicycles just to the south of the city in 1913, William Morris who went on to make motor cars. Much building work went on in Oxford during the living memory of the Territorials: the new Town Hall and Municipal Buildings in St Aldate's Street, the Corn Exchange between George Street and Gloucester Green, Probate Court, Post Office and numerous college buildings. Oxford Cathedral, the smallest in England, was founded in 1525. Oxford's horse-drawn tram service opened in 1881 and operated until August 1914. The terminus of the line was in Cowley Road, just past St Mary and St John's Church on the corner of Leopold Street. The University and St Edward's School in Oxford both maintained OTC contingents. *Territorials:* 2nd South Midland Mounted Brigade, South Midland Infantry Brigade, Oxfordshire Yeomanry, 2nd South Midland Mounted Brigade Signal Troops, 4th Oxfordshire and Buckinghamshire Light Infantry, 3rd Southern General Hospital and Cowley Cadet Corps.

Oxted Small Surrey town at the foot of the North Downs reached by the London, Brighton & South Coast Railway in 1884. Here is St Mary's Church. *Territorials:* 4th Queen's Royal West Surrey Regiment.

Oxton Oxton in north-west Cheshire formed part of the borough of Birkenhead and is noted as being the location of 'many well-built residences occupied by Liverpool merchants'. The railway reached the town in the form of the Lauder Light Railway on 2 July 1901. St Saviour's Church was rebuilt in 1891. *Territorials:* 1st Oxton (Birkenhead) Cadet Corps.

Paddington West London borough and the London terminus of the Great Western Railway. Much, if not all, of the 1950s film classic *The Blue Lamp* was shot in Paddington – see the Regent's Canal; the Coliseum Cinema where the robbery took place; the Metropolitan Music Hall where the alibi was set up, and Paddington Green Police Station outside which the actual blue lamp hung. Opened in July 1888 was the tram service operated by the Harrow Road & Paddington Tramways Company which ran from the Royal Oak Inn at Harlesden, to Loch Bridge just yards from the 10th London Regiment drill hall in Harrow Road. Here, on Paddington Green, is St Mary's Church. *Territorials:* 5th London Brigade RFA, 3rd, 10th London Regiment and Paddington Boys' Club and Naval Brigade Cadets.

Paddock Wood Village in Kent, five miles from Tonbridge on the South Eastern Railway, where brick and titles were made. Here is St Andrew's Church. *Territorials:* 5th Buffs East Kent Regiment.

Padiham Lancashire cotton town on the River Calder, three miles from Burnley, reached by the Lancashire & Yorkshire Railway in 1877. Here is St Leonard's Church. *Territorials:* 5th East Lancashire Regiment.

Padstow Cornwall fishing port and market town on the estuary of the River Camel, sixteen miles from Bodmin, reached by the North Cornwall Railway in 1899. Here is St Petrock's Church. *Territorials:* Cornwall RGA.

Paignton Seaside resort on Tor Bay in Devon, three miles from Torquay and reached by the Devon & Torbay Railway in 1859. Paignton's Christ Church was finished in 1888, St Andrew's in Sands Road opening in 1897. *Territorials:* 4th Wessex Brigade RFA.

Paisley Renfrewshire port and textile manufacturing town on White Cart Water, seven miles from Glasgow and served by the Caledonian and Glasgow & South Western railways. Robinson's, the manufacturers of 'Golden Shred' marmalade, have been in the town since 1864. *Territorials:* Lanarkshire Yeomanry (Royal Glasgow), Renfrewshire Fortress Engineers and 6th Argyll and Sutherland Highlanders.

Palace Colliery Two miles from Bothwell in Lanarkshire. *Territorials:* 6th Cameronians.

Panteg Monmouthshire locality on the Brecon and Monmouthshire Canal, three miles from Pontypool, served by the Great Western Railway. Here is St Mary's Church. *Territorials:* 4th Welsh Brigade RFA.

Pantglas Carmarthenshire seat of the Spencer-Jones family (C J Spencer-Jones a major in the Pembrokeshire Yeomanry) five miles from Llandilo. *Territorials:* Pembrokeshire Yeomanry.

Par Coastal town and port, four miles from St Austell in Cornwall and served by the Great Western Railway. Fishing and the production of china-clay, tin and copper, gave employment to many. Here is St Mary's Church of 1848, the first by G E Street. *Territorials:* Cornwall RGA.

Parkgate Cheshire village and seaside resort on the estuary of the Dee, thirteen miles from Chester, served by the Great Western and London & North Western Joint Railway. *Territorials:* 4th Cheshire Regiment.

Parkham Devonshire village on the River Yeo seven miles from Great Torrington. Here is St James's Church. *Territorials:* Royal North Devon Yeomanry and 6th Devonshire Regiment.

Parkstone Dorset village on high ground above Poole Harbour reached by the Poole & Bournemouth Railway (later London & South Western) in 1874. Here is St Peter's Church. *Territorials:* Dorsetshire RGA and 4th Dorsetshire Regiment.

Pateley Bridge West Riding of Yorkshire market town on the River Nidd eleven miles from Ripon. The North Eastern Railway terminated here, the Nidd Valley Light Railway, which opened in 1907, taking passengers further north as far as Lofthouse-in-Nidderdale. Here is St Cuthbert's Church. *Territorials:* 5th West Yorkshire Regiment.

Pathhead Midlothian village on the River Tyne eleven miles from Edinburgh. *Territorials:* 8th Royal Scots.

Patricroft Lancashire village, five miles from Manchester and served by the London & North Western Railway, where there were ironworks, cotton and weaving mills. Here is Christ Church. *Territorials:* 5th Manchester Regiment.

Patrington East Riding of Yorkshire town, fifteen miles from Hull, served by the North Eastern Railway. Here is St Patrick's Church. *Territorials:* East Riding Yeomanry.

Peak Dale Derbyshire locality three miles from Chapel-en-le-Frith. *Territorials:* 6th Sherwood Foresters.

Peasedown St John Somerset village six miles from Bath and a former colliery settlement. St John's was built 1892–93. *Territorials:* 4th Somerset Light Infantry.

Peasmarsh Sussex village three miles from Rye. Here is St Peter and St Paul's Church. *Territorials:* 5th Royal Sussex Regiment.

Pebmarsh Essex village three miles from Halstead. Here is the church of St John the Baptist, its registers dating from 1648. *Territorials:* 5th Essex Regiment.

Peckham Area in south-east London. *Territorials:* St Mark's Cadet Corps.

Peebles County town of Peebleshire situated at the confluence of Eddleston Water and the River Tweed, twenty-two miles from Edinburgh and served by the Caledonian and North British railways. Woollen garments were manufactured at Peebles, and born here were the Chambers brothers: William (1800–83) and Robert (1802–71), the well known publishers. *Territorials:* Lanarkshire Yeomanry, Lothians and Border Horse and 8th Royal Scots.

Pembroke County and market town on Milford Haven, nine miles from Tenby, served by the Great Western Railway. The Royal Naval Dockyard was transferred here from Milford in 1814. Here is St Michael's Church, restored in 1887, and St Mary's which underwent alterations four years before that. *Territorials:* Pembrokeshire Yeomanry, Pembroke RGA and 4th Welsh Regiment.

Pembury Village three miles from Tunbridge Wells in Kent. Here is St Peter's Church. *Territorials:* Kent Cyclist Battalion.

Penarth Glamorgan town and port, three miles from Cardiff, served by the Great Western Railway. Here on a headland overlooking Cardiff Bay, is St Augustine's Church. *Territorials:* Glamorgan RGA.

Pencaitland Haddingtonshire village on the River Tyne, six miles from Haddington, reached by the railway in 1901. *Territorials:* 8th Royal Scots.

Pendeen Cornwall village seven miles from Penzance. Here is St John's Church which was modelled on the cathedral at Iona from a design by its first incumbent, the Rev R Aitken, and built by the villagers in 1851. *Territorials:* 4th Duke of Cornwall's Light Infantry.

Penicuick Midlothian town on the River North Esk, nine miles from Edinburgh, served by the North British Railway. Important to the town was the production of paper at Valleyfield Mills. The largest in the area and where, during the Napoleonic wars, French prisoners were held. Some 300 died while in captivity and there is a memorial to them. The Esk Mills, once producing cottons. *Territorials:* Lothians and Border Horse and 8th Royal Scots.

Penkridge Small Staffordshire town on the River Penk, six miles from Stafford, served by the London & North Western Railway. Here at St Michael and All Angels Church there are memorials to the Littleton family of Pillaton Hall. *Territorials:* 3rd North Midland Field Ambulance.

Penmaenmawr Carnarvonshire seaside resort on Conway Bay served by the London & North Western Railway. The former prime minister, W E Gladstone, took his holidays here and in 1860 laid the foundation stone of St Seiriol's Church in the centre of the village. *Territorials:* 6th Royal Welsh Fusiliers.

Penrhyndeudraeth Merionethshire village, four miles from Festiniog, served by the Cambrian Railway. Here is Holy Trinity Church. *Territorials:* 7th Royal Welsh Fusiliers.

Penrith Cumberland market town on the River Eamont, eighteen miles from Carlisle, served by the London & North Western and Cockermouth, Keswick & Penrith railways. The town's several breweries (much of their produce being drank in the old Two Lions and Gloucester Arms), iron foundries and saw-mills gave much employment to the population. Six-feet-thick are the red sandstone walls of the tower at St Andrew's Church. *Territorials:* Westmorland and Cumberland Yeomanry and 4th Border Regiment.

Penryn Cornwall market town, two miles from Falmouth, its chief industry being the dressing and polishing of granite. Penryn Station was opened by the old Cornwall Railway Company (later Great Western) in 1863. *Territorials:* Cornwall Fortress Engineers.

Pentre Glamorgan village eight miles from Pontypridd. Here were collieries and engineering works. *Territorials:* Welsh Divisional Transport and Supply Column.

Penygroes Carnarvonshire village, seven miles from Carnarvon, served by the London & North Western Railway. Here many were involved in local slate industry. *Territorials:* 6th Royal Welsh Fusiliers.

Penzance Seaport, market town and holiday resort on Mounts Bay in Cornwall, once important in the tin trade. Here the old West Cornwall Railway terminated – Penzance station opening in March 1852. Born in Penzance in 1778 was Sir Humphrey Davy, inventory of the minors' safety lamp. Here is St Mary's Church of 1835, and built in Clarence Street in 1843, St Paul's. *Territorials:* Royal 1st Devon Yeomanry, Cornwall RGA and 4th Duke of Cornwall's Light Infantry.

Pershore Worcestershire market and former wool town on the Avon nine miles from Worcester and reached by the Oxford, Worcester & Wolverhampton Railway in 1853. Here is Pershore Abbey and St Andrew's Church. *Territorials:* Worcestershire Yeomanry and 8th Worcestershire Regiment.

Perth Busy port on the River Tay served by the Caledonian and North British railways. Here, in Atholl Street, is St Ninian's Cathedral. Once called St John's Town, after its first church, the name lives on in 'St Johnstone', the Perth football team. *Territorials:* Highland Division, Black Watch Infantry Brigade, 1st Scottish Horse, 6th Black Watch and Highland Divisional Transport and Supply Column.

Peterborough Northamptonshire cathedral city and busy railway junction on the River Nene where, as well as boots and shoes, agricultural implements were made. There exists an old railway carriage print in which the artist, from the southern bank of the river, provides an uninterrupted view of the cathedral where lie buried the bodies of Mary Queen of Scots and Catherine of Aragon. *Territorials:* Northamptonshire Yeomanry, 4th East Anglian Brigade RFA and King's School Peterborough Cadet Corps.

Peterchurch Village on the River Dore in Herefordshire's Golden Valley, served by the Great Western Railway. Here is St Peter's Church where a fish with a gold chain around its neck greets you as you enter. Dated 1825, it is a plaster model of a fish said to have been caught in the Dore, complete with gold chain. *Territorials:* Herefordshire Regiment.

Peterculter Aberdeenshire town on the River Dee seven miles from Aberdeen. Here is St Peter's Church and the Culter Mills Paper Company which employed some 350 from the area. *Territorials:* 7th Gordon Highlanders.

Peterhead Aberdeenshire fishing port on Peterhead Bay served by the Great North of Scotland Railway. Two large granite-polishing firms gave employment. *Territorials:* 2nd Scottish Horse and 5th Gordon Highlanders.

Petersfield Hampshire market and former wool town on the River Rother, seventeen miles from Portsmouth, served by the London & South Western Railway. Here at St Peter's Church are memorials to the Joliffe family, and the pulpit stands in memory of Mr Cross who was a surgeon in the town for forty years. Churcher's College in Petersfield maintained a contingent of the OTC. *Territorials:* 1st South Western Mounted Brigade, Hampshire Yeomanry, 6th and 9th Hampshire Regiment.

Petty Inverness-shire village on the Moray Firth five miles from Inverness. *Territorials:* 4th Cameron Highlanders.

Petworth Sussex town served by the London, Brighton & South Coast Railway's branch that opened between Hardham Junction and Midhurst, 1859–68. The station being just over a mile to the south of the town. Guides note Petworth's narrow streets, St Mary's Church having memorials to the Percys who lived in Petworth when not in Northumberland. *Territorials:* 4th Royal Sussex Regiment.

Pevensey Sussex village between Eastbourne and Hastings about a mile inland from the sea. There are two churches: St Nicholas's, off the High Street to the east, and St Mary's, Westham which lies to the west. Much of the Romans' time in Pevensey can be seen, and at Pevensey Bay there are Martello towers. Pevensey station, on the London, Brighton & South Coast Railway, was opened in 1851. *Territorials:* 2nd Home Counties Brigade RFA.

Pewsey Small Wiltshire town on the River Avon, seven miles from Marlborough, served by the Great Western Railway. A short walk from the station is the Kennet and Avon Canal. Here, at St John's Church, the communion rails are made from wood taken from the Spanish ship *San Josef* which was boarded by Nelson off Cape St Vincent in 1797. *Territorials:* 1st South Western Mounted Brigade Field Ambulance.

Phillipstoun Linlithgowshire village, four miles from Linlithgow, where most of the population were employed in a large shale mine. Phillipstoun station was opened by the Edinburgh & Glasgow Railway Company in February 1842. *Territorials:* 10th Royal Scots.

Pickering North Riding of Yorkshire market town, sixteen miles from Scarborough, its station being opened by the Whitby & Pickering Railway Company in May 1836. Here is St Peter and St Paul's Church, well known for its fifteenth-century wall paintings. *Territorials:* 5th Yorkshire Regiment.

Pinxton Derbyshire village, four miles from Alfreton, served by the Midland Railway. Here is St Helen's Church, the area known for its production of soft-paste porcelain. *Territorials:* Nottinghamshire Yeomanry (Sherwood Rangers).

Pitcaple Aberdeenshire village on the River Urie, four miles from Inverurie, served by the Great North of Scotland Railway which arrived in 1854. *Territorials:* 6th Gordon Highlanders.

Pitlochry Perthshire village on the River Tummel, twenty-eight miles from Perth, served by the Highland Railway. Pitlochry is the geographical centre of Scotland and employed many in its production of Highland tweeds, plaids, and whiskey. *Territorials:* 1st Scottish Horse and 6th Black Watch.

Pitmedden Aberdeenshire hamlet sixteen miles from Aberdeen. *Territorials:* 5th Gordon Highlanders.

Pittington Durham mining village, four miles from Durham, served by the North Eastern Railway. Here is St Lawrence's Church. *Territorials:* 8th Durham Light Infantry.

Plaistow Area in Essex and an east London suburb formed out of West Ham. Here is St Mary's Church, opened in 1830, others following as the population grew. The Passmore Edward's Library was opened at Plaistow in 1903. *Territorials:* Given Wilson Institute Cadets.

Plashetts Northumberland colliery village, thirteen miles from Bellingham, served by the North British Railway. *Territorials:* 4th Northumberland Fusiliers.

Plockton Fishing village on Loch Caron, Ross and Cromarty, four miles from Strome Ferry. Plockton station was opened by the Highland Railway on its line to Kyle of Lochalsh in November 1897. *Territorials:* 4th Highland Brigade RGA.

Pluckley Village six miles from Ashford in Kent, reached by the South Eastern Railway in December 1842. Here in St Michael's Church are memorials to the Dering family. *Territorials:* 5th Buffs East Kent Regiment.

Plumstead South-east London suburb ten miles by rail from Charing Cross. Plumstead station was opened by the South Eastern Railway in July 1859. St Nicholas's is Plumstead's ancient parish church. *Territorials:* 2nd and 8th London Brigades RFA, 1st London Divisional Transport and Supply Column and 1st Woolwich Cadet Corps.

Plumtree Nottinghamshire village five miles from Nottingham reached by the Midland Railway in May 1893. Here is St Mary's Church. *Territorials:* Nottinghamshire Yeomanry (South Notts).

Pluscarden In Elginshire, six miles from Elgin. *Territorials:* 2nd Scottish Horse and 6th Seaforth Highlanders.

Plymouth Devonshire seaport, market town and naval station. In the area, several firms involved in the manufacture of chemicals, soap, starch, biscuits and candles gave employment, and down one of Plymouth's cobbled streets, close to the harbour, is the Black Friars Distillery where gin has been made since 1793. The South Devon Railway reached Plymouth in 1849, the Great Western in 1878 and the London & South Western in 1891. Here among Plymouth's many churches is the medieval parish church of St Andrew in Catherine Street – the largest in Devon. At Plymouth College there was a contingent of the OTC. *Territorials:* Royal 1st Devon Yeomanry, Devonshire RGA, Devonshire Fortress Engineers, 5th, 7th Devonshire Regiment, Wessex Divisional Transport and Supply Column, 2nd Wessex Field Ambulance, 4th Southern General Hospital and Plymouth Lads' Brigade Cadet Corps.

Plympton Devonshire village five miles from Plymouth, its station being opened by the South Devon Railway in 1848. Here are two churches: St Mary's and St Maurice's. Plympton, the birthplace of the painter Sir Joshua Reynolds in 1723. *Territorials:* Devonshire RGA.

Pocklington East Riding of Yorkshire market town, sixteen miles from York, producing agricultural implements, rope and twine. Here at All Saints Church there are memorials to the Dolman family, and at the grammar school the anti-slavery campaigner William Wilberforce (1759–1833) was a pupil. The York & North Midland Railway reached Pocklington in 1847. *Territorials:* East Riding Yeomanry, 5th East Yorkshire Regiment and 5th Yorkshire Regiment.

Pollockshaws Renfrewshire town on the River White Cart, two miles from Glasgow, where the main source of employment was weaving. There was also iron foundries, bleach works and paper mills. Pollockshaws had two stations; one opened by the Glasgow, Barrhead & Neilston Direct Company in 1848, and Pollockshaws East, which was started in April 1894 by the Cathcart District Railway. *Territorials:* 6th Argyll and Sutherland Highlanders.

Ponfeigh Lanarkshire colliery village four miles from Lanark. *Territorials:* 8th Highland Light Infantry.

Ponsanooth Cornwall village seven miles from Truro. *Territorials:* Cornwall Fortress Engineers.

Pontefract West Riding of Yorkshire market and industrial town thirteen miles from Leeds. The ancient church of All Saints was partially destroyed in the Civil War and many that fell during the siege of Pontefract Castle lie in its churchyard. Here too is St Giles's Church. The town was once noted for its extensive gardens and nurseries and still, its liquorice Pontefract Cake. Pontefract was served by both the Lancashire & Yorkshire and Midland & North Eastern Joint railways. *Territorials:* Yorkshire Dragoons and 5th King's Own Yorkshire Light Infantry.

Pontesbury Shropshire village seven miles from Shrewsbury on the Great Western and London & North Western branch line that ran down from Cruckmeoe Junction to Minsterley. There were collieries in the area, a brickworks and manufacturer of drainpipes. Here is St George's Church. *Territorials:* Shropshire Yeomanry.

Pontypool Monmouthshire market town on the Afon Lwyd, eight miles from Newport, served by the Great Western Railway. There were important ironworks in the area, and here was made the first tinplate in the world. Here is St James's Church and the Roman Catholic St Alban's. *Territorials:* 2nd Monmouthshire Regiment.

Pontypridd Town in Glamorgan, once called Newbridge, situated eleven miles from Cardiff on the River Taff where it meets the Rhondda. The production of coal and iron built the town, which also held an important position among manufacturers of anchors and chains. The Pontypridd & Rhondda Valley Tramway opened in March 1888. Here is St Catherine's Church and the birthplace of local weaver and poet Evan James who wrote 'Land of My Fathers' in 1856. The Taff Vale Railway served the town. *Territorials:* Glamorgan Yeomanry and 5th Welsh Regiment.

Poole Market town and busy harbour of the Dorset coast served by the London & South Western Railway. The Poole & District Electric Tramways Company, with its Cambridge blue and white trams, began operating in April 1901. Shipbuilding yards and firms manufacturing netting, sailcloth and other fittings for vessels employed many form the area. At the Haven Hotel by the entrance to Poole Harbour in October 1898, Guglielmo Marconi set up one of the world's earliest radio stations and just out at Brownsea Island in August 1907, Lieutenant-Colonel Baden Powell set up the first scout camp. The now collectable Poole Pottery began here in 1875. Here is St James's Church. *Territorials:* Dorsetshire RGA and 4th Dorsetshire Regiment.

Poolewe Fishing village at the head of Loch Ewe, Ross and Cromarty. *Territorials:* 4th Seaforth Highlanders.

Poplar London borough on the Thames once the headquarters of the East India Company. St Matthia's Chapel here has oak pillars said to have been made from the masts of and East Indiamen. Poplar was an important shipbuilding centre from before the time of Henry VIII, the East and West India Docks opening up at the beginning of the nineteenth century. *Territorials:* 17th London Regiment.

Porchester Hampshire village on Portsmouth Harbour served by the London & South Western and London, Brighton & South Coast railways. Here is St Mary's Church. *Territorials:* 6th Hampshire Regiment.

Port Charlotte Village on the east coast of Rhinns of Islay and west coast of Loch Indaal in Argyllshire. Named after the mother of Walter Campbell, laird of Islay. *Territorials:* 2nd Scottish Horse.

Port Ellen Village on the south coast of Islay Island in Argyllshire, founded by Walter Campbell, laird of Islay, who named it after his wife. *Territorials:* 2nd Scottish Horse and 8th Argyll and Sutherland Highlanders.

Port Glasgow Renfrewshire town and important seaport on the south bank of the Clyde, twenty miles from Glasgow, served by the Caledonian Railway. *Territorials:* Clyde RGA and 5th Argyll and Sutherland Highlanders.

Port Talbot Glamorgan town on Swansea Bay served by the Great Western Railway. Port Talbot prospered from the smelting of copper after 1770, the town also growing out of its collieries, rolling mills and tinplate works. *Territorials:* Glamorgan Yeomanry and Glamorgan RHA.

Porthcawl Seaside resort six miles from Bridgend in Glamorgan and served by the Great Western Railway. *Territorials:* Glamorgan Yeomanry.

Portishead Somerset resort on the Bristol Channel twelve miles from Bristol. The dockyard opened for business in 1879 and here is the church of St Peter in which there are memorials to the Mohun and Jenner-Fust families. Off shore was the training ship *Formidable* which was used as a school for 'homeless and destitute boys'. Portishead was served by two railway concerns: the Bristol Pier and Railway Company that opened its station in 1867, and the Weston, Clevedon & Portishead which extended up from Clevedon in 1907. *Territorials:* Somerset RHA.

Portland Peninsular on the Dorset coast four miles from Weymouth. Here the Weymouth & Portland Railway arrived in 1865 which did much to convey the stone quarried locally (Portland stone) used for public and other buildings worldwide. 'Black towers above the Portland light/The felon-quarries stone' (from *A Shropshire Lad* by A E Housman). On the Westside of the island is St George's Church. *Territorials:* Dorsetshire RGA and Dorsetshire Fortress Engineers.

Portlethen Kincardineshire fishing village, seven miles from Aberdeen, served by the Caledonian Railway. *Territorials:* 7th Gordon Highlanders.

Portmadoc Small seaport on Tremadoc Bay in Carnarvonshire where the port dealt mainly with the export of slate produced at the Fesiniog quarries. The Festiniog Railway had reached the harbour in 1865, the Cambrian opening a station two years after that. Here is St John's Church. *Territorials:* 6th Royal Welsh Fusiliers.

Portmahomack Ross and Cromarty fishing village ten miles from Tain on the Dornoch Firth. *Territorials:* 4th Seaforth Highlanders.

Portpatrick Wigtownshire seaport and village seven miles from Stranraer and once the main port for ferries to and from the north of Ireland – Donaghadee just over twenty-one miles away. The Portpatrick and Wigtownshire Joint Committee Railway arrived down from Stranraer in 1862, the line extending from the village to the harbour in 1868. The first submarine cable was laid between Portpatrick and Donaghadee. *Territorials:* 5th Royal Scots Fusiliers.

Portree Village and seaport on the Isle of Skye, Inverness-shire, once well known for its production of tweeds, plaids, yarns and carpets. *Territorials:* 1st Lovat's Scouts and 4th Cameron Highlanders.

Portslade Western suburb of Brighton of which one guide describes as 'an ugly seafaring village on the east arm of Shoreham harbour. But this is Portslade-on-Sea, the old village of Portslade being a mile inland and 'picturesque'. The London, Brighton & South Coast Railway served both. *Territorials:* 6th Royal Sussex Regiment.

Portsmouth No doubt many from the town were once occupied in the construction of the numerous forts and gun positions that appeared as a result of the threatened invasion from France in 1860. And there was the building of the town's Victorian barracks: the Victoria and Clarence, between Alexander Road and Pembroke Road (c1880), and HMS *Victory* Barracks in Queen Street, Portsea (1899–1903). The tower of Portsmouth Cathedral was completed in 1691 and used for many years as an observation post by the navy. At Portsmouth Grammar School there was a contingent of the OTC. *Territorials:* Hampshire Yeomanry, 1st Wessex Brigade RFA, Hampshire RGA, Hampshire Fortress Engineers, 6th, 9th Hampshire Regiment, 3rd Wessex Field Ambulance and 2nd Cadet Battalion Hampshire Regiment.

Portsoy Banffshire seaport, eight mile from Banff, where many were employed in the fish trade. Here too was the source of Portsoy marble which was used in the building of the Palace of Versailles. The Great North of Scotland Railway terminated at Portsoy. *Territorials:* 1st Highland Brigade RFA and 6th Gordon Highlanders.

Poulton Part of Wallasey, Cheshire served by the Wirral Railway at its Liscard and Poulton station. *Territorials:* 1st Poulton Cadet Company.

Poulton-le-Fylde Lancashire market town near the Rive Wyre, five miles from Fleetwood, served by the London & North Western and Lancashire & Yorkshire Joint Railway. Here is St Chad's Church. *Territorials:* 5th King's Own Royal Lancaster Regiment.

Preesall Lancashire town on the Rive Wyre looking across to Fleetwood. Preesall station was opened in July 1908 by the Knott End Railway when the line was extended from Pilling to Knott End. *Territorials:* 5th King's Own Royal Lancaster Regiment.

Prescot Lancashire town, eight miles from Liverpool and served by the London & North Western Railway which opened Prescot station in January 1872. Watches, timepieces and anything to do with their manufacture were made in the town. Here, with its black oak pews and altar rails, is St Mary's Church. *Territorials:* 5th South Lancashire Regiment.

Prestatyn Small Flintshire market town just inland from the sea, but a popular holiday resort since the railway arrived in 1848. The London & North Western served Prestatyn from which many worked in the nearby Goch lead mine. *Territorials:* Denbighshire Yeomanry.

Presteigne The county town of Radnorshire, Presteigne lies on the west bank of the Lugg; the river here forming the border between Wales and England. The railway arrived when the Leominster & Kington Company (later Great Western) opened a branch up from Titley in 1875. Here is St Andrew's Church and the former residence of John Bradshaw (1602–59), one of those that put his name to the death warrant of Charles 1. *Territorials:* Herefordshire Regiment.

Preston Lancashire market and manufacturing town eleven miles from Blackburn on the River Ribble and Lancaster Canal. At Preston there were several iron foundries, biscuit bakeries, engine and steam boiler works. But the town was most important for its cotton. Dominating the town is the 309 ft spire (made from recycled sleepers from the old Preston & Longridge Railway) of St Walburge's Church which was completed in 1854 from a designed by Joseph Hansom – the inventor of the Hansom Cab. Here in Preston, in 1732, was born Sir Richard Arkwright, the inventor of the cotton-spinning machine. St John's Church was built on the site of an earlier building in 1855. *Territorials:* East Lancashire Division, Lancashire Fusiliers Infantry Brigade, Duke of Lancaster's Own Yeomanry, 2nd West Lancashire Brigade RFA and 4th North Lancashire Regiment.

Prestonpans Town on the Firth of Forth, Haddingtonshire, nine miles from Edinburgh and served by the North British Railway. The suffix 'pans' comes from the fact that from the thirteenth century monks paned salt in the area. Also produced here was earthenware, bricks, beer and soap. Prestonpans, the scene of Bonnie Prince Charlie's victory in September 1745. *Territorials:* 8th Royal Scots and Prestonpans Cadet Corps.

Prittlewell Essex locality, and ward of Southend-on-Sea, reached by the Great Eastern Railway in 1889. Here is St Mary's Church which has registers dating from 1645. *Territorials:* 6th Essex Regiment and 3rd East Anglian Field Ambulance.

Prudhoe Small Northumberland town on the River Tyne, nine miles from Newcastle and served by the North Eastern Railway. Here were extensive collieries, Prudhoe's church being dedicated to St Mary Magdalene. *Territorials:* Northumberland Yeomanry and 4th Northumberland Fusiliers.

Pudsey West Riding of Yorkshire industrial town, six miles from Leeds, served by the Great Northern Railway which arrived in 1878. *Territorials:* 8th West Yorkshire Regiment.

Pulford Cheshire village six miles from Wrexham close to the border with Wales. Here is St Mary's Church. *Territorials:* Cheshire Yeomanry.

Pulham Dorset village on the River Lidden eight miles from Sherborne. Here is the church of St Thomas a Becket. *Territorials:* Dorsetshire Yeomanry.

Pulverbach Shropshire village seven miles from Shrewsbury. Here is St Edith's Church, mostly 1853, but the tower dates from 1773. The village is sometimes called Church Pulverbach. *Territorials:* Shropshire Yeomanry.

Pumpherston Midlothian village on the River Almond one mile from Mid Calder. Here were shale oil works. *Territorials:* 10th Royal Scots.

Purton Wiltshire village, four miles from Swindon, served by the Great Western Railway. Here is St Mary's Church. *Territorials:* Wiltshire Yeomanry.

Putney South-west London suburb on the south bank of the Thames. Here is St Mary's Church and, since 1845, the starting point of the annual Oxford and Cambridge Boat Race. *Territorials:* 25th London Regiment.

Pwllheli Carnarvonshire seaside resort on Cardigan Bay reached by railway when the Cambrian Company opened its coastal branch from Portmadoc in 1867. The Pwllheli Corporation Tramways, with its blue and white vehicles, opened for service in July 1899. Here is St Peter's Church which was built in 1887. *Territorials:* 6th Royal Welsh Fusiliers.

Quainton Buckinghamshire village to the north-west of Aylesbury with thatched Tudor cottages, a pond, green and windmill, Quainton was served by two railway companies: the Oxford & Aylesbury Tramroad, which opened in 1872, and the Metropolitan which, running up from London, after

1905 was called the Metropolitan and Great Central Joint. Here, standing next to the Winwood Almshouses of 1687, is the church of the Holy Cross and St Mary. *Territorials:* Buckinghamshire Yeomanry.

Quarles Norfolk hamlet in the north of the county four miles north-west of Walsingham. *Territorials:* Norfolk Yeomanry.

Queen Camel Somerset village, seven miles north of Yeovil, where two bridges, the Wales and Camel, cross the River Cam and a cobbled lane leads to St Barnabas's Church where there are monuments to the Mildmay family. *Territorials:* North Somerset Yeomanry.

Queen Charlton Somerset village clustered around a tiny green near Keynsham and five miles from Bristol city centre. Here is St Margaret's Church. *Territorials:* North Somerset Yeomanry.

Raasay Island within the Inner Hebrides, Inverness-shire. Iron ore was mined here. *Territorials:* 4th Cameron Highlanders.

Rackenford Village on the Little Dart river, eight miles from Tiverton in Devon. Here is All Saints Church. *Territorials:* Royal 1st Devon Yeomanry.

Radcliffe Lancashire market and manufacturing town on the River Irwell seven miles from Manchester and served by the Lancashire & Yorkshire Railway, where many were employed in cotton spinning, calico printing, collieries and papermaking. At St Bartholomew's Church there are memorials to the Radcliffe family. *Territorials:* 5th Lancashire Fusiliers.

Radlett Hertfordshire village six miles from St Albans and served by the Midland Railway. Here is Christ Church. *Territorials:* Hertfordshire Yeomanry.

Radstock Small town, eight miles from Frome, and once the centre of Somerset's coal producing industry. The Bristol & North Somerset Railway arrived in 1873, the Somerset & Dorset the year after that. Here is St Nicholas's Church which was almost totally rebuilt in 1879. *Territorials:* 4th Somerset Light Infantry.

Rainham Essex village on the Thames, five miles from Barking, served by the Midland Railway. Here is the Norman church of St Helen and St Giles. *Territorials:* 4th Essex Regiment.

Rainhill Lancashire village, nine miles from Liverpool, served by the London & North Western Railway. Tools were made here – files, nippers and pliers a speciality. Here is St Anne's Church which dates from 1837. *Territorials:* Lancashire Hussars.

Ramsbottom Lancashire manufacturing town on the River Irwell, thirteen miles from Manchester, served by the Lancashire & Yorkshire Railway. Here were iron and brass foundries, machine shops, printing and spinning works. Here is St Andrew's Church, which was built in 1834, and St Paul's, which dates from 1850. *Territorials:* 5th East Lancashire Regiment.

Ramsey Huntingdonshire market town ten miles from Huntingdon. Two railway companies had lines that terminated here: the Ramsey Railway, which arrived in 1863, and the Ramsey & Somersham Junction which opened its station in 1889. Here is St Thomas's Church, in which many members of Oliver Cromwell's family are buried. *Territorials:* Bedfordshire Yeomanry and 5th Bedfordshire Regiment.

Ramsgate Kent seaside resort and market town, four miles from Margate, served by the South Eastern & Chatham Railway. Here are St George's and St Lawrence's churches, and the St Lawrence College which maintained one OTC infantry company. *Territorials:* Royal East Kent Yeomanry, 3rd Home Counties Brigade RFA, 4th Buffs East Kent Regiment, Kent Cyclist Battalion, South Eastern Mounted Brigade Field Ambulance and Chatham House Cadet Corps.

Rankinston Ayrshire village eight miles from Cumnock. Opened in 1884, Rankinston station was served by the Glasgow & South Western Railway. *Territorials:* 5th Royal Scots Fusiliers.

Ranskill Nottinghamshire village three miles from Bawtry, its station on the Great Northern line being opened in 1849. Here is St Barnabas's Church which was built in 1878. *Territorials:* Nottinghamshire Yeomanry (Sherwood Rangers).

Ratho Midlothian village, eight miles from Edinburgh, served by the North British Railway. *Territorials:* Lothians and Border Horse.

Ravenscourt Park Residential locality of Hammersmith in west London. *Territorials:* 10th Middlesex Regiment.

Rawtenstall Lancashire manufacturing town, eight miles from Bury, where most of the population were employed in cotton and woollen manufacture. Opened in 1846 was Rawtenstall station which was served by the Lancashire & Yorkshire Railway. The Rawtenstall Corporation Tramways, with their maroon and cream trams, opened in October 1908. Here is St Mary's Church. *Territorials:* East Lancashire Divisional Transport and Supply Column.

Reading At the junction of the Kennet with the Thames is the county town of Berkshire. Reading was once important in the cloth industry which, by the time of the Territorials, had disappeared. Now it was biscuits, seeds and sauce: Huntly & Palmers for the biscuits, Messrs Sutton & Sons for the seed nurseries, and Cocks for the sauce. We must thank Mr Martin Sutton for the fine statue of King Edward VII that stands outside Reading station. Oscar Wilde is on record as having visited Huntly & Palmers factory in 1892. He would make another visit to Reading three years later, but for a less enjoyable reason. Reading Goal just across the road from the factory and close enough almost to feel the heat of the biscuits baking. The town's main churches are Christ Church, St Giles, St Lawrence and St Stephen. Both Reading University College and Reading School maintained OTC contingents. *Territorials:* 2nd South Midland Mounted Brigade, Berkshire Yeomanry, Berkshire RHA, 4th Royal Berkshire Regiment, 2nd South Midland Mounted Brigade Transport and Supply Column and Reading Cadet Company.

Rearsby Leicestershire village near the River Wreake, seven miles from Leicester, served by the Midland Railway which arrived in 1856. Here is St Michael's Church. *Territorials:* Leicestershire Yeomanry.

Reay Village close to Sandside Bay, Caithness, ten miles from Thurso. *Territorials:* 5th Seaforth Highlanders.

Redbourn Hertfordshire village on the River Ver, four miles from St Albans. Redbourn station was opened in 1877 and served by the Midland Railway. Here is St Mary's Church. *Territorials:* Hertfordshire Yeomanry.

Redcar North Riding of Yorkshire seaside resort, eight miles from Middlesbrough, served by the North Eastern Railway. Here is St Peter's Church. *Territorials:* 4th Yorkshire Regiment.

Redditch Worcestershire manufacturing town, thirteen miles from Birmingham, served by the Midland Railway. Famous for its production of fishhooks and needles, a very large number of 'skilled artisans', notes the guides, being employed in these trades. Forge Mill, and the Salmon Fly Works, the centre of the town's output. Here at Church Green is St Stephen's Church of 1854–55. *Territorials:* Worcestershire Yeomanry, 2nd South Midland Brigade RFA and 8th Worcestershire Regiment.

Redfields Seat near Fleet, Hampshire. *Territorials:* 4th Hampshire Regiment.

Redruth Cornwall market town, eight miles from Truro, served by the Great Western Railway. The Camborne & Redruth Tramway, with its dark green and cream vehicles, began operating between the two towns in November 1902. Copper and tin was the main source of industry at Redruth; the area said to be the largest producer of the metals in the world. One source notes some 10,000 men, women and children employed. The Mining Exchange was opened in the town in 1880. Here is St Uny's Church. *Territorials:* 4th Duke of Cornwall's Light Infantry.

Reepham Norfolk village, twelve miles from Norwich, where the station was opened by the East Norfolk Railway in May 1881. Here is St Mary's Church. *Territorials:* Norfolk Yeomanry.

Reeth North Riding of Yorkshire village on the River Swale, nine miles from Richmond. *Territorials:* 4th Yorkshire Regiment.

Regent's Park Residential area of St Marylebone, north-west London. *Territorials:* 3rd County of London Yeomanry.

Reigate Surrey market town, six miles from Dorking, served by the South Eastern & Chatham Railway. Here at St Mary Magdalene's Church lies the body of Lord Howard of Effingham who was Admiral of the fleet collected to oppose the Spanish Armada. At Reigate Grammar School there was a contingent of the OTC. *Territorials:* 5th Queen's Royal West Surrey Regiment.

Renfrew County town on the Rive Clyde, seven miles by rail from Glasgow on the Glasgow & South Western Railway. Here, many were employed in engineering works and shipyards. In 1895, Babcock and Wilcox built the largest boiler-making works in the world at Renfrew. *Territorials:* 6th Argyll and Sutherland Highlanders.

Renton Dumbartonshire village on the River Leven, two miles from Dumbarton, served by the North British and Caledonian railways. There were large print works situated on the river bank. *Territorials:* 9th Argyll and Sutherland Highlanders.

Repton Derbyshire village, seven miles from Derby, served by the Midland Railway. Here is St Wystan's Church and Repton School which maintained four OTC infantry companies. *Territorials:* Derbyshire Yeomanry and 5th Sherwood Foresters.

Retford Nottinghamshire market town on the River Idle and Chesterfield Canal, eighteen miles from Nottingham. The town is divided as East and West Retford, the two separated by the river and served by the Great Northern and Great Central railways. Retford is sometimes called East Retford, the church of St Swithin's there being restored in 1855 and referred to by the community as the 'Corporation Church'. St Michael's is in West Retford. *Territorials:* Nottinghamshire Yeomanry (Sherwood Rangers) and 8th Sherwood Foresters.

Reynoldston Glamorgan village twelve miles from Swansea. Here is St George's Church. *Territorials:* Glamorgan Yeomanry.

Rhayader Radnorshire market town on the River Wye, eleven miles from Llanidloes, served by the Cambrian Railway. Here is St Clement's Church. *Territorials:* Montgomeryshire Yeomanry and Herefordshire Regiment.

Rhosllanerchrugog Denbighshire village, three miles from Wrexham, served by the Great Western Railway. Usually called Rhos. Here is St John's Church. *Territorials:* 4th Royal Welsh Fusiliers.

Rhyl Flintshire seaside resort at the mouth of the River Clwyd, four miles from Prestatyn, served by the London & North Western Railway. Here is Holy Trinity Church which was erected in 1835. *Territorials:* Denbighshire Yeomanry and 5th Royal Welsh Fusiliers.

Rhymney Monmouthshire town on the River Rhymney, three miles from Tredegar and served by the Rhymney Railway, where most of the population were employed in collieries or ironworks. Here is St David's Church which was built 1843. *Territorials:* 1st Monmouthshire Regiment.

Rhynie Aberdeenshire village on Bogie Water eight miles from Alford. *Territorials:* 6th Gordon Highlanders.

Richmond (Surrey) Situated on the Thames, ten miles from London by rail on the London & South Western Railway. Here is St Mary's Church. *Territorials:* 6th East Surrey Regiment, Richmond Hill Cadets and Richmond County School Cadet Corps.

Richmond (Yorkshire) North Riding of Yorkshire market town on the River Swale fifteen miles from Darlington. Richmond station was opened in 1846 and formed the terminus of the North Eastern Railway's branch from Eryholme Junction. Here is St Mary's Church and, in the Market Place, Holy Trinity. *Territorials:* Northumbrian Division and 4th Yorkshire Regiment.

Ringwood Hampshire market town on the River Avon and western edge of the New Forest, eight miles from Christchurch, well known for its production of knitted woollen gloves. Ringwood station was opened by the Southampton & Dorchester Railway in June 1847. Bt the Market Place is St Peter and St Paul's Church which was built 1853–55. *Territorials:* 7th Hampshire Regiment.

Ripley Derbyshire industrial town, ten miles from Derby, served by the Midland Railway. Here since 1821 is All Saints Church, and St John's, which was opened in 1894. *Territorials:* Derbyshire Yeomanry and 5th Sherwood Foresters.

Ripon West Riding of Yorkshire market town on the River Ure, twenty-three miles from York, served by the North Eastern Railway. On the Ripon coat of arms there is a stringed bugle horn which represents a town custom said to date from 886. Every evening at nine-o'clock the 'Wakeman' (night-watchman) sounds a horn from the town square. Here, its churchyard sloping down to the river, is Ripon Cathedral. 'For Fountains Abbey', announce the railway poster, 'Travel by rail to Ripon Station'. *Territorials:* Yorkshire Hussars and 5th West Yorkshire Regiment.

Risca Monmouthshire town on the River Ebbw and Monmouthshire Canal, six miles from Newport, served by the Great Western Railway. The production of coal, tinplate, iron and steel gave employment to the area. Here is St Mary's Church. *Territorials:* 4th Welsh Brigade RFA.

Road Somerset village ten miles from Bath. Here is St Lawrence's Church. *Territorials:* North Somerset Yeomanry.

Robertsbridge Sussex village on the River Rother. The church (St Mary's) is across the river at Salehurst. Robertsbridge was served by the South Eastern & Chatham Railway which was joined just to the north by the Kent & East Sussex Light Railway when it opened in 1900. *Territorials:* 5th Royal Sussex Regiment.

Roborough Devonshire village six miles from Torrington. Here is St Peter's Church. *Territorials:* Royal North Devon Yeomanry.

Rochdale Lancashire town on the River Roch and Rochdale Canal, eleven miles from Manchester, served by the Lancashire & Yorkshire Railway. There were collieries, but most important to the town was the cotton and woollen trade. Opened in Toad Lane by the 'Rochdale Pioneers' in 1844, was the first ever cooperative shop. Overlooking the town centre is St Chad's Church which is reached from the Town Hall Square via 122 steps. Born here was the singer Gracie Fields (1898–1979) who gave her first stage performance at Rochdale when the Territorial Force was just two years old. Here are St Chad's and St Mary's churches. *Territorials:* Duke of Lancaster's Own Yeomanry and 6th Lancashire Fusiliers.

Rochester City in Kent, its present cathedral dating from 1077, served by the South Eastern & Chatham Railway. Here is King's School which maintained one OTC infantry company. *Territorials:* West Kent Yeomanry, Kent RGA and 2nd Cadet Battalion Kent Fortress Engineers.

Rogart Sutherlandshire village on the Fleet and Brora rivers, seven miles from Golspie, where some worked in a woollen factory, but most were employed as agricultural labourers. Rogart station, on the Highland Railway, was opened in 1868. *Territorials:* 5th Seaforth Highlanders.

Rogerstone Monmouthshire township, three miles from Newport, served by the Great Western Railway which arrived in December 1850 – the station then called Tydu. Here is St John's Church which dates from 1888. *Territorials:* 1st Monmouthshire Regiment.

Rolvenden Village in Kent, three miles from Tenterden, served by the Kent and East Sussex Light Railway. When the railway arrived in 1900 the station was called Tenterden, but this was changed to Rolvenden when the line was extended to Tenterden proper in 1903. Here, at St Mary's Church, is a memorial to Frances Hodgson Burnett (1849–1924) who lived nearby at Maytham Hall where it is said the walled garden was the inspiration for his novel, *The Secret Garden*, written in 1911. *Territorials:* 5th Buffs East Kent Regiment.

Romford Essex market town, six miles from Brentford and twelve miles by rail from London's Liverpool Street on the Great Eastern. Agriculture was the chief occupation in Romford, but Messrs Ind Coope's brewery employed many from the town. Here is the church of Edward the Confessor, and the St Alban's Mission Church which was opened in 1890. *Territorials:* 2nd East Anglian Brigade RFA and 4th Essex Regiment.

Romsey Hampshire market town on the River Test, seven miles from Southampton, served by the London & South Western Railway. In the area were breweries, corn mills, ironworks a paper mill and jam maker. The Berthon Boatbuilding Company employed many. Here is the Abbey Church of St Mary and St Ethelflaeda. Among its many memorials is the tomb of Alice Taylor, daughter of a local doctor, who died aged two from scarlet fever in 1843. *Territorials:* Hampshire Yeomanry, 4th and 9th Hampshire Regiment.

Rookhope Durham village five miles from Stanhope, once a centre for lead and silver mining. Here is Holt Trinity Church. *Territorials:* 6th Durham Light Infantry.

Rosehall Sutherlandshire estate and seat seven miles from Largs. *Territorials:* 2nd Lovat's Scouts.

Rosehearty Aberdeenshire fishing village four miles from Fraserburgh. *Territorials:* 5th Gordon Highlanders.

Rosemarkie Ross and Cromarty village on the Moray Firth. *Territorials:* 4th Seaforth Highlanders.

Ross-on-Wye Herefordshire town on a steep hill above the River, the spire of St Mary's Church seen for miles around. In and near the town were machine works, a brewery, boot factory and flour mills. Ross station was opened by the Hereford, Ross & Gloucester Railway in June 1855. *Territorials:* Shropshire Yeomanry and Herefordshire Regiment.

Rothbury Northumberland town on the River Coquet eleven miles from Alnwick. Rothbury station was at the termination of the Northumberland Central Railway (later North British) which opened in 1870. Here is All Saints Church. *Territorials:* Northumberland Yeomanry and 7th Northumberland Fusiliers.

Rotherfield Sussex village just over a mile from the railway at Crowborough. Here, at St Denys's Church, there are box pews and wall painting that date from the thirteenth century. *Territorials:* 5th Royal Sussex Regiment.

Rotherham West Riding of Yorkshire industrial town on the River Rother where it meets the Don, six miles by rail from Sheffield on the Midland Railway. Here is All Saints Church and the birthplace in 1901 of Sir Donald Bailey, inventor of the Bailey bridge. *Territorials:* Yorkshire Dragoons, West Riding RHA and 5th York and Lancaster Regiment.

Rothes Elginshire town, eleven miles from Elgin, where many were employed in local distilleries. Rothes station was opened in August 1858 and was served by the Great North of Scotland Railway. *Territorials:* 6th Seaforth Highlanders.

Rothesay Holliday resort on the east side of the Isle of Bute, Firth of Clyde, eighteen miles from Greenock. Herring fishing gave employment to many, as did the town's cotton mills – the first in Scotland. At Rothesay the church is close enough to the seashore to be troubled by sand and ferry boats regularly crossed the Firth of Clyde to Wemyss Bay. One tourist attraction since 1899 is the ceramic-tile-clad lavatories at the end of the pier. *Territorials:* 4th Highland Brigade RGA.

Rothienorman Small Aberdeenshire village, three miles from Fyvie, served by the Great North of Scotland Railway. *Territorials:* 2nd Scottish Horse.

Rothwell Northamptonshire town where many were employed in factories making shoes and clothing. The Midland Railway's station at Desborough lies a mile or more from the town and was renamed Desborough and Rothwell in 1899. Here at Holy Trinity Church, and found when the aisle floor collapsed, is an ossuary containing 1,500 neatly stacked human skeletons. *Territorials:* 4th Northamptonshire Regiment.

Rowland's Castle Hampshire village, three miles from Havant, serve by the London & south Western Railway. *Territorials:* 6th and 9th Hampshire Regiment.

Roy Bridge Inverness-shire village on the River Roy where it meets the Spean, reached by the West Highland Railway (later North British) in August 1894. *Territorials:* 1st Lovat's Scouts.

Royston Hertfordshire market town, thirteen miles from Cambridge, served by the Great Northern Railway. Here at St John's Church there are many memorials to the Wortham and Beldham families. *Territorials:* Hertfordshire Regiment.

Ruabon Denbighshire town, four miles from Wrexham, served by the Great Western Railway. Many from the area were employed in coal mining and at Ruabon's iron, brick and terracotta works. At St Mary's Church there are memorials to the Wynn family. *Territorials:* Denbighshire Yeomanry and 4th Royal Welsh Fusiliers.

Ruardean Gloucestershire village on the River Wye near the Herefordshire border nine miles from Monmouth. Here is St John's Church, much restored in 1873, and again in 1890–91. Of note here is the font. Dated 1657, a time when fonts were forbidden by law. *Territorials:* Herefordshire Regiment.

Rubery Worcestershire hamlet four miles from Halesowen. *Territorials:* 8th Worcestershire Regiment.

Rugby Warwickshire market town on the River Avon sixteen miles from Warwick. An important railway junction and engineering centre from which the town prospered – here met the Great Central, Midland and London & North Western railways. With five bells in the fourteenth-century west tower, and eight in the north-east tower of 1895, this makes St Andrew's, Rugby the only two-towered church with a complete ring in each. Rugby School, always a strong supporter of the Volunteer Force, maintain three OTC infantry companies. *Territorials:* Warwickshire Yeomanry, 4th South Midland Brigade RFA and 7th Royal Warwickshire Regiment.

Rugeley Staffordshire market town on the River Trent and Trent and Mersey Canal, nine miles from Stafford and served by the London & North Western Railway. Here is St Augustine's Church. *Territorials:* 6th North Staffordshire Regiment.

Runcorn Cheshire seaport and market town on the south side of the Mersey, fifteen miles from Liverpool and served by the London & North Western Railway. The prosperity of Runcorn is said to be in shipping and the opening of the Duke of Bridgewater's Canal in 1773. Here is Christ Church, built for their workmen by the Weaver Navigation Company. *Territorials:* 5th Cheshire Regiment.

Rushden Northamptonshire town, five miles from Wellingborough, reached by the railway when the Midland opened its branch to Higham Ferrers in 1893. Here boots and shoes were manufactured. Here is St Mary's Church. *Territorials:* Northamptonshire Yeomanry and 4th Northamptonshire Regiment.

Rutherglen Lanarkshire town on the River Clyde, two miles from Glasgow, served by the Caledonian Railway. Many at Rutherglen were employed at the town's shipyards, chemical and dye works, paper mill and numerous collieries. *Territorials:* Lowland Divisional Engineers and Lowland Divisional Transport and Supply Column.

Ruthin Denbighshire market town on the River Clwyd, six miles from Denbigh, served by the London & North Western Railway. The railway (the old Denbigh, Ruthin & Corwen line) had reached the town in March 1862. Mainly agricultural, the area also had a brick and terracotta works. Here is St Peter's Church. *Territorials:* Denbighshire Yeomanry, 4th Royal Welsh Fusiliers, Welsh Divisional Transport and Supply Column and Ruthin School Cadet Corps.

Ryburgh Great and Little Ryburgh, Norfolk villages on the River Wensum, three to four miles from Fakenham, served by the Great Eastern Railway. Here at Great Ryburgh is St Andrew's Church, and at Little Ryburgh, All Saints. *Territorials:* 6th Norfolk Regiment.

Ryde Isle of Wight seaside resort seven miles from Newport. Here is St James's Church of 1829 and All Saints which dates from 1870. *Territorials:* Hampshire Yeomanry, 2nd Wessex Brigade RFA, 8th Hampshire Regiment, Ryde Cadet Company and 2rd Cadet Battalion Hampshire Regiment.

Rye Sussex town of which one visitor wrote in 1920: 'we walk the streets with a feeling of romance and unreality and find it hard to believe that we have not stepped back several centuries.' Here *for* centuries are St Mary's Church; the Ypres Tower, once a prison; the Flushing Inn, with its thirteenth-century cellar, and its competitor, the Mermaid which is just as old. The South Eastern & Chatham Railway's station at Rye opened in 1851. There was also the Rye & Camber line which began just outside of the town in 1895 and followed the River Rother along to Rye Harbour. It extended to the Camber Golf Links in 1908. *Territorials:* Sussex Yeomanry and 5th Royal Sussex Regiment.

Sacriston Durham mining village four miles from Chester-le-Street. Here is St Peter's Church. *Territorials:* 8th Durham Light Infantry.

Saffron Walden Essex market town, fifteen miles from Cambridge. Once an important wool centre, but later prospered from its production of dye from the saffron crocus. The town's name came from this source, the crocus also featuring in its coat of arms. Here at St Mary's Church, two heroes of the Crimean War are remembered: the Hon H A Neville, killed at Inkerman, and the Hon G Neville who died of wounds received at Balaclava. Both were sons of Lord Braybrooke. *Territorials:* 8th Essex Regiment.

St Albans Hertfordshire market town and cathedral city on the River Ver, twenty miles from London, served by the Great Northern, Midland and London & North Western railways. Perhaps Arthur Melbourne-Cooper photographed the Volunteers of the 1890s; or even earlier, his father who had a studio in Osborne Street. Arthur, who is credited with having began the film industry in Britain, produced an appeal on behalf of the Bryant & May company for donations to supply matches to the troops then serving in South Africa and the Boer War. The town gave employment in its breweries, boot factory and brush works. Here, with its memorial to Sir Francis Bacon, is St Michael's Church; and St Alban's School, which maintained one OTC infantry company. *Territorials:* Hertfordshire Yeomanry, 4th East Anglian Brigade RFA and Hertfordshire Regiment.

St Andrews University and cathedral city in Fifeshire, thirteen miles from Dundee, served by the North British Railway. The Royal and Ancient Golf Club was established here in 1754. *Territorials:* Fife and Forfar Yeomanry, Highland RGA and 7th Black Watch.

St Asaph Flintshire market town, five miles from Denbigh, served by the London & North Western Railway. Here is St Asaph Abbey and the parish church of St Cydey and St Asaph. *Territorials:* 5th Royal Welsh Fusiliers and Welsh Divisional Transport and Supply Column.

St Austell Cornwall market town, fourteen miles from Truro, served by the Great Western Railway. Tin, copper, then china-clay gave prosperity to the town. Here is Holy Trinity Church. *Territorials:* 5th Duke of Cornwall's Light Infantry.

St Bees Cumberland coastal village, four miles from Whitehaven, served by the Furness Railway. Here is the red sandstone church of St Mary and St Bega, and St Bees School which maintained two OTC infantry companies. *Territorials:* 5th Border Regiment.

St Boswells Roxburghshire village on the River Tweed, four miles from Melrose, served by the North British Railway. *Territorials:* Lothians and Border Horse and 4th King's Own Scottish Borderers.

St Buryan Cornwall village six miles from Penzance. Here the church tower rises high above the village square. *Territorials:* Cornwall RGA.

St Columb There is a St Columb Major and, about five miles distant, a St Columb Minor. The principal industry in the area was the mining of clay which brought about the formation of the Cornwall Minerals Railway. A goods line at first, but a later passenger service saw the opening of St Columb Road Station on 20 June 1876. *Territorials:* 5th Duke of Cornwall's Light Infantry.

St Fergus Aberdeenshire coastal village five miles from Peterhead. *Territorials:* 5th Gordon Highlanders.

St Florence Pembrokeshire village three miles from Tenby. The church was restored in 1871. *Territorials:* Pembrokeshire Yeomanry.

St George District of Bristol. *Territorials:* 4th Gloucestershire Regiment.

St Giles Devonshire village three miles from Torrington. The church underwent restoration in 1862–63. *Territorials:* 6th Devonshire Regiment.

St Helens (Isle of Wight) Village four miles from Ryde on the branch built by the Isle of Wight Railway to Bembridge in 1882. Here at the church there are memorials to the Grose family, one of them, Edward, having been mortally wounded at Waterloo in 1815. *Territorials:* 8th Hampshire Regiment.

St Helens (Lancashire) Industrial town, twelve miles from Liverpool, served by the London & North Western and Great Central railways. A major employed at St Helens since 1826 has been Pilkington Glass. *Territorials:* Lancashire Hussars, West Lancashire Divisional Engineers, 5th South Lancashire Regiment and 3rd West Lancashire Field Ambulance.

St Ives (Cornwall) Eight miles from Penzance, St Ives has much to do with the sea and fishing. A vicar once told a visitor that 'the smell of fish is sometimes so terrific as to stop the clock'. All Saints Church, or its spire anyway, is thought to be unlucky. Blown down in 1741, the top thirty feet chopped off of a replacement by an aircraft during the First World War. The Great Western Railway served the town. *Territorials:* Cornwall RGA.

St Ives (Huntingdonshire) 'Strong men have blached, and shot their wives,/Rather than send them to St Ives' (from 'The Old Vicarage, Grantchester' by Rupert Brooke, 1912). Market town on the River Ouse, five miles from Huntingdon, served by the Great Northern & Great Eastern Joint Railway. Here in Market Place stands former resident, Oliver Cromwell. His signature is also found in the account books of All Saints Church, and his ghost in the rooms and corridors of the Golden Lion Inn. *Territorials:* 5th Bedfordshire Regiment.

St John's Chapel Durham locality, seven miles from Stanhope, reached by the North Eastern Railway in 1895. *Territorials:* 6th Durham Light Infantry.

St John's Wood Residential area, much favoured by artists and writers, and part of St Marylebone, London. Here on Ordnance Hill is St John's Wood Barracks, and in St John's Wood Road, Lord's Cricket Ground. *Territorials:* 3rd County of London Yeomanry, Hertfordshire Yeomanry and 9th Middlesex Regiment.

St Just Cornwall market town seven miles from Penzance. The Botallack and other tin mines were in the area. Here at the church are memorials to the Millett and Clenhall families. *Territorials:* Cornwall RGA and 4th Duke of Cornwall's Light Infantry.

St Leonards-on-Sea Sussex seaside resort adjoining Hastings served by the London, Brighton & South Coast and South Eastern & Chatham railways. St Leonard's Church dates from 1831–32, the pier opened in 1891. *Territorials:* Sussex Yeomanry, 2nd Home Counties Brigade RFA, Home Counties Divisional Engineers and St Leonards Collegiate School Cadet Company.

St Mary Bourne Hampshire village on the River Bourne five miles from Andover. Here is St Peter's Church. *Territorials:* Wessex Divisional Transport and Supply column.

St Marylebone West London borough and railway terminus. *Territorials:* 4th London General Hospital.

St Merryn Cornwall village two miles from Padstow. *Territorials:* Cornwall RGA.

St Neots Huntingdonshire market town on the River Ouse, nine miles from Huntingdon, served by the Great Eastern Railway. The St Neots Paper Mill Company, several breweries, flour mills and engineering works gave employment. Here on the edge of town is St Mary's Church. *Territorials:* Bedfordshire Yeomanry and 5th Bedfordshire Regiment.

St Nicholas at Wade Kent village six miles from Margate. The church is set close to a farmyard and has a Jacobean pulpit. *Territorials:* 4th Buffs East Kent Regiment.

St Pancras North-west London borough where the main employers were: in Pratt Street, Idris, who made mineral water; Gilbey, who distilled gin at Oval Road and – the area was within buffer-clanking sound of King's Cross, St Pancras and Euston stations after all – the railway. *Territorials:* Gloucester and Worcester Infantry Brigade, 1st, 3rd, 19th, 28th London Regiment, London Mounted Brigade Transport and Supply Column, 3rd London Field Ambulance, 1st, 2nd London General Hospitals and 1st London Sanitary Company.

St Stephen Cornish village six miles from St Austell. *Territorials:* 5th Duke of Cornwall's Light Infantry.

Salcombe Devon seaside resort five miles from Kingsbridge. A popular yachting centre since 1847. Here, overlooking Baston Creek, is Holy Trinity Church. *Territorials:* Devonshire RGA.

Sale Cheshire town and busy railway junction on the River Mersey and Bridgwater Canal, five miles from Manchester. The guides note that Sale included the residences of many Manchester merchants and businessmen. *Territorials:* Cheshire Yeomanry and 5th Cheshire Regiment.

Salford The River Irwell separates Salford from Manchester on its western side. Unveiled at the junction of Chapel Street and Oldfield Road on 13 July 1905 was George Frampton's memorial to the memory of those from Salford that had served in South African 1899–1902, the inscription particularly mention those of the Volunteer Active Service Companies of the Lancashire Fusiliers.' The painter L S Lowry (1887–1976) lived and worked most of his life in Salford. *Territorials:* 7th and 8th Lancashire Fusiliers.

Salford Priors Warwickshire village, six miles from Eversham, served by the Midland Railway. Here at St Matthew's Church there are memorials to the Clarke (alias Woodchurch) family. *Territorials:* Warwickshire Yeomanry.

Salisbury County town of Wiltshire at the confluence of the Bourne, Avon and Nadder rivers, served by the Great Western and London & South Western railways. The manufacture of carpets and rugs began here in 1889, the town also giving employment in its tanneries, breweries and flour mills. Here is St Thomas's Church which was built for builders working on the nearby Salisbury Cathedral. Thomas Hardy wrote of Salisbury, calling it 'Melchester' in his novel *Jude the Obscure* – Jude working in the cathedral itself. *Territorials:* 1st South Western Mounted Brigade and Signal Troop, Wiltshire Yeomanry, 4th Wiltshire Regiment and 1st South Western Mounted Brigade Transport and Supply Column.

Salsburgh Lanarkshire village three miles from Shotts. *Territorials:* 8th Highland Light Infantry.

Saltash Cornwall market town, five miles from Plymouth, served by the Great Western Railway. An important position during the Civil War, due to its location on the River Tamar, Saltash changed hands a number of times. The town finally surrendering to Fairfax in February 1646. Here is the church of St Nicholas, and Brunel's Royal Albert railway bridge which was opened in 1859. *Territorials:* 5th Duke of Cornwall's Light Infantry.

Saltcoats Ayrshire town and seaside resort close to Ardrossan and served by the Glasgow & South Western and Caledonian railways. One railway poster advertises Saltcoats as 'The finest tidal lake on the Firth of Clyde'. The manufacture of salt employed many until around 1890, the collieries, foundries at Stevenston, others. *Territorials:* 4th Royal Scots Fusiliers.

Saltley Suburb of Birmingham served by the Midland Railway where many were employed in an extensive railway carriage and wagon works. Here is St Saviour's Church. *Territorials:* 8th Royal Warwickshire Regiment and South Midland (Heavy) RGA.

Sand Hutton North Riding of Yorkshire village seven miles from York. Here is St Mary's Church. *Territorials:* 5th Yorkshire Regiment.

Sanday Orkney Isles, nine miles from Kirkwall. *Territorials:* Orkney RGA.

Sandbach Cheshire market town, five miles from Crewe, and junction of the North Staffordshire and London & North Western railways. The chief trade was salt, chemicals and the making of boots and shoes. Here is St Mary's Church. *Territorials:* 7th Cheshire Regiment.

Sandbank Argyllshire village and popular resort on Holy Loch. *Territorials:* Clyde RGA and 8th Argyll and Sutherland Highlanders.

Sandgate Town in Kent, one mile from Folkestone, reached by the railway when the South Eastern opened its branch from Sandling Junction in 1874. There was also a tram service ran by the Folkestone, Hythe & Sandgate Tramway Company which opened in May 1891. Here is St Paul's Church. *Territorials:* Kent Cyclist Battalion.

Sandhurst Village in Kent, six miles from Etchingham. Here is St Nicholas's Church. *Territorials:* 5th Buffs East Kent Regiment.

Sandown Coastal town and resort on the Isle of Wight, six miles from Ryde, reached by the railway in 1864. Here at St John's Church is a memorial to Lieutenant Boxer, RN, who was one of the 483 that perished when the *Captain* was lost during bad weather in September 1870. *Territorials:* 8th Hampshire Regiment and Sandown Cadet Company.

Sandringham Norfolk village seven miles from King's Lynn. Here since 1861 is Sandringham House, a residence of the royal family, and the church of St Mary Magdalene where many of them are remembered. *Territorials:* 5th Norfolk Regiment.

Sandwich Market town in Kent, on the River Stour seven miles from Ramsgate, served by the South Eastern & Chatham Railway. There is a custom in Sandwich whereas its mayors wear black robes in memory of the one killed during a French raid on the town in 1457. Here are St Clement's, St Mary's and St Peter's churches, and Sir Roger Manwood's School which maintained an OTC contingent. *Territorials:* 3rd Home Counties Brigade RFA and Kent Cyclist Battalion.

Sandy Bedfordshire town on the River Ivel, eight miles from Bedford, served by the Great Northern and London & North Western railways. Here remembered at St Swithin's Church is the Crimean War commander of the Naval Brigade, Sir W Peel. *Territorials:* 5th Bedfordshire Regiment.

Sandyway Devonshire location two miles from North Moulton. *Territorials:* Royal North Devon Yeomanry.

Sanquhar Dumfrieshire town on the River Nith, twelve miles from Thornhill, served by the Glasgow & South Western Railway. Here were coalfields and works producing spades, shovels, bricks and titles. *Territorials:* Lanarkshire Yeomanry and 5th King's Own Scottish Borderers.

Sarisbury Hampshire village, three miles from Titchfield, well known for its strawberry production. Here is St Paul's Church. *Territorials:* 5th Hampshire Regiment.

Sauchie Clackmannanshire village, one mile from Alloa, served by the North British Railway. In the area were collieries. *Territorials:* 7th Argyll and Sutherland Highlanders.

Saundersfoot Pembrokeshire resort, three miles from Tenby, served by the Great Western Railway. Once a small location of just three houses, Saundersfoot grew from the coal trade after 1821. *Territorials:* Pembrokeshire RGA.

Sawbridgeworth Hertfordshire town on the former Northern and Eastern line where ancient buildings overhang the streets and the church looks across the River Stort to Essex. At St Mary's Church, a brass tablet remembers Corporal Joseph Vick ('One of the Six Hundred') who, in the Crimean War, charged at Balaclava with the 4th Light Dragoons. *Territorials:* Hertfordshire Yeomanry and Hertfordshire Regiment.

Sawston Cambridgeshire village on the River Cam seven miles from Cambridge. Here, many were employed in an extensive paper mill. At St Mary's Church there are memorials to the Huntingdon and Huddleston families. *Territorials:* Cambridgeshire Regiment.

Saxlingham Norfolk village three miles from Holt. Here is St Margaret's Church. *Territorials:* 4th Norfolk Regiment.

Saxmundham Suffolk market town twenty-three miles by rail from Ipswich on the Great Eastern Railway. Here is St John's Church where there are memorials to the Long family. *Territorials:* 4th Suffolk Regiment.

Scalloway Fishing village on Mainland Shetland, six miles from Lerwick. Here, on the road to Tingwall, is the 'Murder Stone'. If murderers could reach it alive, before their victim's relatives could catch them, they were allowed to live. *Territorials:* Shetland Companies.

Scarborough North Yorkshire seaside resort served by the North Eastern Railway. Here Anne Brontë, who gave us *The Tenant of Wildfell Hall,* died in 1849 and is buried in St Mary's Church, and born here was the actor Charles Laughton who gave us Quasimodo, Henry VIII and Captain Blight. Opening in 1867 was the Grand Hotel. How clever it was of the architect to shape the building like the letter 'V' out of respect for Queen Victoria. And even more ingenious was his plan of: 365 bedrooms (one for each day of the year), fifty-two chimneys (the weeks), twelve floors (months) and on the roof, four turrets to represent the seasons. In 1914 and the early weeks of the war, great damage was caused during the bombardment of the town by the German navy. *Territorials:* York and Durham Infantry Brigade, Yorkshire Hussars, 2nd Northumbrian Brigade RFA, 5th Yorkshire Regiment and Yorkshire Mounted Brigade Transport and Supply Column.

Sconser Village on Loch Sligachan, Skye Island, Inner Hebrides. *Territorials:* 4th Cameron Highlanders.

Scourie Village on Scourie Bay, Sutherlandshire, forty-four miles from Lairg. *Territorials:* 2nd Lovat's Scouts.

Scremerston Northumberland costal village, two miles from Berwick-upon-Tweed on the North Eastern Railway, where many were employed in local collieries, lime, brick and title works. Here is St Peter's Church. *Territorials:* 7th Northumberland Fusiliers.

Scunthorpe Lincolnshire industrial town, twenty-five miles from Grimsby, served by the Great Central Railway. It was the opening of the ironworks in 1864 that saw the growth of Scunthorpe, and again with the steel in the 1890s. All Saints Church was enlarged and restored in 1860. *Territorials:* Lincolnshire Yeomanry.

Seacombe Residential suburb of Wallasey in Cheshire noted by one Victorian guide as containing mostly the residences of Liverpool merchants. Here is St Paul's Church. *Territorials:* Lancashire and Cheshire RGA.

Seaford Sussex coastal town served by the London, Brighton & South Coast Railway to the east of Brighton. Visitors staying at the esplanade hotel, which opened in 1907, will be sure to look at the medieval St Leonard's Church, the iron age hill fort and the Napoleonic Martello Tower. *Territorials:* Sussex Fortress Engineers and Seaford College Cadet Company.

Seaham Harbour The harbour, and the town that grew up around it, were built by Lord Londonderry from 1828 to handle the coal produced in his collieries. There was also large works making bottles and chemicals. Here is St John's Church which was completed in 1841. *Territorials:* 3rd Northumbrian Brigade RFA.

Seaton Burn Northumberland mining village six miles from Newcastle-upon-Tyne. *Territorials:* 5th Northumberland Fusiliers.

Seaton Delaval Small Northumberland mining town, six miles from Tynemouth, served by the North Eastern Railway. Here, in the grounds of the estate belonging to the Vanburgh's, is the little chapel of Our Lady. *Territorials:* Tynemouth RGA.

Seaview Coastal village on the Isle of Wight, three miles from Ryde. *Territorials:* 8th Hampshire Regiment.

Sedbergh West Riding of Yorkshire market town, ten miles from Kendal, served by the London & North Western Railway. There were woollen mills in the area. Here is the church of St Andrew and St Gregory the Great, and Sedbergh School, which maintain an OTC contingent. *Territorials:* 4th Border Regiment.

Sedlescombe Sussex village just over two miles from the railway at Battle. Here is the church of St John the Baptist. *Territorials:* 5th Royal Sussex Regiment.

Selborne Hampshire village four miles from Alton. Here is St Mary's Church where much remembered is the Revd Gilbert White (1720–93) who wrote *The Natural History of Selborne* in 1788. You may miss his grave which is marked simply 'G. W. 1793'. *Territorials:* 4th Hampshire Regiment.

Selby West Riding of Yorkshire market town on the River Ouse, fifteen miles from York, served by the North Eastern Railway. At Selby Abbey can be seen the name of John de Washington, and in one of the windows, the stars and stripes from his family coat of arms. *Territorials:* 5th West Yorkshire Regiment.

Selkirk County town of Selkirkshire, six miles from Galashiels, well known once for its production of woollen goods, tweeds, tartans and shawls. Here are statues to Sir Walter Scott, sheriff of the county 1800 until 1832, and the explorer Mungo Park who was born nearby. Selkirk was at the termination of a branch ran by the North British Railway which came down from Galashiels and opened in 1856. *Territorials:* Lothians and Border Horse and 4th King's Own Scottish Borderers.

Semley Wiltshire village, three miles from Shaftesbury, served by the London & South Western Railway. Here is St Leonard's Church. *Territorials:* 1st South Western Mounted Brigade Transport and Supply Column.

Send Surrey village on the River Wey three miles from Guildford. Here is St Mary's Church. *Territorials:* 5th Queen's Royal West Surrey Regiment.

Settle West Riding of Yorkshire market town on the River Ribble, fourteen miles from Skipton, served by the Midland Railway. Here is the church of the Holy Ascension which was built in 1838. *Territorials:* 6th Duke of Wellington's Regiment and Settle Cadet Battalion.

Settrington East Riding of Yorkshire village, three miles from Malton, served by the North Eastern Railway. Here is All Saints Church. *Territorials:* East Riding Yeomanry.

Seven Sisters Glamorgan mining village, nine miles from Neath, so named after a colliery was opened in the area in 1872; its owner having seven daughters. The Neath & Brecon Railway arrived in 1876. *Territorials:* Brecknockshire Battalion.

Sevenoaks Market town in Kent, seven miles from Tonbridge, served by the South Eastern & Chatham Railway. At the west end of the north aisle of St Nicholas's Church can be seen monuments to Captain Multon Lambarde, an early Volunteer at Sevenoaks, and his family. *Territorials:* West Kent Yeomanry and 4th Royal West Kent Regiment.

Shaftesbury Dorset market town, ten miles from Blandford Forum, well known for its steep cobbled streets – Gold Hill in particular having found its way into films and advertisements. The town was served by the London & South Western Railway's Semley station to the north-east. Here, next to the Town Hall in the High Street, is the fifteenth-century St Peter's Church and at the bottom end of town, St James's which was built 1866–67. *Territorials:* Dorsetshire Yeomanry and 4th Dorsetshire Regiment.

Shanklin Seaside resort on the south coast of the Isle of Wight, nine miles from Ryde, served by the Isle of Wight Railway. Looking for quiet and 'discipline' in his writing, Charles Darwen stayed at Norfolk House in Shanklin for eighteen months and worked on his *Origin of Species*. Here, in Regent Street, is St Paul's Church where you will find the bell from HMS *Eurydice*, sank off Dunnose Point in 1878 and the subject of a poem by Gerrard Manley Hopkins. *Territorials:* 8th Hampshire Regiment and Shanklin Cadet Company.

Shapinsay Island in the Orkneys, four miles from Kirkwall. *Territorials:* Orkney RGA.

Sheerness Holiday resort on the River Medway, Isle of Sheppy in Kent, served by the South Eastern & Chatham Railway. Once a naval establishment and dockyard. Opened in April 1903, with its chocolate and cream vehicles, was the Sheerness & District Tramways service with routes radiating from the town's Clock Tower. Here, on the south side of Broadway since 1836, stands Holy Trinity Church and, at the eastern end, the Roman Catholic St Henry and St Elizabeth's which opened in 1864. *Territorials:* Royal East Kent Yeomanry, Kent RGA and 4th Buffs East Kent Regiment.

Sheffield West Riding of Yorkshire manufacturing city on the River Don, well known for its production of steel. Cutlery and precision tools have been made here since the fourteenth century. Here, at the University of Sheffield, there was an OTC contingent, also at the King Edward VII School. *Territorials:* 3rd West Riding Infantry Brigade, Yorkshire Dragoons, 3rd West Riding Brigade RFA, West Riding Divisional Engineers, West Riding Divisional Telegraph/Signal Company, 4th York and Lancaster Regiment, 3rd West Riding Field Ambulance and 3rd Northern General Hospital.

Shefford Bedfordshire market town on the River Ivel, nine miles from Bedford, served by the Midland Railway. Here are the churches of St Michael and St Francis. *Territorials:* Bedfordshire Yeomanry.

Sheil Bridge Locality ten miles from Lochalsh, Ross and Cromarty. *Territorials:* 1st Lovat's Scouts.

Shelton District of Stoke-on-Trent. Here is St Mark's Church. *Territorials:* 2nd North Midland Brigade RFA.

Shepherds Bush West London district in the borough of Hammersmith. Here is St Thomas's Church. *Territorials:* 7th London Brigade RFA.

Shepshed Leicestershire village, five miles from Loughborough, reached by the railway when the Charnwood Forest Company opened its line between Loughborough and Coalville in 1883. Here at St Botolph's Church there are memorials to the Phillipps family. *Territorials:* 5th Leicestershire Regiment.

Shepton Mallet Somerset market town, five miles from Wells, once important in the cloth trade, and later cider. The East Somerset Railway arrived in 1858, the Somerset & Dorset in 1874. Here at St Peter and St Paul's Church there are monuments to the Strode and Barnard families. *Territorials:* North Somerset Yeomanry, Somerset RHA and 4th Somerset Light Infantry.

Sherborne Dorset market town on the River Yeo, six miles from Yeovil, served by the London & South Western Railway. Long associated with Sherborne, the Digby family of Sherborne Castle have numerous monuments in the town, the Rev Richard H W Digby being and an early chaplain to the local Volunteers. Here is Sherborne Abbey, founded in AD705, and Sherborne School which maintained an OTC contingent. *Territorials:* Dorsetshire Yeomanry and 4th Dorsetshire Regiment.

Sherburn Hill Durham colliery village three miles from Durham. *Territorials:* 8th Durham Light Infantry.

Shere Surrey village six miles from Dorking. Here is the mainly twelfth-century St James's Church where Christine 'the Hermit', her father a local carpenter, was walled up in a cell. The village was served by the South Eastern & Chatham Railway, its station called Gomshall and Shere. Here is St James's Church. *Territorials:* 5th Queen's Royal West Surrey Regiment.

Sheriff Hutton North Riding of Yorkshire village nine miles from Malton. Here is St Helen's Church. *Territorials:* 5th Yorkshire Regiment.

Sheringham Norfolk seaside town and fishing port, four miles from Cromer, served by the Midland & Great Northern Joint Railway. Here is All Saints Church. *Territorials:* 5th Norfolk Regiment.

Shettleston Eastern suburb of Glasgow where the population were mostly employed in collieries. *Territorials:* Lowland Divisional Engineers.

Shifnal Shropshire market town, ten miles from Bridgnorth, served by the Great Western Railway. Here at St Andrew's Church there are memorials to the Briggs family. *Territorials:* Shropshire Yeomanry and 4th King's Shropshire Light Infantry.

Shildon Durham market town, nine miles from Darlington, served by the Stockton & Darlington Railway, where many were employed in local collieries, ironworks and by the railway. Built here was the locomotive *Sanspareil*, which took part in the Edge Hill trials against Stephenson's *Rocket*. Here is St John's Church. *Territorials:* 2nd Northumbrian Field Ambulance.

Shipley West Riding of Yorkshire town on the River Aire and the Leeds and Liverpool Canal, three miles from Bradford and served by the Great Northern and Midland railways. Here is St Paul's Church, and a Roman Catholic church dedicated to St Walburga. *Territorials:* West Riding Divisional Transport and Supply Column and 2nd West Riding Field Ambulance.

Shipston-on-Stour Worcestershire market town at the termination of the Great Western Railway's branch opened from Moreton-in-Marsh in 1889. Here is St Edmund's Church. *Territorials:* 5th Gloucestershire Regiment.

Shipton-under-Wychwood Oxfordshire village on the River Evenlode, seven miles from Chipping Norton, served by the Great Western Railway. Here is St Mary's Church. *Territorials:* Oxfordshire Yeomanry and 4th Oxfordshire and Buckinghamshire Light Infantry.

Shireoaks West Riding of Yorkshire village on the Chesterfield Canal, two miles from Worksop, served by the Great Central and Midland railways. Many from the area were employed in collieries. Here is St Luke's Church. *Territorials:* 8th Sherwood Foresters.

Shirley Suburb of Southampton. *Territorials:* 5th Hampshire Regiment.

Shoreditch District of East London within the borough of Hackney. Here is St Leonard's Church which was rebuilt in 1740. *Territorials:* 4th, 7th London Regiment, London Mounted Brigade Transport and Supply Column and 2nd London Field Ambulance.

Shoreham Sussex coastal town at the mouth of the River Adur and served by the South Eastern & Chatham Railway. Here is Old Shoreham, where a few old cottages are gathered around St Nicholas's Church and the river is crossed by a wooden bridge; and New Shoreham with its busy port and church dedicated to St Mary de Haura. At Lancing College, there were three OTC infantry companies. *Territorials*: 1st Home Counties Brigade RFA.

Shotts Lanarkshire village, seven miles from Motherwell, served by the North British Railway. Here much of the population were employed in the Shotts Ironworks. *Territorials:* 8th Highland Light Infantry.

Shrewsbury Served by both the Great Western and London & North Western railways, the town gave employment in its breweries, iron foundry, tannery, timber yards, saw mills and glass-staining works. Here, on the edge of town, is St Chad's Church, the main part of the building being completely circular. Here too is Shrewsbury Abbey which sits, with busy traffic running on both sides, looking down Thomas Telford's new road of 1836 onto English Bridge and the River Severn. Shrewsbury School maintained three OTC infantry companies. *Territorials:* Welsh Division, Welsh Border Mounted Brigade, Welsh Border Infantry Brigade, Shropshire Yeomanry, Shropshire RHA, Welsh Border Mounted Brigade Signal Troop and 4th King's Shropshire Light Infantry.

Sidcup Kent suburb of London, twelve miles by rail from Charring Cross on the South Eastern & Chatham Railway. Here, on Church Road and built 1899–1901, is St John's Church, and in Main Road, Christ Church which also opened in 1901. Sidcup Hall School, had an OTC contingent of one infantry company. *Territorials:* 5th Royal West Kent Regiment.

Sidmouth Devon seaside resort and market town fifteen miles from Exeter. The Sidmouth Railway Company opened its line in 1874. Here is St Nicholas's Church. *Territorials:* Royal 1st Devon Yeomanry and 4th Devonshire Regiment.

Silchester Hampshire village eight miles from Basingstoke. Here is St Mary's Church. *Territorials:* 4th Hampshire Regiment.

Silksworth Durham village three miles from Sunderland. Here is St Matthew's Church which opened in 1871. *Territorials:* 3rd Northumbrian Brigade RFA.

Silverdale Lancashire village on Morecambe Bay, eleven miles from Lancaster, on the Furness Railway between Arnside and Carnforth. Here is St John's Church which was built in 1886. *Territorials:* 5th King's Own Royal Lancaster Regiment.

Silverton Devon village, eight miles from Exeter, served by the Great Western Railway. A number from the village worked in local paper mills. Here is St Mary's Church. *Territorials:* 7th Devonshire Regiment.

Silvertown Just four miles from London's St Paul's Cathedral, Silvertown's church of St Mark was opened in 1863. The town takes its name from the india-rubber works founded by the firm of Silver. Sugar is refilled there, chemicals and soap were also manufactured. *Territorials:* 7th Essex Regiment and 3rd East Anglian Field Ambulance.

Sirhowy Monmouthshire village with extensive ironworks, one mile from Tredegar and served by the London & North Western Railway. *Territorials:* 3rd Monmouthshire Regiment.

Sittingbourne Port and market town, nine miles from Rochester in Kent, served by the South Eastern & Chatham Railway. In the 1890s, more than 6,000 from the area were employed in the manufacture of bricks and cement. The town was also important in the production of paper. Here is St Michael's Church. *Territorials:* Royal East Kent Yeomanry and 4th Buffs East Kent Regiment.

Skeabost Hamlet at the head of Loch Snizort, Isle of Skye, Inverness-shore, eight miles from Portree. *Territorials:* 1st Lovat's Scouts.

Skegness Lincolnshire town, twelve miles from Spilsby, which developed as a seaside resort in the 1870s. The railway arriving in 1873 after the Wainfleet & Frisby branch of the Great Northern extended the line. Here is the old church of St Clement and, built in 1880, St Matthew's. *Territorials:* Lincolnshire Yeomanry, 5th Lincolnshire Regiment and No1 Company 3rd Lincoln Cadet Battalion.

Skelton North Riding of Yorkshire village five miles from Redcar. Here are All Saints and St Giles's Churches. *Territorials:* 4th Yorkshire Regiment.

Skene Aberdeenshire hamlet eight miles from Aberdeen. *Territorials:* 7th Gordon Highlanders.

Skilmafilly Location seven miles from Ellon, Aberdeenshire. *Territorials:* 5th Gordon Highlanders.

Skipton-in-Craven West Riding of Yorkshire cotton and textile town, nine miles from Keighley, served by the Midland Railway. *Cassell's* notes that extensive mills on the Broughton Road gave employment to some 1,200 in the 1890s. Here is Holy Trinity Church. *Territorials:* 2nd West Riding Infantry Brigade and 6th Duke of Wellington's Regiment.

Slaithwaite West Riding of Yorkshire town on the River Colne, five miles from Huddersfield on the London & North Western Railway, once an important textile producing area. Here is St James's Church. *Territorials:* 7th Duke of Wellington's Regiment.

Sleaford Lincolnshire market town on the River Slea, eighteen miles from Lincoln, served by the Great Northern and Great Eastern railways. Here, at St Denys Church to the east of Market Place, are memorials to the Carr, Seller and Taylor families. *Territorials:* Lincolnshire Yeomanry and 4th Lincolnshire Regiment.

Sledmere East Riding of Yorkshire village, eight miles from Driffield in the heart of the Wolds. Sledmere station (called Sledmere and Fimber from 1859) was opened by the Malton & Driffield Junction Railway (later part of the North Eastern) in 1853. Well known here are the Sykes family who are remembered in St Mary's Church. *Territorials:* 5th Yorkshire Regiment.

Sleetburn Colliery village, three miles from Durham, where the New Brancepeth Coal Company started by Alex Brodie Cochrane in 1856 provided employment. *Territorials:* 8th Durham Light Infantry.

Slough Buckinghamshire market town, two miles from Windsor, served by the Great Western Railway – a new station replacing Brunel's 1841 original in 1886. Here is the red-brick St Mary's Church which was opened in 1876. *Territorials:* Buckinghamshire Battalion.

Smarden Town in Kent, ten miles from Ashford on the River Beult. Here is the large St Michael's Church, called locally 'the Barn of Kent'. *Territorials:* 5th Buffs East Kent Regiment.

Smethwick Staffordshire industrial town on the Birmingham and Dudley & Wolverhampton canals. *Cassell's* notes that in the 1890s 'the glass, chemical and lighthouse works' employed upwards of 2,000 people, with a machine works providing jobs for 2,000 more. The London & North Western Railway served the town. *Territorials:* North Midland Divisional Engineers.

Snaith West Riding of Yorkshire market town on the River Aire, seven miles from Goole, served by the Lancashire & Yorkshire Railway. Here is St Lawrence's Church. *Territorials:* Yorkshire Dragoons.

Snodland Kent village on the River Medway, six miles from Rochester, served by the South Eastern Railway. Here was a paper mill, and at All Saints Church there are memorials to the Palmer, Tilgham and Waghorn families. *Territorials:* 1st Home Counties Field Ambulance.

Soho District of West London. *Territorials:* St Ann's School Cadet Corps.

Sollas Locality ten miles from Lochmaddy, North Uist Island, Outer Hebrides. *Territorials:* 1st Lovat's Scouts.

Somersham Huntingdonshire village, five miles from St Ives, served by the Great Northern & Great Eastern Joint Railway. Here is St John's Church. *Territorials:* Bedfordshire Yeomanry.

Somerton Somerset town, seven miles from Glastonbury, reached by the Great Western Railway in 1906. Somerton had a factory making shirt collars. Here is St Michael's Church. *Territorials:* 5th Somerset Light Infantry.

South Baddesley Hampshire village two miles from Lymington. Here is St Mary's Church. *Territorials:* 7th Hampshire Regiment.

South Bank Locality in North Riding of Yorkshire three miles from Middlesborough. Here is St John's Church. *Territorials:* 4th Yorkshire Regiment.

South Hayling Hampshire village, four miles from Havant, reached by the railway when the London & South Western opened its branch from Havant in 1867. Here is St Mary's Church. *Territorials:* 6th Hampshire Regiment.

South Molton Devon market town on the River Mole, twelve miles from Barnstaple, served by the London & South Western Railway. There was a Civil War engagement here that saw three hours of street fighting on 14 March 1655. Here is the church of St Mary Magdalene and the West Buckland School, which had an OTC contingent of one infantry company. *Territorials:* Royal North Devon Yeomanry and 6th Devonshire Regiment.

South Petherton Somerset town on the River Parret five miles from Crewkerne. Here is St Peter and St Paul's Church. *Territorials:* West Somerset Yeomanry and 5th Somerset Light Infantry.

South Queensferry Small town on the Firth of Forth in Linlithgowshire, served by the North British Railway. *Territorials:* Lothians and Border Horse.

South Ronaldshay Island, part of the Orkneys, ten miles from Kirkwall. Here are the churches of St Peter and St Mary. *Territorials:* Orkney RGA.

South Shields Durham industrial and shipbuilding town on the Tyne, seven miles from Newcastle and served by the North Eastern Railway. There was also a short line that ran out to Marsden and the Whitburn Colliery there. Unveiled on 8 May 1913 in front of the Town Hall in Westoe Road, was Albert Toft's monument to Queen Victoria. Here is St Hilda's Church. *Territorials:* Northumberland Yeomanry, 4th Northumbrian Brigade RFA and 7th Durham Light Infantry.

South Shore Suburb of Blackpool. *Territorials:* Arnold House School Cadet Corps.

South Wingfield Derbyshire village, ten miles from Chesterfield, served by the Midland Railway. Here is All Saints Church. *Territorials:* 6th Sherwood Foresters.

Southall Middlesex market town, six miles from Uxbridge, served by the Great Western Railway. Martinware pottery was produced here 1877–1923. *Territorials:* 8th Middlesex Regiment.

Southam Warwickshire market town seven miles from Leamington, its station being opened by the London & North Western Railway in 1895. Here is St James's Church. *Territorials:* Warwickshire Yeomanry.

Southampton Hampshire seaport and market town. At Southampton, the Cunard offices were opened in 1899 and still remain in the town; as does South Western House, the once South Western Hotel of the London and South Western Railway which was completed in 1872. But dating from 1070, St Michael's Church is the oldest building in the town. The Southampton Tramways Company opened its service in May 1879. *Territorials:* Hampshire Infantry Brigade, Hampshire Yeomanry, Hampshire RHA, Hampshire RGA, 5th, 9th Hampshire Regiment and 3rd Wessex Field Ambulance.

Southborough Town two miles from Tunbridge Wells in Kent, its station opened by the South Eastern & Chatham Railway in March 1893. Here is St Peter's Church, built 1830–31; Christ Church, opened 1871 in Prospect Road, and St Thomas's which was built in Pennington Road 1860–61. *Territorials:* Kent Fortress Engineers and 1st Cadet Battalion Kent Fortress Engineers.

Southend Village on the Kintyre Peninsular, nine miles from Campbeltown, Argyllshire. *Territorials:* 8th Argyll and Sutherland Highlanders.

Southend-on-Sea Essex seaside resort on the Thames estuary served by the Midland and Great Eastern railways. Opening in July 1901 was the Corporation's tramway service which operated from a point close to the railway station. Here is the church of St John the Baptist, built in 1840, and in yellow brick, St Erkenwald's of 1905. *Territorials:* Essex Yeomanry, Essex and Suffolk RGA, 3rd East Anglian Field Ambulance and Southend Technical School (later called Southend High School) Cadet Corps.

Southminster Essex village ten miles from Maldon and the termination of the Great Eastern branch opened from Woodham Ferris in 1889. Here is St Leonard's Church. *Territorials:* 4th Essex Regiment.

Southport Lancashire seaside resort, eighteen miles from Liverpool, served by the Lancashire & Yorkshire Railway. Guides usually note how Southport contained a great number of well-built residences belonging to wealthy merchants and manufactures. Victorian editions refer to Southport's churches as 'modern'. *Territorials:* 7th King's Liverpool Regiment, West Lancashire Divisional Transport and Supply Column and Southport Cadet Corps.

Southwark London borough on the south bank of the Thames, work beginning on Southwark Bridge across to the City in 1912. Here is Southwark Cathedral. *Territorials:* 1st (Queen's) Cadet Battalion London Regiment (later called 1st Cadet Battalion Queen's Royal Surrey Regiment).

Southwell Nottinghamshire market town, seven miles from Newark, served by the Midland Railway. Here is Southwell Cathedral. *Territorials:* Nottinghamshire Yeomanry (South Notts) and 8th Sherwood Foresters.

Southwold Suffolk port, resort and market town, twelve miles from Lowestoft. The railway arrived when the Southwold Company opened its branch across from the East Suffolk Railway at Halesworth in 1879. An extension being made to the harbour in 1914. Here is St Edmund's Church. *Territorials:* 6th Suffolk Regiment.

Sowerby Bridge West Riding of Yorkshire town on the River Calder and at the termination of the Rochdale Canal. Served by the Lancashire & Yorkshire Railway, Sowerby Bridge is four miles from Halifax. Here is Christ Church. *Territorials:* 4th Duke of Wellington's Regiment.

Spalding Lincolnshire port and market town on the River Welland, fourteen miles from Boston, served by the Midland & Great Northern Joint Railway. Here at St Mary and St Nicholas's Church are memorials to the Johnson family, two more recent churches being St John's, opened in 1873, and St Peter's in 1875. The Catholic church in Henrietta Street was built in 1876, then enlarged in 1879. *Territorials:* 4th Lincolnshire Regiment.

Sparkbrook Suburb of Birmingham on the Rive Cole and served by the Great Western Railway. In 1913, Albert Toft's memorial to King Edward VII was unveiled in Highgate Park. Here is Christ Church. *Territorials:* 1st South Midland Mounted Brigade Transport and Supply Column.

Spean Bridge Inverness-shire hamlet of the River Spean, ten miles from Fort William, and the location in 1745 of the first engagement of the Jacobite Rising. The first bridge here was one of General Wade's, built in 1736, the second being by Telford in 1819. Spean Bridge station was opened by the West Highland Railway in 1894. *Territorials:* 1st Lovat's Scouts.

Spennymoor Industrial town, six miles from Durham, served by the North Eastern Railway. One local employer was the Weardale Steel Coal and Coke Company. Here is St Paul's Church. *Territorials:* Northumberland Yeomanry and 6th Durham Light Infantry.

Spilsby Lincolnshire market town eight miles from Alford, the railway arriving in 1868 when the Spilsby & Firsby Company opened a branch between those two locations. In the town is a statue to Arctic explorer Sir John Franklin (1786–1847) who was born in Spilsby. Here is St James's Church. *Territorials:* Lincolnshire Yeomanry and 5th Lincolnshire Regiment.

Springburn Suburb of Glasgow served by the North British Railway. *Territorials:* 3rd Lowland Brigade RFA.

Staddlethorpe North Riding of Yorkshire hamlet, seven miles from Howden, served by the North Eastern Railway. *Territorials:* 5th East Yorkshire Regiment.

Staffin Village on Skye, Inner Hebrides, eighteen miles from Portree. *Territorials:* 1st Lovat's Scouts.

Stafford County and market town on the River Sow where the manufacture of boots and shoes once provided a main source of employment. But before that, it was wool and cloth. Stafford is also an important railway centre. Born here in 1593 was Izaak Walton. Here is St Mary's Church, St Chad's in Greengate Street, and St Thomas's in South Street. *Territorials:* Staffordshire Infantry Brigade, Staffordshire Yeomanry, 3rd North Midland Brigade RFA and 6th North Staffordshire Regiment.

Staindrop Durham village eight miles from Bishop Auckland. Here is St Mary's Church. *Territorials:* 6th Durham Light Infantry.

Staines Middlesex market town on the Thames, six miles from Windsor, served by the Great Western and London & South Western railways. There were breweries here, and a factory making linoleum. Here is St Mary's Church and, in Laleham Road, St Peter's which was built in 1893. *Territorials:* 8th Middlesex Regiment.

Stalbridge Dorset market town, seven miles from Sherborne, once famous for its gloves. The railway reached Stalbridge in the form of the Dorset Central line in August 1863. Here is St Mary's Church. *Territorials:* Dorsetshire Yeomanry.

Stalham Norfolk town, eight miles from North Walsham, its station opened by the Yarmouth & North Norfolk Railway in 1880. Here is St Mary's Church where there are memorials to the Riches family. *Territorials:* Norfolk Yeomanry.

Stalybridge Former Cheshire cotton town, on the River Tame seven miles from Manchester, served by the London & North Western and Great Central railways. *Territorials:* 6th Cheshire Regiment.

Stamford Lincolnshire market town on the River Welland, sixteen miles from Peterborough, served by the London & South Western and Great Northern railways. Stamford had a large works building carts and road wagons. Here, with its 'Arts and Crafts' stained glass, is St Mary's Church where buried in the churchyard is Daniel Lambert who, at fifty-two stone when he died in 1809, is on record as the largest Englishman ever. *Territorials:* Lincolnshire Yeomanry and 4th Lincolnshire Regiment.

Stamford Bridge East Riding of Yorkshire town on the River Derwent, nine miles from York, served by the North Eastern Railway. *Territorials:* 5th Yorkshire Regiment.

Stanhope Large Durham village sixteen miles up the Wear Valley by the North Eastern Railway from Bishop Auckland. Once an important centre for lead mining and iron smelting, one visitor in 1913 noted Stanhope as 'quiet, almost sleepy … a town living in the past'. Here is the medieval church of St Thomas. *Territorials:* 6th Durham Light Infantry.

Stanley (Durham) Mining town, nine miles from Newcastle-upon-Tyne. A major employer in Stanley was the West Stanley Colliery, its Burns Pit being the scene of a disaster on 16 February 1909 in which 168 men and boys were killed. *Territorials:* Northumberland Yeomanry and 8th Durham Light Infantry.

Stanley (Perthshire) Village on the Tay, six miles from Perth, served by the Caledonian Railway. Stanley grew from the several cotton mills that were established in 1785. *Territorials:* 6th Black Watch.

Stanmer Sussex village four miles from Brighton. Here is the seat of the Pelham family, the flint-built church of 1838 having no dedication. *Territorials:* 5th Royal Sussex Regiment.

Stanmore Middlesex village served by a London & North Western branch that opened in 1890 between Stanmore and Harrow (two miles). Here is St John's Church. *Territorials:* 9th Middlesex Regiment.

Stansted Mountfitchet Essex village on the River Stort three miles from Bishop Stortford. Here is the Norman St Mary's Church and, built in 1889, St John's. *Territorials:* 8th Essex Regiment.

Staplecross Sussex village four miles from Battle. *Territorials:* 5th Royal Sussex Regiment.

Staplehurst Kent village, nine miles from Maidstone, served by the South Easter & Chatham Railway. Here is All Saints Church. *Territorials:* 5th Buffs East Kent Regiment.

Starbeck West Riding of Yorkshire hamlet. two miles from Harrogate, served by the North Eastern Railway. Here is St Andrew's Church. *Territorials:* 5th West Yorkshire Regiment.

Staunton-on-Wye Herefordshire village thirteen miles from Leominster. Here is St Mary's Church. *Territorials:* Welsh Divisional Transport and Supply Column.

Staveley (Derbyshire) Large village, five miles from Chester, served by the Midland Railway. Many were employed here in local collieries, there was also a long established brush manufacturer, as well as another firm that made spades and shovels. Here is St John's Church where there are memorials to the Frencheville family, one of them (Peter), had fifteen children with his wife Maud. *Territorials:* 6th Sherwood Foresters.

Staveley (Westmorland) Village on the River Kent four miles from Kendal. Here is St James's Church. *Territorials:* 4th Border Regiment.

Steeple Ashton Wiltshire village four miles from Trowbridge. Here is St Mary's Church, thought to be the most richly decorated in Wiltshire. But still to be seen is damage caused when the spire collapsed in October 1670. *Territorials:* 4th Wiltshire Regiment.

Stenhousemuir Stirlingshire village on the River Carron served by the Caledonian Railway at Larbert station just to the south-west. *Territorials:* 7th Argyll and Sutherland Highlanders.

Stepney East London borough on the Thames. *Territorials:* Rutland Street (LCC) School Cadet Corps.

Stevenage Small Hertfordshire town, four miles from Hitchin, served by the Great Northern Railway. Here is the fifteenth-century flint and stone-built St Nicholas's Church almost isolated on high ground to the north-east of the town. *Territorials:* Hertfordshire Regiment.

Stewarton (Argyllshire) Locality six miles from Campbeltown, Kintyre. *Territorials:* 8th Argyll and Sutherland Highlanders.

Stewarton (Ayrshire) Village on Annick Water, five miles from Kilmarnock, served by the Caledonian and Glasgow & South Western Joint Railway. The carpet industry gave much employment, as did the production of headgear both for civilian and military use. *Territorials:* 4th Royal Scots Fusiliers.

Steyning Sussex town, four miles from Shoreham, served by the London, Brighton & South Coast Railway. Here is St Andrew's Church, late Norman and considered to be the best in Sussex. *Territorials:* 4th Royal Sussex Regiment.

Sticklepath Devon village four miles from Oakhampton. *Territorials:* 6th Devonshire Regiment.

Stirling County and market town on the Forth served by the Caledonian and North British railways. Carpets, tartans, tweeds and shawls were made in the town, two businesses also producing iron bedsteads and carriages. Down the hill from Stirling Castle is the Church of the Holy Rood where, in 1567, was held the coronation of the infant King of Scotland, James VI. Before that, Stirling Bridge was the scene in 1297 of the battle between the Scots and English – a victory for Wallace. *Territorials:* Argyll and Sutherland Infantry Brigade, Fife and Forfar Yeomanry, 7th Argyll and Sutherland Highlanders and Highland Divisional Transport and Supply Column.

Stockport Cheshire town on the River Mersey, it's main employment being in cotton; but there were also foundries, machine works and breweries. On the Lower Peak Forest Canal near Stockport is the Marple Aqueduct which was completed in 1800 after seven years work, seven men being killed during its construction. Here is the medieval St Mary's Church, St Peter's of 1768, and St George's which was completed in 1897. *Territorials:* Cheshire Yeomanry, 6th Cheshire Regiment and 1st Territorial Cadet Battalion Cheshire Regiment.

Stockton-on-Tees Durham port and industrial town ten miles from Hartlepool. The North Eastern Railway employed many at Stockton, there was also shipbuilding yards, iron and brass foundries, brick yards and several firms making maritime equipment. The Royalists, in July 1644, surrender to the Scots at Stockton. *Territorials:* 5th Durham Light Infantry.

Stoke Ferry Norfolk village on the River Wissey, fourteen miles from King's Lynn at the termination of the Great Eastern Railway's branch opened in 1882 from Denver Road Gate. Here is All Saints Church. *Territorials:* 5th Norfolk Regiment.

Stoke-on-Trent Staffordshire town on the River Trent and Trent and Mersey Canal, two miles from Newcastle-under-Lyme and served by the North Staffordshire Railway. The potteries were important to the town, a statue of Josiah Wedgwood being erected facing the railway station in 1863. Here is St Peter's Church where he is again remembered. *Territorials:* Staffordshire Yeomanry, 2nd North Midland Brigade RFA, North Midland RGA and 5th North Staffordshire Regiment.

Stoke Works Worcestershire hamlet, three miles from Bromsgrove, served by the Midland Railway. *Territorials:* 8th Worcestershire Regiment.

Stokenchurch Oxfordshire village on the Buckinghamshire border, seven miles from Wycombe. Here is St Peter and St Paul's Church. *Territorials:* Buckinghamshire Yeomanry.

Stokesley North Riding of Yorkshire market town on the River Leven, ten miles from Stockton-on-Tees. with railway station of the North Eastern line. Here is St Peter and St Paul's Church. *Territorials:* 4th Yorkshire Regiment.

Stone Staffordshire market town on the River Trent and Trent and Mersey Canal, the latter running through the town parallel with its High Street. Here is St Michael's Church which has a memorial to Captain Viscount St Vincent who was mortally wounded at Abu Klea, Sudan, in 1885. Stone station was served by the North Staffordshire Railway. *Territorials:* 5th North Staffordshire Regiment.

Stone Easton Somerset village eight miles from Wells. Here, at St Mary's Church, are memorials to the Hippisley family. *Territorials:* North Somerset Yeomanry.

Stonehaven Port and county town of Kincardineshire on Stonehaven Bay at the influx of the Carron and Cowie. Fifteen miles from Aberdeen, Stonehaven station was served by the Caledonian Railway. *Territorials:* 7th Gordon Highlanders.

Stonehouse Lanarkshire village on Avon Water, eight miles from Hamilton, with railway station on the Caledonian. Here, notes the guides, the inhabitants were mostly engaged in hand-loom weaving and mining. *Territorials:* 8th Highland Light Infantry.

Stoney Middleton Derbyshire village four miles from Bakewell. Here is St Martin's Church with its small octagonal tower of 1759. *Territorials:* 6th Sherwood Foresters.

Stony Stratford Buckinghamshire market town on the River Ouse and border with Northamptonshire, eight miles from Buckingham. Many from the town were employed by the London & Birmingham Railway's works at Wolverton. A tram service to get them to and from work being opened in May 1887. Here is St Giles's Church, rebuilt in 1776 after a fire destroyed much of the eastern half of the town in 1742. Familiar to residents would be the town's two old coaching inns, the 'Cock' and the 'Bull', where stories from travellers grew in the telling. Hence the expression 'a cock and bull story'. *Territorials:* Buckinghamshire Yeomanry and 2nd South Midland Mounted Brigade Field Ambulance.

Stornoway Fishing port on Lewis Island, Outer Hebrides. *Territorials:* 4th Highland Brigade RGA and North Scottish RGA.

Storrington Small Sussex town five miles from Pulborough. Here is the church of St Mary the Virgin. *Territorials:* 4th Royal Sussex Regiment.

Stourbridge Worcestershire industrial and market town on the River Stour, five miles from Dudley, served by the Great Western. The town was known for its manufacture of glass and fire-bricks, many also employed in the production of nails, tools, chains and anvils. Here is St Thomas's Church of 1728–36. *Territorials:* 7th Worcestershire Regiment.

Stourport Worcestershire industrial and market town, four miles from Kidderminster, served by the Great Western Railway. Here the River Severn meets the Stour and the Staffordshire and Worcestershire Canal which was built by Brindley in 1766–71. At Stourport, carpets were made; the not far off Wilden ironworks, owned by the father of Prime Minister Stanley Baldwin, also employing many. Here is St Michael's Church on which work began in 1881. *Territorials:* 7th Worcestershire Regiment.

Stow Midlothian village on Gala Water, seven miles from Galashiels, with railway station on the North British line. Here several woollen producing factories gave employment. *Territorials:* Lothians and Border Horse.

Stow-on-the-Wold Gloucestershire market town on the high Cotswolds, sixteen miles from Cheltenham, with railway station on the Great Western. Here at St Edward's Church during the Civil War, over 1,000 Royalist prisoners were imprisoned. *Territorials:* 5th Gloucestershire Regiment and 4th Oxfordshire and Buckinghamshire Light Infantry.

Stowmarket Suffolk market town on the River Gipping, twelve miles from Ipswich, with railway station on the Great Eastern Line. Stowmarket carried on a considerable trade in corn, malt, coal, slate and timber. Here is the cathedral-like church of St Peter and St Paul. *Territorials:* Suffolk Yeomanry, 5th and 6th Suffolk Regiment.

Strachur Village on Loch Fyne, Argyllshire, five miles from Inveraray. *Territorials:* 8th Argyll and Sutherland Highlanders.

Stranraer Wigtownshire village at the head of Loch Ryan, eight miles from Portpatrick, served by the Glasgow & South Western and Portpatrick & Wigtownshire Joint Railway. *Territorials:* 2nd Lowland Brigade RFA and 5th Royal Scots Fusiliers.

Stratford Eastern suburb of London within Essex, two miles from St Paul's on the River Lea. A railway town, the old Eastern Counties (later Great Eastern) having a works here employing some 5,000 since the 1840s. *Territorials:* Essex Yeomanry, 2nd East Anglian Brigade RFA, Essex and Suffolk RGA, East Anglian RGA and East Anglian Divisional Transport and Supply Column.

Stratford-upon-Avon Warwickshire market town and busy railway junction, eight miles from Warwick. Here is Holy Trinity Church and the tomb of William Shakespeare – but here too are remembered the Clopton family who as medieval clothiers brought much wealth to the town. The Shakespeare Memorial Statue presented by Lord Gower was unveiled in 1888. *Territorials:* Warwickshire Yeomanry.

Strathaven Lanarkshire market town of Avon Water, fifteen miles from Glasgow, served by the Caledonian Railway. Here, silk, cotton and hosiery goods were manufactured. *Territorials:* 6th Cameronians.

Strathbraun Perthshire locality four miles from Birnam. *Territorials:* 6th Black Watch.

Strathcanaird Ross-shire crofting township seven miles from Ullapool. *Territorials:* 2nd Lovat's Scouts.

Strathcarron Ross and Cromarty village seven miles from Strome Ferry. Strathcarron station was opened by the Dingwell & Skye Railway in 1870. *Territorials:* 2nd Lovat's Scouts.

Strathconon Ross and Cromarty locally on the River Conon. *Territorials:* 4th Seaforth Highlanders.

Strathdon Aberdeenshire village on the River Don fourteen miles from Ballater. *Territorials:* 6th Gordon Highlanders.

Strathfieldsaye Hampshire village eight miles from Basingstoke. Here is St Mary's Church and the seat of the Duke of Wellington. *Territorials:* 4th Hampshire Regiment.

Strathpeffer Ross and Cromarty village, four miles from Dingwall, its station opened by the Dingwall & Skye Railway in August 1870. A popular Victorian spar resort – many of the visitors staying at the Grand Hotel – the Pump Room in Strathpeffer dates from 1819. *Territorials:* 4th Seaforth Highlanders.

Stratton Cornwall market town just over one mile from Bude station. Here is St Andrew's Church where both Royalist and Parliamentarian dead from the Civil War are buried in the churchyard. *Territorials:* 5th Duke of Cornwall's Light Infantry.

Streatham South London suburb. Here is St Leonard's Church. *Territorials:* 5th East Surrey Regiment.

Strichen Aberdeenshire village, nine miles from Fraserburgh, served by the Great North of Scotland Railway. *Territorials:* 5th Gordon Highlanders.

Stromness Fishing port on mainland Orkney, fourteen miles from Kirkwall. Here, until the end of the nineteenth century, men from Stromness were used to crew the Hudson's Bay Company and Davis Strait whaling fleet. *Territorials:* Orkney RGA.

Stronsay Island in the Orkneys, twelve miles from Kirkwall. *Territorials:* Orkney RGA.

Stroud Gloucestershire market town on the River Frome, ten miles from Gloucester, served by the Great Western and Midland railways. All along the river cloth mills and factories appeared, *Cassell's Gazetteer* for 1898 noting that the broadcloth produced by 'several thousand persons at Stroud is celebrated all over the world'. Another source notes 150 mills. Here is St Lawrence's Church, almost entirely rebuilt in 1886–88, and Holy Trinity which dates from 1838. *Territorials:* Gloucestershire Yeomanry, 5th Gloucestershire Regiment and South Midland Divisional Transport and Supply Column.

Struy Inverness-shire hamlet at the confluence of the rivers Glass and Farrer, ten miles from Beauly. *Territorials:* 1st Lovat's Scouts and 4th Cameron Highlanders.

Stuckton Hampshire hamlet one mile from Fordingbridge. *Territorials:* Hampshire Yeomanry.

Sturminster Newton Dorset market town on the river Stour, ten miles from Blandford, its station opened by the old Dorset Central Railway in August 1863. Here s St Mary's Church which lies away from the centre of the town at the bottom of a short side street. *Territorials:* Dorsetshire Yeomanry and 4th Dorsetshire Regiment.

Sudbrook Monmouthshire village overlooking the River Severn four miles from Chepstow. Sudbrook grew somewhat from 1873 when work began on the Great Western's Severn tunnel and the subsequent building there of a pumping station to clear water from the workings. *Territorials:* 1st Monmouthshire Regiment.

Sudbury Suffolk market town on the River Stour, sixteen miles from Bury St Edmunds, served by the Great Eastern Railway. The inhabitants here, notes the guides, were chiefly employed in the manufacture of silk, velvet, mats and stays. Born here in 1727, Thomas Gainsborough now stands, brush and pallet in hand, outside of the church. *Territorials:* Eastern Mounted Brigade, Suffolk Yeomanry and 5th Suffolk Regiment.

Summerfield Norfolk village just over one mile from Dorking. *Territorials:* Norfolk Yeomanry.

Sunbury Middlesex village on the banks of the Themes, five miles from Kingston, served by the London & South Western Railway. Here is St Mary's Church. *Territorials:* Sunbury House School Cadet Corps.

Sunderland Durham industrial town at the mouth of the River Wear served by the North Eastern Railway. The great port at Sunderland and the coal trade employed many, as did several works manufacturing anchors and chain cable. Here, the last witches were burnt in 1722. Sunderland's parish church, Holy Trinity, was built in 1719. Here too is St John's of 1769. *Territorials:* Northumberland Yeomanry, Durham RGA, 7th Durham Light Infantry, Northern Cyclist Battalion and Northumbrian Divisional Transport and Supply Column.

Surbiton Surrey residential town on the River Thames twelve miles by rail from Waterloo on the London & South Western Railway. Here, in Maple Road, is St Andrew's Church and, in King Charles Road, Christ Church. *Territorials:* 3rd Home Counties Field Ambulance and Home Counties Clearing Hospital.

Sutton (Cambridgeshire) Isle of Ely village, six miles from Ely, reached by the old Ely, Haddenham & Sutton Railway in 1866. Here is St Andrew's Church. *Territorials:* Bedfordshire Yeomanry and Cambridgeshire Regiment.

Sutton (Surrey) Residential area, four miles from Croydon, served by the London, Brighton & South Coast Railway which reached the town in 1847. Here is St Nicholas's Church. *Territorials:* 5th East Surrey Regiment.

Sutton Coldfield Warwickshire market town, seven miles from Birmingham, served by the London & North Western and Midland railways. Here is Holy Trinity Church. *Territorials:* Staffordshire Yeomanry and 2nd South Midland Field Ambulance.

Sutton-in-Ashfield Nottinghamshire market and industrial town, three miles from Mansfield, served by the Great Northern and Midland railways. The inhabitants here, note the guides, were mostly employed in the collieries and in the manufacture of cotton, thread, silk and wool hosiery. Here are St Mary's and St Michael's churches. *Territorials:* 8th Sherwood Foresters.

Sutton-on-Trent Nottinghamshire village seven miles from Newark. Here is All Saints Church, thought to be one of the finest in the county. *Territorials:* Nottinghamshire Yeomanry (Sherwood Rangers).

Sutton Scotney Hampshire village, one mile from Wonston, its station opened by the old Didcot, Newbury & Southampton Railway in May 1885. *Territorials:* 3rd Wessex Field Ambulance.

Sutton Valence Kent village six miles from Maidstone. Here is St Mary's Church. *Territorials:* 5th Buffs East Kent Regiment.

Swadlincote Derbyshire town, six miles from Burton-on-Trent, served by the Midland Railway. There were collieries in the area, also businesses manufacturing sanitary earthenware, firebricks and Rockingham ware. Here is the church of Emmanuel which dates from 1848. *Territorials:* 5th Sherwood Foresters.

Swaffham Norfolk market town, fifteen miles from King's Lynn, served by the South Eastern Railway. Here is St Peter and St Paul's Church. *Territorials:* Norfolk Yeomanry, 5th and 6th Norfolk Regiment.

Swanage Dorset seaside resort and market town on the Isle of Purbeck, ten miles from Wareham, where much trade was carried on in local stone – Purbeck marble. Swanage station, on the London & South Western Railway, was opened in 1885. Here is St Mary's Church. *Territorials:* Dorsetshire RGA.

Swanley Kent village, four miles from Dartford, served by the South Eastern & Chatham Railway. Here is St Paul's Church and, built 1901–02, St Mary's. *Territorials:* 5th Royal West Kent Regiment.

Swansea Busy Glamorgan seaport and market town situated at the mouth of the River Tawe. Here is St Mary's Church. *Territorials:* Glamorgan Yeomanry, 1st Welsh Brigade RFA, 6th, 7th Welsh Regiment, South Wales Mounted Brigade Transport and Supply Column and 3rd Welsh Field Ambulance.

Swanwick Hampshire village, six miles from Fareham, reached by the London & South Western Railway in 1889. *Territorials:* 6th and 9th Hampshire Regiment.

Swardeston Norfolk village four miles from Norwich. Here is St Mary's Church. *Territorials:* 4th Norfolk Regiment.

Swimbridge Devon village, four miles from Barnstaple, its station opened by the Devon & Somerset Railway in November 1873. Here at the church the vicar gave his name to a new breed of dog. The Revd Jack Russell was at St James's from 1833 to 1879. *Territorials:* Royal North Devon Yeomanry.

Swindon Few in Swindon, Wiltshire, could say they did not work for the Great Western; its locomotive and carriage works by the 1890s employing some 9,000. Once there had been Old Swindon, then when the railway came, New Swindon. The two becoming one in 1900. Opened in September 1904, with its maroon and cream vehicles, was the tram service operated by Swindon Corporation. Christ Church in Cricklade Street was built in 1851, the Great Western giving us St Mark's beside their main line in 1843–45. *Territorials:* Wiltshire Yeomanry, 3rd Wessex Brigade RFA, Wiltshire Fortress Engineers, 4th Wiltshire Regiment and 1st South Western Mounted Brigade Field Ambulance.

Swinton Berwickshire village on Leet Water five miles from Duns. *Territorials:* 4th King's Own Scottish Borderers.

Syderstone Norfolk village six miles from Docking. Here is St Mary's Church. *Territorials:* 5th Norfolk Regiment.

Syston Leicestershire village, five miles from Leicester, served by the Midland Railway. Here is St Peter's Church, and paper mills which employed many from the area. *Territorials:* 4th Leicestershire Regiment.

Tadcaster West Riding of Yorkshire market town on the River Wharfe, nine miles from York, served by the North Eastern Railway. Here is St Mary's Church which during the years 1875 to 1877 was taken down and reconstructed on a higher level – out of the reach of flood water from the river. Arthur Mee noted of the town its 'sprinkling of old houses' and 'big array of brewery chimneys'. Tadcaster a brewing centre since 1341. *Territorials:* 5th West Yorkshire Regiment.

Tain Ross and Cromarty port and market town on Dornoch Firth served by the Highland Railway. Since the Middle Ages, pilgrims have come to St Duthus's Church where the bones of the saint were laid to rest. *Territorials:* 2nd Lovat's Scouts and 4th Seaforth Highlanders.

Tal-y-Coed Seat, five miles from Monmouth. *Territorials:* 1st Cadet Battalion Monmouthshire Regiment.

Talgarth Brecknockshire market town, seven miles from Hay-on-Wye, served by the Cambrian Railway. Here is St Gwendoline's Church. *Territorials:* Brecknockshire Battalion.

Tamworth Staffordshire market town on the River Tame and Coventry Canal, seven miles from Lichfield and served by the London & North Western and Midland railways. Here at St Editha's Church there are memorials to the Ferrers and Frevile families. A large clothing factory employed many at Tamworth in the 1890s. *Territorials:* Staffordshire Yeomanry and 6th North Staffordshire Regiment.

Tankerness Orkney village six miles from Kirkwall. *Territorials:* Orkney RGA.

Taplow Buckinghamshire village on the River Thames, one mile from Maidenhead, served by the Great Western Railway. Here is St Nicholas's Church. *Territorials:* Buckinghamshire Yeomanry and South Midland Divisional Transport and Supply Column.

Tarbert (Argyllshire) Fishing village on Loch Fyne. *Territorials:* 4th Highland Brigade RGA.

Tarbert (Inverness-shire) Village in Harris, Outer Hebrides on Isle of Lewis. *Territorials:* 4th Cameron Highlanders.

Tarbrax Lanarkshire village ten miles from Shotts. *Territorials:* 8th Highland Light Infantry.

Tarland Aberdeenshire village seven miles from Aboyne. *Territorials:* 2nd Scottish Horse and 7th Gordon Highlanders.

Tarporley Cheshire market town, nine miles from Chester, with the Railway (London & North Western) two miles off at Beeston Castle and Tarporley station. Here is St Helen's Church. *Territorials:* Cheshire Yeomanry.

Tarves Aberdeenshire village four miles from Old Meldrum. *Territorials:* 5th Gordon Highlanders.

Tattenhall Cheshire market town, seven miles from Chester, served by the London & North Western Railway. Here is St Alban's Church. *Territorials:* Cheshire Yeomanry.

Taunton Market and county town of Somerset on the River Tone, eight miles from Bridgwater, served by the Great Western Railway. Opened in August 1901 was the tram service operated by the Taunton & West Somerset Electric Railway & Tramways Company, which ran from the depot in East Reach to the railway station. Wool was once important to the area, but the production of cider gives employment now. Factories also produced silk, collars and cuffs, gloves and boxes. Playing an important role in the construction of St Mary Magdalene's church tower in 1852 was a donkey. Daily the animal toiled harnessed to a pulley that took the red sandstone blocks up to the workmen. When the job was complete his fellow workmates took him to the top of the new tower to admire the view. King's College, in Taunton, and Taunton School, both maintained contingents in the OTC. *Territorials:* South Western Infantry Brigade, West Somerset Yeomanry, Somerset RHA and 5th Somerset Light Infantry.

Tavistock Devon market town on the River Tavy, fifteen miles from Plymouth, served by the Great Western and London & South Western railways. Wool, then copper mining, were once Tavistock's main industries – the Great Consols mine being at one time one of the largest in the world. Tavistock had two stations. The Plymouth, Devonport & South Western Junction Railway opening theirs in June 1890, the South Devon & Tavistock having already arrived in 1859. Here is St Peter's Church, and Kelly College which maintained one infantry company in the OTC. *Territorials:* Royal North Devon Yeomanry, 4th Wessex Brigade RFA and 5th Devonshire Regiment.

Tayinloan Argyllshire village on the west coast of Kintyre six miles from Glenbarr. *Territorials:* 8th Argyll and Sutherland Highlanders.

Taynuilt Argyllshire hamlet, fifteen miles from Oban, with railway station opened by the Callander & Oban Company in July 1880. *Territorials:* 2nd Scottish Horse.

Tayport Fifeshire town and port on the Firth of Tay, sometimes called Ferry-Port-on-Craig. Much fishing went on, but many were employed in three spinning factories, an engine works and large timber mill. Tayport is five miles from Dundee and was served by the North British Railway. *Territorials:* Highland Cyclist Battalion.

Tayvallich Argyllshire hamlet seven miles from Ardrishaig. *Territorials:* 8th Argyll and Sutherland Highlanders.

Teddington Middlesex residential district and London suburb on the River Thames, just over thirteen miles by rail from Waterloo station on the London & South Western Railway. The actor and dramatist Noël Coward was born in Teddington in 1899. Here are St Mary's and St Alban's churches. *Territorials:* Home Counties Divisional Transport and Supply Column.

Teignmouth Seaside resort and market town on the Devon coast, fourteen miles from Exeter, served by the Great Western Railway. Here, in the east of the town, is St Michael's Church and, in the west, St James's. *Territorials:* 4th Wessex Brigade RFA, 5th Devonshire Regiment and 1st Wessex Field Ambulance.

Temple Sowerby Westmorland village on the River Eden, six miles from Appleby, served by the North Eastern Railway. Here is St James's Church. *Territorials:* Westmorland and Cumberland Yeomanry.

Templeton Pembrokeshire village, two miles from Narberth, served by the Great Western Railway. Here is St John's Church. *Territorials:* Pembrokeshire Yeomanry.

Tenbury Market town, twenty-two miles from Worcester, where the five-arched bridge that crosses the River Teme takes you from Worcestershire into Shropshire. Tenbury station (called Tenbury Wells from 1912) was served by the Great Western and London & North Western railways. Here is St May's Church. *Territorials:* Shropshire Yeomanry and 7th Worcestershire Regiment.

Tenby Pembrokeshire market town and seaside resort on Carmarthen Bay, nine miles from Pembroke, served by the Great Western Railway. Born here in 1878 was the painter Augustus John. Here is St Mary's Church. *Territorials:* Pembrokeshire Yeomanry and Pembrokeshire RGA.

Tenterden Kent market town, ten miles from Ashford, reached by the Rother Valley Light Railway (later called Kent & East Sussex) in 1900. Here is St Mildred's Church. *Territorials:* Royal East Kent Yeomanry and 5th Buffs East Kent Regiment.

Terling Essex village on the River Ter four miles from Witham. Here is All Saints Church which has memorials to the Strutt family. The registers date from 1538. *Territorials:* 5th Essex Regiment.

Terrington St Clement Norfolk village, seven miles from King's Lynn, served by the Midland & Great Northern Joint Railway. St Clement's Church has a detached bell tower. *Territorials:* 6th Norfolk Regiment.

Tetbury Gloucestershire market town five miles from Malmesbury, its station being at the termination of the Great Western branch opened in 1889 from Kemble. Here at St Mary Magdalene's Church – Norman, but rebuilt in 1777 – are memorials to the Gastrell family. *Territorials:* 3rd Wessex Brigade RFA.

Tettenhall Staffordshire village, two miles from Wolverhampton, served by the Great Western Railway. Here is St Michael's Church, where there are memorials to the Wrottesley family, and the Wolverhampton Waterworks. *Territorials:* 6th South Staffordshire Regiment.

Tewkesbury Gloucestershire market town on the River Avon where it meets the Severn, ten miles from Gloucester, served by the Midland Railway. Here is Tewkesbury Abbey, brought by the town in 1539 from Henry VIII for £453. *Territorials:* 5th Gloucestershire Regiment.

Thame Oxfordshire market town on the border of Bucks, ten miles from Aylesbury, served by the Great Western Railway. Thame station was opened when the old Wycombe Railway reached the town in 1862. Here is St Mary's Church. *Territorials:* Oxfordshire Yeomanry and 4th Oxfordshire and Buckinghamshire Light Infantry.

Thaxted Essex town on the River Chalmer, seven miles from Dunmow, situated at the termination of the light railway branch opened by the Great Eastern across from Elsenham in 1913. Thaxted was once well known for its production of cutlery, but later it would be the wool trade that brought prosperity to the town. Here is the church of St John the Baptist, St Mary the Virgin and St Laurence where for twelve years the composer Gustav Holst was organist. Part of his *Planets* was written at Thaxted. *Territorials:* 5th Essex Regiment.

Thetford Norfolk market town situated at the confluence of the rivers Thet and Little Ouse, the latter forming the border here with Suffolk. The town gave employment in its breweries, brick and lime kilns, chemical works and extensive iron foundry. Thetford Bridge Station was opened when the Thetford & Watton Railway reached the town in November 1875. Here is St Cuthbert's Church; St Mary's, which is just on the Suffolk side of the river, and in White Hart Street, St Peter's. *Territorials:* Norfolk Yeomanry, Suffolk Yeomanry, 4th and 6th Norfolk Regiment.

Thirsk North Riding of Yorkshire market town on Cod Beck, eleven miles from Ripon, served by the North Eastern Railway. A large number of inhabitants were employed in the town's extensive agricultural engineering works. Here is St Mary's Church. *Territorials:* Yorkshire Hussars and 4th Yorkshire Regiment.

Thornaby North Riding of Yorkshire town on the River Tees opposite Stockton, served by the North Eastern Railway. Here, notes one late Victorian guide, many were employed in large yards building iron ships. *Territorials:* Northumbrian RGA.

Thorney Cambridgeshire village, fourteen miles from Wisbech, served by the Midland & Great Northern Joint Railway. Here is St Mary and St Botolph's Church. *Territorials:* Cambridgeshire Regiment.

Thornham Norfolk village five miles from Hunstanton. Here is All Saints Church. *Territorials:* 5th Norfolk Regiment.

Thornhill Dumfrieshire village on the River Nith, fourteen from Dumfries, served by the Glasgow & South Western Railway. The area's employment was mainly agricultural. *Territorials:* Lanarkshire Yeomanry and 5th King's Own Scottish Borderers.

Thornliebank Renfrewshire town, four miles from Glasgow, served by the Caledonian Railway. The town, notes *Cassell's*, owes its existence to the cotton works established there in the latter part of the eighteenth century. *Territorials:* 6th Argyll and Sutherland Highlanders.

Thornton (Fifeshire) Village five miles from Kirkcaldy. *Territorials:* 7th Black Watch.

Thornton (Lancashire) Four miles from Fleetwood. *Territorials:* 5th King's Own Royal Lancaster Regiment.

Thornton Dale East Riding of Yorkshire village, nine miles from Malton, its station opened by the North Eastern Railway in 1882. Here is All Saints Church. *Territorials:* 5th Yorkshire Regiment.

Thorpe St Andrew Norfolk village, two miles from Norwich, served by the Great Eastern Railway. *Territorials:* 4th Norfolk Regiment.

Thorverton Devon village on the River Exe, seven miles from Exeter, its station on the Great Western Railway opened in 1885. Here is the church of St Thomas a Becket. *Territorials:* Royal 1st Devon Yeomanry.

Thrapston Northamptonshire market town on the River Nen, seven miles from Oundle, served by the London & North Western and Midland railways. Here is St James's Church. *Territorials:* Northamptonshire Yeomanry.

Thurso Town in Caithness; its station, opened by the Sutherland and Caithness Railway Company in July 1874, the most northerly in Britain. Once important to the town was its production and export of flagstone. *Territorials:* 5th Seaforth Highlanders.

Ticehurst Sussex village, its station ('Ticehurst Road') laying three miles to the south-west on the South Eastern & Chatham Railway. Here is the mostly fourteenth-century St Mary's Church. *Territorials:* 5th Royal Sussex Regiment.

Tideswell Derbyshire market town six miles from Buxton. Here is St John's Church where there are memorials to the Litton family. *Territorials:* Derbyshire Yeomanry.

Tidworth Hampshire town, comprising North and South Tidworth, its station opened by the Midland & South Western Junction Railway in 1902. Coinciding with the coming of the railway was the British Army which set up barracks and training facilities throughout the area. Here are Holy Trinity and St Mary's churches. *Territorials:* 4th Hampshire Regiment.

Tighnabruaich Argyllshire village on Kyles of Bute nine miles by ferry from Rothesay. *Territorials:* 8th Argyll and Sutherland Highlanders.

Tilford Surrey village on the River Wey three miles from Farnham. Here is All Saints Church. *Territorials:* Surrey Infantry Brigade.

Tillicoultry Clackmannanshire town on the River Devon, five miles from Alloa, served by the North British Railway. Tillicoultry had numerous collieries, the production of woollen garments also providing employment for the town. *Territorials:* 7th Argyll and Sutherland Highlanders.

Tillingham Essex village fourteen miles from Maldon. Here is St Nicholas's Church where there are memorials to the Wyatt family and registers dating from 1652. *Territorials:* 4th Essex Regiment.

Tingewick Buckinghamshire village two miles from Buckingham. Here is the church of St Mary Magdalene. *Territorials:* Buckinghamshire Battalion.

Tipton Staffordshire town one mile from Dudley served by the Great Western and London & North Western railways. At Tipton many great furnaces produced heavy ironwork for the railways, steam boilers, large chains and anchors. There were also cement and brick works. Here is St Martin's Church. *Territorials:* 6th South Staffordshire Regiment.

Tiptree Essex town, seven miles from Maldon, where A C Wilkin farmed, grew fruit, made 'Tiptree' jam and built accommodation for his staff. The railway arrived when the Kelvedon, Tiptree & Tollesbury Company opened a branch off the Great Eastern in 1904. Here is St Luke's Church, which dates from 1855. *Territorials:* Essex Yeomanry and 5th Essex Regiment.

Tiree Island within the Inner Hebrides, Argyllshire. *Territorials:* 2nd Scottish Horse.

Tisbury Wiltshire village, eight miles from Shaftesbury, served by the London & South Western Railway. Here is St John's Church. *Territorials:* 1st South Western Mounted Brigade Transport and Supply Column.

Titchfield Small Hampshire town on the River Meon across from Fareham. Here is St Peter's Church. *Territorials:* Hampshire Yeomanry and 6th Hampshire Regiment.

Tiverton Devon market town on the River Exe, fourteen miles from Exeter on the Great Western Railway, once an important centre of the Devonshire cloth trade. Also in the town was a factory making lace which, in 1898, is said to have employed more than 1,000. Here, at the north end of town, is St Peter's Church, and in Fore Street, the Georgian St George's. Blundell's School at Tiverton maintained a contingent of the OTC. *Territorials:* Royal 1st Devon Yeomanry and 4th Devonshire Regiment.

Tivetshall Norfolk village, six miles from Fakenham, served by the Great Eastern Railway. Here at St Mary's Church are memorials to the Coke family, ancestors of the Earl of Leicester. *Territorials:* 4th Norfolk Regiment.

Tobermory Village and port on Mull Island, Argyllshire, founded in 1788 by the British Fishery Society as a station for fishing vessels. *Territorials:* 4th Highland Brigade RGA.

Toberonochy Village on east side of Luing Island, Argyllshire, fifteen miles from Oban. *Territorials:* 8th Argyll and Sutherland Highlanders.

Tockington   Gloucestershire village, four miles from Thornbury, where much revolved around farming and the ancient Swan Inn. *Territorials:* Gloucestershire Yeomanry.

Todmorden   West Riding of Yorkshire town, nine miles from Burnley, served by the Lancashire & Yorkshire Railway. Situated on the River Calder and Rochdale Canal, here crossed by George Stephenson's Gauxholme railway viaduct with its twin embattled towers, Todmorden prospered from its cotton spinning and weaving. The largest weaving shed in the world was at Todmorden. *Territorials:* 6th Lancashire Fusiliers.

Tollesbury   Essex village on the mouth of the River Blackwater, well known for its oyster beds. The Great Eastern Railway reached Tollesbury in 1904, the line being extended to Tollesbury Pier three years later. At the south end of the village square is St Mary's Church where there is the 'Swearing Font', paid for by an eighteenth-century offender (John Norman) to make up for his unholy conduct in church. The registers date from 1558. *Territorials:* 5th Essex Regiment.

Tollington   Part of the north London borough of Islington. *Territorials:* Tollington School Cadet Corps.

Tomatin   Inverness-shire village on the River Findhorn, nineteen miles from Inverness, with large distillery and Highland Railway station which opened in 1897. *Territorials:* 2nd Lovat's Scouts.

Tonbridge   Kent market town on the River Medway, five miles from Tunbridge Wells, served by the South Eastern & Chatham Railway. There were once gunpowder mills situated on the banks of the river. Here is St Peter and St Paul's Church, and Tonbridge School which maintained an OTC contingent of three infantry companies. *Territorials:* West Kent Yeomanry, Kent Fortress Engineers, 4th Royal West Kent Regiment and Kent Cyclist Battalion.

Tongue   Sutherlandshire village on the east side of the Kyle of Tongue, forty-four miles from Thurso. *Territorials:* 2nd Lovat's Scouts.

Tooting   Area within the London borough of Wandsworth. Here is Holy Trinity Church. *Territorials:* Broadwater Cadet Corps and Upper Tooting School Cadet Corps.

Topsham   Devon fishing port and market town on the River Exe, six miles from Exmouth, served by the London & South Western Railway. Here at St Margaret's Church is a memorial to Admiral Sir John Thomas Duckworth, who died in 1817, and to his son, Colonel George Henry Duckworth, killed at Albuera on 16 May 1811. The church also has memorials to the Ross, Griffiths, Brent and Roos families. *Territorials:* 7th Devonshire Regiment.

Torlam   Location twenty-one miles from Lochmaddy, North Uist. *Territorials:* 1st Lovat's Scouts.

Torloisk   Hamlet on the Isle of Mull, twelve miles from Tobermory. *Territorials:* 2nd Scottish Horse.

Torphins   Aberdeenshire village, seven miles from Banchory, served by the Great North of Scotland Railway. *Territorials:* 2nd Scottish Horse and 7th Gordon Highlanders.

Torquay   Devon market town and seaside resort on Tor Bay, twenty-three miles from Exeter, served by the Great Western Railway. Opened almost a year to the day before the Territorial Force began was the tram service operated by the Torquay Tramways Company. *Territorials:* Devonshire Fortress Engineers, 5th and 7th Devonshire Regiment.

Torre   Western suburb of Torquay, Devon with railway station on the Great Western. Here is Torre Abbey. *Territorials:* 4th Wessex Brigade RFA.

Torridon   Ross and Cromarty hamlet at the head of Loch Torridon ten miles from Kinlochewe. *Territorials:* 4th Seaforth Highlanders.

Torrin Hamlet on the east shore of Loch Slapin, Isle of Skye, Outer Hebrides. *Territorials:* 4th Cameron Highlanders.

Torrington Devon village on the River Torridge, seven miles from Bideford, served by the London & South Western Railway. Here is St Michael's Church, much damaged in 1646 during the Civil War. *Territorials:* Royal North Devon Yeomanry and 6th Devonshire Regiment.

Totnes Devon market town on the River Dart, nine miles from Torquay, served by the Great Western Railway. Here, at St Mary's Church, there is an inscription in Russian. It is to Walter Venning (1781–1821) who died at St Petersburg and founded the Prison Society of Russia. Cider was made at Totnes. *Territorials:* Royal 1st Devon Yeomanry, 5th Devonshire Regiment and Totnes Cadet Company.

Tottenham North London suburb. Here is the c1500 All Hallows Church. *Territorials:* 7th Middlesex Regiment.

Totton Hampshire village near the head of Southampton Water served by the London & south Western Railway. Here is St Mary's Church. *Territorials:* 7th Hampshire Regiment.

Towie Aberdeenshire village on the River Don, twelve miles from Alford. *Territorials:* 6th Gordon Highlanders.

Towyn Merionethshire market town on Cardigan Bay, twelve miles from Barmouth, served by the Cambrian and Talyllyn railways. Here the church is dedicated to St Cadfan. *Territorials:* 7th Royal Welsh Fusiliers.

Toxteth Park District of Liverpool. *Territorials:* Lancashire Brigade RGA.

Tranent Haddingtonshire mining town close to Prestonpans served by the North British Railway. Here, in 1797, a number of miners were shot and killed during a protest about certain conditions set out in the Militia Act. *Territorials:* Lothians and Border Horse, 8th Royal Scots and Tranent Industrial School Cadet Corps.

Tranmere District on the Mersey within the borough of Birkenhead. *Territorials:* 4th Cheshire Regiment and 1st Birkenhead Cadet Corps.

Tredegar Monmouthshire town, seven miles from Merthyr Tydfil, which grew up after ironworks were established on Lord Tredegar's land in 1800. Many were also employed in local collieries. Here are St George's and St James's churches. *Territorials:* 3rd Monmouthshire Regiment.

Treeton West Riding of Yorkshire village on the River Rother, six miles from Sheffield, served by the Midland and Great Central railways. Here at St Helen's Church are memorials to the Vesci, Bradshaw and Lord families. *Territorials:* 5th York and Lancaster Regiment.

Trefeglwys Montgomeryshire village four miles from Llanidloes. Here is St Michael's Church. *Territorials:* Montgomeryshire Yeomanry.

Trefonen Shropshire village two miles from Oswestry. *Territorials:* Montgomeryshire Yeomanry.

Tregaron Small Cardiganshire market town on the Great Western Railway, ten miles north-east of Lampeter, where much revolved around the thirteenth-century Talbot Hotel. Here is St Caron's Church. *Territorials:* Pembrokeshire Yeomanry.

Treharris Glamorgan village, thirteen miles from Cardiff, served by the Great Western Railway. *Territorials:* 5th Welsh Regiment.

Trent Port Lincolnshire location on the river's edge five miles from Gainsborough. *Territorials:* Nottinghamshire Yeomanry (Sherwood Rangers).

Trewern On River Severn and part of Welshpool, Montgomeryshire. *Territorials:* Montgomeryshire Yeomanry.

Trimdon Durham mining village, four miles from Sedgefield, served by the North Eastern Railway. Here is the church of St Mary Magdalene. *Territorials:* 5th Durham Light Infantry.

Trimley Suffolk village on the River Orwell, two miles from Felixstowe, its station on the Great Eastern Railway being opened in 1891. Here, their churchyards adjoining, are the churches of St Mary and St Martin. *Territorials:* 1st East Anglian Field Ambulance.

Tring Hertfordshire market town, seven miles from Aylesbury, served by the London & North Western Railway. Here is St Peter and St Paul's Church. The main industries at Tring were canvas weaving, straw plaiting and brewing. *Territorials:* Hertfordshire Regiment.

Troon Ayrshire town and seaport, six miles from Ayr, served by the Glasgow & South Western Railway. In an Edwardian poster issued by the railway company, we see Troon described as an 'ideal holiday resort with six golf courses...' *Territorials:* 5th Royal Scots Fusiliers.

Trowbridge Wiltshire market and manufacturing town, eleven miles from Devises, served by the Great Western Railway. The Kennet & Avon Canal passed close to the town. There exists a watercolour painting by William Millington (1811–90) which shows a view of Fore Street looking towards St James's Church. Here we see the spire under repair in 1846. The street set out with stalls on market day, people entering the George Hotel, R Walker's shop and a building called Waterloo House. *Territorials:* Wiltshire Yeomanry and 4th Wiltshire Regiment.

Truro Cornwall seaport, eleven miles from Falmouth, served by the Great Western Railway. Here took place the demolition, with the exception of the south aisle, of the old parish church of St Mary to make way for the new Truro Cathedral which was completed in 1910. *Cassell's* notes that in Truro, in the 1890s, could be found tin-smelting works, three small potteries, two brush factories, a large flour mill, three saw mills, a tannery, a jam factory and shirt and clothing manufacturers. *Territorials:* Royal 1st Devon Yeomanry, Cornwall RGA and 4th Duke of Cornwall's Light Infantry.

Tumble Carmarthenshire village seven miles from Llanelli. *Territorials:* 4th Welsh Regiment.

Tunbridge Wells Kent spa and market town, five miles from Tonbridge, served by the South Eastern & Chatham Railway. For visitors to 'drink the waters', the Pump Room at the south end of the Pantiles was built in 1877. Here is the church of King Charles the Martyr, the oldest in the town, and Skinners' School which maintained an OTC contingent of one infantry company. *Territorials:* West Kent Yeomanry, Sussex Yeomanry, 4th Royal West Kent Regiment, Kent Cyclist Battalion and 1st Cadet Battalion Kent Fortress Engineers.

Tunstall Staffordshire market and manufacturing town nine miles from Congleton by rail on the North Staffordshire Railway. The potteries, iron works and collieries in the area gave employment to many. Here is Christ Church. *Territorials:* 5th North Staffordshire Regiment.

Turriff Aberdeenshire town, nine miles from Banff, served by the Great North of Scotland Railway. Here is the Episcopal church of St Congan which was built in 1862. *Territorials:* 2nd Scottish Horse and 5th Gordon Highlanders.

Tutbury Staffordshire town on the River Dove, four miles from Burton-on-Trent, served by the North Staffordshire Railway. Here is St Mary's Church. *Territorials:* 6th North Staffordshire Regiment.

Twickenham Middlesex town on the River Thames, one mile from Richmond, served by the London & South Western Railway. Here is St Mary's Church, and Twickenham Rugby ground which began in 1909. *Territorials:* 8th Middlesex Regiment and the Mall School Cadet Corps.

Twyford Hampshire village on the River Itchen, three miles from Winchester, served by the Great Western Railway. Here is St Mary's Church. *Territorials:* 4th Hampshire Regiment.

Uckfield Small Sussex town on the River Uck (a tributary of the Ouse), eight miles north-east of Lewes, where a window and plaque in the Church of the Holy Cross remembers Lieutenant-General George Calvert Clarke who fought at Balaclava. Another old soldier, Private James Dudeney of the Rifle Brigade, was also honoured when the local Territorials turned out for his funeral in 1910. In the town, which was served by the London, Brighton & South Coast Railway, some trade was carried on in corn, brewing, brick and tile making. *Territorials:* Sussex Yeomanry and 5th Royal Sussex Regiment.

Uddingston Iron foundries and factories making agricultural implements gave much employment in this Lanarkshire town close to the River Clyde and to the south-east of Glasgow. Uddingston was served by the Caledonian Railway and the North British branch line that ran down to Hamilton. *Territorials:* 6th Cameronians.

Uffculme Devonshire market town on the River Culm where many were employed in a large woollen factory and brewery. The Coldharbour Woollen Mill, built in 1799, is now a working museum. Uffculme station was on the old Great Western branch line that ran to Hemyock. Here is St Mary's Church. *Territorials:* 4th Devonshire Regiment.

Uig Fishing village on Uig Bay, Isle of Sky. *Territorials:* 1st Lovat's Scouts.

Ulceby North Lincolnshire village eleven miles to the west of Grimsby served by the Great Central Railway. Here is St Nicholas's Church. *Territorials:* Lincolnshire Yeomanry.

Ullapool Herring fishing was the main dependence of the habitants of this Ross and Cromarty small town and seaport – the place being founded by the British Fishing Society in 1788. Located on the east shore of Loch Broom, a busy ferry trade has always been carried out from the harbour designed by Thomas Telford. *Territorials:* 2nd Lovat's Scouts and 4th Seaforth Highlanders.

Ulverston North Lancashire seaport and market town near the influx of the River Leven to Morecambe Bay and served by the Ulverston & Lancaster Railway. Large ironworks and foundries are noted, the short, but deep and wide, Ulverston Canal that ran down to the bay, also providing employment. Founded at Ulverston in 1111 was the church of St Mary. *Territorials:* Westmorland and Cumberland Yeomanry and 4th King's Own Royal Lancaster Regiment.

Uphall The mining of shale, and its associated paraffin oil production, provided almost total employment for this Linlithgowshire village – the Broxburn oil works being one of several manufacturers in the area. The North British Company provided the rail service. *Territorials:* 10th Royal Scots.

Uploders The River Asker runs through this small west Dorsetshire village which lies three miles from Bridport. *Territorials:* 3rd Wessex Brigade RFA.

Upper Mill Small West Yorkshire town on the edge of Saddleworth Moor, thirteen miles from Huddersfield and served by the London & North Western Railway. *Territorials:* 7th Duke of Wellington's Regiment.

Uppingham Rutlandshire market town at the end of the branch line from Seaton opened by the London & North Western Railway in 1894. Here is the church of St Peter and St Paul, and Uppingham School which maintained three OTC infantry companies. *Territorials:* Leicestershire Yeomanry and 5th Leicestershire Regiment.

Upton Bishop Small Herefordshire village four miles to the north-east of Ross-on-Wye. Here is the church of St John the Baptist. *Territorials:* Herefordshire Regiment.

Upton-on-Severn Worcestershire market town where much trade was carried on via the river. The railway reached Upton when the Midland branch line from Malvern to Ashchurch was opened in 1864. The building of St Peter and St Paul's Church began in 1878. *Territorials:* Worcestershire Yeomanry and 8th Worcestershire Regiment.

Urchfont Small Wiltshire village to the north of Salisbury Plain and seven miles from Devises. Here is St Michael's Church. *Territorials:* Wiltshire Yeomanry.

Usk Small market town on the River Usk twelve miles south-west of Monmouth served by the Great Western Railway. St Mary's Church was much restored in 1899–1900. *Territorials:* 2nd Monmouthshire Regiment and Usk Territorial Cadet Corps.

Uttoxeter Here, at this Staffordshire market town, the Uttoxeter Canal begins its run north-west along the Churnet Valley to near Cheddleton where it links up with the Caldon Canal. Uttoxeter, which lies just a mile from the River Dove and the border with Derbyshire, was served by both the North Staffordshire and Great Northern railways and employed many in Bunting's large brewery and Bamford's factory which made agricultural machinery and implements. Here is St Mary's Church. *Territorials:* Staffordshire Yeomanry and 6th North Staffordshire Regiment.

Uxbridge One guide notes that the River Colne and Grand Junction Canal were 'a great source on convenience' to trade at Uxbridge. Many large corn mills were located on the river, while the canal banks saw wharves where the sawing, planning and moulding of timber was carried on. On the western border of Middlesex, Uxbridge was served by the Great Western Railway and, from 1904, the Metropolitan out of London. Behind the old Market House in the centre of Uxbridge is St Margaret's Church. *Territorials:* 8th Middlesex Regiment.

Ventnor On the south-east coast of the Isle of Wight, visitors have been attracted to the town and its favourable and healthy weather – one guide noted that 'it is visited with less rain than any other place in Great Britain' – since 1841. Ventnor Town Hall was built in 1878, the Albert Hall in Victoria Street in 1887. The town was served by two railway stations. *Territorials:* 2nd Wessex Brigade RFA, 8th Hampshire Regiment and Ventnor Cadet Company.

Wadebridge Cornish market town on the River Camel, seven miles from Bodmin, served by the London & South Western Railway. Here the river is crossed by a bridge built in 1485 by local vicar, Thomas Lovibond. *Territorials:* 5th Duke of Cornwall's Light Infantry.

Wadesmill Hertfordshire hamlet on the River Rib, two miles from Ware. *Territorials:* Hertfordshire Regiment.

Wadhurst Sussex village noted as being the last place to produce Saxon iron. All around St Peter and St Paul's church, iron tomb slabs form much of the flooring. Wadhurst station, which lies just over a mile off to the north-west of the village, was served by the North Eastern & Chatham Railway and was shown in the *Illustrated London* News in 1852. *Territorials:* 5th Royal Sussex Regiment.

Wakefield West Riding of Yorkshire industrial town on the River Calder, seven miles from Leeds, and a cathedral city since 1888. Wakefield changed hands often during the Civil War. One record notes how the Parliamentarians in May 1643 fought their way up the main street and into the Market Place where the Royalist guns were taken in the churchyard of All Saints Church. Here, in the Town Hall, there are seven statues representing the town's past industries: Mining, Iron founding, Spinning, Glass blowing, Agriculture, Engineering and pottery. *Territorials:* Yorkshire Dragoons, 4th King's Own Yorkshire Light Infantry and Yorkshire Mounted Brigade Field Ambulance.

Waldershare Kent village five miles from Dover. Here at All Saints Church there are memorials to the Monin and Furnese families. *Territorials:* Royal East Kent Yeomanry.

Walker-on-Tyne Northumberland industrial and mining suburb of Newcastle. Here is Christ Church. *Territorials:* 5th Northumberland Fusiliers.

Walkerburn Peebleshire wool manufacturing village on the River Tweed two miles from Innerleithen. Walkerburn station on the North British Railway was opened in 1867. *Territorials:* 8th Royal Scots.

Wallbridge Locality near Stroud, Gloucestershire. *Territorials:* Gloucester and Worcester Brigade Company.

Wallingford Berkshire market town on the right bank of the Thames – the river here being crossed by an ancient bridge of nineteen arches – fifteen miles from Reading. Here, Stephen and Henry fought over who should be king. They compromised and signed the Treaty of Wallingford in 1153. A Great Western Railway branch to Watlington was authorized, but the line was to stop short at Wallingford in 1866. Here is the Norman church of St Leonard; St Peter's, which dates from 1760, and on the Market Place, St Mary's of 1854. *Territorials:* Berkshire Yeomanry and 4th Royal Berkshire Regiment.

Wallsend Northumberland town on the Tyne, four miles from Newcastle, served by the North Eastern Railway. The town takes its name from its position at the eastern end of Hadrian's Wall and was once an important shipbuilding centre. Also gone is the Wallsend Colliery, noted in its day as the deepest in Northumberland. Here was the home of George and Robert Stephenson, St Peter's Church being erected in 1807–09. *Territorials:* 5th Northumberland Fusiliers.

Walsall Staffordshire town, eight miles from Birmingham, where many were employed in the manufacture of saddles, buckles and all kinds of horse furniture. A number also helped produce handles, latches, hinges and other architectural ironmongery for William Kirkpatrick's company which was founded in 1855. The local football team is nicknamed the Saddlers. The Walsall Corporation Tramways, with their dark red and cream trams, opened in January 1901. Born here in 1859 was the writer Jerome K Jerome. Here is St Matthew's Church, and the Queen Mary's Grammar School which maintained two OTC infantry companies. *Territorials:* Staffordshire Yeomanry and 5th South Staffordshire Regiment.

Walsingham Norfolk villages (Great and Little) on the River Stiffkey, five miles from Wells, served by the Great Eastern Railway. Here at St Mary's Church are memorials to the Lee-Warner family. *Territorials:* Norfolk Yeomanry and 6th Norfolk Regiment.

Waltham Abbey Essex market town on the River Lea about one mile from the Great Eastern Railway's Waltham Cross station. *Cassell's Gazetteer* for 1898 notes that on the banks of the Lea was a large Government establishment for refining saltpetre and for the manufacture of gunpowder, new works having been erected in 1890 about a half mile from the town for the making of cordite. Percussion caps were also made. Here is the church of Holy Cross and St Laurence. *Territorials:* Essex Yeomanry.

Waltham Cross Hertfordshire village, eleven miles from London, served by the Great Eastern Railway. Here is Holy Trinity Church. *Territorials:* Hertfordshire Regiment.

Walthamstow Suburb to the north-east of London situated on the west side of Epping Forest and the Great Eastern line from Liverpool Street. A tram service was opened by Walthamstow Urban District Council in June 1905, and Forest School had a contingent of the OTC. *Territorials:* 7th Essex Regiment, 3rd East Anglian Field Ambulance, Walthamstow Cadets and Forest Cadet Corps.

Walton-on-the-Hill Surrey village, five miles from Reigate, its station (Tadworth and Walton-on-the-Hill) opened by the Chipstead Valley Railway in July 1900. Here is St Peter's Church. *Territorials:* 5th East Surrey Regiment.

Walton-on-the-Naze Essex seaside resort, seven miles from Harwich, its station on the Great Eastern Railway being opened in May 1867. In 1884, a lifeboat called *Honourable Artillery Company* was presented to the Royal National Lifeboat Institution by the Dramatic Club of the HAC. Here at the junction of the Kirby and Frinton roads, is All Saints Church which was built in 1873 as a replacement for an earlier building that fell into the sea in 1798. The registers date from 1672. *Territorials:* Essex Yeomanry and 5th Essex Regiment.

Wandsworth London borough on the south bank of the Thames, reached by the railway in 1838. Here, on Wandsworth Common, the Emmanuel School maintain an OTC contingent of one infantry company. In Wandsworth High Street since medieval times has stood All Saints Church, and in Heathfield Road from 1849, Wandsworth Prison. The Royal Patriotic Asylum in Trinity Road dates from 1859 and was opened as school for orphaned children of soldiers killed in action. *Territorials:* St Thomas's Cadet Corps and Wandsworth Boys' Naval Brigade.

Wanstrow Somerset village, five miles from Frome, its Great Western Railway station opening in 1860. Here is St Mary's Church. *Territorials:* 4th Somerset Light Infantry.

Wantage Berkshire market town on the Berks & Wilts Canal, ten miles from Abingdon, and birthplace of King Alfred. Opened in 1875, and running down from the Great Western main line, was the Wantage Tramway. Here is the thirteenth-century St Peter and St Paul's Church, and King Alfred's School which maintained one infantry company in the OTC. *Territorials:* Berkshire Yeomanry and 4th Royal Berkshire Regiment.

Warburton Cheshire village on the River Mersey, seven miles from Warrington, served by the London & North Western Railway. Here is the old (timber-built originally) St Werburgh's Church, and a newer replacement which was completed in 1883. *Territorials:* Cheshire Yeomanry.

Ware Hertfordshire town, two miles from Hertford, served by the Great Eastern Railway. There exists an old railway carriage print in which the River Lea is seen passing through the town. Malthouses and barges line the banks. Here is St Mary's Church. *Territorials:* Hertfordshire Regiment.

Wareham Dorset market town on the River Frome, seventeen miles from Dorchester, served by the London & South Western Railway. Here is St Martin's, a Saxon church which dates from c1030 and, located above the river, St Mary's with its lead font on which the faces of the Apostles have been mutilated by Cromwell's men. *Territorials:* Dorsetshire Yeomanry and 4th Dorsetshire Regiment.

Wark-on-Tyne Northumberland village, five miles from Bellingham, served by the North British Railway. Here is St Michael's Church. *Territorials:* Northumberland Yeomanry.

Warkworth Northumberland village and port on the River Coquet, seven miles from Alnwick, served by the North Eastern Railway. Here is St Lawrence's Church. *Territorials:* 7th Northumberland Fusiliers.

Warley Essex village two miles from Brentwood and the nearest station (Brentwood and Warley). Here at Warley, the old St Mary's Church was replaced in 1901 by a new one built from funds provided by stockbroker Evelyn Heseltine. *Territorials:* East Anglian Division, 4th Essex Regiment and Warley Garrison Cadets.

Warminster Wiltshire market town on the River Wylye four miles from Westbury on the western edge of Salisbury Plain. Here, on the western side of town, is St Denys's Church, and all around fine Georgian houses built from the prosperity of the early corn and cloth trade. *Territorials:* Wiltshire Yeomanry, 4th Wiltshire Regiment and Warminster Cadet Company.

Warnham Sussex village to the north-west of Horsham close to the border with Surrey. Served by the London, Brighton & South Coast Railway, Warnham station was a little to the north-east of the village. Here, in the churchyard of St Margaret's, is the grave of Michael Turner, clerk and sexton of the church for fifty years. His headstone tells how 'With nodding head the choir he led / That none should start too soon / The second too, he sang full tune. / His viol played the tune. *Territorials:* 4th Royal Sussex Regiment.

Warrington Lancashire market town on the River Mersey and Manchester Ship Canal, where many were employed in foundries, breweries, chemical and iron works. Glass products were made, as well as soap and borax. Among the towns several churches, St Elphin's has indentations left by cannon balls fired by Cromwell's troops during the Civil War. *Territorials:* 4th South Lancashire Regiment and West Lancashire Divisional Transport and Supply Column.

Warwick Market and county town on the River Avon and Grand Union Canal served by the Great Western and London & North Western railways. Here is St Mary's Church, one of its many memorials being to William Parr, the brother of Henry VIII's last wife, and King's School which maintained one OTC infantry company. *Territorials:* South Midland Division, 1st South Midland Mounted Brigade, Warwickshire Infantry Brigade, Warwickshire Yeomanry, Warwickshire RHA, 1st South Midland Mounted Brigade Signal Troop, 7th Royal Warwickshire Regiment and South Midland Divisional Transport and Supply Column.

Washford Somerset coastal village, four miles from Watchet, served by the West Somerset Mineral Railway which opened in 1865. *Territorials:* West Somerset Yeomanry and 5th Somerset Light Infantry.

Washington Durham village, seven miles from Sunderland, served by the North Eastern Railway. Ironworks, and extensive colliery, and a chemical works employed many. One visitor in 1913 wrote of Washington, that there was little to attract people, especially the 'huge heaps of debris from the chemical works'. Traced to the village have been the ancestors of the American president, George Washington. Here is Holy Trinity Church. *Territorials:* 8th Durham Light Infantry.

Watchet Somerset port on the Bristol Channel. Here were two stations, one operated by the Great Western Railway, the other, the West Somerset Mineral which opened in 1865 and ran to the harbour. Here is St Ducuman's Church. *Territorials:* 5th Somerset Light Infantry.

Waterlooville Hampshire town six miles from Portsmouth. Here is St George's Church. *Territorials:* 6th Hampshire Regiment.

Waternish Locality on Skye Island, ten miles from Portree. *Territorials:* 1st Lovat's Scouts.

Waterside Ayrshire village on the River Doon eight miles from Maybole. *Territorials:* 5th Royal Scots Fusiliers.

Watford Hertfordshire market town on the River Colne, eight miles from St Albans, served by the London & North Western Railway. Here were extensive breweries, one of them Benskin's. At St Mary's Church are memorials to the Morison family. *Territorials:* Hertfordshire Yeomanry, 4th East Anglian Brigade RFA, Hertfordshire Regiment and 2nd (Watford Scouts) Hertfordshire Cadet Company.

Wath-upon-Dearne West Riding of Yorkshire town, seven miles from Rotherham, served by the Great Central and Midland railways. Here is All Saints Church. *Territorials:* 5th York and Lancaster Regiment.

Watlington Oxfordshire town at the foot of the Chiltern Hills eight miles from Thame. Watlington station is situated at the terminus of the Great Western Railway's branch down from Princess Risborough which opened in 1872. Here is St Leonard's Church. *Territorials:* Oxfordshire Yeomanry.

Watnall Nottinghamshire village, five miles from Nottingham, served by the Midland Railway. *Territorials:* Nottinghamshire Yeomanry (South Notts).

Watten Caithness-shire village eight miles from Wick, its railway station being opened by the Sutherland and Caithness Railway Company in July 1874. *Territorials:* 5th Seaforth Highlanders.

Watton (Hertfordshire) Three hundred-year-old houses are a feature of this Hertfordshire village which lies on the River Beane five miles from Hertford. Even older is the flint-built Church of St Andrew and St Mary with its embattled tower. *Territorials:* Hertfordshire Regiment.

Watton (Norfolk) Small market town on the River Wissey, thirteen miles from Thetford by rail on the Great Eastern Railway. Here is St Mary's Church. *Territorials:* Norfolk Yeomanry, 4th and 6th Norfolk Regiment.

Wealdstone Residential district of Harrow, Middlesex, its station opened by the London & Birmingham Railway in 1837. Here is Holy Trinity Church. *Territorials:* 9th Middlesex Regiment.

Wedmore Somerset village four miles from Cheddar. Here is St Mary's Church. *Territorials:* 2nd South Western Mounted Brigade Transport and Supply Column.

Wednesbury Staffordshire industrial and market town, eight miles from Birmingham, served by the Great Western and London & North Western railways. Here, on a hill to the north of the town, is St Bartholomew's Church where there are memorials to the Parkes family. All manner of ironwork was produced in the area including rails, boiler plates and carriage axles for the railways. *Territorials:* 5th South Staffordshire Regiment and South Midland RGA.

Wednesfield Industrial suburb of Wolverhampton well known for its production of keys and locks. *Territorials:* 6th South Staffordshire Regiment.

Weedon Northamptonshire village eight miles from Northampton. Here is St Peter's Church. *Territorials:* Northamptonshire Yeomanry and 4th Northamptonshire Regiment.

Wellesbourne Warwickshire village six miles from Warwick. Here is St Peter's Church. *Territorials:* Warwickshire Yeomanry.

Wellingborough Northamptonshire market town, ten miles from Northampton, served by the London & North Western and Midland railways. Wellingborough was once an important centre for the production of boots, shoes and iron. Ninian Comper's St Mary's Church in Knox Road, on which work began in 1908, is thought to be the finest modern parish church in England. Wellingborough Grammar School maintained an OTC contingent. *Territorials:* Northamptonshire Yeomanry and 4th Northamptonshire Regiment.

Wellington (Shropshire) Market town, eleven miles from Shrewsbury, served by the Great Western and London & North Western railways. Agricultural implements and machinery were manufactured in the town. Here is All Saints Church. *Territorials:* Shropshire Yeomanry, Shropshire RHA and 4th King's Shropshire Light Infantry.

Wellington (Somerset) Market town, seven miles from Taunton, served by the Great Western Railway. Many of the town's fine Georgian houses were built from the prosperity brought by the wool trade. One large employer was Price's wool merchants who became a leading manufacturer of beds. Here is the church of St John the Baptist and Wellington School, which had an OTC contingent of one infantry company. *Territorials:* West Somerset Yeomanry and 5th Somerset Light Infantry.

Wells (Norfolk) Coastal town, ten miles from Fakenham, served by the Great Eastern Railway. Here is St Nicholas's Church which was almost totally destroyed when lightning struck in 1879. *Territorials:* Norfolk Yeomanry, 5th and 6th Norfolk Regiment.

Wells (Somerset) Market town at the foot of the Mendip Hills, twenty miles from Bath, reached by the Somerset Central Railway in 1859 and the East Somerset in 1862. Wells employed a good number in its manufacture of brushes and paper. Novelist Henry James (1843–1916) came to Wells in 1872 and was impressed by the quietness: '… the place seems always to savour of a Sunday afternoon'. Here, with its central tower, is Wells Cathedral. *Territorials:* North Somerset Yeomanry, Somerset RHA and 4th Somerset Light Infantry.

Welshpool Montgomeryshire market town on the River Severn, fifteen miles from Oswestry, served by the Cambrian Railway. There was also the Welshpool & Llanfair Light Railway which opened in 1903. Here is St Mary's Church. *Territorials:* Montgomeryshire Yeomanry and 7th Royal Welsh Fusiliers.

Welwyn Small Hertfordshire town, five miles from Hatfield, served by the Great Northern Railway. Here, in the centre of town and surrounded by fine Georgian buildings, is St Mary's Church. *Territorials:* Hertfordshire Regiment.

Wem Shropshire market town on the River Roden and Ellesmere Canal, ten miles from Shrewsbury, served by the London & North Western Railway. Well known throughout the county was the beer brewed by the Wem Brewery. Here is St Peter and St Paul's Church. *Territorials:* Shropshire Yeomanry and 4th King's Shropshire Light Infantry.

Wentworth Woodhouse Seat of Earl Fitzwilliam (commanding officer of the West Riding RHA) about one mile from Wentworth village. *Territorials:* West Riding RHA.

Weobley Herefordshire town eight miles from Leominster. Here at St Peter and St Paul's Church are memorials to the Birch and Peploe families. *Territorials:* Welsh Divisional Transport and Supply column.

West Auckland Durham mining village, three miles from Bishop Auckland, served by the North Eastern Railway. *Territorials:* 6th Durham Light Infantry.

West Bridgford Nottinghamshire village on the River Trent two miles from Nottingham. Here is St Giles's Church. *Territorials:* North Midland Divisional Transport and Supply Column.

West Bromwich Staffordshire industrial town, six miles from Birmingham, which prospered from its production of coal and iron. Here, on High Street, is Christ Church. *Territorials:* Staffordshire Yeomanry, 3rd North Midland Brigade RFA and North Midland Mounted Brigade Field Ambulance.

West Buckland Devon village three miles from Kingsbridge. *Territorials:* Royal North Devon Yeomanry.

West Calder Midlothian town, sixteen miles from Edinburgh, served by the Caledonian Railway. The area gave employment in its production of coal, iron, shale and limestone. *Territorials:* 10th Royal Scots.

West Croydon Surrey market town, West Croydon station opened by the London, Brighton & South Coast Railway in April 1851. *Territorials:* Surrey Yeomanry and West Croydon Cadets.

West Down Devon village seven miles from Barnstaple. Here is St Mary's Church. *Territorials:* Royal North Devon Yeomanry.

West Haddon Northamptonshire village eight miles from Daventry. Here is All Saints Church. *Territorials:* Northamptonshire Yeomanry.

West Hallam Derbyshire village on the Nutbrook Canal, seven miles from Derby, its station on the Great Northern Railway being opened in April 1878. Here is St Wilfrid's Church. *Territorials:* 4th North Midland Brigade RFA.

West Ham East London district on the north bank of the Thames. The West Ham Corporation opened a tram service here in February 1904. *Territorials:* 6th, 8th Essex Regiment, West Ham Cadets, St Mathew's (Custom House) Cadet Corps and Church of the Ascension Cadet Corps.

West Hartlepool Durham town on Hartlepool Bay served by the North Eastern Railway. Here were extensive iron works, docks and shipbuilding yards. Christ Church was built in 1854. *Territorials:* Northumberland Yeomanry, 3rd Northumbrian Brigade RFA, Durham RGA, 5th Durham Light Infantry and Northern Cyclist Battalion.

West Kirby Cheshire seaside resort on the mouth of the Dee nine miles from Birkenhead. The Great Western and London & North Western and Wirral railways had stations. Here is St Bridget's Church. *Territorials:* 4th Cheshire Regiment.

West Malling Small town, five miles from Maidstone, Kent, served by the South Eastern & Chatham Railway. Here is St Mary's Church where a notice tells how the north porch was built in 1903 from the proceeds of the sale of a jug dated 1581. *Territorials:* West Kent Yeomanry and 4th Royal West Kent Regiment.

West Meon Hampshire village, twelve miles from Alton, its station opened by the London & South Western Railway in June 1903. Here is the church of St John the Evangelist which was built in 1844. *Territorials:* 9th Hampshire Regiment.

West Moor Northumberland colliery village on the North Eastern Railway adjacent to Killingworth. George Stephenson resided at West Moor (1805–23) and a plaque on the wall of his cottage records that his first steam locomotive, *Blücher,* was built in the adjacent colliery wagon shops in 1814. *Territorials:* 5th Northumberland Fusiliers.

West Newton Norfolk village seven miles from King's Lynn. Here is St Peter and St Paul's Church. *Territorials:* 5th Norfolk Regiment.

West Ryton Durham town, four miles from Blaydon, served by the North Eastern Railway. *Territorials:* 9th Durham Light Infantry.

Westbury Wiltshire market town, five miles from Trowbridge, served by the Great Western Railway. Many from Westbury worked in the production of cloth, the old Laverton's Cloth Mills still there in Edward Street, and gloves. Here is All Saints Church. *Territorials:* 4th Wiltshire Regiment.

Westend Hampshire hamlet four miles from Bishops Waltham. *Territorials:* 5th Hampshire Regiment

Westerham Kent market town. There exists an old Southern Region Railway carriage advertisement showing Westerham, its houses, church (St Mary's) and shops gathered around a quiet green. It boasts 'handsome old coaching inns', the place being the birthplace of General Wolfe and just fifty-five minutes from London. Westerham station was opened by the South Eastern & Chatham Railway in July 1881. Erected in 1909 at St Mary's Church, was a William Morris window dedicated to conqueror of Quebec, General James Wolfe. He was born in the parish and baptised at St Mary's. *Territorials:* 4th West Kent Regiment and Westerham and Chipstead Cadet Corps..

Westfield (Caithness-shire) Village five miles from Thurso. *Territorials:* 5th Seaforth Highlanders.

Westfield (Sussex) Village four miles from Hastings where the church is dedicated to St John the Baptist and, notes one guide, two oak doors still swing to and fro after about 400 years. *Territorials:* 5th Royal Sussex Regiment.

Westgate-on-Sea Kent seaside resort, two miles from Margate, its station on the South Eastern & Chatham Railway opened in 1871. Here on Westgate Bay Avenue, is St Saviour's. A church built by C N Beazley 1883–84. *Territorials:* 4th Buffs East Kent Regiment.

Westminster Central London borough designated a city in 1900. Westminster School, in Dean's Yard, maintained an OTC contingent of two infantry companies. *Territorials:* 2nd London Division, London Mounted Brigade, Middlesex Infantry Brigade, Surrey Infantry Brigade, 2nd, 3rd, 4th, 5th, London Infantry Brigades, 2nd County of London Yeomanry, West Kent Yeomanry, Royal East Kent Yeomanry, Hertfordshire Yeomanry, London District Signal Companies, London Balloon Company, London Electrical Engineers, Engineer and Railway Staff Corps, 2nd, 9th, 14th, 15th, 16th, 18th London Regiment, London Mounted Brigade Field Ambulance, 6th London Field Ambulance, Queen's Westminster Cadet Company, Civil Service Cadet Corps (later called 2nd Cadet Battalion London Regiment), Newport Market School Cadet Corps, 'A' (Westminster) Company 3rd Senior Cadet Battalion, Waring Cadet Company and Polytechnic Schools Cadet Corps.

Weston-sub-Edge Gloucestershire village, two miles from Campden, its railway station opened by the Great Western in May 1904. Here is St Laurence's Church, greatly restored in 1861, 1880 and 1888. *Territorials:* Warwickshire Yeomanry.

Weston-super-Mare Somerset seaside resort on the Bristol Channel served by the Great Western Railway and the Weston-super-Mare, Clevedon & Portishead Railway which opened in December 1897. The Weston-super-Mare & District Tramways Company, with its crimson lake and cream overhead electrically operated vehicles, opened in May 1903. Here is All Saints Church. *Territorials:* North Somerset Yeomanry, Wessex Divisional Engineers, 4th Somerset Light Infantry, 2nd South Western Mounted Brigade Transport and Supply Column and 2nd South Western Mounted Brigade Field Ambulance.

Westonbirt Gloucestershire village three miles from Tetbury. Here is St Catherine's Church where there are memorials to the Holford family. *Territorials:* Gloucestershire Yeomanry.

Westwick Norfolk village two miles from North Walsham. Here is St Botolph's Church where there are memorials to the Berney and Petre families. *Territorials:* 5th Norfolk Regiment.

Wetherby West Riding of Yorkshire market town in the River Wharfe, eight miles from Harrogate, served by the North Eastern Railway. Here is St James's Church. *Territorials:* 5th West Yorkshire Regiment.

Weybridge Surrey village on the River Wye, at the point where it joins the Thames three miles from Chertsey, served by the London & South Western Railway. Here is St James's Church. *Territorials:* 6th East Surrey Regiment and Weybridge and District Scout Cadets.

Weymouth Dorset seaside resort and port fourteen miles from Dorchester. Portland stone was exported from Weymouth. Employment was also provided in the manufacture of bricks, titles and maritime equipment. The bathing machine was pioneered at Weymouth, which no doubt encouraged King George III to get his feet wet and in doing so get himself into the record books as the first reigning monarch to bathe in the sea. Thomas Hardy was another frequent visitor, he called the place 'Budmouth' in his novel *The Trumpet Major*. Weymouth Town railway station was opened by the Great Western in January 1857, then the station at the Quay, from where steam packets crossed to the Channel Isles, in 1889. The town was also served by the London & South Western. *Territorials:*

Dorsetshire Yeomanry, Dorsetshire RGA, Dorsetshire Fortress Engineers and Weymouth Secondary Schools Cadets.

Whaley Bridge Derbyshire village on the River Goyt and Peak Forest Canal, three miles from Chapel-en-le-Frith, served by the London & North Western Railway. *Territorials:* 6th Sherwood Foresters.

Whalley Range District in south Manchester. *Territorials:* Duke of Lancaster's Own Yeomanry.

Whimple Devon village, eight miles from Exeter, served by the London & South Western Railway. Here is St Mary's Church. *Territorials:* 4th Devonshire Regiment.

Whissendine Rutlandshire village, six miles from Melton Mowbray, served by the Midland Railway. Here is St Andrew's Church. *Territorials:* 5th Leicestershire Regiment.

Whitburn Linlithgowshire village on the River Almond, three miles from Bathgate, served by the North British Railway. Here were coal and iron mines. *Territorials:* 10th Royal Scots.

Whitby North Riding of Yorkshire port and seaside resort on the River Esk, twenty miles from Scarborough, served by the North Eastern Railway. Here at St Mary's Church are memorials to the Cholmley, Lascelles, Yeoman and Chapman families. *Territorials:* 2nd Northumbrian Brigade RFA.

Whitchurch (Glamorgan) Village on the River Taff, one mile from Llandaff, served by the Cardiff Railway which opened in 1911. Here is St Mary's Church. *Territorials:* Welsh Divisional RE.

Whitchurch (Hampshire) Hampshire town on the River Test, seven miles from Andover, served by the London & South Western Railway (opened in 1854) and the Didcot, Newbury & Southampton which Arrived in 1885. Here is All Hallows Church. *Territorials:* 4th, 9th Hampshire Regiment and 3rd Wessex Field Ambulance.

Whitchurch (Shropshire) Market town, twelve miles from Market Drayton, served by the London & South Western and Cambrian railways. Here is St Alkmund's Church. *Territorials:* South Wales Mounted Brigade, Shropshire Yeomanry and 4th King's Shropshire Light Infantry.

Whitchurch (Somerset) Village three miles from Bristol. Here is St Nicholas's Church. *Territorials:* 4th Somerset Light Infantry.

Whitebridge Inverness-shire hamlet on the River Foyers ten miles from Fort Augustus. 1st *Territorials:* Lovat's Scouts.

Whitehaven Cumberland seaport, market town and busy railway junction twelve miles from Maryport. A large company here made rails for the railways, some of them finding their way to Texas and Alabama in 1872. Here are Holy Trinity and St James's churches. *Territorials:* Westmorland and Cumberland Yeomanry, 4th East Lancashire Brigade RFA and 5th Border Regiment.

Whiteparish Wiltshire village seven miles from Salisbury. Here at All Saints Church there are memorials to the Eyre and St Barbe families. *Territorials:* Wiltshire Yeomanry.

Whithorn Wigtownshire town, eleven miles from Wigtown, situated at the terminus of the Portpatrick & Wigtownshire branch that ran down from Newton Stewart. Whithorn Parish Church as built in 1822. *Territorials:* 5th King's Own Scottish Borderers.

Whitland Carmarthenshire village six miles from Narberth. *Territorials:* Pembrokeshire Yeomanry.

Whitley Bay Northumberland seaside resort, ten miles from Newcastle, served by the North Eastern Railway. Here is St Paul's Church. *Territorials:* Northern Cyclist Battalion.

Whitstable Kent fishing port, well known for its oysters, six miles from Canterbury. In 1830 at Whitstable was opened the first steam-powered passenger railway (the Canterbury & Whitstable) in southern England. Here is All Saints Church. *Territorials:* 4th Buffs East Kent Regiment, Kent Cyclist Battalion and 2nd Home Counties Field Ambulance.

Whittlesea Cambridgeshire market town, six miles from Peterborough, served by the Great Eastern Railway. The 1862 restoration of St Mary's Church included the chapel dedicated to Lieutenant-General Sir H G Smith, GCB who was born in the town and died in 1860. The town of Ladysmith in South Africa was named after his wife. Many from Whittlesea were employed in the production of bricks – Arthur Mee noted of the town that it was 'flanked by the tall chimneys of brickyards rising in mass formation.' *Territorials:* Cambridgeshire Regiment.

Whitwell (Hertfordshire) Village four miles from Hitchin. *Territorials:* Hertfordshire Regiment.

Whitwell (Isle of Wight) Village, four miles from Ventnor, its station opened by the Newport, Godshill & St Lawrence Railway in July 1897. The church here (its really two chapels) is dedicated to The Blessed Virgin and St Radegund. *Territorials:* 8th Hampshire Regiment.

Whitwick Small Leicestershire town, thirteen miles from Leicester, its station opened by the Charnwood Forest Railway in April 1883. Here is St John's Church. *Territorials:* Leicestershire Yeomanry.

Whorlton Durham town on the River Tees three miles from Barnard Castle. Here is St Mary's Church. *Territorials:* 4th Northumberland Fusiliers.

Wick Caithness fishing port once giving employment to hundreds in the gutting and curing of herrings – more handled here than the rest of Scotland together. The Sutherland and Caithness Railway reached the town in 1874, its station being opened on 28 July. *Territorials:* 5th Seaforth Highlanders.

Wickford Essex village on the River Crouch, five miles from Billericay, its station on a Great Eastern Railway branch opened from Shenfield in 1888. Here is St Catherine's Church. *Territorials:* 4th Essex Regiment.

Wickham Hampshire village on the River Meon, twelve miles from Portsmouth, served by the London & South Western Railway. The Wickham Brewery can still be seen opposite Chesapeake Mill (built from timbers of a captured American ship by that name) at the bottom of Bridge Street. Here is St Nicholas's Church. *Territorials:* 6th Hampshire Regiment.

Wickham Bishops Essex village on the River Blackwater, three miles from Maldon, served by the Great Eastern Railway. Here is St Bartholomew's Church. *Territorials:* 5th Essex Regiment.

Widford Hertfordshire village, four miles from Ware, served by the Great Eastern Railway. Here at St John's Church are memorials to the Hamond family. *Territorials:* Hertfordshire Regiment.

Widness Lancashire manufacturing town on the banks of the River Mersey, thirteen miles from Liverpool, served by the London & North Western and Cheshire Lines railways. At Widnes there were iron foundries, chemical and locomotive works. *Territorials:* 3rd West Lancashire Brigade RFA, West Lancashire Divisional Engineers and 5th South Lancashire Regiment.

Wigan Lancashire manufacturing town on the River Douglas, eighteen miles from Manchester, served by the London & south Western and Great Central Railways. Unveiled on 7 February 1903 in Mesnes Park was the Wigan memorial to those Regular, Volunteer and Yeomanry forces that gave their lives in South Africa during the Boer War. Born in the town in 1906 was the entertainer George Formby. *Territorials:* Lancashire Hussars and 5th Manchester Regiment.

Wigston Magna Leicestershire village, four miles from Leicester, served by the Midland Railway who had engine sheds here employing a good number. Here are St Wolstan and All Saints churches, the two leading to a local town nickname 'Wigston two-steeples'. *Territorials:* Leicestershire Yeomanry and 4th Leicestershire Regiment.

Wigton Cumberland market town, eleven miles from Carlisle, served by the Maryport & Carlisle Railway. The principal industries here were the manufacture of cloth, tanning, brewing and the making of spade and shovel handles. Here is St Mary's Church which was built 1788. *Territorials:* Westmorland and Cumberland Yeomanry and 5th Border Regiment.

Wigtown Seaport, fishing and county town of Wigtownshire, eight miles from Newton Stewart, served by the Portpatrick & Wigtownshire Joint Railway. *Territorials:* 5th King's Own Scottish Borderers.

Willenhall Three miles east of Wolverhampton on the road to Walsall, Willenhall was noted for its production of door locks, padlocks, bolts, latches, keys and hinges. Both the Midland and London & North Western railways had stations in the town. The present St Giles's parish church in Walsall Street only dates from 1867, the vicar of its predecessor, William Moreton, being an enthusiast of cock fighting and kept a cockpit at the vicarage. *Territorials:* 6th South Staffordshire Regiment.

Willersey Gloucestershire village, seven miles from Evesham, reached by the Great Western Railway in 1904. Here is St Peter's Church. *Territorials:* 5th Gloucestershire Regiment.

Willesden District and important railway junction to the north-west of London. On the north side of Neasden Lane, the is the old parish church of St Mary's, its registers dating from 1569. *Territorials:* 9th Middlesex Regiment and 1st North Paddington Cadets.

Willington Durham village on the River Ear, four miles from Bishop Auckland, served by the North Eastern Railway. Here is St Stephen's Church. *Territorials:* 6th Durham Light Infantry.

Williton Somerset market town, eight miles from Minehead, served by the West Somerset Railway. Here is St Peter's Church. *Territorials:* West Somerset Yeomanry and 5th Somerset Light Infantry.

Wilmslow Cheshire town on the River Bollin, six miles from Macclesfield, served by the London & North Western Railway. Here is St Bartholomew's Church. *Territorials:* 7th Cheshire Regiment.

Wilton Wiltshire town at the confluence of the rivers Nadder and Wiley, three miles from Salisbury, served by the Great Western and London & South Western railways. Carpets have been made at Wilton since Elizabethan times. Here is the church of St Mary and St Nicholas, built 1841–45 with a detached bell-tower. The church is orientated north-south, rather than the usual east-west. *Territorials:* 4th Wiltshire Regiment.

Wimbledon Residential district in south-west London and between 1860–89 the venue for the National Rifle Association's summer competitions. Wimbledon's Christ Church on Copse Hill dates from 1860; St John's at Spencer Hill was completed in 1875, and All Saints in 1893. King's College School had a contingent in the OTC. *Territorials:* Surrey Yeomanry, 5th East Surrey Regiment and Wimbledon Boys Naval Brigade.

Wimborne Dorset market town at the confluence of the rivers Wim and Stour, six miles from Poole, served by the London & South Western and Somerset & Dorset railways. Here is Wimborne Minster (St Cuthberga's). *Territorials:* Dorsetshire Yeomanry and 4th Dorsetshire Regiment.

Wincanton Somerset market town on the River Cale, five miles from Bruton, served by the Somerset & Dorset, Midland and London & South Western railways. During the Napoleonic wars some 400 French officers were held prisoner at Wincanton. Here is St Peter and St Paul's Church. *Territorials:* North Somerset Yeomanry.

Winchburgh Linlithgowshire village, six miles from Linlithgow, served by the North British Railway. Here most were employed in the production of shale, bricks and tiles. *Territorials:* Lothians and Border Horse and 10th Royal Scots.

Winchcombe Gloucestershire market town on the River Isbourne in the Cotswolds, seven miles from Cheltenham. Winchcombe station was opened by the Great Western Railway in February 1905. Here is St Peter's Church which dates from the late fifteenth century. *Territorials:* Gloucestershire Yeomanry.

Winchelsea Sussex coastal town, eight miles from Hastings, served by the South Eastern & Chatham Railway. Here is St Thomas's Church. *Territorials:* 5th Royal Sussex Regiment.

Winchester Hampshire cathedral city on the River Itchen, twelve miles from Southampton, served by the London & South Western and Didcot, Newbury & Southampton railways. An old barracks known as the King's House was partially destroyed by fire in 1894. In Hyde Street the Hyde Brewery, which employed many in Winchester, can still be seen. Above one of the old city gates is St Swithun-upon-Kingsgate Church, described by Anthony Trollope (he calls it St Cuthbert's) in his novel *The Warden.* Always a strong supporter of the Volunteer Force, Winchester College maintained an OTC contingent of four infantry companies. *Territorials:* Hampshire Yeomanry, 4th Hampshire Regiment, Wessex Divisional Transport and Supply Column, 3rd Wessex Field Ambulance and Peter Symonds School Cadet Corps.

Windermere Westmorland town on the eastern shore of Lake Windermere, its station at the termination of the London & North Western Railway's branch that opened in 1847 from Kendal. Here is St Martin's Church. *Territorials:* Westmorland and Cumberland Yeomanry and 4th Border Regiment.

Windsor Berkshire town on the River Thames twenty-two miles from London. The Slough to Windsor branch of the Great Western Railway was opened in October 1849, the London & South Western also having a station on its branch up from Stains. Here, just along the main road from the castle, is the parish church of St John the Baptist which dates from 1822. At Old Windsor, Beaumont College maintained a contingent of the OTC, as did Windsor's Imperial Service College. *Territorials:* Berkshire Yeomanry, 4th Royal Berkshire Regiment and Windsor Cadet Companies.

Wing Buckinghamshire village three miles from Leighton Buzzard. Here at the Saxon All Saints Church are memorials to the Fynes and Dormer families. *Territorials:* Buckinghamshire Yeomanry.

Wingham Kent village, six miles from Canterbury, at the termination of the South Eastern & Chatham Railway's branch from Eastry. Here at St Mary's Church are memorials to the Oxenden family. *Territorials:* 4th Buffs East Kent Regiment.

Winkleigh Devon village twelve miles from Torrington. Here is All Saints Church. *Territorials:* 6th Devonshire Regiment.

Winscombe Somerset village, two miles from Axbridge, served by the Great Western Railway. Here is St James's Church. *Territorials:* 4th Somerset Light Infantry.

Winsford Cheshire town on the River Weaver, eight miles from Crewe and served by the London & North Western Railway, where many were employed in the production of salt. Here is Christ Church. *Territorials:* Cheshire Yeomanry and 7th Cheshire Regiment.

Winslow Buckinghamshire market town, eleven miles from Aylesbury, served by the London & North Western Railway. Here is St Lawrence's Church. *Territorials:* Buckinghamshire Battalion.

Winston Durham village on the River Tees, six miles from Barnard Castle, served by the North Eastern Railway. Here is St Andrew's Church. *Territorials:* 6th Durham Light Infantry.

Wirksworth Derbyshire market town, thirteen miles from Derby, where lead mines and local quarries once gave employment to the area. Wirksworth station was situated at the end of a Midland Railway branch line that opened in 1867 and ran from Duffield. Here, dating from the thirteenth century, is St Mary's Church. *Territorials:* Derbyshire Yeomanry and 6th Sherwood Foresters.

Wisbech Market town on the River Nene, Isle of Ely, Cambridgeshire, well known for its fruit production. Wisbech was served by the Great Eastern and Midland & Great Northern Joint railways. Here, close to the river, is St Peter and St Paul's Church. *Territorials:* Yeomanry and Cambridgeshire Regiment.

Wiseton Nottinghamshire village one mile from Clayworth. *Territorials:* Nottinghamshire RHA.

Wishaw Lanarkshire town, fifteen miles from Glasgow, served by the Caledonian Railway. Here ironworks and a distillery gave employment to many. *Territorials:* Lanarkshire Yeomanry and 8th Highland Light Infantry.

Wishford Wiltshire village, six miles from Salisbury, served by the Great Western Railway. Wishford station was opened by the Wiltshire, Somerset & Weymouth Railway Company in June 1856. Here is St Giles's Church. *Territorials:* 4th Wiltshire Regiment.

Witchampton Dorset village on the River Allen, eight miles from Blandford, where a paper mill employed many. Here is All Saints Church. *Territorials:* 4th Dorsetshire Regiment.

Witham Essex town on the River Blackwater, fourteen miles from Colchester, served by the Great Eastern Railway. Here is St Nicholas's Church, its registers dating from 1669. *Territorials:* 5th Essex Regiment.

Witheridge Devon village at the confluence of the rivers Sturcombe and Little Dart ten miles from South Molton. Here is the church of St John the Baptist. *Territorials:* 6th Devonshire Regiment.

Withernsea East Riding of Yorkshire coastal village, five miles from Patrington, its station at the end of the North Eastern Railway branch from Hull. Here is St Nicholas's Church. *Territorials:* 5th East Yorkshire Regiment.

Witley (Surrey) Village, four miles from Godalming, served by the London & South Western Railway. Here is All Saints Church. *Territorials:* 5th Queen's Royal West Surrey Regiment and King Edward's School (Witley) Cadet Corps.

Witley (Worcester) Village ten miles from Worcester. Here is St Michael's Church. *Territorials:* Worcestershire Yeomanry.

Witney Oxfordshire market town on the River Windrush, eleven miles from Oxford, served by the Great Western Railway. Gloves were made here and, for centuries, blankets. The whole town owing much to the wool trade. Here at St Mary's Church are memorials to the Wenman family. *Territorials:* Oxfordshire Yeomanry and 4th Oxfordshire and Buckinghamshire Light Infantry.

Wittersham Kent village, five miles from Rye, its station opened by the Rother Valley Light Railway in April 1900. Here is the church of St John the Baptist. *Territorials:* 5th Buffs East Kent Regiment.

Wiveliscombe Somerset market town, eleven miles from Taunton, its station being opened by the Devon & Somerset Railway in June 1871. Slate quarries and a brewery at Golden Hill gave employment to the area. Here is St Andrew's Church. *Territorials:* West Somerset Yeomanry and 5th Somerset Light Infantry.

Wivenhoe Essex town and port of the River Colne, five miles from Colchester, served by the Great Eastern Railway. Here, close to the river's edge, is St Mary's Church which was much damaged in an 1884 earthquake. The church registers date from 1672. *Territorials:* 5th Essex Regiment.

Woburn Bedfordshire market town, fifteen miles from Bedford, served by the London & North Western Railway. Demolished in 1865 was the ancient church of St Mary in Bedford Street, its Bath stone replacement being completed in 1868 at Park Street. Woburn Abbey, the seat of the Dukes of Bedford, is close by. *Territorials:* Bedfordshire Yeomanry.

Woking Surrey residential and market town on the River Wey, six miles from Guildford, served by the London & South Western Railway. Opened here in 1889 was Christ Church, and in the same year, the Shan Jehan Mosque in Oriental Road. The nearby Brookwood Cemetery is one of the largest in the world. *Territorials:* Surrey Yeomanry, 5th Queen's Royal West Surrey Regiment and Home Counties Divisional Transport and Supply Column.

Wokingham Berkshire market town, seven miles from Reading, served by the London & South Western Railway. Here is All Saints Church and, on Reading Road, St Paul's which was built 1862–64. *Territorials:* Berkshire Yeomanry and 4th Royal Berkshire Regiment.

Wolferton Norfolk village seven miles from King's Lynn. At Wolferton the Great Eastern station was the nearest to Sandringham. A station like no other, with no advertisements to offend the royal eye, crowns and royal arms on the lampposts. Here is St Peter's Church. *Territorials:* 5th Norfolk Regiment.

Wollaton Nottinghamshire village on the Nottingham Canal three miles from Nottingham. Here at St Leonard's Church there are memorials to the Willoughby family. *Territorials:* Nottinghamshire Yeomanry (South Notts).

Wolsingham Durham town on the River Wear, ten miles from Bishop Auckland, served by the North Eastern Railway. Wolsingham was well known for its quarries producing fine black-spotted marble. It made shovels, had several saw mills, lead mines and manufactured steel. John Rogerson & Co was a major employer. Here is St Matthew's Church. *Territorials:* 6th Durham Light Infantry.

Wolverhampton Staffordshire manufacturing town thirteen miles from Birmingham. A busy railway and canal junction, the town employed many in its production of locks, keys, locomotive tubing, guns, bicycles, toys and kitchen furniture. The tall, red sandstone, tower of St Peter's Church looks down onto the market place. Wolverhampton Grammar School maintained an OTC contingent of one infantry company. *Territorials:* Staffordshire Yeomanry, 3rd North Midland Brigade RFA, 6th South Staffordshire Regiment and 3rd North Midland Field Ambulance.

Wolverton Buckinghamshire town, two miles from Stony Stratford, founded in 1838 when the London & Birmingham Railway Company set up its locomotive works here. Opened in May 1887 was the Wolverton & Stony Stratford Tramway. Many of the railway's worker were resident in the latter town. Here is Holy Trinity Church. *Territorials:* Buckinghamshire Battalion.

Wombwell West Riding of Yorkshire town on the River Dove and Dearne and Dove Canal, seven miles from Rotherham, served by the Midland and Great Central railways. Here is St Mary's Church. *Territorials:* 5th York and Lancaster Regiment.

Wooburn Buckinghamshire village, four miles from Wycombe, served by the Great Western Railway. Many in the area were employed in local paper mills. Here is St Paul's Church. *Territorials:* 4th Oxfordshire and Buckinghamshire Light Infantry.

Woodbridge Suffolk market town on the River Deben, eight miles from Ipswich, served by the Great Eastern Railway. Here is St Mary's Church and Woodbridge School which maintained an OTC contingent of one infantry company. *Territorials:* Suffolk Yeomanry, 4th Suffolk Regiment and 1st East Anglian Field Ambulance.

Woodburn Northumberland villages (East and West Woodburn), four and five miles from Bellingham, served by the North British Railway. Here is All Saints Church. *Territorials:* 4th Northumberland Fusiliers.

Woodbury Devon village, seven miles from Exeter, served by the London & South Western Railway. Here at St Swithin's Church are memorials to the Haydon family. *Territorials:* 7th Devonshire Regiment.

Woodchurch Village in Kent, five miles from Tenterden on the edge of the Weald. Here is All Saints Church. *Territorials:* 5th Buffs East Kent Regiment.

Woodford Essex residential district and north-east suburb of London. Here is the parish church of St Margaret's. *Territorials:* 4th Essex Regiment.

Woodford Bridge Devonshire village on the River Torridge, four miles from Holsworthy and close to Milton Damerel. *Territorials:* Royal North Devon Yeomanry.

Woodhall Spa Lincolnshire village on the Great Northern Railway's branch to Horncastle which opened in 1855. The story goes that the spa water that brought fortune to the village was discovered when engineers were boring (unsuccessfully) for coal in 1824. Here is St Andrew's and St Peter's churches. *Territorials:* 4th Lincolnshire Regiment.

Woodhay Hampshire village, six miles from Newbury, its station opened by the Didcot, Newbury & Southampton Railway in May 1885. Here is St Martin's Church. *Territorials:* 4th Hampshire Regiment.

Woodhouse Eaves Leicestershire village on Beacon Hill, four miles from Loughborough. Here is St Paul's Church. *Territorials:* 5th Leicestershire Regiment.

Woodlands Dorset village seven miles from Wimborne. The Duke of Monmouth was captured on the Woodlands estate after his defeat at Sedgemoor. Here is Ascension Church, built by G F Bodley for the Countess of Shaftesbury in 1892. *Territorials:* 4th Dorsetshire Regiment.

Woodstock Oxfordshire market town on the River Glyme, ten miles from Oxford, its station (Blenheim and Woodstock) on the Western Railway's branch that opened in May 1890. Woodstock was for centuries known for its glove making. Here is the church of St Mary Magdalene. *Territorials:* Oxfordshire Yeomanry and 4th Oxfordshire and Buckinghamshire Light Infantry.

Wool Dorset village on the River Frome, five miles from Wareham, served by the London & South Western Railway. In the area is a house once the property of the Turberville family, the inspiration for Thomas Hardy's novel *Tess of the D'Urbevilles*. Here is the church of Holy Rood. *Territorials:* 4th Dorsetshire Regiment.

Wooler Northumberland market town, sixteen miles from Berwick-upon-Tweed, its station on the North Eastern Railway being opened in September 1887. The town's population were chiefly employed in agriculture and sheep herding. *Territorials:* 7th Northumberland Fusiliers.

Woolsery Devon village eight miles from Bideford. Here is Holy Trinity Church. *Territorials:* Royal North Devon Yeomanry.

Woolston Locality in Southampton borough with railway station opened by the Southampton & Netley Company (soon absorbed into the London & South Western) in March 1866. Here in Weston Grove Road, and built in 1863, is St Mark's Church. *Territorials:* Hampshire RGA and 5th Hampshire Regiment.

Woolwich London borough on the south bank of the Thames. Here is the Woolwich Arsenal. *Territorials:* West Kent Yeomanry, 2nd, 8th London Brigades RFA, 20th London Regiment, East Anglian Divisional Transport and Supply Column, 1st London Divisional Transport and Supply Column, 4th London Field Ambulance and 2nd Woolwich Scout Cadet Company.

Wootton Village on the Isle of Wight, four miles from Ryde, its station being opened by the Ryde & Newport Railway in December 1875. Here is St Edmund's Church with its Norman south doorway and Jacobean pulpit. Buried in the churchyard is Admiral Sir John Baird who died in 1908. *Territorials:* 8th Hampshire Regiment.

Wootton Bassett Wiltshire market town, six miles from Swindon, served by the Great Western Railway. The Wiltshire & Berkshire Canal passes south of the town. Here is St Bartholomew and All Saints Church. *Territorials:* Wiltshire Yeomanry.

Worcester Cathedral city on the River Severn served by the Great Western Railway. Worcester for some time has been well known for its manufacture of gloves, porcelain and, of course, Mr Lea and Mr Perrins source which is still made in the city. A horse-drawn tram service opened in Worcester in February 1884. Two Worcester schools, King's and the Royal Grammar, maintained OTC contingents. *Territorials:* Worcestershire Yeomanry, 2nd South Midland Brigade RFA and 8th Worcestershire Regiment.

Workington Cumberland seaport and industrial town at the mouth of the Derwent. The port provided employment, other chief industries included the manufacture of steel rails, tinplate, iron bridges and boilers. There was also a paper mill and brewery. Workington's ancient church of St Michael was almost totally destroyed by fire in 1887. Here too, on Washington Street since 1823, is St John's. *Territorials:* Westmorland and Cumberland Yeomanry, 4th East Lancashire Brigade RFA and 5th Border Regiment.

Worksop Nottinghamshire town twelve miles from Mansfield. At Worksop there were iron and brass foundries, saw mils, and a chemical works. Here at the Priory Church of St Mary and St Cuthbert there are memorials to the Furnival and Lovetit families. On display in the church is a scull that has been penetrated by an arrow (the tip still there), found near the porch c1850. Worksop College maintained an OTC contingent of two infantry companies. *Territorials:* Nottinghamshire Yeomanry (Sherwood Rangers) and 8th Sherwood Foresters.

Wormley Hertfordshire village, six miles from Hertford, where the small Norman church of St Laurence is reached via an avenue of oak trees. Here one monument remembers an Elizabethan couple with twelve children. *Territorials:* Hertfordshire Regiment.

Worthing West Sussex town to the west of Brighton served by the London, Brighton & South Coast Railway. Worthing's Pier was reopened after being extended in 1889, then damaged in 1913. Here, in Chapel Road, is St Paul's Church; Christ Church, in Grafton Road; St George's, to the east of the town, and Holy Trinity which, in Shelly Road, dates from 1882. *Territorials:* Sussex Yeomanry, 1st Home Counties Brigade RFA, 4th Royal Sussex Regiment and Steyne School Cadet Corps.

Wotton-under-Edge Gloucestershire market town, twelve miles from Stroud beneath the western edge of the Cotswolds. Here is St Mary's Church and, on the corner of Bear Lane, The British School (1843) at which Isaac Pitman is said to have first taught shorthand. *Territorials:* 5th Gloucestershire Regiment.

Wragby Small town in Lincolnshire, eight miles from Market Rasen, its station opened by the Louth & Lincoln Railway in December 1876. Here is All Saints Church. *Territorials:* Lincolnshire Yeomanry.

Wrexham Denbighshire market town, eleven miles from Chester, served by the Great Western and Great Central Railways. The first lager brewery in Britain was started here in 1881, tanning and coal mining also went on locally. Wrexham District Tramways, with its dark brown and cream vehicles, opened for service in November 1876. Here is St Giles's Church. *Territorials:* North Wales Infantry Brigade, Denbighshire Yeomanry and 4th Royal Welsh Fusiliers.

Writtle Essex village two miles from Chelmsford. When mentioning Writtle, guides of all periods compliment it for its green, pond and cricket pitch which are 'all framed by ancient houses.' Here at All Saints Church, where the registers date from 1631, there are memorials to the Comyns and Petres families, and brasses show a wife with thee husbands and a husband with four wives. *Territorials:* 5th Essex Regiment.

Wroxall Village two miles from Ventnor on the Isle of Wight Railway. Wroxall station opening in September 1866. Here is St John's Church, built by T R Saunders (1875–77) from stone excavated during the construction of the railway tunnel just outside Ventnor. *Territorials:* 8th Hampshire Regiment.

Wye Small market town on the River Stour, nine miles from Canterbury, served by the South Eastern & Chatham Railway. Wye station was opened by the South Eastern Company in February 1846. Born at Wye, and the daughter of a barber, was Aphra Behn (1640–89) who became the country's first professional novelist and a spy for Charles Stuart. Here is the church of St Gregory and St Martin and, founded in 1445, Wye College. *Territorials:* Royal East Kent Yeomanry.

Wymondham (Leicestershire) Village on the River Eye, six miles from Melton Mowbray and close to the borders with Lincolnshire and Rutland. There had been a Midland Railway station serving, and called, Wymondham since 1848, but this was more than a miles away. Opened on 1 May 1884, however, was Edmondthorpe and Wymondham station on the northern edge of the village. Here is St Peter's Church. *Territorials:* 5th Leicestershire Regiment.

Wymondham (Norfolk) Norfolk market town, nine miles from Norwich, served by the Great Eastern Railway. The town had a large brewery, saw mills, and a brush factory. Here is the Abbey Church of St Mary and St Thomas of Canterbury which dates from 1130. *Territorials:* Norfolk Yeomanry and 4th Norfolk Regiment.

Yalding Kent village at the confluence of the rivers Beult and Medway, six miles from Maidstone, served by the South Eastern & Chatham Railway. Yalding, in its time, was the largest producer of hops in England. The headmaster of Cleaves Grammar School at Yalding was the father of Edmund Blunden, the poet attending the school from 1907–09. Here is St Peter and St Paul's Church. *Territorials:* 5th Buffs East Kent Regiment.

Yarm-on-Tees North Riding of Yorkshire market town, four miles from Stockton, served by the North Eastern Railway. The area was often affected by the flooding of the Tees, the water reaching four ft in 1882 at the Market Place. Here, on the brink of the river, is the church of St Mary Magdalene. *Territorials:* 4th Yorkshire Regiment.

Yarmouth Isle of Wight market town at the mouth of the River Yar ten miles from Newport. Yarmouth station was opened by the Freshwater, Yarmouth & Newport Railway in July 1889. Here is St James's Church which dates from c1680. *Territorials:* 8th Hampshire Regiment.

Yate Gloucestershire village on the River Frome, ten miles from Bristol, served by the Midland Railway. Here is St Mary's Church. Yate Court, the fortified mansion of the Berkeley family, changed hands a number of times during the Civil War. *Territorials:* Gloucestershire Yeomanry.

Yateley Hampshire village five miles from Farnborough. Here in St Peter's Church there is a plaque telling how the Colours carried by the 4th King's Own Regiment during the Peninsular Wars and at Waterloo where once lodged there. *Territorials:* 4th Hampshire Regiment.

Yaxley Huntingdonshire village, four miles from Peterborough, its station opened by the Great Northern Railway in May 1890. Close by Yaxley is Norman Cross, the site of a prison purpose-built to hold thousands of French prisoners from the Napoleonic wars. Some 1,770 are said to be buried in the area. Long gone, some stones from the building, however, can be seen at Yaxley's St Peter's Church. *Territorials:* 5th Bedfordshire Regiment.

Yealmpton Devon village on the River Yealm, seven miles from Plymouth, its station at the end of the Great Western branch from Plymouth opened in January 1898. Here is St Bartholomew's Church. *Territorials:* Devonshire Fortress Engineers and Yealmpton Cadet Corps.

Yeldham Essex village on the River Colne, seven miles from Halstead, with station opened by the Colne Valley & Halstead Railway in May 1862. Here at St Andrew's Church are memorials to the Symonds family, the registers dating from 1653. *Territorials:* 5th Essex Regiment.

Yeovil Somerset market town on the River Yeo, twenty-two miles from Wells, served by the Great Western and London & South Western railways. Here at the church of St John the Baptist are memorials to the Harbin, Batten and Newman families. In the area there were breweries and brickfields, but the town was most famous for its gloves. *Territorials:* South Western Infantry Brigade, Dorsetshire Yeomanry, West Somerset Yeomanry and 5th Somerset Light Infantry.

Ynysddu Monmouthshire hamlet, four miles from Risca, with station on the Sirhowy branch of the London & North Western Railway. Many from the area were employed in the colliery at Cwmfelinfach, just a half-mile to the south, the Miners' Institute being built there in 1913. *Territorials:* 1st Monmouthshire Regiment.

York The Scarborough railway bridge crosses the Ouse from where visitors experience a good view of the Minster. In one of Francis Frith's photos of York taken in 1892 we see Lower Petergate with its jettied houses winding on towards the Minster. A coalman's cart is parked up outside Ellis & Kirkby's clothing shop, which is next-door to Merriman the pawnbroker. Across the road the trade sign of Seale's Brush and Mat Warehouses takes the form of a brush large enough to sweep the street from side-to-side in a single action. Here in North Street is All Saints Church, well known for its fine collection of medieval glass, and in Colney Street, St Martin-le-Grand. St Peter's School in York maintained one OTC infantry company. *Territorials:* West Riding Division, Yorkshire Mounted Brigade, 1st West Riding Infantry Brigade, Yorkshire Hussars, West Riding RGA, Yorkshire Mounted Brigade Signal Troop, 5th West Yorkshire Regiment and Yorkshire Mounted Brigade Transport and Supply Column, West Riding Divisional Transport and Supply Column.

Yorkhill District of Glasgow with railway station opened in March 1886 by the Glasgow, City & District line. *Territorials:* Lanarkshire Yeomanry (Royal Glasgow), Lowland Divisional Transport and Supply Column, Lowland Mounted Brigade Field Ambulance, 1st, and 2nd Lowland Divisional Field Ambulances.

Youlgreave Derbyshire mining village on the River Bradford, five miles from Bakewell, once known for its production of lead. Here is the medieval All Saints Church which was restored by Norman Shaw in 1870. *Territorials:* Derbyshire Yeomanry.

Ystrad Glamorgan village, three miles from Treherbert, served by the Taff Vale Railway. Ystrad station opening in February 1861. Here, in Penrhys Road, is St Stephen's Church which was built in 1896. *Territorials:* Welsh Divisional Transport and Supply Column.

Ystradgynlais Breconshire village, nine miles from Neath, served by the Neath & Brecon Railway which arrived in July 1869. Here were collieries, tinplate and ironworks; a major employer in the area being the Ynys-Cedwyn Company. St Cynog's Church, at Ystradgynlais, dates from 1861. *Territorials:* Brecknockshire Battalion.

Further Research

The *Army List* By far the most comprehensive record of officers that served in the Territorial Force is the *Army List*. These record every officer serving as of date of publication – although a *List* dated, eg, January 1909, will only be correct up to the previous month. Here we have names, ranks, dates of commissions which enable the researcher to compile a full record of a man's journey through the officer ranks from his entry into the Territorial Force, through to such time that he retires, resigns of dies. Qualifications are also shown.

Published Unit Records The 'Regimental History'. Until recently, only to be found in secondhand form and expensive. Today, though, most can be found reasonably priced in facsimile reprint form from publishers Naval & Military Press (www.naval-military-press.com). There are libraries of course, but knowing what to ask for is always a problem. I recommend – what the military historian anyway has come to term as his 'bible' on such matters – Arthur S White's *A Bibliography of Regimental Histories of the British Army*. For many years out of print, but thankfully now available as a reprint (ISBN 9781843421559).

Local Newspapers Local newspapers are a must. Items notifying drill nights and annual camps were regular features in most.

The National Archives Few TF records for the period 1908–14 are held at TNA. What there is mostly exists in WO70 and WO32. Awards of the Territorial Decoration are in WO32, those for the Territorial Force Efficiency Medal can be inspected on microfiche in the Open Reading Room.

Regimental Museums and County Record Offices Both can be disappointing when it comes to the auxiliary forces, but both locations are a must for any further research. The latter are often in possession of Territorial Force Association records and correspondence. Details of existing museums can be found at www.armymuseums.org.uk or by writing to the Army Museums Ogilby Trust, 58 The Close, Salisbury, SP1 2EX.

Sources of Information and Recommended Further Reading

Army Orders 1908–1914.

Bradshaw's Railway Guide, 1910 and 1922 editions.

Bulletin of the Military Historical Society. Numerous articles 1948–2010.

Cadet Lists. Various editions.

Cambridge County Geographies. Cambridge University Press, various authors and dates.

Cassell's Gazetteer. Cassell, London, various editions.

Cobb, Colonel M H. *The Railways of Great Britain*. Ian Allan, Shepperton, 2006.

Fielding, James. *Made in Britain*. Summerdale, Chichester, 2007.

Gaunt, Peter. *The Cromwellian Gazetteer*. Alan Sutton, Stroud, 1987.

Kelly's Directories. Numerous editions.

Little Guides. Methuen & Co. Ltd, London, various authors and dates.

Monthly Army List 1908–1914.

Mee, Arthur. *The King's England* series. Hodder & Stoughton, London, 1939–51.

Pevsner, Nikolaus (and others). *The Buildings of England* series. Various publishers and dates.

Regimental and unit histories. More than 200 consulted.

Richards, Walter. *His Majesty's Territorial Army*. Virtue, London, 1910/11.

Territorial Force Return 1913.

Territorial Yearbook. Hodder & Stoughton, London, 1909.

Town guides. More than 200 consulted.

Turner, Keith. *Directory of British Tramways*. Published in three volumes by Tempus and the History Press, 2007–10.

Weinreb, Ben and Hibbert, Christopher. *The London Encyclopædia*. Macmillan, London, 1983.

Westlake, Ray. *A Register of Territorial Force Cadet Units 1910–1922*. Sherwood Press, Nottingham, 1984.

Westlake, Ray. *The Territorial Battalions*. Spellmount, Speldhurst, 1986.

Westlake, Ray. *The British Army of 1914*. Spellmount, Staplehurst, 2005.

Acknowledgements

My sincere ... good friends: Norman Hurst, Mike Jackson, Linda Jackson and Alan Seymour
for their ... his book.

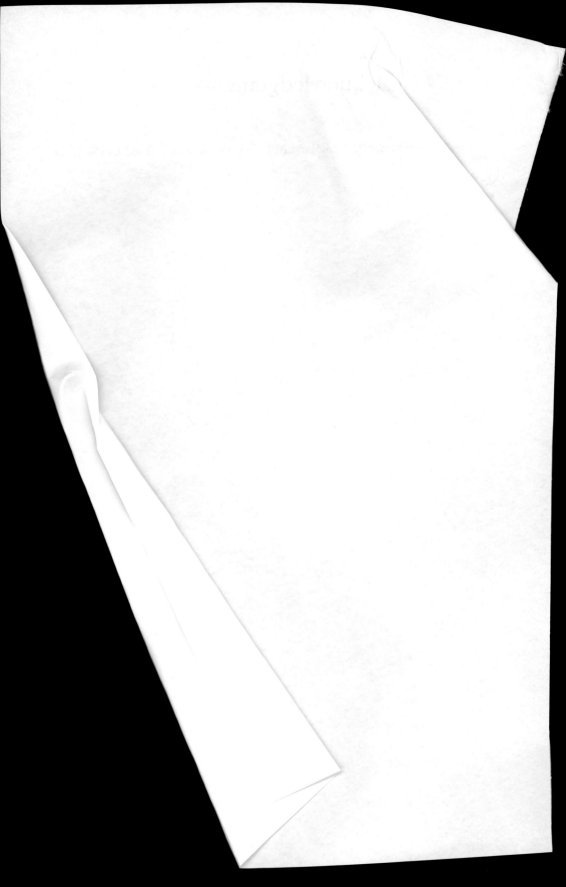